Reasonable Enthusiast
John Wesley and the Rise of Methodism

REASONABLE ENTHUSIAST

John Wesley and the Rise of Methodism

Second Edition

HENRY D. RACK

ABINGDON PRESS
Nashville

Dedicated to
Judith, Elizabeth, Christina and Martin
with love

REASONABLE ENTHUSIAST
John Wesley and the Rise of Methodism

Copyright © 1989, 1992 by Henry D. Rack

First published in Great Britain by
Epworth Press, 1989
Second Edition, 1992

Published in the U.S.A. by Abingdon Press, 1993

This book is printed on recycled, acid-free paper.

Library of Congress Cataloging-in-Publication Data

Rack, Henry D.
    Reasonable enthusiast : John Wesley and the rise of Methodism / Henry D. Rack. — 2nd ed.
        p.   cm.
    Includes bibliographical references and index.
    ISBN 0-687-35625-3 (pbk. : alk. paper)
    1. Wesley, John, 1703–1791. 2. Methodist Church—Great Britain-
-Clergy—Biography. 3. Methodist Church—History—18th century.
4. Methodist Church—Doctrines—History—18th century. I. Title.
BX8495.W5R23   1993
287'.09'033—dc20   93-15360
                                                                            CIP

Typeset by Intype, London

93 94 95 96 97 98 99 00 01—10 9 8 7 6 5 4 3 2 1

MANUFACTURED IN THE UNITED STATES OF AMERICA

Contents

'I . . . think he would have been an enthusiast if he could . . . (but) there was a firmness in his intellectual texture which would not bend to illusion' (Alexander Knox, *Remarks on the Life and Character of John Wesley*)

'*Enthusiasm*: A vain belief of private revelation; a warm confidence of divine favour or communication' (Johnson's *Dictionary*)

Introduction

Shortly before 10 o'clock on the morning of 2 March 1791, in a house in City Road, London, a little old man 'without a dying groan, gathered up his feet in the presence of his brethren'. The slow decays of age had been visible in him for some time, but many people who did not share his particular brand of religious faith had nevertheless been anxious to catch a last glimpse of a man who had become a legend in his own lifetime. Propped in the pulpit by a friend on either side, he had delivered his last sermons in an almost inaudible voice, yet people still seemed to benefit from the sight of his venerable figure and long white hair. As a young man the parson-poet George Crabbe recalled one of several such occasions:

> He was exceedingly old and infirm, and was attended, almost supported in the pulpit, by a young minister on each side . . . He repeated, though with an application of his own, the lines from Anacreon:
>> 'Oft am I by women told,
>> Poor Anacreon! thou grow'st old . . .
>> But this I need not to be told.
>> 'Tis time to *live* if I grow old.'[1]

Thousands are said to have filed past his body lying in simple state in City Road Chapel, and holding the funeral early in the day did not prevent large crowds from attending. Obituarists passed over some highly controversial episodes in his career and concentrated instead on acknowledging that here was a man whose aim had been to do good to his fellow men and women; and his numerous followers found it hard to see any faults in him as he passed from life through death into pious memory.

Yet John Wesley's life had been full of controversy, and the old man known to his first biographers was in many ways very different from the young enthusiast who had shocked his Oxford contemporaries into labelling him as a 'Methodist'. He had aroused infuriated mobs to seek his life; he had been the target of muck-raking scandal as well as of serious theological criticism. Even within the religious revival movement of which he had been an important part, he had been the source of fierce controversy and deep division. The revered old man of the last preaching journeys was still capable of scandalizing contemporaries by taking it upon himself to act as a 'bishop' by ordaining some of his preachers in the 1780s. If, inwardly, he had now attained peace with God and his own nature, his earlier life had been marked by agonizing self-reproach for his lack of true Christianity, and his emotional life had more than once been devastated by the ravages of human love. Moreover, his ideas and his career were full of paradoxes. He had proclaimed, with monotonous repetition, that he 'lived and died in the Church of England' and that his movement was a mere auxiliary to the church, yet he had constantly violated that church's order and it seemed obvious to many that the movement was steadily moving further away from the church. He proclaimed that 'perfection' was possible in this life and urged all good Methodists to look for it, yet never claimed it for himself. He appealed, in the most rational tones of Oxford logic, to 'men of reason and religion' to accept his version of Christianity, yet he had (like many of his followers) a relish for wonders and supernatural stories which most of his educated contemporaries dismissed as superstitions and old wives' tales, no longer fit for an age of reason. He was a thorough autocrat and an old-fashioned 'church and king' man, yet led a movement which many thought was subversive and only too well calculated to lead the lower orders into rebellion against their betters.

The title of this book was suggested partly by the remarks of Alexander Knox quoted on the title page. It has been chosen deliberately to draw attention to some of the paradoxes just mentioned and to try to come to terms with one who remains, despite the large body of literature about him, an enigmatic personality. The problem with John Wesley is not lack of evidence or even of research on many aspects of his career. It is rather the need to penetrate the Wesley legend created by his followers and biographers and the smoke-screen which Wesley himself, consciously or unconsciously, created by his *Journals* and other portrayals of himself and his movement. But it is also partly the problem of the tendency of writers on Wesley to concentrate too exclusively on his personal history, on Methodism to the exclusion of the larger religious movement of which it was part, and on both of these without sufficient attention to the changing society within which their fate was worked out. The sub-title has therefore been chosen as a promise to say rather more than has perhaps been usual about the nature of the early Methodist people whose ideas and activities had a considerable effect on Wesley himself. I have also attempted to sketch, however inadequately, some of the features of contemporary secular and religious life in a way which anchors Wesley and his movement more firmly in their original setting and I have tried to avoid some of the misrepresentations of generations of evangelical propaganda. This is to attempt a great deal – no doubt too much – within the scope of one book. It would have been easier to write a much longer one. Some readers may feel that at times Wesley is almost lost to sight, and certainly the art of historical biography is a difficult one, liable to be neither good history nor good biography. Still, I think this is the right way to try to see Wesley more realistically, and that perhaps others may be stimulated to do better.

I have also given a good deal of thought to the all too familiar problem of balancing narrative with analysis: both are needed in a study of this kind. For various reasons I decided to divide the treatment into three main parts, the breaks being at 1738 and roughly around 1760. By 1760 the basic geography of British Methodism had been established as well as Wesley's regular itinerary; the structures of Methodism had been laid down and all its main problems aired. In secular terms, too, the 1760s marked the beginnings of various political and social changes which would increasingly affect Methodism for the rest of the century. It seemed convenient to sketch the whole eighteenth-century history of Welsh, Scottish and Irish Methodism in the second part of the book, and America (along with other overseas ventures) in the third part, when this became more significant for England and for Wesley himself. I apologize to all these important countries for the slightness of my treatment of them. Partly, with Dr Johnson, I plead pure ignorance; but for the purposes of this book it also seemed right to concentrate on England as being still the scene of the bulk of Methodist activity, including Wesley's own, in this period. In the first part, the Epworth and Oxford sections owe much to the work of Dr Green and Professor Heitzenrater, and I have not attempted to repeat their detailed researches into Wesley's diaries, though I have added some findings of my own. My concern was originally to concentrate on Wesley's later career and on Methodism, though in the event the early period still takes a prominent place.

The post-1760 division of the book contains more analysis and discussion of particular topics and less narrative than the first. I have, however, tried to preserve a sense of movement and change by focussing on what seemed to be the main concerns of successive decades, and briefer references have been made to some of these topics as they arose in earlier years. This has led to some repetitions and cross-referencing which I hope will be helpful rather than irritating. No solution to the problem of arrangement can be perfect, and I can only plead that mine was chosen after much thought and experiment.

This book was originally planned to commemorate the 250th anniversary of John Wesley's conversion on 24 May 1738. Unforeseen delays, sadly, meant that this date was missed. In some ways this is an unfortunate time for essaying a new Wesley biography. A magisterial new edition of Wesley's *Works* has already begun to appear, but will take many years to be completed. My debt to the two volumes of letters so far edited by Frank Baker will be obvious. His inclusion of selections from Wesley's correspondents is a major convenience for reference, quite apart from the meticulous accuracy of the texts. I have read only very selectively in the large body of unpublished theses on various aspects of Wesley's life and thought and on early Methodism; and patchily in the MS material, a good deal of which is in print, though needing cautious use because of past editorial sins. The Wesley problem, as I suggested earlier, lies in the need for fresh interpretations rather than new facts.

I have, inevitably, depended much on my predecessors in this field. All of us remain indebted to the earliest biographers who saved much from destruction or loss and added their first-hand experience of their subject, though naturally of the older rather than the younger Mr Wesley. Of the nineteenth-century biographies, Luke Tyerman's remains a valuable and handy quarry of information, not least for his extracts from anti-Methodist works and press reports. His prejudices are too obvious to be very misleading and his material was presented with a great deal of honest objectivity. Among modern works I have been particularly impressed by Vivian Green's *Young Mr Wesley* and his short but incisive *John Wesley* – the latter seems to me to contain some of the best insights into Wesley's character that have so far appeared, though it should be read alongside Alexander Knox's remarkable essay. Martin Schmidt's *John Wesley. A Theological Biography* has the advantage, unique among Wesley biographies, of a full European dimension, which is especially useful in the first volume. And I confess to a sneaking fondness for Elsie Harrison's *Son to Susanna*, which I fancy first convinced me years ago that John Wesley was actually a real and even interesting human being. Despite its overblown romantic style and cavalier treatment of evidence, it had the great merit of treating Wesley and the early Methodists as subjects for normal biographical analysis. Richard Heitzenrater's *The Elusive Mr Wesley* is a more sober recent attempt to dispel legends by sampling the sources, together with illustrations from contemporary accounts and a full critical bibliography. On points of detail I also owe much to the numerous writings of Frank Baker and I am also grateful for the opportunity of working on his text of the early Methodist Conferences for the new edition of the *Works*. Gratitude is also due for the ninety years' accumulation of material by devoted

Wesley students in the *Proceedings* of the Wesley Historical Society. I hope I have adequately acknowledged these and other conscious debts without seriously distorting the authors concerned, even when I have used their material for my own purposes.

I would also like to offer my thanks to the staff of the splendid John Rylands University Library of Manchester and the Manchester Central Library who have patiently found me material over the years; in the former case, of course, from the Methodist Archives as well. Fruitful help has also been found from the Chester Diocesan Record Office and the always delightful Chetham's Library in Manchester.

I owe a special debt to three living scholars – John Kent, John Walsh and Reginald Ward – which it is difficult to express adequately. Although none of them has written a full life of Wesley (and I can now see why they were wise enough not to try!), each of them could have written a far better one than mine. But their influence through many years of writing and conversation has greatly benefited my own work, and I can only ask them to forgive me if I have misused what I have learnt from them. Several generations of patient students will, I hope, also forgive me for time spent directly or indirectly in acquiring the knowledge and doing the research on which this book is based. At short notice in a busy life the Revd J. M. Turner read over the manuscript and saved me from some misprints and errors as well as making helpful comments, though I must be held responsible for the blemishes that remain. My publisher, John Stacey, has been marvellously patient with a laggard author.

Finally, as always, my wife and family have nobly put up with John Wesley as a guest who often seemed to have overstayed his welcome and to have monopolized too much of my time. But it is their patience, support and amused interest that has kept me going at a seemingly impossible task.

A note on terminology

A few terms frequently used should be explained here. 'Anglican' as an adjective referring to the Established Church of England occurs from the seventeenth century, but as a noun referring to its members scarcely occurs much before the nineteenth century. In the eighteenth century the Church of England was commonly referred to as 'the church' or 'the establishment'; its members as 'Church of England men' or 'churchmen'. I have used all these terms rather indiscriminately, and also (anachronistically) 'Anglican(s)' and 'Anglicanism', simply for brevity's sake. 'Independents' was used (as here) for those usually called 'Congregationalists' in the Victorian period and later. 'Dissenter' rather than 'Nonconformist' was used for the non-Anglican English Protestants, though the Quakers were usually seen as distinct from them.

Following what seems to be now the usual usage, I have used 'evangelical' for all those groups and individuals in all denominations who shared evangelical doctrines and sentiments, including the Methodists, but 'Evangelical' specifically for those evangelicals in the Church of England who would now be seen as the ancestors of the 'Evangelical Party'.

'Methodist' in the eighteenth century was a slippery term. It originated as a term of abuse for the so-called Holy Club in Oxford and was eventually accepted as a label by John Wesley for his followers. However, it was also used at the time for the evangelical groups in Wales associated with Howel Harris and others; and for Whitefield and Lady Huntingdon and their followers in England – all of them Calvinists, unlike Wesley. It was also loosely applied to Anglican Evangelicals and sometimes to anyone who seemed to be religiously 'serious'. I have used the term in this book as generic for the followers of Wesley and Whitefield, for the Welsh, and often for the Huntingdonians. Where it is necessary to distinguish the different groups I have used 'Calvinistic Methodist' for all but Wesley's followers and 'Wesleyan' or 'Wesleyan Methodist' for them. 'Wesleyan' is really a nineteenth-century usage for one part of the then divided Methodist churches, but is a convenient shorthand term for Wesley's followers in the eighteenth century.

Note to the Second Edition

Reprinting has allowed for only limited alterations, and although I have inevitably had further thoughts on various parts of the book, I have as yet not felt it necessary significantly to alter the general lines of argument and interpretation. More should have been said about the role of women in early Methodism, and the rather severe view of Wesley's character could be tempered with more reference to the charm he exhibited, especially in his mellower old age. But these and other matters must await some future occasion.

Alterations have mostly been confined to corrections of factual errors, typographical slips, and uncouth sentences. A few references have been added to the notes together with a brief supplementary bibliography (on p. 561).

I am extremely grateful to friends, correspondents and reviewers for various sorts of corrections, especially to Mr Frank W. Button, Rev. Benjamin Drewery, Ms Elizabeth Hart, Professor Richard Heitzenrater (despite my persistent misspelling of his name in the original edition!), Dr Geoffrey Nuttall and Dr John Vickers. I have used their help as fully as possible within the limits of this revision, though I must accept responsibility for any errors of fact or interpretation which remain.

Henry D. Rack
Manchester, June 1992

Wesley's England: 1. Society and Religion in the Early Eighteenth Century

1. The social order

To think oneself back into Wesley's England is no easy matter. For one thing, he lived to be a very old man, and by the slow-moving standards of his youth the England of his old age had undergone striking changes at least socially and economically, though the structure of church and government remained, to its cost, much the same as earlier. Later images of the period, as well as contemporary reality, present contrasts which are often hard to reconcile. There is the elegance and taste which we still admire in surviving Georgian buildings; but originally these existed not far from hovels long since vanished, in filthy and dangerous streets. Enlightened, 'modernizing' thinking in many spheres co-existed with barbarous punishments for crime and savage repression of the lower orders, soldiers and sailors.

Perhaps the most striking, even the most important, facts to grasp are that this was a country with a far smaller population than today; and that it was predominantly rural. From these facts many consequences followed for the social and religious order. Statistics on these matters will always remain approximate, but one recent estimate at least offers a reasonable order of comparison. This would give the population of England as 5.1 million in 1701, 5.8 million in 1751 and (more accurately from the first national census) 8.7 million in 1801.[1] As will be noted later, the slow and relatively slight rise from 1701 to 1751, in contrast to the much larger and more rapid rise of the next fifty years, is clearly of great significance. What happened during the first half of the century remains a matter of dispute. Although the figures suggest a virtually static situation, overall they also mask local growth as well as variations up and down in time.

The still predominantly rural and village character of England is

1

underlined even when one turns to the 'urban' population. This may be variously defined. Taking a population of 5,000 as the minimum for a town, it has been estimated that only 15% of the population lived in towns around 1750, and though this had risen to 25% by 1800, this was still far short of the situation in 1851, when just over 50% lived in towns of 10,000 or more. If, perhaps more realistically for this period, one takes a town as having only 2,500 or more inhabitants, a recent calculation suggests that in 1700 there were 18.65% townsmen; in 1750, 22.6%; and in 1801, 30.6%.[2]

Equally striking, by contrast with later times, are the size and location of the largest cities. London was, as always, wholly exceptional – the only English city of a size we would think equal to such status. Already in 1700 it held perhaps half a million, and all the rest fell far behind. In 1700 the next largest were Norwich (30,000) and Bristol (20–22,000). By 1750 Bristol had some 50,000 inhabitants, old leaders like York and Exeter as well as Norwich had fallen behind, while Newcastle with Gateshead had 29,000 and Birmingham 24,000 inhabitants. Much greater changes would have taken place by 1800 when Manchester and Liverpool were the provincial leaders, followed by Birmingham, Bristol, Leeds and Sheffield – nearing the modern pattern.[3] But the overall population still remained relatively low, and the areas of substantial growth were still limited, so that the problems they created were still localized. Only London presented the kind and scale of problems which would become familiar and menacing in the cities of the early nineteenth century. For example, it is not surprising that growing London should have foreshadowed the fears of the future about population outstripping church accommodation. In 1711, government money was offered to build fifty new churches (only ten were actually erected) – an expedient not provoked again on a national scale until 1818.

That Bristol and Norwich should be the leading early eighteenth-century cities after London is an indication of where the wealth of England still lay, at least in trade and industry. Norwich was still the centre of one of the major textile areas. Bristol was the outlet for the south-western textile industry and the focus of West Indian sugar and slaves. Still behind them, yet moving up, were the woollens of the West Riding and the cottons of the Manchester area. Newcastle was already important for coal, Birmingham for metal trades. Though already growing, they would not overhaul the older areas until later in the century.

Defoe's famous *Tour through the Whole Island of Great Britain* (1724–6) gives as good a picture as any of the bustling, 'improving' character of many parts of England. What really interested Defoe, himself a (not very successful) tradesman and manufacturer as well as a gifted writer of fiction and what might now be called 'faction', was the evidence of growth, industry and improvements of all kinds. Though he did not overlook agricultural improvements as well as the still important woollen industry in (for example) Wiltshire, what particularly caught his attention were the growing towns and industrial settlements of the Midlands and North, though he noted the survival of older centres too. Exeter had gentry and good company, yet also was full of trade and manufactures. Bristol was hampered, for all its wealth, by the tyranny of its corporation, which prevented newcomers from joining in. (It was, and is, common to contrast the openness of Manchester, a non-corporate town, in this respect.) Ominously, Norwich had had to get an Act to prohibit the use of calicoes to retain the prosperity of its own trade. Of Cheshire Defoe noted that 'there is no part of England where there are such a great number of families of gentry', but also that it thrived by sending cheeses as far as London. London dealers also bought quantities of provisions from Bedford, but this and neighbouring counties had also had a 'wonderful increase' of late in bone-lace manufacture.

However, it is the famous description of the Halifax area which shows what most excited him. Here he found a host of little workshops attached to the houses; plots of land to supplement industry with smallholding; cottages nearby for the workmen employed in the workshops. And so through 'a noble scene of industry and application' to the great marketing centre of Leeds. There would be signal early Methodist successes in these parts. Then, over on the other side of England, Defoe noted how Liverpool had now become 'so great, so populous, and so rich, that it may be called the Bristol of this part of England'. Manchester he famously described as 'one of the greatest if not the greatest mear village in England being neither a city nor a corporation and sending no members to Parliament'. Typically, he claimed its population to be 50,000 (10–12,000 is more likely), and as in Liverpool, building was going on rapidly. As to London, Defoe (like modern economic historians) noted how its devouring needs and influence drew products from all parts of England: the Cheshire cheeses, the coals from Newcastle. Villas and polite society infiltrated the villages nearer to the metropolis. Though trade still depended a great deal on inland waterways and coastal shipping, and Defoe commented especially on the dreadful, impassable, miry ways of the Weald and the heavy Midland clays, he also spoke optimistically about the growth of turnpikes.

Defoe's bias of interest and exaggerations are obvious. Modern historians seem to agree that 'pre-industrial' England was already in a state of preparation for the more spectacular achievements later on. What Defoe was observing was the beginning of a shift from the older textile areas to the newer. The social hierarchy, especially in the older towns, was headed by big merchants, but in towns like Manchester by merchant-manufacturers who, in the days before the rise of great factories, controlled a network of craftsmen working at home or in small workshops; some, like those observed by Defoe near Halifax, supplemented their income by seasonal work in smallholdings. If some worked in towns, many lived in the network of villages around them in the textile area of Lancashire, engaged by the big masters who supplied the raw materials and marketed the finished product. Long before factories became common, children were part of the labour system, and Defoe (like John Locke the bachelor philosopher of education) gloried in the thought of their busy fingers being kept out of mischief. It was among such folk that the Revival would make some of its greatest inroads at the expense of the Church of England, as well as among the clannish communities of miners and fishermen in Cornwall and the North East.

Yet when all this is said, England remained predominantly a land not only of villages but also of agriculture. 'Improvement' applied here too, though among the larger rather than smaller proprietors and tenants. However much industry and trade contributed to England's prosperity and helped to dictate its policy and wars, power lay in land and its owners. And this was where the heart (as well as much of the income) of the Church of England was located, with long-lasting effects on its fate and that of the Revival.

The landed aristocracy and landed gentry were the real holders of power in eighteenth-century society. They supplied the JP's who were the backbone of rural local government and social control, and it was the gentry who supplied the solid core of members of Parliament. Below them lay larger and smaller farmers, some owners but many tenants; and below them again a mass of landless labourers. Eighteenth-century Methodism had some effect on the former, but little on the latter until a later date. Thomas Taylor, a Methodist preacher in Yorkshire in the 1780s, wrote almost like a modern sociologist: 'There is but little trade in any part of the circuit; and where there is little trade, there is seldom much increase in religion.' The tenants were subject to the big landowners 'and dread them much more abundantly than their Maker'.[4] Between the large aristocratic landowners at the top and the landless labourers at the bottom there was a very varied group of middling proprietors and tenants, but ever since the sixteenth century, land-grabbing, enclosure and improvement had squeezed more and more precarious smallholders and cottagers with rights on common land into mere wage-labourers. The more notorious spate of enclosures after 1750 merely accelerated the process. On the bonus side this helped to supply labour to growing industries and fed their workers from a more efficient agricultural sector. England was actually a net exporter of corn during the first half of the eighteenth century, and in fact in 1700 agriculture provided 40% of the gross national product; it was still 33% in 1800 – higher than industrial products.[5]

The social effects of this were marked. Compact villages with a single landowner and a resident parson were much easier to keep free of religious or other trouble-makers. Defoe remarked on 'the famous village of Brightwell (in Oxfordshire) of which it was observed that there had not been an alehouse nor a dissenter from the Church, nor any quarrel among the inhabitants that rises so high as to a riot of law within the memory of man'. Even in his day, though alehouses had arrived, the village was peaceable and without Dissent. The Oxford Diocesan Visitation of 1738 broadly confirms this, for though some 'inconsiderable' persons were absent from church and the youth spent the Sabbath in sport, there had never been any Papists or Dissenters. There was only one family of note and only thirty-five families in all.[6]

One should nevertheless note that at least in larger villages there was a significant category of rural craftsmen, less bound to their betters than labourers. In East Hoathly in Sussex, with only 350 inhabitants, there were innkeepers, tailors, butchers, a chandler, a schoolmaster, excise officer, brickmaker, carpenter, miller and blacksmith.[7] In town and country, too, there was a large army of domestic servants and others living in with their masters.

A much-quoted map of the social hierarchy compiled by Gregory King has been preserved for English society as it was at the time of the Glorious Revolution of 1688; and another by Joseph Massie (based on King, with some revisions) for 1759–60. But both the categories and the statistics given in these tables are often dubious.[8] King was guessing on the basis of inadequate information and reproducing a conservative and static social order as he wished it to be. He omitted any separate category of servants and obscured or omitted or understated rising categories of what we would call industrialists, financiers and civil servants who were symptoms of change. Massie, however, does recognize 'master manufacturers'.[9] What really concerned King was the large part of the population (he thought over half) who were decreasing and not increasing the wealth of the nation – that is, the poor who depended more or less on relief. This was a real problem, though England had begun to escape the cycles of sheer famine which still troubled France.

Certainly this was a very hierarchical society, if hardly a 'class' one in the Marxist sense (though some historians have tried hard to make it so). The language of 'class' does not appear before the 1790s.[10] Contemporaries spoke rather of 'degree', 'order' and 'rank'; of the 'upper ranks', 'middling ranks', 'lower orders'. They did not think of self-conscious economically-based classes engaged in mutual hostility.

People tended to think more in terms of associations by trade, religion, region, family ties and political faction.[11] Nor was England a 'caste' society in the sense of people being fixed in occupations and rank simply by birth – they could readily move or fall lower in the social scale and (less readily) rise higher – certainly within the broad categories below the level of the hereditary aristocracy. How far the aristocracy was really open simply to men with money from trade is open to argument. So is the claim that it was easy and typical for merchants to move into land to better their social status. Yet there seems little doubt that England had a *relatively* open social structure especially for those with money, as compared with the European continent.[12] The real difficulties, it has been suggested, came when one approached the boundaries of a higher social rank.[13] Land always remained the route to real power in this society.

What is very important is the fact that this was a society imbued with the idea and practice and mentality of 'dependence', though it is now thought that even in the minds of the lower orders this was subject to traditional ideas of 'rights' along with 'duties'. Men were expected dutifully to obey their betters and to be content with the lot appointed to them by God, even if they could try to prosper within their sphere.[14] Poverty is ordained by God and is necessary for the well-being of society – the poor must hew wood and draw water. Moreover, William Wilberforce was not simply speaking as an 'Evangelical' when he claimed that the poor had religious advantages since they escaped the anxieties of wealth – this was an old story.[15] However, recent research suggests that even the poor (or indeed the less poor in times of distress) had a sense of what was due to them from their betters in terms of employment, just wages and protection. The century was punctuated by riots against: high corn prices; low wages in the textile industry; turnpike roads; Papists, Methodists and Dissenters; and sometimes against political violations of the 'rights of freeborn Englishmen', as well as poaching affrays and smugglers fighting excisemen. Study of some of these cases has suggested that the rioting mob had its own notions of what was just and directed its anger against specific offenders such as corn-hoarders.[16] Those in authority were sometimes prepared to compromise and conciliate rather than simply to suppress, though in the end they had no scruples about using force if they had to. In this some historians have discerned a conflict between the calculations and imperatives of a market, competitive economy type of mentality and 'the customary moral economy of the plebs'.[17] Problems of authority will often arise in studying the relationship between Wesley, the church and his own followers.

What is equally striking is the extent to which this often unruly and, in many ways, lightly governed society was kept in a state of relative control and equilibrium. A recent social historian sums up three of its leading characteristics: the fundamental strength and resilience of the social hierarchy; the possibility of movement up and down the hierarchy despite inequalities; and the attempt by the ruling class to secure consensus in the society by influence, persuasion and religion, though ultimately by force if necessary.[18]

How, in fact, was England governed? By modern standards there was remarkably little government, and most of it exerted locally rather than nationally: through JP's, parish vestries (and the clergy), and town corporations. Apart from the statutory poor law, social welfare was largely left to charity (endowed or individual) and voluntary societies. So, too, was education. The national government was limited and distinctly non-interventionary in its attitudes, anxious to avoid the unpopularities of taxation except when forced by war. The House of Commons essentially represented the men of property (and overwhelmingly of landed property), elected on a limited franchise which was uniform in the counties but variable in the boroughs, many of the latter being notoriously controlled by aristocratic patrons, or representation being divided between two great families who only rarely had to contest elections.[19] Although the monarch still had an active role and could influence the choice of ministers, he had to have men who could manage the House of Commons, and indeed the Lords. Management meant a mixture of influence, family and personal connexions, persuasion, pensions and jobs, but also oratory to persuade a substantial section of the House, which included men who prided themselves on being 'independent'. Much modern research and controversy on the party history of this period has led to revisions and re-revisions of what the traditional labels of 'Whig' and 'Tory' meant at various times and how far they represented real divisions. Even though elections and government were carried on (and had to be) by what to modern eyes looks like mere corruption which men out of office liked to denounce as such at the time, it is increasingly recognized that various degrees of ideological reality did exist to fortify the old party labels. They had a powerful reality under Queen Anne, when parties differed on policy and strategy about the French wars, on the influence of city financiers and (not least) on attitudes to the church and Dissent.

The accession of George I in 1714 led to a dramatic change in party fortunes. The Tories were smeared, rightly or wrongly, as Jacobites under the skin and proscribed from office for nearly fifty years. Government fell into the hands of Whig groups, and the opposition during this period became a matter of Tories and dissident Whigs out of office. After 1760, in a period of political instability, with a king wishing to avoid rule by a permanent oligarchy, there was opportunity for the proscribed gradually to get into office, and though sentiment and tradition often determined what labels men adopted, from the time of the younger Pitt's premiership in the 1780s a transition was beginning to take place. Tories came to office and Whigs, some of a reforming cast, were ousted for many years.

The divisions, influence and 'spoils' system of political life also affected the church. Bishops sat in the Lords and in a small House often had vital votes, while clergy could be useful at election time locally. Patronage and influence was as important in the church as in every other aspect of public and private life. The church was systematically exploited for political advantage. The Duke of Newcastle, one of the arch-manipulators of patronage, stated his rules for the appointment of bishops thus: 'First, to recommend none whom I did not think most sincerely affected to his majesty and his government and to the principles upon which it is founded . . . The next rule has been, to recommend none whose character as to virtue and regularity of life would not justify it.' It is fair to say that despite the order of priorities, the second maxim was generally observed, and the bench was free of some of the grosser scandals of churches elsewhere. But Newcastle's correspondence and that of aspiring clergy and bishops shows that anxious and intricate calculations and the balancing of family and factional interest pervaded all appointments of this kind. Virtue without influence was never likely to go very far.[20] When John Wesley confessed that he was a Tory and the son of a Tory, bred as a High Churchman in strict non-resistance principles, he revealed his and his father's grounding in the divisions of the late seventeenth and early eighteenth century, for which religion and politics were almost inseparable. Father and son transferred their loyalism to the Hanoverian monarchy, though Wesley's mother did not. Old Samuel ceased to progress up the ecclesiastical ladder as his Tory patronage ceased to be effective, though John got his fellowship of Lincoln in Tory Oxford partly through his family political traditions. Not even pious Evangelicals could escape, nor indeed wished to escape, the needs and possible advantages of patronage.

Comparisons between eighteenth-century England and under-developed countries today are tempting and to a degree apt, though they need to be balanced with a realization that England already had developed some of the conditions for what some historians have seen as a take-off into sustained economic growth later. But some of the comparisons hold good, for example in communications, health and (up to a point) in education as well as law and order. Thus health and life-expectancy were much like those in India today – about thirty-five years, with a very high infant mortality. This was a very youthful society. Then there was literacy, a subject on which only very rough estimates are possible, based partly on the evidence of marriage registration. It is thought that, on the evidence of signing one's name, this was a skill acquired by about 1715 by 45% of men and 25% of women; by 1760, by 60% of men and 40% of women.[21] This covered great variations between town and country, the higher and lower orders. Common sense suggests that reading was a more common skill and may well have been under-estimated. It could be acquired not only through a variety of schools but also more informally or by oneself, and was worth doing as the key to possible advance and, importantly for the Revival, as a road to religious improvement. Indeed serious religious movements like Puritanism and Methodism usually stimulated ambitions to read among their members and fostered the skill.

No brief description can do justice to the variety of eighteenth-century life. The older books of social history dwelt on the contrasts referred to at the beginning of this chapter, strongly marked by the literary sources, satire and caricatures, to create a picture – true as far as it goes – of stark contrasts between the elegance of upper-class life and the horrors of Gin Lane and Tyburn. But a mixture of Capability Brown, Horace Walpole's letters and Hogarth's caricatures has given way to the rather more desiccated calculations of the new social historians, though also to dedicated attempts to recover the life and mentality of the 'common people'.[22] More important, perhaps, and not least for the subject of this book, is the broad spectrum of the 'middling sort of people' down to the craftsmen. These often sober folk, as distrustful of the spendthrift aristocrat as of the feckless poor, were the real target of Methodism (or at least the backbone of its membership). This was a world in which strands of commercial modernity (like the 'commercialization of leisure') jostled uneasily with an upsurge of philanthropy, in which compassion was mixed with calculation, improving sentiments and fear of the lower orders as well as with religious concern.[23] Not least, this was a period when religious toleration grew, though tempered with restrictions and sometimes poisoned with the recurrence of anti-Popish fears. For all its dirt, brutishness, barbarity – the more shocking when set beside elegance, rationality and humanitarian idealism – this was an improving society: free of war during Walpole's rule; more prosperous and more tolerant than the seventeenth century and justifiably anxious not to return to that time of division, instability and fanaticism.

John Wesley was not an impartial witness, but his constant travels and mixing with varieties of people made him one of the best-informed observers of his time, though he had an unusual tenderness for the poor and a jaundiced opinion of the aristocracy and 'gentlemen'. His view of the condition of England, we shall see, was on the whole optimistic. If he deplored poverty, he thought that the country was generally increasing in population and wealth. Nor did he deprecate this; and while in his later years he inveighed against the dangers of wealth to Methodist souls, he still urged them to 'gain all you can, save all you can', so long as this was to enable them to 'give all you can'. He was also optimistic about the growth and spread of religion. His theological creed centred on a vision of cumulative holiness, issuing in love and service to God and man. For all his old-fashioned ideas on political and social questions, as well as on religion, he was very much a man of the optimistic, improving eighteenth century, and his 'enthusiasm' was clothed in the garments of 'reason.'

2. The religious order

(i) The established church

(a) The working of the establishment

Throughout the century, the Church of England was the dominant church in the country and had at least the nominal allegiance of 90% of the population. It was dominant not only in numbers but also in legal rights and privileges, social weight and influence, and as a recognized part of the constitution along with King, Lords and Commons. Fielding's Parson Thwackum was rather more than a caricature of Anglican attitudes when he proclaimed: 'When I say religion, I mean the Christian religion . . . the Protestant religion . . . the Church of England.' Anglicans saw it as the best-constituted church in Christendom, with the best liturgy, avoiding (as one seventeenth-century churchman put it) 'the meretricious gaudiness of the Church of Rome and the squalid sluttery of fanatick conventicles'.[24]

Anglican privileges, coupled with a wider range of social duties than can easily be imagined today, reflected the old idea that to support its religious role a church must have independent endowments and the social and legal duties which go with them. In a lightly governed society lacking most official social services, the clergy were the expected sources of education, charity, even medical care, as well as being among the natural leaders and guides of village communities. All the bishops were in the House of Lords; Parliament was closed to Catholics and contained few Dissenters. Office holders under the Crown and in corporations were supposed to qualify by a sacramental test. The universities were Anglican and largely staffed by clergy. In lieu of civil registration, the clergy performed and recorded the majority of baptisms and burials and married all but Quakers and Jews after 1753. Church courts continued to have business over wills and marriage disputes as well as church dues, though their spiritual discipline gradually decayed.

Formidable though this engine for religious and social control seemed to be, the eighteenth-century church has had a black reputation among religious historians. This has been strongly coloured by later theological and other prejudices. Evangelicals have found it lacking in the sovereign doctrine of justification by faith; Anglo-Catholics have found it lacking in sacramental zeal and a sense of priestly ministry; nineteenth-century reformers saw it as inefficient and worldly. Critics at the time complained of the unfair distribution of clerical incomes and the pervasiveness of pluralist and absentee clergy, holding more than one living and paying starveling curates to do duty in their absence. The truth is that most of these practical evils were older than the eighteenth century, mediaeval in origin though aggravated by the Reformation, and were beyond the power of the clergy to rectify. The holy heroes of Evangelical and Anglo-Catholic biography benefitted from the anomalies and abuses as much as anybody. Only compelling circumstances of loss of pastoral control on a large scale could force Parliament to reform the system, and it is significant that this situation did not finally come to a head until the 1830s.

The twenty-six dioceses and ten thousand parishes and their clergy varied enormously in size and income, and in a manner related to ancient endowments and lay raids on church property and revenues rather than to the size of population. In 1762 the Archbishop of Canterbury had £7000 per annum, the Bishop of Bristol only £450, though this was topped up, with a canonry of St Paul's and a London living, to a total of £1550.[25] Cathedral canons were a notoriously well-heeled class with minimal duties. As one of them put it: 'The life of a prebendary is a pretty easy way of dawdling away one's time: praying, walking, visiting and as little study as your heart could wish.'[26]

As to the parochial clergy, they occupied a range of posts from a few plums with £1000 a year or more through a much larger number of £150–£300 which may be taken to be the area of tolerable to modest comfort. But below this was a large array of benefices and a larger army of anxious curates at £50 a year or often much less. It was the prevalence of such posts as well as the belief that able men needed incentives that were urged in defence of pluralities and consequent non-residence. But though small neighbouring livings of low income were quite often justifiably held together by custom or luck, the main truth was that it was influence and connection which built up many of the most far-flung and affluent connections. Yet it was also this that gave the jostling ranks of anxious curates their first (and too often their last) rungs on the ladder of preferment.

This untidy and (as contemporaries often recognized) unfair system of uneven rewards had always existed because of the historical accidents of private endowment. It had been aggravated by the Reformation, when many livings belonging to monasteries had been acquired by laymen as 'impropriators', drawing the major tithes and leaving only the minor ones to the clerical 'vicar' who performed the duties. By 1603 some 4,000 out of over 9,000 livings were in this situation, and the laity seldom disgorged them.[27] By the early nineteenth century the extent of non-residence amounted to over 4,800 clergy. In York diocese in 1743 it ran to 393 out of 711 surveyed, with 335 pluralists.[28] Most of these had their places supplied by curates; the rest were served by clergy residing nearby and this in fact often enabled the rather minimal duties to be performed which were expected.

The lot of the poorest clergy probably improved somewhat during the eighteenth century. Queen Anne's Bounty from 1704 used some of the dues stolen by Henry VIII to help low incomes and in some areas this helped to stabilize Anglican ministry.[29] In 1714 curates' stipends were stipulated to be in the range of £20–£50 per annum and bishops tried to enforce this. It has been suggested that a fair number of incomes did improve after the hard times of war taxation and party strife and anti-clericalism during the period from 1690 to 1714.[30] The clerical profession was attractive to the younger sons of aristocrats and gentry with the necessary influence for promotion, but influence also carried a number of tradesmen's sons as high as the episcopal bench. However, the largest single category was that of clergy sons like the three Wesley boys. If they could scrape their way through university (for this was now mainly a graduate profession), they could enter the only gentlemanly profession open to a poor man's son.

Like every other aspect of eighteenth-century religion, the working of the establishment was deeply conditioned by seventeenth-century events. The civil wars of the 1640s had been fought partly over the question of what kind of religion and church should be established. By 1662 bishops and Prayer Book had been restored, and those refusing to conform had been expelled (nearly 2,000 in all). James II had been expelled in 1688 because he seemed to threaten England and its church with arbitrary royal rule and 'popery', but the church had lost six bishops and some 400 clergy, as well as an unknown number of laity who could not stomach the deposition of a monarch divinely ordained. In 1689 separate worship by those dissenting from the Church of England had been allowed. The reign of Anne (1702–14) had seen furious faction fights between High Church Tory clergy and Whiggish or moderate bishops. Then came the Hanoverians, the proscription of the Tories and pressure on the lower clergy to conform if they hoped for promotion. These events had divided loyalties, created crises of conscience, and subtly and profoundly affected the complex ties of sentiment and custom which fortified the church's hold on the community, as well as materially affecting its resources and means of discipline and the support it could expect from the state.[31]

The Establishment ideal was that all should be members of a single church, supervised by the clergy in their parishes and overseen by the bishops in their dioceses. This was to be done by a mixture of pastoral care backed by the sanctions of spiritual or financial penalties through the church courts – a system largely untouched by the Reformation. For collective deliberations the Convocations of Canterbury and York should have acted as forums and legislative bodies, subject to Parliament. Convocation did not sit for effective business after 1717, and this has often been seen by historians as a fatal blow to the effectiveness of the church in this period. But its record of ineffectiveness and subordination to Parliament during the Reformation period and its divided state under Anne make this very doubtful. The church courts continued to have plenty of business during the eighteenth century, but their role in imposing penalties for religious and moral offences in this period has never been systematically investigated. It seems that they did not simply decline after the Restoration in 1660. Given backing from the government under Charles II and again under Anne one can see the old sanctions working to curb sexual offences, force attendance at church and sacrament, and punish working on Sundays and the like. Patchily the system continued to be applied up to perhaps the mid-eighteenth century, and in some places even beyond. But it seems clear that this was conditioned by government attitudes, official toleration of Dissent, the decline of High Church Tory influence in positions of power after 1714, anti-clerical lay influence and the rise of ill-controlled industrial areas. In these last, discipline declined early, and by mid-century many returns from churchwardens were simply an unconvincing '*omnia bene*' ('all is well').[32]

In response to this situation, it has been suggested, two different reactions can be discerned – 'policy' would perhaps be too strong a term.[33] One might attempt to reconstruct the old order of coercion with the essential backing of the government. This was the vision of the extreme High Church Tory Bishop Atterbury, who in 1710–11 proposed reinforcing the church courts, licensing all schools by the bishops, protecting clerical incomes, simplifying the creation of new parishes and government money for church building. One of the few effects of this was the building of a few new churches in London, as has been noted earlier. There were also short-lived attempts to curb Dissenting schools and academies and to keep Dissenters out of office. But the church courts' power over religious observance and morality gradually declined. In the 1730s Bishop Gibson was still hoping to strengthen them, but it is noticeable that by the end of the century Bishop Watson simply ignored the subject in his numerous reform proposals.

What was the alternative? This seemed to be to improve pastoral care and supervision by bishops and clergy and to supplement the official organs of the church with voluntary organizations, enrolling lay help. Several bishops stepped up their visitations, discouraged plurality and non-residence, and increased confirmation services. A famous example of this is Bishop Burnet's description of his pastoral ideals and practice, though it should be noticed that he drew on his Scottish background and piety and met with much resistance.[34] As to voluntary aid, part of the prehistory of the Revival seems to be the rash of devotional Religious Societies which began as early as the 1670s and continued with varying fortunes into the 1730s. The Society for Promoting Christian Knowledge (SPCK, 1698) was a promoter of cheap religious literature and charity schools; the Society for the Propagation of the Gospel (SPG, 1701) promoted missions overseas in which the SPCK was also concerned. The Societies for the Reformation of Manners (SRMs) from the 1690s to the 1730s represent a compromise between official coercion and voluntary suasion, since they hoped to stir up the lay magistracy to prosecute blasphemy, drunkenness, swearing and brothel-keeping.[35] But it should be emphasized that there was no concerted overall policy here for an alternative system of church management to meet what some have seen as an emerging situation of 'religious pluralism'.[36] It was rather the effort of a few enthusiasts to supplement official means. The ordinary parish staggered on basically unaltered. Yet 'stagger' is perhaps a misleading word. The old system could cope well enough so long as population growth was slow and stability was maintained. In the broad stretches of rural England the church retained its hold and at least a passive loyalty. The problems lay not so much in the defects in the system or in the quality and outlook of the clergy as in economic and social changes and consequent changes in outlook. These were still limited, and in limited areas, even late in the century.

What in fact were the characteristics of the bishops and clergy and how effective were they? So large a body of men defies generalization, and any attempt to describe them is hampered not only by lack of detailed research but also by the black legends created by later partisans. It has already been observed that bishops were political appointees, though they were normally of good character and often men of learning and even devotion. But Parliamentary duties kept them from their dioceses for many months in the year, and poor communications restricted them during the rest.[37] Their stock duties of confirmation, testing and ordaining of the clergy and a triennial 'visitation' of the diocese were generally performed with fair efficiency. This last function was largely performed through questionnaires about numbers of services, residence, schools, numbers of Papists and Dissenters and the like. The eighteenth-century bishop was essentially a remote figure, seldom seen by his clergy and only intermittently troubling them. He was very different from the busy episcopal dynamo, the man of many committees and public pronouncements, who emerged as the Victorian ideal. The difference in outlook, expectation and function was at least as important in determining the eighteenth-century style and performance as physical and administrative difficulties.

It was the parochial clergy who really mattered for the working of the establishment, and here the same limitations of circumstance, personality and expectation obviously applied even more. Once again, generalization is impossible about 10,000 parishes and perhaps 15,000 men, though some day a thorough examination of visitation returns and local studies will give us a more precise picture.[38] The strong and weak points of the system may be illustrated by examples from the dioceses of York and Oxford. In Hexham with a population of about 3,500 there were about 380 Presbyterians and 200 Roman Catholics (17% non-Anglicans). There was no parsonage house; the endowment was only £30 per annum, so the resident parson was only a curate. There had been no confirmations within living memory and only 22% of those qualified attended Easter communion. Similarly in the textile town of Wakefield: 160 of the 1400 families were Dissenters (11%); and of some 4000 communicants only 400 at most (10%) took the sacrament. Yet in Todwick near Doncaster, with only 32 families, mostly poor, there were no Dissenters and most adults attended communion. In other places of similar size there were cases of over 80% attendance. Topcliffe parish contained ten villages – a situation often productive of non-attendance and Dissenting inroads. Yet in this case there were few Dissenters; there were ten communion services a year, with almost everybody attending and others receiving at home. But the clue here may be that the parson resided and was extremely active in catechizing and visiting. In Oxfordshire there are numerous examples of small village communities, some looked after by visiting dons from Oxford. Some were like Defoe's Brightwell example mentioned earlier, where the church had a secure hold and non-attendance at church was low, though so, very often, was communion attendance. The village of Heath contained only forty-nine persons, mostly labourers but a few craftsmen. They included a few Papists and Dissenters (the latter being shoemakers), but even one of the Dissenting families attended church. The town of Henley, on the other hand, was claimed to contain a population which was one-third Dissenting.[39]

Though many local accidents (including the residence and energy of incumbents or lack of them) help to explain these variations, some more general patterns have been suggested in terms of size, settlement history and distribution and landholding. Certainly, in general, towns and industrial settlements show more Dissent and lower communion attendance than small and compact agricultural villages. It was also important to have a harmonious relationship between the parson and the main landowners. There is a telling illustration of early eighteenth-century attitudes in Addison's fictional Sir Roger de Coverley, the idealized Anglican squire. He was on good terms with his parson, curbed non-attendance at church and sleeping during the sermon (except his own!), and rewarded the virtuous with flitches of bacon. This is contrasted with the next village, where squire and parson are at loggerheads; the squire has made his tenants 'atheists and tithe-stealers' and the parson has threatened to 'pray for him in the face of the congregation'. Addison revealingly comments that such feuds are very damaging in the country where there is more deference to men of property than learning and where people will not believe a truth if it is opposed by men of £500 a year.[40]

What is important to realize is the general view held of the clerical position and its duties, not only by the clergy themselves but by other people. The dutiful parson ideally held two services on Sunday, preaching two sermons; and theoretically read morning and evening prayer daily or at least on Wednesdays, Fridays and feast days. He would catechize the young, apprentices and servants and visit the sick (systematic visitation of the whole parish seems to be a later Evangelical invention). Communion would be administered at least three times a year. For the rest, the parson conducted baptisms, marriages and funerals and acted as a fount of charity and local administration and welfare. But his way of life, his strengths and weaknesses, were closely related to, and coloured by, his status and role as a minor landed gentleman and a direct or indirect farmer. If there were poor vicars or curates, their graduate and ordained status as 'gentlemen' could easily slip below the level of respect and obedience.

The well-known and often quoted example of Parson Woodforde probably gives a fair example of the better sort of decent, uninspired, semi-secularized yet conscientious and paternalistic country clergyman. His celebrated dinners were particularly in evidence at his tithe 'frolic' for the local farmers (the parish clerk relegated to the kitchen and his niece to her bedroom). Poor men were dined on Christmas Day and given a shilling apiece. His dog Hector 'performed incomparably' at hare-coursing on Boxing Day. That day, too, he gave tips to the tradesmen who did his brewing and blacksmithing. Young people were duly prepared for confirmation and entertained with cake and wine. He visited the sick, and on Good Friday read prayers with some pride ('there used to be none that day, which I think was very wrong').[41]

The picture is of a farmer-parson fitting comfortably into his place in the established order of things, his authority seldom questioned at least until after 1800 at the end of his life. He was also supervising a simple religious pattern which was, like its pastor, part of the immemorial order of things, especially in the countryside. The combination of pigs, preaching and sacraments was customary and traditional. It is as obvious in the seventeenth-century diary of Ralph Josselin as in that of Woodforde. What one misses, however, in Woodforde, is Josselin's vivid sense of a personal Providence, as active in the accidents to his livestock and family as in his religious life, though occasional survivals of this sense occur a century later and would become prominent among Evangelicals.[42] That other well-known eighteenth-century parson, William Cole of Bletchley, shows a more marked High Church predilection for sacraments and holy days, but in essence shared the same outlook and way of life.[43] We shall see that the father of the Wesleys, Samuel Wesley of Epworth, was in many ways an excellent example of the best kind of provincial clergyman, trying to uphold the old discipline on evildoers and eagerly welcoming the new initiatives of the voluntary societies. What marred his ministry was the savage strife of the early years of the century which Woodforde, in a later generation and a quieter parish, escaped. The more lurid examples of hard-drinking, fox-hunting and careless clergy (some of which in any case probably reflect the frustrations of educated men sunk without congenial company) should be set against the dutiful if dull conduct of the silent majority. It has always to be remembered that the clerical profession *was* a profession which many adopted as the best and most natural available without seeing the need for the divine call thought essential by later Evangelicals and Anglo-Catholics.

The real weakness of the system was that it had grown up in a rural and relatively slowly changing society. It was already visibly ineffective in new and rapidly growing areas where the flexible, lay-centred system of Methodism had early successes which multiplied later as these areas multiplied, and with them a less dutiful and less easily controlled population.

There were, in fact, many reasons why the eighteenth-century church was difficult to reform and adapt to changing conditions. Politicians did not like to stir up controversy, and some anti-clerical Whigs were more anxious to restrict than increase clerical influence. Financial help was only likely to come by redistribution of existing resources, which meant raiding the property of existing wealthy clergy. There were legal difficulties as well as vested interests militating against division of swollen dioceses and parishes. There was more church-building in the eighteenth-century than has usually been recognized, but most of this was in the shape of 'proprietary' churches financed from pew rents and not open to the poor. Moreover, reform proposals reflected traditional ideals and expectations. Thus Bishop Gibson of London in Walpole's day thought first of carrots to tempt Tory clergy to be loyal to the government. When, in the 1730s, he turned to structural reforms, he suggested changing diocesan boundaries, using suffragan bishops, redistributing incomes, and increasing the powers of church courts.[44] None of this happened, and it was all designed with the ideal of the settled parish and parish priest in mind. This was suitable to a settled, slow-moving society and to the conventional religion of the majority. But it was indeed more acceptable to the tastes and felt needs of the greater part of the nation than contemporary evangelicals of all sorts as well as later critics have generally allowed.

(b) Worship and spirituality

Assessments of the spirituality of this period have been coloured by the same partisan assumptions as have been applied to the rest of its religious life. Moreover, histories of worship and spirituality have been dominated by particularly rigid models of what is 'correct'. Indeed little serious research has been devoted to the works of private piety in this period at all. A more objective and more historically orientated view seems to be needed, which would recognize different styles of piety and the contexts in which they arise and from which they take their meaning.

So far as public worship is concerned, it is not difficult to discern from the visitation returns the frequency of some basic observances such as Sunday and daily services, sermons, eucharistic celebration and attendance.

Over seventy years ago Wickham Legg, in his *English Church Life from the Restoration to the Tractarian Movement*, sought out signs of the survival of 'Catholic' practice in this notoriously dark age: daily prayers, frequent communion, vestments and ritual. A recent much more systematic and sophisticated analysis by F.C. Mather should be the starting point for a more realistic and discriminating picture of eighteenth-century piety. Mather, for example, brings out well the regional variety and strength of conservative High Church tradition especially in some areas in the north as well as the better known examples, probably sustained by the Religious Societies, in London. The variable persistence and late eighteenth-century decline in High Church practice may well relate to social variations, as Mather suggests, and local conservatism helped to keep old traditions in being. The High Church tradition in Manchester centred on the Collegiate Church (which had a weekly communion from the 1730s against the will of its 'low' warden) seems to have established a tradition of monthly communion in all the other Manchester town churches old and new and of all shades of opinion throughout the century.[45]

The church had inherited a large stock of mediaeval buildings, and despite a surprising amount of mediaeval ornament (which testifies to the uneven and incomplete nature of the English Reformation), the prevailing taste now moved in favour of light, plainness and enlightenment rather than darkness, ornament and mystery. Whitewashed walls relieved by boards with the Ten Commandments and the Lord's Prayer at the East End and memorials to the gentlemanly dead along the walls of the church replaced images of saints. Most striking is the way in which the nave and even the chancel were packed with private pews, the best near the pulpit. Although the symbolic obscuring of the altar by massive three-decker pulpits may not have been as common as is often alleged, the churches did become more like boxes for prayer and preaching than arenas for the eucharistic mysteries.

Daily prayers were a rare survival, chiefly in cathedrals, some large town churches and a considerable number of London churches. Wednesday and Friday prayers were more common where High Church traditions and endowments persisted. Prayers at the great festivals and holy days were not uncommon.[46] But attempts to introduce more were liable to meet the plea in the country that folk had to go to work early and could not come.[47]

Communion observance in the eighteenth century has often been taken to be infrequent and a sign of 'low' views or indifference.[48] The facts are less simple and less easy to interpret than this view implies. Most cathedrals and a few town churches had a weekly eucharist, and in fact it looks as though the weekly observance in some cathedrals was actually an innovation in the late seventeenth century. The notorious 'Latitudinarian' Tillotson as Dean of Canterbury introduced a weekly eucharist there in 1683 and Chester had only had six a year in the early seventeenth century (two very recently added to commemorate James I's escapes from assassination)![49] The general pattern seems to have been for country churches to have three or four communions a year at the great festivals, while most towns had at least one church with a monthly celebration. Places with five or six celebrations were usually adding extra ones at Easter to get maximum attendance over the season. Bishop Secker's Oxford Charge of 1741 has often been quoted, urging incumbents to add a fourth celebration at Michaelmas to celebrate

harvest and optimistically hoping they would rise to a monthly eucharist.[50] Few did, unless they were keen High Churchmen like Samuel
Wesley or those who initiated the Manchester tradition.[51]

Frequent celebrations can as easily be misinterpreted in the light of
later, anachronistic ideals as infrequent ones. The Prayer Book laid
down a norm for reception of three times a year, one to be at Easter,
and this often seems to have been taken to mean that no more were
necessary. Similarly, Easter communions were always the most numerously attended. Where celebrations increased, attendance often fell.
More frequent celebrations in fact seem often to have been designed
simply to allow more to attend at least occasionally and to relieve the
clergy of large numbers on a few occasions.[52] Actual attendance numbers
vary in a bewildering fashion which defy easy explanation and should
be carefully distinguished from the number of celebrations; neither
should be seen as a simple indication of high or low views of the rite or
of seriousness in approaching it. It is very likely that the eighteenth
century did not differ much, if at all, in the incidence of frequency of
celebration from earlier periods – there is some evidence that it had a
legacy of increase since the late seventeenth century. Attendance is
another matter, for here it does seem that the high level of attendance
(at least at Easter) characteristic until the late seventeenth century had
generally fallen off. This is alleged to be due to the decay of discipline
and of the church courts – if so, it throws an interesting light on the
instincts of the laity when not coerced.[53] Earlier non-attendance may be
commoner than has sometimes been thought, and in any case was
influenced by the resistance of Catholics and Puritans for their own
reasons (disapproval of the Prayer Book) and not merely a dislike of
eucharistic worship as such.[54]

The reasons for infrequency of celebration and attendance are certainly varied and complex. They could include the reluctance of
churchwardens to pay for the elements or of parsons to subject poor
people to communion collections. Then there was the very common
belief that communion was only for the well-prepared, or at least those
beginning to take up religion in earnest, as well as fears persisting since
New Testament times that to be unprepared and careless might actually
be dangerous. The popularity of 'Week's Preparation' handbooks
fostered the impression that one must prepare carefully, and many felt
they were unable to do this. Even devout High Churchmen seem
generally to have thought 'frequent communion' meant monthly; and
one of John Wesley's sisters thought excessive frequency lessened the
effectiveness and seriousness with which the rite was received.[55] It was
against these various objections that divines of all schools of thought
from the extremely 'low' Bishop Hoadly to the most devout High

Churchmen argued, saying that the only absolutely necessary 'preparation' was to come willing to receive what Christ offered. John Wesley's sermon on 'Constant Communion' was typical in its arguments here, and not even peculiar to advanced High Churchmen. What emerges from all this is the fact that the place of the eucharist in eighteenth-century devotion was quite different from that which was developed by the nineteenth-century Tractarians and the modern Liturgical Movement. It was not seen as the norm and centre of weekly devotion but as an occasional, special and (one might say) festival occasion or one which was taken as a sign and instrument of special concern and devotion. The significance of this for interpreting the alleged 'sacramental revival' in Methodism will be considered later.[56]

Preaching was certainly the most obvious centre-piece of ordinary worship. Archbishop Tillotson (who died in 1694) enjoyed a posthumous popularity through his published sermons, which were not only popular Sunday afternoon reading but a handy source for adaptation by less talented men. Tillotson, it will be shown, deliberately set himself to emphasize plain and simple Christianity, centred on moral duty, though his celebrated sermon (almost a self-caricature) on 'His Commandments are not Grievous' should be read in the context of an attempt to persuade the worldly at least to attempt an approach to Christianity. Morality, effort, duty were the watchwords, and the fact that bishops as distant from evangelicalism as Gibson and Secker found it necessary to warn their clergy against preaching mere morality without reference to the atonement suggests that evangelical complaints about a 'religion of works' and 'Pelagianism' were not simply the product of excessive prejudice. But we shall see that there were intelligible historical and practical reasons for the emphasis on good works and duty. John Wesley (unlike most of the Anglican Evangelicals) did not despise these discourses, though Methodism added fresh passion as well as doctrine to them. Yet even the sober Bishop Butler acknowledged that reason was not enough, but rather 'reason joining with the affections which God has impressed upon the heart'.[57]

Private piety in this period remains an unstudied area. Pious people at the time still drew on the classics of an earlier period, much reprinted, though new ones also appeared. A mass of little books of devotion, often distributed by the SPCK and charity schools, were produced, which await their historian.[58] There were guides for poor men and gentlemen, and more general guides like the seventeenth-century Puritan Bishop Lewis Bayly's *Practice of Piety* and above all the anonymous High Church manual *The Whole Duty of Man*, first published in 1657. This book has often been misrepresented as a typical 'Latitudinarian' product, which it emphatically is not. It was produced from a circle originally concerned to combat excessive emphasis on justification by faith alone, taken to imply the lack of need for moral concern and effort. It was in fact admirably calculated to offer minute guidance, week by week, in the cultivation of self-examination about specific outward and inward faults. By the 1740s a *New Whole Duty* was produced to remedy what was felt to be its dangerous lack of doctrinal guidance. Then, in 1763, the Evangelical Henry Venn produced his *Complete Duty of Man*, to lay a 'proper foundation' of grace and faith; but it must be said that however successful he was in doing this, as a detailed guide to meditation and morality it was greatly inferior to the original. John Wesley was again the odd man out in printing a condensed version of the old *Whole Duty* with a preface implicitly rejecting Evangelical criticisms of it.[59]

Traditional pictures of the eighteenth century as an age divided between men of taste and the gin-soaked mob tended to ignore the importance of the respectable middling ranks of tradesmen and self-improving artisans. These produced an increasing reading public often seriously if sporadically concerned with religion. The diary of the Sussex tradesman Thomas Turner is very revealing of a man involved in local administration and the small beer of parish life. Or rather, not so small beer, for Turner, like many of his contemporaries, drank too often and too well, but unlike others frequently repented of his vice and spent sober Sunday afternoons with Tillotson and the *Whole Duty*. His incidental reflections on his life show his religion to be a reality.[60] It is curious to note that at the other end of England a very similar pattern emerges in the diary of a Manchester wig-maker: drinking to excess, repentance and serious reading, though in his case from the more distinctively High Church authors natural to that town.[61] Dr Johnson recalled how his mother, the wife of a provincial bookseller, told him at the age of three of 'two places, to which the inhabitants of this world were received after death, one a fine place filled with happiness, called heaven; the other a sad place, called hell'.[62] We shall see how many future Methodists had a firm religious upbringing.

Much of the devotional literature read in this period (like the *Whole Duty*) seems to be the product of a diffused High Church or Puritan piety. The most famous of the newer works was the Nonjuror William Law's *Serious Call to a Devout and Holy Life*, which was admired by men as diverse as Gibbon, Johnson and John Wesley. It was written in a pleasing style and enlivened by character-sketches of various types of religious or worldly people. Though commonly seen as an exception to conventional religion of the period, it is marked by the same concern for 'reasonableness' and 'duty', but in the service of a highly ascetic life. Indeed the most serious criticism of it is that it was too obviously fitted only for people of leisure and independent means. Law himself was financially supported by two devout ladies and later became a channel for the theosophic mysticism of Jakob Böhme.

One of Law's contemporaries was the engaging figure of the genial giant, John Byrom of Manchester. He was the inventor of a shorthand system used by the Wesleys, a minor poet ('Christians Awake'), and a compulsive student of mystical writers. His circle in London and Manchester included people as various as Methodists and Deists.[63] His correspondence and diaries reveal an unexpected category of those – some dilettante, some more serious – with similar religious tastes. To a degree still not fully explored there existed a kind of theosophic 'underground' feeding on Behmenist and Quietist ideas which influenced some of the more wayward spirits of the Revival and, more directly, formed an audience later for Swedenborgianism.[64]

One important aspect of early eighteenth-century piety was the development of the devotional Religious Societies which were mentioned earlier. These developed as early as 1678 and survived into the 1730s as recruiting grounds and reception points for the Revival. By then they had spread from London to the provinces.[65] As originally developed in the 1670s they seem to have arisen from the need felt by pious London tradesmen and apprentices for something more than public worship and purely individual piety, and at first helped to fortify the church against the feared inroads of Popery. They met under clerical supervision to read good books, say prayers, attend communion frequently and collect for charity. Personal problem-sharing was optional. That they continued even after Methodism had colonized many of their members shows that they had their own distinctive appeal and were not simply part of the prehistory of Methodism.[66]

Finally, there was a world beyond the formal beliefs and provisions of the church which still awaits a historian to continue the story revealed up to 1700 in Keith Thomas's classic *Religion and the Decline of Magic*. It is already clear that this world of folklore, magic and traditional beliefs and practices attached to conventional Christianity survived the impact of science and enlightenment. If this was partly at the cost of sinking from being part of the mental world of the educated and uneducated alike to being confined to the lower orders (as has been suggested), this is not the whole story.[67] Certainly evangelicalism at all levels was characterized by a revived sense of the supernatural. We shall see that in some areas (notably Cornwall) and at some social levels the Revival fed on, and at the same time partially refined, the traditional world of the supernatural among those it converted. Those convulsed by fears of hell in the early days of the Revival were probably having awakened into vivid life doctrines which were still part of the conventional framework of belief. After all, they were still not far away from a century soaked in religious propaganda and sectarian conflict. Religious observances, however conventional, were still practised by the greater part of the population, and religious publications, as in the previous century, were a substantial part of total publishing.[68] A recent writer has warned that the historian's temptation to concentrate on change and early signs of 'modernity' tends to obscure the persistence of more traditional and customary modes of thinking.[69] Belief in the supernatural even among the educated classes was by no means dead; nor was hell, despite the gradual increase of private doubts about it and the cooling of its fires.

Both the minority response to the Revival and the majority rejection of it testify to the fact that this was still a religious age. What its critics have complained about is really that its religion was not to their taste.

(c) Theology

What was the condition and nature of Anglican theology at the beginning of the Revival in the 1730s? To characterize it as 'Latitudinarian' in blanket terms is inadequate. Nor was the theology of the time exclusively occupied with the Deist controversy, as unwary readers may be led to suppose. It is better to think of a spectrum of traditions ranging from High Church attitudes inherited from the seventeenth century (some more extreme, some less); through more moderate men, whose relaxed and comprehensive notions of Christianity became more common over time; and so to the minority of Deistic extremists who, if small in numbers, were large in a capacity to alarm the more 'orthodox'. By the 1740s, of course, there would have to be added to these the new school of evangelicals readily labelled 'Methodist' indiscriminately by their critics. A moderate High Churchmanship was common among the lower clergy at least in the early years of the century and, as we have seen, pockets of mystical piety also existed.

'Latitudinarian' is a vague term and changed its value over time. As it appeared in the 1660s in *A New Sect of Latitude Men* by 'S.P.' (probably Symon Patrick), it offered a plea for concentration on essentials and toleration on other matters; a taste for the benefits of science and reason but also for episcopacy and the beauties of the English Liturgy. Doctrinal authority was to be found in a balance of scripture, reason and the Fathers. Freewill was upheld against predestination.[70] Clearly this attitude was conditioned by a reaction against the warring sects of the recent Puritan régime. At this stage, too, there was an affinity with the Cambridge Platonist group.[71] That group's watchword of 'reason' as the 'candle of the Lord' which judges natural and revealed religion had a mystical quality associated with the guidance of the Holy Spirit within the soul. But in the longer run the 'candle' of reason became a purely 'natural' quality.

Reflecting this change in a more general way, 'Latitudinarian' in the eighteenth century came to be a term applied to those who stressed reason as the touchstone of Christian truth with morality as its content; a reduced notion of 'essential' doctrines, playing down the more mysterious, more controversial and less 'practical' doctrines; and a broadly tolerant attitude to theological differences and to Dissent. Often they were suspected of being unorthodox on doctrines such as the Trinity and person of Christ, as well as having 'low' views on the sacraments.

Among the more notorious exponents of this simplified Christianity were Archbishop Tillotson, the philosopher John Locke and Bishop Hoadly, Whig place-seeker, hammer of Nonjurors and author of a notoriously 'Zwinglian' work on the Lord's Supper. Hoadly's sermon on 'Christ's Kingdom Not of this World' seemed to teach so low a view of the church as to reduce it to a creature of the state, and the row over this led to the suspension of active Convocations, but there is more to be said for him than is usually allowed.[72]

It is clear that Tillotson and Locke, however much they stressed the necessity for Christianity to be 'reasonable', still believed in the fact and necessity of special revelation through the Bible for things we could not know by reason alone. Thus Tillotson told his biographer Thomas Birch 'that Christianity, as to the practical part of it was nothing else but the religion of nature, or pure morality, save only praying and making our addresses to God in the name and through the mediation of our Saviour and the use of the two sacraments'. When he chose to do so he was perfectly able to assert the necessity of the atonement, grace and faith for salvation, but he chose in his much-read sermons to stress practical morality.[73] Locke, in his *Reasonableness of Christianity* (1695), reduced it to a few essentials. We believe in Jesus as Messiah on the evidence of fulfilled prophecy and his working of miracles. Especially revealing is his definition of 'faith' as 'a firm assent of the mind', 'belief in Jesus as the Messiah'. Salvation is obtained by those who 'make a sincere endeavour after righteousness by obeying God's law'. This faith in Christ is counted in place of perfect obedience, and the work of Christ makes up what is lacking in our own efforts.[74] This view of grace, faith and works reflects a significant shift away from the Protestant Reformation doctrine of justification: it was widely held in the eighteenth century, as we shall see, and the Revival was fundamentally opposed to it, though John Wesley's attitude here was more equivocal in the long run.

There is, at first sight, a strong contrast between this minimalizing and reduced view of traditional doctrine and that of the High Churchmen. This term, too, is subject to variation and abuse. At root it meant 'extreme' – in terms of a stance in which religion and politics were fused together, though distinctive theological positions can be discerned. High Churchmen, especially in the early eighteenth century, were marked by extreme claims for the rights of the church and clergy, for example in Convocation; for restrictions on Dissent; for 'passive obedience and non-resistance' towards the monarch, though on this last of course the deposition of James II had divided and confused their loyalties. If some were Jacobites in their hearts, some transferred similar sentiments to the Hanoverian dynasty in the end. In varying degrees they stressed the apostolic succession as the source of authority of the episcopate; a priestly quality in the ministry; a sacrificial element as well as a real presence in the eucharist; the birth of the Christian in baptismal regeneration. An ascetic piety and relatively frequent communion and sometimes the practice of confession, together with a special reverence for the teaching and practice of the 'primitive' church of the first five centuries, were other marks, taken to the greatest extremes by Nonjurors and those close to them. High Church views, to a greater or lesser extent, were perhaps the most prevalent sentiments among the lower clergy in the early eighteenth century; they were strongly marked in the early career of John Wesley as they were in his father and brothers; and his mother at least was a Jacobite. Wesley's original pursuit of 'primitive Christianity' was very much in the High Church and indeed Nonjuror mode.[75] The High Church tradition persisted even later in the century more commonly than has often been recognized, and as has already been suggested it continued, if in attenuated forms, to colour devotional literature.[76]

That traditional theology still had life in it is shown by the work of a man like Daniel Waterland (d. 1740), who may be classed as a moderate High Churchman (though some would label him 'central'). He wrote a number of works on the eucharist with an impressive command of ancient and modern learning. To read Waterland's footnotes is to realize the existence and persistence of a whole world of forgotten theologians, concerned with very different issues from those which obsessed the fashionable Deists and their critics, and makes one wonder how much we really know of the staple fare of reading clergymen of the period. Waterland produced a well-argued case for an Anglican way on eucharistic doctrine, avoiding the extremes of Rome and the Zwinglians as well as those of the more quirky Nonjurors. At the end of his life he produced an equally balanced treatment of justification, apparently with the Methodists in mind.[77]

The least conspicuous type of Anglican theology in this period until the Revival began was that inherited from seventeenth-century

Calvinism and Puritanism. Calvinism had, in one form or another, been the prevailing Anglican mode in the early seventeenth century, and Puritan sentiments had survived within the church even after the great ejection of 1662. But these traditions seemed to their few early eighteenth-century adherents within the church to be out of fashion, surviving only among a beleaguered and dwindling minority; and the Revival did not in fact originate with them. John Wesley was an Arminian High Churchman, and Whitefield and other evangelical Calvinists had to learn their creed afresh.[78]

Anglican beliefs about justification by faith and the role of works in salvation require further comment, since these became key issues between the new evangelicals and the rest of the church. The evangelical charge was that the bulk of the clergy and laity had sunk into 'Pelagianism', meaning that they trusted in their own efforts for salvation instead of the grace of God by faith alone. This was too simplistic, yet it did point to a tendency deplored and condemned by a number of non-evangelical bishops and others. As early as 1716 a Dr Bisse claimed that 'of late years a caution has been dinned into the ears of the clergy that they would do well to let alone the doctrinal and mysterious parts of religion, as nice, useless and oftentimes contentious speculation, and instead thereof to preach to the people only good, plain, practical morality . . . enforcing such from the reasonableness and nature of things'.[79] In the 1730s Bishop Gibson felt he was fighting on three fronts: against those rejecting special revelation; those 'trusting in Christ as their whole duty and so excusing themselves from the moral law'; and those who 'affirm that observance of the law is sufficient and so will forego the benefit of Christ's redemption'. His own teaching was that 'faith in Christ is the foundation of a Christian's *title* to heaven' but that 'repentance and good works are necessary conditions of *obtaining* it.'[80] In 1758 Archbishop Secker (who dwelt much on moral duties in his own sermons) complained that the clergy neglected distinctive Christian belief. 'While we urge on our hearers the necessity of universal holiness, we must urge equally that of the being "found in Christ, not having our own righteousness but Christ's by faith".'[81]

From his new evangelical perspective in 1739 John Wesley said he differed from those clergy who speak of justification 'as the same thing with sanctification' or speak of our own holiness or good works as the cause of our justification, or see sanctification in merely outward terms.[82] James Rogers, before his conversion to Methodism, recalled how he discussed salvation with his friends. The general opinion was that at the day of judgment we were judged by the balance of our good deeds over our bad ones. Others thought that 'God was merciful and had sent His Son to die for sinners, and that the best way would be to amend their lives and do all they could, and Christ would make up the rest'. The parson of the parish agreed.[83] Biassed though these sources are, the bishops' complaints suggest they have a ring of truth as reflecting common sentiments. To a dying relative anxious about her soul, the virtuous Lord Egmont urged that she should think of Christ's dying for us 'and that we are able to apply his merits to ourselves by faith in Him which she could do as having lived so good a life'.[84] The artist Thomas Gainsborough probably spoke for many when he remarked that 'I trust if I do my best, all will be well through the merits of Christ who hath promised to make good our failings if we try sincerely'.[85] It is not surprising that an elderly Whitefield convert, a churchwarden, found 'the new birth, the want of free will in us to do good works without the special grace of God and the like' was a 'new language', though he later found it in 'an old exposition of the Catechism, the Church Articles and the Book of Homilies'.[86] So, at more sophisticated as well as less sophisticated levels, the old Reformation doctrine of justification by grace through faith had been eroded into a variable balance between grace and works. At its most sophisticated, there is the work of Bishop Bull in the later seventeenth century, who in effect produced a version of the Council of Trent's view of these matters – strongly attacked by John Wesley later.[87] Most clergymen probably also saw the Christian life as a gradual product of religious nurture, for High Churchmen the 'new birth' being the washing away of original sin in baptism. To speak of a sudden 'new birth' and conversion later in life seemed to them to deny the baptismal work of grace and dangerously to underplay the need of constant good works.

How had this situation come about since the Reformation? C.F. Allison, in a rather neglected book on *The Rise of Moralism*, has drawn attention to the dry and intricate niceties of the seventeenth-century doctrinal debate on justification. Here he sees two schools of Anglican thought in conflict over the 'formal cause' of justification; this ultimately resulted in a separation of doctrine and morality and thus in a 'rise of moralism' which 'masqueraded as faith'. He sees this development as destroying a 'classical' Anglican balance or synthesis of doctrine and morality, faith and works – an aspect, too, of T.S. Eliot's famous late seventeenth-century 'dissociation of sensibility'. One may, perhaps, doubt the 'synthesis', which owes more to later perceptions of what counts as the true 'spirit of Anglicanism' than to seventeenth-century realities which to the historian look more like rival parties struggling to control the Establishment, with one form of 'Anglicanism' finally winning.[88]

Moreover, although the technical debates described by Allison were real enough to the participants, and continued a conflict which has

Augustinian and mediaeval as well as Reformation roots and became a
live issue once again (using some of the same traditional terms) during
the Revival, it may be doubted whether the change described can be
explained simply in terms of scholastic debates. More potent were the
effects of such indecisive debates in convincing an increasing number of
people that they were profitless and even dangerous, not least among
the lower orders. Here the crucial factor was the experience of the
Interregnum, when sectarianism seemed to have run rife and excessive
stress on salvation by faith had led to a neglect of practical morality
with dire results, religious and social as well as moral. If theologians
justified a reaction against this in technical terms, plain preachers of
morality like Tillotson conveyed the message in a simpler, more direct
fashion. It may be surmised that once the exacting doctrinal screws of
pure Reformation doctrine were slackened, many people reverted to the
kind of commonsense view of decent effort made up by a merciful God
as sufficing for salvation which was reflected among Rogers' friends. In
a curious way the High Church reaction against Calvinist antinomianism as reflected in the *Whole Duty* coincided in its practical emphasis on
'works' with the Latitudinarian simplifications of Tillotson and the
ethical instincts of the laity. All gravitated gradually towards a common
concern for morality without mysteries and a religion on which men
could agree: a religion which would also reunite a church and nation
riven with dissension for generations. Indeed, one can hardly over-
emphasize the extent to which the seventeenth-century horrors haunted
the inherited memories and fed the fears of eighteenth-century people.
As late as the 1790s the old war-cries of 'Church and King' and
'Down with the Rump' current in the 1650s could be repeated against
Dissenters.

Tillotson, who had grown up during the mid-seventeenth-century
crisis, is a good example of its effects. He thought that theological
uncertainties had driven people to the false securities of Popery. The
proper response was to stress the 'reasonableness' of Protestantism and
to avoid speculation about 'sublime mysteries' like the Trinity and
person of Christ. Above all, 'the great design of Christianity was the
refining men's natures, and governing their actions, the restraining their
appetites and passions'. Birch says that Tillotson saw Christian doctrine
as 'a system of principles all tending to this'.[89] When evangelicals like
Whitefield condemned this as no better than Mahometanism it did them
no good, since Tillotson had become required reading for the devout.[90]

Some critics thought that the trend to 'bare heathen morality' had a
specific origin in the reaction against the antinomian tendencies of the
Interregnum when faith was preached up to the exclusion of works: so
thought Gibson, Secker and, later, Wilberforce.[91] This was certainly the

original context of the *Whole Duty of Man*, and it was changing times and different dangers which led to criticisms of it later (see above, p. 22).

The trend towards emphasizing reason, 'natural religion' and morality was no doubt also reinforced by the achievements of science and philosophy in the seventeenth century. Newton and Locke and their popularizers seemed to have produced a clearer, more plausible, more certain picture of the workings of the universe and the workings of the human mind than the wrangling of the theologians over insoluble mysteries. Devout scientists and divines (and not a few men combined both roles) saw these discoveries as illuminating God's activities and enhancing his glory, yet they also created problems for traditional theology. Regularity and law made a personal providence and miracle more problematical. If reason brought clarity and enlightenment, revelation seemed to offer mysteries insoluble by theologians and not always of obvious use. To an important degree the philosophers of the seventeenth century had been engaged in a search for certainty in knowledge and had seemed to achieve it by defining the degrees of certainty and knowledge appropriate to various aspects of experience and reality.[92] It is significant that Locke's apparently purely philosophical work on epistemology in his *Essay* should have been provoked by a discussion among friends with a view to finding a basis for the 'principles of morality and revealed religion'.[93] We have seen how his *Reasonableness of Christianity* reduced it to plain simplicity, though based on an interpretation of the Bible and defending special revelation. To do this, and to assert reason as a test for revelation (bearing in mind the 'revelations' of the fanatics of his youth) Locke had to allow for truths 'beyond' reason.[94]

The religious and intellectual pressures of the time, in short, affected the evaluation of two abiding concerns of the religious mind: the quest for a sure knowledge of God and religious truth which was now weighted heavily in favour of what was 'natural' and 'reasonable'; and the quest for a sure knowledge of the way of salvation, now weighted heavily in favour of morality. Both tendencies were liable in some minds to lead to a discounting of 'mystery' and distinctiveness in Christianity. The orthodox nevertheless clung to special revelation and the special work of Christ in salvation, and supported these claims by appealing to Christ's miracles and the fulfilment of prophecy. It was only the radical minority of 'Deists' who denied the truth of these 'proofs' of the Bible and saw the Bible itself as fallible and its 'revelation' as at best a 'republication' of the immemorial, unchanging 'natural religion' which is known to all men if their minds are not corrupted by bad nurture and the deceitful wiles of scheming priests. Behind such notions lay ultimately an optimistic, benevolent reading of the nature of God, an implicit denial of original sin in favour of man's natural goodness. It followed that the traditional reading of the need for the sacrificial death and atonement of Christ was unnecessary as well as morally dubious. Notions of his divinity and therefore of the Trinity were incredible, and in a law-bound universe miracles, let alone the resurrection of Christ, were incredible. Though small in numbers, these radicals caused great alarm and there were many attempts to disprove their case. They were, after all, challenging fundamentals of Christianity which had been common ground to the warring Catholics and Protestants. This is why the Deist controversy and the need to fight it in terms of its own rational tone coloured so much of the controversial theology of the period and has led historians to overlook the persistence of more traditional themes.

It has also been suggested that Deism and other types of rationalizing, moralizing theology in the early eighteenth century have a social and political significance.[95] A certain parallel can be seen between the spectrum of religious attitudes on the one hand and social and political ones on the other. For example, the most extreme High Churchmen and Nonjurors were politically inclined to divine right Jacobitism and an important role for the clergy in society. The Deists were politically ranked among the more extreme Whigs: more hostile to the power of the monarchy and strongly lay and anti-clerical. In between, the 'Latitudinarian' divines and men like Newton were aware of a relationship between the law-bound world of nature; a moderate, rational and moral religion; and an orderly, stable political system. Late in the eighteenth century Tom Paine's vulgarized version of Deism was attractive to the same radicals who liked his politics. One cannot press such an analysis too far (what can one make of the deistic but Jacobite Bolingbroke?). But politics and religion ran in close harness in this age, and the social as well as political divisions between High Churchmen, Latitudinarians and Dissenters were equally marked. However, just as one aspect of the eighteenth century was a search for political stability, so another was a search for religious stability and peace in what has been called a 'civic religion', a lowest common denominator on which all could agree and which would banish the spectres of the past. The Revival was savagely attacked at least partly because it seemed to raise those spectres again and to by-pass or deny the appeals to common reason and morality into the bargain.[96]

It is within this larger context that the particular question of Deism should be viewed, for this rocked the boat alarmingly in the opposite direction. It seemed like a caricature of what in more moderate men was combined with a degree of traditional appeal to revelation, the work of grace and the supernatural power of God. It is notoriously difficult to define a body of men who did not form a sect or party and whose very name was often no more than a term of abuse.[97] Yet the brief summary of the nature of their challenge given earlier (above, p. 30) seems to me to represent the essential tendency of the writers usually labelled in this way. It is also worth observing that the weight of traditional accounts ascribing victory to the 'orthodox' champions mainly on the grounds of superior qualities of argument and the notion that Deism then suddenly collapsed, perhaps at the blast of Bishop Butler's trumpet in his *Analogy of Religion* (1736), overstate the case. Certainly William Law, Butler and Berkeley in very different ways raised the argument above the pedestrian 'Old Bailey' theology (of which Dr Johnson complained) – a theology in which the 'evidences' of miracle and prophecy were tediously deployed and defended on the credit of the apostles. But the Deists did not simply fade away; nor were all their arguments manifestly inferior to those of their opponents. They made damaging points about the credibility of the Bible; the inconsistency of believing biblical miracles and disbelieving most others; the moral problems raised by traditional views of the atonement (though for reasons of social security they tended to shrink from a too enthusiastic denial of the ultimate sanction of hell). Anthony Collins partially anticipated Hume and others on the fundamental question of the difficulties of basing revelation on the uncertainties of history. If the orthodox retained a stronger and more realistic sense of the tragic and 'fallen' qualities of human nature on which the traditional 'plan of salvation' rested, the Deists invoked a powerful sense of the benevolence of God which was too often clouded over in the cruel arbitrariness of some traditional presentations.[98] It may be added that one powerful argument in favour of eighteenth-century English religion as a whole is that despite limitations and prejudices it became strikingly more tolerant than in the previous two centuries. The Smithfield fires were not re-lighted, and Tyburn was reserved for secular crimes. As one historian has remarked, Englishmen 'may have become less religious but also more Christian'.[99]

Finally, the relationship between 'Enlightenment' and 'Revival' in this period is more complex than is allowed for by simple notions of the latter being a 'reaction' against the former. Evangelicals and their historians encouraged this picture of stark contrast, but they had more common ground with the reasonable, moral Christianity of their day than they liked to recognize. They accepted the same 'evidences' against the infidel Deists, and 'Latitudinarians' like Locke and Watson were not only concerned to defend revelation but believed that they were drawing their Christianity from a 'reasonable' reading of Scripture and not from reason alone.[100] No English evangelical approached the achievement of the American Jonathan Edwards, who drew on Locke as well as Calvin to construct a picture of God, the world, man and the way of salvation which continues to impress by its intellectual virtuosity. The English evangelicals drew more on the 'practical piety' of the Puritans. But strong though their revulsion was against 'works' religion, they did not escape the accents of their time.

This was most conspicuously true of John Wesley, who in many ways was not a typical 'evangelical' at all and became less so as he grew older. In strictly philosophical terms we shall see that he was an empiricist disciple of Locke even though with some important limitations. In religious terms his idea of 'perfection' has been described as an expression of the 'optimism of grace', though Calvinists thought him little better than a Pelagian man of 'works'. Like his Latitudinarian contemporaries, Wesley wanted to concentrate on a few agreed truths of Christianity with toleration of differences on other matters. His view of what constituted conformity to the Church of England was in the end a long way from the stiff High Churchmanship of his youth. His views on toleration were thoroughly those of his time. In what follows we shall be studying the paradox of a man who had absorbed some of the values and style of an 'age of reason', but used them to defend a supernaturalist view of the world which went well beyond what was generally acceptable to his educated contemporaries. He was a 'reasonable enthusiast', combining religious values in some ways as radical as anything in the sixteenth-century Anabaptists and seventeenth-century Puritan Separatists with aspects of High Church piety, and clothing the whole in the language of Locke as well as that of the Bible.

(ii) Dissent

The more remote origins of English Dissent lay in the circumstances of the sixteenth-century Reformation and the divisive views it produced of what a properly constituted, reformed Protestant church should be.[101] Right up to 1662 and in some respects until 1689, the final form of the Established Church of England had not been settled, but was the subject of recurring disputes and the changing fortunes of various parties. In so far as the Civil Wars of the 1640s were fought about religion (and much else was involved), it was the proper shape of the church's government, doctrine and worship which was at stake. By the 1640s what is loosely called 'Puritanism' had produced some who wanted to remove the 'rags of Popery' from the Prayer Book and to develop a more pastoral episcopate; while others wanted to abolish both in favour of an established Presbyterian hierarchy. Others again preferred to separate from the Establishment altogether and establish 'gathered' churches of true believers on Congregationalist or Baptist principles. In the aftermath of the Civil War new sects proliferated, the main later survivor being the

Quakers, devotees of the Inner Light, though also vigorous evangelizers with a strong sense of community.

When, after the failure of political and religious experiments by 1660, the monarchy was restored, and with it episcopacy and the Prayer Book, nearly 2,000 ministers resigned or were expelled. Vigorous attempts were made to compel all to conform to the restored church by law and persecution, though there were also abortive attempts by Charles II to allow Catholic and deviant Protestant worship by royal prerogative, and schemes were canvassed to relax the establishment's requirements sufficiently to 'comprehend' some of the dissidents within it. A final attempt at 'comprehension' was made in 1688/89 on the accession of William III and Mary, together with toleration for those unwilling to comply. The failure of the 'comprehension' half of the scheme meant that the so-called Toleration Act of 1689 produced a much larger body of Dissent than had been expected or intended.

The Act of 1689 may be seen as a triumph for Dissent in the sense that it was an acknowledgment that it had become impossible to incorporate all the English people in one church. This was partly the result of the Dissenters refusing to conform; partly a reward for supporting the Glorious Revolution of 1688; partly from a sense that it was politically safer and perhaps more profitable to tolerate them and from a slow increase in the principles of toleration for its own sake.[102] But the grant of toleration was also the mark of a defeat, especially for Presbyterians and others who had hoped to capture and remould English religion and indeed the social order, and had had no intention of tolerating the sects either. This defeat and the very limited terms of toleration marked the beginnings (or perhaps rather the final confirmation and consolidation) of religious, social and political divisions in England which would have a considerable influence on its later history, as well as helping to determine the shape and fate of the Evangelical Revival.

Toleration was only intended to apply to separate worship by Trinitarian Protestants, under various conditions. Only the penalties of the penal laws were suspended, not the laws themselves – a symbol of Anglican hegemony. Dissenters were kept out of the universities, and receiving the Anglican sacrament remained a test for crown and civic office in corporate towns. Under High Church Tory ministries in Anne's reign an attempt was made to stop 'occasional conformity' (taking the sacrament for office but continuing Dissenting worship) and to restrict Dissenting education to an elementary and artisan level. Although these Acts were repealed under George I, the intention – to reduce Dissent to a dwindling, low-class minority – was clear. In fact the social stigmas and limitations, the sense of belonging to a defeated party, ensured that those sections of the aristocracy and gentry who had supported them and split the ruling class in the mid-seventeenth century soon deserted their ranks.

Few Dissenters became members of Parliament – though there was no legal bar here, they usually lacked the necessary landed wealth and connections.[103] In some corporations they did better. They are said to have dominated Bridgewater for generations and were prominent also in Bristol and Norwich, where the meeting house had brackets for the civic mace.[104] Though no town was dominated by Dissenting voters, it appears that in some they were sufficiently important to be courted by MPs.[105] But attempts to repeal the Tests, culminating in a public campaign in 1787–90, failed, and the 1790s saw a fierce Anglican and Tory backlash (see below, p. 320).

The actual numbers of Dissenters remain a matter for speculation and guesswork except for estimates based on a survey and other information available just before 1720. A recent calculation based on this material has produced a total of 338,120 (some 6% of the population), but very unevenly distributed both in terms of Dissent as a whole and of its constituent denominations. Dissenters made up nearly 20% of the population of Bristol, but less than 2% in Shropshire.[106] These variations appear to be due to long-standing patterns derived from events and fortunes as far back as the sixteenth century and perhaps even earlier in some cases. Once fixed, they remained for generations, and Dissent became a static, ingrown, hereditary (though also declining) creed. The fact of decline seems certain, though impossible to quantify exactly. Estimates for the 1740s suggest anything from 150,000 to 250,000, with a hard core perhaps much smaller.[107] Its strength is generally held to have been in towns and among the commercial and industrial classes, and though some have emphasized that it had also a considerable rural following, the urban proportion of Dissent was well above the overall urban proportion of the population and scattered rural Dissent was very vulnerable to losses.[108]

Although there was considerable variety in the social composition of congregations in different places, the range was essentially within the middling ranks of society and down into the skilled artisans, with some farmers and craftsmen in rural areas, but mere labourers were not common among them. The Presbyterians were the most numerous body in the early eighteenth century, and long remained the most wealthy and influential. Next came the Independents, while the two sorts of Baptists (Calvinistic and 'General' or Arminian) contained more of humbler rank, including some ministers who also had secular occupations. Some Quakers had notoriously prospered in banking, brewing and industry, though there were humbler members too. A wealthy city

Presbyterian chapel might support a minister as comfortably as a good many Anglican clergy, but rural ministers might have to supplement their incomes with teaching or medicine.[109] There has been speculation since Max Weber on the alleged connection between Protestantism and the rise of capitalism, and Weber's notion of ascetic Calvinist virtues feeding the capitalist spirit has been extended to explain the alleged prominence of Dissent in the rise of industrialization. Was it something to do with their education in the 'modernizing' Academies; or their childhood upbringing? Or was it, perhaps more plausibly, the fact that commerce and industry were among the few occupations open to them and that success was reinforced by their tight family and chapel networks?[110]

Though to some extent united by a shared second-class citizenship and antipathy to the Established Church, and able to act together (for example through the lay 'Dissenting Deputies') for legal defence of its liberties, Dissent was not a unified force, and eighteenth-century developments tended to divide it further. All of them except the Quakers tended to centre life in the local church – even the English Presbyterians had failed to sustain the kind of national and regional hierarchy familiar in Scotland. County and regional associations for consultation, some of them merging Presbyterians and Independents, did exist, but local churches jealously guarded their autonomy.[111]

Doctrine was what divided them most. A London 'Happy Union' of Presbyterians and Independents in the 1690s soon broke up over an antinomian controversy, and in 1718–19 a conference at Salter's Hall in London over suspicions of heresy on the person of Christ and so on the Trinity revealed a division which proved prophetic of things to come.[112]

When they were asked at Salter's Hall to subscribe to 'orthodox' formulas, it was noticeable that the majority of Independents and Particular (Calvinistic) Baptists did so, but the majority of Presbyterians and General Baptists did not. Although this reflected in part an old tradition of reluctance to subscribe to anything beyond the words of Scripture, it has generally been thought significant that it was mainly the non-subscribing denominations which were now to move into anti-trinitarianism, denial of a penal substitutionary atonement and an optimistic view of human nature as against the dark doctrine of original sin. Various suggestions have been made to account for this. Presbyterian churches were subject to ministers and trustees, but Independents to their church meetings. Learned Presbyterian ministers were perhaps 'infected' by heterodoxy in Scottish and Dutch universities as well as in their academies. Certainly Baptists and Independents were very prone to lay down strict doctrinal and practical guidelines for their members.[113] It is also noticeable that a number of heterodox Presbyterian chapels suffered secessions of members who then founded severely orthodox and Calvinistic Independent churches, a number of which developed evangelical convictions later (see below p. 326).

The initial reaction to the Revival by Dissenting ministers was generally as hostile as that of their establishment counterparts, though this was not always true of their humbler members. Dissenting worship is indeed often seen as being as dull, its sermons as dry and moralistic as those of the Church of England without the redeeming glories of the Prayer Book. Matthew Henry's routine at Chester in the early eighteenth-century may be typical. In the morning: Psalm 100, a 'short' prayer, reading and exposition of the Old Testament, another psalm, a 'long' prayer (up to half an hour), an hour's sermon, more prayers, singing and a blessing. In the afternoon the same except for reading and exposition of the New Testament.[114] The Puritan custom of a weekday 'lecture' or exposition of Scripture continued in some places, and a monthly communion was preceded by a service of preparation in the old style.[115] It is well known that the introduction of hymns alongside metrical psalms was controversial, since the former were seen as 'human' compositions, though the seductive songs of Isaac Watts eventually won their way and were adopted by the evangelicals of all parties. Discipline, except among Presbyterians, was often severe, and members could be expelled for heresy, immorality and marrying out of the society, and bankrupts were suspect, particularly among the Quakers.

Watts and Philip Doddridge have often been cited as exceptions to the dullness of eighteenth-century Dissent and as examples of the survival of something of the old Puritan virtues, a bridge from Puritan to evangelical piety.[116] Watts was a considerable scholar as well as hymn writer; Doddridge an attractive personality, minister and Dissenting tutor, and ecumenical in his range of personal relationships and supporters. Watts was reserved and indeed hostile to the new Methodists and Moravians, but Doddridge had friendly relationships with them, though he suffered losses to them from his own church. Like Richard Baxter's before him, Doddridge's orthodoxy was suspect in some quarters, but Roger Thomas has happily described him as a man who was 'moderately orthodox' – 'where the moderation consists not so much in a reduced orthodoxy as in a reduced dogmatism'.[117] It is not surprising that he should have had friendly relationships with that other 'moderately orthodox' man, John Wesley.

The Dissent of this period has suffered from uneven coverage by historians, their views much coloured by the long-term consequences of the religious changes they were describing. Some of the best, it has been pointed out, were of the Presbyterian-Unitarian tradition and tended to concentrate on 'rational' Dissent and its more 'modernizing' tendencies.[118] But there was more to Dissent than heterodoxy or pernickety orthodoxy. Geoffrey Nuttall has pointed out that some of the ministers, and more of the ordinary laity, lived uneasily with the decay of the old Puritan imperatives to personal salvation. Some found their way to evangelical-type conversion independently of the new Methodists; some welcomed them when they arrived. The impact of the Revival on the old Dissent was indeed very complex and not confined to its later stages. Michael Watts has remarked that although the Revival in England and Wales began in the Established Church, it was Dissent that benefitted most from it in the end.[119] But the shadow of the seventeenth century lay as heavily over Dissent as over the Church of England. Free-ranging evangelism was difficult for bodies under legal limitations, without the respectable and self-assured place in society of Anglican clergy, and with dark smears of 'enthusiasm' and 'republicanism' all too easily sticking to them. It is not surprising that John Wesley, a High Churchman and the son of a High Churchman (though the grandson of Dissenters on both sides), should have had a lifelong distaste for Dissent, for what he saw as a hole-in-the-corner, static, localized form of religion, tainted by heterodoxy and disloyalty (see below pp. 308f.).

(iii) Roman Catholicism

The history of Roman Catholicism in England during the eighteenth century has tended to be neglected by historians attracted by the martyrs of the sixteenth century or the spectacular results of the Irish immigration of the nineteenth. But fresh perspectives on the period are beginning to appear, and despite the small numbers of the Catholic community and its deprived status, it is of more importance for the study of English religion in this period (including the Revival) than appears at first sight.[120]

The 'old religion' of England had indeed been pruned down to small dimensions, very uneven in distribution, as a result of the Protestant triumph. Yet during the sixteenth and seventeenth centuries this minority had usually been regarded with fear and horror by Protestant Englishmen and subjected to severe restrictions in law and savage persecution in practice, though in an erratic way. The reasons for this were partly religious, partly political, though in the case of Catholicism these two motives were peculiarly and tragically entwined with each other. Religiously, Protestants had mostly regarded Catholicism as a horrid perversion of Christianity; politically, it was regarded with the darkest suspicion not only because all religious deviation was a form of disloyalty but also because Catholics owed allegiance to that 'foreign potentate', the Pope. Had he not excommunicated Queen Elizabeth and invited her subjects to rebel against her, stirred up foreign invaders and taught that Catholics need not keep faith with heretics? Foxe's *Book of Martyrs* and tales of the Inquisition burned an indelible image of Catholicism in the English imagination as a heretical, cruel and treasonable religion.

These fears were repeatedly refreshed during the seventeenth century by religious or partly religious wars, the sufferings of continental Protestants and the erratic religious behaviour of the Stuart kings. They were seen as 'soft' on Catholics, favoured them at court, intermarried with them. Charles I's Archbishop Laud seemed to be infiltrating popish practices into the Church of England; Charles II wished to tolerate them; James II was an open Catholic who seemed bent on subverting the Protestant establishment as well as exercising arbitrary power like his French contemporary Louis XIV. Fears of this kind, justified or imaginary, coloured many aspects of English religious life in the later seventeenth and early eighteenth century. As we have seen, the rise of the Religious Societies and the tone of Tillotson's sermons had been partially due to attempts to counter the popish menace.[121] These fears were repeatedly reinforced by the ambitions of Louis XIV; the real or supposed plots of Jacobites to restore the Stuarts after 1688; the advance of the Catholic powers in Central Europe and their persecution of Protestant minorities whose plight excited much English sympathy. Closer to home there was the permanent anxiety of Catholic Ireland, its Protestant rulers always liable to invasion as England's back door.

As a result of these inherited and contemporary fears, Catholics had been oppressed by ever more severe penal laws, and the 1689 Toleration Act naturally did nothing for them. Locke's *Letter on Toleration* was typical in excluding Catholics on political grounds as a menace to civil security. Had all the penal laws been implemented, Catholics would not only have been excluded from all civil offices but also prevented from bearing arms or serving in the armed forces, or buying or selling land. They might lose their inheritances to Protestant relatives; they could be punished for educating their children as Catholics; they could suffer for being priests or celebrating mass or joining a religious order; and they were subject to extra taxation.

Nevertheless, the eighteenth century saw a general growth in practical toleration, a revulsion against persecution simply for the sake of religion, and Catholics shared in the benefits of this mood. As early as 1710 an Italian claimed that apart from the taxation and ban on military service, Catholics effectively had freedom of religious practice. They attended mass at Catholic embassies; Catholic gentry had chaplains and services; a Benedictine kept a kind of open chapel for visitors to Bath; and 'a kind of convent of nuns' maintained a school near London.[122] This toleration was precarious and easily disturbed, for example during the invasion fears of the 1740s. Informers could cause trouble at other times, and formal attempts at legal relief could cause a popular Protestant backlash. Thus in 1778 the needs of the American War led to various relaxations in the law, partly to facilitate recruitment of Catholic soldiers. But Scottish opposition prevented the extension of this north of the border, and in England Lord George Gordon's Protestant Association helped to touch off the Gordon Riots in 1780 and embroiled John Wesley in some embarrassment as we shall see (below pp. 311f.). Although further concessions were made in 1791, political emancipation was delayed until 1829, and only then compelled by the need to conciliate Ireland.

Yet against these ugly incidents and hardened prejudices should be set the extent to which Catholics managed to worship discreetly and to live in peace with their Protestant neighbours. What is more, they seem to have grown in numbers. The venerable tradition according to which Catholics in England were a dwindling minority until they were rejuvenated in numbers and enthusiasm by Irish immigrants and converts from Anglo-Catholicism in the nineteenth century has received a significant check from recent research. By Professor Bossy's calculations there were about 60,000 in 1640, a figure which hardly changed until after 1700 (so by that time they represented about 1% of the population as against some 6% for Protestant Dissenters). But then they probably increased in numbers, until by the 1770s they had reached about 80,000. After that they increased more rapidly, and this was a growth in English Catholics quite apart from the large accessions of the Irish from then onwards.[123]

Bossy also adds precision to what was already known about their distribution, which was very uneven. Until the 1770s they were most numerous in certain areas of Lancashire; in parts of the North-east; in the West Midlands; the southern Welsh Marches; in Hampshire and parts of the neighbouring counties; in the Thames valley; in parts of East Anglia and in London. When the Irish came they naturally clustered in Lancashire and London, but some parts were scarcely affected by them at all for years to come.[124]

Socially speaking, there are no real surprises until the 1770s. Up to then, it seems that a very great deal depended on the surviving, faithful Catholic aristocracy and gentry families in the areas named. They provided centres for Catholic life, homes and staging points for the ministry of priests. Catholic communities, then, were generally made up of aristocratic and gentry families with their tenants and household servants, and Catholic priests were often in effect acting in terms of a kind of extended domestic chaplaincy role. The survival of the community probably owed a good deal to the feeling that interference with a gentleman's domestic arrangements was hardly decent. Moreover, Catholic worship and devotional habits had a sober, English flavour very different from the 'meretricious gaudiness' of the Continent.[125] It also meant that with the important exception of London (where Catholic tradesmen were naturally a more prominent category), the community was predominantly rural with a rural social profile.

But by the 1770s and increasingly thereafter, things began to change. The first signs of change were certainly not due to Irish influence, but to the same developments in population, urbanization and industrialization that helped to swell the ranks of Methodism and Protestant Dissent. There were more Catholics in the Lancashire towns (at first rural immigrants in search of work); and in due course an increase in the numbers of modest business and professional families natural to an urban setting. This in turn helped to emancipate the priesthood from its dependence on the aristocracy and gentry, though the new urban Catholics in some places were beginning to flex their muscles and to desire to help to run the churches they were financing. There is interesting evidence, too, that in some of the towns Catholics were beginning to play some role in public life alongside their Protestant neighbours. In Manchester, the Catholic priest sat on the Infirmary Trust like his Anglican and Dissenting brethren; and in the 1780s the town committee for servicing Sunday schools included Catholics.[126]

It was really only from the 1790s that the Irish influx permanently changed the character of Catholicism in England, and by the 1820s the old English community in the areas affected by immigration was overwhelmed by them. Even here, however, one can see differences of degree between different chapel communities in the same town. Professor Bossy's startling thesis is that until then there were signs that the English Catholic community was beginning to become part of the spectrum of English Dissent rather than a distinct and alien religion. One can see the force of this claim from a sociological point of view, though it must be subject to some doubts in other respects. Quite apart from the persistent Protestant mythology about Catholicism, there were real theological differences, and both sides could all too easily be made aware of them.[127]

Although there were many reasons for the recrudescence of anti-Catholicism from the late eighteenth century onwards, not least the increasing Irish dimension with its economic, political and racial overtones, the Revival also played an important role. Evangelicalism helped to refuel ancient religious antipathies to hysterical proportions, and Methodist and Evangelical connections with Protestant Ireland made matters worse. We shall see that John Wesley himself had an ambiguous role in this process (below pp. 309ff.). At the same time,

Methodism itself was subject to charges of 'Popery', partly because of Jacobite scares, partly because of some of its leader's and its own devotional practices (below pp. 274, 280). What counted most in the uneasy relationship between Catholics and evangelicals of all sorts was not so much the realities of developing Catholic life in the towns as the black Protestant legend which was all too easily revived in the inflamed imaginations of evangelical zealots.

PART ONE

'Primitive Christianity': The Young John Wesley (1703–38)

I

A Country Living: Epworth (1703–20)

John Wesley's birthplace was in one of the more isolated areas of early eighteenth-century England. Epworth was a straggling market town of no more than 1500 inhabitants, sited on a small hill rising from the fenny Isle of Axholme in north Lincolnshire.[1] The parsonage in which he was born had probably not changed much since it was described in 1607 as three-storied, built of timber and plaster and thatched with straw.[2] In 1702 it was partly burnt and repaired; then wholly burnt in the more famous fire of 1709 which so deeply impressed itself on the future evangelist's mind. It was then replaced by a substantial brick building which still stands.

In the early seventeenth-century the Isle had often been covered with water, and although the drainage schemes of Cornelius Vermuyden in 1626 uncovered fertile land, winter continued to bring floods from the rivers which surrounded the Isle on three sides and access was always difficult. The drainage scheme left another legacy of importance for the discomfort of the Wesley family. Like all such schemes in the seventeenth century it brought profit to the contractors, while creating loss and resentment among the traditionally-minded inhabitants. Riots against the loss of common land rights took place in the early 1640s, and Epworth parish produced a company of recruits for the Parliamentary forces in the Civil War. Riots of this kind continued to occur into the early eighteenth century, and resentment short of riot, but still violent and brutal in its effects, was suffered by the Rector of Epworth.[3]

To these rough independent fenmen, people like Samuel Wesley were foreigners, their intrusion aggravated by demands for tithes and, for some at least of the inhabitants, by the very fact that they were clergymen of the established church. For there was a minority of Dissenters in the parish, up to a hundred in all, the majority Baptists, the rest Quakers.[4] In the contested election of 1705 for the county of Lincoln, Samuel 'supposing there was a design to raise up Presbyterianism over the Church and that Whichcote and Boston were favourable to it (in consequence of which the Dissenters were all in their interest) espoused the other party', supporting the late members Sir John Thorold and Mr Dymoke (the Tory candidates). Samuel described the sequel in a letter to the Archbishop of York. 'During the election night our Isle people kept drumming, shouting and firing of pistols and guns under the window where my wife lay; who had been brought to bed not three weeks.' At Lincoln a clergyman told him he had heard 'near twenty' of the Isle people say 'if they got me in the castle yard they would squeeze my guts out'. Back at home the mob with drums and guns 'complimented' him till after midnight and one cried out to his children: 'O ye devils! we will come and turn ye all out of doors a begging shortly.' As he owed money to some of the opposition, they were able to have him jailed for debt in 1705 through the agency of one of Whichcote's relatives. While he was in jail his cows were stabbed, the rectory door forced and his dog wounded. Some have suspected that the rectory fires of 1702 and 1709 were kindled by the same hostile hands; and perhaps (though this is a mysterious subject) the Epworth ghost 'Old Jeffery' owed something to the same agency.[5]

No doubt the hostility of Samuel's parishioners was in some cases aggravated by the fact that he was an ex-Dissenter turned fierce opponent of Dissent. His *Letter from a Country Divine* (1703) severely criticized the conduct of the Dissenting Academies (in two of which he had himself been educated).[6] If John Wesley is to be believed, Samuel was also part-author of the defence speech of Dr Sacheverell, the furious Tory High Churchman, when he was prosecuted by the government in 1710.[7] In Samuel's own mind, at least, most of his persecutions were due to his loyalty to church and state and the hostility of the Dissenters.[8] To compound his offences he was, or at least tried to be, a strong disciplinarian in his parish. Formal penance was still imposed for sexual offences as in some other Lincolnshire parishes. At the mass confirmation for 800 candidates at Epworth in 1712 he told Bishop Wake that it would have been more proper 'for my parish to have come by themselves and none to have been confirmed but those whose names had been given in by the minister'.[9]

Samuel Wesley's troubles at Epworth were undoubtedly in consider-able measure the product of the political and religious party strife of the time. Yet it is hard to doubt that they were aggravated by his own personality and were the culmination of a career which had already included some stormy episodes.

He was the son and grandson of able and dedicated Dissenting ministers, both of whom had been victims of the Great Ejection of nonconforming clergy in 1662. His wife, Susanna, was the daughter of an even more distinguished Dissenting minister, Dr Samuel Annesley, who had ministered until his death in 1696 to a congregation of Presbyterians in Spitalfields, London. Both Samuel and Susanna, however, had joined the Church of England from conviction while still young (Susanna in her teens and Samuel at the age of twenty-one in 1683). As sometimes happens with converts, both reacted against their inheritance by becoming High Church. Samuel's conduct as already described, as well as his patronage connections, mark him out as a High Church Tory, though his conduct from William III's reign onwards shows that he was no Jacobite. But Susanna, as a later incident would reveal, was Jacobite in sympathy, though probably on religious rather than political grounds – so far as such a distinction can be made in this period.[10]

Some have felt that the Puritan inheritance of piety nevertheless remained strong in both parents, especially Susanna, and that this was transmitted to their son John. Dr Newton, Susanna's latest and best biographer, sees her Puritan inheritance as having left a lasting stamp on her piety and as being vital for understanding her mode of family management. And Methodists have liked to quote Samuel's alleged dying words about 'the inward witness'. But it has been pointed out that at the devotional level there was much common ground between pious people of the early eighteenth century, and the young John Wesley at Oxford was heavily under High Church and indeed Nonjuror influences so far as his piety was concerned.[11]

Samuel, after beginning his education under Dissenting auspices, slipped away on foot to Oxford in 1684 and enrolled himself as a servitor at Exeter College – a menial status in which poor boys were educated in return for waiting on other undergraduates. There is more than a suspicion that he was guilty of paying his debts from Dissenting funds, and he later enraged his old associates by allowing an attack on them by himself to be published anonymously in 1703 at a time when it would do them maximum damage.[12] In August 1688 he was ordained deacon and in February 1689 priest. After temporary curacies divided by a spell as a naval chaplain he was appointed in 1691 to the Lincolnshire country living of South Ormsby with about 200 inhabitants at £50 per annum through the influence of the Marquis of Normanby – a nobleman of vacillating political allegiances, mostly Tory. In the meantime he had married Susanna in November 1688. John Wesley asserted that his father was forced out of this living by the opposition of the Marquis after Samuel had shown his resentment at that nobleman's mistress forcing her company on Susanna. Although the basic story is plausible enough (and by no means unique), the nobleman in question was apparently the Earl of Castlebar.[13] Normanby in fact continued to favour Samuel and later his sons. In 1694 he recommended him to the Archbishop of Canterbury for an Irish bishopric but nothing came of this. Instead, Samuel received the Crown living of Epworth in 1695 as a reward for loyalty, and there he remained until his death in 1735, despite vain hopes for further promotion.[14] He had not done well in the lottery for livings, but he had had sufficient of the all-important 'influence' to be saved from the lifelong insecure curacies of many of his contemporaries.

At Epworth most of his children were born and a considerable number died. Susanna herself was the last of Dr Annesley's numerous children by two wives: the Doctor was not sure whether he had had 'two dozen or a quarter of a hundred'.[15] Samuel and Susanna were almost equally prolific. Traditionally they have been credited with nineteen children, though Samuel himself was uncertain and a recent count suggests between seventeen and nineteen. John Wesley was the thirteenth or fourteenth and the second of only three sons to reach maturity. It was to be a predominantly female household in which he grew up.[16]

John Wesley was born on 17 June 1703 (old style). (The tradition that he was baptized John Benjamin, though still occasionally repeated, was due to an early nineteenth-century confusion with earlier children who died young.)[17] Very little is really known about his life at Epworth until his surviving correspondence and diaries begin in the 1720s. The gap is partly filled by family recollections and papers which help to recreate the atmosphere and in a few cases cast a more direct light on Wesley himself; but pious anecdotes and Wesley's own confident memories when an old man need to be treated with caution.

The ill-will of the Epworth parishioners has already been illustrated, though the rectory family did enjoy better relationships with some of their more gentlemanly neighbours.[18] But the political aspect of these divisions extended into the family itself. The most striking example of this, and one which had a direct bearing on John Wesley's birth, was an incident in 1702. Both parents were Tories, but whereas Samuel accepted William of Orange as William III, Susanna regarded him as a usurper. James II was the true king by divine right, and although she allowed that one should submit to the new king, this did not extend to 'praying for a usurper, and vindicating his usurpation after he came to the throne'.[19] John Wesley described the dramatic climax to the conflict to Adam Clarke. "'Sukey', said my father to my mother one day after family prayer, "Why did you not say *amen* this morning to the prayer for the King?" "Because," said she, "I do not believe the Prince of Orange to be King". "If that be the case," said he, "you and I must part; for if we have two Kings, we must have two beds."' Wesley added that his mother was 'inflexible'; his father set out for London and as a

Convocation proctor remained there for the rest of the year (1701). In March 1702, at the death of King William, since both agreed on the legitimacy of Queen Anne's title, 'the cause of their misunderstanding ceased. My father returned to Epworth and conjugal harmony was restored.'[20]

Correspondence discovered in the 1950s corrected this account, showing that the conflict was even more intense and agonized on Susanna's side, and less easily resolved than tradition allowed. Samuel had sworn an oath which he would not retract unless she begged 'God's pardon and his' and the death of William did not change his mind. Susanna consulted the Nonjuror Bishop George Hickes on the case of conscience and he thought the oath invalid. She refused offers of mediation by the Archbishop of York and the Bishop of Lincoln, and eventually a neighbouring clergyman persuaded Samuel to return. Meanwhile the rectory fire of 1702 was taken by Susanna to be the 'finger of God' in judgment on Samuel's oath.[21] The whole story is a telling illustration of the atmosphere of church life at the time: the power of traditional ideals and the continuing sense of divine intervention which would find many expressions in John Wesley's later career. It is also, of course, a testimony to the tough characters and adherence to principle of his parents. It seems appropriate, finally, that the fruit of the reunion should have been John Wesley's birth.

Samuel had some good qualities. He was learned, zealous, pious, affectionate when his prejudices were not aroused; but also, as Dr Green says, 'obstinate, passionate, partisan and pedantic'.[22] He diverted himself from his numerous troubles with literary work: verses like his odd collection of *Maggots* (whimsies), journalism in his brother-in-law John Dunton's *Athenian Gazette*, a *Life of Christ* in verse and a massive and learned commentary on Job, presented to George II's Queen Caroline after his death.

One fault which deeply affected John Wesley's family and conditioned his life until he attained security as a Fellow of Lincoln was Samuel's chronic state of debt. The 'real value' of the Epworth living was supposed to be £160 per annum, to which was added, after 1724, £60 from the curacy of nearby Wroot. Samuel himself sometimes put the nominal value higher, though saying that he often received much less.[23] He was actually jailed for debt in 1705, but as the result of an appeal to his old university and the Archbishop of York, supporters of the government rallied, paid his debts and obtained his release.[24] But this was only one in a series of misfortunes. Susanna described an interview with Archbishop Sharp during her husband's time in jail. Sharp asked her 'whether you ever really wanted bread?'. With her usual clear-sighted honesty she answered: 'I will fairly own to your Grace that, strictly speaking, I never did want bread. But then, I had so much care to get it before it was eat, and to pay for it after, as has often made it very unpleasant to me. And I think to have bread on such terms is the next degree of wretchedness to having none at all!'[25] Samuel's critical physician brother Matthew once took him to task for his improvidence, not least in saddling himself with so many children – 'a black account; let the cause be folly, or vanity or ungovernable appetite'. To which Samuel replied with a rather jocular account of his finances, his misfortunes and expenses.[26] When all allowances are made for the uncertainties of modest ministerial incomes, the ravages of nature and the persecutions of enemies, he was certainly a hopeless manager. Susanna acknowledged to her brother, when Samuel had mismanaged some business for him, that she had been mistaken when she thought him fit for 'worldly business'. 'He is one of those who, our Saviour saith, are not so wise in their generation as the children of this world.'[27]

Susanna, on the other hand, was competent, businesslike and possessed of a cool, rational mentality which contrasted strongly with Samuel's emotional and 'poetic' temperament. She confessed to John that "Tis an unhappiness almost peculiar to our family, that your father and I seldom think alike.' Samuel Wesley junior, the eldest son, mentions that he wishes his parents 'were as easy in one another and as little uneasy in their fortunes' as himself and his wife.[28] It has been pointed out that conflicts were mitigated by the parents' different spheres of influence: his the church, the parish, the study; hers the kitchen, the nursery, the classroom. In general Susanna conformed to traditional and contemporary expectation that a wife should acknowledge her husband's authority unless, as in rare cases, her conscience intervened. Samuel, unfortunately, did not always keep to his sphere, for it seems that he was liable to fly off the handle and beat the children for their faults and so drove them to lying. Susanna thought that they should be spared this if they confessed their faults and that this avoided lies.[29]

Temperamentally, it seems painfully clear, they were poles apart. Rash and hasty, Samuel was a man of principle and courage but prone to self-dramatization. He also romanticized his married life when he referred to it in his *Life of Christ*.[30] Susanna was the very opposite. Her very competent manuscript exposition of the Apostles' Creed, her private meditations and her later correspondence with son John show a cool and rational as well as a devout mind.[31] In different circumstances, perhaps in a different period of history, she might have become an able devotional writer or practical theologian. Plagued with an impoverished and disturbed household and almost annual pregnancies she had to devise a severe, precise régime to survive. But one cannot help suspecting that she had a personality not really contented with motherhood and domestic occupations. Her managing instinct might have been better fulfilled as a headmistress or college principal.

Everyone who has studied the Wesley family has been struck by the extent to which the character of the father seems to have been inherited by Charles Wesley and that of the mother by John. Charles always remained more of the formal High Churchman than John, but in temperament he was not only poetic but also emotional, hasty, self-dramatizing, at times almost manic-depressive. John possessed the cool intelligence and passion for neatness and orderliness of his mother, though time and necessity took him a long way from his High Church origins. It was clearly his mother's influence which counted most for him in the last analysis, in some ways with fruitful, in others with fateful results. But indeed most of the family were marked for life by parental influence, though a good deal must also be allowed for the restrictions of poverty and the physical and social environment which the girls could escape less easily than the boys.

The eldest son, Samuel Junior, though a true High Church son of his parents and indeed with Jacobite connections, was probably less damaged than the others – like Charles he married happily. As Green points out, he was twelve years older than John, and his position in the family 'imposed on him a responsibility and sense of obligation of which he never divested himself'.[32] He took on increasing responsibility as his father aged, and pressed John in the 1730s to take over the Epworth living for his parents' sake. On the other hand he had a wife and family of his own and a teaching post in the distant West Country which released him from the Epworth cocoon more than the others.

The rest of the family were much more directly dominated by their parents. For the girls the effects were almost uniformly disastrous. They were mostly lively, literate and clearly torn between a desire for independence away from Epworth and the difficulty of making a permanent break. Something of their attitudes to their environment comes through in a verse by Hetty on the Epworth opposition:

> High birth and virtue equally they scorn,
> As asses dull on dunghills born;
> Impervious as the stones their heads are found;
> Their rage and hatred steadfast as the ground.[33]

It must be said that they did not choose their men well, but their choices were limited and not always of their own making. It has been fairly pointed out that one of the roots of the problem was the familiar one in that age of finding decent marriages for the too-numerous daughters of a poor man.[34] But it is hard to acquit Samuel in particular of aggravating and even brutalizing a difficult situation.

Emilia, after an abortive attempt at teaching, wished to marry a clergyman but was frustrated by her brother Samuel and her mother. Instead she married an apothecary, as unbending a Whig as she was a Tory. She was later left a widow.[35] Mary was a cripple who married Samuel Wesley's curate John Whitelamb at Wroot. Perhaps predictably, she died in childbirth, and Whitelamb lived on to disapprove of John Wesley preaching on his father's tombstone in 1742. He felt the family had neglected him, though he had shown a doglike devotion to the Rector as his benefactor.[36] The younger Susanna married a man who was 'common, coarse and uncultivated, morose and too much inclined to despotic sway', and later separated from him.[37] Mehetabel (or Hetty) was the most tragic of all. She was the most sprightly and witty of the girls and a constant worry to her parents. About 1724 she was to have been married to a lawyer but her father prevented it. Hetty would have persisted, but apparently her suitor refused to do so, and according to Clarke she vowed either never to marry or to take the first man who offered that her parents approved of. This led to a highly unsuitable marriage to a drunken plumber. What in fact happened was that she was seduced by an unknown lover and hastily married to the plumber to cover the consequences: a short-lived child was born four months later. Hetty expressed her subsequent sorrows in some poignant verses.[38] John Wesley, though he defended her against his parents, did so with a characteristic lack of tact by preaching against his father's conduct in the face of the parish.[39] Martha Wesley's tragedy was almost equally distressing. Secretly courted by and informally engaged to Westley Hall, a member of the Oxford Holy Club, she was jilted in favour of her sister Kezziah, then taken up again more publicly by Hall. This led to her being blamed by the family for stealing her sister's lover. Hall married her but later became a shameless theoretical and practical antinomian, inflicting his mistresses on his long-suffering wife. This was particularly distressing to John Wesley, who was fond of his sister and deeply embarrassed by the effects of Hall's conduct on the reputation of Methodism.[40] Kezziah, having luckily escaped Hall, fell into ill-health and died young.

This sorry and extraordinary catalogue speaks for itself, though it is fair to add that Epworth Rectory was not a scene of unrelieved gloom. The children carried on a lively correspondence and shared their affairs of the heart, and at least when John Wesley was at home, his diary reveals 'a flourishing social life, of dinners, dancing and visits which brought the Wesleys into contact with the richer yeoman families of the district'.[41]

In justice to Samuel Wesley it must be emphasized that outside his troubled household he was in many ways an admirable example of the best kind of early eighteenth-century parish priest. In his *Letter to a Curate* he details the aims, studies, duties and discipline of the ideal minister which conform closely to his own practice. He was not only a strict disciplinarian but also a diligent pastor. He held two services every Sunday and observed daily prayers on Wednesdays, Fridays and feast days. Catechizing was held at first all the year round, though later only in Lent. Holy Communion was administered monthly in Epworth, six times a year in Wroot. His *Pious Communicant Rightly Prepared* advocated frequent communion, and he even offered a weekly communion to a visitor, paid for by himself if the parishioners objected.[42]

That book included an appendix on the Religious Societies which he defended as aids not only to their members but also to clergy working in large parishes. This was originally written in 1699 and a year earlier he had preached for a Society for the Reformation of Manners in Westminster.[43] Other evidence makes it clear that Samuel was doing his best to involve himself in supporting the various initiatives and organizations which, as we have seen, made up the High Church movement for religious renewal at the turn of the century. He even had a characteristically grandiose plan to offer himself as a missionary overseas, and the Wesley family were acquainted with the initiatives of the Halle Pietists.[44] From 1699 he was a correspondent of the SPCK, and letters to them show how, after despairing of founding a Society for the Reformation of Manners, he had managed to start a Religious Society on the Woodward model with some variations of his own. They had begun with eight, added twenty more 'inconsiderable men' and hoped to increase. They met for prayer, reading and edifying conversation. They intended to help the poor and to correspond with similar societies abroad and translate their tracts. The parent body of what he visualized as a chain of societies would also tackle 'reformation of manners'.[45] It looks as though Samuel's persistence wore down some of the opposition, though we do not know what became of his Society. In 1701 he records that he had lately set up a monthly communion with only 20 attenders but in 1733 had 100.[46] John Wesley claimed later that some had indeed been influenced by his father.[47] It seems reasonable to claim that one of the sources at least for the audience of the Revival was earlier activity of this type.

Church attendance was also increased for a time by Susanna's experiment of a house meeting during her husband's absence at Convocation in 1712, which has often been seen as a prototype of later Methodist activity.[48] This began as a session of prayers and sermon reading and religious conversation for her family in the absence of a Sunday afternoon service, but in the end 200 of the parishioners crowded in. Apparently readings of the Danish Pietist missions in India were a particular attraction. Samuel had some reservations when she dutifully informed him. She responded sharply to the charge that it looked 'particular' (peculiar and eccentric) and said that no one would have objected to the much more questionable practice of Sunday visiting. Though she had some qualms about leading, being a mere woman, she really did not care if people thought it scandalous, for 'I have long since shook hands with the world'.

When the curate aroused Samuel's alarm by charging her with holding a 'conventicle', she responded robustly. He should not be moved by the clamour of the 'worst of your parish'. Far from being a conventicle, the meetings had brought two or three hundred more to church and 'wonderfully conciliated' the people and improved their behaviour. If the work was stopped it would prejudice people against the curate and drive them from church once again. What happened next is not known, though presumably the meetings stopped on Samuel's return. Once again, and perhaps especially in a parish with a Dissenting minority, societary experiments identified a class of pious people not touched by the ordinary church routine, and Susanna, like her son later, showed that she had few inhibitions about formal restrictions if she thought souls were at stake.

But generally her influence was confined to the family circle and here something needs to be said about her often-described system for rearing her children.[49] This began with 'regularity' in everything they were capable of from birth – first in sleeping and then by the age of one 'they were taught to fear the rod and cry softly' so that 'that most odious noise of the crying of children was rarely heard in the house, but the family lived in as much quietness as if there had not been a child among them'. They whispered for what they needed at meals, ate what was set before them and were left alone to fall asleep without attendance. They were given nothing they cried for but were to ask the servants politely and address each other as 'Brother' and 'Sister'. They learnt the Lord's Prayer as soon as they could speak and all but one learnt to read from the age of five. No loud talking or playing were allowed, but they were run as a miniature school. Susanna complacently observed that 'it is almost incredible what a child may be taught in a quarter of a year by vigorous application'.

All went well until the family was dispersed after the fire of 1709, when they were allowed to talk to servants, neglect the Sabbath and play with bad children, but she restored the régime later. She devised byelaws, such as the one about confessing faults, which was spoilt by Samuel's impatience. Private possessions should be respected; promises strictly observed; attempts to please 'kindly accepted'. The girls were taught to read as well as sew. In all this Susanna evidently assumed that, given the right method and environment, all children, regardless of character, could be moulded to the same degree of attainment, very much in the spirit of Locke's theory of knowledge.

What is also very important is her basic belief and principle that to form the minds of children, the first essential is to 'conquer' or 'break' their wills, the sooner the better. Only then can the slower process of cultivating the understanding be developed. Otherwise they will become stubborn, and subduing the will by force will then become painful. Without this initial conquest of the will there can be no foundation for religious education – precept and example are not enough. Once it is done, however, they can be governed by the reason and piety of their parents until their understanding comes to maturity. Self-will is the root of sin and misery; a mortified will produces piety and happiness. Hence the early 'fearing the rod and crying softly', for it saves more pain later. 'Let none persuade you it is cruelty to do this, it is cruelty not to do it.' The careful and 'enlightened' scheme of balanced behaviour, politeness and respect for each other all presupposed that this initial subjection of the will had been carried out.

How far was this attitude and regimen unusual at this time? Was it something peculiar to Susanna or characteristic of certain groups in society or perhaps (as many have supposed) from her Puritan background? Recent and controversial attempts to write the history of family life, marriage and child nurture still falter for lack of adequate evidence, and Susanna's case has attracted some attention because of its rare detail. For example, Lawrence Stone has claimed that belief in original sin fostered a stress on repression in educational theory and that Puritans and Dissenters were particularly prone to this. He then alleges that there was a change in child rearing practice and relationships between parents and children in the period 1660–1800 towards a more affectionate and permissive mode. The child was seen (as in John Locke's view) as a creature open to moulding by environment and experience. The wise parent begins with a degree of severity but proceeds to love and friendship as the child becomes able to respond. There is a move also away from corporal punishment (seen as being widely prevalent until the eighteenth century by a number of theorists). Stone also speculates that the old views of original sin and repression persisted longest among the lower middle class, transmitted from the Puritans to the nineteenth century via the Evangelicals. Susanna Wesley he sees as a mixture: 'fear the rod', but also the use of rewards for doing well, rather like Locke. But he observes that she differed from Locke in that her object was to please God. The result was the adult John Wesley's compulsive perfectionism, conformity to authority but also a sense of his own role in society as one of the chosen of God.[50] Philip Greven, writing of the American experience, has an interesting model of three modes: the 'evangelical', 'moderate' and 'genteel'; the first including the breaking of the will, with Susanna Wesley cited again as an example.[51] But he plays down the element of corporal punishment, and Linda Pollock's study of children in this period casts doubt on the Puritan stereotype of obsession with original sin in children and a desire to break their wills.[52]

Greven sees Locke on balance as one of his 'moderate' type with some elements of the 'repressive' evangelical, since he emphasized early constraint followed by compliance. It is indeed possible that Susanna was influenced by Locke or the attitude he represented, and certainly Charles Wesley (who was much influenced by Susanna in his approach to his own children) wrote later that the most important of Locke's rules was 'that in which the whole secret of education consists' – that is, 'make it your invariable rule to cross his will'.[53] Locke was against flogging except for obstinacy, but he believed that the first thing was to 'bend' the will: only later could children be won by reason and duty. Esteem or disgrace in the eyes of their parents should be major incentives to obedience.[54] There are striking resemblances between Locke and Mrs Wesley: on the treatment of servants, crying infants, older children teaching the younger, lying.[55] Both begin with subduing the will, but Susanna is more authoritarian. The will is to be 'broken', not 'bent', and the rod can be used at first to do it. Nor did she allow for play in education as Locke did. She is, to use Greven's model, more 'evangelical' and less 'moderate'. What is clear is that John Wesley's views on child nurture exactly follow his mother's, and his writings on the subject often quote her exactly.[56] Moreover both, unlike Locke, clearly see the whole matter as aimed at instilling early principles of religion: 'break the will that you may save their souls'. Religion is a matter of breaking our wills to make us submit to God's will, and so to subdue sin and to prepare the way we are to submit to the will of parents first.[57] Psychologically, it could be argued, this provided a model and prepared the way for evangelical conversion.[58]

Certainly there was a marked effect of this upbringing on John Wesley's personality. When upwards of thirty he still felt subject to his father, and if this was not unusual, it is still more significant that during his forties he felt that he would be as much bound to obey his mother 'in everything lawful' as when in leading strings (though she was now dead).[59] At the same time he developed an authoritarian character of his own over others. The influence of his mother and the predominantly feminine atmosphere of Epworth rectory may be held to help to explain his troubled relationships with women for the rest of his life.

The most famous incident of his childhood, and one which has been seen as having a decisive influence on his future career, was the Epworth rectory fire of 1709.[60] In view of the myths and exaggerations which have grown up around this story, it is worth summarizing the events in Susanna's sober account. She says that the fire started 'by what accident God alone knows'. John thought that it was by wicked parishioners and Elsie Harrison gratuitously guessed that it was the Rector's carelessness. She also, inaccurately, portrays Susanna, pregnant and half-naked, as saving the children, while Samuel fatuously commended John to God and more practical men got the boy out of a window. In fact it seems clear that Samuel evacuated the family downstairs and out of the back of the house; Susanna escaped from the front. Only after failing to reach John did the Rector fall to prayer. At the age of seventy-five John Wesley claimed to have a distinct recollection of the events himself, down to the words of his rescuers and his father's thanksgiving afterwards. The next day, by one of those 'providences' which Methodists loved to recount, Samuel picked up a scorched leaf of his Polyglot Bible which read, in Latin, 'give up all that you have and take up the cross and follow me'.

Both parents do seem to have felt it providential that all their children had been saved. Hitherto all had been brought up by the same régime, but in a meditation dated 17 May 1711, Susanna wrote of 'Son John' that she intends 'to be more particularly careful of the soul of this child that thou hast so mercifully provided for, than ever I have been, that I may do my endeavours to instil into his mind the disciplines of thy true religion and virtue'.[61]

After Wesley's death biographers coupled this remark with a 'providential' interpretation of the fire of a special kind.[62] By about 1737 Wesley adapted for himself the biblical phrase of a 'brand plucked from the burning', and the phrase became part of the Wesley legend, indicating not only his providential deliverance from the fire but also a divine dispensation pointing to some extraordinary mission for him. After his death biographers coupled this with Susanna's meditation. In fact there is no sign that she interpreted this as a sign of special mission, and Wesley himself denied that he thought himself singled out in this way. Like many evangelicals he could see the finger of God acting in apparent accidents to preserve him to the day of conversion, though this is not the same as a sense of special calling to a particular work.[63] Yet there is a good deal in his *Journal* and other writings to suggest that he did come to feel that the rise of Methodism and his own part in it was seen in a 'providential' light.

Beyond this dramatic episode and the likely effect of his mother's upbringing, the slender store of anecdotes about his childhood has not been increased since Tyerman's biography a century ago. Between the ages of eight and nine he had smallpox, borne 'bravely, like a man, and indeed like a Christian, without complaint'.[64] Wesley later claimed that he had been 'serious in religion' since he was six years old, and he is said to have been admitted to communion by his father at the age of eight.[65] The control of the emotions by reason and the habit of offering rational or apparently rational arguments about all decisions seems to have shown itself early. According to his own recollection, when asked to accept food between meals (against Susanna's rule) he would answer politely, 'I thank you; I will think of it.'[66] And already this habit excited exasperation in others. His father once responded, very sensibly: 'Child, you think to carry everything by dint of argument, but you will find how little is ever done in the world by close reasoning.'[67] It is doubtful, indeed, whether Wesley ever really learnt this lession. On one famous occasion, too, the Rector was provoked into saying to his wife: 'As for Jack, he will have a reason for everything he has to do. I suppose, he would not attend to the most pressing necessities of nature unless he had a reason for it.'[68]

On 28 January 1714, at the age of eleven, John was entered as a foundation scholar at the Charterhouse in London on the nomination of the Duke of Buckinghamshire, Lord Chamberlain of the Household and in fact none other than Samuel's old patron for South Ormsby, the former Marquis of Normanby.[69] Only a few trivial and dubious stories survive from this period. If, as was claimed, the older boys stole the youngers' share of meat, one may think of him as involuntarily experiencing a form of self-denial which he adopted voluntarily later. He is also said to have followed his father's advice to preserve his health by running round the school grounds three times every morning.[70] One suspiciously appropriate story has it that when he was asked why he was so often with younger boys than himself, John replied 'Better to rule in hell than serve in heaven'.[71] This Miltonic assertion very probably reflects the later charges of ambition.

As to John's religious life at school, in 1738 he claimed that he 'had not sinned away the washing of the Holy Ghost which was given me in baptism until the age of about ten'.[72] This sounds very like the remembered impact of the transfer from the sheltered home environment to that of an eighteenth-century public school. But he adds (in his very severe self-criticism of 1738) that he was guilty of outward sins, even though they were not scandalous in the eyes of the world, and he still read the Scriptures and said his prayers and hoped to be saved as a consequence. This is a familiar example of evangelical self-condemnation of the period before conversion. Very probably he appeared a pious if not priggish boy to contemporaries, and in 1750 he himself wrote: 'I have not found God so present with me for so long a time since

I was twelve years old.'[73] In any case he was at least partly under the eye of his brother Samuel who was at Westminster School (where Charles was later a pupil) and for a time lodged with him. More or less compelled to send the boys to these schools to give them a chance of reaching university and respectable employment, their parents probably thought it worth the moral risk. Samuel Jr reported that 'Jack is a brave boy, learning Hebrew as fast as he can'.[74]

It was during the Charterhouse period, from December 1716 to January 1717, that the famous Epworth ghost 'Old Jeffery' appeared. John was not present, but he took a keen interest in the affair and eventually published an account of it in the *Arminian Magazine* for 1784.[75] The contemporary evidence is remarkably full: a diary by Samuel Wesley as well as letters and other accounts. The phenomena were those usually associated with poltergeists: groans, knockings, banging doors, fear shown by the dog, latches lifted and doors pushed open, a bed raised under one of the girls and the Rector feeling himself pushed by an unseen force. Rather more eccentric were sounds of gobbling like a turkey-cock, the turning of a windmill and the winding of a jack. A creature like a badger or white rabbit was seen and (allegedly) a human form. Jeffery also had Jacobite prejudices, for the knocking was loud when the Rector prayed for King George. The phenomena ended abruptly for no apparent reason, though Emily Wesley claimed a supernatural visitant in 1750.

No completely convincing explanation has been offered for this, and it is worth noticing that the family needed some convincing at first that the noises did not have a natural explanation – perhaps rats, mischievous neighbours or even one of the girls (Hetty was suspected). Mrs Wesley then thought it might be a portent of the disappearance of her brother in India. But John Wesley (though he was not present) confidently asserted that it was a messenger of Satan to punish his father for the rash vow back in 1702. Indeed he had an experience himself with a closing door at the Rectory in 1726.[76] Joseph Priestley, as a philosophical materialist, naturally saw it as a prank of servants and neighbours, and indeed Samuel had been preaching against a local 'cunning man' (white witch).[77] Some of the early nineteenth-century Wesleyans were reluctant to dismiss the supernatural so readily.[78]

Dr Green, noting that there was much in the circumstances that is nowadays associated with poltergeists (however these are to be explained), concludes, however, with the point that matters for Wesley's biographers. The events 'served to arouse his interest in similar phenomena, to buttress his natural credulity; to confirm his awareness of the unseen world'.[79] No doubt the primitive world of Lincolnshire reinforced this outlook, and this world was still very much alive over a century later.[80] But Wesley was able to invoke respectable, if old-fashioned, learned opinion as well on these matters, and we shall see that his supernatural beliefs had an important bearing on his relationship with his later Methodist followers and on the general character of the movement which he led.

The effects of Wesley's upbringing can only be judged by cautious speculation in the light of his later character and behaviour. Not only child-rearing methods but the whole methodical, serious-minded ethos and the overt religious aim lived on to colour the rest of his career as the proper approach to life. If Oxford opened the way to mild flirtations with worldliness, within a few years asceticism reasserted itself and was shaped more by High Church and Catholic models than the Puritan ideals that some have seen reflected in Epworth piety. These influences, as we shall see, were to be modified rather than simply replaced by 'evangelical' influences later. Wesley had seen the method of the conscientious parish priest but also the mixed and often hostile response of rough parishioners. Whatever doubts he may have had about his own achievements, he was never free of the sense at least of the demands of God which indeed haunted many of his converts from an early age.[81] The sequel will show that for Wesley both in his spiritual quest and in his relationships with other people, perhaps especially with women, it was above all his mother's influence which would mark his personality and emotional life. Psychologically as well as religiously he was indeed 'a son to Susanna', even though his father's influence was not negligible. Wesley's long-drawn-out religious development was also a kind of delayed and extended adolescence which culminated in some sense in the religious experience of May 1738 and was, perhaps, resolved by his absorption into his public missions which emerged in 1738–9. If this resolved or at least helped him to come to terms with the problems of his inner life, it did not solve all his emotional ones.

But it is likely that it was with pleasant expectations of a less restricted way of life that the young John Wesley went up to Christ Church, Oxford, in June 1720 with a Charterhouse exhibition of £20 a year to support him.[82]

II

A Holy Experiment: Oxford (1720–35)

The reputation of the eighteenth-century universities has suffered at the
hands of later critics almost as much as the church of which they were
important arms. Oxford has perhaps been particularly unfortunate not
only because of its unfashionable Tory High Churchmanship but also
because of the entertainment value of some of its diarists and memoirists.
Thomas Hearne, the splenetic and garrulous Nonjuror, provides all too
many quotable profiles of Whigs and others whom he disliked, though
also some grudging tributes to the learned, industrious and moral
(including some from John Wesley's Lincoln College). Gibbon's famous
account of his short stay is also all too memorable and may be quoted
here as an example of what has often been taken to be an adequate
summary of the university and its teachers in the 1750s.

'I spent fourteen months at Magdalen College: they proved the
fourteen months the most idle and unprofitable of my whole life.' He
reveals the basis of his judgment when he says that: 'The schools of
Oxford and Cambridge were founded in a dark age of false and barbarous
science' and 'they are still tainted with the vices of their origin . . . the
government still remains in the hands of the clergy, an order of men
whose manners are remote from the present world and whose eyes are
dazzled by the light of philosophy.' The 'public professors' have 'these
many years given up altogether even the pretence of teaching'. 'The
fellows or monks of my time were decent easy men who supinely enjoyed
the gifts of the founder; their days were filled by a series of uniform
employments: the chapel, the hall, the coffee house and the common
room, till they retired, weary and well-satisfied, to a long slumber. From
the tasks of reading, and thinking or writing, they had absolved
their consciences.' Their 'conversation stagnated in a round of college
business, Tory politics, personal anecdotes, and private scandal: their
dull and deep potations excused the brisk intemperance of youth, and

their constitutional toasts were not expressive of the most lively loyalty to the House of Hanover.' After some mildly approving remarks about his first tutor, Gibbon said of his second that 'he well remembered that he had a salary to receive and only forgot that he had a duty to perform'. In religion they 'united the opposite extremes of loyalty and indifference' and the Thirty-Nine Articles 'are signed by more than read, and read by more than believe them'. Gibbon then drifted into Roman Catholicism and so out of the university.[1]

'Learning,' said Hearne in 1729, 'is at so low an ebb at present, that hardly anything of that kind is sought after, except it be English, Scotch or Irish history'.[2] The consensus of later historians is summed up by Sir Charles Mallet: 'For a great part of the eighteenth century Oxford was a world of drab ideals, a small society where disillusioned Jacobites and half-hearted Hanoverians contended with each other, where scholars disinclined for study encountered teachers as indifferent as themselves, where dreamers found enthusiasm discouraged, education deadened, endowments ill-applied.'[3]

More recent scholarship has been concerned not only to soften these harsh judgments and to lighten the gloomy picture by examples of diligence and devotion, but also, and perhaps more importantly, to explain the peculiar circumstances in which the university operated and to clarify the contemporary understanding of its role in society.[4]

Gibbon, like some continental visitors, judged the university as a centre of scholarship and energetic teaching and modern thought. In these respects it often compared unfavourably with overseas or indeed Scottish universities in this period. But many English contemporaries did not conceive of the university's functions in this way. They saw it as *intended* to be a conservative rather than innovative institution. Its role was to provide 'a body of traditional learning on which religious orthodoxy, political and social order were thought to depend . . . few imagined that a university ought to be concerned with pure research or disinterested scholarship'.[5] As a Vice-Chancellor at the end of the century put it: 'The sole purposes of our Academical Institutions' are 'maintainance of order, the Advancement of Learning, and the furtherance of Religion and morality'.[6] The university was to pass on received wisdom and maintain the established order in church and state. Above all it was the trustee of orthodoxy in the church: it trained the clergy and defended the church intellectually against the subversive religious and political opinions of Roman Catholics and Dissenters. The college Fellows filled in their time until country livings or other offices were found for them by college patronage or the Tory squires of the South or Midlands. In this way Oxford's role in the national life was extended. From this point of view Gibbon's criticisms were beside the point, indeed a misunderstanding of the university's functions.

There was a further major complication of the university's position in this period which may go far to account not only for some contemporary criticisms but also for its reluctance to change and its unedifying internal quarrels. This was the political context. Oxford's Tory High Churchmen became identified with the defeated Stuart cause. They were smeared as Jacobites and suffered from the proscription from court favour and office common to the Tories after the accession of George I. How far they, like other Tories, were really hardened Jacobites remains a matter of dispute among modern historians; a good deal has to be allowed for the effects of contemporary Whig propaganda. The Jacobite smear tended to make Oxonians, deprived of the opportunity of co-operation with the government, the victims of self-fulfilling prophecies. Most of the colleges were dominated by Tories of various shades of opinion; a few were, or became, Whig in complexion (Exeter, Jesus, Wadham and from the 1730s Christ Church under Dr Conybeare). The heads of houses tended to be more moderate, the junior members more extreme and Jacobite. The result was a series of unedifying squabbles within and between colleges, aggravated by religious fears, personal antipathies and the claustrophobic atmosphere of senior common rooms.[7] Schemes for university reform were opposed when, as often happened, they were designed as instruments for Whig government control and patronage, and in the 1730s churchmen were alarmed by Deism and attacks on church patronage.[8]

The university therefore reacted with suspicion towards change; its Jacobite reputation deterred Whig families and contributed to the decline in numbers, at their lowest by the 1750s. Socially speaking, the range of undergraduates narrowed: the very aristocratic and very poor became less conspicuous and the majority were described as 'gentlemen', a category becoming less precise during this century. They tended to be the sons of country squires and parsons with a smattering of merchants, lawyers and tradesmen; and the colleges had stronger regional connections than today.[9] Scholars by the end of the seventeenth century were no longer likely to be poor and clever boys, but rather men committed to orders and hoping to go on to fellowships. A high proportion of clergy sons were commoners whose parents were prepared to make sacrifices to give them a chance of a fellowship later and to avoid the drudgery of servitor status. Servitors still existed, though they declined in numbers later. Such men earned their keep by waiting on the better-off, and included men as considerable as Dr Johnson or George Whitefield. At the other extreme, 'gentlemen-commoners' had special privileges, and most of them like noblemen attended university for social reasons rather than intending to proceed to a degree. The Wesleys were fortunate to obtain the status of scholars and to enter the wealthy and prestigious society of Christ Church by way of their Westminster and Charterhouse connections.

College Fellows generally came from gentry or professional backgrounds, and were young unmarried men destined for holy orders and mostly heading for church livings in the long term. In estimating the academic and religious quality of the university one has to bear in mind the peculiar nature of the Oxford collegiate system. The university had a limited corporate existence and was still more limited in the provision it made for teaching. The importance of the colleges had steadily grown since the Middle Ages and the most important part of teaching and religious instruction was in their hands and that of their tutors. Hence much depended on the tone, traditions and personnel of particular colleges at particular times.

The curriculum, system of instruction and examinations were still formally those of the Laudian statutes of 1636, much being inherited indeed from the Middle Ages.[10] Work for the BA took three to four years and was based on a limited number of classical authors and the Aristotelian 'sciences' of logic, rhetoric, morals and politics. These were studied through a mixture of lectures, scholastic disputations and oral exercises at specified intervals. The formal examinations had become stereotyped, and reputedly the subjects chosen for disputation were often repeated and stock responses could easily be learnt. Much use was made of compendia. There were indeed few failures at the end of the course. The strong features of the system were not the perfunctory lectures of professors nor the equally perfunctory university examinations, but the quality of college instruction along the way, which seems quite often to have been done with fair conscientiousness. John Wesley's systematic concern for his tutorial duties was far from unique. At Christ Church and Queen's, too, there is evidence of college exercises, disputations and written work being carried out for a long period. The MA exercises were of a similar character but less instruction was given; residence was more difficult to enforce and often reduced, and notoriously one of the requirements – the delivery by the candidate of 'solemn lectures' – had degenerated to 'wall lectures' delivered to an empty room.

The curriculum was not only highly traditional but often suffused with Oxford's long-standing veneration for Aristotle. Yet in practice, if not officially, changes were under way in the early eighteenth century. In the 1720s Amhurst said that it was not infrequent for 'the tutors in their lectures upon many points of philosophy to tell their pupils that in the schools they must hold such a side of the argument, but that the other side is demonstrably the right side'. In 1726 he says that change was creeping from the colleges into the schools in that 'Locke, Clarke and Sir Isaac Newton begin to find countenance . . . and that Aristotle seems to totter on his throne'. These great men certainly gained earlier and more official countenance in Cambridge. Locke's *Human Understanding* was not much favoured at Oxford, and a meeting of Heads in 1703 was pledged to follow 'Aristotle and the entire peripatetic doctrine' and was prepared to censure the reading of Locke. But the indications are that individual undergraduates and some tutors were more liberal.[11] The latest study of Oxford logic shows that much of the instruction depended on compendia of Aristotelian and later scholastic logic: Wesley studied Aldrich's version. These were geared to formal disputation and point-scoring, and Wesley's controversial writings show the effects of this. The newer logics like those of Watts (1725) were influenced by Locke and probably displaced Aldrich and the rest as the century went on. The Lockeian tradition was more concerned with discovering truth in scientific and religious matters; and truth for Locke comes through experience and observation.[12] We shall see that Wesley, though he kept the capacity for the older kind of point-scoring and clever syllogisms which annoyed more than they convinced, was also much influenced by Lockeian empiricism. The way in which he combined this with a more traditional supernaturalism is important for any estimate of his outlook and character.[13] It may be added that outside the formal curriculum there were many opportunities for the acquisition of polite culture and that educated men were accustomed to indulge in Latin and English versifying. Here, too, Wesley reflected the habits of his contemporaries, sometimes with a tone which shocked his later Methodist biographers.[14]

The effectiveness or otherwise of this system of education depended very largely on the capacity and dedication of college tutors. The Laudian statutes laid down their duties as being not only to 'read' to their pupils but also to attend to their discipline, conduct and religion. Rules for tutors' duties suggested or laid down by would-be reformers like Prideaux in 1715 or the new statutes of Hertford College in 1739 may suggest that reform was needed here.[15] Yet there is a good deal of evidence to suggest that a number of colleges and individuals lived up to the ideal. George Fothergill of Queen's in the 1720s wrote that his 'reverend tutor is very careful' of him and that he believed he was 'diligent in his own studies'. He was also kind to George and helped him with his finances (an old tutorial responsibility). Jack Leybourn of Brasenose (aged thirteen in 1728) was submissive to his tutor who was cousin to his mother and had much correspondence with her.[16] George Whitefield's tutor helped him when he fell ill through his ascetic excesses.[17] John Wesley's own experience of his tutors at Christ Church seems to have been a happy one, and his own conduct as a tutor was scrupulously active both academically and religiously. His conduct in the latter respect became bound up with his ideals for the 'Holy Club', and hence caused resistance in some quarters, but in general he represented the best tutorial standards of his time.

Undergraduate behaviour, so easy to characterize in terms of a few lurid examples (then as now), was in fact subject to a predictable variety. The chief offenders, whose antics tend to be taken as typical of the whole, were noblemen and gentlemen commoners with special privileges and money to burn. Erasmus Philipps of Queen's dined with other smart gentlemen, did some reading, but was occupied chiefly in a round of amusements and race meetings, fox-hunting and cock-fighting. His diary contains much about horses and little about work.[18] Richard Morgan Senior wrote of his son Richard at Lincoln to John Wesley that 'he fares as well-rigged and with as great a quantity of all sorts of apparel as I believe a gentleman-commoner needs to be provided with'.[19] Such examples were indeed sometimes rashly followed by those of lesser means. But the scholar sons of middling folks and clergy were a different matter. Richard Graves in 1732 recalled a set of men at Pembroke who were 'jolly, sprightly young fellows . . . who drank ale, smoked tobacco, and sung bacchanalian catches the whole evening' as well as a 'flying squadron of plain, sensible men' who had 'come to the university on the way to the Temple, or to get a slight smattering of the sciences before they settled in the country'. But his own 'set' was 'a very sober little group who amused themselves in the evening with reading Greek and drinking water'.[20] It was on sober men like these that Wesley would graft the disciplines of 'Methodism' in Oxford.

As to the dons, Gibbon's picture of their social life is no doubt true as far as it goes, centring on the common room where, as Dr Green charitably observes, time must often have hung heavily on their hands, even when they were conscientious tutors. Many of them had as their ultimate ambition the hope of reaching their turn for a college living or other patronage which would lead to the life of a country parson along with marriage. Thomas Warton's whimsical picture has often been quoted:

> These fellowships are paltry things,
> We live indeed like petty kings.
> But who can bear to waste his age
> Amid the dullness of a college,
> Debarr'd the common joys of life,
> And that prime bliss – a loving wife! . . .

Would some snug benefice but fall,
Ye beasts, ye denizens, farewell all! . . .
Come joys, that rural quiet yields,
Come tythes and houses, and fruitful fields.[21]

Most Fellows were in holy orders, and a number held curacies in the Oxford area. If, like Wesley, they ventured further afield into unlicensed eccentricity, they could still draw their Fellowship stipends until they married, as Wesley did, with important effects for his independence as a roving evangelist. It should be noted that a developed sense of personal vocation was not required or perhaps common among the eighteenth-century clergy. 'The notion of being members of a clerical profession was much more common among the clergy than any high concept of priesthood.' Many simply followed their fathers in the profession, and indeed there was often not much else for them except teaching. Doubts usually crept in among the better-off when they felt forced into orders against their wills. As one wrote in 1699: 'I have no particular call to that holy profession, besides a good resolution which I took very lately to enter into it, and I have had the grace to keep it.'[22] John Wesley was following a common pattern as a clergyman's son by taking orders, and few would have shared his doubts about doing so to 'eat a piece of bread'.

Yet religion did form an important part of the framework of Oxford life at both university and college level.[23] The university was, from one point of view, a seminary of the Church of England. It should be remembered that there were no theological colleges and indeed no undergraduate degrees in theology, while only a very few proceeded to the higher degrees of BD and DD. Preparation for orders was left to the conscience of the individual; examinations by bishops' chaplains were not formidable and bishops often complained of the low attainments of candidates for orders. At Oxford, it was only later in the century that Secker and others tried to develop divinity lectures for ordinands. The real framework for religious nurture – as for so much else – was provided by the colleges.

Official provision included compulsory attendance at chapel, lectures on the Greek Testament (which Wesley performed at Lincoln) and instruction in divinity for undergraduates. Communion was celebrated each term and at the great festivals, though it seems from Wesley's account that it was weekly at Christ Church (which was the cathedral church of Oxford). There is, as usual, some evidence for devout men going further. The Hertford statutes provided for Sunday lectures to undergraduates, and in 1731 Queen's had disputations in divinity. On the other hand there is evidence of slackness in conforming to college prayers. The immediate background to John Wesley's return to Oxford in 1729 and the development of the Holy Club throws some light on the university's attitudes. High Church orthodoxy was maintained not only against Dissent but also against heterodoxy. Thus in the 1690s there was a scandal when the Rector of Exeter was ejected for his Socinian *Naked Gospel*, though there are suspicions that political partisanship was involved.[24] There were also Deist fears in the late 1720s which produced a pamphlet from Samuel Wesley junior and a circular from the Vice-Chancellor and Heads of Houses in 1729 (despite some opposition), urging college tutors to explain the articles of religion to their pupils and recommending the reading of the scriptures and orthodox books. This appears to be part of the background to Charles Wesley's personal reformation, in which some have seen the origins of the Holy Club, and it was probably this that led the Rector of Lincoln to summon John Wesley back to his college duties.[25] The Holy Club itself was in part a response to a sense of the need for a more intense and personalized religious commitment in the university.

A university characterized politically by a firm Toryism, with Jacobite overtones; its religion firmly rooted in the ideals of seventeenth-century High Church divines; its scholarship, traditional rather than innovative, was in many ways an appropriate and indeed congenial setting for the sons of Epworth Rectory. The combination of a framework of formal discipline and piety which he could exploit and embroider if he wished, together with larger opportunities for intellectual and social life than were available at home, provided Wesley with an almost ideal setting for his holy experiments as well as a degree of freedom which he could develop if he wished. It would be several years before his private conscience and peculiar brand of High Church ascetic discipline finally went beyond what was acceptable to most of his Oxford contemporaries.

John Wesley entered Christ Church in June 1720. His Charterhouse education served him well, for it gave him the opportunity of acquiring an exhibition and later a Studentship (scholarship) at Christ Church, which saved him from his father's menial status as a servitor.[26] His life in Oxford was not entirely detached from Epworth, for he paid long visits there – sometimes to act as his father's curate – and the ties with his mother were shown by his habit of corresponding with her on his spiritual reading. But Oxford inevitably became the centre of his interest, and his inner feelings, so far as he recorded them, were confided to his diary rather than his mother.

Wesley's career at Oxford could be analysed in terms of three distinct yet overlapping areas of activity and concern. There was, first, his academic career as undergraduate and college fellow and tutor, to which also was related his decision to take holy orders. There was his social life – recreations and friendships which included the delicate and disturbing development of relationships with women. Finally, there was his religious development in terms of his personal quest for holiness and his attempts to influence his contemporaries. Gradually he came to understand the pursuit of holiness in ways which restricted or at least coloured the other aspects of his life, though this took longer that might have been expected to persuade him into cutting out 'worldly' recreations, and in his relationships with women he ingenuously persuaded himself that heavenly and earthly love could be combined to the profit of his soul.

It will be convenient to divide Wesley's Oxford life into three periods: at Christ Church as an undergraduate followed by ordination in 1725; from the election as Fellow of Lincoln in 1726 to the beginnings of the 'Holy Club' in 1729; and finally the period of intensifying 'Oxford Methodist' activity which concluded with the expedition to Georgia in 1735.

Not much can be said about Wesley's life as an undergraduate, since little is known about him until the diaries and surviving letters provide a record from 1724 to 1725.[27] Christ Church was a rich and Tory college, though by the end of Wesley's stay there the Deans were beginning to edge it towards greater conformity to government interests. Earlier, during his time there, Samuel Wesley junior had been friendly with the furious high Tory Dean Atterbury.[28] John appears to have had friendly relationships with his tutors George Wigan and Henry Sherman, and as a student and son of a poor clergyman he was expected to proceed to his Bachelor's degree (1724), and did so in a conscientious fashion. Even the atrabilious Hearne acknowledged that Sherman was 'a great and very good tutor . . . a disciplinarian, a sober, studious, regular and learned man'.[29]

His own and family letters suggest a cheerful and dutiful son with no pressing religious problems. Not surprisingly, he was sometimes in debt. An Oxford gentleman had his cap and wig snatched off in the street, but 'I am pretty safe from such gentlemen; for unless they carried me away, carcass and all, they would have but a poor purchase'. This was in 1724, and in the same letter he shows his acquaintance with Dr Cheyne's commonsense book on 'health and long life' in which much is ascribed to 'temperance and exercise'. This was to have a considerable influence on Wesley's own practice and his advice to others. His own health at Oxford was variable, and in 1731–2 he evidently feared (not for the last time) that he was contracting consumption. There may have been a psychosomatic element in some of these bouts of illness (the consumption scare was at the time of attacks on the Oxford Methodists, and Wesley's health improved as his religious stability increased). The other point about the few letters before 1725 is the appearance once again of an interest in the supernatural. He reports a seventeenth-century Irish story about a boy carried through the air, an apparition to Lincoln College men, and thoughts on a haunted house. To his brother Samuel he sent verses, translated or imitated from Latin of an artificially erotic cast, like one on Chloe and the flea:

> Now on her panting breast he leaps,
> Now hides between his little head;

and, following Horace, verses to:

> The cruel queen of fierce desires.[30]

Analysts of Wesley's early development have always fixed on 1725 or thereabouts as the point when he began to be more seriously religious. This was also the point when he took the decision to enter holy orders, and it is natural to suppose that preparation for ordination was at least one factor in this spiritual awakening, which for some has been seen as his real 'conversion'. It is also significant that he first began to keep a diary in April 1725. From about this time, too, he appears to have become acquainted with some clerical families and their womenfolk in the Cotswolds, notably the Kirkhams of Stanton. Robert, the son of the family, became one of the Oxford Methodists, but more interest has centred on his sisters, particularly on Sally ('Varanese'). If Elsie Harrison's romantic reconstruction is to be believed, disappointed hopes of marrying Varanese promoted Wesley's turn to seriousness in 1725 and perhaps also the decision to take orders.[31]

Although Mrs Harrison's picture is superficially attractive, if only because it follows a similar pattern to that of a later love affair in Georgia, it certainly cannot be sustained as it stands. In his retrospect of May 1738 Wesley portrays himself as only formally religious and without any notion of 'inward holiness'. He supposed that he must have expected to be saved by 'those transient fits of what many divines taught me to call repentance'. Of the change in 1725 he wrote in the same account that: 'When I was about twenty-two, my father pressed me to enter into holy orders. At the same time, the providence of God directing me to Kempis's *Christian Pattern* (i.e. the *Imitation of Christ*), I began to see that true religion was seated in the heart, and that God's law extended to all our thoughts as well as words and actions . . . and meeting likewise with a religious friend, which I had never had till now, I began to alter the whole form of my conversation (i.e. behaviour) and to set in earnest upon a new life . . . I began to aim at and pray for inward holiness.'[32] But we have to be wary of Wesley's later recollections of fact and chronology, as well as the influence on them of his later religious perspectives.

Although proceeding to orders was the natural course for Wesley to take, there probably was parental pressure. In September 1724 his mother expressed a wish that he were in orders so as to help to serve his father's churches, but Wesley's letters for the rest of the year say nothing directly about this, and the diary, beginning in April 1725, throws no light on the matter either. In January 1725 his father wrote: 'As for what you mention of entering into Holy Orders, 'tis indeed a great work', and Samuel proceeded to give him advice about motivation which will be noticed later.[33] The implied doubts about vocation could have arisen either in reaction to pressure from the family or from Wesley's own desire to find a suitable profession. The decision, which soon followed, to seek a college fellowship, was an equally natural course for a poor parson's son to take, and one obvious route for a man with little hope of patronage. It could open the way eventually to a living, and in the meantime would not prevent him from acting as his father's curate. It did not necessarily imply a desire for an academic life.[34] Nor is it plausible to see it as being provoked by speculative hopes of marriage to Sally Kirkham (as Mrs Harrison suggested), for Wesley as yet had no prospect of a living, and the Fellowship would be forfeited on marriage. Samuel Wesley's answer to John's apparent doubts about taking orders 'to eat a piece of bread' was that 'It is no harm' to do so, 'though a desire to live a strict life is a better reason, and the chief motive should be the glory of God and the service of his church in the edification of our neighbour'.

Mrs Harrison's theory centres on the undoubted fact that at the end of 1725 Sally was married to the Rev. Jack Chapone, though she and Wesley persisted in a close and affectionate relationship long after this, and she interprets a mysterious entry in the diary for 14 April 1725 as indicating a marriage proposal from Wesley which failed. The diary began on 5 April, and on 14 April he wrote: 'First saw Varanese [this word in cypher]. Let it not be in vain!' This entry is squeezed in, evidently at some later date. Since the question of ordination had already been raised, if it was not settled, it can hardly have been precipitated by a disappointment in love. If he did have hopes of marriage to Varanese, they must have come later in the year, and if so might have provoked the inserted remark as a retrospective reflection on the first meeting, though this could equally well refer to hopes of spiritual edification. What adds seeming force to the Harrison theory is that on 7 April Wesley's sister Emily had written to him in the light of her own unhappy love life: ' . . . whether you will be engaged before thirty or not I cannot determine; but if my advice is worth listening to, never engage your affections before your worldly affairs are in such a posture that you may marry very soon . . . I know you are a young man encompassed with difficulties that has passed through many hardships already . . . but believe me if you ever come to suffer the torment of a hopeless love all other afflictions will seem small in comparison of it.'[35] To clinch the case Mrs Harrison quotes Emily again: 'Had you not lost your dear Mrs Ch-n, where had your love been fixed? on heaven, I hope, principally; but a large share, too, had been hers: you would not have been so spiritualized, but something of this lower world would have had its part in your heart, wise as you are; but being deprived of her then went all hope of earthly happiness: and now the mind, which is the active principle, losing its aim here, has fixed on its Maker for happiness.'[36] Seductive though the psychology of this observation may be, it should be noted that it was written ten years later, in 1735, and it is not evidence for an abortive proposal, though it may well suggest one part of Wesley's motives for the plunge into holy discipline during 1725 in addition to his preparation for ordination. When Emily wrote to John in the Spring of 1725, she can hardly have been referring to Varanese, since he did not meet her until a week later (at least if he got his date right – and possibly he did not), though he may well have been thinking of marriage in a more general way. Something of Wesley's state of mind during 1725 may be gathered from his first set of 'General Rules', apparently before the diary began, and a passage dated 26 March about 'unclean thoughts' and their remedy in avoiding 'idleness, freedom with women and high seasoned meats' or from a set of self-reviewing statements in January 1726 which included 'I have loved women or company more than God.' But these are only a small part of a more general ascetic self-examination.[37] All we can be certain of is that Varanese did come to play an important part in Wesley's emotional and religious life after her marriage, though the precise nature of her role remains obscure and open to more than one interpretation.

Wesley was ordained deacon on 19 September 1725 and priest in September 1728. In comments on his preparation for ordination, it has been usual to contrast his father's advice for scholarly work with his mother's for practical divinity. But as we have seen, his father certainly emphasized the importance of a spiritual call, and his mother's advice was in response to a specific request from John himself. But she did emphasize the study of practical divinity as 'of all other studies I humbly conceive to be the best for candidates for orders'; and she did add, rather sharply, that it was an 'unhappiness almost peculiar to our family that your father and I seldom think alike'. She went so far as to say indeed that he should be ordained quickly as an inducement to studying practical divinity. And she hoped it might make him apply his mind 'to things of a more sublime and spiritual nature . . . now, in good earnest, resolve to make religion the business of your life', and 'enter upon a strict examination of yourself that you may know whether you have a reasonable hope of salvation by Jesus Christ'.[38]

In Wesley's retrospect of May 1738, he saw his vision of the holy life as having been inspired and deepened by spiritual reading in à Kempis, Taylor and William Law, and by the help of a 'spiritual friend', but in this and various other later accounts his chronology is often muddled.[39] The contemporary evidence of letters and diaries seems to show that he was reading à Kempis by May 1725 and discussed that writer's severities in letters to his mother and father. If the claim in the preface to the first extract of the *Journal* is correct, he read Taylor before à Kempis and drew from him the idea of keeping a devotional diary; again he corresponded with his mother about points he disliked about him.[40] The reading of William Law came after these, and much later than Wesley implied in his later accounts. He probably began reading the *Serious Call* at the end of 1730 and *Christian Perfection* after meeting Law himself in 1732.[41] It was à Kempis and Taylor who deepened his sense of 'inward holiness' and provoked in him considerable resistance to some of their severities.

The identity of the 'religious friend' is uncertain. There is no indication whether it was a man or woman, but Varanese is often supposed to be the person in question. It may be thought significant that Wesley does not name the person to his mother; and in referring to Taylor's *Holy Living and Dying* in June 1725, Wesley refers to the opinion on him by 'a person of good judgment' that '*she* [my italics] would advise no one very young' to read the book.[42] But there is no clear evidence that she actually introduced him to these books, and Robin Griffiths has also been suggested as the 'religious friend' – Wesley was close to him at this time and upset by his early death in 1727.[43] At all events the general turn to seriousness is shown by the correspondence with his mother, which contrasts strongly with that in 1724. Starting a diary is another sign, as is a 'General Rule in All Actions of Life', apparently drawn up in August 1725, probably in preparation for his ordination as deacon the following month.[44]

Wesley's various retrospective surveys of his development at this time agree in their picture of a concern for inward religion and the subjection of all thoughts, feelings and action to the pattern of Christ, to what he came to refer to as holiness or 'perfection', and (though not always consistently or correctly in chronology) in the importance of the role of the work of à Kempis and Taylor.[45] Correspondence with his mother and occasional interjections from his father show the points which troubled him. À Kempis seemed to think that we should be miserable in this world, but Wesley thought cheerfulness should be allowed to break in. Susanna agreed, though laying down the rule that 'whatever weakens your reason, impairs the tenderness of your conscience, obscures your sense of God, or takes off your relish of spiritual things' – whatever, in fact, 'increases the authority of your body over your mind, that thing is sin to you'.[46] Again, Wesley found Taylor's recipes for humility excessive and perverse in their deliberate seeking for humiliation. Susanna, with her usual good sense, thought that true humility is 'the mean between pride, or an overvaluing ourselves on one side, and a base, abject temper on the other'; it comes from a sense of the glory of God and our own unworthiness. We should not court to be little esteemed.[47]

Following on this, Wesley worried away at problems of knowledge and faith. Faith, from some of his reading, he saw as 'a species of belief, and belief is defined, an assent to a proposition upon rational grounds. Without rational grounds there is therefore no belief and consequently no faith.' He thought that there could be no absolute certainty of final pardon of our sins because we could not be sure of 'final perseverance'. But we can know that we are '*now* in a state of salvation'. So what about predestination? He cannot believe in this because it affronts God's justice and mercy and makes him the author of sin. He used to think that there was a divine decree of election of a remnant yet that all have power to become part of it, but unfortunately Article 17 will not bear that sense. In response to this, Susanna made a penetrating thrust about Wesley's character. She took him to task for his ratiocinations about things which troubled him personally. 'But this I perceive much affronts you, and you can't well digest it. Therefore you employ your wit in making distinctions and general arguments.' On faith she thought Bishop Pearson the best guide, and John finally agreed that 'saving faith (including practice) is an assent to what God has revealed, because he has revealed it, and not because the truth of it may be evinced by reason'. On predestination his mother agreed with him in rejecting it in its Calvinist form. She believed that 'God elects some from eternity to everlasting life', but this is founded on his foreknowledge, seeing those 'who would accept of his proffered mercy'. She also dissuaded John from giving way to the subtle idealist philosophy of Berkeley.[48]

On the face of it Wesley's concerns at this time seem to be less with the existential state of his soul than with purely theoretical theological problems. No doubt this reflects in part the fact that he was studying with a view to ordination, and even his devotional reading was partly approached with such interests in mind. Yet Susanna's discerning comment was probably correct. The points he chose to discuss were those which touched him on what were becoming personally sensitive spots. This is particularly true about the questions concerning humility and faith, and his views of the latter are of interest in the light of his later development. It seems doubtful whether predestination was of the same order of concern for him at the personal level; like his mother, he instinctively adopted the anti-Calvinist stance which was now normal for Anglicans. As an intellectual problem it recurred occasionally later, but Wesley never wavered in his revulsion against it, and we shall see that for practical as well as theological reasons he would react violently against its resurgence among evangelicals.

We can therefore picture Wesley as developing a more intense intellectual and practical seriousness about religion, perhaps in the first instance because of the reading needs of his preparation for ordination. This was deepened by the picture of inward Christianity given by à Kempis and Taylor, even if the circumstances of his introduction to them remain obscure. Perhaps the conflict between this and what now seemed to him to have been a merely outward and conventional religion was sharpened and at the same time sweetened by the charming yet alarming friendships with the Stanton ladies and others.

We may now consider the various aspects of Wesley's development from 1725 to 1729; first, his academic progress.

After taking his BA in 1724, Wesley remained at Christ Church to perform the exercises for his MA, and soon began to hope for a Fellowship. The family were already discussing this by January 1725, and Samuel began canvassing support on his son's behalf. Thus he tackled Dr Morley, the Rector of Lincoln College, and the Bishop of Lincoln as College Visitor; also Sir John Thorold of Gainsborough, the father of the Fellow whose place John hoped to fill and a relation of the MP championed by Samuel in the stormy election of 1705. There was much talk of their hopes and fears and the shortage of money.[49] In fact, for once, the Wesleys were lucky. The College and the Fellowship had Lincolnshire connections, as did those whose influence was invoked on their behalf; and shared political prejudices no doubt helped. Lincoln was a well-run college and a serious young man like John Wesley – though not yet too serious to be sociable – no doubt seemed a reasonable candidate. So he was elected to the Fellowship on 17 March 1726. Naturally, the family was delighted. Susanna glorified God and Samuel, after reciting his financial troubles, concluded more cheerfully: 'Wherever I am, my Jacky is Fellow of Lincoln.'[50] And indeed, apart from anything else, at least one financial burden was on the way to being lifted.

Lincoln College was a late mediaeval foundation, created in 1427 specifically to combat Lollardy or, as Wesley later described it, 'to overturn all heresies and defend the Catholic faith'. He remarked on this when defending his freedom from parochial restraints in preaching.[51]

It was perhaps peculiarly fitted for his needs, since apart from the Lincolnshire connections all but one canon-law Fellow were supposed to be students of theology and to be ordained priest when of canonical age. On the other hand, 'student of theology' in this context meant proceeding to the BD within nine years of the BA and six years after this to the DD unless excused. In 1736 Wesley moved to a Fellowship for which this was not required, but for unknown reasons, in 1739 (along with Charles) and again in 1741 he did consider doing the exercises for the BD. Perhaps it was as well that he did not act in 1739, as he planned to attack Bishop Bull's views on justification.[52] But he continued to hold his fellowship until he forfeited it by his marriage in 1751.

The financial security which this gave him continued to be important long after he left Oxford. The income came from a variety of endowments and allowances; fees for pupils; and free rooms or rents if they were let as well as food and other allowances. It has been calculated that from 1730 to 1750 the yield varied between £18 and £80 per annum, but was most often about £30.[53] This was comfortable enough for a young bachelor.

The governing body of the college consisted of a Rector and twelve Fellows, many of them non-resident. In 1731, Dr Morley was succeeded as Rector by Euseby Isham, of a substantial Northamptonshire family. Both of them were moderate, non-Jacobite Tories, fairly typical of the heads of houses. With both Wesley had happy relations at least until his 'Methodism' became excessive. Morley he described in 1731 as 'one of the best friends I ever had in the world', and Isham actually supported the early Oxford Methodist activities and had subscribed to Samuel Wesley's *Job*.[54] The Common Room has been described as peaceable, conservative but free from the animosities of some other colleges at this time. Some of the Fellows seem to have found Wesley an agreeable companion at first. A new Fellow wrote to him in 1727 saying that he was 'infinitely desirous of making your acquaintance. And when I consider those shining qualities which I heard daily mentioned in your praise, I cannot but lament the great exasperation we all suffer in the absence of so agreeable a person from the College.'[55] Most came from Lincolnshire, Northampton or Yorkshire, and most were youngish men who eventually proceeded to country livings. Most of the undergraduates came from gentry or country clergy families, and few were sons of noblemen.[56] Within the customary conventions of college life Wesley did his duties conscientiously: as lecturer in logic (1726–30), in Greek (1726–7 and 1729–34) and in philosophy (1730–35).[57] Religious instruction and pastoral care of undergraduates were part of the traditional duties of conscientious tutors, but although the rise of Oxford 'Methodism' from 1729 might be seen as a development from this, it was taken to an extreme, which made his tutorial care seem excessive and oppressive indoctrination to some.

Once Wesley was ordained priest in 1728, his prospects for a career as a conventional clergyman were only moderate. He might continue as a bachelor fellow for life, probably serving curacies near the city like others. Or he might wait for a college living and perhaps then marriage, but Lincoln's patronage was limited and not very lucrative. In March 1727 he actually thought of taking up a schoolmaster's job in Yorkshire: not an uncommon course for a clergyman to take, and in his case partly in hope of paying his debts, but also in hope of little company but that of his own choosing – a romantic foretaste, perhaps, of his later picture of his hopes for the Georgia expedition.[58] Nothing came of this, so he settled for Oxford, and once ordained began preaching in the Oxford area.[59] In long vacations and at other times he spent long periods at home, helped his father with *Job*, and acted as curate at Wroot until he was summoned back as tutor in 1729.

What was his social life like at this time? The diary in 1725–27 (after which there is a gap for two years) shows his life expanding in three directions: intellectual, social and spiritual. These various interests do not always seem easily compatible, and indeed Wesley himself evidently found them creating tensions which in the long run he tried to resolve by subordinating everything to religion. But this only happened gradually, and his practice in any case did not always accord with his theory. The ideals which he embraced in 1725 (at least according to his later account) did not make him a single-minded ascetic, and he now had more money for recreation.

Wesley's academic reading naturally continued not only for formal tutorial needs but also in pursuit of personal interest. Thus he read Homer, Juvenal, Virgil, Xenophon, and in theology a number of seventeenth-century and more or less contemporary divines: men like Bull, Atterbury, Beveridge; the Nonjurors Hickes and Spinckes; but also Berkeley and Clarke and devotional works by Norris and Fénelon as well as à Kempis. A good deal of miscellaneous literature is also listed with no evident plan or purpose in the selection. This included poetry, history and science, but also a considerable number of plays, including some of the risqué Restoration dramatists. It would be a few years yet before this category of reading was dropped.[60]

What is more, the diary shows much social relaxation. Wesley found the company of the Fellows 'both well natured and well bred'.[61] There are fairly frequent references to playing cards and sometimes to chess; also to dancing (a curious note of directions for formal entry and bows). When at home in Epworth he sometimes went shooting and at least once indulged in hunting.[62] At home, too, there were other rural pursuits: visits to feasts and fairs; picking currants; the erection of an arbour.[63]

Much of this relaxation was in company with his sisters, but both in Oxford and at Epworth there were friendships with more uneasy overtones. Relationships with attractive and intelligent women seemed to bring together in a delightful if disturbing way the various sides of Wesley's nature: his intellectual curiosity, spiritual aspirations and a desire for close friendship which did not lack an erotic element. Sex was the serpent in Wesley's Eden, for the pattern of his relationships with women in this period, as later in his life, showed how difficult he found it to come to terms with this side of his nature beyond a certain point. From 1725 the main focus of his affections was evidently on the Kirkham girls at Stanton and especially Sally ('Varanese' or sometimes 'Sappho'), whose problematic connection with the religious change of 1725 has already been discussed. Later, there was a high-flown correspondence, in accents of religion mingled with romance, with Mrs Pendarves, later to be the famous bluestocking Mrs Delaney. (Unfortunately the Varanese correspondence has not survived.) The circle used classical pseudonyms: Mrs Pendarves was 'Aspasia', her sister Anne 'Selima', Charles Wesley 'Araspes' and John Wesley 'Cyrus'. Possibly Mrs Pendarves invented some of these names, and she also nicknamed John Wesley (appropriately enough) 'Primitive Christianity'.[64]

Wesley's strongly affectionate friendship with Varanese continued after her marriage in December 1725, and it looks as though he was in love with her, though in a sense not easy to define. They joined in spiritual reading and discussion of the spiritual life, and Wesley evidently felt that in the company of these high-spirited, intelligent, charming and apparently spiritually-minded ladies he was being guided through human affection to heavenly love. But perhaps, unwittingly, the process was really operating in the reverse direction. There are unmistakable erotic overtones to these relationships, and it is a measure of Wesley's naïvety that he should have continued with this highflown and emotional relationship with Varanese after her marriage. 'I would certainly acquit you,' she said, 'if my husband should ever resent our freedom but the esteem I have to you . . . as it is grounded on reason and virtue and entirely agreeable to both, no circumstance of life shall ever make me alter.' And that evening he lay on her breast and clasped her hands in his while she said 'many obliging things' in the presence of her sister.[65] On another occasion she said to him: 'Methinks 'tis almost a sin to prostitute those expressions of tenderness to others which I have at any time applied to you. I can't think it expedient nor indeed lawful to break off that acquaintance which is one of the strongest incentives I have to virtue. I never read over your letters without . . . it animates my soul anew and gives it fresh vigour in any good design I have in view.'[66] Wesley himself told Mrs Pendarves that Varanese had shown him 'what he ought to have been, though not what I was'. To this he owed 'both the capacity and the occasion of feeling that soft emotion with which I glow even at the moment while I consider myself as conversing with a kindred soul of my Varanese'.[67]

Wesley's sister, as we have seen, thought that there was more than spirituality to all this. His mother was suspicious too. No doubt he gave her a more severely edited picture than to his sisters, but there was enough to make her write: 'I heartily wish your converse with your friend may prove innocent and useful; but old folks are scrupulous and much given to fear consequences. May God preserve you from sin and danger.' Or again: 'I have had many thoughts of the friendship between V. and thee, and the more I think of it the less I approve it.' In a particularly pointed biblical metaphor she averred that many 'seek to enter the Kingdom of heaven but are not able . . . because there is some Delilah, some one beloved vice, they will not part with'. Reflecting on youthful mistakes and sins from the perspective of her advancing age on eternity she wrote that 'sensual pleasures, the desires of sexes and pernicious friendships of the world' would look very different in later life.[68]

Susanna was probably right to suspect that the friendship was not quite as heaven-pure as Wesley imagined. It seems that he was also attracted by Sally's sister Betty.[69] He was also entangled with Kitty Hargreaves, a neighbour at Epworth, and in June 1726 his father sent her away 'on suspicion of my courting her'.[70] Wesley appears to have been struggling between love of God and love of woman in a meditation on 3 July 1726 when he wrote that: 'As we would willingly suffer a little pain or forgo some pleasure for one we really love, so if we sincerely love God we should readily do this for him . . . Christ therefore puts the matter on the right issue where he says If you love me keep my commandments . . . Begin in small things first: Never [in cypher] touch Kitty's hand again.' In August he resolved 'never to touch any woman's breasts again'.[71]

From August 1730 he began his correspondence with Mrs Pendarves, which also continued for several years. The style was high-flown, and quite unlike his normal one with other people: a kind of pseudo-classical gallantry, a mixture of sacred-profane affection, discourses on spirituality and philosophical discussion as in his abridgement of Peter Brown's version of Locke.[72] It is hard to judge precisely what was happening here. At one level he was trying to repeat the relationship with Varanese (who often figures in the letters), and some have felt that as the letters went on, the convoluted and rather artificial language became informed with a more urgent and existential note. If so, it was not shared by Mrs Pendarves. On leaving for Ireland she found excuses for failing to reply, and Wesley clearly felt that he was being fobbed off. If not exactly a bore, he was, intellectually and perhaps emotionally, investing more capital in these ladies than they could comfortably return with interest.

To interpret these relationships remains problematical.[73] There is no evidence that Wesley ever proposed to any of these ladies, and in any case Varanese was married. Financially, Wesley was years from being able to marry, and if he had, few eighteenth-century women would have thought the pleasures of romantic religious friendship with an earnest young clergyman a fair exchange for actually marrying him. For Varanese at least, it looks like a case of having her cake and eating it: she had a husband and a religious friend, too.

How obtuse Wesley could be in handling personal relationships was revealed by events at home in the troubled summer of 1726. Early in the year Hetty had been seduced, married to her drunken plumber and lost her baby. The family was divided in its attitude to her. Samuel was implacably hostile; John advocated charity. But he spoilt this admirable attitude by preaching a sermon plainly intended as a not very oblique rebuke to his father. Samuel predictably flew into a rage and was estranged from John for some weeks. John then wrote to his brother Samuel junior a letter in which with painstaking detail he explained how correctly he had behaved at every stage. Not only was he sure that he was right, but he also appeared to think that personal relationships could be conducted and estrangements settled by the methods of theological or legal controversy.[74] It was a habit which he never entirely lost, and very revealing of his character.

Where women were concerned Wesley could be warmer. But was the elaborate language not simply a matter of convention, but also a device (like the theologizing of spirituality to his mother) to express while also partly concealing troubling feelings? Though he was capable of some physical expression of his feelings (with periodic qualms and repentance), he seems, some have thought, to have been happiest if intimacy stopped short of marriage. What gives colour to this is the pattern, well documented and strikingly similar, of two subsequent love affairs followed by a disastrous marriage. But before and after that marriage there was an affectionate string of correspondence with favoured female religious friends. More can be said of the reasons for these failed love affairs later. The situation in the 1720s is less clear. On the one hand one may suggest that the later pattern of hesitancy was already present; but on the other some of the more striking examples of self-reproach ('I have loved women and company more than God') are only items in longer catalogues of self-examination. Perhaps what he really liked was an intimacy of heart and mind, religious dedication with a considerable 'tutorial' element through the medium of romantic friendship, but stopping short of marriage. But before the end of the Oxford period he had been influenced by some of his friends to see celibacy as best for the holy life, and at a later stage for many years he believed that marriage (for sexual reasons) was incompatible with perfection.[75] And on the eve of the Georgia voyage in 1735 he rather sourly criticized the usefulness of conversing with religious women, though he found himself unable to resist the temptation.[76] If relationships with women were only one of the experiences which provoked inner conflicts between duty and feeling, they were among the most seductive and difficult for him to handle.

We turn now to spiritual and theological developments in 1725–29. The evidence seems to be of a gradually deepening seriousness. In March 1726, after John's election as Fellow of Lincoln, Susanna expressed the belief that 'the Holy Jesus . . . seems to have taken the conduct of your soul into his own hand, in that he has given you a true notion of saving faith, and, I hope, an experimental knowledge of repentance'.[77] The focus of their discussion at this time was the work of the late Cambridge Platonist John Norris, and the language does not convey the 'evangelical' meaning which it would later have for Wesley. In January 1727 he told his mother that after taking his MA he would draw up a scheme of studies; that he agreed with her that there are many books which it is not worth while to know; and that mere curiosity was no justification for indiscriminate study and speculation. He spoke with disgust of a contemporary theological controversy. It is perhaps significant that he showed much emotion at the death of his friend Robin Griffiths and recalled that he had recently asked him 'to let me have the pleasure of making him a whole Christian'.[78] It was then, too, that Mrs Wesley expressed her anxieties about 'Delilahs'.

In March 1727 there are further signs of a new seriousness and discipline. To his mother Wesley writes that he will organize his finances better; he is glad he is 'little and weak' as a good dispensation of Providence; and a mysterious 'habit of sin' also providentially stirs him to the pursuit of virtue. He is cutting down on the pleasures of company, and sees the need of developing good habits 'before the flexibility of youth is over'. In this mood he romantically visualized the possibility of the Yorkshire schoolmastership as an opportunity for living a retired life with select acquaintances. Mrs Wesley naturally approved of this, but his habit of ratiocination continued. In her next letter Susanna expatiated on the nature of love and warned John against elaborate definitions in preaching: 'For it does not answer the true end of preaching, which is to mend men's lives, not fill their heads with unprofitable speculations . . . Every affection of the soul is better known by experience than any description which can be given of it' – a lesson which Wesley took a long time to learn. To his brother Samuel, after defending some of his biblical exegesis, John ended rather grandiosely with one of his most famous aphorisms: 'Leisure and I have now taken leave of one another. I propose to be busy as long as I live, if my health is so long indulged to me.'[79]

If this was a declaration of intent rather than of absolute achievement, the diary shows that Wesley was trying to implement it. One sign of seriousness and 'method' was the attempt to develop a systematic scheme of study; this may go back even earlier than 1725, for an example appears in the cover of his first diary dated 1722.[80] Mixed with earlier and later, post-conversion, material in the first few pages of the book there is also a set of 'Rules' and 'Resolutions' which appears to belong to 1725.[81] They include 'A General Rule in all Actions of Life': 'Whenever you are to do an action, consider how Christ did or would do the like and do you imitate his example.'

Then, 'General Rules of Employing Time'. There are nine of these, concerning beginning and ending each day with God; sleeping not immoderately; being dutiful in his calling; employing spare hours in religion; avoiding drunkards and busybodies; avoiding curiosity and useless employments and knowledge; 'avoiding all manner of passion'. On 26 March he adds, perhaps in reference to this last, that he 'found a great many unclean thoughts arise in Chapel, and these temptations to it'. He analysed the causes and listed the remedies: avoiding idleness, freedom with women and high seasoned meats.

Then came 'General Rules as to Intention':

1. In every action reflect on the end.
2. Begin every action in the name of the Father, the Son and the Holy Ghost.
3. Begin every important work with prayer.
4. Do not leave off a duty because you are tempted in it.

Under Taylor's influence, according to his own account, Wesley began his diary the next month, and this may be seen as reflecting the more inward side of the intellectual arguments with his mother. The rules seem to reflect that concern, expressed in his later accounts, for a more intense inward holiness. They record the use of time, and special signs twice a day appear to show praise, prayer, 'intention', thanksgiving. On 20 September, the day after his ordination as deacon, he resolved to review his life always twice a day; and on 24 October he resolved on a weekly review. It is not clear whether all of these reviews were kept up, though there are occasional 'resolutions' on particular points such as 'despise nobody's advice'. On 1 December he resolved on fasting every last Wednesday to remedy lax discipline. During his first year as an ordained man he reviewed the past week every Saturday night with prayers for help and mercy. It was at the beginning of one of these, early in 1726, that he included the statement, 'I have loved women and company more than God', though also questions about pride, indolence, intemperate sleep. The remedy for this last was to rise at 5.00 a.m. – a practice only gradually achieved, despite his later claims that he managed it at once.[82]

On 24 September 1726 Wesley drew up a plan of study reflecting his MA preparation, but also that for the ministry: divinity on Sundays; classics on Monday and Tuesday; the science of logic on Wednesday; languages on Thursday; the sciences of metaphysics and physics on Friday; oratory and poetry, writing sermons and letters on Saturday. The letter to his mother about a scheme of study after his MA, which the diary for 27 January shows him beginning together with financial reviews from March, was followed by a period of two years for which the diaries have been lost. The letters of this period suggest that, despite his resolutions, there was no comprehensive cutting off of recreation and conversation.

But it is striking that when the diary reappears late in 1729, it leaves out the earlier longhand records of conversations, notes on light reading and so on, though other records show him still reading plays until the end of 1731, when they disappear. The classics, serious reading and above all devotional works bulk large.[83] Yet as late as May 1731, Wesley was tempted to play cards on Sunday, and in July 1733 he danced with a lady friend.[84] However, if the drive to holiness was a gradually evolving affair and did not mark a clean break with the past, the development of a personal, individual discipline for study as well as piety was an essential preliminary to the organization of the so-called 'Holy Club'. This extended and diversified as well as intensified a passion for an organized life of piety which gradually became more inward and more world-denying. It gave a corporate dimension to what had hitherto been largely an individual quest, thought not in quite so simple and unitary a fashion as has often been supposed.

What were the origins and characteristics of the 'Club'? Wesley gave varying accounts of the rise of his movement on different occasions, including his activities in his Oxford period. The best known and most influential originated in an apologia to the father of William Morgan who had died mad (it was alleged) as a result of the ascetic excesses of the pious group which Wesley led. This letter was written in October 1732, and the account which it contained was read by Wesley as an explanation and defence of his activities to various groups. A version of it was used by the anonymous author of *The Oxford Methodists* (1733), which helped to publicize the term 'Methodist' for the group. The account reached a wider audience and established itself as part of Methodist history when Wesley published the letter to the elder Morgan as an introduction to the first instalment of his *Journal* in 1740.[85] According to this account, 'In November 1729, at which time I came to reside in Oxford, your son (William Morgan), my brother, and myself and one more[86] agreed to spend three or four evenings in a week together. Our design was to read over the classics, which we had before read in private, on common nights, and on Sunday some books in divinity.' Later, the group added more social work and observance of the fasts of the church through the influence of the Manchester man John Clayton. In the meantime they had acquired a variety of nicknames, especially from Christ Church and Merton men. These included: 'Sacramentarians', 'Enthusiasts', 'Supererogation Men', 'The Reforming Club', 'The Godly Club', 'Methodists'. This last term, which Wesley later at least recognized as from an ancient school of physicians, had several precedents.[87] Eventually he came round to accepting it as the title for his followers in his post-conversion period, though for some time he was very conscious of it as a nickname which at least needed explanation against critics. It was widely used in the eighteenth century as a general label for evangelical enthusiasts as well as, more specifically, for the followers of Whitefield and Welsh revivalists like Howel Harris. The 'Holy Club' term was current by the end of 1730, when old Samuel Wesley said that if John was the father of the Holy Club, he was its grandfather by virtue of his own pious activities in Oxford a generation before.[88] Though this was only one of several derogatory terms used by critics at the time, it is as 'The Holy Club' that the early Oxford Methodists have been pictured in many later accounts. Perhaps the picture was sharpened by engravings taken from a painting by a not very successful Victorian painter, Marshall Claxton, showing John Wesley directing a group in his rooms at Lincoln. The impression given is of an organized club with rules, meeting at set times in one place for devotional purposes and expanding into social work, though with a strong religious purpose behind this as well.

Certainly this is very probably how its enemies saw it. But 'club' had unwelcome connotations of a secular, if not conspiratorial, kind. Samuel Wesley junior objected to it for this reason.[89] Wesley himself often spoke of the group as the 'company', but he did not reject the term 'society' ascribed to it by the Morgans, and indeed he spoke of the prospect of the younger Morgan son's becoming 'a member of our little society'.[90] This was in 1734, and in July 1733 he had evidently been proposing to Clayton that they should 'avow themselves a society and fix upon a set of rules', to which Clayton objected on the grounds that this seemed to be setting their own rules above the customs of the church.[91]

Since the origins of the later 'evangelical' phase of the Methodist societies have often been associated with the earlier religious societies which began in the 1670s, it is as well to say at once that the 'Holy Club' never at any time followed their exact pattern and certainly did not begin in their manner.[92] When work by the Oxford 'Methodists' extended to the townspeople, however, societies more like the old type do seem to have been developed.[93] Their activity was not even primarily a religious meeting in origin but, as Wesley's letter to Morgan indicated, an informal meeting for studying the classics plus a book on 'divinity' on Sundays. In later accounts Wesley rather misleadingly spoke of studying the Greek Testament. The study was really an exercise in academic discipline by mutual self-help of the kind that other serious young Oxford men like Richard Graves indulged in.[94] Its later, quite rapid development into something very different and its relationship to later Methodism obscured this fact. Its original nature was very probably influenced by alarms about infidelity in the university, which lay behind the summons to Wesley to return to duty, as we shall see.

The traditional picture also implies a group dominated by Wesley himself, though his own account to Morgan indicates that at least the extension of the group's activities owed much to initiatives by his colleagues. Wesley does, however, plainly see them as beginning in November 1729, though it has often been said that the real originator of the 'Holy Club' was Charles Wesley, who collected a devotional group earlier in the year, which John took over as leader on his return. This was certainly what Charles himself claimed at least in later life. He wrote to Doctor Chandler in 1785 that after his own turn to seriousness in 1729 'I went to the weekly sacrament and persuaded two or three young students to accompany me, and to observe the method of study prescribed by the statutes of the university. This gained me the harmless nickname of Methodist. In half a year my brother left his curacy at Epworth, and came to our assistance. We then proceeded regularly in our studies, and in doing what good we could to the bodies and souls of men.' Charles's letters at the time recount his 'reformation' which seems to have begun by January 1729, and also show how he was responding to the university authorities' concern for discipline, so we may see his initiative as being partly dictated by personal needs, partly by other pressures. John was evidently advising him also, as for example on diary-keeping.[95]

Charles had come up to Christ Church from Westminster School in 1727, and his early letters reflect his father's ebullient and whimsical temperament, with no sign of religious concern. It looks as though

Charles, even more than John, found Oxford life a pleasant change and a release from the seriousness and restrictions of Epworth. He seems also to have had excursions to London and to have had emotional entanglements with London actresses. To his brother John he protested: 'What! would you have me be a saint at once?'[96] But by January 1729 he was disillusioned with the 'pretty creatures' in London, proposed to 'reform', and asked John's advice about a 'system'.[97] One may suppose that the conflict of Epworth ideals with fashionable Christ Church ways was brought to a head by the problems with the 'pretty creatures' to create a crisis of conscience, and it was characteristic of Charles that he then plunged enthusiastically if erratically into a more serious way of life, though he felt that Christ Church was 'the worst place in the world to begin a reformation in'. He was probably encouraged, and his sense of standing for a good though unpopular cause strengthened, by the attempt of the Heads of Houses to recall tutors to their duties at the end of 1728 in face of signs of infidel problems. Charles quoted their letter, and noted that there was opposition to it in Christ Church, where the Dean refused to publish it.[98]

By May 1729 Charles was trying not only to reform himself but to influence Bob Kirkham (Sally's brother) and Morgan. Kirkham was not entirely satisfactory, and it may be added that Charles was more wary than John of the seductive charms of the Stanton ladies.[99] There is really no suggestion here of an organized society, which was perhaps how Charles saw it over half a century later; in his Chandler letter he was, of course, anxious to put the original 'Methodists' in a very different light from the organization which his brother had made of it by the 1780s, by now including the American ordinations which Charles furiously opposed. At the time, in 1729, Charles was simply trying to influence a very few friends in an informal way.

John visited Oxford in the summer of 1729, following Charles's 'reformation', and the brothers began meetings, together with Kirkham and Morgan, to read pious works together, such as the life of De Renty, the pious seventeenth-century Catholic who had also founded little 'companies' and whose *Life* became one of Wesley's favourite books.[100] In October 1729 Dr Morley, the Rector of Lincoln, evidently trying to implement the Heads' proposed reformation, summoned John back to act as tutor.[101] In March 1730 the group began to meet more regularly. As Wesley recalled it in his letter of 1732 to Mr Morgan, it consisted only of the Wesley brothers, Morgan and 'one more', usually identified as Kirkham, though there is some uncertainty about this.[102]

As we have seen, the original 'design' was to read the classics on weekdays and divinity on Sundays, as a study group to do collectively what was already being done individually by Wesley according to his study plan drawn up in 1727. By March 1730 a regular pattern emerged by which they met on particular days in each other's rooms. Their reading included devotional works like Norris and De Renty, but this was not what they 'chiefly read', as Wesley claimed in a later account.[103]

The picture of a single, tightly-knit 'club' led by Wesley under fixed rules and meeting in one place has dissolved in the light of recent research.[104] As the association developed, it consisted of several small groups in separate colleges, varying in the closeness of their association with Wesley himself. Some people did meet regularly with him for study and prayer; but they also met separately with other friends at other times. A larger circle joined in some of the charitable activities; and others merely sympathized or subscribed money. In part this shifting network reflected both the collegiate structure of the university and (even more) its shifting membership of students and dons, as well as the rising and falling enthusiasm of the participants. At the same time the history of Oxford Methodism both during and after Wesley's time of residence shows that though he learnt and adapted much from his associates, he did tend to acquire a leading position among them. For his own part he gained from his friends something of that sense of a holy company to stimulate his own devotion and to further his hopes of influencing others which he would later develop in the mature Methodist system. They also gave him an opportunity to exercise his instincts to be a spiritual director.

But the development of the Oxford 'Methodism' was related to, and complicated by, his tutorial duties. From one point of view Wesley, from his return to college in November 1729, set himself to be the best kind of Oxford tutor.[105] He lectured on classics, logic and divinity and from June 1730 began to take private pupils, one of whom was later to teach Gibbon and be given the grudging compliment that he was a 'learned and pious man'. He kept lists of the books he had read with them, and fifty years later recalled that he had not only told them what books to read but also had ordered them to read no others.[106] One has to remember that traditionally tutors were supposed to supervise the religion and morals as well as the instruction of their pupils, and that Morley intended him to tighten up supervision of this kind. The suspicion was, however, that though Wesley may not have put pressure on his pupils to 'join the Holy Club' (and he denied it in the case of the younger Morgan brother), he was inclined to impose parts of his private disciplines upon them, such as early rising and communion. Some, like his future brother-in-law Westley Hall, or John Whitelamb his father's curate, were more amenable than others, who were criticized by Wesley for falling by the wayside.[107] The best-documented case is that of Richard Morgan, whose brother William had been an early and influential member of Wesley's circle and whose tragic death and the charge that Wesley had driven him mad had led to the apologia already mentioned.

Morgan's father was evidently a man of decent piety, who was prepared to place Richard under Wesley's charge despite what had happened to William, though with reservations. He wished him to live a sober and virtuous life and attend church and sacrament according to college rules, but 'for young people to pretend to be more pure and holy than the rest of mankind is a dangerous experiment'. Richard was not to use his father's money for Wesley's charities, and he should 'live as decently as the gentlemen of his station.'[108]

Richard wrote to his father in January 1734 complaining of the devotional reading and exercises that Wesley was forcing on him, and that Wesley had thereby provoked mockery of him as a 'Methodist'. The Rector had said that Wesley was putting people off from entering the college. It is revealing that Wesley accidentally found a copy of the letter, did not scruple to read it, and then defended himself to the father. He saw religion as 'a constant ruling habit of soul; a renewal of our minds in the image of God; a recovery of the divine likeness'. Morgan replied temperately, avoiding theological argument, agreeing with the need of religious discipline, especially for a boy with a rather lax previous history, but warning again against excess. It seems that despite his revolt the young Morgan succumbed to Wesley's personality, also came under the influence of the Evangelical James Hervey, and so became a 'Methodist' while he was at Oxford. Wesley met him again many years later in Ireland.[109] There is an interesting parallel here to the charges of proselytization and the abuse of the tutorial function made against Newman at Oriel during the later Oxford Movement, and one may feel that Mr Morgan had a better sense of the best way of dealing with young people. Wesley's defence shows his usual dogmatism, sense of his own rightness and lack of sensitivity to the varieties of human nature which was characteristic of him at this time and in many ways much later.

Wesley's development from the end of 1729 shows how his personal discipline and relationships related in a kind of complicated counterpoint to the development of the more corporate experiment of Oxford Methodism: though closely connected, they cannot simply be identified with each other. He continued to correspond with his mother about Taylor as before, and from August 1730 with Mrs Pendarves about theology and spirituality mixed with ambiguous professions of affection. In 1732 he drew up a set of 'General Rules' for self-examination to become ever more elaborate in later versions. Though originally for Wesley alone, the 'club' could use them. The description of 'real Christianity' given to Mr Morgan in 1734 shows clearly enough his ideal of a total inward and outward patterning of the Christian's life on Christ. Such ideals

Wesley certainly wished to impose upon others, and some of the means of inculcating such ideals were fed gradually into Oxford Methodism. But some of the members had their own ideas of Christianity and its rules which influenced Wesley at least for a time. Their corporate activities in fact owed much to the initiative of others than Wesley.

At the end of August 1730 there was an important new development. William Morgan had accidentally visited a condemned criminal in the Castle prison and thought it would be useful to visit debtors there, so others began to accompany him regularly in this work. The same month, again following Morgan's lead, they began sick visiting in the town with the permission of the incumbents. Wesley consulted his father about the propriety of this, and received in answer the revelation that the old man had done the same years before. He also obtained approval from the Bishop, and indeed there were precedents for such work.[110]

In answer to the gibes of the young men of Christ Church and Merton, Wesley drew up a series of questions about the beginning of 1731 concerning their activities.[111] These in effect affirmed that Christians should imitate Christ in going about and doing good: feeding the hungry, clothing the naked, visiting sick and prisoners and making 'all these actions subservient to a higher purpose, even the saving of souls from death'. They should influence their neighbours to be Christians and therefore scholars by 'method and industry'; encourage frequent communion; guide them to read good authors and adopt resolutions from those authors. They should do good to the needy with material help and the distribution of Bibles, Prayer Books and the *Whole Duty of Man*, teach their children and guide them in devotional exercises. Finally, they should do the same for prisoners as well as helping the release of small debtors and setting them up in trades.

In face of threats to 'blow up the Holy Club' and increasing opposition, Wesley was led to fortify himself further by consulting 'a clergyman of known wisdom and integrity', a Lincolnshire neighbour Joseph Hoole, later to be associated with the High Church and Nonjuring circles who would influence Wesley through his friend John Clayton.[112]

Early in 1731 the names of new recruits began to appear in Wesley's diary – Hall, Hervey and John Gambold – though they did not all join the group at once. Gambold says he first met Charles Wesley in March 1730 and was introduced to John some time later. He portrays John as 'always the chief manager', being 'blest with such activity as to be always gaining ground and such steadiness that he lost none'. Though retaining authority, he yet allowed all to speak and regarded their words as well as his own. Gambold portrays the group as meeting most evenings for prayers (chiefly on charity) and the study of books. 'But the chief business was to review what each had done that day, in pursuance of the common design, and to consult what steps were to be taken next.' The impression is of a group for study and social action rather than cultivating devotional life, though Gambold adds that for some years they had read the New Testament together and discussed problems arising from it. Wesley, says Gambold, 'directed' his friends on systematic study and the organization of daily routine. They were to pray twice daily, keep the fasts and communicate weekly. Wesley stressed self-examination as in his *Collection of Prayers*, and the keeping of a diary record to maintain in their minds a sense of God's presence.[113]

Though this description was written some years later, and at some points reflects a slightly later stage of development (Gambold probably joined the group early in 1732), it is probably a fair picture.

It was in fact about this time that some of the devotional practices which Gambold mentions were introduced by an important new recruit, John Clayton, a Manchester man at Brasenose. Clayton was a more important influence on the Oxford Methodists and on Wesley himself than has perhaps always been recognized, and in a number of different directions. For one thing he reinforced Wesley's determination to be a 'Primitive Christian', a protean concept which for late seventeenth-century High Churchmen meant conforming to the practices as well as the doctrines of the church of the first five centuries. The concept would later take more varied and divisive forms, including those of heterodox Deists and Arians, and for the new-style Methodists of the 1740s something closer to the 'apostolic' patterns of the New Testament.[114] Wesley had already absorbed High Church ideals of doctrine and piety from his reading of the seventeenth-century divines and the moderate Nonjuror Robert Nelson, but through Clayton and Clayton's friendship with the Manchester Nonjuror Dr Deacon he now received more advanced and eccentric ideas from the so-called *Apostolic Constitutions*, which were taken to be a 'primitive' authority for discipline and devotions. These practices included compulsory Wednesday and Friday fasts ('station fasts'), baptism by immersion, and various eucharistic observances. To this was added use of certain mystical writings, a taste reinforced by Wesley's encounter with William Law in July 1732.[115]

Clayton also helped to enlarge Wesley's circle of acquaintances by introducing him to the SPCK men in London and Sir John Phillips. But even more important for the work of the Oxford Methodists was Clayton's interest in charity and the education of the poor, and the extension of the group to Brasenose. A letter from Clayton in August 1732 gives an account of the group's work.[116]

Wesley himself, in his account to Mr Morgan, singled out the addition of 'the fasts of the Church of England and the Church Catholic' as

Clayton's distinctive contribution to the work of the group.[117] To Clayton, also, may perhaps be attributed the increasing tendency for the group to talk about devotional matters during their meetings, for about this time Wesley was engaged in collecting prayers which were to be used for his first published work. The members were urged to follow Wesley's practice of making sets of 'General Rules' to guide their lives.[118] As to social work, Clayton was much concerned with education, and it was perhaps to further this that Wesley wrote to his mother in July 1732 for an account of her Epworth system.[119] Clayton also urged the Methodists to visit a workhouse, and he showed a certain concern for discriminating between idle and worthy beggars which would show itself more forcefully in later years in his criticism of the Manchester poor. On this point Wesley would show himself a truer son of 'Catholic' Christianity than Clayton or other evangelicals.[120] It is in fact a nice question to ask how far the charitable activities were at least in part an expression of Christian discipline and a demonstration of commitment to the world, and a means to saving the souls of those aided rather than 'pure' charity. The Wesley questions about the propriety of their work and Gambold's comments on it leave this at least an open question.[121]

But while these developments were taking place, the company received a severe blow which was particularly damaging to Wesley himself. William Morgan, who had contributed so much to the Oxford Methodist initiatives, became physically and finally mentally ill; by March 1732 his father was speaking of 'this ridiculous society', and William's use of his allowance for its charities; and in August William died.[122] A common view seems to have been that his illness had been aggravated, if not caused, by his Methodist excesses, and that in fact Wesley's ascetic demands had driven him mad. Wesley of course indignantly denied this, and his letter to Morgan's father in October 1732 was essentially an apologia for his work. What made matters worse for the Methodists' reputation was the fact that Wesley tried to help a man called Blair who was in prison on a charge of homosexuality. This was a measure of Wesley's charity and courage, but confirmed the bad opinions of critics.[123] As to poor Morgan, the truth is hardly now recoverable. Probably the Methodist disciplines did no more than aggravate his illness and he was the kind of earnest, sensitive man who might well have ended as he did without Methodism. Methodism was a vehicle for his concerns, but Wesley was hardly the best guide for a man who perhaps needed restraint rather than encouragement.[124] Yet it is also worth noting that Morgan's father, with whatever cautions, was prepared to entrust his other son to Wesley's care.

At all events the tragedy fuelled hostility still further, and in December 1732 popular feeling and suspicions were well expressed in an article in

Fog's Weekly Journal and in reply to this a pamphlet (often attributed erroneously to William Law) called *The Oxford Methodists* (1733). The latter did not unequivocally favour them, especially in the first edition, and Wesley himself thought it might be satirical.[125]

The *Fog's Journal* attack was illuminating in its way. Methodism was seen as an example of the famous English tendency to melancholy but similar to Continental Pietism. Nothing in life is indifferent to Methodists and so they condemn much that ordinary people find innocent. They starve their bodies and even let blood to cool their animal spirits. Indeed it is claimed in thinly veiled terms that they admire Origen's sacrifice of his manhood as a means to this. In short they are 'enthusiastic madmen'. The attack is a mild version of the kind of traditional attacks on mysterious and suspect sects which have occurred throughout history and would be applied to Methodism in later years.[126]

The author of *The Oxford Methodists* had gained access to the Morgan letter and used it for a factual account of their work, which he found 'edifying'. The charge of enthusiasm would be answered as time and good conduct did their work, and though he thought them excessive in some things, this was perhaps unavoidable in the young.

The underlying ideals of the Oxford Methodists, at least in Wesley's eyes, were no doubt those of the total imitation of Christ as expressed to Mr Morgan and more at large in a sermon on 'The Circumcision of the Heart' preached in January 1733. It was in fact a description of Wesley's ideal of 'Christian perfection', and he cited it as such in his *Plain Account* of that doctrine in the 1760s, as proof that he had never changed his mind on it, though in fact there was at least one important change in later editions about faith as the way to perfection.[127]

Public opposition as well as individual difficulties led to members falling off, though others joined, such as Benjamin Ingham, who later ran an Oxford Methodist type of society at home in Yorkshire and founded an evangelical sect.[128] There was also a falling off when Wesley was absent, for example in 1733 to consult Clayton in Manchester. It was perhaps in hopes of stabilizing the group by more formal rules (his favourite expedient for his own problems) that Wesley asked Clayton for his opinion on such a scheme; he received a negative answer from the Manchester circle, which preferred the wisdom of the 'primitive church'.[129] In the event Wesley's active supervision probably counted for more, though he offered a guide to piety by his first published work in *A Collection of Forms of Prayer* (January 1734).

This consisted of prayers for the morning and evening of each day of the week, linked with specific virtues and vices, together with a scheme of self-examination. They appear to be drawn from Wesley's accumulated reading of a variety of High Church and Nonjuror authors, particularly the so-called Spinckes collection of *Private Devotions*. The scheme of self-examination owed something to his father's *Pious Communicant*, but more to Robert Nelson's *Practice of True Devotion*.[130] The introduction to the book indicated Wesley's ideal that 'Christ liveth in me' is the 'fulfilment of the law'; 'he that being dead to the world is alive to God . . . who has given him his whole heart'. But to achieve this ideal Wesley was also recommending to his pupils at this time the Pietist Francke's *Nicodemus or The Fear of Man*.[131]

During 1734, partly under the influence of Clayton and his circle, partly through William Law, Wesley was studying the mystics and pondering the precepts of the 'primitive Christians'. Clayton in general wished to pursue a course between the 'monkish mysticism of the fourth century and the lukewarm indifference of the present age'.[132] But the imposition of some practices as rules met doubts from Wesley himself and opposition from some of the others. By the beginning of 1735 he was becoming concerned about the 'beliefs of the gospel' and questioning the supposed 'apostolic' rules advocated from the pseudonymous *Apostolic Constitutions* by Clayton and the Nonjurors. In the end he decided that practices like the 'station days' of fasting were useful but not obligatory. Yet on the eve of his departure for Georgia he still advocated fasting, at least on Fridays, as a sign to the self-indulgent world of the high table, and believed this to be at least near-apostolic.[133]

But the time was now approaching when for Wesley himself Oxford would cease to be the scene of his path to piety. In 1734–35 two possible decisions for a change dominated his mind, and these bore not only on his possible future career but also on his conception of personal piety. The first was the proposal to succeed his father as Rector of Epworth, and the second was the invitation to become a missionary in the new American colony of Georgia and so to begin his quest all over again in a new world.

The Epworth proposal came as a result of his father's poor health, which led Samuel to wish to resign the living in John's favour so as to secure a home and support for Susanna on his death.[134] The proposal was made in October 1734, and John did in fact take over his father's duties during the final illness and for a time after his death in April 1735. To ease his father's dying anxieties he finally, reluctantly, agreed to succeed him if this could be engineered. Epworth was a Crown living, and through Thomas Broughton of the SPCK and Sir John Phillips approaches were made to men in high places, even to Walpole. It is in fact unlikely that in face of the usual scramble for places and Wesley's dubious reputation for his Oxford Methodism this move could have succeeded.[135] The chief interest, indeed, for Wesley's biographers, is the evidence that the episode affords of Wesley's character and motives at this time. In elaborate letters to his father and brother Samuel junior he resisted their pressure and arguments in favour of the obligations of parochial ministry and filial piety, by spelling out at great length the arguments in favour of staying in Oxford. They can be reduced to a simple sequence of Oxford logic: our duty is to follow a course of life which tends to the glory of God; the glory of God requires a holy life; I can follow a holy life best in Oxford; therefore I must stay in Oxford. Only there could he obtain the right company, conditions and ability to pursue a holy discipline – not in bucolic, barbarous Epworth.[136]

Both the mode and content of the argument are familiar examples of the Wesley style to get his own way. He even invoked the authority of the Bishop to support his legal position.[137] Although he argued that he could actually only do good to others by being in conditions that allowed him to make himself good, few have doubted that in this Wesley was pursuing what suited his own inclinations and the cultivation of his own soul rather than the good of his family or of others generally, under the specious guise of doing the will of God. It was a highly self-regarding stance. As Samuel junior bluntly wrote: 'I see your love to yourself but your love to your neighbour I do not see.'[138]

Wesley's acceptance of the Georgia appointment was also, ultimately, bound up with his concern for saving his soul in the way that he thought suited him best, though again the ostensible purpose of the post was concern for others. The motivation here was, however, rather more complicated. In his review in January 1738 he pictured himself as having gone to convert the Indians without having been converted himself. The actual circumstances and purposes of the mission will be examined later; here it is sufficient to say that those behind the project, Oglethorpe and Dr Burton, were already acquainted with the Wesley family who were, as we have seen, themselves interested in missionary work (there is Samuel's romantic dream about himself and the East, not to mention the news of the Pietist exploits). It is significant that when John spelled out his reasons for accepting the post in a letter to Burton in October 1735, he once again emphasized that his primary motive was to save his own soul, 'to which all the rest are subordinated', though he added that he hoped to offer the gospel to the Indians. He then spelled out his hopes of finding an unspoiled country and community in which he would not be distracted by the seductions of civilization (including civilized women!). It would be like Eden before the Fall.[139] The apparent *volte face* from his arguments in favour of the necessity of staying at Oxford instead of going to Epworth is noteworthy. It looks as though the arguments for Oxford had really been mostly a way of getting out of the Epworth trap, and that in reality Wesley was already feeling that the holy experiment of Oxford Methodism had been a failure for him personally so far as his private struggle was concerned. Still clinging to his old methods, he now blamed the failure on the worldly and distracting Oxford environment and hoped that in the Georgian Eden as it was before the Fall he could at last succeed.

Before assessing what Wesley had achieved at Oxford and what he had given and received from it, it is necessary to turn from his 'Methodist' organization to his spiritual development as it had unfolded during the ten years before his departure for Georgia.

The Oxford Methodist organization no doubt helped to develop Wesley's sense of leadership and his lifelong love of supervising and guiding other people's spiritual progress, but although it began as a study group, developed into an agency for good works and added to this experiments in spiritual discipline, Wesley's own personal discipline was much more exacting. It can be traced mainly in his diaries and notebooks, whereas his interpretation of what he was doing and with what aims can be seen partly in his various later retrospective reviews of his life and partly in letters written at the time. The former have to be read with due regard to their purposes and the perspective Wesley had when he wrote them.

His private discipline gradually became more complex, intense and obsessive. In 1730 he began a set of General Questions which was several times extended and revised.[140] They are designed to check the prayers and activities of the day for their purity of intention so as to sanctify every thought and action to God. In all this, even when doing good to others was the work in hand, the ultimate aim was stated to be to do all things with 'a present or previous perception of its direct or remote tendency to the glory of God'. But what may well strike the reader is the way in which everything seems to centre on Wesley's own condition and motives. The most striking manifestation of this is the development of a kind of spiritual temperature chart. In April 1732 it was fairly simple: a form for analysing religion, study, correspondence, travel, pupils, the 'accidents' of life.[141] These schemes were not displaced by the interest in mysticism (which seemed to promise more direct access to intimacy with God) and experiments in meditation from 1732. From the end of 1733 the intensification of his self-interrogation increased and resulted in an extraordinary, almost neurotic 'grid' system on which he listed his activities hour by hour and rated his 'temper of devotion' on a scale of 1 to 9 as well as recording resolutions kept or broken.[142] It was in 1734, too, that he began to talk of celibacy, and early in 1735, as we have seen, he was doubting the value of female religious conversation. Clayton's notion that one should steer between 'monkish' excess and modern laxity is also reflected in a memorandum by Wesley in 1734/35 which questions how frequent self-examination should be; how to steer between 'scrupulosity' and 'self-indulgence'; and between 'niceness in marking my progress and carelessness in it'.[143] If this partly reflected the more relaxed approach of some mystics and certainly a degree of disillusionment with his achievement by the methods so far used, his tone about the proper stance for a Methodist to take on fasting, and behaviour in hall before he left for Georgia, was stern enough.

What religious and theological ideals informed this behaviour? Wesley's retrospective surveys in January 1738, May 1738 and in the *Plain Account of Christian Perfection* in 1767 are far from objective, but the second has been especially influential in later analyses. In the *Plain Account* he was concerned to trace the steps by which he evolved his mature doctrine of perfection while claiming that he had not in essence changed his mind since 1725. This was a defensive operation against charges made during the perfectionist revival of the 1760s. He quoted his 'Circumcision of the Heart' sermon of 1733 as showing how he then understood the Christian life after following the injunctions of Taylor, Law and à Kempis. The 'circumcision of the heart' was defined as 'that habitual disposition of soul, which in the sacred writings is termed holiness . . . the being cleansed from sin' and 'so "renewed in the image of our mind" as to be "perfect as our Father in heaven is perfect"'. He also emphasized that 'Love is the fulfilling of the law, the end of the commandment.' In sum, all designs and desires must be centred on God with a pure intention of heart.[144] If this is a true account of Wesley's ideals at the time, it has still to be said that the contemporary evidence shows considerable uncertainties about the means of achieving it.

In other accounts he was more concerned to show how his ideas of religion in general had developed in the light of his subsequent sense of failure, and in the case of the famous review of 24 May 1738 in the light of his newly-acquired doctrine of justification by faith. Here he dwelt on his sinful life of bare outward piety before 1725, followed by the discovery of the need of inward holiness and total dedication of our thoughts and motives. But he concluded that, despite all his efforts, he could not find comfort or a consciousness of acceptance by God. Then a 'contemplative man' convinced him that 'outward works were nothing' and instructed him on 'how to pursue inward holiness or a union of the soul with God'. This, Wesley later thought, led him to neglect outward works in favour of 'mental prayer' for 'purifying the soul and uniting it with God'. But he now thought that this was just as much an effort of his own works and righteousness. And so he proceeds to recount how the Moravians taught him about justification by faith.[145] From that perspective, plainly everything he had attempted hitherto was of the nature of sin and a vain attempt to save himself by his own efforts.

A little earlier, on 25 January 1738, Wesley wrote a memorandum headed (in Greek): 'Not tossed to and fro by every wind of doctrine'.[146] This is a strictly doctrinal account under the significant heading: 'Different views of Christianity as given (1) by the Scriptures (2) the Papists (3) the Lutherans and Calvinists (4) the English Divines (5) the Essentialist Nonjurors (6) the Mystics.' Then he reviewed these answers to his long-standing question 'What must I do to be saved?' He had early been warned not to lay too much stress, like the Papists, on outward works or on faith without works. Then he fell among Lutheran and Calvinist authors (a phase apparently not noted elsewhere), who confused him by an extreme emphasis on faith. Then the 'English writers' (such as Taylor and Nelson) 'a little relieved him' from this. But he was worried about their varying interpretations of Scripture. Then he was advised (obviously by the 'essentialist' Nonjurors) to trust the test of 'antiquity': what was believed by everyone, everywhere and always. But he thought that they exaggerated by making antiquity a 'coordinate rather than subordinate rule' with Scripture, by taking antiquity too far and making temporary rules binding on all ages. Finally, the mystics gave him noble pictures of union with God and inward religion which made all else seem mean and insipid, but they also seemed to play down good works and faith in favour of love being all. All other commands are to be used only so long as you find them useful to you. This confused him further.

This account focusses on doctrinal problems of authority and faith and works, and though this is obviously relevant to what was shortly to happen to him, there is no sign of the Moravian solution already explained to him in Georgia. It rather represents the confusion of mind already evident on the eve of the voyage, though no doubt sharpened and, so to speak, finalized by his traumatic experiences there and the failure of the experiment of the old ways in a new environment. The common ground and differences in the various accounts reflect later perspectives and the occasions for writing: they are not simple transcripts of what Wesley thought and felt at the times described. A word of caution is also necessary here, as elsewhere, about laying too much stress on the books Wesley read and their original religious pedigree and meaning. Too many analyses of Wesley's experience and theology have proceeded in this bookish way. It is true that the books mentioned did influence him, some of them (even the mystics) long after his conversion. But he read and abridged them very selectively and built them into patterns of his own. He omitted 'Popish' and other material that he disliked. He valued the books for aspirations and aphorisms about holiness and for descriptions of its effects. His selection was conditioned and his interpretations coloured by his own needs and experiences and those of his followers. They become part of his own synthesis of piety and are very much eighteenth-century documents. Martin Schmidt (who himself is perhaps over-inclined to dwell on the literary influences on Wesley in terms of the authors' original characters) is certainly right in stressing that what Wesley especially valued was the personal models of piety (suitably edited indeed) of a selection of varied saints like the Mexican hermit Gregory Lopez or De Renty or the Presbyterian Thomas Halyburton.[147] Even the loving union of Madame Guyon with God often sounds very like the perfection experiences of early Methodists, and pictures like this could easily be taken up, shorn of their original contexts and unwelcome accompaniments.

To gauge Wesley's state of mind up to 1735 it is often better to rely on more strictly contemporary evidence uncontaminated by later ideas, and especially on his letters, allowing for a degree of intellectual distancing from his feelings (as his mother suspected) or at times perhaps self-dramatization. The diaries reveal anxieties and frustrations, but less about his overall understanding of what he was doing. So even here they may be held to conceal as much as they reveal – which is even more true of the famous (and often misleading) published *Journal*, as we shall see later. The ever-increasing complexity of the disciplines recorded in the diaries at least tend to confirm that his mother's suspicion was correct: that the theological niceties raised in his letters to her in fact were intellectual projections of existential anxieties.

The letters broadly confirm the idea that Taylor and à Kempis were making Wesley think seriously about the demands of a holy life and its inwardness from 1725, and when responding to his queries about difficulties raised by his spiritual guides his mother uses the language of 'pressing after greater degrees of Christian perfection'.[148] There arose out of this reading a dislike on the part of Wesley for the morbidity and distrust of pleasure in his guides. 'Holiness and happiness' became twin aspirations for Wesley and indeed other evangelicals later, and although happiness was not to be sought in 'worldly' things, it is noticeable that it took a few years before the cards and dancing and the rest faded out.[149] Wrestling with Taylor, as we have seen, also led Wesley on to questions about the meaning of faith and the nature of predestination. On faith he was weaned from an almost Lockeian rationalism to belief in revelation as revelation, but this was a long way from the more complex and existential meaning it later acquired for him.

Although the development of the private disciplines testify to the search for inward holiness, they are also evidence of the difficulty of achieving it. There is also a suggestion of a gap between what Wesley believed or hoped and what he felt and experienced which would become a major problem later. In a letter to his sister Martha in 1730 he had apparently written that: 'If God sees I sincerely desire devotion in prayer, and that I can do no more than desire it, why does not he do the rest?'[150]

Wesley liked Taylor's definition of the 'pardon of sins in the gospel as sanctification'. 'As we hate sin, grow in grace and arrive at the state of holiness, which is also a state of penitence and imperfection, but yet of sincerity of heart and diligent endeavour; in the same degree we are to judge of the forgiveness of sins . . . Forgiveness of sins is . . . a state of change effected upon us.' This was in February 1730, and in October 1731 he said that 'our hope is sincerity, not perfection, not to do well, but to do our best'. Of St Paul he says: 'Perfect, indeed, he was from sin, strictly speaking, which is a voluntary breach of a known law, at least from habits of such sin.' He allows for involuntary wanderings of thought in prayer: he knew of few but De Renty who had been free from these. Following a common idea of the time, he argued that 'sincerity' was sufficient.[151] But 'perfection' was certainly his aim, and the language of perfection was already appearing, as we have seen, in 1725. The ideal, repeated in letters as to Mrs Pendarves and in the 'Circumcision of the Heart' sermon, is what he offered to Mr Morgan as a justification for his tutorial disciplines over Morgan's younger son: religion is 'a constant ruling habit of soul; a renewal of our minds in the image of God; a recovery of the divine likeness; a still increasing conformity of heart and life to the pattern of our most holy redeemer'.[152]

But that Wesley was not achieving this is made clear in a letter to his mother in January 1734. Rather ironically, in view of Westley Hall's later moral delinquency, Wesley marvels at that man's achievements as 'the very picture of M. De Renty'. His own case was different. 'Although to perceive God as he is be a blessing, which may not be vouchsafed to some not yet made perfect, and although the lively and uninterrupted apprehension of his presence with even embodied spirits be vouchsafed only to a few choice souls, yet is there not an inferior sort of attention to his person which all Christians ought to aspire after? May not any who seriously endeavour to obey him hope to advert more and more to those truths: "He besetteth me behind and before and layeth his hand upon me." "I come to do Thy will O God." "I seek not myself but Christ crucified." This is that perception of the presence of God which I desire (Alas, how faintly!) to attain to! This is that recollection which I study to advance in day by day; this seems to me one stair of "the ladder to heaven," one degree of Christian simplicity.' Susanna herself had problems. She had written that: 'I still continue to pay my respects to an unknown God. I cannot know him. I dare not say I love him – only this, I have chosen him for my only happiness, my all, my only God . . . And when I sound my will, I feel it adheres to its choice, though not so faithfully as it ought.'[153] It seems likely that this was

Wesley's experience also, and it was one which would trouble him for years to come.

In his attempts to reach this happy state of the mind that was in Christ, Wesley seemed to be relying on a firm belief in God as seen in his revelation, Mrs Wesley having urged him away from reasoning too much about this. But in February 1734 she strikes a deeper and more personalized note about faith. 'By faith I do not mean an assent only to the truths of the gospel concerning him [Jesus], but such an assent as influences our practice, as makes us heartily and thankfully accept him for our God and Saviour, upon his own conditions.' She goes on to emphasize that 'without the great atonement there would be no remission of sins' and that 'no man can qualify himself for heaven without that Holy Spirit which is given by God Incarnate'.[154] This accords with much contemporary thinking about salvation as being not merely by works but based on the prior work of Christ (see above, pp. 27f.). Wesley's striving for 'holiness' was implicitly dependent ultimately on this, despite his later disclaimers. Moreover, Mrs Wesley emphasized that, as regards faith, he must not judge his achievements by his feelings but 'rather by a firm adherence of your will to God', which most of what he said and did also suggested. But she added that he should take God for his only good, cleave to him, put his soul 'into the hand of Jesus Christ your Saviour' and trust him wholly by faith, since Christ had redeemed him. In the 'Circumcision of the Heart' sermon, Wesley himself speaks of 'that faith which alone is able to make thee whole . . . the one medicine given under heaven to heal their sickness'. It is 'that faith which is set only on an unshaken assent to all that God hath revealed in Scripture – especially that Christ is the propitiation for our sin'. But in his post-conversion period he added at this point a passage about assurance in our hearts, a sure evidence or conviction of his love.[155] This betrays his new 'evangelicalism' and modifies the claim that he had never changed his views even of perfection.

By Wesley's own account, the next stage in his development was the influence of the mystics, who led him to a 'refined way of trusting to my own works and my own righteousness', which lasted until the Georgia voyage. So he saw it in the self-review of May 1738. In the more theological account of January that year he distinguishes the influence of the 'essentialist Nonjurors' and the mystics. The Nonjuror appeal to antiquity and imposition of binding customs from it is a stage lost in the May account, though clearly important at the time, as the debates with Clayton show; as we have seen, they affected Oxford Methodist practice. Though Wesley retreated from the rigidity of fasts and developed doubts about the *Apostolic Constitutions*, some of the sacramental practices acquired from the Nonjurors remained with him long after his conversion, and his baptismal practice and discipline obtained from them caused trouble in Georgia and in the early stages of the Revival.[156]

The encounter with the mystics was more important for Wesley's views of salvation.[157] The contemporary evidence shows that the effects he ascribed to them later were more or less correct. As we have seen, he did not give up his disciplines, but he developed doubts about their rigidity and pondered on 'Christian liberty'. But perhaps we should see him as maintaining the old framework, while wistfully hoping for a more direct apprehension and sense of the image of Christ within him.

Who were these authors, and who introduced Wesley to them? Clayton's influence was of some importance here, too. At an intellectual level he wrote to Wesley about Norris (the late Cambridge Platonist already known to Wesley) and the French metaphysician Malebranche. These were among the seventeenth-century writers anxious about contemporary tendencies towards mechanistic materialism. Malebranche's philosophy of 'seeing all things in God' attracted Byrom and his circle.[158] Clayton also wrote about William Law; about Poiret (who was a kind of one-man clearing house for Continental mysticism), Scougal (whose *Life of God in the Soul of Man* influenced Wesley and Whitefield) and the Quietist Madame Bourignon. Clayton had reservations about 'mental prayer' as against vocal prayer, and it was partly in this context that he advised steering between the extreme of the ancients and the lukewarmness of moderns.[159]

Wesley was in fact already acquainted with some of the writers loosely classed as 'mystics': à Kempis, of course, but also Fénelon (as early as 1726/7); De Renty for religious societies, and his vision of the Trinity which influenced several Methodists later; Law from late 1730 and Scougal in 1732 or earlier.[160] But from 1732 (and here perhaps we may suspect the influence of Law as well as Clayton) Wesley certainly read these and other writers more extensively and intensively, and there is no doubt that they influenced his thinking. The 'contemplative man' mentioned as guiding him in this direction has not been certainly identified. One candidate is Joseph Hoole, a neighbour of the Wesleys in Lincolnshire and later in Manchester. Rather more likely is James Garden, a man linked with the Nonjuring mystical circles of North-east Scotland and with the Byrom circle as well as a Lincolnshire neighbour. It might even be William Law.[161]

Among the writers who attracted Wesley and helped to form his model of 'perfection' was Castaniza (Scupoli), whose *Spiritual Combat* was also read by Susanna and perhaps appealed to them by its concentration on will and intelligence rather than feeling.[162] Wesley's attraction to the 'primitive church' and his quest for a quasi-mystical sense of perfect communion with God perhaps accounts for his liking for the ascetic Ephraem Syrus and 'Macarius the Egyptian' (really a Syrian whose spirituality derived from Gregory of Nyssa). Both continued to figure in Wesley's post-conversion reading, and Macarius appeared in the Christian Library in the 1750s. Albert Outler has attributed a special influence to these men on Wesley in terms of perfection as a dynamic process rather than a static state in the manner of the Roman writers.[163] Through them, he says, Wesley unconsciously acquired a dose of Eastern spirituality. But it is doubtful whether too much should be made of this or of the peculiarities of these two writers. Wesley continued to use the Westerners indiscriminately and, as has already been noted, absorbed what he fancied from these eclectic sources into a synthesis of his own, regardless of context or pedigree.

So far as his complaints about the bad effects of the 'mystical writers' are concerned, he was evidently referring to some particular group which was new to him, or at least newly enforced by his anonymous 'contemplative man' around 1732 and after. The sources, the picture given and the objections can best be seen in a letter to his brother Samuel from Savannah in November 1736.[164] This was a short scheme of their doctrines, professedly drawn from writers like Tauler, Molinos and the *Theologia Germanica*. The diary shows him reading these between 1732 and 1736. These authors were certainly read by Byrom and his circle, and the objections Wesley made to them are a more elaborate version of those made in his review of January 1738.[165] He particularly objected to their cavalier attitude to 'means', which were to be chosen, taken up and dropped according to what helped the individual. So long as you reach the end of love, there is no need to stick to any particular system of rules. The means of grace are played down. You cannot do any good to others until you are converted yourself. But only do works of charity when they do not damage your own spiritual life. There was much in this that contradicted Wesley's favourite methods and indeed Oxford Methodism generally. It is not surprising that he revolted against a way which was temperamentally alien to his activist character. But Henry Moore was probably right in observing that what attracted Wesley temporarily to this way was that these writers at least 'taught the necessity of the crucifixion of the world'.[166] Perhaps even more attractive at the time, and indeed later, was the promise of a way which might give him that direct and unbroken communion of love with God which was at the heart of the practical experience of Christian perfection as Methodists came to understand it. At the time, in the mid-1730s, he revolted against this because of their slighting of the means of grace: one may suspect that his long-term pursuit of holiness by means of rigorous discipline was too deeply rooted to be eliminated. But if he quarrelled with them about means he was still attracted by the end.

Even the severe perspective of May 1738 from which he dismissed the mystics as adrift for advocating a version of salvation by works was not his last word on the matter. Somehow he wished to reconcile the use of discipline with the spontaneity of a direct experience of God. The way of faith seemed to offer this, but the ideals of the simple and easy way of the Quietists had something to offer as well. The language of 'pure love' and the state of perfection as one of uninterrupted love between God and man remained. Faith would now be the means – but also the old discipline in a simpler form (see below, pp. 156f. 400f.).

It has been common for Methodists to write off Wesley's pre-1738 experience as a futile exercise in trying to obtain salvation by works. After all, Wesley himself on 24 May 1738 reviewed his past life in this sense, though (as we shall see) he had reservations later about this. Early as well as later Methodist biographers have said the same.[167] But quite apart from Wesley's own changing views, it has to be said that an assessment of his development should not be confined to 'evangelical' perspectives. Some alternatives will be considered later when reviewing the meaning of his 'conversion' (below, pp. 145ff.). For the moment it is worth observing that the most recent thorough reviewer of the Oxford period, Professor Heitzenrater, though in fact viewing the subject from an 'evangelical' perspective, feels constrained to argue that the 'good works' of the Oxford period were not 'unevangelical'. They were not only good in themselves but also means to religious achievement, indeed a religious exercise. They cannot be written off simply as a vain attempt at salvation by 'works'. Wesley here, as in his specifically religious disciplines, was trying to realize a vision of 'the mind that was in Christ'.

Though Wesley's decision to stay at Oxford and then to go to Georgia was dictated primarily by a desire to save his own soul, he at least had the grace to see that this was supposed to be so as to be able to serve his neighbour. Heitzenrater is prepared to see Wesley as not far from Aldersgate Street, citing a remark in a letter to Burton about the Georgia project to the effect that: 'nor indeed till he does all he can for God, will any man feel that he can himself do nothing.' Wesley advised Whitefield in 1734 or early in 1735 'to resume all your externals but not to depend on them in the least'.[168] The problem, as Heitzenrater sees it, was that his ascetic practice of the Christian life could not be completely realized from the theological perspective Wesley had adopted. A tension was created in some of those who followed the High Church way of perfection adumbrated by men like William Law, which for future evangelicals perhaps had the role of driving men to despair of the doctrine and means proposed.[169] The ideal of a perfect realization of the mind and life of Christ which Wesley so often described was not achieved by the discipline, and indeed the discipline simply made him more aware of the gap between the ideal and the reality. Yet he needed to go through the Oxford experiment, Heitzenrater concludes, to prepare himself for the crisis and experience of Aldersgate Street.[170] Yet there is more to the Oxford period than this. Much of what Wesley learnt there was in fact subsumed into the mature Methodist synthesis as he saw it, even (as is suggested here) the despised 'mystics'. Wesley's perfectionism – the real heart of his message – could only have emerged from his peculiar background and experiences in Oxford, even though it was partly remoulded by what he learnt from the Moravians. Wesley was never to be quite a typical 'evangelical' for this reason.

As has already been noted, Wesley's terms of acceptance for Georgia, especially coming so soon after he had opted for Oxford in preference to Epworth, suggest that the Oxford system had come to be seen at last as spiritually bankrupt. His hope was still to save his soul, and indeed by the same methods. Perhaps, he thought, it was the setting that was wrong: after all, this had been his reason given for rejecting Epworth. It could be said that he was in the first stage of another transition. To leave the university was, consciously or unconsciously, to move from one of the centres of the English ruling order, especially in the church, to the very periphery, to the provinces, indeed literally to the frontier. Like the Religious Society movement of High Church renewal, Wesley's Oxford Methodists had in their own way been assaulting the heartland of the establishment. From now on, and increasingly, Wesley would be engaged in a movement to reform the church from a position away from the centre, from below rather than from above. This would become ever more obvious after his return from Georgia and the failure of his only experiment as a parish clergyman.

It remains to ask what Wesley gave to Oxford and what Oxford gave to him, that is, apart from his spiritual development. So far as what he gave to Oxford is concerned, the Methodist group was really a minor and ephemeral phase in the history of the university. Methodism was not in anything like the sense of the later Tractarians an 'Oxford Movement' at all. Of course it left a mark on individuals. For some it was a prelude to settling down as a parish priest, in a few cases more serious than the generality. For others it was the beginning of some strange spiritual pilgrimages through Methodism to other groups such as the Moravians. The Oxford Methodist group itself had always tended to wax and wane in accordance with the presence or absence of leading personalities as well as because of the shifting nature of a university population. The Wesleys and Whitefield occasionally visited later and found the work of devotion and charity continuing in a modest and variable way. Societies of townspeople were also begun in Wesley's time in Oxford, some apparently evolving into the later, 'evangelical'

Methodism. Wesley occasionally returned for academic occasions, and in the 1760s there was a celebrated row over the expulsion of the St Edmund Hall 'Methodists', but they were Calvinists and not adherents of Wesley. All in all, Methodism in its earliest form and original home was a failure.[171]

What Oxford gave Wesley is less easy to assess beyond what has already been said. But there were gains other than the purely spiritual which made their mark on his later work. He carried with him, despite his eventual radical change in his relationship to the church, certain things which he could have obtained in no other way: the manners, culture and status of a gentleman, and a clergyman; the status, too, of a Fellow or 'late Fellow' of Lincoln College, which regularly appeared on the title pages of his books. One could not dismiss such a man as easily as a mere layman or Dissenter. Oxford logic served him well in his numerous controversies; and in his relationships with his preachers and his favoured correspondents (male and more especially female) he revived the tastes and habits of an Oxford tutor, suitably scaled down to his audience. He could argue, however legalistically and dubiously, that his ordination on the college title gave him a roving commission to preach where he liked. And in one very material way his Fellowship served him well. Until his marriage he had a regular if variable stipend which gave him a degree of financial independence. This saved him from some of the dangers of dependence or the appearance of dependence on the offerings of his followers, though not from suspicions that he was making money out of his gospel ramblings.

Wesley's later attitude to Oxford was rather equivocal. He paid a few visits there in later years, though he had severed himself from formal invitations after his critical University Sermon of 1744 there. In 1772, perhaps in a rare moment of depression or simply from spiritual nostalgia, he burst out to Charles: 'I often cry out, *Vitae me redde priori.* Let me be again an Oxford Methodist! I am often in doubt whether it would not be best for me to resume all my Oxford rules, great and small. I did then walk closely with God and redeem the time. But what have I been doing these thirty years?'[172] With a very different kind of nostalgia, and in a more mellow mood, he recorded a visit in 1778. Having an hour to spare, he 'walked to Christ Church, for which I cannot but still retain a peculiar affection. What lovely mansions are these! What is wanting to make the inhabitants of them happy? That without which no rational creature can be happy – the experimental knowledge of God.'[173] It is a comment very like that on his visits to country houses: a human pleasure he could not repress, along with a correct moralizing on its eternal insignificance. But there is a special nostalgia here, for Oxford was for Wesley a symbol of a religious ideal which he never lost, despite later modifications. And there were also the feelings of an old man who was also an old Oxford man. It was the same feeling which made Newman dream of returning and Matthew Arnold invoke the last echoes of the Middle Ages.

There were indeed rougher moods. Wesley condemned the university's failures in morality and discipline in his last University Sermon. And although he sometimes compared continental and Scottish universities unfavourably with his own, in his scheme for higher education at Kingswood and on some other occasions he criticized the defects in the Oxford curriculum.[174] It is nevertheless pleasant to think that Wesley, for all his attempts to methodize everything into Christian perfection, was no more immune than so many others to the lifelong claims of Oxford on the heart.

But in 1735 Wesley was certainly disillusioned with his life there, and prepared to cast anchor on a rougher shore.

III

Serpents in Eden: Georgia (1735–37)

As one of its recent historians has recorded, Georgia's colonial history is 'a case study in the persistence of historical mythology'.[1] By this he meant that popular and textbook accounts stress its origins as an illustration of English humanitarianism and utopian idealism. Even those more sober historians aware of the realities have portrayed its inception in these terms. Daniel Boorstin remarked that 'something about the fabled lushness and tropical wealth of Georgia inspired both extravagance and rigidity in the plans of those who wished to develop it. The supposed prodigality of the land seduced men to believe that they could cut the colony to their own pattern. These early planners combined a haziness about the facts of life in Georgia with a precision in the scheme for that life.' These 'London philanthropists were trying to make Georgia fulfil a European dream. They were less interested in what was possible in America than in what had been impossible in Europe.'[2] This would in fact stand very well as an epitaph for the dream of Wesley and its death.

Whatever the dreams (and certainly the promoters, like most colonial founders, gave highly-coloured pictures of the prospects), Georgia was never really the haven for debtors which it has often been portrayed as being, nor was it settled by them. Few such actually came, and even in the Trusteeship period before it became a Crown colony, Georgia was largely peopled by the 'worthy poor' and indentured servants, along with self-financed settlers from England or the Carolinas. The Trustees were often moved less by philanthropy than by practical concerns for imperial defence, improving relationships with the Indians, the promotion of trade, and exotic experiments in silk production and viniculture. In short, these were the preoccupations of a frontier settlement with some special trimmings. After becoming a Crown colony in 1752, Georgia developed as a land of small farmers, frontiersmen and planters;

slavery spread; rice plantations were established and social divisions emerged. Here it shared many of the characteristics of the middle colonies.

Yet this is not quite the whole story. The Trustees did have idealistic plans for the colony which had included for some of them the settlement of debtors; optimistic ideas for its economy and social structure; and paternalistic ideas for its organization. These concerns bulked larger in their London discussions than on the ground in the colony, though they also affected some of their agents' reports. As so often happened in America, the land as well as the people compelled change from the ideal. James Oglethorpe, who figured prominently in the establishment of the colony (and in the Wesleys' fate), offers an interesting example of the mixture of idealism, paternalism and realism which actually marked the early years. In considering this early stage during which the Wesleys were involved it seems fair to balance the rough realities with the strength of idealism shown by the promoters, including their religious hopes – which Oglethorpe shared. Of course the Methodist pioneers had only a small part in the colony's story and an ephemeral one. For Wesley's biographer, however, the episode has a special interest as a phase in his holy experiments. Here he can be seen as a would-be foreign missioner, the subject of an unlucky love-affair and the uneasy discoverer of a new way of faith.

If the Georgian reality never matched up to the expectations of the more idealistic promoters, the reasons lay partly in circumstances on the spot, partly in the mixture of motives for the foundation, and partly in the characters and motives of the settlers. The project grew out of two sets of circumstances. These were: first, English philanthropic and religious ideals of freedom and betterment; secondly, national and practical considerations felt in England and in the Carolinas. These included imperial concerns to improve English trade at the expense of Europe and the provision of a bulwark against French and Spanish threats to the southern frontier of the existing colonies by founding a buffer state in the 'Debatable Land'. Attempts had already been proposed of this kind, and now these efforts coincided with religious concerns to combat Popery, which was always as much a political as a religious obsession.[3]

The immediate occasions of the foundation were Carolina's need for defence and a desire to settle the unlucky deserving poor, with debtors at first primarily in mind. The emphasis was on 'deserving'; there was no intention of shipping off criminals. Some, like Oglethorpe, had indeed been moved and disgusted at the state of prisons, more particularly as they affected debtors. He and another Trustee, Lord Egmont, are good examples of the mixture of idealism and realism which informed some of those concerned.

James Edward Oglethorpe came from a notoriously Jacobite family, though he himself seems to have abandoned this unprofitable cause by 1720 and in 1722 became an MP. In Parliament he took a special interest in the fate of debtors and other humanitarian causes and was chairman of a parliamentary inquiry into prison conditions in 1729. He was also concerned with the Spanish threat; as a strong Protestant was indignant about Catholic persecution of its Protestant minorities; and took an interest in trade. In character he was an aggressive, masterful man, keen on discipline and order but also ambitious and susceptible to flattery. His interests, then, nicely came together for fulfilment in the Georgia scheme.[4]

Percival, later Earl of Egmont, was an Irish peer, rather conscious of his aristocratic status, a courtier on good terms with the Royal Family and for a time with Walpole. He fell out with the Prime Minister when he thought Walpole had used his interest to prevent Egmont's son from taking his father's seat at Harwich. More significant, perhaps, for the Georgia affair is the fact that he was a strong Protestant, meticulous in religious observances and while not above recording scandal in his diary, a man unhappy about sexual immorality. He was also critical of political corruption and the influence of the city money men – familiar opposition targets. He was critical of episcopal behaviour and thought the morals of the Prince of Wales a scandal to 'all sober and religious folks', so it is not surprising that he associated with members of the SPCK.[5]

The idea of settling debtors and others in a new colony was given its opportunity by fears of the French and Spanish. The charter of the colony was granted in the spring of 1732 with three stated purposes: to settle the poor; to strengthen the colonies by increasing trade; and to protect the southern frontier. The Trustees would control it for twenty-one years after which it would revert to the Crown. It would be governed by a Council, and although no provision was made for a legislative assembly, the Council could make laws and set up courts. Council members could not, unusually, hold office or land in the colony. Foreign nationals could settle and have freedom of religion except for Roman Catholics. The English mainly in mind were not debtors but tradesmen down on their luck.[6] The ideal was for a colony of shopkeepers, traders and small farmers. To that end there was a limit on the size of landholdings and there were rules to ensure descent of inheritance in families and to prevent the accumulation of large estates – rules which were much resented and later had to be altered. The aim was to create a sturdy body of stable settlers able to defend the colony.[7] With the same ends in mind, Oglethorpe had three laws passed which also provoked much opposition and later repeal. They were to prohibit rum and black slaves and to regulate the Indian trade. Oglethorpe's nightmare was that of an effete, unhealthy population open to Catholic corruption through the slaves and so to collapse.[8] The colonists did not live up to expectations and in 1750 the laws were repealed, opening the way to a more normal southern colony, but the vision of a kind of idealistic expediency is worthy of note. One modern commentator has even speculated that with more efficient and tactful management Georgia might have been saved from slavery and so altered the history of the later United States![9]

For the Wesleys' time in Georgia it is necessary to bear in mind that Oglethorpe had the difficult task of guarding against possible invasion, creating settlements from scratch and subduing an unruly population to discipline and, if possible, to morality and religion. The private obsessions of the Oxford clergymen with missions, pastoral care or personal piety had to be subordinated to these larger ends. There was in any case ample material for conflict. Thomas Causton was a leading figure in the colony as storekeeper, and so the main channel for the colony's supplies as well as being a magistrate. He was a controversial figure, and it has never been clear whether he was dishonest or simply a bad keeper of accounts.[10] For that matter, Oglethorpe himself exasperated the Trustees by his failure to keep and transmit accounts, and it is a tribute to his personality that although holding no clearly defined official position in the colony, he was effectively a kind of governor in the early years.

The first batch of colonists arrived in Charleston in January 1733, 116 in all, and soon began work on the new town of Savannah. Several other settlements followed, often located for defensive purposes, including Frederica. Both places were to be the scenes of Wesley's labours and misfortunes. Religion played a significant part in the provisions which the Trustees, and not least Egmont and Oglethorpe, thought necessary for the health of the colony. Religious liberty, as against Anglican hegemony, was an attraction for the Salzburgers and the new Moravians. The latter did not make a favourable impression on the Trustees. Egmont saw them as 'a lot of enthusiasts' under the protection of 'a Baron Sindersdorf (sic) himself an enthusiast,' and he lamented the mentality of those who think that 'everything that comes uppermost in the mind is inspired by the spirit of God'.[11] It was intended that the SPG should pay temporarily for four ministers until a glebe should be granted for their support, but the anti-clericalism of Georgian gentlemen showed in the fact that the Trustees kept the land in trust.

The first shipload of colonists had included a volunteer clergyman who soon died, and the first duly appointed man was one Quincy whose variegated background and controversial character reflected the uncertain quality often felt to be typical of those Anglican clergy who sought their fortunes in the colonies.[12] Egmont had 'an indifferent character' of him though also of the religious discipline of the colony. Maybe ill-health and colonial conditions undid the poor man. Certainly John Wesley thought so, and found him good-natured enough.[13] Such conflicting reports were typical of personalities in the colony, especially as viewed from distant London.

It was Quincy's unsatisfactory ministry that led to hopes of someone better as early as July 1735. Dr Stephen Hales of the Trustees was hopeful of Dr West's good pupils at Lincoln College, but in the event the Wesleys' friend Dr Burton 'informed us that two gentlemen, one a clergyman, bred at the University, and who have some substance, have resolved to go to Georgia out of a pious design to convert the Indians. They are brothers and their name Wesley.' On 24 September Egmont recorded: 'Appointment of Charles Westly (sic) MA to be Secretary of Indian Affairs. He being a very religious man and good scholar will take orders and occasionally officiate in the church till we can get a settled minister. The elder Westly is in orders and a Fellow of Lincoln College. The third gentleman (worth £3000) yet being seriously disposed he goes with the elder Westly to assist him in the conversion of the Indians.' Finally there was 'one Mr Hall of Oxford' who had just taken orders so as to replace Quincy. Egmont added, rather strikingly, that he took this 'sudden resolution' of the four gentlemen to go to 'help the cause of religion as a particular providence and mark of God's favour to our designs' – a remark almost worthy of a Methodist.

Later, the plan changed. Charles Wesley would be secretary to Oglethorpe and for Indian affairs and minister of Frederica for the time being. Westley Hall – for it was indeed Wesley's erratic brother-in-law who had volunteered – found reasons for withdrawing.[14]

For Wesley himself, as we have seen, the Georgia project represented a possible solution to his disillusionment with progress in Oxford. In an idealized wilderness he would revert to a spiritual state of nature and start primitive Christianity all over again. Whatever he may have said to the SPG and the Georgia Trustees, he was frank enough to Dr Burton about the fact that saving his own soul was his primary motive.[15] It is also worth noting how the letter is packed with scriptural phraseology beyond the level customary with him. When challenged from within or without he was liable to react with logic-chopping arguments, but he was also liable not only to use scriptural language but to dramatize his position and prospects in terms of biblical situations and persons, to assume a kind of 'apostolic' role. In this case it was the Pauline role of turning to the 'Gentiles' instead of the 'Jews'. Further examples of this will be seen in the early days of the Revival, especially in the face of persecution. Before leaving England, too, Wesley rather arrogantly gave directions for behaviour to those left behind, like Richard Morgan and the Oxford Methodists. Brother Samuel junior was sharply lectured about the immoralities of the classical writers and the duty of religious instruction in schools.[16] Once again one has the impression that the way of salvation for all must be what Wesley thought right for himself at a given time. This may well have been a way of fortifying his confidence in his own prescriptions, especially if they succeeded with others.

Before receiving Wesley's exalted letter, Dr Burton had written him a letter of advice on the basis of priorities directly the reverse of those Wesley had in mind. That is to say, for Burton the salvation of others took priority over Wesley's own. He sketched a programme of religious work for him including 'the apostolic manner of preaching from house to house'. He warned him that 'the generality of the people are babes in the progress of their Christian life, to be fed with milk instead of solid meat'. He should preach simply in the manner of Christ's parables rather than with 'laboured discourses on a subject in which men think themselves not immediately concerned'. He should adapt his behaviour and 'manner of address' to different circumstances and people, becoming all things to all men, like St Paul. 'Here is a nice trial of Christian prudence. Accordingly in every case you would distinguish between what is essential and what is merely circumstantial to Christianity . . . what is of divine and what is of human authority. I mention this because men are apt to deceive themselves in such matters . . . singularities of less importance are often espoused with more zeal than the weighty matters of God's law. As in all points we love ourselves, so especially in our hypotheses.'[17] It was in response to this moderating advice that Wesley adopted his high apostolic tone. Burton clearly knew his man, and Wesley might have avoided much grief if he had taken his advice.

The first shipload of emigrants to Georgia was joined early in 1734 by the refugee Salzburgers. In March Oglethorpe returned to England with some Indians who provided exotic publicity for the project.[18] Then, in October 1735, the Wesleys joined a mixed group of English, Salzburgers and Moravians, some 700 in all, 257 of them with the Wesleys on the *Simmonds*.[19] The Wesleys were joined by Benjamin Ingham of Queen's and Charles Delamotte, son of a Middlesex sugar merchant and magistrate. Charles Wesley, by his own account, had intended to spend his life at Oxford, but had been persuaded by John into the post of secretary. Ordination he 'exceedingly dreaded', but John had persuaded him into this as well, and he was ordained deacon and priest on 22 and 29 September 1735.[20]

At this point, with the voyage to Georgia, John Wesley's famous published *Journal* begins its record, continued almost to the end of his life. It is important to be clear from the outset about what the nature and apparent purpose of this published record was, and its relationship to other personal records, for studies of Wesley's life from 1735 have naturally relied heavily on it.[21] It must be distinguished from the private diaries (still not all published) which began in 1725. These began in a mixture of cypher and clear and at first contained a good deal of personal matter. Later they became bare and impersonal shorthand records of his occupations during each day and as such appear to have continued until shortly before his death, though the volumes from 1741 to 1782 have disappeared. The published *Journal*, commencing with the Georgia voyage, appeared in the form of a series of what Wesley called 'extracts' from his 'journal', the first probably early in 1740. Thereafter they appeared in instalments published a few years after the events they recorded. His motive for publishing the first extract was evidently to defend himself against the various hostile accounts and rumours about his behaviour in Georgia and flight from the colony. The next extract was primarily to give his version of the break with the Moravians and to defend and publicize his view of them. Thereafter he seems to have felt it to be useful to give the general and Methodist public a continuing view of his activities and opinions. For Methodists it was a kind of account of his stewardship, but also to defend his behaviour and opinions to hostile Methodists and non-Methodists and to correct mistakes and dispel scandals. At the same time it acted as a kind of history of the Revival from his point of view, a panorama of the movement and a collection of exemplary specimens of piety. It also enabled him to publicize the signs and wonders which he saw as verifying the divine action in the world (and not least in Methodism) as an answer to sceptics, as well as allowing him to publicize his own opinions on events and books. In this way it already fulfilled some of the educative role for Methodism later taken up by the *Arminian Magazine* from 1778. What is clear from all this is that the *Journal* was essentially a vehicle for apologetic and propaganda, a selective and slanted account, and not the objective record it is often treated as being.

It is natural to suppose from Wesley's talk of 'extracts' that in addition to his private diary he was keeping a much fuller narrative 'journal' from which the 'extracts' were being taken. It seems unlikely that any such continuous record was ever kept except perhaps for short periods (as on the voyage to Georgia) and special episodes – Wesley seldom had leisure for such a record for much of his later life. Fragments of what may appear to be such a record which survive seem generally to have been either 'journal letters' written up to report his activities to friends and colleagues from time to time, pieces written up to defend his behaviour or record his own feelings about some sensitive episodes, or first drafts for the published version. The published 'extracts' appear to be worked up from such accounts and from his private diaries. Quite apart from apologetic considerations, it was natural that he should slant his accounts of events differently for different correspondents or audiences and for the published 'journal' omit sensitive personal material. His love-affair in Georgia and expulsion from the colony led him to give more than one such variously slanted account to different audiences, and it is unfortunate that Curnock in his 'Standard' edition of the *Journal* chose to weave material from these accounts into a continuous narrative, thus obscuring the exact sources used. Some earlier episodes in Georgia, moreover, were recorded more fully by Charles Wesley in his journal in shorthand and omitted from the Victorian edition, though partly restored in a version of the early 1900s. Alternative versions of some events can also be found in Moravian sources. In short, to reconstruct Wesley's history and particularly his behaviour and motivation, one has constantly to be aware of the status and bias of the sources, including the variable nature of his own accounts.

Georgia, for Wesley, was an experiment in 'primitive Christianity', and that in more than one sense. It was a way of starting all over again in a virgin land with the prospect also of creating Christians from scratch so far as the Indians were concerned. In April 1736 he was reading Fleury's *Manners of the Ancient Christians*. In the event he spent far more time with the settlers, who did not prove very amenable to Prayer Book religion interpreted in the light of antiquity. The Moravians, however, provided another model of primitive Christianity, closer to the apostolic age than the Fathers, and the two versions of 'primitive' Christianity jostled uneasily together in Wesley's mind. All these problems were complicated by his unhappy love-affair and its aftermath.

The voyage was delayed by contrary winds until December and they finally reached Savannah in February 1736. On shipboard the pilgrims kept up the Oxford disciplines and Wesley gave up the use of flesh and wine. They also ministered to the settlers as Dr Burton had enjoined them. A regular routine developed of prayer (including extemporary prayer for the first time), worship, study and instruction, and Wesley thought this had some impact. Even a 'gay young woman . . . appeared to be much surprised and affected', though only for a time. This was Mrs Hawkins who caused Oglethorpe and the Wesleys much trouble later. Wesley was reading Johnson and Brevint on the eucharist and noted that a sick person recovered after communicating.[22]

During a stormy sea voyage Wesley was depressed to find that he was beset by fears of death and noted that religious feelings induced by such fears were ephemeral. He was all the more impressed by the calmness of the Moravians – even the children – in the midst of storms.[23] Soon after landing he met the Moravian leader A.G. Spangenberg, who asked him disquieting questions about his spiritual condition. When he asked, 'Does the Spirit of God bear witness with your spirit that you are the child of God?', Wesley was 'surprised and knew not what to answer'. Spangenberg went on: 'Do you know Jesus Christ?' 'I know He is the Saviour of the world.' ' "True," replied he, "but do you know He has saved you?" I answered: "I hope he has died to save me." He added: "Do you know yourself?" I said, "I do." But I fear they were vain words.' But Spangenberg's own record of the conversation concludes on a very different note: 'I observe that grace really dwells and reigns in him.' On dealing with the dubious Mrs Hawkins, Spangenberg quoted à Kempis's advice: 'All good women avoid and commend them to God', or at least converse sparingly with her. Soon came the first encounter with the Indians who had visited England with Oglethorpe. They welcomed ministers who would 'speak the good word' to them, but they 'would not be made Christians as the Spanish make Christians: we would be taught before we are baptized'.[24] Finally, on 7 March 1736, Wesley entered on his ministry in Savannah.

The colony and town were, of course, still in their infancy: Egmont recorded in June 1734 that there were 437 persons in the colony, 259 of them in Savannah. In July 1737 Wesley calculated that there were 518 souls, 149 of them under sixteen years of age. About 180 of them were at least nominally of the Church of England, evidently only a minority, which had a significant bearing on what was to follow. Burton had indeed warned him that he would have to deal with more than one denomination.[25] Plots had been neatly laid out for the settlers, many as yet unoccupied; Wesley had no proper church and parsonage and lived initially with the Moravians, holding services in the court-house and meetings elsewhere. In an account from notes made during his stay and later published in his journal, Wesley described the colony – its settlements, climate, vegetation, Indians and so on – in a fairly realistic fashion. Of the Indians he gives a much more hostile account than appeared in his first impressions of them, as we shall see.[26] Though intending to be an Indian missionary, all too soon for his own taste he was forced into being minister of Savannah only, though with something of an informal itinerant ministry elsewhere.

To a significant degree the pattern of Wesley's ministry was influenced by Oglethorpe's policy for the colony as well as by his personal relationships with the Wesley brothers. On board ship Wesley had formed a favourable impression of him and his regulation of the passengers.[27] But there followed a difficult period in which relationships were poisoned by the intrigues of Mrs Hawkins and Mrs Welch.[28] Charles Wesley thought they were both in love with Oglethorpe (a man not given at all to sexual gallantries), though it is also possible that the women resented his puritanical discipline and thought the parsons were encouraging him in it. Charles, they sensed, had seen through Mrs Hawkins's ostentatious religious raptures on the ship and hated him for it. But Charles was at first not much less naive than John or indeed Oglethorpe in his belief in their scandalous tales. They told him they had committed adultery with Oglethorpe and he believed them. Then they told Oglethorpe that Charles was spreading scandal about him and *he* believed them, with the result that he was estranged from Charles until John disabused him.[29] But unfortunately both brothers half believed that Oglethorpe had sinned with the women until Charles had an emotional talk with Oglethorpe, during which both men postured as dying men abandoning all worldly hopes. Charles was so shattered by physical illness and emotional stress that he resigned his post and left for England in July 1736.[30]

The hostility of the women to John did not end there. They complained that he scandalized them as adulteresses and Mrs Hawkins attacked him with a pair of scissors and had to be restrained by force.[31] The whole episode suggests murky undercurrents of sexual jealousy and hysteria of which these idealistic and inexperienced clergymen were more or less innocent victims. But it was an unfortunate start to have been estranged in this way from the dominant personality in the colony. Oglethorpe was reconciled and evidently thought well of Wesley's good character and essential sincerity, but he had much on his mind and was not inclined to sacrifice what he saw as the overall well-being of the colony to Wesley's schemes. It looks as though he would have liked him to have married and settled as minister in Savannah to help to civilize and stabilize the settlers; and so on various pleas he prevented him from developing his Indian mission. As for Wesley, perhaps he never quite lost the suspicion that Oglethorpe had misbehaved, though he thoroughly shared his ideals for the colony and warned him about hostility and intrigues against him in London. It may be added that Wesley already showed himself no respecter of the great, a characteristic that would become more marked as his evangelical career developed. To Oglethorpe himself he ingenuously wrote that if his designs were of God they would prosper, but 'If on the contrary (as I shall hope, till strong proof appear) your heart was right before God . . . the God whom you serve is able to deliver you.' Then, in his best style of high biblical rhetoric, Wesley exhorted him to fulfil his role as God's deliverer and father to his people.[32]

Despite Wesley's professed aim to save his own soul, on being forced to stick to parish work in Savannah, he spoke of the Indian work as being his 'main design'.[33] Since it formed only a minor part of what he actually did in Georgia, it can be dealt with fairly summarily here. Protestant overseas missions notoriously lagged behind those in Catholic lands and scattered efforts in the seventeenth and eighteenth centuries, or indeed much later, were the product of voluntary work and not part of an integrated colonial policy like (for example) the Spanish in the Americas. For this various reasons can be given, some theological, some political and economic, as also for the noticeable increase in missionary interest from the late eighteenth century which clearly owed much to evangelicalism and will be discussed in a later chapter.[34] The modest designs of the SPG which had sent Wesley to Georgia included a concern to save the Indians from Popery for colonial security reasons as well as religious ones.

Oglethorpe was at his best in dealing with the Indians. Not only did he show considerable skill in maintaining good relations with them (which was essential for security reasons) but also he had a genuine liking for them and appreciation of their culture, even though he hoped for their conversion. He believed that 'there is nothing wanting in their Conversion but . . . to explain to them the system of Religion; for as to the moral Part of Christianity, they understand it and answer to it'. Thus they abhor adultery, disapprove of polygamy and murder, and the Creeks do not practise theft. In a letter to Samuel Wesley he persuaded himself that they had a tradition of the deluge, belief in the immortality of the soul and 'expect an instructor and Mediator'.[35]

Wesley's first impressions were also favourable, as we have seen in his encounter with those Indians who had been with Oglethorpe to England. But his desire to see more of them was frustrated by his other duties, and it seems that disillusionment was already setting in, at least about the character of those closest to the settlers. In June 1736 he 'hoped a door was opened for going up immediately to the Choctaws, the least polished, that is, the least corrupted of all the Indian nations'. In July he had a meeting with the 'Chackasaws' about their religion. Their notion of One who 'lives in the clear sky' and 'Two' with him and that 'the souls of good men go up', though mixed with other ideas, evidently impressed Wesley with hopeful thoughts of their openness to conversion. This may suggest to the modern reader rather that in fact they had already been influenced by Catholic missionaries and had syncretized something of what they heard with their own traditions.[36]

Wesley certainly came to his task with notions of noble savages, an unspoiled state of nature and intimations of natural religion in these people. He saw the Chickasaws at least as having a sense of Providence, of looking up to the Supreme Being and so as being ready to receive the gospel.[37] By the end of his stay, though he had not seen more at first hand, he had collected material from traders and was much more hostile and pessimistic. He concluded: 'What is the religion of nature, properly so called?' By their fruits 'the gods of these heathen too are but devils'. Their rule is 'to do what he will and what he can'. They are 'gluttons, drunkards, thieves . . . implacable, unmerciful'.[38]

In the event Oglethorpe kept him to his post in Savannah, though Wesley still hoped to be a missionary by proxy through Ingham and Delamotte, who indeed did a good deal of work among them. He shared Oglethorpe's concern to curb the traders from corrupting them.[39] He also had some contacts with negroes and Jews, and was particularly taken by some of the former he met in Carolina.[40] The blend of 'primitive', utopian and biblical ideals gave way to harsh reality in this as in other areas of Wesley's Georgia life, though it was replaced by an optimism of grace. His mission field and heathen audience turned out to be in England (and he saw it in these terms). It was characteristic of the process by which Methodism developed that when overseas missions once again became part of the Methodist prospectus it was by a series of accidents which gradually persuaded Wesley to allow pioneer initiatives by his followers to be developed.

Savannah and the settlers became Wesley's real field of labour. By May 1736 he was already saying that there were heathen enough there and asked Burton whether he ought to preach the gospel to 'other nations' until he had dealt with them. 'Even this work is indeed too great for me.'[41] Parish work was in any case new to him, and his problems were vastly increased by the nature of the settlers and his own exalted ideas of Anglican piety and discipline. He wrote to Egmont that Savannah was already too large for his care, and he wished there were more Christians in it, yet he thought there were more than in towns of that size in England. As regards morality, ironically in view of what happened later, he praised Causton and the other magistrates for repressing 'open vice and immorality' and promoting the glory of God. Here was the ideal of the SRMs coming to life.[42] No doubt this was in part to impress the Trustees with the fruits of his stewardship. Charles Wesley on his return to England gave a more sombre picture. Quincy had neglected the people; only three take communion; the people go shooting on Sundays (which Oglethorpe tried to prevent). Before Charles left, however, John had forty to communion; he 'preaches by heart (extempore) and has a full assembly'. Wesley himself commended his clerk as 'a sober industrious man'.[43]

To his personal friends in England Wesley wrote in a taut, 'apostolic', almost millennarian strain. To Mrs Chapman in March 1737 he repeats his old concern for being remade in the image of God and the need to 'be an example to my flock'. All his parishioners were 'in your sense of the word, unlearned, and most of them of low understanding'. Echoing Burton's advice he claimed 'we have no need of nice distinctions; for I exhort all and dispute with none'. To James Hutton he hoped the Lord was 'lifting up his standard against the flood of iniquity which hath long covered the earth'. To the secretary of the SPG he wrote that the adage about the blood of the martyrs being the seed of the church had not been followed in America; and to Dr Cutler of Boston he said that he must first learn how to attain to being 'crucified with Christ'.[44] This certainly reflected his idealized 'primitive' vision, but the reality, if more mundane, did include some successes as well as failures.

Wesley maintained some of his Oxford disciplines and some practices he had learnt from the Nonjurors. Yet it should be recognized that much consisted of a strict rendering of the Prayer Book discipline enjoined upon him by the SPG. This was quite sufficient to make him seem a rigorist, if not a Papist, to those who had not been exposed to such rigour in England and did not expect it in Georgia. That a considerable number were Dissenters made matters worse. Twice-daily prayers were observed as well as prayers on Sundays. In May he revived the custom of dividing the prayers 'according to the original appointment of the church': morning prayer at 5.00 a.m.; communion and sermon at 11.00; evening prayer at 3.00 p.m. Communion was celebrated every Sunday and holy day 'according to the rule of our church'. If Wesley's claims on Mrs Williamson later were typical, he also expected attenders at communion to give notice of their intention: a discipline which had certainly fallen into disuse in parts of England. More eccentrically, Nonjuror fashion, he insisted on triple dipping of infants in baptism; refused it to those whose parents disagreed; and refused private baptism except to the sickly.[45] In visiting systematically from house to house and not simply the sick he was probably going beyond contemporary convention.[46]

Then came a development which has always been seen as foreshadowing the future Methodism. In late April to early May 1736 Wesley devised a plan '(1) to advise the more serious among them to form themselves into a sort of little society, and to meet once or twice a week in order to reprove, instruct and exhort one another. (2) To select out of these a smaller number for a more intimate union with each other, which might be forwarded, partly by our conversing singly with each, and partly by inviting them all together to our house; and this, accordingly, we determined to do every Sunday in the afternoon.' On 10 June, he developed a similar but more limited plan for Frederica. Here, 'on Sundays in the afternoon and every evening after public service, to spend some time with the more serious of the communicants in singing, reading and conversation'. They sang a psalm and Wesley read from Law's *Christian Perfection*. Six days later he began to meet another group on Wednesdays and Fridays – the 'primitive' fasting days.[47]

Wesley himself saw this later as a stage in the development of Methodism, at least in his *Ecclesiastical History*. It was a sequel to the meetings from November 1729 and was followed by evening meetings from 1 May 1738.[48] Curnock saw this as the origin of the class meeting, and the inner circle of the select bands as a result of plans after consultations with the Moravians: 'a Moravian graft upon the "Oxford Methodist" stock'.[49] It is wise not to try to force back the origins of the later precise Methodist system here. The Georgia episodes were simply part of a series of *ad hoc* experiments to meet varying circumstances (as the difference between the Savannah and Frederica groups shows). Unlike the Oxford groups, they were not for study and charity but devotion; unlike the old Religious Societies they included women, who, at least at Frederica, would meet together with the men. The inner group at Savannah does sound like the Moravian 'band', though its purpose is not made clear. Plenty of partial precedents can be found for various versions of the societary idea anyway: De Renty, and Spener of course, as well as the Moravian and English experiments. As Schmidt says, one striking difference here is that Wesley's groups were not voluntary associations but chosen by him 'from above' out of the church congregation; and the subdivision into two tiers also differed from the English precedents.[50]

The reactions to Wesley's régime varied. One was typified by a Mr Horton: 'I like nothing that you do. All your sermons are satires upon particular persons, therefore I will never hear you more; and all the people are of my mind, for we won't have ourselves abused. Besides, they say they are Protestants. But as for you, they can't tell what religion you are of. They never heard of such a religion before.' He added that Wesley's behaviour had caused all the quarrels that had happened since his coming. Reactions like this culminated in the formal indictment in August 1737 for non-Anglican practices.[51] Yet it is also clear that some individuals were keen to accept his guidance: it was a paradigm of the later reaction to Methodism in England.[52]

As to the Moravians, whatever influence they had on his societary experiments, the effect on his personal life was considerable and increasing. Before meeting them he had known nothing of their teaching or ecclesiastical position. His reading and spirituality at Oxford had been dominated by High Church, Catholic and patristic models, though he was acquainted with some of the Pietist Francke's work, and his selective imagination was always able to distil and synthesize visions of holiness from diverse sources. What really obsessed him within the framework of ascetic, High Church observances was the vision of 'primitive

Christianity' and the holy life it promised. He had still not quite shaken off the promise of the mystics and was attracted by the example of 'disinterested love' he found in an old man in Georgia.[53]

One characteristic of Wesley which would have a profound influence on the later development of Methodism was already beginning to show itself spasmodically in Georgia: his ability to respond to the test of experience even against his own inherited prejudices, especially when experience appeared to show religious reality in unexpected places. Thus he was first favourably impressed by the calm behaviour of the Moravians (so different from his own) in face of the storms on the voyage to Georgia. This was what made him seek their company and be willing to listen sympathetically to their teaching. When Spangenberg told him of Zinzendorf's testimony that he had been so full of the love of God that he had never felt the love of the world for so much as the part of an hour, Wesley was reminded of his beloved Mexican hermit Gregory Lopez. This led him to correspond with the Count and eventually to elicit from him a statement of Moravian doctrine and practice.[54] Impressed by their practical signs of Christian experience, yet still in the grips of his patristic and High Church vision of 'primitive' order and piety, Wesley persuaded himself by conversations with Spangenberg soon after landing in Georgia that the Moravian faith and order were all 'agreeable to the plan of the first ages'. But we may perhaps glimpse the first signs of a new conception of 'primitive Christianity' in his reaction to witnessing a Moravian ordination to the ministry. 'The great simplicity as well as solemnity of the whole, almost made me forget the 1700 years between, and imagine myself in one of those assemblies where form and state were not, but Paul the tent-maker and Peter the fisherman presided, yet with the demonstration of the Spirit and of power.'[55]

It is doubtful in fact whether Wesley understood the full complexities of the Continental Pietist tradition. He was about to be exposed to two distinct and conflicting examples of this in the shape of the Moravians and the Salzburgers.[56] The Salzburgers were under the influence of Francke's Halle, but the Moravians under Zinzendorf were highly suspect in their eyes. To make matters worse, Baron von Reck, who had conducted the first party of Salzburgers to Georgia, had been attempting a reconciliation of the two bodies at home and had been firmly told by Halle that this would not do. Worst of all, Spangenberg had himself been a teacher at Halle and had been dismissed for his separatist tendencies. Wesley liked both groups but saw a difference between them. The Salzburgers were Lutherans without episcopacy in the apostolic succession, but the Moravians seemed to have not only bishops but bishops in the succession, a view which the Moravians persuaded other Anglicans to take to secure their position in England.[57]

The Moravians were well aware of Wesley's peculiar views which Spangenberg saw he held strongly, 'since he drank them in with his mother's milk'. He noted the strict views that non-episcopal sacraments were invalid and that Lutherans and Calvinists must be rebaptized. Wesley recognized Moravian orders and thought the Moravians wrong to accept baptism from Rothe, the Lutheran pastor of the Moravian settlement at Herrnhut back at home. Above all, Scriptures of doubtful interpretation on various points of practice should be settled by the writings of the first three centuries.[58] Ingham and Wesley would actually have liked to join the Brethren, but Spangenberg thought they should do so only if cast out by their own church for their discipline. Zinzendorf at this stage in fact liked to see the Moravians as a 'seed' in all the churches, rather than as a separate denomination. The Moravian Töltschig, moreover, made it clear to Wesley and Ingham that admission to communion among the Moravians depended on an experience of grace, peace and reconciliation with God through Christ – the point Spangenberg had been probing in Wesley's experience by his questions about personal faith.[59] In due course Wesley received from Zinzendorf a statement of the Moravians' highly christocentric faith and their views on the church and sacraments.[60] Wesley did not reply, and he must have found much of it baffling but perhaps also disturbing in its demand that to receive communion one must at that moment have a sense of acceptance with Christ. It was Spangenberg's probing of his personal knowledge of Christ as Saviour that had disturbed him from the first.

Wesley either misunderstood or hoped he misunderstood the Moravian view of the way to salvation, for on 31 July 1737 he had another conversation with Spangenberg in which he was told that conversion meant 'passing from darkness to light, from the power of Satan unto God'; that this 'passing' can be gradual, though sometimes wrought in a moment. Wesley asked whether faith is 'perfected by good works or only shown thereby?' and was told: 'By works faith is made perfect.' He also asked about scriptural rules of conduct: on magistrates, oaths, exclusion from communion, extempore prayer and fixed fasts.[61] The questions reflect Wesley's old concern with 'primitive' practice coupled with the newer anxiety about grace, faith and conversion. The apparently 'primitive' if simplified practices of the Moravians, including their episcopate, seemed to link them with the patristic and indeed apostolic age of the church, and this predisposed Wesley to take their uncomfortable salvation doctrines seriously.

One other important practice Wesley learnt from the Moravians, and this was the use of hymns. For various reasons hymns had never been an accepted part of Anglican worship. For Puritans at least this had been seen as the use of human compositions, and the prejudice against them had been carried into the Dissenting tradition and was still controversial for some even after Isaac Watts helped to sanctify them. Instead use was made of metrical psalms. Wesley and his companions seem to have used psalms on shipboard, but the Moravians introduced him to the varied resources of German hymnody, including their own, and it was perhaps their most powerful permanent legacy to Methodism along with the concept of personal conversion.

Wesley was introduced to the hymns on shipboard, and they were one medium for his learning of German. (It is curious that Charles Wesley does not seem to have been involved in either concern.) Singing was one of the activities of the Savannah society, and private hymn-singing punctuates his diary. By May 1736 he was beginning to translate German hymns, and it was perhaps with the needs of societies in mind that he finally produced his first hymnbook in Charlestown, SC, in the spring of 1737.[62] This book was arranged on a quite different pattern from the *Hymns for the Use of Methodists* of 1780 (see below, p. 414). It is in three parts: for Sunday; Wednesday and Friday; and Saturday. Nuelsen sees it as designed for public worship, but it looks more like an instrument for society devotion on 'primitive' lines. Of the seventy-eight hymns, about half are from Watts and a few others are by Herbert, Samuel Wesley senior and junior, and Addison. There are eight translations by John Wesley, five from the German and the others from the French and Spanish. The German hymns represent the subjective tradition of German devotion, though Wesley omitted some of the more erotic imagery which appealed to the Moravians.[63] It is interesting to note that despite its personal appeal to him, Wesley chose to minimize the German element, though it stood first in the book. A second 'Collection' followed in 1738, arranged in the same way for the use of the London Religious Societies. In 1739 *Hymns and Sacred Poems* included Charles Wesley's hymns for the first time. Here Wesley noted that some reflected his former love of the 'mystics'. He condemned their teaching in favour of 'faith working by love', though it is to be observed that he did not reject them wholly if placed in this context. The contents of these books is a reminder that the Moravian influence certainly did not replace or overwhelm the other complex strands in Wesley's development.

All this time, while Wesley was attempting to be a missionary and parish priest and exploring the Moravian way, another aspect of his personal life was causing him increasing mental and emotional tension until it finally brought together all his problems in an explosive manner. This was his relationship with Sophy Hopkey, the worst of all the serpents in his Eden.

One of the advantages that Wesley thought he would find in Georgia (so his letter to Dr Burton suggested) was that there would be no women to distract him – at least none eligible enough to attract him. But he was in trouble very soon with Mrs Hawkins's intrigues, and to Charles in March 1736 he wrote (in Greek): 'I am in danger every hour. There are two or three God-fearing, refined young women. Pray that I know none of them after the flesh!'[64] Spangenberg had urged him to keep his distance even from godly women. Oglethorpe remarked to Charles Wesley before his return to England: 'On many accounts I should recommend to you marriage, rather than celibacy. You are of a social temper, and would find in a married state the difficulties of working out your salvation exceedingly lessened and your helps as much increased.'[65] Very probably, as the sequel showed, he thought the same of John or at least hoped that marriage would divert him from Indian adventures, but here he was dealing with a more elusive candidate.

In judging what then happened as a result of Wesley's entanglement with Sophy Hopkey which led directly to scandal and his flight from the colony, we are dealing with an episode which was of considerable importance for Wesley's development. It created scandal over the circumstances of his departure and so blackened his character in the public eye for some years afterwards. For Wesley's personal life it was not only emotionally wounding but deepened his religious problems and so contributed to the crisis of May 1738. For his biographers it is revealing of various aspects of his character, but understanding of the episode is made more difficult by the various versions of it produced by Wesley himself, though the variations are also revealing.

The story as critics and less partial observers and enquirers at the time viewed it tended to be that Wesley had been emotionally involved with Sophy (more or less scandalously according to taste) and had probably wanted to marry her, but that she had rejected him in favour of a Mr Williamson. After her marriage Wesley, driven by jealousy, found excuses to repel her from communion, which naturally offended her husband and her uncle (Thomas Causton the shopkeeper and magistrate), who then had him indicted by a Grand Jury for this as well as other charges about his eccentric and oppressive conduct as minister. Wesley then fled the colony.[66] Some of Wesley's early biographers also suspected on the basis of imperfect information that something like this had happened. Thus Hampson, knowing only the *Journal* account, could not judge the truth of the charge that Wesley had repelled Sophy from communion because she had rejected his proposal of marriage. If true, it was probably 'from a phrenzy of disappointed love'.[67] Whitehead knew more; thought Wesley had proposed and been rejected, and surmised that this was because she was put off by his 'slow procedure in the business' or his 'rigid manner of life'. Certainly he showed disappointment.[68] Henry Moore had access to the same material, fortified by the aged Wesley's conversation with him on the affair. He acknowledges the effect on Wesley of an attractive and apparently pious girl, especially as (so Wesley had told Moore) 'till then he had never before familiarly conversed with any woman except his near relations' – which was certainly not true in view of the Kirkham and other episodes. Moore goes on: 'I know that she ultimately broke it off; but I know also that he did not at any time determine on marriage. I had the whole account from himself, as I do not know that he ever told it to any other person.'[69] What Moore was anxious to reject was the idea that there was a formal proposal and he was anxious also to play down the possibility of a jealous reaction afterwards. Though he was probably right about the lack of a formal proposal, it is almost certain that Wesley did consider marriage with her, and Hampson and Whitehead were nearer the truth about his reactions than Moore wished to believe or the ageing Wesley was able to admit or recollect.

The published *Journal* naturally omitted the private passages with Sophy and represented Wesley as the innocent victim of rough colonists and resentful relatives against the righteous discipline of an honest pastor. But Wesley also wrote other accounts of the affair and its aftermath. Though often coinciding in detail, they vary in their pictures of motive and in their judgments of Sophy herself according to the time, purpose and audience for which they were written.[70] The account closest to Wesley's own candid view of what happened is one apparently written only two weeks after Sophy's marriage, though the extant copy is dated a year later. It was probably intended only for his family and intimates – perhaps his mother. In this Sophy is seen in a favourable light, with allowances made for her behaviour. Later, when he thought she had been deceiving him and that her behaviour in any case was religiously and morally dubious, he represented her as a deceiver and himself as an innocent. This was in an account drawn up in preparation for the threatened court case. He portrayed himself here as a much abused pastor. There are also two manuscript journal accounts explaining his departure from Georgia which were the basis for the later published *Journal*.[71]

There is certainly enough here to reveal Wesley's turmoil of mind, even if his motives and objectives are less clear. He first met Sophy Hopkey on 13 March 1736.[72] She was then seventeen years old, the niece of Thomas Causton the Savannah storekeeper, and had had an emotional entanglement with an unsatisfactory suitor. No doubt Wesley felt that he was saving her for better things, though she may have been among the young women against whose temptations he was urging Charles to pray about shortly afterwards. The relationship began decorously enough with devotional reading and conversation, and Wesley's later representation of it as essentially pastoral was no doubt a sincere appraisal of his original attitude. He was in fact drifting into the same mixture of high-minded converse, tutorial supervision, spiritual guidance and interchange and human affection as he had enjoyed with the Cotswold ladies. As he himself acknowledged, at first he only spoke to her on 'topics pertaining to God', but by July 'I saw there was a mixture in my intention, though I was not soon sensible of it'. By October Causton was telling Wesley that she 'will never be easy till she is married' and that he 'gave her up' to Wesley, who for his part said that Sophy was 'too much afflicted to think of it'. Finding that Sophy at Frederica along with his other disciples there had drifted into worldliness, he bombarded her with Law and Ephraem Syrus, and to his distress found that she was talking of going to England, though she was upset when he asked her if she might stay for friendship's sake. Wesley asked Oglethorpe whether it would be proper to travel in his boat to Savannah, and Oglethorpe asserted that it was, no doubt to further the relationship. Wesley was in fact still possessed of the idea that he ought to stay celibate, but was afraid of being shaken: hence his fears for the journey, and not without reason. During the voyage they faced danger and distress, and Wesley was impressed by her conduct. Their conversation was a touching mixture of the devotional and emotional. Lying by the fire one night he asked her if she was engaged to Mr Mellichamp and she answered: 'I have promised either to marry him or to marry no one at all.' 'I said (which indeed was the expression of sudden wish, not of any forward design), "Miss Sophy, I should think myself happy if I was to spend my life with you." She burst into tears and said, "I am every way unhappy. I won't have Tommy; for he is a bad man. And I can have none else." She added, "Sir, you don't know the danger you are in. I beg you would speak no word more on this head." And after a while, "When others have spoken to me on the subject, I felt an aversion to them. But I don't feel any to you. We may converse on other subjects as freely as ever."'

Wesley had virtually been betrayed by his feelings into a proposal or perhaps worse. Indeed he confessed: 'I can never be sensible enough of the exceeding goodness of God' during the journey. 'I know that in me there was no strength; God knoweth if there were more in her. To him alone be the praise, that we were both withheld from anything which the world counts evil.' He then gives a glowing and minute account of her character, conduct, intelligence and spirituality. She was neat and indefatigable in hardship; had an 'unformed' yet 'deep and strong understanding'; was 'teachable in things either of a practical or speculative nature'; the 'temper of her heart towards God' was a 'deep, even reverence'. Whatever her real character may have been, Wesley was obviously determined to see in a rather ordinary girl of no great sophistication or education a paragon comparable to his earlier friends (or perhaps his mother?); in fact the ideal wife whom he wished yet feared to possess.

There ensued a conflict between desire, duty and inhibition. He was resolved on a single life, but his resolution was deeply shaken. He began a routine of meetings with her, reading Hickes's *Devotions* and Ephraem Syrus 'with a single eye' (to her spiritual good), but 'I found it a task too hard for me to preserve the same intention with which I began, in such intimacy of conversation as ours was'. For their reading he had to sit close to her, and 'unless I prayed without ceasing . . . could not avoid using some familiarity or other which was not needful. Sometimes I put my arm round her waist, sometimes took her by the hand, and sometimes kissed her.' To stop this he told her that he 'resolved never to touch you more', at which she seemed 'surprised and deeply serious'. But he soon renewed his caresses.

By February he was in great straits and again hinted at marriage without a direct proposal. Indeed he thought that the obstacle was on his side, not hers, and that if she had 'closed with me at that time' he would have made 'but a faint resistance'. However, she said she thought it best for clergy not to marry and that she was resolved to remain single.

Consultation with his friends led to Töltschig the Moravian seeing no objection but Ingham raising doubts about her piety. Confused by this, Wesley wrote to Sophy that he found that 'I can't take fire into my bosom and not be burnt', so he proposed to retire with prayer to decide what to do. While doing so he had what may have been a near-visionary experience – a measure of his agitation. God seemed to guide him to seek resignation to the divine will and so, momentarily, he obtained peace. As he recorded it in his private account, the decision turned on three points: he believed Sophy's resolution never to marry; and he believed that it was not expedient for him to marry for two weighty reasons. One was because it would frustrate his design of going to the Indians; the other was that 'I was not strong enough to bear the complicated temptations of a married state'. Perhaps the third was in the end decisive – as always he was adept at finding excuses for what he more instinctively felt he wished or did not wish to do. His informal vow of celibacy was bound up with his 'primitive' notions of the conditions of perfection, but it was also bound up with all his hesitancy before the physical and emotional 'complications' of the married state.

Yet still he hesitated, telling Sophy that if he married at all it would be after he had been to the Indians. Sophy was now beginning to retreat or rather, perhaps, to put pressure on him to make a decision. She complained that people were talking about them, but was upset when he talked of going to England. Wesley wavered again, and Delamotte and Ingham, distrustful of her character and alarmed at the breaking up of their fellowship, were averse to a marriage. In March they fell back on drawing lots between 'Marry', 'Think not of it this year' and 'Think of it no more'. The lot fell on the last. Wesley's reflections on this were painful: he had lost the prospect of 'such a companion as I never expected to find again'. But he still could not leave well alone. He persuaded Sophy not to take any step in anything of importance without consulting him, and persuaded himself that he could not leave her alone and yet that the slightest temptation would break his resolution.

But on 9 March 1737 all his hopes and fears were confounded and his belief in Sophy shaken by the news that she wished him to publish the banns of her marriage to Mr Williamson. He wondered whether this was a device to force his hand, and resorted to seeking guidance from the *sortes biblicae*, with indecisive results. Sophy herself seemed to leave matters uncertain by saying she would marry Williamson unless Wesley objected, and in a tearful encounter he again barely escaped from proposing. And Causton said he might have her if he would. Williamson understandably objected to Wesley's continuing interference, and in the event he and Sophy, instead of waiting for the banns to be called, went to South Carolina to be married on 12 March. This was at least irregular, and was one basis for Wesley's later strictures on Sophy's conduct. Indeed he made formal protests to the Anglican Commissary about such breaches of his jurisdiction.[73]

In his diary he still referred to her as 'Miss Sophy', though in public as Mrs Williamson, and perhaps the most revealing expression of his real feelings at the blow is not so much the considered private narrative as the broken, agonized phrases in his private diary at the news of the engagement: 'Miss Sophy to be married! . . . Amazed, in pain, prayed, meditated . . . Necessary talk (religious) with her; I quite distressed! . . . Necessary talk (religious); confounded! . . . Took leave of her . . . At home, could not pray! Tried to pray, lost, sunk! . . . little better . . . easier!' And, finally, 'No such day since I first saw the sun! O deal tenderly with thy servant! Let me not see such another.'[74]

There followed a pattern not unlike that already shown in the case of Varanese. Marriage was not to interrupt intimate conversations, spiritual guidance and direction of Sophy's conduct. Williamson objected and said it made her 'uneasy'. In this case at least there was the excuse of his pastoral responsibility and authority as her parish minister – or so at least Wesley persuaded himself. At the least this was naive and unwise, and worse was to follow when he proceeded to formal disciplinary action.

To cauterize his wound Wesley plunged into intense pastoral duty, but nevertheless selected Sophy for special attention. What helps to explain the varied accounts he gave of the affair is that after her marriage he discovered what he thought was evidence of her insincerity and hypocrisy even during her period of intimacy with him. He persuaded himself that her neglect of fasting and morning prayer were culpable in her more than her neighbours because she had promised to observe both. He also fell foul of Causton over charges against the storekeeper's conduct.

In July he wrote plainly to Sophy of his complaints against her conduct as regards services and her relations to her former lover, himself and Williamson. Finally, on 7 August he repelled her from communion because of her conduct and failure to give notice as required by the Prayer Book rubric.[75] It seemed plausible to Wesley's enemies, as it has to more sympathetic biographers since, to suppose that Wesley's behaviour here, however correct ecclesiastically, looks suspiciously like retaliation for his despised love. Henry Moore, though always defensive of Wesley, had a valid point when he noted that Wesley in fact did not repel her from communion at once but at first received her, and only repelled her after he had obtained evidence which convinced him of her bad conduct.[76] Such discipline in general was, of course, part of Wesley's whole method at this time.

Against Wesley's claims in his various accounts that he had behaved honourably, if in a vacillating manner, Sophy later issued an affidavit claiming that he had tried to persuade her to live with him for the good of her soul, proposed marriage, offered to give up his ascetic demands and to settle instead of going to the Indians. Before and after her marriage he had pressurized her by saying her soul was in peril unless she submitted to his discipline.[77] There is not much doubt that this was coloured by her own resentment and bewilderment, but even more by Causton's desire to use all means to destroy Wesley and his influence in the colony. Wesley's changed views of Sophy's sincerity were partly the product of gossip (though not all of it was hostile to her), but it is hard to escape the impression that his willingness to believe it and to punish her with full rigour were reinforced by the pangs of despised love. In fairness to both parties it may be said that they were the victims of Wesley's personality and of his impossible expectations of the perfect Christian combined with the perfect wife, which also conflicted irreconcilably with his notions of clerical celibacy and perhaps with his underlying uneasiness about marital intimacy. As to Sophy herself, she need not be charged with hypocrisy without qualification. She was naturally attracted by a strong personality who was also a good match in terms of the colony's social hierarchy. At the same time she was understandably bewildered by Wesley's scruples, his blowing hot and cold, as well as being oppressed by his asceticism and intellectualism mixed with more tender passages. What is striking is that whatever the truth about the earlier Varanese affair, years later Wesley would become involved in almost exactly the same confused triangular relationship with Grace Murray and John Bennet, with the same problems of idealism and vacillation. It is this which strengthens the case for seeing the roots of the problem in Wesley's personality as well as in his principles and circumstances.

In Georgia there were indeed further complicating circumstances which helped to produce the final débacle. At the personal level Causton and Williamson were understandably furious at the rejection from communion, which seemed to be a direct insult to Sophy's character. Wesley was cited to appear before the magistrates for defaming Sophy and refusing her communion without cause, in £1000 damages. In response Wesley denied the first charge and said that the second was ecclesiastical and therefore not subject to the secular power. Causton took Wesley's conduct also as an insult to himself and intrigued vigorously to blacken him in the eyes of the public as well as packing the Grand Jury; and Sophy herself produced the damaging affidavit already referred to. According to Wesley at least, the Grand Jury was a motley crew including many Dissenters, a Papist and an infidel.

In August the Grand Jury made a presentment which at least shows the ways in which Wesley's peculiar disciplines had offended a section of the colony, represented as deviations from the Church of England.[78] He had altered the liturgy, and added unauthorized hymns and customs like dipping infants. He had refused communion without notice to some but allowed it to boys. He had imposed mortifications on wives against their husbands' wills and in general had meddled in the affairs of private families.

Then, Wesley thought, God intervened; for having first endorsed the indictment, the jury then turned to Causton's conduct. As to Wesley's conduct, biassed though the account was, they were referring to real irritations. Moreover, they were not simply objecting to Wesley on personal grounds, for later on Delamotte suffered the same treatment for the same objectionable practices.[79]

In all this there were more factors at work than Wesley's personal offence or even his ecclesiastical practices. One clue is the Grand Jury's turning to Causton's conduct. Another is Causton's comment to Wesley that: 'Perhaps things would not have been carried so far had you not said that afternoon, "You believed if Mr Causton appeared, the people would tear him to pieces; not so much out of love to you as out of hatred to him for his abominable practices."'[80] Causton's multiple roles and influence in the colony had made him many enemies and provoked charges to the Trustees of financial malpractice. The Grand Jury to indict Wesley gave the opposition their chance. What they resented was not simply possible corruption but the attempt by Oglethorpe and the Trustees to impose an idealistic régime on them, and some of this of course rubbed off on Wesley as its ecclesiastical arm. Causton's charges against Wesley, however, though no doubt supported by others, also put Wesley in the position of 'my enemy's enemy is my friend'. And if Causton's remark and some other sources are correct, Wesley may have consciously exploited this to his own advantage.

In October 1737 William Stephens as representative of the Trustees made a visit to Georgia to inquire into the troubles following Mrs Williamson's marriage. Although he collected views on the Wesleys along predictable lines, he also identified a political conflict at work. He had heard that, a year before, Causton had persuaded John to write to the Trustees representing the colonists as a lawless lot, and that Wesley was now publicizing this story. Hence a crowd had 'come into the court in a menacing manner, crying out Liberty, calling the people to remember they were Englishmen etc., and that Mr Wesley was generally the principal speaker, to harangue the people, though he had no sort of business or any call there'. Stephens heard Wesley preach on the obedience of people to the magistrates, but also say that it was 'consistent with Christian liberty for people to insist on their rights, when they found themselves oppressed by inferior magistrates exercising discretionary authority which exceeded their commission'. Reporting to the Trustees at the end of the year, he was judicious on the speculations about Wesley's motives but saw Savannah as full of conflict about his stance. Most of the malcontents against Causton and the régime acceded to Wesley, but many others ('I must say of the best note and distinction') to the magistrates. So the town was split, and he was grieved to see Wesley abetting 'an angry sort of people against the civil magistrates, whom they appeared determined to overthrow (if possible) at any rate'. As they resorted to Wesley's house for advice, and he was 'openly . . . espousing an opposition' to the proceedings of the court, this showed that he was 'the head of the party'. When he finally fled he went with 'obscure' men – the common by-word is 'he is known by his companions'.[81] Even if Wesley was not as consciously political as this account implied, and may simply have taken up with those whom he thought were supporting his just claims, one does receive a vivid picture of how all forms of opposition used Wesley as an opportunity to assault the ruling élite. It is an intriguing contrast with Wesley's scathing attacks on 'sons of liberty' in the 1770s.

Wesley and his friends debated what he should do. At first he thought that he should stay to face his accusers, then that he could best defend himself and even help the Indians by going to London to give the Trustees his version of events in the colony. Meanwhile he was challenged by a troublesome Carolina parson, Dison, who held services attended by the Caustons and Williamsons.[82] His friends still thought that the departure should be delayed, but as the pressure built up he gave public notice that he was leaving. On 2 December the magistrates forbade him to leave and commanded that none should help him to do so. In fact no one tried to stop him, and it may well be that the magistrates hoped that he would leave, as the best way out of a situation that was disrupting the colony. And so, 'I shook off the dust of my feet, and left Georgia, after having preached the gospel there not as I ought, but as I was able, one year and nearly nine months.'[83]

The scandal surrounding his going, and hostile versions of it, dogged him for years. A Captain Williams charged him with 'great familiarities' with Mrs Williamson and with jumping bail. It was this that provoked the publication of the first 'extract' of the *Journal*. Others charged him with plans to introduce Popery into the colony, and he was still being smeared with the Grand Jury proceedings by his literary opponents Church and Warburton in the mid-1740s.[84]

Wesley certainly wished to put his case to the Trustees as soon as possible. He had already, earlier in the year, had to justify his expenses against rumours of embezzlement, though his usual careful keeping of accounts was his best defence against such smears and the Trustees do not seem to have doubted him.[85] The Trustees discussed the Grand Jury charges in December, some weeks before Wesley's return. His baptism and communion discipline were defended as correct by Dr Busby, and the Trustees resolved to send the charges to Wesley to answer. Egmont's conclusion was that: 'It appears to me that he was in love with Mrs Williamson before she married and has acted indiscreetly with respect to her and perhaps with respect to others, which is a great misfortune to us; for nothing is more difficult than to find a minister to go to Georgia who has any virtue or reputation.' He also noted the charges against Causton 'long and I think malicious'.[86]

Wesley landed at Deal on 1 February 1738, the day before Whitefield departed to take up his own Georgia ministry. He gave the Trustees an account of himself on 18 February, with an account also of the state of the colony 'not a little different' from those that they had received before. There were further meetings when he explained his departure. Egmont's account of Wesley's defence was that 'it appeared indeed that he was guilty of indiscretion but that Causton our head-bailiff was much more to blame, and he charged upon him many particulars of gross mis-administration which must be inquired into'. The Board were probably more concerned with this than with Wesley's misfortunes, and resolved later to dismiss Causton as storekeeper though not as a magistrate. On 26 April Wesley left his documents of appointment to Savannah with the Trustees 'as having no more place in those parts', and in this curiously oblique way in effect resigned. The Board took this to be so and revoked his commission. 'In truth,' wrote Egmont, 'the Board did it with great pleasure, he appearing to us to be a very odd mixture of a man, an enthusiast and at the same time a hypocrite, wholly distasteful to the greater part of the inhabitants, and an incendiary of the people against the magistrates.'[87]

This verdict was understandable, indeed justifiable from the point of view of the Trustees and their concern for the colony. Wesley's own verdict on his Georgia ministry was, in a different way, equally severe. By the time of his resignation he had deepening personal religious anxieties on his mind, and his verdict in his published *Journal* after his conversion is well known. 'It is now two years and four months since I left my native country, in order to teach the Georgia Indians the nature of Christianity. But what have I found myself in the meantime? Why, what I least of all suspected, that I, who went to America to convert the Indians, was never myself converted to God.' He then recorded in 'Pauline' style his gifts and graces, but saw all these as worthless without faith.[88] This, of course, was written in the first high phase of teaching hard justification by faith alone after his conversion in May 1738. Later in life he added some significant footnotes to this passage such as that he did have 'the faith of a *servant*, though not that of a *son*'. In any case this was a verdict on his own state and not on the effects of his ministry.

That ministry has generally been judged to be fruitless and, read in the light of his personal condition, significant chiefly for its role in bringing him to spiritual bankruptcy in terms of salvation by works and so preparing the way for salvation by faith. But of the effects of his work Wesley himself was less sure. In the published *Journal* for 3 February, he was perhaps putting the best face on it he could by noting that even spiritually he had been usefully humbled, had lost his fear of the sea, and had met holy men among the Moravians and holy literature through new languages. Some in Georgia had 'believed and begun to run well', and some work was begun among the heathen.[89] Other observers, though not unprejudiced, thought that he had achieved more. Whitefield in Savannah thought that not only had Delamotte done well, but that 'the good work Mr John Wesley has done in America, under God, is inexpressible'.[90] More impressive was Commissary Garden who, though troubled at Wesley's misadventures and perhaps anxious for professional solidarity, wrote to the Bishop of London at the end of 1737 that 'no one could be more approved, better liked and better respected of, by all the people of Georgia. He was innocent of anything criminal, and after all Quincy had had much the same treatment.'[91] Wesley's journals and letters show that he did have a following of devout people, even if they tended to fall from his more exacting disciplines once he was away. As to the longer-term effect of his work in Georgia, it has to be said that although Whitefield followed it up, that gospel wanderer had his own problems to face and much of his concern was invested in his orphanage; he was temperamentally unfitted as well as handicapped by his roving career to consolidate a 'Methodist' presence in Georgia. Calvinistic Methodism can indeed be said to have provided through some tenuous and obscure personal connections part of the contributory pre-history to the Wesleyan version of Methodism in America, but the origin of this was essentially later and much further north, and not due to Wesley's initiative either before or even after his conversion.[92]

But can Wesley's negative estimate in the *Journal* about his personal state be sustained, written as it was in the light of his later conversion? Some of his other later retrospects rather play down the contrast in favour of his unchanging views of perfection or the steady deepening of its meaning through the Bible, though now emphasizing justification by faith.[93] The review of 24 May naturally emphasizes that he was still vainly seeking salvation by works and that this was the mixture as before, despite what he learned from the Moravians. In this account he claims that on the voyage home he saw his need of faith, but not its true nature through Christ.[94] The self-critical published accounts of his state of mind during the voyage can be checked to some extent by manuscript material noted at the time. On 8 January he wrote: 'By the most infallible of proofs, inward feeling, I am convinced: Of unbelief, having no such faith in Christ as will prevent my heart from being troubled . . . Of pride . . . Of gross irrecollection as in a storm I cry to God every moment; in a calm, not; Of levity and luxuriance of spirit . . . Lord, save or I perish! Save now. 1. By such a faith as implies peace in life and in death. 2. By such humility as may fill my heart from this hour for ever . . . 3. By such a recollection as may cry to Thee every moment . . . 4. By steadiness, seriousness, gravity (in Greek).'

He decided to attempt to mitigate his problems by preaching to those on the ship. On 24 January he again reproached himself for his 'summer religion' and could only think of what a wise man had said to him, 'Be still and go on'.[95] This was written at the time and copied into the published *Journal*; however, there follows a passage not so included but which apparently belongs here – the theological review already quoted (above p. 97) which deals in turn with his successive views of authority and faith and works as derived from the various Christian traditions.[96]

If the retrospect after his conversion led him to believe that he had never had faith in God, never been a Christian, the more exactly contemporary reflections, though troubled and severe enough, suggest something less clear-cut theologically but more practical and experimental. What haunted him was the fact that he had only a fair-weather religion, and the fear in storms had not in fact been dispelled. He persisted in his discipline and the ideal of complete dedication of life and thoughts and feelings, but felt he lacked peace of mind in face of trouble, danger or emotional disturbances: the Hopkey affair confirmed this above all. It was lack of the feeling of peace except in untroubled circumstances that convinced him of essential unbelief, or at least of defective faith. He did not have a settled temper of belief and virtue, and he exaggerated this into the notion that he had no faith at all. As yet he could only mitigate this by seeing it as his 'cross' and persist in religious work. Perhaps already he sought comfort in the evidence of fruits obtained in others which he did not share himself – an expedient which would recur in the post-conversion period to combat doubt.

The shipboard meditations show some effects of the Moravian teaching, for the 1725 notions of faith as intellectual 'belief' had been portrayed by the Moravians as inadequate. Rather, faith should be more personal and inward and accompanied by assurance – something Wesley was now conscious he lacked, at least as a settled habit. In the January review of doctrine faith still appears as belief, but a belief evidenced by an experienced sense of confidence and peace with God. A search for assurance, confidence and joy was evidently on the way. It is not surprising that on his return to England Wesley anxiously inquired of the Moravians what the way of faith really was. Martin Schmidt is perhaps right to see Wesley as already showing signs of the beginning of an important theological and spiritual change, though he reads it too much in the light of the later published *Journal* version and from a markedly Lutheran perspective.[97]

Georgia, then, was certainly important in Wesley's career. He had experienced what he badly needed, a dose of parish work in a particularly difficult setting; and he had tested by experience how far the Oxford Methodist methods would really work, not just for a few choice spirits but also for the generality of people. He had also tested a 'primitive' and 'natural' environment as the theatre for the individual life of piety. As many hermits and monks had found before him, this was not liable to make the task easier but rather more difficult, throwing a man back on his naked self, face to face with his inward problems. The problems of celibacy and marriage had appeared once more in their most acute form and found him even less able to resolve them. The Moravians had offered a version of 'primitive' Christianity which was at once an encouragement to simplicity and a disturbing challenge to what he lacked himself, and this led to the first signs of a modulation from one mode of faith and salvation to another, yet without totally replacing his earlier notions of method and holiness, though he was to think for a time that they had done so.[98]

It was therefore with a sense of unsolved problems and a resolution simply to live with them as best he could that Wesley approached the uncertainties of what to do next – as a clergyman in process of losing his living and as a would-be Christian.

IV

The Road to Aldersgate Street: The Wesleys' Conversion (1738)

What would John Wesley do next? He must have been very uncertain. One possibility was to return to Oxford where, after all, as a Fellow of Lincoln he had his only formal appointment in the church and where he could, presumably, take up once again the life of an Oxford Methodist. John Hutchings (an old Oxford Methodist) would have liked him to do so: 'God formerly put his seal to your labours of love in this place and I hope He will be pleased to bless your endeavours once more.'[1] The thought recurred to Wesley himself occasionally during the next few years – hence perhaps the abortive plans to take the BD, unless (as is more likely) this was simply to be a platform for voicing his views. On 17 February he still thought of returning to Georgia, but thought that the Trustees would stand in his way and opted for plans to visit the Moravian settlement of Herrnhut instead.[2]

Oxford Methodism still naturally interested the brothers Wesley.[3] The fellowship had always needed committed leaders to keep them up to the mark, but these were only spasmodically forthcoming. Whitefield helped for a time, but he soon moved into a wider world: to Gloucester in 1735, where he founded an Oxford-style religious society; after his ordination to a popular preaching of the 'new birth'; and finally to Georgia early in 1738. Charles Kinchin and John Gambold moved into country livings, and although Gambold was keen enough to help, he was attracted by mysticism and gravitated in the end to the Moravians.[4] Charles Wesley had galvanized the Oxford Methodists into activity in his usual bustling fashion during a visit in February 1737, when voting for the Tory parliamentary candidate, as well as later in the year.[5] Writing to Lady Cox in March 1738 John took care to refute highly-coloured stories about their claims to special revelations, miracles and tongues.[6]

In fact what was left of Oxford Methodism was changing its nature.

Mixing town and gown, with more and more of the former element, the groups became more and more concerned with the search for personal salvation and gradually evolved in the same Methodist or Moravian ways as some of the older Religious Societies would do.[7]

Whatever plans may have been in Wesley's mind, it is noticeable that on his way from Deal to London he seems to have dosed himself with the prophylactic for doubt which he had proposed in his self-review of January: to 'take no thought' of his worries but 'gently go on "in the work of the Lord"'. Thus he regularly forced himself to speak about religion to all those he met on his journeys of the next few weeks. He 'renewed' his rules to nerve himself to 'absolute openness and unreserve' and to say and do nothing but what was to the glory of God. This looks very like the old Oxford method, rather than a 'Puritan' expedient, as Schmidt suggests.[8] Once back in London he lodged with the Huttons, the Nonjuror family already active in religious societies, and known to him in his Oxford days. Here, on 7 February, he first met the Moravian Peter Böhler, who was so greatly to influence him during the next few weeks. Already the Hutton group had become remarkably excited. As young James had written to Wesley: 'The London and Oxford Methodists come . . . and sing Psalms audibly against the peace and quiet of the neighbourhood. I am stigmatized as mad, Presbyterian, fanatic, but I bless God I mind not the foolish words of simple men. I pray they may be converted.' He actually congratulated Wesley on his sufferings in Georgia and wished him 'the red cross of martyrdom'.[9]

The next few weeks were spent by Wesley in preaching in London churches and visiting his family and friends. Gradually, under Böhler's influence, his preaching included talk of justification, faith and the new birth, and the churches began to be closed against him. The process of this change can be traced in his journal, letters and Böhler's alternative account in his journal. Peter Böhler (1712–75) had come under Pietist and Moravian influence at Jena and was converted through Zinzendorf. He became a minister and later a bishop in the Moravian church. On the way to Oxford in February 1738 he grew fond of Wesley and, though convinced that Wesley did not really 'know the Saviour', thought that he was willing to be taught and would become 'completely ours'.[10]

In fact Böhler had great hopes for the Moravian way in England, both at Oxford and in London, though success in the university would be especially desirable for the hope it offered of infiltrating the Anglican clergy.[11] The confrontation between his simple ways and the style of pious High Church Anglicans is particularly instructive. He thought that they placed an excessive emphasis on ordination and 'are even more essentially churchly and liturgical than the Lutherans'. In the meetings he held with them he found it hard to endure their insistence on praying 'from the printed book'. Böhler was in fact an educated man who had taught at the University of Leipzig, but he preferred primitive simplicity and was mocked by the undergraduates when with Wesley: 'My brother, it does not even stick to our clothes.'[12] Yet by his own account he had considerable success in attracting university as well as townspeople to meetings. Probably he exaggerated, for in his own way he was as obstinate in his principles as John Wesley, and what he wanted to achieve was not only individual conversions to Moravianism but also the imposition of the Moravian order of spiritual discipline. His diary shows that on one occasion he had scruples about receiving communion with Gambold and Charles Wesley, and by the time he had drawn lots the celebration was over. He was intent on organizing Moravian-style 'bands' which had begun in Herrnhut in July 1727. These were very small groups for intensive fellowship and mutual examination of the soul. They were organized by sex and marital status as were the other, less intense Moravian groups. Böhler actually began such groups in Oxford, though apparently they did not persist long at this time. A more permanent success was achieved with the Fetter Lane Society a little later.

However, it was Böhler's influence on John Wesley that was most important in the end. At Oxford on 18 February Wesley 'conversed much' with Böhler but 'understood him not, and least of all when he said . . . "My brother, my brother, that philosophy of yours must be purged away."' No doubt this is a reference to Wesley's usual logic-chopping when faced with ideas and demands which disturbed him. But it may also reflect Böhler's rejection of 'natural' knowledge in favour of the Bible and Christ as the standard of Christian knowledge.[13]

On 5 March Wesley acknowledged that by Böhler's arguments, 'I was clearly convinced of unbelief, of the want of that faith whereby alone we are saved', and he thought he could not preach to others that which he did not possess himself. Böhler then counselled him with the famous words: 'Preach faith *till* you have it; and then *because* you have it you will preach faith.'[14] His first effort to do so was to a condemned criminal under sentence of death, something he had felt unwilling to do before, since like many eighteenth-century moralists he doubted the repentances of those at the point of death. Later, Charles Wesley and some other Methodists like Silas Told became specialists in the art of snatching such sinners from hell at the last moment.[15] Incidentally, Böhler's advice is of interest in that some Pietists and evangelicals doubted whether unconverted ministers could be effective at all. He also differed from the Moravian 'still brethren' encountered by Wesley later, who did not recognize degrees of faith.[16]

On 14 March Wesley set off with Kinchin to Manchester, testifying

on the way, and there consulted with Clayton and the other High
Churchmen. Before long Clayton was expressing disquiet at his
behaviour. Meeting Böhler again, the Moravian 'amazed me more and
more by the account he gave of the fruits of living faith – the holiness
and happiness which he offered'. He tested it out in his Greek Testament.
Böhler says that the brothers brought up objections, especially from à
Kempis (no doubt this was part of the counsel from Clayton). Böhler
talked of 'living in the Saviour', which Wesley thought was a 'new
gospel', but what most struck him was the promise of his old ideal of
'holiness and happiness', neither of which he possessed.

By 2 April Wesley thought that he should wait for the far-off promise
in 'silence and retirement', so he went with Kinchin to his country
parish. However, he was soon summoned to London and had further
talk with Böhler. By now he had no objection to Böhler's view of the
way of faith, for which he found support in words from the Anglican
homily *Of Salvation*: 'A sure trust and confidence which a man hath in
God that through the merits of Christ his sins are forgiven and he
reconciled to the favour of God.' Happiness and holiness, he admitted,
are the fruits of this faith. He further confirmed it by New Testament
texts about the witness of the Spirit: that whoever is born of God does
not commit sin and that whoever believes is born of God. His only
remaining doubt was about the claim that this work is instantaneous,
but this he now found to be the norm in the *Acts of the Apostles*. His last
expedient was to claim that this was only so in the early years of
Christianity – a basic conventional Anglican response to unwelcome
manifestations of primitive 'enthusiasm' in the eighteenth century and
also the source of a nice compromise between allowing miracles in the
Bible against the Deists and denying them to Papist and contemporary
prophets, including Methodists. This would be a vital point in some of
Wesley's later controversies (see below, p. 276).

But on 23 April Wesley was convinced by 'the testimony of several
living witnesses' and could only cry out, 'Lord help my unbelief'.[17] The
witness of old friends in Oxford convinced him that 'God *can* (at least if
He *does* not always) give that faith whereby cometh salvation in a
moment.'[18]

From Böhler's account of Wesley's confrontation with the 'living
witnesses' it seems that John asked how he could attain that faith, and
he pleaded that he had not sinned as gravely as some. Böhler said that
he had sinned enough in not believing in the Saviour: to be lost is not a
matter of specific sins to be overcome (perhaps) by discipline but a root
sin of not having faith in Christ. And, as Schmidt remarks, the idea of
sudden conversion meant a completely new creation by God and not
merely the restoration of the divine image, as Scougal and Taylor

claimed. Faith, moreover, had 'now been raised from the rank of the theoretical into that of personal reality'.[19]

Before Böhler left, he helped to initiate a significant development. On 1 May, along with Wesley and other Anglican clergy, he founded what Wesley termed 'our little society . . . which afterwards met in Fetter Lane'. Wesley then listed the 'fundamental rules' (which were developed further during the next few months). Members would meet weekly to confess their faults and pray. The society would be divided into several 'bands' of five to ten people. It would have a conference every Wednesday with singing and prayer. New members would be put in bands on trial. A general intercession would be held every fourth Saturday and a general lovefeast once a month. Individual members would not be allowed to act in anything 'contrary to any order of the society'.[20]

Opinion on the nature of this society has varied. It was once seen as a Moravian society, but Curnock's claim that it was a Church of England Religious Society has often been repeated since. In fact it was not quite either. Although it was certainly not a Moravian society, the addition of bands and lovefeast and the emphasis on confession of faults to one another make it very different in organization and ethos from the unitary Religious Societies. In fact a new crop of societies was beginning to emerge, and these as well as some of the old ones would be infiltrated by the Moravians and Whitefield converts, reflecting the doctrine and priorities of the 'new birth'.[21]

That same day, 1 May, John Clayton had written a disturbed letter to Wesley. He and 'all your Lancashire friends' have 'great uneasiness' about John and are 'afraid' for him. They rejoice at his 'sincerity and zeal', but he needs prudence, the 'light' of the gospel as well as the 'heat' (ironical in view of Wesley's later complaints that he had more light than heat). The problem for Clayton centred on the fact that 'few or none were edified by Mr John's preaching, because they were offended with his manner. And your using no notes, and so very much action has with the generality established your reputation for self-sufficiency and ostentation.' Byrom thought that he should 'preach by book' and cut off his hair. And Clayton added a comment very much to the point in considering Wesley's spiritual life – that he needed a 'director' to save him from self-will.[22] In fact Wesley was already beginning to show some of the marks of the emerging kind of newer Methodist. He found he could not confine himself to set forms of prayer and had resolved on 1 April to used fixed or free prayer to suit the occasion.[23] This move into the extempore for preaching and praying (not to mention the long hair) is more striking and radical than is always appreciated – it made the old High Churchman begin to look like an Interregnum enthusiast.

The change was further underlined by a sharp correspondence with

William Law. On 14 May Wesley wrote in his most aggressive and
authoritarian style 'in obedience to what I think the call of God . . . I
reckon not praise of men'. The essence of his complaint was that he had
been proceeding after the model of Law's tuition but found that though
it was 'great and wonderful' he could not follow it, not even with all the
means of grace. But now he was directed by a 'holy man' (Böhler) who
taught him to believe and be saved, strip oneself of one's own works and
righteousness and fly to Christ. Why had Law not given this scriptural
advice? Why did he scarcely ever hear Law name the name of Christ?
And never 'so as to ground anything upon faith in his blood?' and so on.
Is the reason that 'you had it not yourself'? Wesley concluded by asking
Law to consider 'Whether your extreme roughness, I might say, sourness
of behaviour . . . can possibly be the fruit of a living faith in Christ.'

Law replied by saying that Wesley had read à Kempis and been given
the *Theologia Germanica* by Law, who had been governed in all he wrote
and did by the two fundamental maxims of Christ: 'Without me ye can
do nothing' and 'If any man will come after me let him take up his cross
and follow me.' The exchanges continued, on Wesley's side with high
indignation, on Law's with a certain injured dignity. In his last letter
Law said he had never set up to be Wesley's tutor, and Wesley had
come to him as he pleased.[24]

A number of writers on this exchange have felt compelled to judge
which side was in the right. Evangelicals have naturally felt that Law
was lacking in the true doctrine of salvation, and even Anglican admirers
have found it hard to reconcile Law's early exclusive High Church
views with his later Behmenist universalism, which seemed to some to
undermine the atonement. But Wesley in the first hard phase of his
evangelicalism was a harsh judge. Even those who have agreed with his
theological stance have felt that he was ungracious and arrogant to an
older man who responded in a measured and temperate tone, though
tinged with his customary irony. It was the arrogance of the new convert
to the 'unsoundness' of his old mentor which showed here, and Wesley
would think differently in later years, when he was even prepared to say
that men like Law who formally denied justification by faith might still
possess the thing itself. But for the time being the confrontation was
stark indeed.[25]

During the first weeks of May Wesley described himself as going on
in 'constant sorrow and heaviness'. Then, on 21 May, he heard the news
that brother Charles had been converted. Charles, temperamentally so
different from his brother, emotional and easily exalted or depressed,
had at first reacted in a hostile manner to John's discovery of the truth
of justification by faith, yet he reached the experience itself first. Ever
since his return from Georgia, despite bouts of illness, he had been busily

travelling and conversing on the old lines. Then, from July to November 1737, there are frequent references in his *Journal* to 'the new birth' or 'inward change'. On 7 July young Charles Graves told him that 'he first felt the beginning of the change, and was convinced of the reality of what he only believed before upon my brother's and my teaching. He appeared full of joy and love.' (He was seen by his friends as 'stark mad'.) To his sister Hetty, Charles spoke about 'the inward change', and to sister Kezzy about the 'new creature'.[26] This language requires explanation, for Charles was certainly not yet influenced by the Moravian teaching. Perhaps, as Luke Wiseman suggested, he was speaking of realizing the gift of God given in baptism.[27] But it is significant that he was recommending the reading of Law and Scougal's *Life of God in the Soul of Man*. The language of the 'new birth' is in fact used by Law himself, and talk of this and 'conversion' occasionally occurs in the Wesleys earlier. Thus Law speaks of the two great truths of 'the deplorable corruption of our Nature and its new Birth in Christ Jesus'.[28] It is also of interest that Whitefield had experienced the 'new birth' around Easter 1735 and from early in 1737 was preaching on 'the New Birth and Justification by Faith in Jesus Christ (though I was not as clear on this as later)'. He added that it 'made its way like lightning into the hearers' consciences'. By the end of July he had met Ingham and Charles Wesley at the Huttons. (Ingham had been converted in Georgia early in 1737.)[29] What Whitefield did was to heighten and sharpen the contrast between the 'old' and 'new' man, and it was this felt change of life which Charles seems to have observed happening under the old terms. But justification by faith was not yet seen by him as the means.

Lying ill in Oxford in February 1738, Charles met Böhler, began to teach him English and was challenged about his trust in his 'best endeavours to serve God' instead of in faith. On 25 April he was shocked to find his brother contending for instant conversion, though he grudgingly acknowledged that the *Life of Halyburton* (one of John's favourite books) was 'one instance, but only one' of this in modern times. From 28 April he was examining Böhler's doctrine to see whether it was true and whether he had it. Before Böhler left, he was persuaded that he would 'receive the gift before I die'.[30] At 'Old Mr Hutton's' on 11 May he met 'Mr Bray, a poor ignorant mechanic, who knows nothing but Christ; yet by knowing him, knows and desires all things'. He then encountered Luther on Galatians, and like John began to see his language as being that of the *Homilies*.[31]

Charles's conversion was, as one might expect, marked much more than John's by those extraordinary signs of supernatural agency which would become common among rank-and-file Methodists later. He was ill with pleurisy when he heard someone come into his room and say:

'In the Name of Jesus of Nazareth arise and believe, and thou shalt be healed of all thy infirmities.' He thought that it was a Mrs Musgrave, but finding she was not in fact in the house he hoped that this was indeed Christ speaking. He felt 'a strange palpitation of heart' and 'said yet feared to say, "I believe, I believe"'. In fact Bray's sister, Mrs Turner, admitted that she had spoken the words, inspired by a dream, yet 'the words were Christ's'. Bray assured him that he did believe, and Charles found himself 'convinced, I knew not how nor when'. Fortified by this wonderful sequence of events, Charles 'found myself at peace with God, and rejoicing in hope of Christ'.[32]

As to John, on 24 May his published *Journal* gives an elaborate analysis of his spiritual development up to that date. He concluded by describing how Böhler had convinced him that 'a true living faith in Christ is inseparable from a sense of pardon for all past and freedom from all present sins'. This faith 'was the gift, the pure gift of God, and that He would surely bestow it upon every soul that earnestly and perseveringly sought it'. So he resolved to pursue it by 'absolutely renouncing all dependence, in whole or in part, upon *my own* works or righteousness'. But he would add constant use of all the other means, praying for that very thing 'justifying, saving faith, a full reliance on the blood of Christ shed for *me*; a trust in Him, as *my* Christ, *my* sole justification, sanctification and redemption'. On 24 May he was certainly in a highly-wrought frame of mind, and a letter to a friend that day (probably Gambold) shows in a mixture of scriptural and personal epithets how conscious he was of sin, of the need for personal fruits of faith and of his lack of them.[33] In the published *Journal* he recorded a series of encouraging, providential words – from opening the Bible, from an anthem in St Paul's.

And so, at last, to the much-quoted climax:

> 'In the evening, I went very unwillingly to a society in Aldersgate Street, where one was reading Luther's preface to the Epistle to the Romans. About a quarter before nine, while he was describing the change which God works in the heart through faith in Christ, I felt my heart strangely warmed. I felt I did trust in Christ, Christ alone for salvation; and an assurance was given me that He had taken away *my* sins, even *mine*, and saved *me* from the law of sin and death.'

He then began to pray for all those who had persecuted him and 'testified openly' to what had happened. Then the question came 'from the enemy': 'This cannot be faith; for where is thy joy?' He was then taught that 'peace and victory over sin are essential to faith in the Captain of our salvation but that, as to the transports of joy – that usually attend the beginning of it especially in those who have mourned deeply –

God sometimes giveth, sometimes withholdeth them, according to the counsels of his own will'.[34]

What was the meaning and significance of this event for Wesley? The issue has been much debated, not only in terms of its meaning for Wesley at the time but also, and perhaps more importantly, in terms of its significance for his subsequent career and teaching. The question is complicated by the ambiguities of the word 'conversion', which has different connotations in different Christian traditions; and the partisans of those traditions have a vested interest in applying their notions of conversion to Wesley's experience. It is significant, for example, that writers of 'Catholic' sympathies, or those unsympathetic to evangelical notions of defining real Christianity in terms of a sharp transition from salvation by works to salvation by faith, have played down the significance of 24 May in favour of the earlier landmark of Wesley's turn to seriousness in 1725. Those of evangelical views have predictably seen 24 May as all-important and determinative of his whole subsequent career. This has been customary among Methodist biographers.[35] The interpretations given are also influenced by the extent to which one takes account of Wesley's views and conduct for the rest of his life or confines attention to the period up to 1738. Wesley himself complicates the issue because, despite the self-review of 24 May, which suggests a sharp break with his earlier life and opinions, in other places, especially when discussing the rise of Methodism or his ideas of perfection, he stresses continuity or only limited changes from 1725 onwards.

The contrast between the 'Evangelical' and 'Catholic' views may be illustrated at once by examples from two non-Methodist scholars. Schmidt believes that the highly critical self-review of 24 May is in itself decisive evidence for the importance Wesley attached to the event of that day and against the notion that the essential change was in 1725. The essence of Schmidt's view is that Wesley 'brought his whole situation under the Pauline antithesis between law and grace' and saw his whole development in terms of the leading ideas of the Epistle to the Romans: the result of Böhler's teaching on justification and reconciliation, although not only of this. The objective perception of this became a matter of personal assurance through the reading of Luther's preface. The motifs of law, sin and spiritual experience as essential features in justification resemble Luther's. But it was personal assurance which was brought into being by his conversion, and so justification as an experience of man rather than an act of God was placed in the central position, influenced by Böhler's emphasis, though both men were close to Luther in relating faith to promise. The emphasis on faith led to greater importance being attached to its psychological features. Here

Wesley and Böhler diverged from Luther in the direction of Pietism. Wesley wanted to see the power of Christ living within us, the new man as a demonstrable effect, and he wanted actual dominion over sin. A final difference from Luther is the desire for 'holiness and happiness', for Wesley a long-held view, derived from a long English tradition and very characteristic of later Methodism. 'The English heritage and the German contribution found in John Wesley a true and authentic alliance.'[36] As an analysis of Wesley's beliefs at the time from a continental Protestant perspective too often lacking in Methodist interpretations, this is valuable; but it is less satisfactory as an appraisal of Wesley's mature position later.

For a contrast we may take an Anglican view from Vivian Green.[37] The 1738 experience, he thinks, gave Wesley a feeling of reassurance about his faith and so an inner dynamic which had previously been lacking. He emerged in some sense a changed man, though in many respects his personality was much the same in its characteristics. The experience added to, rather than subtracted from, the personal faith that he had acquired earlier. It did not so much change his character as confirm the truth of the message he delivered. It was less the beginning of a new phase than a stage in the long development since Epworth days. Green does reject the theory of a 1725 'conversion' as oversimplified. 'If there was one precise moment which crystallized Wesley's spiritual development, then it occurred in May 1738, but the moment may not be detached from what had gone before nor should it be seen as a final and irreversible experience.'

Green then emphasizes Wesley's inherited High Church theology and piety within which he pursued his ascetic methods at Oxford with a view to individual sanctification; this set up tensions because of his troubled personal life and lack of achievement. The conversion, Green thinks, did not in fact alter his theological standpoint (at least in any final way) because in his later years he modified his sharp views on justification exhibited in 1738 (a point which will be developed later). Apart from the new stress on justification by faith 'for which there were ample precedents in Anglican formularies', there was no significant difference between what he taught before and after 1738. He had never believed in justification by works, nor that he could be saved by some form of Christian ethical idealism. The beliefs he held later, their rigidity mellowed by age and spiritual insight, were essentially those he had before he left Oxford for Georgia. Green allows *some* significance to the May experience. It cannot be identified simply with a turning towards God, and it meant far less to him than the Moravians thought it should. 'What John Wesley's conversion provided, even if in form and actual experience the terminology was spiritual and theological, was a psychological reassurance.' He gained a confidence in the truth of what he was preaching that gave him the strength and dynamic confidence for his life of evangelism.

These judgments obviously differ considerably. Schmidt sees a definite and decisive theological change, though including a psychological element. Green sees only a psychological one, and although he rejects the idea of an essential 1725 'conversion', the theological perspective he offers does not differ much from those who see the earlier date as decisive. Schmidt sees the change in a Pietist Lutheran perspective; Green in a High Church Anglican one.

In considering these and other interpretations, the beginning of wisdom (as in the assessment of literary and other 'influences' on Wesley) is to avoid one-sided, doctrinaire, unitary interpretations and to allow for eclectic and if necessary inconsistent positions on Wesley's part, subject also to changes in the light of his subsequent experience.

There are in fact really two areas of dispute. One is the content of the experience and what it meant to Wesley at the time. The other is the place of the experience in his religious development, the effect it had on his later career and the way in which he viewed it in later life. Some of the conflicts of interpretation arise because an understanding of the conversion which fairly represents what Wesley thought in 1738 and for some time after is then taken to have been what he continued to believe for the rest of his life. Of the two areas of dispute the first is the more intractable and subject to uncertainty. The second should be more amenable to factual verification, and but for the theological interests already referred to need not be too difficult to settle. A better historical perspective may also help to clarify the first problem. To these problems, indeed, a third has to be added in the shape of some recent attempts at psychological interpretations of the conversion in the light of Wesley's upbringing and his relations with his parents. The difficulty here, despite the unusually plentiful evidence for a man of his period, is the uncertainty and controversy attached to the whole notion of 'psycho-history'.

It has been customary for evangelicals to see Wesley's 1738 conversion as one of a select number of historical models of conversion experience, part of an 'evangelical succession' including St Paul, St Augustine and Martin Luther. Whatever truth there is in this perspective, it ignores important differences between the problems which 'conversion' solved for these great men and the historical circumstances in which they were placed.[38] The particular tradition of conversion of which Wesley's was an example had a much more recent history than such a 'succession' picture allows for, and one has also to consider Wesley's personal history and temperament in approaching the event.

'Evangelical' conversion, in fact, really originates no earlier than the

very end of the sixteenth century, at least in England, and may almost
be said to have been invented by some late Elizabethan Puritans, notably
William ('Drunken') Perkins.[39] The early sixteenth-century Reformers,
in recounting their personal spiritual histories, dwelt chiefly on the shift
in their theological understanding from Romanism to Protestantism,
concentrating on the doctrine of justification by faith as an objective
fact of divine action. Perkins, and other Puritans after him, was able to
take the truth of this doctrine as an accepted fact and was more concerned
to identify the existential, experiential change from living by works to
living by grace and faith. Above all, as predestinarians, this group was
anxious to identify the signs by which a person might be assured that
he was indeed one of the elect and to analyse the stages by which one
might recognize the development of God's work in the soul, through
which it was prepared to receive grace. In American and English
Congregationalism after about 1640 there was a further imperative for
such analyses, for aspirants to full church membership and admission
to communion were expected to produce acceptable evidence of conversion. The result of these developments seemed to be to focus attention
less on the mystery of the divine election and more on what the would-
be convert could and should do by way of preparation for the reception
of grace and on hopeful signs that he had received it.

By the early eighteenth century some American descendants of the
Puritan fathers, alarmed at the decreasing numbers of people professing
conversion, preached intensively to produce the experience and some,
like Solomon Stoddard, induced local outbreaks of what in retrospect
look like previews of the Great Awakening of the 1740s.[40] How far
Wesley, in 1738, was conscious of this history, is more than doubtful,
but the story is relevant to the origins of the English Revival. What is
certainly relevant to his own experience is the parallel development in
Germany. Here, seventeenth-century Pietists had also produced a
concern for personal conversion or 'new birth' of an instantaneous and
conscious type. One famous model for this was the conversion of A.H.
Francke, the Pietist leader in Halle (of whose celebrated educational
and philanthropic institutions the Wesley family had read years
before).[41] And from Pietism the tradition was transmitted to the eighteenth-century church of the United Brethren, the Moravians whose re-
presentatives Wesley met in Georgia and England with such dramatic
effect.

Given their Lutheran background (and despite their stress on practical piety and the religion of the heart rather than mere theological
correctness as regards the doctrines of grace and faith), it is not surprising
that the Moravians should have stressed that salvation cannot come by
'works' but only by faith. And the transition from works to faith was

seen by them as producing a 'new birth', typically experienced in an instantaneous conversion. This was what Böhler and his friends taught Wesley. Before the end of April 1738 Wesley had accepted intellectually that salvation was by faith alone, through an instantaneous experience, on the testimony both of Scripture and living witnesses. But he had not actually experienced this happening to himself. The event on 24 May appears to represent this truth becoming a part of his own experience. It also appears to have been combined with an explicit 'assurance' of the change having happened – if anything, this is perhaps the dominant aspect of the experience. In any case, Wesley seems to have felt that the fact of the change and an assurance that it had happened had occurred in the same moment of experience. (In later reflection he and other Methodists often seem to have seen the two experiences as happening on separate and successive occasions, and Wesley's own doubts after the May experience led him to seek the reassurance of the Moravians that assurance could be delayed.)[42]

Postponing for the moment strictly psychological explanations of the experience, there are at least two complicating factors to be borne in mind when studying Wesley's account and the analysis he gives himself in his *Journal* of the process leading up to it, quite apart from the presuppositions brought to the interpretation of it by later scholars. One is the attitude of the newly-converted in this mode, which Wesley very evidently shared at the time, along with most of his followers in their autobiographies. Typical is the harsh valuation of their religion before their conversions: all apparent moral and religious achievement is written off as devoid of merit; apparent virtues are only splendid vices, partaking of the nature of sin. A character not obviously vicious, perhaps even outstandingly virtuous in the eyes of the world, but still more a character with defects in respectable behaviour, is liable to be described in terms of lurid immorality.[43] This was true of Wesley's assessment of his pre-1738 behaviour and achievement, at least in the main published text of his *Journal*, though we shall see that there is evidence of second thoughts later. It is also a common feature of new converts of this tradition that doubts and depressions are liable to creep in soon after conversion. This is certainly true of Wesley at least up to January 1739, and they were accompanied by characteristically logical arguments to prove that the evidence of his feelings showed that he was not a Christian.[44] Why these self-excoriations then ceased except for one extraordinary outburst of the old sort in 1766 is a problem which will be discussed later, but the doubts in the months immediately following May 1738 are a common enough phenomenon in this tradition. In Wesley's case we shall see that there may have been aggravating psychological factors.

The other problem about the *Journal* evidence is that it represents a synthesis for public consumption of what Wesley had experienced, believed and taught in the early months immediately following his conversion, presented in a particularly stark form. As such it obviously has evidential force for his state of mind then, though it is not a simple transcript of his exact feelings immediately after the event. It is very important to realize that it was not his own last word on the subject either in terms of doctrine or experience, as can be seen by certain footnotes added many years later and other later evidence.[45]

If the arguments of Böhler and the Moravians convinced Wesley intellectually in 1738 that salvation could not come by 'works' but only by grace and faith and, at least for a brief period with interruptions, he believed that he had subjectively experienced the 'new birth' and assurance they promised, this was not solely due to their arguments and testimonies. It is obvious that their arguments appealed and their testimonies convinced because Wesley, after the heroic efforts in Oxford and the traumatic events in Georgia, found that his methods and assumptions had proved bankrupt in terms of delivering the spiritual goods he sought. As has already been hinted, one cannot at this point evade the challenge or, perhaps, avoid the seductive prospect of psychological explanations. No modern biographer can really ignore the suggestive patterns of parental pressures already noted in the Epworth home. It is much more difficult to sort out the details of the results in view of the variety of psychological schools of thought and the even greater hazards which accompany psycho-history. One is not encouraged by the fact that some of the supposed 'facts' on which these interpretations are based turn out to be hoary Wesley legends (such as the arcane significance of his supposed christening as John Benjamin or misunderstandings of 'providential' interpretations of the Epworth fire of 1709).[46]

Still, the general principle may be accepted that even if no psychological interpretation of the conversion is entirely plausible, and certainly none is a complete 'explanation' of what happened, psychological factors must be coupled with more intellectual, theological and spiritual ones in an attempt to explain what happened to Wesley. Three may be mentioned here as illuminating in various (perhaps not mutually exclusive) ways. Källstad has used the notions of 'cognitive dissonance' and role-taking to explain how Wesley's upbringing predisposed him to attempt to understand and live his life in terms of biblical images and models which led to conflicts between what he felt and what he thought he ought to be. There were further stresses induced by the conflicting models of Anglican and Moravian ways of salvation and the personal conflicts between the ideal of celibacy and the emergence of sexuality.

The conversion of 24 May can then be seen as a stage in the cognitive process which reduced the dissonance between the Anglican and Moravian models by an appeal to experience in favour of the Moravians because Wesley felt he had received the gift of justifying faith. Dissonance remained as he found a lack of full joy, but this was reduced by Moravian explanations in Germany. The recurring self-criticisms of 1738/9 are seen as due to conflicts between his celibate ideals and attractions (hitherto unnoticed) to the Hopson sisters in London. The remaining dissonances were reduced as a result of responses to his preaching which appeared to confirm the truth of the message.[47]

J.W. Fowler sees the 1725 turn to seriousness and the conversion of 1738 as stages in Wesley's development to adult maturity, the establishment of an independent identity. In this a crucial part was played by the fact that his was a personality dominated by patterns shaped by a superego created by the standards imposed by his parents. The conversion of 1738 brought a measure of release through the idea of justification by faith, and the post-conversion anxieties were resolved when he became concerned with the salvation of others from 1739 onwards. Fowler adds some interesting reflections in similar terms about Wesley's later modifications of his views about justification and sanctification and the universality of salvation. He sees this as a reflection of a further integration of the self and its conflicts in middle age.[48]

Fowler draws on studies by R.L. Moore which offer one of the more elaborate attempts to interpret Wesley's development from a psychological point of view.[49] In particular an essay of 1974 attempts to show the connection between his childhood experiences, conversion and the effects of field preaching in 1739. The contrasting personalities of Susanna and Samuel had imposed upon Wesley a compulsive perfectionist personality along with a sense of providential calling (from the escape from the fire) with a strong sense of maternal authority which was firm yet just. Against this was the capricious and inconsistent authority of his father. Oxford and Georgia provided him with opportunities for transferring the safely structured moral world of Epworth into a wider world, and at the same time the refusal to take on the Epworth parish and the attempt to be a missionary in Georgia showed resistance to his father's authority, atoned for by labours on *Job*. Georgia also fulfilled his father's failed dreams to be a missionary and, Wesley hoped, would be an escape from the fear of the love of women. In the event it only brought further conflict over the failure of the mission and further female entanglements. This led Wesley to see the need to submit his self-will to the will of God and confirmation was provided by the Moravians, who also taught him the need for the faith of a son. He found a God in whom there was not only a demand for righteousness but also an image of the heavenly father, and love which echoed something of his mother's justice and avoided the caprice of his father. He had returned to the maternal moral order of the nursery. He was able to call no man master but God alone – hence his later ability to stand against church authorities.

Wesley was aided in his growth in confidence by identifying with the roles of various scriptural figures, even Christ himself, and by becoming a travelling preacher; this fulfilled, in a sense, his Dissenting maternal grandfather's itinerant life and even his father's missionary ambitions. The doubts about his failure to sustain a sense of joy and assurance after May 1738 were resolved by seeing the fruits of conversion in others. 'Now he had preached faith until *others* had it, and the assurance which he could not gain through a sensible change in himself he now gleaned from that which his ministry was facilitating in the lives of others.[50] In leading a movement of this kind he thus fulfilled the providential call to an extraordinary ministry which Susanna had expected for him after the fire. For good measure, Moore speculates on the reasons for the ecstatic response by people like the Kingswood miners. Had they shared a similar upbringing to that of the Wesleys? On the contrary, they probably experienced parental neglect or casual brutality. Now they had the offer of a loving heavenly Father, hence their emotional response.

In view of the difficulties already mentioned, it would obviously be rash to adopt these theories without question. It seems reasonable to accept that Wesley's spiritual development was entwined with his psychological development. A prolonged adolescence and recurring difficulties in attaining autonomy and maturity might be a reasonable summary of the situation, and in some ways, especially in relation to women, one might argue that maturity was never fully attained. The conflicting personalities of his parents and the severe Epworth régime were important factors here. Together with the actual teaching and discipline taught or otherwise acquired in the strictly religious field, these influences help to account for the pattern of ideals and the problems that they created in Wesley's religious development. The tendency to think in terms of biblical models for life is important, but so is the continuing and even strengthening tendency to follow the teaching of experience. The sense of a 'providential' role is, however, one which seems to have developed later in life as a result of the Revival experience – the idea that it was instilled by Susanna seems at best not proven. The idea that Wesley failed to gain a permanent inward sense of joy and assurance and that the problem was resolved by observing the fruits of faith in others (which occurs in all these theories) appears to be soundly based, and more will be said about this later in considering the future course of Wesley's spiritual life. In sum, though it is possible to produce apparently coherent explanations of the conversion and its effects solely in terms of psychology or of theology or of styles of spirituality, it seems more satisfactory to suggest that Wesley's religious problems and the solutions he found for them were conditioned by his upbringing and psychological development. The theological explanations he offered and the spiritual solutions he found were a personal synthesis of elements drawn from a variety of sources and confirmed by experience – that of others even more than his own at some important points.

The other main issue – how Wesley regarded his 1738 experience and its theological significance for his mission in later years has been the subject of a good deal of controversy and sharply opposed views. As has already been indicated, these tend to reflect with suspicious accuracy the theological and ecclesiastical presuppositions of the writers. The truth in this case seems to lie not so much between the extremes as in a position embracing elements from both of them.

Generally speaking, Methodists and other evangelicals to this day have seized upon the conversion of 1738 and its theology of faith and instantaneous conversion as the key to the whole of Wesley's subsequent activity as a revivalist. This has often led to a very sharp contrast being drawn with his pre-1738 theology and piety, and to the claim that this was almost totally abandoned after 1738. His High Church piety and theology, influenced by Catholic and mystical writers, is dismissed as salvation by works, and this is replaced by an uncompromising form of Protestant justification by grace through faith. Wesley's own self-review on 24 May and his teaching in the early 1740s seem to confirm this.

In contrast with this tradition, various non-Methodist writers, especially those of a 'Catholic' bent (though also some Methodists), have expressed doubts about this picture even to the point of rejecting it almost entirely. The more extreme versions of the alternative view generally claim that Wesley's 'conversion' really occurred in or about 1725, perhaps with a further stage of deepening perception and commitment in 1729 when he came to see that inward as well as outward holiness must be achieved.[51] In any event, from this perspective the 1738 'evangelical conversion' has been at least greatly exaggerated in its significance. It is alleged that so far as it mattered at all, it was a short-lived emotional moment which induced a temporary adherence to a full-blooded Protestant evangelical view of salvation, but that this was gradually replaced by a reversion to his previous pattern of the disciplined pursuit of holiness and left no lasting mark on him.

The second view is certainly a valid protest against the more simple-minded pictures of Wesley as a convert to conventional evangelicalism, the writing off of his previous achievements, the ignoring of later changes in his views, a survival of pre-conversion habits and some evidence of

post-conversion doubts about his condition. Part of the problem lies in
the ambiguities of the term 'conversion', which in Catholic tradition
may be understood either in the technical sense as 'entering religion'
(i.e. becoming a member of a religious order) or, more generally, as a
conscious decision to take up a commitment to a serious pursuit of a
Christian life. In this sense it is perfectly reasonable to see Wesley as
being 'converted' around 1725, with a further stage of change in 1729.
This is indeed what is suggested by some of Wesley's own accounts of
the development of Methodism, which mention these dates and stages
and sometimes omit 1738 altogether.[52] Yet this does not exclude the
possibility of a further change in belief and an experience associated
with it, which is precisely what Wesley's self-review of 24 May 1738
suggests. He then certainly seems to have taken the 'evangelical' view
that he was becoming a Christian for the first time.

The more important question, perhaps, is whether he changed his
mind later to the point of rendering the 1738 event unimportant. And
here neither of the interpretations seem quite to fit the facts. For it is
easy to show that whatever Wesley subsequently thought about the
lasting significance of 1738 for his own Christian life, he certainly
regarded what he learnt then as the beginning of his distinctive doctrine
and mission. Time and again to the end of his life he harks back
approximately to this date.[53] There is also much in the general character
and specific content of his preaching of justification by faith and
assurance, together with his observations on converts, to show that he
regarded this way of salvation as the norm. Moreover, many of his pre-
1738 High Church practices and prejudices were gradually abandoned
or modified: apostolic succession; the invalidity of Dissenting ministries;
and of course a wholesale breaking of High Church ideals of church
order in his use of field preaching, lay preaching, infringing parish
integrity and in the end ordination.

Yet before we revert to a strict 'evangelical' view of 1738 and its
consequences, we must recognize another set of facts which severely
modifies any picture of Wesley as a typical 'evangelical'. In some matters
he changed his mind and habits not at all. His eucharistic doctrine and
practice remained that of the late seventeenth-century High Churchmen
(though for a fuller appreciation of the significance of this for Methodism
at large more will be said later about a subject which has been generally
misunderstood). The Oxford disciplines persisted in a less complex
form, as the surviving diaries show. The holiness aim persisted, though
it took some significantly new forms.

In the early years of his newly-found doctrine of justification by faith
Wesley certainly spelled out the doctrine and its implications with
uncompromising fervour, together with its implications of the new birth

and assurance, despite the doubts he had about his own experience. This can be seen, for example, in the careful expositions of 'what we teach' in the first Conferences of 1744–7.[54] This leaves no doubt that in the 1740s the conversion had led to a sharp change in doctrine. Yet there is equally no doubt that in the succeeding years there were gradual, piecemeal modifications of its rigour. At first he taught that a man was not converted unless he had a clear assurance of the fact from God (which incidentally explains why into 1739 he doubted his own conversion).[55] Yet later he reluctantly acknowledged that although this was an 'ordinary privilege' of the reborn, it could be interrupted or lacking for a variety of reasons.[56] He also came to doubt the emphasis that many Methodists laid on feelings and various psychological disturbances as signs of the work of God. They were to be regarded rather as accidental accompaniments of the rebirth; neither their presence nor their absence were decisive proofs of their state before God.[57] In later years Wesley went further, astonishingly far for an 'evangelical'. He conceded that a man might be justified who did not clearly understand the doctrine or even (like William Law) actually denied it.[58] It was the reality, the results of what the doctrine stated that really mattered – a life of 'faith working by love'. These concessions were dictated partly by the light of continuing experience of converts, partly by controversies with opponents, above all by the threat of Moravian 'stillness' and Calvinist antinomianism. Controversy with the latter in particular led to painstaking and controversial re-statements of the earlier pronouncements on faith, works and sanctification in a manner which was not always consistent.[59] Formulas like 'faith working by love' also point to the emergence of a major change in the placing of justification by faith in the scheme of salvation, which has a bearing on the question of whether Wesley retreated from his 'evangelical' views of 1738 (see below, ch. XI.1, for discussion of theological evolution).

Can it be said that after a brief flirtation with classic justification by faith Wesley then gradually reverted to his earlier views? This is not the case. Two distinct if related points are involved here. It is true that he scarcely afterwards refers specifically to 24 May and his own experience then; why, is not clear, though it has been suggested that he did not wish to dwell on the Moravian influence after the break with the Brethren and his attacks on their errors.[60] And if he continued to press for conversion, he did not dwell so much later on the details. On the other hand, we have seen that he frequently implied that his distinctive mission and teaching had begun about that time. Even the 24 May account and analysis was allowed to stand in editions of his *Journal*. However, there is some evidence of second thoughts about the harsh phrases on his lack of faith and lack of salvation. In the edition of his

Works in 1774 and after his death in 1797 there are footnotes added to some of these phrases including the admission that he had the 'faith of a servant but not of a son'. Doubts have sometimes been expressed as to whether these are Wesley's own emendations, but they seem groundless: they have the Wesley pungency; and there would be no reason for a Methodist to tone down what was really a typical statement of the worthlessness of pre-conversion piety for salvation.[61] The toning-down accords with his later more generous and less doctrinaire views of justification already noted.

Wesley did not abandon the doctrine of justification or the idea that it was normally received in a decisive experience of conversion and new birth. It remained the foundation of the holy life, but the picture he favoured more and more was that it was the beginning of a process of sanctification culminating in perfection – a perfection which could be received in a moment (exactly parallel to justification) but was also susceptible of further growth by faith and discipline. This shifted the traditional Reformation emphasis on the all-importance of justification and the 'evangelical' emphasis on the moment of conversion towards progress in sanctification. And when talking about sanctification and perfection, Wesley plainly drew much more on Catholic than Protestant sources; he revived (though selectively as always) his love for the works of Law, à Kempis, even some of the mystics so strongly condemned in 1738. But he combined this with the view derived from the Moravians that spiritual changes could be wrought in a moment by faith, and now applied this to perfection as well. Given these gradual shifts of emphasis and the combining of such diverse religious and theological traditions, it is not surprising that eighteenth-century Moravians and Calvinists should have thought Wesley was not a converted man; was a man of works and theologically unsound. But then, what else could be expected from an Arminian, they implied? It is the same shifts and combinations that help to account for the opposing interpretations of Wesley's conversion and its aftermath.

Whether the result can really be regarded as a harmonious synthesis is open to debate. G.C. Cell, in a paradoxical work designed to show that Wesley's theology was very unlike the relaxed humanism of the 1930s, tried to demonstrate that he had reverted to what he saw as 'Calvinism' in essence. But Cell says that Wesley added to this a strong, but healthy and controlled, eighteenth-century element of empiricism in his appeal to experience. Cell's final conclusion was startling (in view of some strong words on the way about the snares of Catholic mysticism and salvation by works). Wesley had worked a miracle by taking the two great principles separated at the Reformation, 'the early Protestant doctrine of justification by faith and the Catholic appreciation of the idea of holiness or Christian perfection', and joined them 'in a well-balanced synthesis'.[62] The formula has often been quoted and often doubted, if only because holiness ideas are not absent from the Protestant tradition, and to suppose that they could only be found in Catholic theology may be a product of an unnecessary inferiority complex on the part of Protestants.[63] It is also true that though Wesley owed much to Catholic writings, he understood them in his own way, and no Catholic writer could have seen 'perfection' in Wesley's way as an instant gift. Yet his placing of justification as the gate to the sanctification process was a long way from Luther and the sixteenth century. The formula certainly has the merit of highlighting the unusual nature of Wesley's doctrine and the way in which it tried to meet a persistent problem in post-Reformation Protestantism, and also the shift away from the simple certainties of 1738.

Further discussion of Wesley's mature theology must be postponed to a later chapter. For the moment it is sufficient to say that the conversion of 1738 was neither a temporary hiccup in an otherwise Catholic-style pilgrimage of holiness, nor an all-determining rejection of that model in favour of a simple Protestant evangelical pattern of justification by faith. If attempts to see him as having achieved a unique 'synthesis' of the two traditions overstate his success in drawing on both, they nevertheless point to his peculiar position as a man who avoided both extremes. His adoption of justification by faith experienced in conversion was a real change in his theology and the style of his ministry, but he modified its terms later without reverting simply to his earlier High Church beliefs, though some of those earlier values concerning the disciplined pursuit of holiness were reasserted. In the 1740s he was much influenced by 'evangelical' models of justification, and for a time was concerned with his own lack of the expected inward evidence of receiving it. The pressure of events and experience – that of his converts' rather than his own – forced him to modify his theology more than once. His own experience never fully corresponded to what he taught his converts to expect, yet theirs seemed to him to confirm the truth of what he preached, including perfection. And the task of interpreting the events of 1738 offers an exacting exercise in analysis of a religious event which resulted from the combined effects of biblical models, patterns derived from inherited religious traditions, the stresses of personal psychology and the persistent force of experience felt in the self and observed in others.

Converting Fires: The Origins of the Evangelical Revival

1. The concept of revival

'Revival' implies a renewal of something once possessed in a full and lively manner, but now in weakness and decline. It has a certain air of nostalgia, a touch of the myth of the golden age, like the variable Anglican versions of 'primitive Christianity'. The golden age to which nineteenth-century writers on revival tended to look back was in fact the Evangelical Revival itself, for then (it seemed) great preachers had attracted thousands of hearers and converts; whole new religious groups had been created and old ones lifted to a higher plane, while many individuals were marvellously converted. What was to be 'revived' was a high and concentrated level of conversions, usually with more or less strong signs of excitement. This would be based on the preaching of the key doctrine of justification by faith as against salvation by conventional religious observance seen as mere 'works'. The change wrought by justification could expect to be known through a more or less instant experience of 'new birth' or 'conversion'.[1]

But this was 'revival' seen in retrospect: for those involved in the eighteenth-century movement itself the perspective was bound to be rather different. They believed that they were experiencing a renewal of the truth and life of primitive Christianity as in the apostolic age, and saw this doctrinally as a renewal of the salvation doctrines of the Reformation. In more general terms they expressed a concern for 'vital' and 'inward' religion, and in John Wesley's case a concern for 'holiness' or 'perfection'. The phenomena of instantaneous conversions and a mass following really took them by surprise, and even the doctrines that produced them were often only found by painful search.

Reflecting in 1779 on what had happened, Wesley wrote that: 'The remark of Luther that a revival of religion seldom continues above thirty years has been verified many times in several countries.' Yet there are exceptions. 'The present revival of religion in England has already continued fifty years. And, blessed be God, it is at least as likely to continue as it was twenty or thirty years ago.' Indeed he thought it more likely, since it was spreading deeper as well as wider than ever, and more people are able to testify to the experience of perfection. So he hoped it would continue to the last day. Here at least he evidently saw the movement as beginning with the Holy Club, and he liked to contrast this long-lasting movement with short-lived revivals elsewhere.[2]

But Wesley also recognized another type. In 1771 he commented on the pattern of Methodist development in Weardale where, after a gradual increase, the society was static for ten years; then had a revival; then settled back; then 'the work of God revived' again, culminating in scenes of religious excitement like those in the early days of Methodism.[3] Thus a religious 'revival' could be seen in two different forms: as a more or less long-term movement of religious renewal and growth (Methodism being exceptional here according to Wesley); or as a much more localized and short-lived outbreak with intense religious excitement and a concentration of conversions in a single community of people who were formally Christians in an evangelical sense. In some cases it might spread elsewhere, though still not lasting for more than a year or two.

The prototype of the second type of revival is to be found in America, occasionally even before 1700 and more frequently later. The New England Congregationalists expected individual conversion as a mark of justification and election, and this qualified people for church membership. But only a minority experienced this, and the lack of it was particularly worrying for converted parents of unconverted children. Within these small Puritan-influenced communities it was possible for preachers sometimes to create short-term waves of conversion, and it has been remarked that such 'collective hysteria' resembled that producing witch scares, and that 'revivalism grew as belief in witchcraft declined'.[4] There was little sign of anything like this in English Dissent of the period, probably because it never gained the social and political grip of communities which had been obtained in New England Puritanism. Revival in England came initially mainly from the dominant Church of England. The rare exceptions tend to prove the rule by their isolation.[5]

The New England revivals were generally local and short-lived, like the famous one under Jonathan Edwards in Northampton, Mass., in 1736. Even the 'Great Awakening' of the early 1740s, when Whitefield's visits helped to link up local outbreaks, only lasted for a short period compared with the long wave of English Methodism. American-style revival was, then, a matter of intense but rather localized and short-lived excitement, though by the nineteenth century it was liable to ebb and flow in a cyclical pattern in some communities.

Yet localized excitements of this kind can also be recognized as occurring within the long wave of Methodist overall growth, as well as in non-Methodist evangelical communities. This was what happened in Bristol with scenes of charismatic excitement at the beginning of the movement in 1739. The Weardale example in the 1770s, as Wesley described it, looks very like the American pattern of revival within a more or less believing community, and there were other cases in Cornwall, Yorkshire, Lincolnshire and elsewhere in the 1780s and 1790s, though they were largely confined to the Methodist minority of members or at least adherents. The exception was, perhaps, Cornwall, where Methodism has been seen as being more nearly a 'religion of the people' than elsewhere. It is certainly not the case (as has often been claimed) that the charismatic outbursts were confined to the early days of Methodism or where it was breaking new ground (see further below, p. 195). It is also, in the light of his remarks on the Weardale case, not quite true to say that Wesley had no notion of 'revival' as a localized burst of religious frenzy.[6] It is probably true that when Methodist Conferences asked 'What can be done to revive the work?', they spoke of religious renewal within the existing church membership rather than of a programme to stimulate such local events within the community at large. But in fact at Weardale something of the kind had been going on which was also true of the local outbreaks in the 1780s and 1790s. However, much of the effect was within the existing membership (for the later period see below, pp. 491ff.).

The important point here, however, is that the late eighteenth-century development in English Methodism of hopes of revival through prayer meetings and in some cases the help of specially gifted revival preachers like William Bramwell seems to mark a transition to a different approach to the nature of revivals. In early Methodism, revival (whether short and local or prolonged and extensive) was seen as an unplanned, unpredictable act of God. It could not be created by human effort, even human effort directed according to the promises of God. This was probably still true of the late eighteenth-century cases already mentioned. But during the early nineteenth-century, special methods to create revivals were developed (the prayer meeting for revival; the 'protracted meeting', the 'anxious seat'), which some believed would infallibly induce a revival.[7] These were liable to be most successful among those already within or connected with the evangelical world, and it is significant that in the Methodist revivals of the 1780s a large part of the converts were already members, as were all those perfected through 'entire sanctification'. Nor is there much sign of the outside world being affected, as could happen in terms of public morality in some New England towns – Cornwall perhaps excepted.[8]

But if we go back to the original Methodist movement of the 1740s, we are faced with a special problem. This movement, it has been said, 'did not revive the existing local parish or Dissenting congregations on the American model; local churches were the end-product not the takeoff point of the Wesleyan connexion'. It did not strengthen existing religious institutions, but tended to weaken them, and to 'found new ones out of men and women who had no deep sense of having belonged to a religious community before, even though they may have attended parish churches and Dissenting chapels'.[9] Moreover, as Wesley observed, the growth of Methodism seemed to be through a long wave rising for years, quite unlike the short, local revivals even though these punctuated the longer-term growth. In the early 1800s it was still possible for the new Primitive Methodists to repeat the earlier pattern in much the same style. Of course as time went on Methodists were faced with the American problem of unconverted children within the community and sometimes with similar results, and we shall see that a number of early Methodists were certainly not without a religious background, even though not tied closely to the existing churches. But taken as a whole and especially in its Methodist form, the English Revival of the eighteenth century remains a phenomenon which defies simple and unitary explanations.

Before reviewing some of the possibilities it is, however, necessary to appreciate that the English case is part of a much wider international phenomenon.

2. The international scene

The Evangelical Revival in England was only part of a much more extensive international movement of a similar general character, yet it is still all too common for English treatments of the subject to take little if any account of this fact; and there is still no general modern history of the movement as a whole. Yet even to understand the English part of it requires some knowledge of the wider movement. For one thing, if we attempt to explain the sources of the movement, the fact that it was not confined to one country at once raises at least three possibilities: that it originated in one country and was transmitted to others; that it arose independently in each place for similar or perhaps related reasons; or that both processes took place in varying degrees. One assumption often made should be contradicted at once by a biographer of John Wesley. Wesley did not begin the Revival, not even in England, whatever his role in it was to be later.

What was the geographical spread and chronology of the Revival? It is hard to know where to begin. It is possible that in some ways still not properly traced it began or at least was previewed in Germany. In seventeenth-century German Lutheranism a complicated and many-sided movement of religious renewal developed which is broadly charac-terized as 'Pietism', its most notable leaders being P.J. Spener and A.H. Francke.[10] They reacted against the official stress on formal theological correctness and merely conventional churchgoing and what they felt to be the impoverished state of spiritual life. Instead, they wished to create a more personalized and inward type of piety and stressed the importance of good works, a concern which had always been theologically suspect in orthodox Lutheranism. These aims they pursued with the help of private religious societies (the contemporary development of religious societies in the English church may not be simply a coincidence). For Francke especially, true Christianity comes in a process of 'new birth' or conversion – and he had had a sudden experience of this himself. In some ways this movement resembled English Puritanism (indeed was influenced by the reading of Puritan works), and like Puritanism it soon developed into different types, some working within Lutheran state churches (and in Francke's case at Halle with favour from the govern-ment), others separating into sects and some indeed influenced by mystical piety. Similar groups developed within the Reformed (Calvin-ist) churches of the Netherlands and North-West Germany. During the early years of the eighteenth century one can also find Lutheran groups in Central European Catholic territories which existed in difficult and often persecuted conditions without much formal church life. In these circumstances they had to depend on travelling preachers, lay helpers and informal meetings. Sometimes, especially in periods of anxiety and persecution, these groups produced spiritual and physical manifes-tations remarkably like those of future Methodists.[11] Some of them were also helped by ministers and literature from Pietists like Francke; some emigrated to Lutheran areas of Germany and some eventually to England and America, in the latter case at least with some effect on the later American Awakening.[12]

Then, still in Germany, there were the renewed Moravian Brethren. The original Moravians had been a kind of Protestantism before the Reformation in what is now Czechoslovakia, a radical fragment of a conservative mediaeval revolt against Rome. Very little remained of them after persecution in the seventeenth century, but a few refugees were given sanctuary in Germany in the 1720s by Count Zinzendorf on his estate. Zinzendorf had been brought up under Pietistic influences, and out of the Moravian refugees and other followers he created a new society marked by a belief in salvation by faith, personal conversion as 'new birth', and an intense, personal devotion to Jesus which at times took very sentimental and bizarre forms. Most striking is the fact that the new society also created a number of settlements for communal living of a highly organized kind. Colonies of Moravians were planted in England and America, and this is the one foreign influence whose impact on the English Revival is well known, for it was Moravians who taught John Wesley the secret of justification by faith experienced in a personal conversion and 'new birth'. But this was not until 1738, and the Moravians were already in England by then and preceded Wesley's journeys to the north of England.

America must be considered next. The roots of what Americans call the 'Great Awakening' are complex. Continental Pietist influences have to be considered here.[13] Some of the refugees from Europe already mentioned had certainly come under Pietistic influence and were concerned for inward religion and the new birth. Most of them worked among their own people, but one at least has been credited with a wider influence. He was T.J. Frelinghuysen, who in the 1720s is claimed to have produced intense conversions by his preaching.[14] He helped to inspire a Presbyterian ministerial family called Tennent to follow his style of preaching by 1730. Then in 1734–5 the celebrated Calvinist Congregationalist theologian Jonathan Edwards evoked a brief but spectacular and famous revival in his New England parish of Northampton which temporarily moved a large part of the community to seek conversion. Edwards was important partly because he was a profoundly learned Calvinist, a philosopher influenced by Locke; but also because he was a skilled analyst of the religious emotions and the processes of conversion in the light of his philosophical and theological teaching. A few years later, in 1739–40, the English preacher George Whitefield (who had experienced the new birth in 1735) began his series of prolonged visits to America. Here his popular preaching seems to have done much to join up the scattered local revivals in New England and to give them a sense of belonging to a movement which is known as the First Great Awakening. American historians have given this movement the kind of serious study and sophisticated analysis which has generally been lacking for England, and recent work has tended to stress the economic and social as well as the religious roots of the movement.[15]

These do seem to have at least influenced the degree to which different colonies and churches responded to revivalism (for example Congregationalists in New England but Presbyterians elsewhere). In New England the movement appears to be related to a sense that the high ideals of the Puritan tradition had been eroded by the growing prosperity and complexity of society; and evangelical conversion could resolve the conflicts between the ideal and the sinful reality in individual cases, especially in small communities. It was only later that British Methodists began to introduce their work among the Episcopalians, who had hitherto been immune to such influences.

Next, Wales. Wales had been strongly influenced in some areas by Puritan preachers in the seventeenth century, but it was also an area where the Church of England was poor and not very effective, and suffered from a language barrier, particularly among the higher clergy. It seems that an important preparation for the Revival can be found in the system of charity schools which spread literacy and moral and religious concern before the Revival began.[16] As early as 1714, for a few years a minister called Griffith Jones was preaching to crowds in the open air and intruding on other men's parishes. Then in 1735 two crucial Church of England men were converted, a layman called Howel Harris and a clergyman called Daniel Rowland, the latter being influenced by Griffith Jones. They became the leading figures in what was to be the Connexion of Welsh Calvinistic Methodists, though it suffered from divisions, and Harris in particular had a rather erratic career. The Connexion only finally separated from the church at the end of the eighteenth century. Harris was important in another way: he was in touch with Whitefield, may have inspired him into open-air preaching, and later helped to run Whitefield's loose Connexion for a time.

In England the Revival developed out of an untidy series of local revivals, eventually consolidating into several distinct bodies and influencing existing churches. There are some possible previews in the 1690s, notably Richard Davis, a Congregationalists' church in Northamptonshire, and perhaps the work of the cousins Mitchell and Crossley in Lancashire and Yorkshire (Crossley actually lived long enough to welcome Whitefield's work in the 1740s.)[17] But these movements were localized and short-lived. Nor did Dissenting and Scottish Presbyterian contacts with, and knowledge of, American developments seem to have much immediate effect until Whitefield began his English work after his first American visit.[18] Whitefield had in fact been an associate of Wesley's at Oxford, but experienced the 'new birth' in 1735 and drew large crowds with his preaching before going to America. In February 1739 he began to preach in the open air and became a spectacular popular preacher and an important link between the revivals in England, America and in Scotland. Although he later had a loose Connexion of English Calvinist Methodist societies, these moved into Congregationalism after his death. Whitefield himself remained in the church, but as a Calvinist he had an uneasy relationship with the Wesleys and this became a serious split in the English Revival as a whole – the followers of Wesley were in fact the odd ones out for their opposition to Calvinism.

Whitefield's chief patron and supporter was the Countess of Huntingdon, a kind of godmother to many of the Revival leaders.[19] She, too, was converted in the 1730s, and for a good many years supported the Wesleys as well as Whitefield, but she was closer to Whitefield, and under her patronage he preached to the aristocracy at her famous 'spiritual routs'. She built chapels, protected preachers as her chaplains and founded a college to train preachers at Trevecka. In the 1770s there was a furious row between the Countess's preachers and the Wesleyans over Calvinism, and in the 1780s she separated from the church, but after her death her Connexion lost much of its following to Congregationalism.

While at Oxford, Whitefield had been a member of the circle of devout churchmen nicknamed the 'Holy Club' or 'Methodists' which developed from 1729 under the leadership of the Wesley brothers. The group included a number of people who later were very far from following the Revival way, but some contributed to various branches of it. Moravianism attracted one or two, including Benjamin Ingham, Wesley's companion to Georgia. Ingham was converted by the Moravians in 1737 and on his return to England began founding societies in Lancashire and Yorkshire.[20] He submitted to the Moravians for some years, but later the Inghamites had a small connexion of their own, a few churches of which still survive. As we have seen, it was only in 1738 that the Wesley brothers were converted, and at first they worked with the Moravians in societies which were still a modification of the old-style Religious Societies. It was the split with the Moravians in 1739 that led to the organization of separate Wesleyan societies and the emergence of a connexion which was to become the largest of all: the new evangelistic bodies which by the time of Wesley's death in 1791 were poised (against his will) to become a new church or rather group of churches after later secessions.

This does not exhaust the list for England. The Revival, we shall see, was made up of many local revivals under local leaders: men like David Taylor, a servant in Lady Huntingdon's family, who preached in the North and North-west; or John Bennet, who was converted by Taylor and whose societies in the latter area were absorbed into Wesley's connexion.[21]

Meanwhile, beginning in the 1730s in a few places, but generally rather later, there developed a scattered crop of converted Anglican clergymen, mostly parish priests.[22] Their conversions were usually highly individual and seldom owed anything to the Methodists, though in the loose usage of the time they were often labelled as such (like others who struck their critics as being unusually pious). Some itinerated outside their parishes, and a few (like Grimshaw of Haworth) assisted the Wesleys. But some opposed the irregularities of Methodism from the first, and nearly all did so in the end, as well as falling out with Wesley over his Arminianism and perfectionism. Most were Calvinists in the moderate terms of the Thirty-Nine Articles. Later in the century they included some important lay activists with humanitarian concerns, like William Wilberforce, for they were able to influence higher ranks in society than the Wesleyans were able to reach.

Some individual Dissenters were influenced early by Methodism, chiefly in the lower ranks, for Dissenting ministers were generally hostile. But by the 1770s Baptists and Congregationalists were becoming part of the Revival. A few had sustained the old Puritan ways; more drifted in through conversion by Whitefield or the Wesleys and created new evangelical churches. Some, too, seceded from old Presbyterian churches which had become unorthodox on the divinity of Christ and the atonement. Generally these founded severely Calvinist but evangelical churches. A new kind of Baptist community was also created: the General Baptists of the New Connexion – which was orthodox but Arminian, and had been influenced by Methodism. There was much fluidity of allegiance between these groups in the early heat and confusion of revival, and sharp party lines took time to develop. Some individuals had long spiritual pilgrimages through several homes. Some ex-Methodists also helped to feed unusual sects which cannot be described as 'evangelical' – such as the tiny Shaker sect which emigrated to America and the visionary Swedenborgians. Even the Unitarians, who evolved from the old and now unorthodox Presbyterians, produced individuals who thought that their creed could be given popular appeal by using Methodist preaching techniques.[23]

Some Quakers were converted to Methodism, and eventually some felt the pull of evangelical teaching while remaining within the Society.[24]

In Scotland, the revival seems to have drawn partly on native traditions and partly on influences from outside, including an important stimulus from Whitefield's visits. Wesley had few followers here, and the Scots generally experienced evangelicalism within the various Presbyterian churches, established or otherwise. The first signs were in the early 1740s, among bodies created by earlier secessions from the Presbyterian Establishment, but the Establishment itself developed a powerful evangelical party which would eventually be one of the forces behind the great Disruption of 1843.[25]

Finally, there is Ireland, where the sources seem mainly from outside. Whitefield visited from 1738, Cennick (a former Methodist turned Moravian) in 1746 and Wesley himself from 1747. Although Wesley made it part of his regular tours, much was done by individuals, clerical and lay, who had been converted by a variety of means, including visits to England. In this predominantly Catholic land the Revival added a new dimension to the various Protestant churches, but also had some success in converting Catholics, and some leading preachers of Irish origin had a considerable influence on the Wesleyan Connexion in England.

The Revival, then, had a remarkably extensive international spread and was made up of many different groups, even though in terms of numbers only a minority were affected.

These groups certainly were not uniform, and indeed sometimes violently disagreed. They sometimes transformed a church from within and intended to do no more; but in a number of important cases (such as the Wesleyans) they eventually drifted away to form new churches. In Germany they affected sections of the Lutheran and Reformed churches; in Scotland the Presbyterians; in America Congregationalists, Presbyterians, Baptists and continental immigrants. But in England and Wales they began within the Church of England and only later affected Dissent extensively – though as Michael Watts has remarked, it was Dissent which gained most in the end from them.[26] It is in fact a common feature of the Revival in most places (though not all) that it began in established churches (of different sorts in different places). Some historians have wished to emphasize the distinctiveness of the movement in different countries – for example some historians of the American Great Awakening.[27] But there is in fact a striking degree of common ground.

Thus, as against the common bias of the time in favour of rational religion, the Revival stressed revealed, biblical, supernaturalist religion. At the popular level this could be anti-intellectual and anti-rational, and their religious experience expressed itself in dreams, visions, particular providences and healings; some of their leaders (like John Wesley) shared their outlook, though without, however, abandoning the rationality of their education.

The contemporary bias of a religion heavily stressing morality was challenged by the Revival's central emphasis on the traditional Reformation doctrine of justification by grace through faith as the only foundation for good works. This was to be experienced in a new birth, for many a distinct moment of conversion of an emotional kind. For many contemporaries, this contrasted strongly with the gradualness of the usual process of salvation, and especially for High Churchmen with the notion of the Christian life as beginning in baptism. The Anglican Evangelical John Berridge's self-composed epitaph neatly summarizes the expected pattern and contains no mention of baptism: 'I was born in Sin Feb 1716. Remained ignorant of my fallen state till 1730, Lived proudly on faith and works for salvation till 1754 . . . Fled to JESUS alone for refuge 1756.'[28]

Behind this lay a reversion from rather optimistic contemporary views of human capacity to traditional notions of the fallenness and helplessness of sinful human nature. But there was also a great divide in the Revival between Calvinists and Arminians. Evangelical Calvinists in America were aware of the solid and impressive Calvinist theological tradition which had decayed in England. The English seem to have relearned this creed by experience fed by old practical works of divinity. They preached for conversion, but ultimately saw it as the fruit of election, even when they preached as if all who showed signs of real repentance could be saved. The Arminians horrified them by speaking as if men might be saved and then fall away: for Calvinists the elect were guaranteed final perseverance. Worst of all, and highly untypical of the Revival as a whole, John Wesley and his followers preached a controversial doctrine of perfection as in some sense achievable in this life. Calvinists rejected this, though most of them strongly emphasized growth in holiness, and in practice few fell into the trap of antinomianism (rejection of the moral law) which Wesley claimed was the fate of Calvinists. There is a kind of spiritualized eighteenth-century optimism (but about the power of God rather than of man) in Wesley's views here which will be examined later.

Another common characteristic of the Revival, though varying in degree from one group to another, was the stress on an active lay piety. Laymen (even, in some degree, laywomen) could preach, lead in prayer, and exercise pastoral care. They did not simply attend means of grace provided by the clergy but were encouraged to meet in more informal groups for the intensive mutual cultivation of spiritual experience. The late Gordon Rupp once remarked that the original sixteenth-century Reformation affirmed two great dimensions of church life: Word and Sacrament. To this, in the period 1560–1660 (he said) was added a stress on a third dimension, 'the discipline of Christ', which can be seen variously in Calvinist Geneva, English Puritanism and elsewhere. The next period, he suggested, saw the addition of a 'fourth dimension': the church as *koinonia* or fellowship, the Christian cell meeting for prayer and mutual guidance and edification.[29] The examples Rupp cited were German Pietism and Moravianism, and English Methodism. Though such cells were especially important for these, and in fact an integral part of their organization as well as a useful means of grace, one can find the same impulses expressed in more limited and cautious ways among most of the Revival groups.

The use of these groups and the participation of active laymen is also related to the development of a great variety of special means of grace and new forms of worship. The extent and variety of these means varied from group to group. Anglican Evangelicals kept close to the Book of

Common Prayer, but Moravians and Methodists developed a rich variety of special services as well as a liberal use of hymns and extempore prayer. The experimental and informal note was prominent until the new spontaneity hardened into a new routine.

Finally, most of these groups showed a concern for philanthropy, developed voluntary institutions to express their concern in action, and in some cases later pressed for legislative change as well. This impulse was evidently related to older and newer debates about the problem of poverty and the marked rise of philanthropic concern during the later eighteenth-century. It was not simply a peculiarity of evangelicals, though they added their own special glosses to such concerns.

The Revival was very obviously a Protestant phenomenon, and indeed it has been argued that the whole movement originated, at least in part, as an anxious response to the religious and political threats of the Catholic powers of Europe.[30] Yet there are certain parallels worth mentioning within the Roman Catholic world. The desire for what was often called 'inward religion' and for laymen to meet in groups for mutual comfort and not simply in the formal services of the church is one which can be seen in the Catholic world as well; so is the desire to reach the unchurched and to stir up the indifferent. A remarkable passage in a report from a Moravian synod in 1741 seems to suggest that the parallel is more than accidental. 'The difference between those zealous servants of God, who, in Germany by some are called Pietists, in England Methodists, in France Jansenists, in Italy and Spain Quietists, in the Roman Church in general often known by the character of preachers of repentance and asceticism, but in the Protestant Church generally thought mystics on the one side, and our [Moravian] economy on the other, is this: the former strive either for an alteration in the religious worship; or even for abolishing the external part [of worship]; we preach nothing but the crucified Christ for the heart . . . '[31]

Although it need not be assumed that the Moravians had correctly stated the difference between themselves and the other groups they mentioned, the striking point is that they felt that it was plausible to compare the evangelical Protestant groups with ascetic and mystical groups in the Roman Church. Some modern scholars have also noted the parallels. Owen Chadwick has commented on developments within the tradition of Catholic Quietism which produced widespread meetings of laity in Spain and Italy of a type which, he says, would have been labelled 'Pietist' in German Protestantism. Contemplative mysticism had here reached beyond the religious orders, even beyond the educated middling ranks to lesser folk. 'This was probably because the method was supposed to be very simple and easy' (so the title of one of Madame Guyon's books). Official inquiries claimed that these people had separatist tendencies; allowed laymen to preach; and believed that extempore prayer was alone necessary, public prayers and sacraments being unnecessary.[32] It should be remembered that there were individual Pietists, Moravians and Methodists who read the writings of Madame Guyon and Antoinette Bourignon, though some of them did so with less discrimination than John Wesley and caused divisions as a result.[33] It is perhaps best to see this strain of Quietism in Catholicism and Protestantism as a distinct tradition in contemporary piety which in fact helped to produce a fresh crop of Protestant sects at the end of the century.[34] Yet it also helped to feed a much wider desire for 'inward religion' and the fellowship group to supplement and even supplant formal worship which was expressed in one particular way by the evangelical movement for renewal through justification by faith and new birth, and in another way by mystical communion with God.

A Catholic parallel of a different kind, at a more acceptable and official level, can be found in the feeling among some good bishops and clergy that the conventional parish work of the church was failing to Christianize the lower ranks. This concern led to special missions by travelling clergy in areas of low practice to arouse people to a sense of sin and drive them to confession and communion, often in a highly emotional way. Jean Delumeau has, controversially, suggested that the real Christianization of the masses and curbing of their superstitions took place in the seventeenth and eighteenth centuries and not before. He compares these Catholic missionaries with the early Quaker preachers and the Methodist itinerants, who may be seen as doing unofficially for the half-Christian lower orders of the Church of England what Catholic missionaries were performing officially for Catholics elsewhere.[35]

Further than this it would be unwise to go. One cannot ignore the deep divide on the theology of grace, faith and works which is so prominent in the preaching of the Revival and which consciously set it in opposition to Tridentine Catholicism, conventional Anglicanism and the Enlightenment. Yet even the Revival was not exempt from the intellectual fashions of the time. We shall see that John Wesley was in many ways what his contemporaries regarded as an 'enthusiast' in his supernaturalism. Yet he was a rational enthusiast and appealed in terms of 'reason' as well as religion. Worries about materialism in public and social life; a concern for inward rather than merely conventional religion; spirituality rather than mere morality; a desire to remedy defects in official church organization, are features of a great variety of initiatives for religious renewal in the West in this period which influenced minorities deeply and gradually helped to alter the tone of a larger public.

3. The problem of origins

Early evangelicals, as we have seen, tended to see the Revival as a mysterious act of God, and later evangelical historians have been prone to agree. So far as a more mundane historical explanation has been offered, it has often been in general terms of a 'reaction' against what has been taken to be the manifestly sub-Christian religious and moral tone of church and nation. In the more optimistic versions of this picture one is given the impression that laxity, infidelity and Latitudinarianism were defeated by the movement, though its work had to be completed by the addition of the Tractarians' teaching on the nature of the church and sacraments. In reality, evangelicalism was a minority movement which failed to capture most of the church and excited much hostility, while leaving large stretches of what it regarded as 'works' religion unaltered.

There have been few attempts so far at a comprehensive modern analysis of the origins and causes of the Revival.[36] So far as Methodism is concerned, some mention deserves to be made of the remarkable essay by Halévy which first appeared some eighty years ago, for though it has not attracted much comment since and can be shown to be seriously flawed, it nevertheless suggests a mode of analysis which deserves to be explored further. Halévy is more famous for his notion that Methodism – or rather evangelicalism as a whole – helped to save England from a French-style revolution in the early nineteenth century. His earlier essay was an attempt to give it a similar role at its outset in 1739–40.[37] He pictured England in the early eighteenth century as imbued with a deep but latent Puritan seriousness which the existing religious bodies could not release or embody. But by an accidental conjunction of secular and religious circumstances at the end of the 1730s this release took place. The Wesleys were taught salvation by faith by the Moravians, and Whitefield learnt the secret of field-preaching from the Welsh. At the same time there was an explosive and potentially revolutionary economic and political situation in the West country and elsewhere which the Wesleys exploited, turning these fiery passions into the harmless ecstasies of religious conversion. Thus Methodism was born.

Unfortunately Halévy's thesis was riddled with errors and improbabilities. There was no 'revolutionary' situation, and the disturbances he described were purely economic and continued to occur later. Methodism captured only a minority, and on the religious side Halévy placed too much stress on the peculiar case of Wesley. In any case he did not attempt to explain the origins of other branches of the Revival.[38] And yet there remain fruitful ideas for exploration in his picture: latent religiosity including the Puritan strain; the possibility of special factors in the 1730s; and perhaps especially the attractive 'model' of a causal analysis which combines the secular and the religious, the long-term factors and short-term 'trigger' events.

Much more research is needed before a more effective general explanation can be attempted. Here it will only be possible to survey some of the piecemeal explanations which have been suggested for various sorts of causes.

One factor which has struck several observers is what may be termed 'ecclesiastical geography', that is to say, the pattern at least of Methodist success and failure which seems to correspond to the areas of weakness and strength respectively in conventional Anglican parochial ministry. The areas of Anglican weakness and Methodist strength tend to be where parishes were large, especially where settlements were scattered: in industrial areas; in towns; where single landowners did not dominate; where churches and clergy were lacking or inactive. In southern agricultural parishes with compact territory, single landowners and resident clergy Methodism was much less successful. It has been calculated that well over half the Methodists were in areas where the organized religion was weakest.[39] Whitefield and Wesley certainly felt they went to 'sheep without a shepherd' and sometimes were stared at as if a clergyman were a strange animal: 'Why did not you come before?' said miners to Wesley in the North-east.[40]

Social, economic and political factors tend to bulk large in modern accounts of religious history, though analysis of the Revival in these terms remains at a rather elementary stage. Evangelicals tended to be apolitical, tacitly or openly to endorse the scriptural injunction to 'obey the powers that be' as given by God, no doubt an implicitly 'conservative' stance. In moral terms there are some signs that for their own reasons evangelicals shared the impression purveyed by opposition politicians out of office that government and society were corrupt and immoral and irreligious. The Wesley family was Tory with Jacobitism on the female side, as we have seen. Methodism was tarred with the Jacobite brush in the 1740s, and there is the possibility that here and there it appealed to a section of the aggrieved and proscribed Tory population as a form of opposition to the established order. But it also offended mobs as an enemy of the church and local community (see further, below pp. 372f.).

More obviously, Methodism appealed very selectively in terms of occupation and social status. Thomas Taylor, it will be remembered, thought that where there was little trade there was little religion (in his sense), and it has often been observed that Methodism did seem to attract more of the craftsmen and industrial workers than the less skilled and agricultural labourers.[41] This also helps to account for the geography of distribution. Miners and fishermen were apparently also especially responsive to the message. Explanations have been offered for this in terms of fears induced by dangerous occupations and a general susceptibility to supernatural beliefs among such workers. More generally, industrial migrants have been seen as finding their disorientation healed by Methodist fellowship, which was indeed close and valued, though not necessarily for this reason.[42] It has been generally thought that those in crafts, industries and towns were less deferential and less bound to their employers, pastors and masters than mere labourers and agriculturalists, and therefore more open to deviant religious movements.

Was the Revival or, perhaps more realistically, were some of the more spectacular local outbreaks of excitement touched off by natural or man-made disasters? Debates about the effect of economic fluctuations on later Methodism and revivals have been somewhat inconclusive in deciding whether the ebb and flow of revival is simply related to prosperity and distress or vice versa. The revival tradition had its own internal cycles, and distress may have done no more than heighten these effects.[43] The initiation of a new religious movement may be another matter again, but despite local distress the period from 1730 to 1750 seems to be one of relative prosperity and stability.[44] Was this indeed what made it feel safe to launch a deviant religious movement? Though Methodism suffered from the mob, Wesley appealed confidently to the protection of the law for religious liberty, and to the end of his life had optimistic views of the economic improvement of the country – and the progress of God's work.

What more obviously alarmed people and sometimes scared them temporarily into religion individually or collectively were natural rather than man-made disasters, for these appeared more like acts of God. This might be true of epidemics and certainly of earthquakes: the latter regularly produced scares, sermons and penitents; nor were these confined to evangelicals: a sense of providential and judgmental acts of God remained strong among others too. War sometimes produced similar results.[45] Personal misfortunes often produced individual crises, but in all this one can hardly see a general cause for the Revival.

The spectacular if usually short-term outbreaks of cries and convulsions which marked Wesley's early preaching in Bristol and elsewhere, as well as on later occasions, have naturally attracted psychological explanations in terms of crowd pressures and 'contagion' or brainwashing.[46] The Wesleys themselves were not unaware of this, but it should be recognized that many conversions took place in much more private struggles. At the individual level, indeed, one may detect adolescent conflicts and sexual tensions, but it was a striking feature of this revival that it affected all ages and both sexes (the notion of conversion as an adolescent phenomenon tends to be coloured by research on late nineteenth-century inherited evangelicalism).[47] The more spectacular outbreaks had nothing peculiarly evangelical or even Christian and religious about them since similar phenomena occur in other contexts (the witchcraft parallel has already been noticed) and indeed in other cultures. What is significant is the strongly supernatural-ist character of the evangelical mentality, natural at the social and cultural level to which it chiefly appealed, but evident also in the educated leadership, including Wesley himself. Even among its enemies, 'enlightenment' was only skin-deep or at least restricted and selective (see further, below pp. 431f.).

Somehow none of these 'explanations', singly or collectively, seems to explain enough. They suggest favouring circumstances and possible mechanisms, but not much more. What they plainly do not explain is why, from what may seem to be (so to speak) vulnerable groups, only a proportion was affected by the Revival and a still smaller part of this was recruited permanently. Indeed many people were extremely hostile. The factors so far suggested may therefore be seen as a necessary part of an explanation, but hardly as sufficient.

In studying an ostensibly religious movement it seems excessively sceptical, if not perverse, to fail to consider at least the *prima facie* case for a religious explanation as a key factor differentiating converts from the mass of the susceptible and suggestive. One thing is in fact obvious from the surviving biographies of converts – that a high proportion of them had a more or less marked religious background. Suggestions have been made, indeed, that this is quite specific in one or other of three directions: a reaction against Deism; a renewal from High Church sources; or a survival and revival of the old Puritanism.[48]

As to Deism, there is not much to be said for this as a series of personal reactions, though there are a few cases of individuals passing through a Deist phase, or of occasional confrontation with Deists and a natural hostility to Deism. Episodes of unbelief and temptation to blasphemy are more common, but have psychological roots often related to Calvinism, rather than springing from intellectual scepticism.[49] Deism and evangeli-calism really operated in different worlds and continued without either affecting the other very much. What evangelicals obviously reacted against much more was the more pervasive tendency towards rationaliz-ing and moralizing in religion and in contrast with this they certainly stressed supernatural power and faith. Whitefield notoriously dismissed Tillotson's religion as little better than Mahomet's.[50]

What about the High Church tradition? It is possible here that Wesley's example has been taken to be more significant and typical than was in fact the case, although in fact a number of others (such as

Henry Venn and indeed many a country clergyman) came from a similar background.[51] It was common enough for them to read devotional literature of this school, and we have seen that 'new birth' language could come through William Law as well as the Moravians. The search for 'primitive Christianity' began, often enough, with anxious asceticism and sacramental piety, and in London and Bristol among members of the old Religious Societies from which some have seen a strong continuity into Methodism.[52] But the contrasts between High Church and Methodist attitudes to church order are dramatic (if less so in the case of Anglican Evangelicals), and if Wesley in his sacramentalism and perfectionism clearly retained much from his earlier period, this was not true of many of his followers. It is probably best to follow Dr Walsh in seeing the most important effect of the High Church tradition on some future evangelicals as consisting in a process by which their methods drove people to despair, so making them ripe for the way of grace and faith 'alone' (very like Luther's despair of the mediaeval penitential system.)

The possibility of Puritan roots is perhaps the most intriguing. A number of contemporaries saw Methodists as a 'new sort of Puritans', recalling features of the Interregnum horrors and not intended as a compliment. A man like Grimshaw at Haworth looks very like the old northern Puritan clergy, and the Calvinism and personal piety of Anglican Evangelicals recalled the same tradition in Anglicanism, though Wesley came to appreciate it only some years after his conversion.

But if there was a relationship, was this a 'revival' based on surviving tradition or something less direct? Undoubtedly a number of 'Puritan' clergy remained within the Church of England after the Restoration, and the type must have persisted here and there much later: William Burkitt, whose *Expository Notes on the New Testament* was used by Wesley, has been described as an 'evangelical churchman' who used extempore prayer and was vicar of Dedham, notorious for 'presbyterianism' in Elizabeth's reign.[53] Family traditions of this kind could be important and some of the High Church Religious Society supporters of Oxford Methodism were of old Puritan families.[54] But Calvinist theology seems to have become an obscure and beleaguered category of early eighteenth-century Anglicanism, and it has been suggested that it was moral rigour rather than conversion by faith that survived best.[55]

Survival should have been strongest in Dissent, and though Methodism is generally seen as an Anglican product, there were considerable accessions from Dissent, which was perhaps not as moribund as has always been supposed.[56] Several Methodist preachers had this background, and a fair number of followers were acquired by revolt from Arianizing Presbyterian churches.[57] There is also rather a striking category of men of Huguenot families who turned evangelical, like Delamotte, Wesley's companion in Georgia, and the Perronets.[58]

The most striking links, however, seem to be literary rather than personal. Works like Alleine's *Alarm* and Baxter's *Call to the Unconverted*, Bunyan, and a number of others turn up frequently in the process of conversion in evangelicals of all types, and this helps to explain the Calvinism of Evangelicals, as in the case of Whitefield. This legacy may have been kept alive by pious bequests, as in the village of Myddle, where there was an annual distribution of Alleine's *Alarm*, but most seem to have been acquired by what were seen as the providential 'accidents' of finding dog-eared volumes in bookshops or rectory attics.[59] What was inherited was evidently the Puritan tradition of 'practical piety', not its scholastic divinity or its political and ecclesiological concerns.

Perhaps, after all, what is striking in all this is not so much the influence of distinct strands in the Anglican tradition as the influence of what they had in common. If the Puritan literature just referred to could convey ideas of conversion, it could also coincide with High Church and indeed Latitudinarian stresses on moral concern and discipline, which induced in some minds anxieties about failures in achievement and so prepared the way for salvation by faith alone. It is characteristic of the first generation of Methodists that they seem to have had great difficulty in finding this formula at all: it was as if this was a lost secret which had to be painfully rediscovered by trial and error. What does stand out is the frequency with which in the biographies the subject has had a more or less strong religious background and nurture through home or school (see further, below p. 424). There are also indications that these converts (as the existence of the biographies shows) were the most stable.[60] Wesley's *Journals* also contain a number of examples of 'old' Christians converted before the Revival.[61] What is more problematical is the unrecorded and perhaps less stable anonymous mass of converts whose background may have been more like that of the tradition of unchurched 'harlots and publicans and thieves' of whom Charles Wesley sang.[62]

The growth of the Revival is perhaps less mysterious than its origin. This is perhaps where speculations about the appeal to certain areas and sectors of the population is most relevant, for Methodism and other groups boomed in the later eighteenth century as the pace of population growth and industrialization quickened in the Midlands and the North. Nor should organization and technique be overlooked. Wesley's connexional system, the mobile deployment of travelling preachers with a degree of collective loyalty, and his passion for rule and guidance with institutions to follow up the initial impact of preaching, all helped to sustain growth. Polemic and publicity (good or bad) also helped – the role of the Whitefieldite *Christian History* is often overlooked here.[63] Moreover, as we shall see, Wesley's movement was to a significant degree the product of cannibalizing a number of localized evangelical networks originated by others into a national organization.

More problematic is the point of take-off in the late 1730s. This, at least, is what it looks like if one focusses on Wesley and Whitefield, though in an international perspective, or even taking into account other British groups, it looks less decisive; and in any case it tends to exaggerate the size of Methodism in its first few years. A less Wesley-centred observer, like William Batty in his history of the Inghamites and Moravians in the north, saw the beginning of a 'general awakening' as taking place in 1737, in the light of Ingham's work in Yorkshire and Whitefield's in London.[64]

Yet it can be suggested that the 1730s was a decade when good Anglicans and others felt that religion was particularly threatened: by anti-clerical Whig attacks on tithes and church property; by Deism; by Bishop Gibson's loss of favour with Walpole; and the threat of heterodox appointments to the episcopal bench. It was not only disgruntled 'country' politicians out of office who voiced criticism of the Walpolean régime as corrupt and as undermining religion and morals.[65] Wesley took up this theme of national degeneracy in his apologias for Methodism, and though this was not a disinterested comment, it may be significant that Whitefield's early preaching in the 1730s received an enthusiastic response until he showed signs of 'enthusiasm' and 'fanaticism'. Wesley's opponent John Lewis acknowledged that God might have raised up Wesley for the work. He might have 'permitted this new spirit to arise and press through the land, to witness against the wickedness of the age, against deism and infidelity, and against the remissness of church discipline and of the pastoral care'.[66] Finally, the search for general causes should not be allowed to remove the force of personality. If Wesley and Whitefield would have been ineffective without a receptive audience, the accident of their conversions (and those of Welsh revivalists) between 1735 and 1738 provided leaders of special gifts and determination who drew together and focussed isolated groups and individuals within a relatively short space of time.

In attempting to make sense of the various possible causes, it must be repeated that the state of research makes generalization hazardous and single-cause explanations implausible. The international connections have to be borne in mind while due weight is allowed to the influence of different traditions and histories in each area. Although Professor Ward noted how 'Methodist' phenomena such as field-preaching, lay-preaching and emotional conversions had already occurred in central Europe early in the eighteenth century, it would be rash to assume that this simply came to England from the Continent.[67] Should one rather look for similar forces working in all the areas concerned, though producing variable results at different times in different national circumstances? Professor Ward has pointed to the widespread Protestant fears of the advance of Popery and absolutism. Others have seen a reaction against the Enlightenment, though if Pietism is seen as a parent of revivalism, the chronology will not fit for Germany and might rather suggest Pietism as a parent of the Enlightenment.[68]

One fundamental concern common to all groups seems to be a sense that the life of the church and of the individual needed to be revived from within, and that an 'inward' Christianity needed to be substituted for mere outward observance. It is also striking that all began as movements within established churches, the establishment naturally varying in eccesiastical complexion according to the country concerned (Lutheran, Anglican, Presbyterian, Congregationalist).

For England the crucial point here was the failure of the attempted Puritan 'revolution' of the seventeenth century, which had been not merely religious, but also political and social. Politically, socially and psychologically as well as religiously, this crippled any prospect of a concerted religious renewal led by Dissent.[69] The High Church party had also been deeply damaged by the loss of divine-right monarchy and the Whig proscription of the Tories after 1714. The bid for semi-voluntary renewal and moral reform through the Societies' movement foundered partly because it still looked to patronage from above, if not official backing for its moral reform programme.

The seventeenth century had in fact left a legacy of civil and religious strife, yet without destroying the sense that religion was a major source of social cement and stability if rightly understood and organized. The only solution seemed to be to combine an establishment capable of comprehending the majority with toleration for worship which did not allow full civil rights to the irreconcilable minority, since 'comprehension' of all in the established church had failed. The political stability achieved by one-party rule after 1714 needed to be accompanied by (if possible) a one-party church, which Bishop Gibson laboured to accomplish. In religious terms this also meant a more comprehensive, less dogmatic creed, which in fact a good many Dissenters came to share as well, with a major emphasis on practical morality in which all good men could agree. The result, for Anglicans at least, has been aptly described as a 'civil religion'.[70] Adopting a more unkind formula used by a historian of the Elizabethan Settlement, it was 'designed to appeal to the lukewarm multitude, and it enlisted their lukewarm support . . .

The fact that it also kindled no flame in men's hearts, if hardly a merit, was less of a defect in that most men's hearts were not inflammable'.[71] Of course the new phase of Anglicanism was even less planned than the earlier one, and it was a great deal more tolerant. But in both cases it had to reckon with the more 'inflammable'.

The problem was that consensuses of this kind take time to achieve and always leave some groups out: the religious enthusiasts (high and low); those out of office and favour; disadvantaged social groups. The reform movement from above by decorous semi-voluntary effort had failed. The Evangelical Revival in its various forms was a projected new, if ill-coordinated reform movement, which failed in its objective to reform the church as a whole. Although in some places it drew initially on members of older groups, it was essentially a movement from below, led by mere parochial or unbeneficed clergy without patronage (except in the rare and eccentric case of Lady Huntingdon), and before long, in the Methodist case, using 'ordinary' laity outside the parish system. It also worked from the circumference, not the centre; from the provinces more than from London, and was especially successful in remote areas like Wales, Cornwall, or the new industrial areas.

Wesley's well-known desire that Methodism should merely be a society within the church to renew it was never more than half-true about Methodism as a whole, though it left its mark on later Wesleyanism. His motives here were not simply conservative, for he feared the localized isolation of the parish clergy and Dissenting ministry as a damper on evangelism. Pressure from below, however, as well as his own irregularities, ensured that Methodists found their real life within their own societies and steadily moved away from the church. As for Evangelicals, they conformed more and more to the parish and became scattered sectarians within the broad structure of civil religion. In neither case was there any prospect of capturing the establishment or even of gaining substantial patronage within it.

In Methodism, at least, the evidence to be related later suggests that Wesley almost unwittingly captured types of people who were plainly unhappy with the régime of conventional 'civil religion' in church or Dissent and were not too patient, either, with Wesley's autocracy and his refusal to allow Methodist autonomy under a recognized ministry of its own. Their desire for this may well testify to other, more secular aspirations for freedom from the 'deference' society of the eighteenth century, and certainly this became apparent by the end of Wesley's life, and even more later. In religious terms it is a mistake to identify Methodist beliefs and feelings too exclusively with Wesley's own preferred patterns, though it was no mean achievement to impose as much unity of aim and organization as he did, despite much opposition. The passions he unleashed were only imperfectly controlled by his discipline, and if he inspired a cadre of devoted perfectionists, there were plenty who doubted this and other parts of his 'Catholic' legacy.

A recent treatment of the sources of the Revival has stressed that a movement plainly of a minority anyway was a really a rearrangement of 'the religious sub-culture' rather than the triumphal progress towards the transformation of the nation beginning with the church, which Wesley intended it to be.[72] It was, on this reading, primarily a reconstruction of part of the existing religiously-minded public, with new vehicles for individual and communal expression, rather than the creation of a new religious public. The unanswered question is how far it affected those hitherto little affected by organized religion at all (which the same writer earlier suggested may have been the case). It remains possible that in certain circumstances Methodism had a wider role as a 'popular' religious movement beyond its formal membership, at least in certain areas, notably Cornwall.[73]

PART TWO

John Wesley and the Rise of Methodism
(1738–60)

V

'A New Species of Puritanism': The Emergence and Expansion of Methodism (1738–51)

1. A movement emerges: Whitefield, the Wesleys and the Moravians

Wesley's appearance at this stage of his career has been recorded in some descriptions, and in 1741 by a rather striking portrait by John Williams. He was rather short, about five feet three inches in height (1.53m.), slim but muscular, and without superfluous flesh. The most striking feature of his face was a prominent, pointed nose. His eyes were blue, sharp and piercing, and according to one account a slight cast was sometimes visible. He wore his own hair, which according to an observer in Georgia (writing many years later) was auburn, though a contemporary description a few years later says it was black and the Williams portrait suggests black with brown highlights. He disdained wigs and wore his hair long, which certainly looked odd to contemporaries, though it gave him a patriarchal appearance in his white old age. All agree on his neatness and his passion for tidiness in his person and surroundings. The Williams portrait gives him a convincing look of an austere, rather authoritarian Oxford Methodist.[1]

As we have seen, at the point when Wesley began to be 'evangelically' active, a scattered movement of religious renewal in this style was already beginning to show in America, Germany and Wales. In England there were reception points for the preaching of the 'new birth' among old Oxford Methodists like Kinchin and Gambold, the Moravian-influenced circles in London, and the hearers of Whitefield in the Religious Societies and elsewhere. Here and there were solitary pilgrims who had found their own way to conversion, like John Cennick in 1737, who was soon to become an associate of Wesley, then of Whitefield and finally of the Moravians.[2]

The experience of 24 May did not, as we have seen, solve all Wesley's problems. His first lesson, before the end of that day, was that though peace and joy and victory over sin are essential to faith, yet 'transports of joy' at the beginning are sometimes given, sometimes withheld by God. He comforted himself with the thought that although he still felt temptations, he was now always and not just sometimes 'conqueror' over them. Yet he was haunted by the doubt whether he should not have a more 'sensible' change. It was a problem which would trouble him for many months and perhaps was never entirely solved. He was impressed with the strength of the faith of others compared with his own, and could only reassure himself with the notion that faith could be real yet present in varying degrees. Inquiries and arguments about this would also be prominent in his early ministry.[3] Whatever his own doubts, he shocked some old friends by his claim that he had not been a Christian until now. Mrs Hutton wrote to Samuel Wesley junior that John had 'turned into a wild enthusiast and fanatic'. 'If you was not a Christian ever since I knew you,' she told him, 'you was a great hypocrite, for you made us all believe you was one.' Old Hutton feared he was despising the two sacraments by his talk of faith alone and said that by Christ's teaching works are also necessary. It also appears that some of the new converts were despising all teaching but that in dreams and visions – a phenomenon which would haunt the revival and belie Wesley's claims of its 'reasonableness'.[4]

It was to clarify his doubts about the need for 'sensible' evidence of real faith by questioning 'living witnesses' at the source of his Moravian mentors that Wesley made his way to Germany in June 1738. The *Journal* account was part of a section designed to justify Wesley's break with the Moravians, and in the preface to this Wesley identified their errors as the teaching that justification was only genuine if a person was free from doubt and fear; and that the 'ordinances' should not be used until this had happened. Yet the account of the German visit shows no criticism of the Moravians. It looks as though he was implicitly saying that the authorities at home disagreed with the trouble-makers in London.[5] It is in the light of the later break and Moravian attempts to explain it that two anecdotes not recorded in the *Journal* should be explained. One was that at Marienborn Ingham was admitted to communion but Wesley rejected as a '*homo perturbatus*' whose 'head had gained an ascendancy over his heart', though they also thought that admission might interfere with his work of doing good as an Anglican clergyman. Ingham would in fact later assimilate his societies to the Moravians. The other story is that Zinzendorf set Wesley to work in the garden, and when he had worked up a sweat sent him on a visit without changing his clothes to a nearby nobleman, saying 'You must be simple, my brother'. Though Curnock doubts the stories, they are consistent with Moravian and Zinzendorfian behaviour on other occasions, and might help to explain Wesley's later criticisms.[6]

At the new settlement of Marienborn Wesley began to collect testimonies of conversion to salvation from 'inward as well as outward sin', and in conversation with Zinzendorf was told that a justified man might have peace without joy and that assurance of his condition might follow justification at a later date. Wesley contrasted this with Böhler's teaching.[7] Similarly, at Herrnhut, as well as inspecting the Brethren's organization, Wesley heard from Christian David about the intermediate state of those who are justified but have not yet received a new, clean heart and the 'constant indwelling of the Holy Ghost' and 'full assurance of faith'. The same point was emphasized in other persons he met.[8]

One case is of particular interest, that of Arvid Gradin, for although Wesley seemed to be looking for evidence of a separate experience of assurance to reassure himself that he was really justified despite his lack of the correct feelings, there are hints in some of the conversations which seem to become clear in the Gradin case that the converts were also speaking of a condition of being cleansed from all sin. Gradin spoke of a condition of 'deliverance from every fleshly desire and from every outward and inward sin', as well as of peace. In his *Plain Account* nearly thirty years later Wesley in fact quoted the Gradin testimony as referring to the state of 'perfection', which he had searched for over several years and now met for the first time in a living man.[9] It looks very much as if Wesley had expected his old vision of perfection to be realized in the act of conversion; that his experience made him doubt this; that he saw the hope of the feelings of joy and peace coming in a subsequent experience; but that he also now associated this with the gift of 'perfection'. He would discover later that the Moravians were not at one with him here, and later still his own views developed further, but his notion of instant perfection would always show the marks of the Moravian way. His views of assurance as being of one's present state and not of 'final perseverance' were expressed in controversy with Arthur Bedford in September 1738.[10] Wesley also inspected the schools and orphan house at Herrnhut, as well as the more famous one at Halle of which he also had read. These experiences, too, in addition to the Moravian societary systems, would leave marks on Methodism. The atmosphere of his travel letters exudes the enthusiasm and romantic vision of one who is seeing primitive, apostolic Christianity in action. He evidently felt 'apostolic' himself in writing to Charles Wesley and Hutton, for he adopted a 'Pauline' style.[11]

Yet despite all this, two years later, after the break with the Brethren, Wesley says that he wrote a letter of mixed praise and criticism after his visit which he had set aside since he doubted his judgment. If the version quoted in the *Journal* later is correct, he criticized their lack of seriousness, elements of worldliness, and secrecy and dissimulation. This was certainly his later view. A letter to Zinzendorf in October 1738 does hint mildly at his intention to speak of a 'few things which I did not approve', though he admits he may have misunderstood them. Probably these doubts were sharpened in the light of later experience.[12]

The period between Wesley's return from Germany in September 1738 and the call to join Whitefield in Bristol in March 1739 is aptly labelled by Curnock 'With the Religious Societies'. From the Moravian enclaves through the Societies and so into field preaching he moved to the position where in March 1739 he proclaimed in a famous aphorism that 'I look upon all the world as my parish'.[13]

The old Religious Societies were described earlier, and their relationship with Methodism has always been a matter for some debate. Samuel Wesley's association with them, and Wesley's own experiments at Oxford and in Georgia, suggest variations on an old theme. But the Methodism which was later to emerge did not simply develop out of the old societies. For that matter, neither Oxford Methodism nor the Georgia experiments were exactly on the Horneck and Woodward model. The Fetter Lane society, we have seen, already showed Moravian influence. Moreover, the picture of Methodism emerging from the matrix of the religious societies has been heavily influenced by the early evidence in London and Bristol; elsewhere developments were often very different. Certainly Whitefield and Wesley worked extensively among the societies in London and Bristol and recruited from them; but some were entirely new, the fruit of Whitefield's preaching, and even the older ones were, by his account, marked by extempore prayer, the teaching of justification by faith and converse on the soul. Some were also influenced by the Moravians. Methodism brought further changes: the inclusion of non-Anglicans and women and sub-divisions for those seeking conversion and perfection which were foreign to the ethos of the old societies.[14] Still, for the original scenes of their labours, the societies (old or new), were an important field of labour, as the churches were closed to the evangelists and the fields were not yet open. Indeed Wesley seems at first to have been a kind of agent of the Fetter Lane society, whose members were supposed to do nothing without consulting their brethren.

The activities of Wesley and his associates in this period can be examined from three angles: public ministry; the controversies this aroused; and Wesley's inner life.

As regards the first, the pattern of Wesley's activity consisted of a busy round of preaching in churches, and meeting and preaching in the societies, especially Fetter Lane. He took several excursions to Oxford and a few farther afield, for example to Reading, where he first met Cennick. Some clerical friends, old or new, were working with him, like Gambold or Stonehouse at Islington.[15] This hints at clerical leadership of a loosely associated 'movement'. Wesley knew of ten such men so far, including one or two Presbyterians. Fetter Lane now had fifty-six men in eight bands, though only eight women in two. Sometimes he was addressing five or six hundred people, and he even talks of a 'general awakening': there was a 'great awakening' at Oxford in November 1738. The language recalls that of the Americans: Wesley had read Jonathan Edwards's account of the Northampton revival the previous month.[16]

Already Wesley was observing some strange events which would become more common the following year. Mrs Hutton had already complained of visionaries, about whom John was always less sceptical than Charles. In Oxford and London there were cases of troubled spirits written off as mad by relations and physicians, but seen by Wesley as in the throes of the salvation struggle and ripe for spiritual healing.[17] Then, as later, he was confident that he could distinguish such cases from natural hysteria or 'enthusiasm'. He and Charles had several encounters with 'French Prophets', members of a section of Huguenot refugees who spoke in tongues, claimed revelations and used healing gifts. Charles met one who 'gobbled like a turkey-cock', but thought little of her because of her 'lewd life and conversation'. John tested the spirits and found them wanting because they were 'enthusiasts' who 'wanted the end without the means' and did not follow 'the Law and the testimony'.[18] The problem became more difficult when his own preaching produced convulsions, and already there were claims to visions which he felt less willing to reject. Some of them reflect Moravian phraseology about the fountain opened in the side of the crucified Saviour.[19] The truth is that at this time and later Wesley was moving in a highly-charged charismatic atmosphere in which he thought he saw the scenes of the Acts of the Apostles, reproduced with all the strange gifts of the apostolic age, repeated: not only instant conversion but visions, demon-possession and healing. His opponents thought that he was claiming miracles, and despite his disclaimers and his careful investigations, he believed that much that he saw was indeed the work of the Spirit, whose work of this kind was not confined to past times, as educated contemporaries thought. On 1 January 1739 Wesley himself was caught up in a scene at Fetter Lane reminiscent of the day of Pentecost. While they were singing at three o'clock in the morning, 'the power of God came mightily upon us, insomuch that many cried out from exceeding joy, and many fell to the ground'. On recovering a little 'from that awe and amazement at the presence of His majesty we broke out with one voice "We praise Thee O God; we acknowledge Thee to be the Lord"'.[20]

Yet with another side of his personality Wesley was maintaining part of the old Oxford discipline. He fasted on Wednesdays and Fridays and would have liked the Fetter Lane members to do the same. In Christmas week he received the sacrament daily. Old and new ways met when he baptized a group of adults in January, noting that only one was born again 'in the lower sense' of receiving remission of sins and some, he thought, not born again in either sense.[21] A suggestive gap was opening up between his High Church ideals of rebirth in baptism and the new way of faith. Before long he would be finding that the eucharist was not only a 'confirming' but also a 'converting' ordinance.

His notions of the Anglican norm for apostolically authorized ministry (and perhaps, his own sense of authority) were put under strain when Hutton proposed a leadership structure for the societies. The Moravians would always maintain that the reason for Wesley's break with them (apart from his lack of a true 'new birth') was that he wished always to be the leader and could not bear to be led. In fact Wesley at first submitted to the Fetter Lane rule of consulting the brethren before making decisions (as over the move to Bristol), and he told Whitefield that they must not set up their own 'will and judgment against that of our whole society'.[22]

But this conflicted with Wesley's sense of authorized ecclesiastical authority (and perhaps his own sense of authority by virtue of the personal call of God). In November 1738 Hutton and others proposed a tighter supervision of the bands and especially the settling of the females in separation from the men. He himself should be appointed as 'register'. A lot should be cast on whether to have a 'president'. Monitors should be chosen to tell everyone their faults. It was a further measure of 'Moravianization'. Wesley disagreed, partly on pragmatic grounds, but also because: 'A general monitor commissioned by God to reprove every one of his brethren you have, so long as you have any priest or deacon among you.' He added later that 'I believe bishops, priests and deacons are of divine appointment', so he was tender of any approach to 'pastors appointed by the congregation'. Yet he confessed to his 'weakness', thought that it should be referred to the brethren, and said that he was not bigotted either to the 'ancient church' or the Church of England.[23]

Wesley was in fact beginning to find himself in a position which would become familiar in future years: pressed by those on one side wishing to substitute their own church order for that of the Church of England and those on the other side condemning him even for his own 'irregularities', which he saw as consistent with an overall loyalty to the church. For already, if Wesley suspected Hutton was violating apostolic order, some of his friends thought Wesley himself was equally guilty. In December 1738 Wesley's old Oxford friend James Hervey wrote in disturbed tones about his 'setting forth strange doctrines' and encouraging 'honest tradesmen' to leave their occupations to 'turn preachers'. Samuel Wesley junior had heard that he allowed an 'Anabaptist' into one of 'our pulpits'; that he had preached in unconsecrated buildings and prayed extempore. To Hervey, Wesley allowed that honest tradesmen could not be 'public preachers' unless formally 'called', though they should witness in their own sphere.[24] But he was involved in a movement which would soon throw up preachers of its own accord.

In one respect, indeed, Wesley was already taking a high ground of principle on 'irregularities' by March 1739. He wrote to an unnamed friend (perhaps Hervey or Clayton) who had advised him to return to college or to sit still and not to interfere with souls in other people's parishes as this was contrary to 'Catholic principles'. Wesley responded that 'scriptural principles' alone weighed with him and *they* commanded him to 'instruct the ignorant, reform the wicked and confirm the virtuous'. Since he was unlikely ever to have a parish, forbidding him to work in others' parishes meant not doing this work at all. And so to: 'I look upon all the world as my parish . . . This is the work I know God has called me to.'[25]

Finally, in this period, there is the question of Wesley's inner life. Later in life he said that he wondered that the people had not stoned him and his brother Charles when they taught that without full assurance there was no salvation; and he certainly came, though reluctantly, to admit that such assurance might be lacking for psychological reasons. His inquiries in Germany, as we have seen, were directed towards reassuring himself that the assurance might be delayed and that there were degrees of real faith without it. In the *Journal* of this period there are several severe self-examinations which with inexorable logic conclude that because he does not possess settled joy (though he has some other marks of faith) he does not possess the 'full assurance' of faith though he has a 'measure' of it. He worried himself with the thought that even this conclusion was the result of judicious reasoning and that he did not 'feel' as he judged. Finally, on 4 January 1739, there is a ruthless self-analysis (in the *Journal* recorded as of 'one who had the form of godliness many years', but the diary shows it was himself). He says he had received (obviously on 24 May) 'such a sense of the forgiveness of my sins as till then I never knew' but had apparently not sustained it. He analyses the fruits of the Spirit (love, joy and peace) and since, for example, he does not *feel* the love of God, he believes that he does not possess it. So, he concludes, 'I am not a Christian'.[26]

It is curious that after having collected so many reassurances that faith might be real without full assurance and that the assurance could be delayed, Wesley should have concluded on such a totally negative note. If his later recollection was correct, he was just as uncompromising in his preaching. What is equally striking is that this is the last of these self-analyses and confessions of unfaith in his *Journal*; nor are his letters much more forthcoming, with the exception of one remarkable outburst to Charles in 1766 and a narrative of an unhappy love affair closely parallel to that made of the Hopkey one in Georgia. The famous *Journal* is a much less self-revealing document than it is often taken to be, but from this point it ceases even to record these studied analyses. It would be rash to suppose that Wesley suddenly ceased to have doubts, though the beginning of field preaching and the spectacular effects of his work soon began and may have reassured him. He may also have been warned by Whitefield's example not to give hostages to fortune by revealing too much of his inner state.

It is possible that his condition was complicated by further female attractions. Hutton wrote to Zinzendorf in March 1740 of the Wesley brothers: 'Both of them are dangerous snares to young women; several are in love with them. I wish they were once married to some good sisters, but I would not give them one of my sisters if I had many.' This is likely enough, though no indication of Wesley's own feelings. Källstad, in the psychological analysis mentioned earlier, speculates that Wesley was attracted by the Hopson sisters in London, this (he claims) would help to explain the last sharp self-analyses and Wesley's reluctance to leave for Bristol. There is no direct evidence of this, but the recurring desire for close female friendship which had characterized Wesley before may well have once again sharpened the sense of conflict between affection and dedication and deepened the sense of failing to achieve holy peace in believing.[27]

But a fresh and, as it turned out, momentous decision was about to be forced on Wesley. On 3 March 1739 Whitefield wrote from Bristol about the 'glorious door opened among the colliers. You must come and water what God has enabled me to plant.' Then, much more insistently on 22 March: 'If the brethren after prayer for direction think proper, I wish you would be here the latter end of next week.' He should come before Whitefield leaves and 'many are ripe for bands'.[28]

According to the *Journal* and other evidence, there was great uncertainty among the brethren and on the part of the Wesley brothers whether John should go. The *sortes biblicae* and the 'lot' pointed different ways – the former intimated danger of death; Moore says that Wesley thought much of death, and believed that his 'course was nearly finished', since his constitution would not stand the strain of his labours. One may well suspect that what Whitefield was doing alarmed him.[29] Field preaching was likely to be dangerous as well as irregular. When he came to write up his *Journal* for publication, Wesley pictured this as a 'new period of my life', and printed the long, logic-chopping letter he had written to his father to justify staying at Oxford rather than taking over Epworth. This was, on the face of it, a curious choice, but probably the old decision between Oxford retirement and the rough and tumble of Epworth seemed to be a parallel to the new choice between the routine of the London societies and the prospect of the Kingswood 'frontier'. (The choice between Oxford and Georgia might seem even more relevant here.)

Wesley's first reactions to field preaching are well known. 'I could scarce reconcile myself at first to this strange way of preaching in the fields; having been all my life (till very lately) so tenacious of every point relating to order, that I should have thought the saving of souls almost a sin if it had not been done in church.' But he soon reflected, while expounding the Sermon on the Mount, that this was 'one pretty remarkable precedent of field-preaching, though I suppose there were churches at that time also'.[30]

But before a description of Wesley's work in Bristol, which involved him in extraordinary scenes and a major controversy which split the emerging Revival and precipitated the development of a distinctive Wesleyan 'connexion', something must be said about his predecessor in field preaching, George Whitefield (1714–70). This is the more necessary since Wesley and his biographers never really did him justice and indeed tended to obscure the fact, very obvious in contemporary accounts, that Whitefield and not Wesley was seen by the public as the real leader of the movement at this stage. Lady Hertford wrote in 1739 of a 'new sect who call themselves Methodists. There is one Whitefield at the head of them.' Continental observers heard of the Revival early and said the same, though by the 1750s Wesley and Whitefield were apparently seen as equally prominent and in theological rivalry on the question of Calvinism.[31] Wesley scored over Whitefield in the long run because he organized a connexion which perpetuated his own name and his own voluminous *Journal*, and accounts of the Revival gave the impression that his brand of Methodism as well as his own career were the source and centre of the whole movement. Whitefield's Connexion and the English Calvinistic version of Methodism have tended to be forgotten because they dissolved after Whitefield's death and fed mainly into evangelical Independency. But Methodist historians need to be reminded that to this day those in the Calvinistic tradition naturally regard Whitefield and not Wesley as the standard-bearer of true evangelicalism and as the real leader of the Revival. The lack of an adequate edition of Whitefield's writings and of critical modern biographies has not helped.[32]

Whitefield was brought up in an inn, and by his own account had a period as a mere 'pot-boy' before going to Oxford as a menial servitor. The contrast between this and his spectacular success as a preacher, together with aristocratic contacts through Lady Huntingdon, created conflicts over pride and ambition in his mind. Towards Lady Huntingdon his conduct could be remarkably servile. Though it is often overlooked that the family had clerical connections and had only recently come down in the world, no doubt Whitefield's early humiliations counted for more than this.[33] His religious development at Oxford from 1732 proceeded by the usual fits and starts, and it is noticeable that he was influenced by much the same kind of 'holiness' literature as John Wesley had been. He also became a member of the Oxford Methodist group, and his fasting and mortifications became so extreme as to threaten his health. Then, soon after Easter 1735, he felt a great thirst and 'it was suggested to me, that when Jesus Christ cried out "I thirst" His sufferings were near to an end'. So he cried out 'I thirst, I thirst' and soon afterwards found himself delivered. At home in Gloucester he 'awakened' some young people and formed them into a society. Then, he says, God 'was pleased to enlighten my soul and bring me into the knowledge of his free grace and the necessity of being justified in His sight by faith only'. Various Puritan writings helped him here, and probably help to explain his developing Calvinism.[34] After his ordination as deacon in 1736 he began to preach the 'new birth' with great success, especially in the period early in 1737 while he was waiting to go to Georgia. He spoke of the new birth and justification by faith, though he says that he did not understand this as clearly then as later.[35] There was evidently no Moravian influence here, and his conversion did not follow the stock Methodist pattern. For the rest of the year he worked with the religious societies and acquired public fame, which revived again on his return from Georgia at the end of 1738. But his 'enthusiasm' created hostility; the churches were closed to him, and he turned to field preaching, beginning in the colliery area of Kingswood near Bristol in February 1739. His Calvinism, which seemed 'antinomian' to critics, was credited to the whole of the new-style Methodists (much to Wesley's indignation), and would soon lead to a split in the Revival.

Even allowing for retrospective exaggerations, there is little doubt that before his departure for Georgia Whitefield had lifted the movement for awakening from an eccentricity of a few friends into something more extensive and public. If he alienated the respectable, he soon found an appeal to the less sophisticated when he went into the open air. The step may have been dictated by the closing up of the churches and the (literally) stifling atmosphere of the society rooms. He may also have been inspired by Howel Harris's example.[36] He was certainly moved by the Kingswood colliers' situation as 'sheep without a shepherd', though a rather mysterious clergyman called Morgan (surely Welsh in origin) had tried the experiment of preaching in the open air there before him.[37] But it was something little known since the seventeenth century, not countenanced by the Church of England, and arguably illegal.

The crowds soon gathered, and the impact was startling. How did Whitefield do it – and for many years – both in Britain and America? Despite the famous squint (which was much caricatured), many seem to have found him an attractive personality, 'almost angelical' in appearance to his admirers.[38] As usual with sermons, the printed versions are only a faint, skeletal ghost of the originals, which were undoubtedly laced with illustrations, the use of incidents during preaching and above all enlivened by a fine voice and dramatic manner. Like most great preachers, Whitefield had the gifts of an actor, as several well-worn anecdotes show. A man who could charm money out of Benjamin Franklin's pocket and move Bolingbroke to compare him favourably with the bishops clearly had uncommon powers. As always with this type of preaching, especially if not followed up by a tighter organization than Whitefield ever developed, the results were bound often to be ephemeral, and the fashionable male world came mainly out of curiosity. Still, there was a loose Calvinistic Methodist Connexion in England, and preachers and 'tabernacles' who looked to Whitefield for leadership.[39] But what now appear as the dull commonplaces of evangelical theology, it should be remembered, were new, sometimes welcome, sometimes terrifying to their first audiences, especially when presented by a master preacher. Even Wesley, as we shall see, could be electrifying with a much more reasoned approach. The sense of sin and hell was clearly still close to the surface of the imaginations of a section of this society, and the revivalists brought it vividly to their consciousness and consciences. Moreover, Whitefield (and Wesley, too) seems to have been able to revivify a latent strain of moralism (too loosely called 'puritan', though it included this) in some English minds. Whitefield was disgusted by the maypole and dancing in Kingswood. The only way of stopping such things, he thought, was by 'going boldly and calling the people from such lying vanities in the Name of Jesus Christ'. He added the striking comment that 'That reformation which is brought about by a coercive power, will be only outward and superficial; but that which is done by the power of God's Word will be inward and lasting.' The contrast with the SRM approach is instructive. Somehow he was managing to 'internalize moral imperatives'.[40]

Wesley first tried this new way of field preaching ('submitted to be more vile' as he put it) to 3,000 people in a brickfield near Bristol on 2 April 1739 and a few days later did the same in Kingswood. No doubt he felt it significant that it was here that he recorded the first of several occasions on which the rain 'providentially' held off for his benefit.[41] He then followed much the same routine as Whitefield: preaching, meeting societies and forming 'bands' of the more devout. Whitefield was also concerned to form schools like the one in Kingswood, which would later cause trouble between himself and Wesley. But for the moment it is clear that he recognized his own gifts and inclinations as being those of an 'awakener', and more or less deliberately left Wesley to consolidate the results in an organized way. 'Dear Mr Wesley was left behind to teach them the way of God more perfectly' and to 'confirm those who are awakened'.[42] A potential alliance was emerging, but it was one which from the first tended to favour Wesley's control. Unlike Whitefield he stuck to Britain, and his incessant travels, as well as the body of his carefully-stationed preachers which was soon to emerge, meant that he kept a developing network of societies under his own control. It is not surprising that, like the Moravians, the Whitefieldites felt that Wesley was an ambitious man who must have all in his own hands. There was truth in this, though the result was more accidental and less conspiratorial than they supposed. But what really poisoned the relationship between the two men and their followers was a split on doctrine.

Before proceeding to this, however, some further consideration has to be given to what struck many observers in the early days of the Revival and caused puzzlement and controversy: the strange psychological phenomenon of 'convulsions' under the preaching of Wesley and some others. On 17 April 1739 Wesley visited the Baldwin Street society in Bristol and while expounding Acts 4 'called upon God to confirm his word. Immediately one that stood by (to our no small surprise) cried out aloud, with the utmost vehemence, as in the agonies of death. But we continued in prayer till "a new song was put in her mouth".' Then two people of good reputation were 'seized with strong pain' and 'roared' with disquiet of heart. A few days later people dropped to the ground as if 'thunderstruck'. Many others followed, most notably John Haydon, a man of 'regular life and conversation' who regularly attended church and sacrament and was a strong churchman and hostile to Dissent. He saw the convulsions as delusions of the devil, but then himself fell 'raving mad' after reading Wesley's sermon on 'Salvation by Faith'. He showed symptoms of demon-possession, cursing the devil, but was relieved by prayer.[43]

Other charismatic phenomena were occurring at this time. The dreams and visions complained of by Mrs Hutton certainly occurred.

Wesley himself was impressed particularly by cases of 'God making good his promise daily', 'very frequently during a representation (how made I know not, but not to the outward eye) of Christ either hanging on the cross or standing on the right hand of God'. He knew this to be of God because those experiencing it had become 'new creatures'.[44] There would be many more such cases as Methodism developed. With dreams, visions, healing, demon-possession, only tongues seemed lacking to complete the apostolic picture. The French Prophets certainly seemed to have them, and some of the other cases observed by Wesley appeared to speak in other languages without benefit of having learnt them. The strange sighs and cries during a convulsionary outbreak under the eccentric Evangelical John Berridge twenty years later have been interpreted as unrecognized glossolalia.[45]

Though an early Wesley biographer like Moore allowed for the supernatural here, as in the case of 'Old Jeffery', later biographers have found early Methodist supernaturalism embarrassing, and not least when Wesley believed in it. The convulsions are alleged to have been confined to the early years, or to places and times where Methodism was first introduced. This is certainly not true, even though they were commonest in such circumstances. Wesley speaks of them in 1744 as being frequent in Europe and America when people are first convinced of sin. An account of Berridge's spectacular outbreak at Everton in 1759 read by Wesley at York provoked a case there. Similar scenes were enacted in Weardale in 1771 and in several places in the 1780s and 1790s during revivals in old-established societies.[46] Nor were they confined to Wesley himself. Cennick describes how in Bristol in 1739 the people were convulsed by a thunderstorm, rushing up and down and crying 'The devil will have me; I am his servant'. One cried 'That fearful thunder is raised by the devil; in this storm he will bear me to hell'. Cennick judiciously concludes that conviction of sin did not simply come from God or the devil: the work of the Holy Spirit raised a struggle from the devil and so led to the convulsions, and he probably thought the storms were raised by the devil.[47] James Robe observed convulsions at Kilsyth in Scotland and answered the objection that the French Prophets (or 'Camisards') showed similar symptoms. The Camisards are proved wrong by their false prophecies and their claims of being affected by supernatural power, including utterances they do not remember or understand after the fit. Robe said that bodily agitation is not in itself a proof of possession by the Holy Spirit or by bad spirits. All that he claimed was that the people's minds are seized 'in a natural way' from the 'great fear of God's wrath' when they are convicted of unbelief. They remember what they said afterwards, and the symptoms go when they are delivered from fear by conversion.[48]

These occurrences were not new: there had been many such cases, variously interpreted in the sixteenth and seventeenth century. The symptoms of demon-possession and of those influenced by witches were very similar. Natural explanations in terms of epilepsy or hysteria had been ventured, and those who opted for supernatural explanations disagreed on whether they were from God or the devil in the case of conversions, though the devil was naturally seen as responsible in others. Even 'natural' causes could be seen as secondary: the primary cause was the devil, who could still use apparently 'natural' causes for his own ends.[49] For Wesley in 1739 the issue was complicated by the fact that the French Prophets were operating at the same time and that the convulsionaries he met included those in the throes of conversion and those with symptoms of demon-possession; the line was not easy to draw.[50]

Reactions to the phenomena and interpretations of them followed earlier and predictable lines. Sceptics and critics saw them as hysteria or enthusiasm or perhaps as fakery, though at least one physician came to see them as the finger of God.[51] But Wesley himself was in doubt. He wrote to various sympathizers for news and views of similar cases. James Erskine in Scotland knew of some and thought that they might be Satan's work to hinder God, or else God testing a sinful generation – but what mattered was whether they issued in conversion. Joshua Read, a Congregational minister, cited past cases, including that of Richard Davis in the 1690s (see below, pp. 325f.). Some cases he had had: they could be natural or diabolical or divine, but conduct was the true test.[52] Charles Wesley fairly quickly came to the conclusion that the devil was at the bottom of it, though he recognized cases of contagious hysteria and cannily dealt with them by putting the offenders out, after which they soon recovered. But of course the devil might use this to discredit the work in the eyes of the respectable. Cennick thought there was something diabolical in it, but noticed that when he prayed God to show signs the antics soon began.[53] He was probably correct in suspecting that Wesley was partly responsible for creating some cases, for John at least once was 'insensibly led' to ask God in public to 'bear witness to his word' of universal redemption against the Calvinists and the convulsions duly began.[54]

After investigating, Wesley concluded that though nature and Satan might have a part in the cases, the Holy Spirit convicting of sin was the main agent. He thought that the symptoms clearly differed from those of epilepsy.[55] In the North-east in 1743 he thought them diabolical, in opposition to Christ trying to save souls. But in 1744 he allowed for God or the devil; even the latter's work might be used by God. Reflecting on the Everton case in 1759 he allowed that God might work like this.[56]

Good results in conversion and conduct seemed to be the final test, but he remained reluctant to rule out the possibility that this might be a work of God – and a good knock-down proof of the divine work in the world, even though conversion was neither proved by its presence nor disproved by its absence.

Modern psychological interpretations of course strengthen the naturalistic suspicions of the earlier period. Crowd psychology and imitative hysteria seem plausible in the light of some of the evidence, and were suspected even by some of the revivalists. Whitefield, like Cennick, thought that Wesley wrongly encouraged it, and though he found that it happened once under his own preaching, it is suspicious that Wesley was present.[57] It is the case, however, that Whitefield often induced cries and tears himself, and the suggestion that his results differed from Wesley's because Wesley originally preached that men were not saved without a definite assurance is not plausible when convulsions were produced by some Calvinists as well.[58] Brain-washing by hell-fire preaching breaking down and re-forming the personality is not entirely plausible, though Sargent's cultural parallels are a reminder of how little specific to Christianity is present in these cases.[59] The problem in all this is that the phenomena were selective, and the evidence scarcely suffices to identify what the social or psychological specifics were. Wesley's own investigations suggested that the effects could be gained in people with or without a strong religious background. What is common to them all is often a strong sense of hell, and this seems to be induced less by hell-fire preaching than by the subjects' own innate belief and conscience which appear to have required little to arouse them.[60] They created their own hell. However, some may have been more open to this than others. Bristol had a large Quaker population, and there were things in early Methodism which recalled primitive Quakerism.

What is certain is that supernaturalism was rife in early Methodism quite apart from the convulsions; that its original character and impact as well as the character of Wesley himself cannot be understood without taking full account of it; and that at the same time such things constantly recalled to mind seventeenth-century excesses – political and social as well as religious – which helped to discredit it with some while it popularized it with others.

Controversial though these phenomena were, Wesley faced other problems within the emerging revival movement itself which were soon to break up the band of brothers and precipitate the formation of a separate organization of his own. This came about all the more rapidly because the conflicts occurred more or less simultaneously. They were over predestination, Moravian 'stillness' and Wesley's violations of church order. All in a sense involved questions of authority, and the first two were linked by fears of antinomianism on Wesley's part. This was always the dark underside of revivals with a strong doctrine of grace and faith.

Wesley's journal-letters to Hutton show more clearly than the published *Journal* that the predestinaton controversy began virtually as he started work in Bristol – indeed he had been warned not to raise the question there as the people were so 'deeply prejudiced' for it.[61] Soon he was invoking the evidence of convulsions or at least conversions as proof that he was right when he preached against the doctrine and for 'free grace', and Charles did the same in London where the problem also occurred. It divided the society in Bradford-on-Avon; and at Deptford Wesley expelled a Mr Acourt for dividing the society by disputing about it.[62] (As usual he claimed that he did not expel for 'opinions' but only when they were forced on people and divided them.) In Bristol in July 1740 Charles was pestered by an appropriately-named Mr Wildboar who called for damnation upon his own soul if Christ's death was for all.[63] For his part Whitefield was shocked that Wesley preached against predestination, as he feared it would divide the people. He counter-attacked by claiming that the work was the 'result of the doctrine of election and final perseverance'.[64] Although Whitefield's preaching may have helped to popularize the doctrine, it is a mistake to see it as being simply a matter of dispute between himself and Wesley. Clearly it was the product of deep passions at all levels of the societies and pushed to extremes from below as much as from above. It was this practical threat of splitting the Revival as much as doctrinal indignation which made the two chief protagonists at first reluctant to proceed to extremes and then anxious to get the upper hand as a break became unavoidable.

In August 1740 Wesley wrote to Whitefield in a temperate fashion that there were bigots for and against predestination. God is sending a message to both sides, and 'for a time you are suffered to be of one opinion and I of another'.[65] But during the next few months attitudes hardened; Whitefield claimed he had love, peace and joy in believing but that sin remained in him, and he deplored the Wesleys' preaching of sinless perfection. Charles (tactlessly or aggressively?) preached on universal redemption at the death of William Seward, a Calvinist. Howel Harris, who had tried to be on good terms with both sides, hardened against the Wesleys. More seriously, John Cennick, who had been looking after the Kingswood societies in the Wesleys' absence, threatened to separate if they spoke against final perseverance and on the possibility of the justified falling from grace. All the societies agreed with him, he said. Charles told John that they designed to 'have a church within themselves, and to give themselves the sacrament in bread and water' – an interesting sidelight on the role of the 'lovefeast' (see below, p. 411).[66]

In February 1741 matters came to a head. Wesley had preached a sermon on 'Free Grace' the previous August and published it along with a hymn on 'Universal Redemption' by Charles. Whitefield had begged him not to do so, but John drew a lot in favour of doing so and actually published after Whitefield left for America. Whitefield replied in an open letter, published early in 1741. It seems clear that he was reluctant to do this, but felt that Wesley had forced his hand by making the dispute public. In a private letter he had complained of Wesley's conduct, and Cennick or others had printed and distributed it at Wesley's Foundery chapel in London. Although Wesley ostentatiously tore it up in front of the congregation, saying that this was what Whitefield would have done had he been present, the damage was done. Cennick became a strong protagonist for the Calvinists and his followers formed a separate society in Bristol; the Londoners were in conflict too. In a confrontation at Kingswood Wesley accused Cennick of dividing the society and Cennick accused him of preaching Popery. The society finally split, ninety seceding with Cennick and fifty-two remaining.[67]

This split was of great significance in the history of the Revival, much more so than is easily grasped by later generations, for whom the Calvinist issue has become unimportant and almost unintelligible. The long-term effects of the Revival were to weaken the Calvinist tradition practically, even among its own supporters, but at first this did not seem to be the case. Wesley's *Journal* represented him as the injured party upholding a necessary truth against innovators teaching a creed that undermined morality and the honour of God. The Wesleyan case has tended to be accepted, not least because it was the version of the long-term winner. Yet most sections of the British and American revivals were in fact Calvinistic. As has already been observed, renewals of strong doctrines of grace always tend to produce predestinarian and indeed antinomian doctrines. The eighteenth-century revival was no exception, and controversy and individual struggles on the question continued to characterize all sections of the movement for the rest of Wesley's life. We shall see that this intensified into a pamphlet warfare in the 1770s after Whitefield's death (below, ch. XII.1).

The question was, of course, an old one – as old as Augustine and Pelagius and older. The protagonists in the eighteenth century were largely innocent of the intricate scholastic structures of theology which had been evolved by Calvin's successors and their Puritan disciples. It is far from clear how much Wesley or Whitefield knew at first hand of these writers or of Arminius, the father of the opposition. It seems likely that many of the eighteenth-century Evangelicals learnt their

'Calvinism' by experience: the sense of being damned sinners mysteriously chosen for salvation. This was reinforced by Puritan practical
divinity. Only Toplady, one of the main protagonists in the 1770s, seems
to have had a fair knowledge of the historical theology behind the
tradition. Some Methodists and others imbibed the tenets by contacts
or inheritance among the Dissenters. Wesley, as we saw earlier, reacted
against the doctrine of predestination instinctively in the 1720s by virtue
of his High Church inheritance. But behind the polemics there was an
issue deeper than predestination. Though both sides saw humanity as
sinful and in need of salvation by grace, Wesley had been imbued with
the vision of perfection as possible in this life and never lost it, even
when he added 'evangelical' views of salvation by faith to it. Why not
perfection by faith too? And why not preparation for it by disciplined
effort? Calvinists were suspicious of this optimistic view, denied perfection in this life and suspected Wesley of stressing human effort and
potential. Wesley in return thought that predestination dishonoured
God, was unjust and undermined all moral effort. Both sides appealed
to Scripture selectively and with inevitably inconclusive and mutually
unconvincing results. We shall see that the situation was aggravated by
the fact that Wesley was simultaneously engaged in controversy with
the Moravians, who seemed to him to be fostering inactivity and
antinomianism.

As to Wesley and Whitefield themselves, their positions were expressed clearly enough in Wesley's sermon on 'Free Grace' and Whitefield's
'Letter' in reply.[68] Wesley argued in terms which did not really vary
throughout his numerous subsequent controversies on the issue. All
versions of predestination (he claimed) teach that by an unchangeable
decree of God, one part of mankind is infallibly saved, one part infallibly
damned. Preaching is therefore vain; nothing we can do makes any
difference to our fate, hence all motive for pursuing holiness is removed.
Predestination tends to poison relationships between people; it destroys
the happiness of Christians. The doctrine contradicts Scripture and,
worst of all, it implies blasphemy, making Christ's 'come unto me all ye
that are weary and heavy-laden' a mockery and destroying God's
attributes of justice, mercy and truth, making him worse than the devil.

Whitefield is often seen as little more than an emotional preacher with
no intellectual gifts, yet his 'Letter' is not a contemptible performance. It
is a well-reasoned, if simplified, presentation of the traditional Calvinist
arguments since Calvin himself, in answer to the obvious knock-down
common sense displayed by Wesley. (For Wesley did not approach a
notoriously difficult problem with any subtlety.) Whitefield complained
about Wesley's obstinacy in publishing the sermon and his reliance on
a 'lot' for doing so. He taught that God saved some and left the rest in

their sins (the milder form of the doctrine), and was on strong ground in claiming (correctly) that here he followed the Thirty-Nine Articles. As we do not know who the elect are, we must preach to all as an appointed means to salvation; here, of course, he differed from the hyper-Calvinists who thought that such appeals derogated from the divine initiative. (It was this which insensibly led to an erosion of hard Calvinism and made hyper-Calvinists feel that Whitefield spoke with an 'Arminian accent'.) Even the non-elect might be restrained from sin by this. The elect do perform works of holiness without hope of reward, and such holiness is a mark of election. Without the assurance of election and final perseverance men would despair. Perhaps, Whitefield riposted, Wesley's attacks on election and teaching of perfection had prevented him from receiving assurance. Like Calvin he claimed that all deserved condemnation for original sin and could only be grateful that God saved some: did Wesley 'believe original sin aright?' As to God's character, sinners are justly condemned to satisfy law and justice. How can one claim Christ died for all when, as Wesley admits, not all are saved?

Fundamentally, Calvinists felt that Wesley made salvation depend not on God's 'free grace' but on human free will, a denial of the basic premise of the Revival message. In terms of biblical texts, both sides could appeal to some for their own ends. At least Whitefield and Wesley were courteous to each other, and despite Wesleyan propaganda it appears that Whitefield was certainly the more reluctant of the protagonists to engage openly in controversy and that he had grounds for believing that Wesley had provoked it by his actions – a pattern that was to be repeated on other occasions, despite Wesley's disclaimers.

Wesley's opponents often charged him with an ambition to control any organization that he was involved in, and certainly it must often have looked like this to those who suffered from his activities. Whitefield had in fact suffered in this way, which probably sharpened the controversy just described. As one of his admirers says, he had left England in 1739 as the leader of the Awakening and returned in 1741 to find that Wesley had supplanted him.[69] This was especially mortifying when he had left Wesley to consolidate the work he had begun. A particular point of contention was over the school Whitefield had founded for the Kingswood colliers' children. He now found that Wesley had not only taken over control of the school but had altered the plan to include lodgers 'as at Herrnhut'.[70] There are indeed signs that Wesley may have been influenced by this model, and we shall see later that he had even more radical 'community' ideas for a time. Whitefield evidently resented this takeover, but what he felt especially was the neglect of the colliers. In reply, Wesley pointed out that he had had to take over the financing and managing of the project, including personal responsibility for the debt, as well as another school in Bristol. He had also taken on the 'new room' in Bristol at the urging of Whitefield and others, to secure the pulpit from trustees.[71] It might be argued on Wesley's behalf that Whitefield had left matters unsettled and that without Wesley there might have been no school at all; but in the atmosphere of theological controversy an impartial judgment was scarcely possible.

It says something for both men, though perhaps particularly for Whitefield, that despite doctrinal suspicions they managed to co-operate on later occasions at a personal level and from time to time deliberately preached for each other. Whitefield was welcomed in the northern preaching houses established by Wesley – an area where there were none attached to himself. As early as November 1741 Whitefield expressed his and Wesley's affinity in doctrine by saying that he offered Christ freely and that Wesley could push holiness as far as he liked, only he (George) could not agree on the ending of the 'in-being' of sin in this life.[72] Their followers were often less tolerant, however, and the existential pressures of the experience of grace, as well as inherited or acquired theological tenets, ensured that the Calvinist controversy would be a running sore in the bowels of the Revival as well as a source of pain for individuals. It is clear that this was no mere clash of personalities to be resolved by their personal reconciliation. Whitefield was often absent, but the conflict went on. In Bristol Wesley had to contend with Cennick and shuttle to and fro between London and Bristol to assert his control. The split was of importance not only for defining the future tone of Wesley's brand of Methodism but also for its coherence and Wesley's control over it. It helped to precipitate the formation of its separate existence and 'connexional' character.

While all this was happening, another and equally serious split was emerging, which in Wesley's eyes had a similar potential for damaging theological and moral consequences and had similar effects on the emergence of a distinct 'Wesleyan' body. This was the outbreak of 'stillness' in the Fetter Lane society and elsewhere, influenced by some of the Moravians. It was an affair which to this day is subject to difficulties in understanding and differences of interpretation, in which Wesley's presentation of the case has tended to dominate.

There were already signs of division at Fetter Lane early in 1739. Wesley had objected to Hutton's schemes for organization at the end of 1738, and in April 1739 Charles was complaining about a Mr Shaw who attacked the 'Christian priesthood' and claimed to be able to baptize and administer the Lord's Supper 'as well as any man' – a claim of which more would be heard later from Methodist preachers.[73] There are hints during 1739 of rival leaders and perhaps disquiet at the convulsions, and by September of neglect of the 'ordinances'.[74]

This may have prepared the way for the influence of the controversial Moravian Philip Molther, who arrived in London in October 1739 en route for Pennsylvania. In the event he stayed until September 1740. Molther had studied theology in Jena and joined the Moravians as early as 1738. But it may also be significant that he originated from French Alsace – an area subject to Quietist mystical influence. It is interesting to note that even while in controversy with him, Wesley submitted his translation of Rothe's hymn 'Now I have found' for correction; and Molther rendered one passage 'O Love, thou bottomless abyss', a phrase reminiscent of the mystical *Abgrund*.[75]

According to Molther's account, the Fetter Lane society had been under the Wesleys' care since Böhler left and: 'The good people, not knowing rightly what they wanted, had adopted many most extra-ordinary ways. The very first time I entered their meeting, I was alarmed and almost terror-stricken at hearing their sighing and groaning, which strange proceedings they called the demonstration of the Spirit and of power.' It was apparent to him that they were groaning for salvation, and he addressed them (in very imperfect English) on 'free grace in the blood of Jesus'. Molther then says that Wesley attacked the society during 1740 and finally separated from it because he could not get his way.[76]

Wesley, however, says that even before Molther addressed the meeting Mrs Turner, 'whom I left strong in faith and zealous of good works', had been convinced by Molther that 'she never had any faith at all' and that till she received it she should be 'still' and leave off all 'outward works'. Others followed, and as it happened Hutton had recently returned from Germany determined to conform the society more closely to Moravian ways; Molther seemed to be a ready instrument to hand.[77] It has to be remembered that this section of Wesley's *Journal* was intended to explain and justify the break with the Moravians.

Fetter Lane had been influenced by the convulsions and Molther's approach was partly a reaction to this, but he went to the opposite extreme. Wesley's old Georgia friend Spangenberg also spoke of 'looking unto Jesus and exhorted us all to lie still in his hand'. Some of the brethren claimed that none of them had true faith and until they had it they should be 'still', abstaining from the means of grace, especially the Lord's Supper; and that the ordinances 'are not means of grace, there being no other means but Christ'. But Wesley argued for degrees of faith and the use of the ordinances to strengthen it. He was encouraged to find a woman (it may have been his mother) who had actually been converted through receiving the Lord's Supper, and it was this which made him teach the unusual doctrine that the Supper is a 'converting', not simply a 'confirming', ordinance. This experiential, evidential reply to the Moravians was emphasized strongly and became a special feature of his teaching (see below, pp. 405f.).[78]

Shuttling to and fro between London and Bristol, Wesley dealt alternately with the predestinarians and 'still' brethren. Conferences with Molther merely repeated and hardened the entrenched and opposite opinions of the two sides on degrees of faith and the way to obtain or strengthen it.[79] In April 1740 Wesley found that Molther was ill and in his *Journal* said that he believed 'it was the hand of God that was upon him' – a claim to judgmental 'providence' common in early evangelical circles, though later Wesley claimed, not very convincingly, that he had not intended to mean that it was because Molther had opposed him.[80] The infection spread to the Islington church of Stonehouse, an Evangelical clergyman, and in face of the growing threat Wesley delivered addresses on degrees of faith and using the 'means', including the Lord's Supper as a 'converting ordinance'.[81] A further clue to the underlying sources of the teaching appears in discussions on a book called *The Mystic Divinity of Dionysius* – here was the old enemy of the Oxford struggle in the mid-1730s.

Finally, on 20 July, Wesley confronted the Fetter Lane society with an ultimatum, 'gave them up to God' and asked those who agreed with him to follow him. He then withdrew, followed by eighteen or nineteen of the society. A few days later they met at the old King's Foundery which Wesley had acquired and fitted up for preaching since the previous November. At this point there were about twenty-five men and forty-seven or forty-eight of the fifty women 'in band'. It is usually claimed that Ingham and Lady Huntingdon were among the company, though this is not certain.[82] The Foundery had the advantage of being in Wesley's own hands, and along with the New Room in Bristol formed the nucleus of his own following. Wesley often traced 'Methodism' back to 1729, but in the later 'Rules of the United Societies' traced their origin to 'the latter end of 1739'. In terms of an independent organization which grew into his 'connexion' this was correct. He was now free of the Fetter Lane constraints and of Whitefield. Fetter Lane itself gradually became a Moravian society.

'Stillness' problems, however, like predestinarian and antinomian ones, did not disappear. For years there were local outbreaks and periodic purgings. Some were due to Moravian influence, some more likely the effect of their roots in Quietist mysticism. In Manchester in the 1750s there was an outbreak influenced by the local devotees of Law and Böhme, and Wesley expelled these, as usual claiming that it was not for their opinions but for disturbing the society. John Byrom called him 'Pope John' for this.[83] In the early months after the secession from Fetter Lane it looked as though the still brethren might gain a distinguished recruit, for the evidence suggests that Charles Wesley wavered, gave up preaching and retired to Oxford to meditate. Lady Huntingdon took him to task and he recovered.[84] Whitefield would have liked to keep up friendly relations with the Moravians and asked to use Fetter Lane, but they refused for fear of conflicts. In Wesley's eyes there was all too much similarity between his two current bugbears in their excessive stress on grace alone.[85]

Did Wesley exaggerate? It has been argued that Molther's poor English may have led to misunderstandings, and that the later teaching of Molther and Spangenberg shows that they allowed for degrees of faith and did not neglect the sacraments. But the Moravians had already shown that they admitted only those with full assurance of faith to the sacrament, and the Moravian sources show that there was indeed a dispute of the nature that Wesley described. The most one can say is that this was an aberration of a section among them and that it was not permanent.[86]

These disputes in fact helped to clarify Wesley's mind about his distinctive theology. There are signs of an emphasis on 'perfection' which offended, yet was also provoked by, the predestinarians and 'still brethren'. At the same time he was busy on another front – defending justification by faith against contemporary Anglican views on salvation by a mixture of faith, works and sincerity.[87] Here he sharply distinguished justification and sanctification. He reacted violently to a reading of Luther's *Galatians* with its decrying of reason and good works, seeing it as the root of the Moravian error. Yet in June and July 1740 he was considering sermons for his BD exercises and a university sermon which would have included a scathing attack on Bishop Bull's quasi-Catholic notions of justification. In the sermon he did preach ('The Almost Christian'), Wesley nevertheless emphasized that faith must produce good works.[88] Talking to Böhler and Spangenberg he found them picturing the 'new man' as still not eliminating the 'old man' of corruption, but he shows that he still had a vision of an achievable perfection.[89]

The root of this conflict was, according to Schmidt, the conception of faith. Molther thought in a dogmatic way: only faith involving renewal of the whole man is real faith. But Wesley thought psychologically: there are degrees of faith in progression from justification to the indwelling of the Holy Spirit, following his own experience in 1738. Schmidt also allowed for an element of ambition, exaggerated in the Moravian tradition, yet real. Moreover, Wesley saw the contest as being not between himself and Molther but between Molther and Böhler. It was a matter of defending classic Protestantism, the Lutheran idea of justification represented by Zinzendorf and Böhler, against the younger generation of Herrnhuters; and of the difference between piety nourished in the church by the Bible and prayer and free, silent mysticism. Schmidt finally allows for the Moravian tradition of conveying doctrine by half-truths and dissimulation as against the openness of Wesley.[90]

This does not go far enough, for in fact it turned out that there were deep differences between Wesley and Zinzendorf as well. There was a conflict between the Lutheran tradition as a whole and Wesley's inherited High Churchmanship, which on the question of salvation as holiness had not been replaced completely by Moravian ideas of faith. Behind the stillness affair lay two traditions which tended to reinforce each other: the Lutheran notion of justification by grace through faith which had always tended to produce pathological suspicions of anything that might allow for an element of 'works' in salvation; and the Quietist tradition of mystical waiting on God in a state of effortless dependence. Wesley's long-term devotion to 'perfection' and his practical fears of antinomianism combined to make him react strongly against any tendency to eliminate preparation for the reception of faith. And he was beginning to suspect that the Moravian promise of true faith as bringing complete cleansing from sin was not quite what it seemed. This was confirmed in a remarkable Latin conversation with Zinzendorf in Lincoln's Inn Fields on 3 September 1741.[91]

Zinzendorf claimed that Christians in this life are 'miserable sinners' and have no 'inherent perfection' – 'Christ is our only perfection'. Christian perfection is only 'imputed', not inherent; we are perfect only in Christ, not in ourselves. What Zinzendorf meant, it seems, was that the Christian is 'entirely sanctified' from the moment he is justified and cannot become more or less so later. However, this is only sanctification 'by imputation'; a person is viewed by God as being 'covered' by the merits of Christ. For Wesley, there is an actual inherent holiness possible which can grow further or indeed be lost. Wesley developed his views more clearly, if not necessarily more consistently, later, but there was already a confrontation here between the underlying Lutheranism of Zinzendorf and the underlying 'Catholic' Anglicanism of Wesley. In the Moravian way of faith Wesley thought he had found the secret door into the perfection of which he dreamed; now he saw (or thought he saw) that he had been mistaken in their meaning. But he did not give up the dream, and in his usual eclectic way he managed in due course to develop a two-stage view of salvation in which faith would bring first justification, then entire sanctification, with his old disciplines built in to prepare for these successive experiences and improve upon them. Though he never abandoned justification by faith and enforced it strongly against his Anglican opponents in the 1740s, already he had a vision of a second stage which would seem to him to be experimentally verified by outbreaks of perfection in the 1760s.

Wesley owed much to the Moravians, though he characteristically adapted and changed what he learnt from them. Quite apart from the clarifications about faith, works and holiness which he developed in conflict with them, he also borrowed a good deal in terms of the use of 'bands', though he developed the inner groups within the society in a different way from theirs because of his doctrine of perfection. Then there were the lot, the lovefeast and some elements in the watch night, though the covenant service came from Puritanism and much else from accident and experiment. Some of this could in any case be found or further justified from the early church. Whitefield, too, borrowed in a similar way. The influence of Moravianism, then, was more extensive on the English Revival than can be measured by its small membership.[92]

The third area of controversy in this period, which in many ways lasted for the rest of Wesley's life, was conflict over doctrine and order with the Church of England. From start to finish here he was really fighting on two fronts. On the one hand he wished to adhere to the church and avoid separation and the slur of Dissent. On the other, he wished to be free to proclaim his gospel and to organize its fruits in whatever ways he thought necessary. But a third and very important factor was pressure from below, from the rank and file of his followers. Along with the exigencies of events and the light of experience this pressure led Wesley to modify his thinking and practice.

Clashes with the Anglican clergy and hierarchy were common enough, and although Wesley discouraged his followers from attacking the clergy, he could be critical enough of them himself on occasion. His published *Journal*, however, tended to play down the element of conflict with the hierarchy.[93] A fuller account of Methodist relationships with the Church of England will be given at a later stage (below, ch. VIII.3), but the three main charges made against the Methodists appeared early: 'enthusiasm', doctrinal aberrations and violations of church order. 'Enthusiasm' meant the manifestation of convulsions, visions, healings and the like which seemed to suggest that Wesley, Whitefield and their followers were claiming special powers like those of the apostles, and were reviving the wild times of the Interregnum. Though Wesley played down claims to special revelations, the charges were not easy to refute. Whitefield's and Wesley's early journals gave colour to the charges.

The doctrinal charges centred on justification by faith and the suspicion that this led to the neglect of works; so did claims about predestination; and the prominence of Whitefield led to Methodism as a whole being seen as teaching this doctrine, despite Wesley's protests.

The third set of charges concerned church order. The changing character of the religious societies soon created problems. They had had a chequered character from the start, and had sometimes been charged with being conventicles or nests of Jacobites. They seem already to have been under lay control in some cases before Methodism began; then had come Moravian infiltration and the new doctrines and practices described by Whitefield in his 'Letter'. Dissenters were joining them, although Wesley baptized Quakers and Baptists and, controversially, rebaptized other Dissenters.[94] In April 1739 a pious Dissenter asked to be admitted to the Bristol society; this led to an anxious *sortes biblicae*, drawing of lots, and talk of reference to London – it is not known with what result. But in August 1739 a Dissenter called Joseph Humphreys formed a society of Whitefield converts in Deptford. The Rules of the United Societies in 1743 made it clear that men of all denominations could join, which casts a curious light on Wesley's claim that Methodism was a mere auxiliary to the Church of England.[95]

To a staunch churchman like Samuel Wesley junior, even extempore praying and preaching denoted schism, and both suggested the habits of Dissent. Preaching in other men's churches, even with permission from the incumbent, soon raised questions from bishops and opposition from churchwardens. Whitefield and Wesley were barred from the pulpit in Islington, and Piers of Bexley (a clerical associate of Wesley's) was expressly forbidden by ~~Bishop Gibson~~ *Abp. Potter* to allow them to preach in his church.[96]

But it was field preaching which raised the most tricky legal problems at this early stage. It seemed to violate the rights of the regular clergy, highlighted the problem of unbeneficed clergy like Wesley and Whitefield, and arguably violated civil as well as canon law. It was Whitefield who first fell foul of the authorities. At Bristol in February 1739 he was summoned by the Chancellor of the diocese, who asked why he was preaching in the diocese without a licence and in private houses. Whitefield claimed that the custom of getting a licence had grown obsolete; that the canons about house preaching applied only to Dissenters; and counter-attacked by asking why other clergy violating the canons by tavern-haunting and card-playing had not been attacked.[97] Whitefield further argued that custom appeared to allow clergy to preach by the same general licence which rectors thought sufficient for their curates; and in London pleaded that his post in Savannah covered him, as this was in the province of the Bishop of London. But on field preaching he also took a higher ground: they only went to those excluded from the churches, and 'has not God set his seal on our ministry in an extraordinary manner?' – by conversions.[98]

Charles Wesley, always more of a High Churchman than his brother, had much greater qualms about field preaching at first, though he was led by Whitefield's example to try it from 29 May 1739. He had 'scrupled' doing it until expelled from the churches, and even then had to be urged on by Whitefield and his brother, who argued that the commands of God and needs of souls override the commands of men.[99]

John Wesley had fewer hesitations, and his attitude and arguments resembled Whitefield's: a mixture of legal niceties, the higher ground of God's will and the needs of souls, with side-swipes at unsatisfactory clergy. The most famous confrontation was with Bishop Butler at Bristol (the author of the *Analogy*). Wesley tactfully omitted this from the published *Journal*, but a very characteristic manuscript account has long been known, and another has recently turned up which shows that three meetings took place.[100]

Wesley explained 'justifying faith' in terms echoing his 24 May experience about personal assurance and the Anglican Homilies. Butler quoted Whitefield's *Journal* and said: 'Sir, the pretending to extraordinary revelations and gifts of the Holy Ghost is a horrid thing, a very horrid thing' (i.e. 'enthusiasm'). Wesley characteristically disclaimed any responsibility for Whitefield's views and used his regular argument that he claimed only the common privileges of Christians. When Butler said Wesley had no licence to preach in the diocese, Wesley said that his mission was to do good where he could and that his ordination was a commission as a priest of 'the Church Universal'; as Fellow of Lincoln he was not licensed to a particular cure but to preach in any part of the Church of England. He believed he had broken no law, but if he had, he must obey God rather than man. This was to be his regular line in the future. How far he was legally correct in his claims as a Fellow of Lincoln is unclear; perhaps Whitefield was on stronger ground in claiming customary irregularity and undue prejudice against Methodists. But certainly in terms of custom and probably of law, their field preaching and systematic violation of parochial rights placed them on dubious ground and caused understandable offence.[101] Like the rebellious priests of the Oxford Movement, though in a different ecclesiastical direction, Wesley thought he knew the priorities of the gospel and church better than the bishops, and those who portray Wesley as a good churchman should observe that he early took the higher ground of obedience to God and the imperative of soul-saving as his appeal of last resort. That he was able to argue legalistically to avoid the final break is typical of his mode of argument to avoid unwelcome and awkward challenges, but that he was not expelled speaks volumes for the weakness of contemporary Anglican discipline. Writing to Hervey in August 1739 Wesley shows his impatience with the parochial system; but equally significantly, to Charles in June of that year he spoke of his sense of an 'extraordinary call' over-riding the ordinary call authorized by the church. He was always able to speak more candidly to his brother than to anyone else about his real feelings in such matters, and here he revealed, not for the last time, a sense of providential mission which to others could only be clothed in legalistic arguments or Oxford logic.[102] In his belief that the irregularities did not mean separation from the church so long as he attended her worship and preached her doctrines he was, as we shall see, aided by a very low and bare definition of the church and of conformity to it which was common among Latitudinarians but remarkable in an old High Churchman.[103]

Already there were signs that irregularity was taking a further and even more controversial form, for which no shadow of canon law could be found. This was lay preaching. The Welsh revivalist Howel Harris had been the pioneer. Harris never obtained orders, though he often tried to do so, but he preached all the same, and Wesley and Whitefield did not condemn but rather supported him. Who the first 'Methodist' lay preacher was has been a matter for rather tiresome argument, and is partly a matter of definition. In 1790 Wesley recalled that 'the first lay preacher that associated with me in England in 1738' was Joseph Humphreys. But earlier he had spoken of Thomas Maxfield, who 'came and desired to help me as a son in the Gospel; soon after came a second, Thomas Richards; and then a third, Thomas Westell'. He claimed that they asked him and that he dare not refuse them.[104] This was in the context of justifying his authority over them. Elsewhere he ingenuously spoke of 'permitting' rather than authorizing them, thereby minimizing the 'irregularity'.

Of Maxfield as the first Methodist lay preacher a picturesque story is told. He had been left as a kind of pastoral supervisor at the Foundery and had taken to preaching. Wesley descended in anger and was confronted by his mother, who told him that Maxfield 'is as truly called of God to preach as you are. Examine what have been the fruits of his preaching and hear him yourself.' Lady Huntingdon also supported him. Wesley observed and concluded: 'It is the Lord, let Him do what seemeth Him good.' Of Thomas Westell, too, a pious lady said: 'Stop him at your peril. He preaches the truth and the Lord owns him as truly as He does you or your brother.' Henry Moore claimed to have had the Maxfield story from Wesley himself, and it has an authentic ring in the test of experience and fruits which would guide Wesley increasingly in these matters as well as sheer necessity. The incident can probably be dated early in 1741.[105]

Wesley's reluctance to allow lay preaching is understandable in terms of its clear irregularity, its odour of schism and Dissent and its social offence, for which there is much evidence. The clergy were outraged at this challenge to their professional status by 'unlettered mechanics'. It is very obvious that lay preachers were forced on Wesley not only by the growing demands of the work, since the clergy were seldom joining him, but also, and even more significantly, by pressure from below by converts who could not be silenced – the 'problem of the eloquent convert'.[106] From personal testimony they moved to commenting informally on scripture and so, almost insensibly, to formal preaching. After all, Wesley himself had privately confessed to an 'extraordinary call' – why should not they? The pressure from below to go further and claim sacramental rights had already occurred in the clash noticed earlier between Charles Wesley and Mr Shaw.

Wesley's account of the first three preachers was really a reference to those first subject to him as 'sons in the gospel' in his own organization. They were not the first to be associated with him before the break with the Moravians. Joseph Humphreys was a Dissenter, and as a Dissenter began preaching independently in 1738. In 1739 he became associated with Whitefield and the Wesleys and ran a society of Whitefield converts in Deptford. In September 1740 he began preaching and acting as an assistant at the Foundery, but his hereditary Calvinism reasserted itself, and he joined Whitefield in 1741.[107] Cennick was another spontaneous preacher emerging 'from below'. He was urged by a member of the Society in Bristol to preach in an emergency in June 1739, and Wesley accepted him as a lay assistant there.[108]

All the Revival leaders had doubts about the practice, but their hands were forced by necessity and their inability to stop it. Wesley already had plans for concerted action including laymen. In a meeting on 12 November 1739 not referred to in his *Journal* he described how he, Gambold and Robson agreed to meet annually in London. They would fix their business for the year ('where, when and by whom'); meet quarterly; send a monthly account to each other of what God had done 'in each of our stations'; inquire whether seven other clergymen (including Ingham) would join them with three laymen (including Cennick), along with other friends.[109] This looks like the embryo of the Conference which would begin in 1744 (Whitefield's 'Associations' began in January 1743). But it was also the first of several vain attempts at concerted action by all the 'evangelical' clergy. Nothing seems to have come of this first attempt.

Lay help was in fact unavoidable. In April 1741 Wesley confessed that he could not do without Maxfield: the clergy had 'miscarried' as much as the laity and he doubted whether the Moravians were not laymen – in any case he did not trust them. Whitefield had doubts about Harris, and some objected to his lay preaching, but even Charles Wesley forbore to condemn him because of his good character.[110] 'Fruits' and necessity effectively settled the issue.

The controversies and splits had the effect of producing a separate organization subject to Wesley. This was an untidy, unplanned process, like most of what Wesley did. So far there were only two main centres, London and Bristol, with a few places in between, and the allegiance of some members and societies remained uncertain. The clearest signs of a distinct 'Wesleyan' organization were Wesley's two 'rooms' in his own hands in London and Bristol, and the purging of those societies and that at Kingswood which began in February 1741.

In May 1739 Wesley took a piece of land in the Horsefair in Bristol, where he built a 'room' big enough to contain two societies and others who might wish to join them 'at such times as the Scriptures was expounded'. This suggests that it was intended to be more than a society room, but for preaching as well. It was later enlarged and developed into a preaching house with rooms to accommodate Wesley and his helpers. It survives as the most elegant and unspoilt of early Methodist chapels. As we have seen, Wesley was advised to take it off the hands of the original trustees for fear they would control the pulpit. In the same way he took on the Foundery and refurbished it as a preaching place to hold 1500 people, plus a 'band-room', school room and home for several people including his mother until her death in 1742. (After early doubts she had supported him, allegedly being converted during a sacramental service.)[111]

Early in 1741 there were clear signs that Wesley was taking a grip on his societies. In quick succession he purged Bristol, Kingswood and then London. Thus at Bristol in February he met the bands and 'read over the names of the United Society, being determined that no disorderly walker should remain therein'. Those he approved of were given 'tickets' – the first mention of this mark of membership. The rest were put on trial unless they 'voluntarily expelled themselves'. At Kingswood he did the same, but Cennick and others took offence, thinking rightly or wrongly that they were being disciplined for their opinions, and withdrew. Then to London to do the same. In April John wrote to Charles: 'I must go round gleaning after George Whitefield. . . . The bands and society are my first care. The bands are purged; the society is purging.'[112]

Thus by April 1741 an organization was emerging. There were major societies in London, Bristol and Kingswood, with some others under Wesley's influence. There was a hard core of bands within the societies on the old Fetter Lane model. Members were subject to discipline over their conduct, and although there was ostensibly no doctrinal test, they were pursuing faith and good works were expected, while the notion of a later perfection experience was being explored. A 'Wesleyan' version of the common doctrines of the Revival was slowly emerging. The language of the 'United Societies' originated in the simple fact that the two met in the New Room, but was becoming a description of the whole chain under Wesley's supervision. Writing the Rules for them in May 1743, Wesley described the process as beginning with a few people coming to him about advice on how to 'flee from the wrath to come' late in 1739. To this he added 'evidence of the same' in life and conduct. By that time another sub-division had been devised, the class meeting; but the original inner group was the band for which he had devised rules dated December 1738.[113]

Obviously things were less clear-cut, and the organization was less extensive in the spring of 1741; Wesley's description of its origin is misleading. He had taken possession of a section of an untidy sprawl of societies which had been thrown up by a movement in which he was only one of several leaders. As yet, the only links between the societies were the Wesley brothers themselves and a few lay helpers. They were held together by the restless shuttling to and fro of the journeying brothers, and the attempt to devise an overall organization with the help of other clergy in November 1739 had evidently failed. It was only in 1744 that the series of 'Conferences' began.

The scope of the Revival was still limited, though less so than a mere description of the Wesleys' work would suggest. Their coverage was still limited to the London-Bristol axis, though they had made a few sorties into Somerset and Wales. But Wales, as we shall see, had already been largely pre-empted by Harris and the Calvinists. Even within this limited geographical area numbers were still small, despite the large crowds for open-air preaching, of which Wesley and Whitefield gave very exaggerated accounts.[114] As to full 'members', there were only 90 at Kingswood in March 1741; an early list of the Bristol society suggests about the same; and at the Foundery in July 1740 there were 73 or 74.[115]

Yet Wesley had travelled a long way from the days of Oxford Methodism. He had moved from Eden into the world without forgetting Eden. He had moved from the decorous university holiness groups to the strife-torn urban religious societies, and beyond them to the rough world of the colliers. He had come to see how these unchurched or half-churched people could be organized in an alternative manner to that of the parish system. Yet he had also retained the vision of a select band of brothers – and sisters – seeking for the elusive goal of inward holiness.

The peculiar world of Methodism was haphazardly emerging as a perfectionist group within the world yet not of the world. And already there were signs that this would disrupt Wesley's inherited ideals of ecclesiastical order, and unleash an aggressive lay piety which would lead him into paths that would be hard to reconcile with conventional Church of England ways.

2. Northern lights and Celtic fringes

Wesley, particularly in Bristol, was reaping where he had only been one of many sowers, and this was even more true elsewhere. Readers of his various sketches of Methodist history and even unwary readers of his *Journal* might easily gain the impression that Methodism and indeed the Revival as whole were the result of a campaign beginning in Bristol and London and subsequently spread by his evangelistic journeys to the North and elsewhere. Yet in truth only a small part of the completed national network was the product of his pioneering work, though much was due to his subsequent organization and supervision. Much was begun by freelance 'evangelicals', Anglican clergy, Moravians and lay Methodists. It could be argued that the Wesleys' role was really to weld parts of heterogenous local revival groups and small local or regional networks into a coherent national 'connexion'. This was done amid much competition and charges of sheep-stealing; some individual converts had very devious spiritual pilgrimages, while some societies were very unstable.[116] Wesley, to put it rather brutally, was a great cannibalizer.

Excellent examples of this process can be seen from Wesley's advance into the North and North west. Both areas developed evangelical groups before Wesley's arrival: in fact he was invited in to help existing work. It is indeed salutary to view the course of events in this large area through the eyes of the early protagonists rather than simply through Wesley's *Journal*. It is true that the Wesleys soon had an optimistic eye to the northern barbarians like the colliers of the North-east, so similar to those of Kingswood. Charles Wesley in October 1742, about to go to Yorkshire, wrote prophetically that 'Neither London nor Bristol will yield such a harvest of souls as the rude populous north'.[117] He was quite right, as it turned out. The northern counties contained one quarter of the population of England, but the Anglican church gave it only one-eighth of its pastoral resources. By the end of the century the population was in the same proportion, and Methodism had half its chapels, half its preachers and 54% of its members in the seven northern counties.[118]

Wesley himself can have known little of the area at first. Apart from his Epworth upbringing his only personal contacts had been with the Clayton circle in Manchester, which he did not visit again after early

1738 until 1747. His first venture beyond the Bristol-London axis was to the Midlands in June 1741. This was probably at Lady Huntingdon's request, though he does not say that he met her. Instead, he accompanied her preaching servant David Taylor to Leicester, Nottingham and elsewhere.[119] It is very obvious that he was not pioneering here, but on the contrary visiting societies established by others and troubled with 'stillness'. In Leicestershire the work was probably begun by Taylor and there had been a 'great awakening', but a Mr Sympson, apparently a former pupil of Wesley's, had 'put them to sleep'. He had been influenced by the Moravians. At Nottingham there was a society founded as a result of preaching by a Mr Howe in 1740 who had brought a hymn book of Wesley's from London. The Moravians had infiltrated them, too, and although Charles Wesley visited 'Mr Howe's society' in May 1743, soon afterwards he founded a new and it would seem distinctively Methodist one.[120]

In May 1742 John Wesley visited Lady Huntingdon at Donington Park, but this time preached through Yorkshire to Newcastle and back through Yorkshire, Epworth, the Midlands and so to Bristol. The immediate occasion for this was to see Lady Huntingdon's friend Miss Cowper before she died, but something of the kind had already been in the Wesleys' minds. John had written to Charles saying that one of them 'must soon take a journey into Yorkshire' (he does not say why), and Lady Huntingdon was also concerned about David Taylor's intention to 'build himself a room and . . . become a lay teacher'. How contact points in new areas could be found is illustrated by a letter of Henry Piers, Vicar of Bexley, to John about the journey north. Piers had formerly been curate of Winwick in Lancashire and had written to 'my man Pierce Stirrup, who is now in Lancashire, together with two or three well-disposed young men in his neighbourhood, to give you the meeting at Wakefield'. He was acquainted with a clothier's wife there or at Halifax, and through her he might bring 'salvation to the house'. He had known her when at Winwick.[121]

Wesley took Taylor with him, and at Birstall they met John Nelson, a travelling stonemason who had been influenced by Wesley in London, drifted into preaching at home and for a time cooperated with Wesley's old Oxford friend Ingham. And so to Newcastle-upon-Tyne, where Wesley recorded that 'one Mr Hall' had been a year before but with no apparent fruit; nor did anyone care to have him again nor appeared to care for such matters'. This was in fact his brother-in-law, the unstable Westley Hall, whose own account shows him to have been in Newcastle in 1740 – why, he does not explain.[122] There was an old-style religious society in the town, some of whose members met Wesley and asked him to stay, but they seemed mostly concerned with pride in their library and in being 'well spoken of by all men'. There is no indication that Wesley colonized them or indeed founded a society at all on that occasion. But a journey of Charles to Newcastle in October 1742 saw the start of it, and when John returned shortly afterwards he spoke of 'the wild, staring loving society'.[123] It was successful enough for John to proceed forthwith to buy land and build a so-called 'Orphan House.' The Pietist-Moravian echo is obvious, but the Orphan House seems to have been much like the Bristol and Foundery chapels, and became his headquarters for the North. In March 1743 he came again and purged the society there like those elsewhere, recording an interesting variety of reasons for their backslidings.[124] His reception among the colliers of the North-east was warm, and here he was certainly pioneering. In Newcastle itself he was working an area of the city which had an unruly population.[125] On the way back south he preached at Epworth on his father's tombstone since the church was closed against him, and here, too, he found a 'little society', disturbed by 'stillness' emissaries from Fetter Lane.[126]

So it is clear that everywhere except in the Newcastle area Wesley was meeting people already well worked over by others, elements of a religious renewal movement affecting part of the Midlands but especially Yorkshire. If Wesley regarded them as part of his 'parish', those already in the field understandably regarded him as an interloper, sheep-stealer and 'troubler of Israel'. The Moravian accounts, for example, of how the Revival spread from the South to the North, picture it as a movement which had been begun by Whitefield in the South and Ingham in the North (which is broadly correct, though one should add Taylor in the Midlands and farther north). The Moravians themselves, who had commissioned workers to go to Yorkshire in May 1742 and sent them off a few weeks later, were going in response to an invitation from Ingham to take over a group of societies he had founded. The 'general awakening in England' as they saw it had begun with Ingham in September 1737 and Whitefield's preaching in London.[127]

Ingham had been the focus of one of the overlapping 'Holy Club' groups in Oxford and later had accompanied Wesley to Georgia. In 1734 he had already established a kind of society in his home at Ossett in Yorkshire.[128] In Georgia early in 1737 he found 'rest to his soul' and his 'heart was united with Jesus', but 'the Lord manifested himself' to him 'in a particular manner' on 24 August 1740, and in allusive scriptural language he described what appears to have been a 'full assurance of eternal salvation'.[129] In the meantime, though already ordained, he felt what was evidently a special call to evangelism in September 1737. Sitting on a hill near Wakefield he 'surveyed the whole country where he was now called to be an instrument for calling many souls; and there and then he was commissioned and ordained by God to be a preacher of the gospel and was anointed of the Holy Ghost for the works'.[130] By the end of 1738 he had already held meetings in some thirty places, in 1739 forty, and in that year he began preaching in barns and the open air as the pulpits were closed to him. In 1740 he was preaching in over fifty places, many with organized societies, including Leeds, Dewsbury, Wakefield, Halifax and Birstall.[131] This was in Yorkshire, and although his biographer says he first entered Lancashire at Colne in response to the invitation of Joseph Gawkroger and about that time met old Grimshaw at Haworth, in fact he had already preached at Manchester in May 1742 at the request of John Bennet, the apostle of the North-west. Manchester, however, would have to wait another five years for its first evangelical society.[132]

In 1741 Ingham claimed 2,000 'constant hearers' in about 60 places, and about 300 whom he believed were united with Christ, with several hundreds seeking him. He preached through these places once a month and had a monthly 'general meeting' – a miniature 'connexion'.[133] But Ingham lacked the iron will and single-mindedness (or 'ambition') of a Wesley. In July 1742 he placed himself and his societies under the Moravians, invited from London, though in 1751 he broke with them only to fall under the influence of the Sandemanians – a sect with intellectualist views on faith. Only one or two of his societies have survived to this day.

Ingham had other connections. In December 1738 he preached in Cambridge, where there existed a now largely forgotten group of 'Cambridge Methodists' parallel to the more famous Oxford one. A number of these also eventually landed up in Moravianism, and through members like Francis Okely and Jacob Rogers influenced a religious society founded in Bedford in 1736; this led to a strong Moravian influence there. Rogers is said also to have started a 'meeting' in Nottingham in July 1739.[134]

Ingham was not the only northern pioneer. A more elusive, less well-documented figure is David Taylor, already observed as a protégé of Lady Huntingdon in the Midlands. He seems to have been converted by Ingham in 1737; certainly from about 1740 he was founding societies in parts of Leicestershire, Yorkshire, Lancashire, Cheshire and Derby-shire.[135] He appears and disappears, an uneasy, unstable figure, in the diaries and memoirs of most of the 'evangelicals' in these areas. Thus, early in 1741, John Nelson found him preaching in Ingham's society in Birstall: 'a dry morsel his sermon was', not to be compared with John Wesley's, for he had 'not stayed long enough in the large room at Jerusalem' and was not 'endued with power from on high'. Taylor, hearing of this comment, 'could have stabbed him', but having preached Wesley's doctrine obtained converts till the 'Germans' got at him.[136]

But Taylor's journeys did have important consequences in Derbyshire and Cheshire, for he founded several societies which became the basis for other people's work, in rivalry with Taylor himself. Moreover, one of his converts was John Bennet, in January 1742. Bennet was a Presbyterian from Chinley in Derbyshire, and one of several such who were drawn away from this Arianizing congregation, much to the disgust of its minister, James Clegg, who saw Taylor as a dangerous antinomian. And Bennet was the creator of more societies which became the basis of Methodism in the North-west.[137]

The cases of Bennet, John Nelson and William Darney are good examples of how Wesley expanded his connexion. Nelson was a native of Birstall, but a travelling stonemason whose business often took him to London. He had early intimations of God, like many Methodist preachers, and with stops and starts undertook a work of self-reformation which came to a crisis when he heard Wesley preach in London in June 1739. 'He stroked back his hair and turned his face towards where I stood, and I thought fixed his eyes upon me' so that 'my heart beat like the pendulum of a clock'. Wesley appeared to penetrate the secrets of his heart and at the end of the year Nelson finally knelt down and prayed: 'Lord, thy will be done; damn or save!' He then had a vision of Christ 'as evidently set before the eyes of my mind as crucified for my sins, as if I had seen him with my bodily eyes'. This set him free.[138] Back home he began testifying and drifted into preaching, encountering Taylor's 'dry morsel' and hesitations from Ingham and his societies. Nelson, in his downright Bunyanesque language, was very scornful of Moravian eccentrics like one who 'had got into the poor-sinnership, who held his neck on one side and talked as if he had been bred up on the borders of Bohemia'.[139] He had a vivid premonitory dream of Wesley coming to visit him, which was fulfilled in May 1742 when Wesley passed through Birstall on his way to Newcastle.[140] Nelson developed his Yorkshire societies and travelled elsewhere, becoming one of Wesley's sturdiest itinerants.

William Darney was a more eccentric figure and, like Taylor, he appears as an awkward element in many of the records. Known as 'Scotch Will', he was a product of the Scottish Revival, felt a call to preach in 1741–2, and by the end of 1743 (if not earlier) was active in Lancashire and the West Riding. Like Taylor he established some societies and by 1744 was vacillating like several others between Methodism and Moravianism, especially as Nelson had objected to his preaching. So did others, though perhaps even more criticism was made of his doggerel hymns which he insisted on publishing. His societies were known as 'William Darney's Societies' – an independent regional group – and in 1747, largely under the influence of William Grimshaw, the Evangelical Vicar of Haworth, they were taken under Wesley's control. Darney himself was recognized as a 'preacher to assist us only in one place' – his gifts were felt to be too limited for more, and his Calvinism was distrusted. He finally left the Methodists in 1768.[141]

Perhaps, like Taylor, his most important contribution was his influence on another man, in this case William Grimshaw. Grimshaw, even allowing for legend (and he was the kind of man around whom legends gathered), was a remarkable figure – a kind of rough reincarnation of the old northern Puritans in an area that had changed little since their day. His path to conversion was long and painful and reputedly finally brought on by reading John Owen on justification. When he first laid hands on the Puritan classic he was struck by a 'blast of heat' in his face. Later, he practised the old Puritan habit of personal covenants with God.[142] Darney influenced him in the use of hymns and lay preachers, and although Grimshaw ruled and evangelized his wild moorland parish with 'Methodist' methods, he also travelled elsewhere in what became the 'Haworth Round' – another section of the Methodist network – and as far as Manchester. It was he who presided over the first 'Quarterly Meeting' for a Methodist 'Circuit' in 1748. He was to have been the leader of the Methodists in succession to the Wesleys, but died in 1763, too early for the experiment to be tried.[143]

John Bennet has already been mentioned as one of Taylor's converts. As we have seen, he was a convert from Presbyterianism (not a very common type among the Methodist preachers) and had been designed for a learned profession but took to trade.[144] He was converted in January 1742 after a rather remarkable vision of Christ after leaving Taylor. By May 1742 he had begun preaching and developed a 'round' of societies extending into Cheshire and South-east Lancashire, with occasional journeys elsewhere, including Sheffield. He first heard Wesley preach in June 1742, and by the spring of 1743 he had become more or less formally associated with Wesley's network. He was one of the small group of lay preachers who joined Wesley in his first Conference in 1744. It seems to have been he who devised the Quarterly Meeting system and was used by Wesley to introduce it elsewhere.[145] It is unjust to Bennet to remember him only as the man who stole and married Grace Murray, 'Wesley's Last Love', (for this story see below, ch. VI.2). He failed to qualify for the usual biography because he fell out with Wesley over predestination as well as over the Murray affair, and finally broke with him in 1752.[146] Despite his efforts to retain his old 'round', most of it was retained by Wesley – a signal testimony to Wesley's capacity for tight control. Bennet finally settled down as an Independent minister in Cheshire. Here he was friendly with other Independents, some of them also ex-Methodists, for though he would have liked to have come under Whitefield's wing, that evangelist was too elusive and had no base in the North.[147]

The Moravian contribution to the Midlands and the North has repeatedly appeared in this survey. Böhler and William Delamotte (brother of Charles and a Cambridge Methodist) appear to have been the first to go North in 1739, and it is significant that they went by invitation to Ingham's societies.[148] Casual infiltration can also be seen in the 'stillness' outbreaks troubling other societies on the Wesleys' travels. But the Moravians resembled Wesley in advancing by taking over the work of others – in this case especially the Ingham network from 1742. They also founded a settlement at Fulneck in Yorkshire, and mopped up the remnants of some of Taylor's societies, for example at Dukinfield, in Cheshire. However, it is evident from this last case that they did so at least sometimes by the will of the members. The Dukinfield leader was another ex-Arian from the old chapel there.[149] The Moravians were, indeed, serious competitors with the Methodists for capturing the scattered local societies and small networks in the Midlands and North, and promised to be a more extensive group than turned out to be the case in the end. They had problems with German control and with Zinzendorf's reluctance to allow his followers to become a church instead of a 'seed' in all the churches.

In many places there was constant competition for souls between the various evangelical groups, many individual cases of moving from one group to another, and much instability. Thus at Roughlee in Lancashire in 1746 it appears that the Inghamist Moravians had established a society, but William Darney, as part of his deal with the Wesleys, urged the Wesleyan preachers to start work next door to them.[150] Grimshaw had much trouble with the Baptists – and all revivals of this kind tend to produce individuals developing such principles from reading the New Testament.[151] In Manchester the Methodist society emerged in 1747 with a mixture of Anglican and Dissenting members, and in the 1750s was subjected not only to 'still brethren' (probably of local manufacture) but also to rivalry with a new evangelical Independent church, itself drawn from ex-Baptists, ex-Presbyterians, Scotch immigrants and (almost certainly) unstable Methodists. At least one of the first Methodist trustees turns up later as an Independent deacon.[152]

To sum up: Methodism in the North was to a large extent feeding on and absorbing a heterogeneous scattering of local renewal movements and societies under local leaders and travelling evangelists. What had produced this movement is a matter for speculation. Certainly there were some prime examples here of the vulnerability of large Anglican parishes to interlopers – there had been several examples of Puritan curates hanging on to their posts for years after the Restoration in Lancashire.[153] In the Derbyshire Peak district, too, the Church of England's hold had been weak and William Bagshawe ('the Apostle of the Peak') had founded a chain of Presbyterian churches. This was the legacy which Bennet exploited, and in some of these old Dissenting communities memories of evangelical Puritanism may well have been revived in reaction to Arianism, as was the case in at least one Manchester family.[154] The old religious societies seem to have played less of a preparatory role here than in the South, though there are some exceptions. Richard Cawley, an ex-Baptist turned Anglican, ran one in Alpraham in Cheshire with results, Wesley thought, very like his Oxford Methodism. It was then made evangelical Methodist by influences from outside.[155] But there were others which look very like old Taylor societies or new creations by Bennet, Ingham and Nelson. It was, then, to a people prepared that the Wesleys travelled, and this helps to explain the relatively rapid spread and consolidation of Methodism in these areas.

At much the same time there was expansion to the extreme South-west. The background to the Methodist approach in this area was very different from that in the North. At first sight it might seem that here at least the Wesleys were approaching almost virgin territory. Early in 1743, so the story goes, a Methodist sea captain called Joseph Turner of Bristol found a religious society at St Ives. He 'reformed' the society and told them of Wesley's work, which produced a request for help. A preacher was sent to them, and apparently this led to the Wesleys themselves visiting.[156] By the time Charles Wesley came to Cornwall in July 1743 some work had already been done, for he made for St Ives and was met on the way by the lay preachers Thomas Williams and William Shepherd: they stayed at 'brother Nance's' where they met 'the society'. At Morna Charles took the names of those 'desirous of joining in a society'.[157] Much of his ministry was among the tin miners, who proved to be the most receptive among the Cornish. There was considerable mob violence during the early visits, though this was aggravated by Jacobite scares and fairly soon eased off. One early encounter already showed the element of supernatural feeling which was to form a strong bond of union between the Cornish and the Methodists. When Charles won over a section of the mob in the St Ives preaching house, one man was overheard to say: 'I think the desk was insured; we could not touch it or come near it.'[158]

Although one or two religious societies may have formed a nucleus for the work, the Wesleys were now accustomed to open-air preaching and were able to proceed to this immediately, with the result that they quickly gained a mass audience. John Wesley followed his brother in August 1743, accompanied by Shepherd and John Nelson and following the same route as his brother along the North Cornwall coast. But during his next visit in April 1744 he met the Revd John Bennet of Laneast and in January 1745 the Revd George Thomson of St Gennys.[159] Charles had already been accompanied by these clergymen on his visit in 1744, and at St Gennys there was a curious scene when Charles declared from the pulpit that by so-called 'harmless diversions' he had been 'kept dead to God, asleep in the devil's arms, secure in a state of damnation for eighteen years'. His companion Mr Meriton 'added aloud, "And I for twenty-five"; "And I," cried Mr Thomson "thirty-five"; "And I," said Mr Bennet, "for above seventy."'[160] This holy competition is a reminder that these who would later be called 'Anglican Evangelicals' had in fact preceded the Methodists and had been converted (as so often) quite independently of them.[161]

Thomson's conversion seems to have occurred around 1733–34, initially as the result of a dream. He had been in touch later with Isaac Watts and with Whitefield in 1739. (Whitefield indeed visited Cornwall in 1743.) Bennet, a very aged clergyman, had apparently known Samuel Wesley Senior at Oxford and had been converted by Thomson, probably in 1742.[162] The best known of the group was Samuel Walker of Truro, converted about 1747, probably through the influence of the rather mysterious figure of a Scottish schoolmaster called George Conon. Walker would figure importantly in Wesley's life in the 1750s, when he complained about Wesley's interference in Evangelical parishes and accused him of schism for his use of lay preachers. In fact at first Wesley seems to have avoided founding societies in Thomson's and Bennet's parishes. One further early Evangelical in Cornwall should be mentioned as a link with Oxford Methodism. This was James Hervey, who had preached at St Gennys in 1738 and was a curate at Bideford until 1743 and left a religious society there. In 1743 there were three societies there visited by Thomson.[163] But apart from these efforts, Methodism in Cornwall was substantially starting from scratch, without the extensive preliminary work characteristic of the North of England.[164]

In each of the other Celtic lands the circumstances and background of the Revival were different, and so the fortunes of the intruding English evangelists were different as well. It is not possible to give even a concise history of each area's experience, but only enough to indicate how the indigenous versions of evangelicalism inhibited Methodist or at least 'Wesleyan' growth in Wales and Scotland, though it had less competition of that kind in Ireland.

Wales, as we have seen, had been the first area of Britain to experience revival and had been the first scene of the novelty of field preaching.[165] The prospects for English Methodism in Wales were unfavourable from the first, partly for linguistic reasons, partly because the revival was well under way before the Wesleys were even converted. Here they could not 'cannibalize' scattered local revival groups, nor, it seems, did they attempt to do so. For once they appear to have been willing auxiliaries to an existing movement, and only circumstances forced them into considering independent work against almost insuperable difficulties.

Daniel Rowland and Howel Harris had begun work independently of each other after their conversions in 1735, but Harris gradually learned about the Oxford Methodists and Moravians and made contact with Whitefield and the Wesleys. Whitefield visited Wales in March 1739 and met Harris at Cardiff. He describes how Harris had become 'a burning and shining light', had been refused holy orders, but for three years had been at work preaching and had 'near thirty societies in south Wales'.[166] Harris was already anxious to co-operate with other evangelicals, and as a layman probably felt the need of more clerical help. In June 1739 he met John Wesley in Bristol, and despite those who had 'said all manner of evil of him' found that Wesley's preaching pleased him. In October Wesley finally took a short preaching trip into Wales and went again in April 1740 'at the pressing wish of Howel Harris'. In October William Seward, who had helped Harris on a preaching tour, was assaulted so violently by a mob that he died as the 'first Methodist martyr'.[167]

Charles Wesley first met Harris in London; providentially, he thought, because Harris had 'blundered to the Foundery' by accident. Here, too, Harris' prejudices against the Wesleys were overcome: his 'conscience in the Holy Ghost bore witness to the truth I spoke', Charles claimed. Charles found Harris a 'son of thunder and consolation', and he stood with Charles against the Moravian menace, challenging their 'stillness' with an account of how he had actually been converted while taking the Lord's Supper. In November 1740 Charles in his turn took a preaching tour in Wales, where he found the people divided over predestination like those in Bristol, but he tried to moderate their fervour and wrote to Harris pleading for unity as 'your second self.'[168] Both brothers made brief visits in 1741, dashing to and from Bristol and arguing about predestination in both areas, with Harris trying always to act as a moderating influence. Wesley met Daniel Rowland, with whom he was 'knit together in love'. Their chief lay supporter was Robert Jones JP, of Fonmon Castle, which became a centre for English Methodist influence.[169]

No doubt the Wesleys would have liked to enlist Harris on their side in the predestinarian controversy, but even if this had been possible, the strength of the indigenous Welsh movement would have been too strong to allow for a significant 'Wesleyan' presence in Wales. The Welsh Revival had roots deep within the previous religious history of the Principality, and some of the revivalists' habits had significant precedents in Puritan times. Itinerant preaching, for example, had already been a matter of complaint in the days of Archbishop Laud, and under the Commonwealth it had been allowed as an expedient for enlightening the 'dark places of the land'.[170] A connecting link between this and the later period was Griffith Jones, Rector of Llandowror in Carmarthenshire. In 1714–18 he had taken to preaching in the open air and in other parishes as well as his own. He was supported by Sir John Phillips, with whom the Wesleys would later be acquainted through Oxford Methodism and the SPCK. It was Jones who converted Daniel Rowland in 1735.[171] John Wesley saw Wales as 'ripe for the gospel' in the sense that 'they are earnestly desirous of being instructed in it'. Though ignorant of 'gospel salvation', 'many of them can say both the Lord's Prayer and the Belief (the Creed). Nay, and some add the Catechism.'[172] The latest study of religious life in Wales from 1660 to 1730 makes it clear that the traditional picture of the Revival as a simple reaction against a dead and corrupt church, emerging miraculously from the efforts of a few prophets working upon a lost and sinful people, is even less true of Wales than of England.[173]

One important influence was that of the charity school movement. The SPCK had made efforts in Wales since its foundation in 1699, though its impact was limited by its reluctance to teach in Welsh. It really preferred to teach in English as a cultural medium for 'civilizing' the Welsh, rather like the policy of the British in India in the nineteenth century. But from 1737 Griffith Jones launched a series of 'circulating schools' with itinerant teachers for instruction in Welsh. What is more, the main point was to teach reading, not writing, as a means to Christianizing the people. It has been pointed out that despite giving a kind of preview of the Revival, Jones had an uneasy relationship with its leaders, though it is equally true that they had a close relationship with his work. Harris was actually a superintendent of the schools in 1737, and many of the teachers indulged in preaching against Jones's will. The schools and the Methodist societies in Wales significantly both flourished in the same areas of South Wales. It has also been plausibly suggested that the literature used in the schools was likely to create the same kind of uneasy, anxious consciences as those which led members of the Religious Societies in England to welcome the evangelical gospel of release through salvation by faith.[174]

The Welsh Revival was precipitated by the conversions of Rowland

and Harris in 1735. Both preached in the open air and founded societies, though temperamentally they were very different and later clashed over doctrine. In 1750 Harris retired to his estate in Trevecka where he founded a community influenced by the example of Halle and Herrnhut. By then there were 433 religious societies in Wales, and in 1768 a further ingredient was added when Lady Huntingdon founded her 'school of the prophets' at Trevecka to train evangelical preachers. It was of fundamental importance that these were Calvinistic Methodists, and by far the largest sector of them: in 1750 the English branch connected with Whitefield had only twenty-nine preachers and twenty-three preaching places.[175]

The origin of the society idea for Harris is open to some debate. They may well have been a spontaneous development from 1736 under the name of 'private societies'. He may have heard of the English Religious Societies through Griffith Jones, though he seems not to have known of the Woodward book before 1739. Other influences came later still. By 1739 he had organized nearly thirty societies, with Bible-reading, hymns, prayers and exhortations and then personal spiritual conversation.[176]

Harris was as concerned as the Wesleys not to break with the Church of England, and it has been pointed out that he was a curious combination of the 'enthusiast' and the High Churchman. He was very reluctant to drift into outright Dissent.[177] A complex organization developed for associating and supervising the societies, with confusing overlaps of function and terminology. In addition to the weekly meetings of the 'private societies' there were monthly, bi-monthly and quarterly meetings, and from January 1743 a series of 'associations', drawing in ministers and exhorters from a wide area. This first association was notable for the presence of Whitefield, Cennick and Humphreys from England – a reminder of an important link with the English Calvinists and of the distinction from the 'Wesleyans'.[178] Attempts to reconcile the Calvinistic and Arminian Methodists in 1743 and 1749 were a failure.[179] Although Whitefield was elected Moderator of the first association, he was never willing to be tied down and preferred a roving commission. In his absence his Tabernacle in London and the English societies associated with it were run by Cennick until he left for the Moravians in 1745; then Harris added the English branch to his labours until 1749 – through all this Whitefield was never more than a nominal Moderator and often absent.[180] Signs of Moravian influence can be seen in some of the Tabernacle institutions, but the Welsh organization drew much on Scottish and even American as well as Welsh Presbyterian and Congregationalist patterns.

In face of this indigenous Revival, and doctrinal and language problems, it is not surprising that 'Wesleyan' Methodism remained a small and stunted plant, a scattering of a few societies. But doctrinal differences ensured that some separate organization would emerge. A few societies were founded, though in 1745 it was allowed that preaching could be done without forming societies, and this may have persisted in Wales after 1748 when it was frowned on for England. In 1746 a Welsh Circuit appeared in the Minutes of Conference, but it still had only seven societies in 1749, all in the south. Wesley only visited occasionally, but in 1761 Thomas Taylor opened up a more vigorous work, and some progress was made into North Wales from Chester. But there were only 600 members in the whole of South Wales at Wesley's death. Moreover, these were English-speakers: Welsh-speaking Wesleyan work only began after 1800.[181] One Welsh gift to English Methodism should, however, be mentioned. Sarah Gwynne, the daughter of Marmaduke Gwynne JP, married Charles Wesley in 1749, and family cares were an important factor in Charles's gradual abandonment of regular itineracy.

The situation facing Methodism in Scotland was very different, yet also marked by a Revival with indigenous roots. The special features here included the final triumph of Presbyterianism as the Established Church of Scotland from 1690 and the relegation of Episcopalians to sectarian status and the taint of Jacobitism because most of the clergy followed the English Nonjurors in refusing to swear allegiance to William III. The Union with England in 1707 and the abolition of the Scottish Parliament made the Church of Scotland along with the separate legal system focuses of national feeling and identity. What was missing from the Scottish religious scene was the English type of Dissent; Baptists and Independents only penetrated Scotland (and even then not very numerously) as a result of the Evangelical Revival much later on.

Presbyterianism dominated the scene, for even dissidents and seceders from the Establishment (unless they were already Nonjuring Episcopalians or Roman Catholics) almost always maintained versions of the Presbyterian tradition in theology and polity.[182] The disputes which led to these schisms were mainly over the relationship between church and state, usually arising over the use of patronage; the doctrinal purity of the church in face of creeping rationalism and moralism which tended to erode traditional Calvinism; and in some degree tensions induced by 'evangelical' attitudes before and after the onset of the Revival.

Patronage was often the occasion of conflict, for after 1712 the theoretical right of the congregation to 'call' the minister had been in effect overridden by the power of a few influential members. This led to complaints that unsound and unedifying men were intruded, and in principle raised questions about the spiritual rights of the church. Doctrinally, traditional Calvinism was subtly or openly undermined by the same intellectual fashions as in England. In Scottish terms, 'Moderates' (roughly equivalent to English 'Latitudinarian' as a 'bogy' word) overbore those who would become known as 'Evangelicals'.

One of the most important of these schisms was that of the Associate Presbytery or Seceders, which originated in protests against private patrons imposing 'uninspired' ministers on parishes. Led by the Erskine family, the rebels organized themselves into the Associate Presbytery from 1733 and were noticeably supported by people of modest social rank like shopkeepers, tradesmen, artisans and peasants.

The sources of the Evangelical Revival in Scotland remain somewhat unclear. There was probably some direct or indirect knowledge of continental Pietism and a considerable interchange of ideas and concerns as well as personnel with the American colonies. There are signs of concern about the decay of piety and suggestions for combating it on both sides of the Atlantic.[183] But there was also much within the Scottish tradition to explain what was to happen in the early 1740s. As far back as 1630 Kirk O'Shotts had seen a revival very similar to the later, more famous ones. Oral tradition of this wonderful outpouring of the Spirit kept its memory fresh, but probably more important was the tradition of small 'praying societies' which had occurred in 1630 and were maintained into the eighteenth century. The Seceders favoured such exercises, too.[184] Conversion was indeed one of their spiritual concerns, and mass outbreaks of weeping marked some of their preaching and sacramental services.[185]

Praying societies had a role in the famous Cambuslang Revival of 1742, which shows how old traditions could live on to be galvanized into violent life in suitable conditions.[186] Cambuslang was a Clydeside parish with a population at odds with their patron. In 1731 their unwanted minister was replaced by the Revd. William McCulloch, a much more congenial man who favoured the praying societies. Though the accounts of him suggest a solid, slow, cautious and not at all 'popular' preacher, he was a faithful and dedicated one. He encouraged the societies to pray for revival; read accounts of the New England Awakening and Whitefield's work; and preached on conversion and the experience of being born again.[187] At the beginning of 1742 a revival developed which affected all classes, sometimes with considerable emotional accompaniments and (it was claimed) with marked moral effects on the whole community, very much as in New England. Writing to Whitefield in April 1742, McCulloch claimed that 300 were already convicted and 200 converted. Whitefield himself preached there, it was claimed, to crowds of 20,000 to 30,000 people, with 3,000 taking communion. Though as usual the more ecstatic accompaniments declined in a year or two, the communion attendance in 1751 was still higher than it had been before the revival.[188]

Nor was Cambuslang an isolated case. James Robe, the minister of Kilsyth, began to preach for conversion in 1740 and experienced very similar scenes. Like Jonathan Edwards he wrote a *Faithful Narration* of the work (in 1742), and carefully defended it against comparisons with the discreditable French Prophets.[189]

These events, it should be pointed out, took place within the established church and, especially in the larger towns, eventually became the source of a distinctive Evangelical party within the church.

Whitefield made his first visit to Scotland in July 1741; it was natural that he should be a more congenial visitor than Wesley by virtue of his Calvinism. But as an Anglican minister from a church which the Scottish Presbyterians felt had greatly damaged them in the past, he excited some suspicion. More important, the Erskines and their Associate Presbytery wanted to keep him to themselves as the only true church. But Whitefield, as always, wished to be an awakener to all. The Erskines had been in correspondence with Whitefield for the previous two years, and on his arrival in Scotland he did give the Seceders priority, but they wished him (he said) to confine himself to them as the Lord's people. He soon fell foul of them by his visits to others, and as in England attracted some of the nobility.[190]

At Cambuslang he produced very similar effects to those experienced under Wesley's preaching in England: people wept and cried aloud, 'mourning over a pierced Saviour'. An observer noted that some fell down as if dead. Nor did this happen only when 'men of warm address alarm them with the terms of the law, but when the most deliberate preachers speak of redeeming love'.[191]

This tour had important effects very similar to those in America, in that while it built on existing Scottish work, it helped to link up the places concerned with evangelism, giving them a sense of common concern and a concerted movement and almost certainly also raising the spiritual and emotional temperature.

John Wesley's first contacts with Scotland, as we have seen, were through correspondence about the meaning of the convulsions in Bristol in 1739, and through Whitefield he was put in touch with Ralph Erskine. It is remarkable that Erskine convinced him in 1740 that every congregation has a right to choose its own pastor: a pet doctrine of the Seceders, but a startling thought for a Church of England man. In 1741, though still on friendly terms, Erskine was disapproving of Wesley's notion of the Lord's Supper as a 'converting ordinance', for Erskine saw it as a 'confirming ordinance' for the converted only. Moreover, he had heard that Wesley wrongly held that the sins of believers after conversion 'flow no more from the remains of corrupt nature . . . but merely from natural temptations'. Wesley was soon aware that Erskine had been attacking Whitefield as a 'tool of Satan' for his open ways; if he was too Calvinistic for Wesley he was not Calvinistic enough for them.[192]

With other Scots Wesley had happier relations. His most congenial correspondent was Lord Grange, who had also befriended Whitefield. Grange was a devout and ecumenical Presbyterian, much concerned to promote toleration and cooperation between Christians. He also passed on letters to Wesley from James Robe. He hoped for a 'concert for prayer and praise, for the revival of true Christianity'. Like Wesley in his *Character of a Methodist*, he thought that those who agreed in 'practical religion' should work together and not divide over 'opinions'.[193]

Yet Wesley first visited Scotland only in April 1751.[194] This was not of his own volition, but at the request of Captain Gallatin, a Methodist army officer stationed at Musselburgh. Neither Charles Wesley nor Whitefield were keen on the experiment. Charles quoted a Methodist preacher as saying: 'You may just as well preach to the stones as to the Scots.' Whitefield feared that Wesley's well-known hostility to predestination would prevent his obtaining a hearing and lead to conflict.[195] Wesley's motives for going are not clear. One early historian of Methodism thought that it was to combat Arianism and Socinianism, though this was a more obvious target in England. Wesley may well have seen Gallatin's invitation as 'providential', and his quite friendly reception may have seemed to him to confirm this, though in any case it was reasonable enough to try the one country in Britain which he had not yet explored. He was to pay some twenty visits to Scotland during the rest of his life.

Dr Skevington Wood suggests that Wesley's main objective in Scotland seems to have been to establish societies in the main cities.[196] Here, too, he made some good friends such as John Gillies, the early biographer of Whitefield and historian of revivals and also a man of ecumenical spirit. Some noble ladies also supported Wesley, notably Lady Maxwell with whom he had correspondence on spiritual matters, and who was one of the select band experiencing trinitarian visions in the 1770s. Wesley generally received a friendly welcome in the Church of Scotland, but his view of the Scots was coloured by English prejudices as well as religious differences. He thought their universities mean, and (disagreeing with Whitefield) that the General Assembly of the Kirk was shocking rather than solemn in its behaviour. He thought that Scottish sermons 'contained much truth, but were no more likely to awaken one soul than an Italian opera'. The Scots, he thought, 'hear much, know everything and feel nothing'. They are the 'best hearers in Europe' but 'only on the Lord's Day'.[197]

In any case Wesley himself could do much less than the men on the spot. He attracted a few Scots as preachers, but those few of high quality like Alexander Mather. Mather had been well educated and drilled in piety in the Scottish tradition, but clearly found difficulty in coping with Wesley's favourite demand for the pursuit of the experience of Christian perfection.[198] In accord with Wesley's itinerant principles there was no question of Scots ministering to Scots. Chapels were slowly established by local initiative, but by the time of Wesley's death in 1791 there were only eight. Although there were more societies than chapels, the total of 1179 members and sixteen preachers was a very modest achievement. Coke had grandiose plans in 1786 for a mission to the Highlands and Islands including Erse speakers, but nothing came of this.[199]

One obstacle was certainly ingrained Scottish Calvinism. Yet another Erskine, Dr John Erskine of Edinburgh, engaged in controversy with Wesley over this after reprinting James Hervey's Calvinistic *Aspasio Vindicated* in 1765, and in 1770 Lady Glenorchy, one of Wesley's aristocratic supporters, left him over the issue.[200] John Pawson thought the trouble was that the Scots had been imbued with doctrine, 'mixed with Calvinism' from their youth, but 'in general they know little or nothing of Christian experience', and so it needed a 'far higher degree of the Divine influence' to 'awaken a Scotchman out of the dead sleep of sin than an Englishman'. They were also too bigoted in their own opinions, church government and ways of worship so that Methodist preachers were unlikely to do much good among them.[201]

Pawson was probably right. Even Scottish Methodists tended to approximate their ways to the native Presbyterian culture. In 1766 Wesley contrasted his Church of England ways with theirs: he used a short private prayer before worship; stood to sing; knelt for prayer; used the Lord's Prayer in worship. In 1774 he attacked the Glasgow preachers for staying in town for three or four months at a time, preaching on Sunday and three or four days in the week. They could not, he said, 'preserve either bodily health or spiritual life like this'.[202] In 1789 he was furious at the way in which Pawson had given way to Scottish habits by allowing the Glasgow society to persuade him to ordain seven elders who formed a disciplinary court in which the preachers had no vote.[203] In the end he gave way so far as to ordain some preachers for Scotland, and the use of communion tokens marked 'MC' (Methodist Church) implied a formal separation of the kind he would not countenance in England but had already tacitly authorized in America. He allowed this on the ground that in a country where the Church of England was not established he was not infringing its rights. Pawson thought that this might have been helpful earlier on but was now too late. He and others were much offended when Wesley followed his own logic by ordering the new Methodist ministers to remove their gowns and bands when they re-entered England.[204]

It has been surmised that Wesley intended to inaugurate a distinct Methodist Church in Scotland conforming in some externals to the Church of Scotland, while within this framework the Methodist societary structure would be retained. But in 1793, after Wesley's death, the Conference stopped the ordaining of ministers and wearing of gowns and bands.[205] Wesley did not make his intentions clear here any more than in America, though interpretations of his 'plan' are best discussed in the light of the general situation in Methodism in his last years (below, ch. XIV.2, 3). Certainly his actions tended to spring from practical motives to meet each situation as it arose. As to Methodist impact in Scotland, it has to be seen as limited to an auxiliary role to the native traditions.

Ireland, inevitably, was a different story again, heavily influenced by its miserable history. Here Methodism had its greatest success in the Celtic lands after Cornwall, though its scale should not be exaggerated: 14,158 members at Wesley's death in 1791, a much smaller proportion of the population than the 58,318 from that in the rest of Britain.[206]

Given its history of colonization, exploitation and civil war as well as religious divisions, it is not surprising that the Protestantism of England and the Anglo-Irish had not been accepted by the mass of the people. The Irish branch of the established church was part of this originally alien culture and, as in England, tied to the political establishment, but with much more slender physical resources and active or passive membership. By comparison with England the Irish hierarchy appeared very top-heavy, with four archbishops and eighteen bishops. For political reasons, patronage over the higher and better-paid posts tended to be exercised in favour of English rather than Irish-born clergy, and sometimes men who were not found tolerable in England were promoted into Ireland. Despite the efforts of some devoted bishops, Irish livings were often remarkable for the pluralities and non-residence of the parish clergy as well as for their miniscule congregations. Thus in the early eighteenth century the diocese of Ferns had 131 parishes but only thirteen beneficed clergy (mostly under £100 per annum) actually serving, with nine curates at £30 per annum. In the Diocese of Clonfert (a strongly Catholic area) in 1722 there were only ten beneficed clergy, half of them non-resident; in that of Elphin only twenty clergy, and here the bishop estimated that the Catholics outnumbered the Protestants by fifty to one.[207] The financial problems were partly due to ancient lay depredations on clerical income, and some bishops worked hard to improve the lot and conduct of the clergy. In Raphoe in the 1730s six out of seven clergy were resident; buildings were in reasonable repair; services, catechizing and quarterly communion were much as in rural England.[208]

But nothing could alter the fundamental weakness that in most areas outside Ulster the Church of Ireland was the religion of the minority.[209] There were extremely severe penal laws against Catholics, though persecution was most likely in times of national alarm. A survey of 1732 showed some 900 Catholic chapels, 1445 priests, 500 schools and some 50 friaries.[210] Nor did the Church of Ireland have a monopoly even of Protestantism. In Ulster, for historical and geographical reasons, there was an important minority of Presbyterians of Scotch-Irish descent who had their own reasons for hostility to the established church and suffered from the sacramental test for public office as in England, though restrictions were eased as the century moved on. In this situation the prospects for an evangelical movement were not very promising. The Ulster Presbyterians were not likely to be more amenable to Methodism than their relations in Scotland; the Church of Ireland would react to 'enthusiasm' and irregularities like their brethren in England; and the Catholics, so much more numerous than in England, were likely to be impervious to Protestant revivalism. The best hope would be in neglected areas of the Establishment and, as it turned out, certain special categories like garrison towns and continental immigrant communities.

In Ireland, as elsewhere, Wesley was not the pioneer of evangelicalism, though in this area the preparation was slight and there seems little sign of an indigenous renewal movement even in terms of Religious Societies; such other activity as there was seems to have occurred only shortly before his arrival. Whitefield had visited briefly in 1738 on his way from Georgia and received a cordial reception from the bishops and the usual crowds in churches.[211] But the first evangelical preaching with lasting effect was that by John Cennick, who was by now a Moravian and from 1746 began preaching in Dublin at the invitation of some Quakers. His subsequent visits brought considerable success but he died, worn out, in 1755.[212] In Dublin he founded a society and acquired a former Baptist meeting house in Skinner's Alley which would be a subject of dispute with the Methodists later. One curious legacy he left for the Methodists was the nickname of 'Swaddlers', allegedly from an Irish priest's misunderstanding of Charles Wesley's preaching on 'the babe wrapped in swaddling bands', but perhaps rather from Moravian religious 'baby talk'.[213]

The first Methodist preaching was also in Dublin, by Thomas Williams, a preacher who had fallen out with the Wesleys. Nevertheless, in 1747 he went to Dublin, founded a society and invited Wesley to come to Ireland to follow up the work. He subsequently went to Northern Ireland, became associated with Whitefield and finally obtained Anglican orders through Lady Huntingdon's influence.[214] But his activities in Dublin ensured that Methodist relations with the Moravians, always likely to be difficult, were poisoned from the start.

Wesley arrived in Dublin in August 1747. His stay was short but he observed that all his hearers were Protestant and that the Irish were 'more teachable' than the English and therefore needed the more care as they would be 'equally susceptible of good and bad impressions'.[215] Charles, coming soon afterwards, found that the preaching room had been wrecked by a mixed Catholic and Protestant mob, opened another and had a 'great awakening' in an outlying rural area. Here, John found on his next visit that there were already 100 members, including several Quakers, but only nine Catholics.[216] For the rest of his life he made regular visits about every two years. From 1748 Ireland was regarded as a separate circuit and from 1752 Conferences were held in Ireland, usually in Wesley's presence. He was very conscious of the Catholic presence, which quite often led to mob violence, though some heard him in the open air. After a riot in Cork in 1749 he issued an open 'Letter to a Roman Catholic' of a remarkably conciliatory spirit, though on other occasions he attacked Catholic doctrines and practices in conventional Protestant terms and he played an equivocal role in the Protestant Association which led to the Gordon Riots in 1780. His general attitude to Catholicism will be discussed at a later stage.[217]

In Dublin at least these early visits produced respectable results. In August 1748 John wrote to Charles that they had 350 members in the countryside but they are 'raw, undisciplined soldiers and without great care will desert to their old master'. But in Dublin in August 1749 he was pleasantly surprised to find that, despite hostile Moravian claims, the society had not suffered much and in fact amounted to 449 even after purging.[218]

The main difficulty with the Moravians was a rather unedifying quarrel about possession of the Skinner's Alley meeting house. The dispute illustrates all too clearly how easily each side thought the other guilty of duplicity, quite apart from their doctrinal differences.[219] As Cennick rightly pointed out, the trouble stemmed initially from the action of Thomas Williams, who had organized a society himself and then persuaded the agent for the owners of the room to let it to him instead of the Moravians by offering a higher rent. Charles Perronet took over the lease on behalf of Charles Wesley and the Moravians were evicted. Charles Wesley tried to be conciliatory and John obviously had qualms, for he took over the lease and offered to let the Moravians have it back if they paid for the expenses incurred. There followed much correspondence and mutual suspicions of bad faith. It is hard to judge the rights and wrongs of this. Wesley evidently felt he had acted generously, but Cennick and the Moravians felt that he had quietened his conscience very easily by making an offer he chose to regard as rejected when the Moravians did not answer quickly. In the end they moved elsewhere. It has to be said that in this as in other cases Wesley had a naive but irritating habit of supposing not only that he was always in the right but also that he alone was dealing plainly and straightforwardly.

Of all the evangelical groups in Ireland, Wesley's did best. Whitefield seldom visited, and although some of his followers founded societies, for example in Dublin in 1752, they received little encouragement from him. That society was helped by John Edwards, a man who also for a time helped Wesley in England, but fell out with him over Calvinism and founded an Independent church in Leeds. In the end Whitefield's Irish, like his English, followers were mopped up by other groups.[220]

Some Evangelical Anglicans began to appear in Ireland in much the same accidental and individual way as in England and experienced the usual conflicts with the Methodists over Calvinism and church order. In Wesley's later years this helped to aggravate an important case in Dublin of pressure by some Methodists to hold their services in church hours.

One of the central figures in this affair was a hot-tempered Irish Evangelical clergyman called Edward Smyth. Smyth was a man who had had great expectations as the nephew of Archbishop Arthur Smyth of Dublin, a man chiefly remembered, it seems, for having accumulated £50,000.[221] Unfortunately for Edward the Archbishop died intestate, and so Smyth took up a country curacy. His brother William was converted by William Romaine, a leading English Evangelical, and through contact with the Wesleys and Lady Huntingdon, Edward was converted too and in the 1770s lost his curacy through his 'Methodism' and for rebuking the misconduct of his patron.[222] He worked for the Wesleys on and off for some years, and amongst other things offended the lay preachers in Bath by insisting on taking their place in the pulpit. Later he acted for a time as a kind of paid 'curate' for John Wesley himself.[223] In 1786 he finally became minister of a proprietary chapel called Bethesda in Dublin belonging to his brother. Wesley was surprised to find 'uncommon liberty' there among 'the rich and great' (his usual bugbears). But there was tension between this essentially Anglican chapel and the Methodists, probably reflecting social divisions as well as the question of the relationship of Methodism with the established church.[224]

In May 1788 there was pressure from Dublin Methodists for services in church hours which was settled by an uneasy compromise. Smyth, though once hot for separation, objected. His chapel is said to have drawn off over a hundred of the Methodists including the richer members.[225] Smyth himself soon fell a victim to faction. Unusually for an Evangelical Anglican he was an Arminian; he fell out with his Calvinistic assistant at Bethesda and eventually concluded his career in Manchester, where he built two proprietary churches and had friendly relations with the Methodists there.[226]

But what exactly was the extent and character of Methodist impact on Ireland? The old stereotypes of lively and flexible evangelism competing successfully with an effete and moribund church has given way more recently, as we have seen, to more sociological approaches. A recent application of such analyses to Ireland by Dr Hempton takes full account of Methodist flexibility, Arminian theology, use of the laity and conversionist zeal, all in strong contrast with the prevailing habits of the existing churches.[227] But, as Hempton points out, this does not explain the variations of Methodist growth in time and place and the fact that these differed markedly between Ireland and England. Increases and decreases of membership in certain years were much more marked than those in England, and they varied also in different regions.

The strong Methodist areas in Ireland were mainly in the larger towns; smaller market towns with good communications and their rural hinterlands; and certain self-contained communities such as the refugees from the Palatinate and garrisons of English soldiers. In 1770 55% of them lived south of a line drawn between Sligo and Dundalk, but in 1815 68% lived north of this line. The reason seems to be the attractive power by the later date of the 'linen triangle' of Ulster and an area around Lough Erne, because of economic changes. Methodism appealed most to people in Anglican areas loosely attached to existing churches and to the more literate in urban areas; but least to Roman Catholics, despite some distinguished converts who became Methodist preachers. Dr Coke estimated in 1802 that only 72 out of 1209 Methodists in one circuit were Roman Catholics, and this was regarded as a high proportion.[228] Roman Catholics who swelled open-air crowds did not translate into secure members. Wesley encouraged Thomas Walsh, a devout, even mystical Catholic turned Methodist preacher, to preach in Irish, but it is doubtful whether he had much success.[229]

Even in favourable areas there were limitations to the appeal of Methodism in Ireland, as in England. The affinity between its supernaturalism and that of the lower orders which stood them in good stead in Cornwall and elsewhere had to compete in Ireland with the supernatural world of popular Catholicism.[230] The entrenched denominationalism of Anglicans, Presbyterians and Catholics was also hard to crack in Ireland.

Two important contributions were, however, made to Methodism at large by the Irish. One was a disproportionate contribution of personnel to overseas missions. The other, more fateful, was the influence of some leading Irish preachers who worked mainly in England. This contributed to the notoriously anti-Catholic stance of Wesleyan Methodism in the early nineteenth century.[231]

To recapitulate the chronology of the extension of Wesley's mission. Wales was first penetrated by John Wesley in October 1739 and by Charles in November 1740. The Midlands had been briefly visited in June 1741 and through them the North was reached as far as Newcastle in May 1742. In 1743 both Wesleys reached Cornwall. Ireland was added in 1747 and finally Scotland in 1751. If the heart of the work can be regarded as being in England, then we can visualize the basis of Wesley's annual journeyings as being roughly defined by the triangle formed by London, Bristol and Newcastle, in each of which cities he had chapels with accommodation for himself and his preachers; and all were places of which he was particularly fond – not least the last. Annually he worked round this triangle, clockwise or anti-clockwise, and by doing so he could take in the Midlands and usually the North-west and Lancashire as well as Yorkshire. Wales and Cornwall were usually taken in from Bristol. Ireland was usually approached through Wales via Holyhead or sometimes through Lancashire and Chester. Scotland could be taken by the western or Newcastle routes. The winter was generally spent in London with short excursions to the home counties, and leisure for writing.

Thus, for example, in 1748 Wesley went to Ireland, back to London and Bristol, on to Newcastle, back through Yorkshire and Lancashire, London and Bristol again, down to Cornwall, back to Bristol again and so to London for the winter. In 1753 he went from London to Bristol, then to Birmingham, Cheshire, Lancashire and so to Scotland by the western route, back via Newcastle and Yorkshire to London. Then followed an unusual trip to the Isle of Wight and so to Cornwall and back via Bristol to London for the winter. This frequently repeated type of itinerary might be varied and interrupted by emergencies, though it is noticeable that even the gravest seldom diverted him for long from the major visits. But longer-range plans might be dropped. In 1751 he agreed with Charles to visit Cornwall, Ireland and the North each year and in 1760 regretted that he had not stuck to this plan. Cornwall had become out of order when he failed to visit it for three years.[232] Certainly much depended on constant monitoring by the chief.

The numbers of members acquired by all this work are not known nationally before 1766–7, but a few local figures for 1743 are of interest.

After much purging the London societies stood at 2,200; Bristol at some 700; Newcastle at 800. It is striking that Newcastle, though the newest, already had a larger proportion of Methodists to the population than Bristol, and Bristol more in proportion than London.[233] The first national figures in 1767 show a total of 25,911: 22,410 for England, 232 for Wales, 468 for Scotland and 2801 for Ireland.[234] The developing structure of societies and circuits, held together by the annual Conference of preachers and their local journeys, will be described in the next section.

'Mr Wesley's Connexion' had emerged as a result of a complex process of revival and controversy. Wesley had been insensibly led into defining his position and drawing societies under his sole control by doctrinal disputes sharpened by rivalries for leadership. The chief antagonists here were Moravians and predestinarians. This led him to define his doctrines but also his disciplines more clearly – hence the preoccupations of the first few Conferences. Control and stabilization of the societies came by a variety of devices including travelling preachers. Expansion had been rapid partly because of a series of accidents by which local networks of evangelicalism had been absorbed into Wesley's connexion; and this in turn made more organization and supervision necessary. If Whitefield was still the star preacher, Wesley's attention to detail and control (which made his critics feel rightly or wrongly that he was ambitious and domineering) virtually ensured that his would become the largest section of the Revival. His success tended to obscure the extent to which this was the fruit not of one man's work but of a large number of forgotten local leaders.

3. 'Mr Wesley's Connexion': the organization and structures of Methodism

The organization of Wesley's 'Connexion' was strikingly different from that of most other eighteenth-century churches and religious associations, at least in its fully-developed form.[235] That development, however, was certainly not planned from the start but emerged through a series of accidents and improvisations. Wesley always maintained that this was so and he was right.[236] The various institutions were developed by a process of trial and error, borrowing and adaptation, occasionally outright invention. A fundamental principle which emerged in controversy with Anglican critics of his 'irregularities' was his view that 'order' in the church should be simply what is expedient and necessary for sustaining the preaching of the gospel and fostering its fruits. No *a priori* principles of 'correct' order can be laid down; no man-made canon laws can be allowed to interfere; and on the ministry Wesley was already implying in the 1740s that there was no divinely-ordained pattern revealed in the New Testament, though it took him some time to free himself from the traditional Anglican pattern, if indeed he ever entirely did so. The religious priorities of converting but above all of perfecting souls were the real imperatives behind his piecemeal and sometimes inconsistent ecclesiastical expedients. He maintained all his life the principle that Methodism was a mere religious society auxiliary to the church, and although this looked more and more like a polite fiction as the years went on, it probably helped to make him feel free to improvise and his 'low', minimal, eighteenth-century definitions of 'church' and 'conformity' to it helped too.[237]

If the Methodist organization emerged piecemeal in response to circumstances, it is also the case that it was neither simply imposed by Wesley from above nor simply forced on him by pressure from below. Both processes combined to produce the end-result, as can be seen, for example, in the way in which lay preachers first 'happened' and then were authorized, or the famous class meeting was suggested by a lay member and then adapted by Wesley for his own purposes. Once adopted by him, however, the various structures did tend to become fixed and sacrosanct and part of a form and discipline to be obeyed.

By the end of the 1740s the structure was essentially complete in outline, though still subject to further enforcement and a number of later refinements, as well as various legal measures to ensure its perpetuation after his death and provide for the transmission of his authority to his preachers. It will be convenient first to describe the completed structure and then to trace its evolution.

It consisted, first, of a large number of local 'societies', large and small. These societies were in turn grouped in larger or smaller 'circuits' to which one or more travelling preachers would be appointed for a period of one or two years during which they travelled round the various societies. There was a 'quarterly meeting' of the circuit officials to administer its temporal and spiritual affairs under the supervision of the senior travelling preacher (the 'assistant'). Each year a 'Conference' was held of Wesley and his travelling preachers and others, which settled the doctrine and discipline of the whole connexion. Two changes took place after Wesley's death. In place of Wesley as head the Conference elected a president and secretary each year; and a further tier of government was added in the shape of districts under a travelling preacher as chairman. The district consisted of a number of circuits, and the district meeting twice a year helped to fill the supervisory gap between the annual Conferences.

Each society contained smaller groups. All full members were placed in 'classes' of about a dozen members under a leader which met weekly for spiritual conversation and guidance. Membership of the connexion was defined by membership of a class. The more spiritually advanced members were also placed in 'bands' to pursue the gift of perfection. Those who appeared to have achieved it were placed in 'select societies' or 'select bands'. Finally, for a time there were also groups of 'penitents', apparently of those who had fallen back from the bands and there were also experiments in classes for children. The class meeting persisted as the core of the Methodist system, but the more select groups were always more difficult to maintain and appear to have faded away during the early nineteenth century.[238]

How had this structure developed? The society emerged first and had the least specific origin. There are too many precedents and parallels for any one to be singled out as the origin of the Methodist variety. As we have seen, there were the Anglican Religious Societies, the Pietist and Moravian ones and of course the Oxford 'Holy Club'. This last was the beginning of Wesley's own experiments, but he acquired further elaborations from elsewhere and by experiment such as the subdivision into bands and the admission of women and of non-Anglicans. The colonized religious societies of his early post-conversion ministry were marked by the teaching of justification by faith, extempore prayer and intense spiritual self-searching. His own developed sub-divisions reflected his teaching on progressive perfection, and the end-result was very much marked by his own ideals.[239] The borrowings from the Moravians and others were utilized for, and subordinated to, his own peculiar designs.

The societies began to become distinctively 'Wesleyan' as they emerged, under Wesley's control, from the links with the Moravians and Whitefield. He termed them, in 'Rules' drawn up for the purpose in 1743, 'The United Societies'. As first used the term simply referred to the two Bristol societies meeting in the Bristol New Room from 1739, but soon it came to cover the others under his supervision in the ever-widening area. The 'Rules' made it clear that this was an organization on different lines from the older societies, for they were simple and made no mention of denominational restrictions. There were only two qualifications: a desire to 'flee from the wrath to come' and evidence of the same in conduct. They were not even required to show proof of conversion, so there was no question of a 'gathered church' membership. All sincere seekers after salvation were welcome, and did not cease to hold their denominational tenets so long as they did not make them matter of dispute. This of course co-existed uneasily with Wesley's equally persistent claim that Methodism was merely an auxiliary to the Church of England from which it should not separate.[240]

Then there were the bands. These, certainly, were a Moravian import. A form of them had appeared in Georgia, then at Fetter Lane, and they were retained by Whitefield and Wesley alike. At first they seem to have implied no more than a category of people especially in earnest, but when the Wesleys adopted the idea of justification by faith and conversion, the basis of membership of the bands became the possession of conversion, if not yet of the 'full assurance' of faith. Membership therefore became a device not merely for intensifying the pursuit of holiness but also for defining the stages in its achievement. The intensity of the spiritual pressure placed upon members of the society can be gauged from a piece by Charles Perronet in the *Arminian Magazine* on the right method of meeting the classes and bands. Some of the topics for the bands are: whether they *now* believe, aim at being wholly devoted to God, see God's hand in all that befalls them, take up their cross daily, humble themselves in every way, and so on. This was warmly endorsed by Wesley.[241] The 'Rules' drawn up by Wesley himself in December 1738 also emphasize separation from sin.[242] The rules developed further later, and by 1750 the members of bands had a 'ticket' distinct from that of other members.[243] The 1744 Conference made the distinction between ordinary and band members clear. The former are 'awakened persons' but 'part of them, who are supposed to have remission of sins, are more closely united in the Bands'.[244]

In 1744, too, the description of the different groups included the select societies and penitents. The select societies consisted of those who 'seem to walk in the light of God'.[245] At the Foundery that year there were 77 members of select societies, only one tenth of the number in the bands. It is not certain when they were created, but one was certainly in being by December 1740 in Kingswood under the name of 'select bands'.[246] What 'seem to walk in the light of God' meant at the time is hard to say: probably perfection, though this would be clarified later. In his *Plain Account of the People Called Methodists* (1749) Wesley saw their members as examples of holiness to their colleagues and a group whom he could 'direct how to press after perfection', but also very interestingly, as 'a select company to whom I might unbosom myself on all occasions without reserve'. It is a pity that we do not know more about how far this happened in practice. In later years Wesley certainly saw the select bands as being of those who 'appeared, so far as we could judge, to be partakers of the same "great salvation"', i.e. perfection; and the bands as of those seeking for it.[247]

As to the 'penitents', they are those who 'have made shipwreck of the faith', and Professor Baker states that they were backsliders from the bands and not from the ordinary society members, though this is not clear from the *Minutes* of 1744.

One problem in the system so far was that apart from the weekly society meeting there was little supervision of the ordinary members not in the bands. Characteristically, the solution to this problem came about by accident.[248] Money was needed to pay for the debts on the New Room in Bristol, and in February 1742 a Captain Foy suggested that every member should subscribe a penny a week. When it was pointed out that some were too poor even to pay this, Foy offered to take on the pennies for eleven other members himself. He would call on them weekly and make up any deficit. Other members took this up, and the system began of dividing up the whole society into 'classes' of about a dozen each. Wesley soon noticed that the visits tended to include help with personal problems, and seized on this as the way to supervise all the members, especially those not in bands. Before long the visiting system was changed to a weekly meeting of the whole group. The leaders were to give 'advice or reproof' and question the members about their current condition. Membership was signified by a quarterly ticket, and it was customary to pay a further shilling when it was given.[249] Members were first placed on trial for two to three months, and absence for three consecutive meetings without good cause entailed expulsion as 'ceasing to meet'. Wesley in fact often purged the societies ruthlessly on his visits – he preferred a smaller group of the committed to a large group of the lukewarm.

The class meeting became so vital and integral a part of the Methodist polity and seemed so clearly to express its values of a mixture of individual and collective piety and 'fellowship' that it achieved an almost mythical status as a picture of true Methodism. An early preacher found that the Methodists in class 'lived as the Christians of old, having all things common'.[250] As this was also the mark of being a member of the Methodist Connexion it caused great embarrassment in the nineteenth century when it decayed and became unpopular.[251] There were no doubt many devoted class members and leaders – a letter to Wesley in 1742 gives a rare glimpse of the self-examination of one such by Wesley's rules and the problems he found.[252] But there were many casualties from the start, and Wesley's idyllic description in the *Plain Account* should be read along with his records of complaints about members who seldom met and complained that it did them no good when they did; the frequent purges tell their own tale.[253]

An early example of reasons for 'ceasing to meet' shows some of the problems and vividly illustrates the tensions between the way of life demanded of Methodists and their other associations with people 'in the world'.[254] Wesley listed seventy-six people in Newcastle in March 1743 who had left: fourteen (chiefly Dissenters) because their ministers refused them the sacrament; nine because husbands or wives were not willing they should stay; twelve whose parents were against it; five because masters or mistresses would not allow them to come; seven because 'their acquaintances' dissuaded them; five because people 'said such bad things of the society'; nine because they 'would not be laughed at'; three because they would not lose the poor's allowance; three because they 'could not spare time'; two because it was too far off; one for fear of falling into fits; one because people were rude in the streets; two 'because Thomas Naisbit was in the society'; one because he 'would not turn his back on his baptism'; one because we 'were mere Church of England men'; one 'because it was time enough to serve God yet'. There were also sixty-four expulsions: two for cursing and swearing; two for habitual Sabbath-breaking; one for beating his wife; three for habitual lying; four for 'railing and evil speaking'; one for idleness; and twenty-nine for 'lightness and carelessness'.

Wesley, by his own account, saw the class meeting as a means for closely assessing the spiritual lives of members, but it had other functions as well. A modern analysis of the reasons for its decline emphasizes that its basic priorities were evangelism and conservation – the recruitment and assimilation of new members. Since the qualification for Methodist membership was not conversion but the desire for conversion, it followed that many were converted after they joined the society and class. 'Assimilation' included the acceptance and living out of the Methodist virtues and culture, which were often in sharp contrast with the respectable world of the eighteenth century as well as with its rougher side. The backsliding Newcastle members revealed this very clearly. The perfectionist aim widened the gap with the ordinary world even further. But there are signs long before Wesley's death that prayer meetings were more popular than class as a converting agency, and his perfectionism always met resistance even within Methodism.

Until 1744 Methodism was held together primarily by the personal supervision of the Wesleys with a little help from one or two Anglican clergy and a good deal more from the travelling lay preachers, who numbered about forty by 1744. Wesley was soon conscious of the need for more co-ordination in the work, especially given the conflict-ridden nature of the little revival groups. It is in the light of this that we should see the meeting and plan already described (above, p. 211) in November 1739 for some clergy and lay preachers to meet regularly and allocate areas of work. Though nothing came of this, it is a pointer not only to the form and purpose of the later Conference but also to vain efforts over several years to harmonize the work of the evangelical clergy. In the event the Welsh Calvinists partly anticipated Wesley by the associations beginning in January 1743.

The first Methodist Conference met in June 1744 and consisted of the Wesley brothers and four other clergy, who soon agreed that they should be joined by such 'lay brethren' (travelling preachers) 'as we shall judge proper'. Four were invited, including Bennet and Maxfield.[255] They were feeling their way at this stage, and in the agenda spoke of what they might learn from 'Zinzendorf, Whitefield, the Kirk and the Quakers'.[256] The matters to be discussed were said to be 'what to teach, how to teach and what to do, i.e. how to regulate our doctrine, discipline and practice'. As befitted what was literally a 'conference' and not yet a formal governing body, they would meet as those with 'everything to learn', speak freely what was in their hearts, and submit to the collective judgment in 'speculative things' only so far as they were individually convinced. In practical matters they would submit only so far as their consciences allowed; and all the proceedings would be confidential. The method of procedure would be by question and answer (as they are to this day) and (unfortunately for historians) only conclusions would be recorded and not the debates that led to them.[257]

At this first Conference, doctrine was dealt with first. They discussed faith, justification, assurance, sanctification. Then followed a debate on discipline and an outline of organization, the purpose of the various groups and the roles of various leaders. There was talk of reunion with the Moravians and Whitefield. Finally, they agreed to meet during the next three quarters at Newcastle, Bristol and London respectively. In the event this did not happen, for the Conference became basically an annual affair, though in some years there were special and occasionally regional meetings *ad hoc* for emergencies. A selection of Conference decisions (the 'Large Minutes') was later drawn up as a code of discipline and periodically revised.[258]

Already the various groups were being led and serviced by a variety of officers. There were leaders of classes and bands; stewards for the societies to look after 'temporal things', but also to ensure that the discipline was observed. They were to be subordinate to the 'helpers' (travelling preachers). As preaching houses multiplied they required trustees for legal purposes.[259]

At the time of the first Conference Wesley used the term 'helper' and 'assistant' indifferently for his lay preachers, the 'help' and 'assistance' being in relation to him.[260] Nor was there yet any distinction between travelling (itinerant) and 'local' preachers. In fact in Wesley's lifetime the status and role of the preachers was often variable. Since they were not ordained, he judged them by their fruits and employed or dropped them at first as he thought fit.[261] Two main categories of preachers emerged: travelling, full-time men posted to different circuits (groups of societies); and 'local' preachers, who worked in their spare time in their own localities. A category of 'half-itinerants' also existed in the eighteenth century – men who lived in one area but periodically travelled elsewhere (there were twelve, for example, in 1755). Men often moved from one category to another as finance, family problems or health dictated. There were also 'exhorters', especially early on (eighteen in Cornwall in 1747). They addressed informal meetings, technically not 'preaching' unless they formally expounded a text, though the line was inevitably a narrow and fluid one.

In this connection it is worth observing the phenomenon of women preachers. Despite public prejudices and the usual seventeenth-century memories against them, they too could feel a 'call', find gifts and graces, and often considerable local popular acceptance. Wesley himself was equivocal about them. Clearly this was another movement from below, and in 1780 he condemned one and ordered the local itinerant to stop her.[262] But he always had a tenderness for holy women as well as a persistent sense of special providences, leading of the Spirit and 'extraordinary calls'. Thus one of his favourites, Sarah Crosby, moved into 'exhorting' and, as so often with her male predecessors, into preaching. Wesley merely counselled her to take things gradually step by step as the guidance came.[263] In effect he was quietly permitting her to preach. Mary Bosanquet he allowed to have an 'extraordinary call' in this direction.[264] In the 1780s women in Fakenham in Norfolk proved to be popular open-air preachers, and one was listed in 1785 as a local preacher. In 1787 the senior minister of the Norfolk circuit formally authorized a woman to preach on Wesley's instructions.[265] Though the practice always had its defenders, it tended to cause scandal, and after Wesley's death the Wesleyans eventually banned it. But in the early nineteenth century the new 'Primitive Methodists' and Bible Christians used it considerably, and a recent study has shown how effectively these women expressed the special social and spiritual values of domestic, family-centred piety in their environment.[266]

Within the ranks of the full-time itinerants two types emerged. Originally Wesley termed them indifferently 'helpers' or 'assistants', but as the system of 'circuits' (groups of societies) emerged, Assistant became the title of the senior, supervising preacher in each circuit. This first occurred in 1749, though the term had been confined to full-time preachers since 1745.

There was a high wastage rate among preachers for all kinds of reasons: personal circumstances, simply falling out with Wesley, or a desire for ordination. In 1741–65 it has been calculated that some 200 preachers had been called, but only 81 were still in the work at the end of the period.[267] Wesley came to take great pride in them; he tried to discipline them and educate them, and was tolerant of their sometimes limited gifts – far more so than his brother Charles, as we shall see. Although he resisted recurring pressure to treat them as full ministers and to ordain them to administer sacraments until events forced his hand in some cases late in his life, he certainly regarded them as more than mere preachers, and constantly urged them into pastoral work as well.[268]

The growing complexity of the connexion and its sheer size brought further problems. Some preachers, like John Nelson, had independent means or supported themselves with a craft. Otherwise they depended on the charity of stewards, who doled out casual payments for clothes, horses, even wigs.[269] As the first Conference laid it down, these were to be 'apostolic' gifts in kind, not money. But from 1752 there was a yearly clothing allowance of £12 and £10 for a wife. Eventually a regular scale of allowances was laid down, though it was difficult to enforce it locally. There followed in 1768 a ban on paid preachers engaging any further in trade.[270] In 1763 a Preachers' Fund was begun, to give allowances to retired preachers and their widows and families. It is revealing equally of the growth of professionalism, the pressure of humanity, and the original idealism of the movement, that this move was regarded with amazement by young John Pawson, who thought 'ministers' trusted to God for support and that John Wesley 'did not greatly approve', 'as he always thought it worldly and not Christian prudence, to provide for a rainy day'. He was always prone to judge others' needs by his own where such matters were concerned.[271]

The Conference appointed preachers to a particular area, in the early days sometimes only a few months at a time, later for longer. From 1746 a system of 'circuits' or 'rounds' (both equally expressive of the itinerant pattern) was developed. Some of them originally reflected earlier networks, like Grimshaw's around Haworth or Bennet's in the North-west. There were seven enormous ones in 1746, nine in 1748, and by Wesley's death in 1791 114. By then the maximum stay for a preacher had been fixed at three years. Wesley thought that if it were any longer they would preach themselves and their hearers into boredom; this perhaps reflected earlier circumstances rather than the more settled reality of his later life.[272]

Although the circuit emerged in 1746, it was a further two years before the mode of administering it became clearer.[273] The 1748 Conference expressed a wish that the societies should be 'more firmly and closely united together', and a year later it was revealed that what was in mind was a 'general union'. London should be 'accounted the mother church' and its stewards 'consult for the good of all the churches'. The assistants would collect information for them, and the London stewards would operate a kind of clearing house for debts and aid. As a step towards this one of the helpers would be regarded as the assistant in charge of the circuit.[274] Whether or not this rather ominous threat of centralization was fully carried out, circuit administration was stabilized by the quarterly meeting, an institution fathered by John Bennet. As early as May 1743 he had used monthly meetings of stewards from his original societies and for further organization there is reason to believe that he had learnt something from the Quakers (he noted material from one of their meetings in his letter-book in 1749 and they held monthly and quarterly meetings).[275] In October 1748 Grimshaw presided over the first quarterly meeting of leaders and stewards at Todmorden Edge for Lancashire, and two days later Bennet held a similar one for Cheshire.[276] Bennet then recommended them elsewhere, and in 1749 the Conference asked for his 'plan' and that he should travel around promoting it.[277] Bennet's monthly meetings did not catch on, but the quarterly ones did.

The trustees who administered the chapel property posed a problem for fear that they should control the pulpit, keep out preachers they did not like and thereby fragment the connexion. As we have seen, Wesley was early warned to take property into his own hands to avoid this. The solution in principle was found by various versions of a 'model deed' from 1746 which all preaching houses were supposed to follow. It secured that the Wesleys and their named successors and ultimately the Conference should appoint the preachers and define the doctrines preached by reference to certain of Wesley's writings. But there would be more trouble about this in Wesley's later years.[278]

In the end it was Wesley's authority, with or without the Conference, that mattered. There is in fact disappointingly little evidence about what really went on in that body. Wesley's *Journal* and the preachers' autobiographies, though occasionally referring to divisions, tend to give the impression that miraculous harmony emerged in the end. We shall see that there certainly were deep divisions – as over separation from the church in the 1750s – and individual preachers could oppose Wesley. Thomas Walsh, in 1755, answering charges that he was 'making light' of Wesley's directions, said that he desired, next to his duty to God, to follow them.[279] There were complaints that in Conference Wesley did all the business himself, though in at least one case a preacher who stood up to him received his grudging respect.[280] In one or two cases emotional appeals by others carried the day. In 1763 some preachers questioned Wesley's authority and Howel Harris dissolved them into tears; and on a later occasion the saintly Fletcher of Madeley had the same effect. Wesley himself was not above the simple device of omitting to invite trouble-makers who opposed his policies, for he kept invitations firmly in his own hands.[281] He kept control of the Conferences during his lifetime, and we shall see how in the 1780s he took action over the succession after several tentative proposals earlier. In this period, too, certain committees emerged for finances, books, buildings, and other affairs. A small 'cabinet' apparently existed to assist him and plan business.[282] These were really the inevitable products of Wesley's old age and the increasing size and complexity of his connexion; yet also of the increasing weight and maturity and *esprit de corps* of the travelling preachers, who to most Methodists were ministers in all but name. The late and controversial ordinations complicated the question of their authority, but this is best discussed in the context of the 1780s as a whole.

Despite a degree of power-sharing, then, Wesley kept holding the reins in his own hands to the end. How did he gain this authority, and whence did he think it derived? Notoriously, he was an authoritarian leader, and several of those who fell out with him thought that he was ambitious for power and would brook no superior. Nor did he believe that power, either secular or ecclesiastical, came from below. In 1790 he wrote: 'As long as I live the people shall have no share in choosing either stewards or leaders among the Methodists. We have not and never had any such custom. We are no republicans, and never intend to be.'[283] The Conference of 1766 actually debated the complaint that Wesley had too much power, and his response explaining the source and nature of this power is as revealing as it is ingenuous.[284]

By Wesley's account it all started when a few people in London in November 1738 asked him to advise them and pray with them, and others followed elsewhere. They asked him, not he them, and from this came his power to appoint and organize. Similarly with the preachers: they asked him to be allowed to be his 'sons in the gospel'. The Conference began when he asked people to advise him – not govern him. In all this he sought no power, but simply followed Providence and the good of the people. Like others in positions of power, he claimed that it was a burden to him which he would gladly lay down if any could be found to take it over. Some had complained that this was 'shackling free-born Englishmen', and requested rule by a Conference of all the preachers and by majority vote. Maybe this would happen after his death, but until then they were engaged to obey him; and in any case, he added realistically, 'To me the people in general will submit, but they will not thus submit to any other'. No one needed to stay with him; but if they did, they must submit in accordance with the terms on which they first joined him.

Underlying this is a kind of contract theory based on the original terms on which people asked Wesley for guidance. It took no account of the very complicated circumstances in which his power had evolved as the Methodist societies developed, and still less of the development of the band of preachers into *de facto* ministers. One explanation for Wesley's attitude to his authority and one source of the broad acceptance of it was the hierarchical 'dependency' nature of eighteenth-century society which was described earlier.[285] This could indeed co-exist with elements of resistance, and a sense of customary rights and the paternal duties of masters. In many ways Wesley's mode of running his connexion fitted into this pattern, and his authority benefitted from it. As a clerical gentleman he was, for most of the time, dealing with social inferiors as accustomed to obey as he was to command. But the resistance also reflected contemporary trends, and it is noticeable that the feelings and language of those wanting a greater share in the control of the connexion mounted and acquired secular echoes as Wesley grew older. His lay associates were drawn from precisely those categories in society most open to some independence of mind. Their choice of Methodism was itself a declaration of independence of the clergy, and their experience in the connexion gave them a taste for more independence.

But Wesley's authority was also highly personal. He was the founding father, and generations grew up having known no other leader. His authority was cumulative, like that of long-lived Popes, with whom he disliked being compared. Moreover, he was constantly in touch with the whole movement at all levels. This was one reason why the people and preachers would listen to him more readily than to Charles, who had ceased to itinerate, and certainly knew far less of Methodism as a whole than did his brother. But there were also more subtle bonds. John was able to value the gifts of the humble and those of limited talents; he shared their taste for the supernatural, their belief in 'providences' and extraordinary calls. Taken together, these factors go far towards explaining his unique position, which everyone (including himself) recognized could not be handed on to any other individual. Despite minor secessions and individual losses, the remarkable thing is how many were retained in the movement.

The Methodist organization was strikingly different not only from most contemporary churches and religious organizations in England, but also from secular government. English government was local more than national, and most churches reflected a similar ethos. The Baptist and Independent view of the church emphasized its primary location in the local gathered church, and county, regional and national associations were weak and consultative rather than with ruling authority. The English Presbyterians were more like Independents in the eighteenth century in this respect than their Scottish relations.[286] Even the Church of England, shorn of an effective Convocation, operated in terms of disconnected dioceses, and in some ways indeed amounted to a parochial 'Independency' ruled by local clergy. Among the evangelical groups, Wesleyan Methodism also stood out as a tighter, more hierarchical body than the looser 'Associations' of the Calvinistic Methodists or

Huntingdonians. It was also more firmly subordinated to Wesley and his preachers at every level.

In structural terms Methodism was closer to the Scottish Presbyterian hierarchy than to English Dissent, but perhaps even more it resembled the Quakers; some have seen it as taking on the role of early Quakerism as an enthusiastic, evangelizing force.[287] The very word 'connexion' is instructive. In secular use it could be applied to a tradesman's clientèle, and even more to a politician's personal following, and so to the personal, religious following of a Wesley, a Whitefield, or a Lady Huntingdon. But it also implied a chain and a network rather than a merely local cluster of adherents. The ethos was not merely that of religious individualism, the individual quest for salvation. Wesley and his followers certainly pursued and emphasized this, but added to it a collective approach: the lines 'Help us to help each other Lord, Our little stock improve' in Charles Wesley's hymn expressed this, and the whole structure embodied and furthered this vision. Despite strong and persistent localizing and 'congregationalizing' tendencies in Methodism, the remarkable thing is that the connexional spirit was also strong. Few other contemporary religious organizations had so strong a sense of a collective national identity and loyalty. And at the local level it adapted better than the Church of England to physical geography and population shifts, which had made nonsense of inherited parochial geography.

What was the ultimate purpose of the organization? Wesley, in his periodic reviews of its history, often pictured it in terms influenced by his original Oxford quest, as the pursuit of inward and outward holiness, in the last analysis the hope of perfection. This, as an expression of his own vision, is essentially correct, and in the account given here of the society and its subdivisions it has been emphasized that it was this which determined the peculiar Methodist structures as against those of their rivals. In some respects early Methodism was a 'holiness sect', though also something more. Some of the classic marks of a 'sect' are there: the charismatic leader, the demarcations from the world, the conversionist teaching. But against this there is the persistent if strained relationship with the Church of England. It was the sectarianism as well as the localism of Dissent that Wesley feared and resisted. Methodism has never fitted easily into the 'church or sect' analysis.[288] Wesley in any case balanced conversionist zeal with the Oxford Methodist passion for spiritual nurture, and his complex notion of perfection made him at once very different from typical 'evangelicals' and from later perfectionist sects. It has to be allowed, however, that Wesley was not the whole of Methodism. His 'reasonable enthusiasm' was balanced by the obsession of many of his followers with the ecstasies of conversion alone and with strong separatist tendencies as well (see below, ch. XI.1).

Ecclesiologically, Methodism was a curiosity, and in some ways strongly marked by the mental climate of the time, as well as by Wesley's personal idiosyncracies. Since he did not admit to himself that he was founding a church, he felt free to experiment in ways that might otherwise have been more inhibited than they were by his High Church inheritance. 'Order' in canonical terms could then be subjected to the expediency of promoting his mission. For apologetic purposes he retreated from his early, exclusive High Church views to a more typical eighteenth-century, almost 'Latitudinarian', view of conformity to the church. 'Conformity' simply meant not contradicting its doctrines and not deserting its worship; and to this he added a rather selective interpretation of the Articles' definition of the church which made it almost a left-wing Reformation 'gathered church'. More interesting is the logic of what he actually practised and his basic principle in doing so. With all his inconsistencies he ultimately viewed the church in a highly pragmatic manner. The priorities are right doctrine and right practice. No ecclesiastical arrangements have been laid down by divine *fiat* in the New Testament as binding on future generations: they are to be improvised as the exigencies of mission dictate. Though Wesley ostensibly took this line for his societies as auxiliary to the Church of England, he was in fact laying down a plausible and healthy approach to church order, as his cavalier attitude to Anglican 'order' clearly implied. One of the tragedies of nineteenth-century Wesleyanism was that it fossilized his pragmatism into a new ecclesiastical orthodoxy as dogmatic as the old ones.[289]

VI

Brothers in Love

1. Charles Wesley: sweet singer and uneasy colleague

Every biographer of John Wesley has to face the question of what to do about brother Charles, for from the days of the Oxford Methodists into the mid-1750s John and Charles were often working more or less in concert, though in different places, and engaged in the same struggles and contentions. Charles has even been credited with being the 'first Methodist', founding the Holy Club and beating John to conversion by a few days. His contributions to Methodism were indeed considerable, and not only by his famous hymns. It is more difficult to estimate his contribution to the spread and consolidation of Methodism, though this was certainly less than that of his brother and, especially in later years, he often seemed to be more of a hindrance than a help to him. Yet there was considerable affection between the brothers, and Charles never actually abandoned his brother or Methodism. In early life at least he tended to give way to John as the elder and more inflexible personality, and John, despite disagreements, always tended to be more candid about his inner life in his letters to Charles than to anyone else.

There are in fact considerable practical difficulties in the way of recontructing his career. Compared with John Wesley's *Journal*, Charles's is often seen as a disappointment. He can be vivid and detailed, but the main manuscript of the journal was only preserved by a near-miracle and survives only from 1735 to 1756 with several gaps; it has never been satisfactorily edited as a whole.[1] His letters also lack a modern critical edition, though Professor Baker's admirable short life of him includes a substantial selection. This is a pity, since the letters are often more lively than John's. Nor has Charles received a satisfactory modern biography: the fullest remains that of Jackson in 1847.[2]

Charles was born in Epworth in 1707, the youngest of the three male children to survive to manhood, and he had a less robust constitution than John, which may help to account for some of his later vacillations of behaviour. It has often been pointed out, and rightly, that he inherited more of his father's temperament than his mother's, and indeed he seems almost a manic-depressive personality, prone to rise to the heights in times of success, only to fall into depression when he was physically or mentally under pressure. Yet it is fair to say that after his conversion he could be as bold as John in standing up to mobs and opposition. Henry Moore allowed that he was 'odd, eccentric and what is called *absent* to a high degree'. John once told Moore that he 'always dreaded him (Charles) visiting him, notwithstanding their great love to each other – knowing well the derangement of books and papers that would probably ensue'. This has an authentic ring, and is unconsciously very revealing of John's own obsessively neat personality. One can see why less tidy personalities found him exasperating.[3] In the 1730s John Gambold was entertained by an acquaintance with an account of 'the whimsical Mr Wesley, his precocious and pious extravagances', though his impression was that in their 'Methodism' at least, Charles had a 'constant deference' for John and 'followed his brother entirely'.[4] Charles himself confessed during his religious struggles at Oxford that 'my head by no means keeps pace with my heart', and this was a permanent characteristic in contrast with John, who realized that his heart did not keep pace with his head.[5]

Charles went to Westminster School in 1716, and by virtue of this connection was elected Student (scholar) of Christ Church, Oxford, in 1727, when John was already Fellow of Lincoln. He was much influenced in his outlook by his elder brother Samuel, that strong High Churchman with Jacobite connections.[6] Some account has already been given of his spiritual struggles and the over-simplified claim that he founded the Holy Club (above, pp. 85f.). Then came the Georgia episode and the conversion in London in 1738.

Once launched on his 'evangelical' career, Charles was as active as John and in much the same manner: preaching in the societies and then in the open air. He played a full part in the struggles with the Calvinists and Moravians, though he seems to have been briefly influenced by the 'still' brethren. The pattern that emerges until the 1750s is of a close colleagueship with his brother. Sometimes they were together, but more often they succeeded one another in the paths of their travels; sometimes one went first into new areas, sometimes the other. The routes around the 'great triangle' and its offshoots were much the same.

But in one important and perhaps fateful respect they differed. This was in their marriages. It will be recalled that General Oglethorpe thought that Charles would do better spiritually and in other ways if he were to be married. At Oxford Charles had had an entanglement with a London actress, and in Georgia had been the dupe of the egregious Mrs Hawkins. Hutton thought that he and John were both in danger from emotional young women. The danger for men in his position in an emotional religious movement was indeed considerable. In 1745 Charles was defamed to the Bishop of London by a woman 'charging me with committing or offering to commit lewdness with her'. In rejecting the charge Charles solemnly professed his innocence of all such misbehaviour or even the thought of it, and there is no reason to disbelieve him.[7] John Wesley sometimes had the same problem, as we shall see.

Charles's approach to marriage was, as one might expect in view of their very different characters, less tortuous and ultimately much happier than his brother's. He first met Sally Gwynne during a visit to Wales in August 1747. She was nearly twenty-one, nineteen years younger than him, and the daughter of Marmaduke Gwynne JP of Garth, a convert of Howel Harris. As is the way of such things, a correspondence which began and indeed continued on a religious plane developed through the language of passionate heavenly love into something more personal and human. For early Methodists, indeed, heavenly and earthly love were often hard to distinguish. By September 1748 at latest there must have been an 'understanding', for Charles was beginning to express his love in verse:

> Two are better far than one
> For counsel or for fight.
> How can one be warm alone
> Or serve his God aright?[8]

There can be no doubt that this was a love-match. Though sincerely glossed with religious concern and bound up in Charles's mind with the love of God, there is a straightforwardness about his courtship which is in telling contrast with John Wesley's hesitant and self-questioning love-affairs. Nor was it marked by the distrust and low expectations of the married state found in some other evangelicals. Whitefield, after being disappointed once, married a widow for the sake of being more useful in God's work and not from that 'foolish emotion that the world calls love'. John Berridge thought of taking a 'Jezebel', but retreated very readily when texts dipped from the Bible seemed to warn him off. Notoriously, he dismissed Mrs Whitefield and Mrs John Wesley as a 'brace of ferrets', which was perhaps unfair to the former though less so to the latter. But Charles was less guilty than some of his brethren of subordinating domestic life to the exigencies of gospel ramblings.[9]

The obstacles to his marriage were in fact external rather than internal. The brothers had agreed on their return from Georgia that they would not marry without consulting each other. John actually proposed three names to Charles and fortunately agreed to Sally, whose name appeared last. Charles consulted other friends, and their support encouraged him to think, 'THIS IS THE LORD'S DOING! THIS IS THE WILL OF GOD CONCERNING ME'. It was the need for assurance about this rather than any psychological uncertainties that made him hesitate, though he did ask Sally to agree that he should continue to 'regulate diet and travelling'.[10] As it turned out, the real obstacles came from Sally's earlier lovers and then from her family, who were understandably anxious to secure the financial stability of this apparently penniless and unbeneficed clergyman.[11] In the end Charles's hopeful promise of £100 a year had to be guaranteed by John Wesley on the security of the sales and stock of the brothers' publications.[12]

And so they were married by John in August 1749, and 'not a cloud was seen from morning till night'. 'We were cheerful without mirth, serious without sadness. A stranger, that intermeddled not with our joy, said "It looked more like a funeral than a wedding".'[13] After preaching in the neighbourhood for a fortnight, Charles began as he intended to continue, and 'cheerfully left my partner for the Master's work'.

The marriage was happy and harmonious despite the strains of itineracy and family tragedies. In 1754 Sally was permanently disfigured by smallpox; her first child died of it, and other deaths were to follow. In some Methodist eyes, including John's, the fate of his surviving sons Charles junior and Samuel seemed more tragic, or at any rate questionable. These boys were musical child prodigies, and in the next generation Samuel Sebastian Wesley was an outstanding composer of church music. Charles tried to educate his children on Susanna's method (he distrusted public schools and did not try Kingswood, his brother's school). He was certainly concerned that they should be good Christians, but he also took great pride in their musical talents and was keen to enable them to cultivate their gifts. He realized that they could not be stopped and that they might be able to train for an honourable profession. To this end he crossed Methodist prejudices by having them perform 'concerts' at home to publicize their performances: at least, he said, it was better than mixing with bad musicians. But good Methodists were not convinced.[14] On the whole Charles comes well out of this. Despite his obvious care for their souls and perhaps some special pleading before his critics, he had a sense that the boys had a right to a life of their own and (more unusually) was equally solicitous for his daughter Sally junior.[15]

More serious for Charles's Methodist connections was his gradual withdrawal from full itinerary. It has been generally supposed that his marriage and family had much to do with this. Old Berridge commented in 1770 that 'Matrimony has quite maimed poor Charles', but if so, the problem went back a long way.[16] Professor Baker underlines the state of his health, which had certainly been chancy ever since his bad time in Georgia, but Tyerman was perhaps right to stress the equally important point that he was increasingly at odds with the preachers and societies over their attitudes towards the established church and critical, too, of the preachers' quality. They repaid his distrust with interest, as their criticisms of his preaching in his later years showed.[17] The prolonged tale of these disputes and Charles's growing alarm at his brother's laxity and tendency to give way to the preachers' demands for autonomy from the church (as he saw it) will be told in the context of Anglican-Methodist relationships generally. Here it need only be said that Charles was all too prone to believe the Methodist gossip, to fly to the worst and most pessimistic conclusions, and actually to intrigue and muster opposition to his brother. John was right to assert that he knew the state of the connexion and its needs better than Charles, and that somehow men had to be found to carry on the work.[18] In effect Charles meddled when he saw things going in directions he disapproved of, but was not prepared to carry on the day-to-day burden of supervising the connexion.

Already in October 1753 John wrote to Charles urging that he 'either act really in connexion with me: or never pretend to it'. By this John meant 'taking counsel with me once or twice a year as to the places where you will labour'. 'At present you are so far from this that I do not even *know* when and where you intend to go.' He accused Charles of simply following 'those impressions which you account divine' rather than reason. He claimed that for the past ten years Charles had no more been 'in connexion' with him than Whitefield had been.[19] If so, then even Charles's itinerant period had been at his own whim. In 1756 Charles took his last full nationwide journey, and then desisted from travelling, as Tyerman suggested, to avoid unpleasant clashes with the preachers. Henceforth he confined himself largely to Bristol, and then from 1771 to London, in which places he acted as a kind of resident minister for the main chapels, resisting John's occasional attempts to stir him into travelling again. Nor, one supposes, had Charles's part in the traumatic affair with Grace Murray made John trust him; and John took care to keep his own counsel when he proceeded to conduct ordinations in his last years – action which reduced Charles to helpless fury (for these episodes see below, pp. 258ff. 518ff.).

In the end the traditional view that Charles's chief contribution to Methodism was in his hymns is probably correct. As a preacher he was, as one would expect, impassioned and dramatic. John Wesley hit off the difference between the two brothers: 'In connexion I beat you; but in strong, pointed *sentences* you beat me.'[20] Like many lay Methodists, in his early days Charles preached as the spirit moved him, sometimes with spectacular effects. Later in life some thought he offered poor and erratic fare in London.[21]

Hymns were another matter. The significance of the hymnbook of 1780 and Methodist attitudes to hymns will be discussed later in connection with Methodist piety, but something may be said here about the special qualities of Charles's own contribution.

No doubt he indulged in verse-making like so many of his contemporaries at Oxford, though his first extant piece of religious verse dates from 1728.[22] He must have heard the Moravian hymns in Georgia, but it seems as though his own gift was released by his conversion, as in the 'Conversion Hymn' beginning 'Where shall my wondering soul begin? How shall I all to heaven aspire?', which already has his characteristic tone of voice. He became prone to express his hopes and fears and thoughts on all manner of things (domestic matters, politics) in verse. Some have forgotten polemical and apologetic contexts in lines like 'For all, for all, my Saviour died' (against the Calvinists). It may be added that John had no scruples about altering his brother's and other people's hymns to what he thought was correct.

Part of the significance of Charles Wesley's hymns was that they were designed by a classically-educated and quite well read Church of England clergyman for congregations of very ordinary and only sketchily educated or illiterate people. In this respect he resembled Isaac Watts, whose hymns were also much used by the Methodists. Watts had consciously set himself to imitate the Psalms and Christianize them, and then to write independent hymns in such a way as to make them suitable for ordinary Dissenting congregations. Literary critics have never found it easy to discuss hymns as literature because of their peculiar role and limitations. It is therefore a considerable compliment to Watts and Wesley that their work has attracted some attention and appreciation as verse from some recent writers on eighteenth-century poetry. Donald Davie, for example, has noted how Watts (a well-educated and in some respects learned man) successfully adapted his language for a common auditory without losing a sense of style and dignity. Through language which was essentially simple, he yet contrived to express profound religious ideas coupled with intense yet controlled religious feeling. Much the same is true of Charles Wesley so far as language and ideas are concerned, but Davie thinks that as used by Methodists, at least, the emotion is less restrained and liable to get out of hand.[23]

Charles Wesley differed temperamentally from Watts and had an even less sophisticated audience. Yet it is also fair to say that he educated his readers as well as releasing their emotions. As well as voicing their favourite themes of conversion, holiness and heaven, he could encapsulate a theology in 'Our God contracted to a span, Incomprehensibly made man', or express a complex typological symbolism in his mystical poem 'Wrestling Jacob'. Some themes Wesley dealt with in common with Watts, but he concentrated more (and with greater emotional abandon) on themes like personal conversion. Both wrote feelingly on heaven: the theme perhaps most remote from modern taste. But Watts had a vision of God in creation, combining eighteenth-century notions of space with a Calvinist sense of the immediacy of God's presence in creation, which is less evident in Wesley.[24] In his sacramental hymns Charles was a full-blooded High Churchman who did not shrink from the most startlingly realistic language about the presence and sacrifice in the eucharist. Much of the language of the hymns reveal a mind so steeped in the Bible as to use its language without conscious quotation. Like his brother, Charles often seems to be reliving the life and mind of the apostolic age and revivifying that apparently remote and lost experience for his own day. In their journey from conviction of sin through conversion to perfection, the early Methodists were taught and led as much through hymns as through sermons and Wesley's pamphlets. From them, too, they absorbed a measure of theology and even of culture.

2. John Wesley and women

If Charles Wesley, after the first few years of the Revival, was as much a liability as an asset to his brother's mission, in one part of John's life he acted as a deliberate if well-intentioned wrecker. This was in the affair of Grace Murray, and as an indirect consequence he may perhaps also be held to be partly responsible for the subsequent disaster of John Wesley's marriage. Like all matters concerning Wesley's relationships with women, the Murray affair is one which has rather embarrassed Methodist biographers, and Charles's role in it has appeared particularly disreputable. It is still difficult to unravel the process by which this sad affair muddled its way to catastrophe. For the student of Wesley's character, however, his conduct of the affair and his private account of what happened so closely resembles the earlier episode with Sophy Hopkey as to give rise to the suspicion that this was not simply a tragedy of errors but further evidence of some deep-rooted psychological disability in his nature as regards relationships with women. Although much of the evidence comes from John Wesley himself and is subject to obvious doubts about its reliability and objectivity, there is some material from the other protagonists with which to balance his account.

We have seen that the fragmentary evidence for the early relationship with Varanese is insufficient to support the notion that it was a failed proposal of marriage which precipitated a spiritual crisis. The most that one can say is that John seems to have been, in some sense of the word, in love with her and pursued a dangerously affectionate relationship with her after her marriage to Jack Chapone. There are also signs of similar entanglements with others in the Oxford period, including Aspasia (Mrs Pendarves).

The Sophy Hopkey affair in Georgia is a much clearer case. Here, even if there was no formal declaration, there can hardly be any doubt that Wesley was in love and would have liked to marry Sophy, but was torn by conflicts between love, duty, notions of the value of celibacy and more obscure difficulties with his own nature which led him to blow alternately hot and cold until the bewildered girl married elsewhere. There followed the attempts to keep up the relationship, to impose his standards of piety upon her; the scandal of rejecting her from communion and the flight from Georgia. He had also impossibly idealized her character and was correspondingly mortified to find it wanting.

Now, twenty years later, a remarkably similar pattern repeated itself. However much one may blame the débacle on his rival for Grace's favours, John Bennet, and the bustling intervention of Charles Wesley, it can hardly be denied that here, as in the earlier case, John Wesley made his proposals so obliquely and with so many hesitations and reservations, allowing so many chances to his rival, that he must share the blame for his own disappointment. Curnock comfortingly saw his conduct as proof that he subordinated his personal happiness to the work of God, and even the more sceptical Léger concluded that in the last resort Wesley's love for God overcame all other loves. But his meticulous arguments in favour of the marriage, followed by his careless-ness in securing his prize as well as his passion and pain when he lost her, suggest that the situation was less simple.

It is not too difficult to reconstruct the general course of events, though the details and chronology and certain legal points are more difficult. The published *Journal* understandably says nothing directly of the affair, but its record of incessant activity coupled with the more private information has its own poignancy as the context within which the private pain was being experienced.[25] The bare outline of the story is this.

Wesley was in love with Grace Murray, a widow and trusted Method-ist female helper. He intimated his intention to marry her and thought he had bound her to marry him. But he did this in so convoluted and hesitant a manner and with so many delays that Grace was left in uncertainty. Meanwhile she was approached by a more determined lover, John Bennet, the apostle of the North-west. Not only was Grace torn between the two men, but there was hostility and jealousy among other Methodist women; Charles Wesley thought Grace unsuitable for his brother, and claimed that marriage to her would split the societies. He therefore hustled her into marriage with Bennet. In doing so it seems that he wrongly supposed that in any case Bennet had the prior claim and that John was the interloper, whereas the opposite was true.

Grace Murray was born in 1716 and became the wife of a Scottish sea-captain. She was converted in 1739, partly through the preaching of Whitefield and partly through that of John Wesley.[26] The first sign of her acquaintance with John comes in an account of her experience which she wrote to Charles Wesley and which John printed in his *Journal* for 2 May 1740. She was made a band leader at the Foundery after her husband was drowned at sea in 1742. At the end of 1745 she was appointed housekeeper at the Newcastle house. It was there, early in 1746, that she first met a 'gentleman dressed in black', John Bennet in fact, whom she nursed through an illness. She thought that he was dying, but after she had prayed for him he began to recover. Bennet later claimed that he took this to be a sign that she was to be his wife. Although they corresponded for the next two years, Grace claimed that 'I never gave any answer concerning love affairs, for I thought that I would not marry again.'[27] Grace's spiritual experience, like that of many other early Methodists, was highly charged with emotion, and like John Bennet she was prone to vivid dreams. She shows signs of much tension and guilt over the conflict between love for her husband and for Methodism, and later felt guilty over refusing a suitor who then married another and fell away from Methodism. This probably made her more vulnerable to emotional and spiritual blackmail when Bennet claimed that the health of his soul depended on his marrying her.[28]

John Wesley certainly valued her highly, especially for her work among the female bands. Then, in August 1748, he too fell ill and was nursed by Grace in Newcastle. Here there is a major clash of evidence. According to Wesley it was on this occasion that he brought himself to say that, 'If I ever marry I think you will be the person'. Soon afterwards, he said, he proposed to her 'more directly' and she gave him a 'voluntary and express promise' to marry. In his own mind at least he seems to have thought that he had entered into a formal contract *de futuro*, i.e. a promise of marriage. As in much that followed, it is doubtful whether Grace realised the implications of this, and in any case the formal and legal stages claimed by Wesley in retrospect (complex in any case in the state of English marriage law at the time) were part of his portrayal of himself as an honest and injured man.[29]

At the end of August Wesley took Grace down to Chinley and left her with Bennet. No sooner had he left than Bennet began to press his own suit, telling her that his healing at Newcastle meant that God had given her to him. That night Bennet had a dream or vision of Grace in distress with Wesley approaching her tenderly and saying, 'I love thee as well as I did, on the day when I took thee first.' But she put him away from her. Bennet took this as supporting his suit and said, 'Take care that you do not fight against God.' Wesley naturally thought that Bennet misunderstood the dream, and indeed next morning Bennet asked Grace, 'Is there not a contract between you and Mr Wesley?' From love of Bennet or fear of exposing Wesley she answered 'No'. She then agreed to marry Bennet if Wesley consented. This could be regarded as another contract *de futuro*.[30] Bennet apparently corresponded with Wesley, jibbing at having to abide by his advice; claiming he 'did not want a woman' but thought it God's will he should marry; and criticizing Wesley for carrying Grace around to the damage of her soul.[31]

Bennet did not know that Wesley had carried Grace off to Ireland for several months (a course of action highly damaging to her reputation) and according to her Wesley did not say much about the correspondence with Bennet. In July 1749 Wesley entered into a contract *de praesenti*, which before the Marriage Act of 1753 counted as a private marriage ceremony. Either Grace thought Bennet had abandoned her or, as Wesley claimed, he convinced her that the Newcastle proposal rendered her promise to Bennet not binding.[32]

But on returning to Bristol that month, Grace was seized with jealousy through gossip about Wesley's relations with another woman.

On 1 September the three parties met at Epworth, and according to Grace, 'Mr Wesley declared his passion for me, which he had concealed too long.' She claimed that she had hitherto seen him only as a father and blamed him for concealing his feelings. She was as surprised by his declaration as if 'the moon had dropped out of her orbit'. She felt 'between two fires'. After many words to no purpose they parted, and she went to Newcastle and married Bennet.[33] But Wesley's account may be believed here as showing a less simple course of events. The scene at Epworth was impassioned, tearful and confused. Grace wanted to marry Wesley, but felt Bennet would go mad if she refused him. He and another preacher browbeat her until she promised to marry Bennet, but when she told Wesley this, she said she still felt contracted to him, and when he said 'Which will you choose?', she replied that she was 'determined to live and die with you'. He then left for Newcastle and wrote a stinging letter to Bennet.[34] In this he asserted Bennet's duty of obedience to him and his own prior claim to Grace.

This letter never reached Bennet, but Charles Wesley was sent a copy. In great agitation Charles resolved to stop his brother marrying

Grace, but John at last seemed to have made up his mind. Having argued the pros and cons, he renewed his contract *de praesenti* at Grace's request, with Christopher Hopper, one of the preachers, as a witness.[35] The brothers met at Whitehaven, and although Charles still opposed the marriage, he agreed to arbitration by Vincent Perronet. Although John attempted to explain the moral and legal status of his claim, Charles either misunderstood or wilfully misinterpreted the situation in his frantic desire to stop his brother marrying Grace. He carried her off to Newcastle while John continued his work at Whitehaven. John must have known the risks of allowing Charles to take Grace away and prayed for a sign in a dream or vision. A dream duly occurred, of Grace dying, which he took to mean she was dead for him. On 3 October 1749 Charles married Grace to John Bennet. That day John Wesley met Whitefield in Leeds, who said that he was persuaded that Grace was John's wife but that Charles Wesley had carried all before him. Whitefield engineered a tearful reconciliation of all the parties at which Charles was enlightened as to his error. Until then he had regarded John as a 'heathen man and a publican' for unjustly brushing aside Bennet's prior claim; but now he blamed Grace.[36]

Wesley could scarcely reconcile himself to Bennet, whom he thought had not only grievously injured him personally but had also sinned before God. Bennet was suspicious of Wesley and jealous that he wanted still to remain in contact with Grace and might alienate her affections from him. Charles was suspicious, too. It was the story of Sophy Hopkey and Williamson all over again.[37] In fact the breach with Bennet was never really healed. He was already moving towards Whitefield and Calvinism, and before long a crisis built up in his 'round' over the Calvinist question, sharpened by deteriorating personal relations. By 1752 he had broken with Wesley, though he failed to carry most of his old societies with him (see above, pp. 219f.).

Wesley's own view of the course of events and his strong feelings about his disappointment are made clear in an account comparable to the first and most private one he had given of the Hopkey affair. The main outline of his case is also given in a letter to Charles, and his feelings are confirmed in another to Thomas Bigg. The letter to Charles is additionally interesting for a review of his changing views on marriage.[38] To Charles, John listed his objections to marriage. At the age of six or seven he used to say he would never marry 'because I should never find such a woman as my father had'. Between about 1720 and 1730 he had no thought of marriage as he could not keep a wife. He was then persuaded from the example of the primitive church that it was unlawful for priests to marry. Next he concluded that marriage was a less perfect state as it might entail a 'taint upon the mind, necessarily attending the marriage bed'. Nor could a married man be so single-minded towards the Lord as a single one. It would also hinder his giving to the poor and his special mission generally. But these objections were removed one by one. A mixture of books, experience and the example of friends convinced him that there was no primitive law against it and that he might even be less distracted by marriage than without it. In Grace Murray, moreover, he thought he had found one in all ways 'meet for me': a helper in his work, a nurse for his 'shattered carcase', a neat housewife, a faithful friend with 'some knowledge of books and men'. In short, this was a vision of that not impossible she whom he had envisaged long ago and had once imposed on Sophy Hopkey, too. In this case, however, he had of course seen Grace in action at home and on journeys as a Methodist female helper. He also acknowledged more openly than before that she would be a protection against 'unholy desires and inordinate affections – which I never did entirely conquer for six months together before my intercourse with her': 'It is better to marry than to burn.' She would guard him against the danger of the affections of other women in the society.

The objections urged by others against the marriage are also revealing. It would alienate the preachers, split the societies, be a scandal to the world: all this apparently because Grace was said to be 'low-born'. To this Wesley answered that her gifts mattered more and that he despaired of finding a spiritual 'gentlewoman'. She is really his 'servant' (they said) but that is all the better as he knows her well. Her travelling with him will make people say she is his mistress, but they will say so anyway, and travel has tested her capacity for helping him. He concluded that he had every reason to marry and 'I know no person so proper as this'.

It looks very much as though Wesley was near to overcoming his old theological and psychological hindrances to marriage. If Susanna's formidable shadow had inhibited him earlier, it was perhaps beginning to fade. He seemed to be acknowledging sexual desire and the legitimacy of its expression, and observation seems to have convinced him that it was not after all an obstacle to perfection. Morever, he needed protection against scandal and female jealousy in the societies. The fact that he did marry within a couple of years of the failure of the Murray affair does seem to prove that the obstacles in his mind and feelings had been removed.

Yet doubts remain. Wesley in his own mind, at least in what amounted to apologetic retrospects in his usual manner, thought that he had made his intentions clear and had even entered into successive and binding legal agreements, so clear indeed that a modern scholar has been able to make a case for claiming that he committed bigamy in marrying Mrs Vazeille later![39] To Grace, at least by her own account, this was not clear at all. He seemed to be half-promising and delaying, and in any case she was the prey to conflicting emotions and Bennet's emotional blackmail to an extent that Wesley did not really grasp. Moreover, the fact that he allowed Charles Wesley to carry Grace off to Newcastle and then resorted to lots and prayers for visions from God suggests that in reality he was much more uncertain than his methodical arguments suggested. This, too, was an old pattern reasserting itself. Like any enthusiast he really wanted a direct voice from God; or perhaps one should say that he hoped that events would decide the issue and this could be taken as divine guidance.

Of course there were other factors. Charles Wesley easily persuaded himself that it was Grace Murray's scheming that had deceived them all. This was the tradition that descended in his family, but was a face-saving device which let Charles off too easily.[40] It is true that he always said that John was easily deceived in people's characters, and there was some truth in this. John also idealized women whom he thought he loved, as we have seen, and Grace Murray was a more confused woman than John realized: we may well believe that she was overawed by one she saw as a spiritual father, and was certainly put under great pressure by Bennet, whose own rather insecure character and need for marriage is plain enough from his diary, despite his denial that he 'wanted a woman'.[41] Grace may well have felt that he needed her more than Wesley did.

Charles's case was ostensibly that the woman was unsuitable and that marriage to her would split the societies. It is as well to realize that the problems of the affair were exacerbated by poisonous Methodist gossip which distracted Grace, and to which Charles was always too prone to listen anyway. Some Methodist women were certainly prone to fall in love with their leader (a familiar hazard for revivalists) or at any rate to resent a sister who seemed likely to catch him. Charles's personal case against Grace was that she was not as spiritual as she seemed, but above all, apparently, that she was too mean in status for his brother and that this would cause division and scandal. This was a real problem in the eighteenth century, though misalliances not much short of Dukes marrying dairymaids did occur.[42] John Wesley, however, was singularly free of prejudice about status: he placed grace and gifts above worldly considerations; indeed his prejudice was strongly *against* the gentry and upper classes. In fairness to Charles he saw the scandal as centring on the supposed fact that John would be ousting Bennet who had the prior claim to Grace. But there was a social prejudice too.[43] And one may also wonder whether Charles was entirely disinterested in his analysis of the risks. It is perhaps unduly suspicious to note that with the loss of his fellowship on marriage John would have to fall back on the publishing profits which were supporting Charles. But it cannot have escaped Charles's notice that if John, despite his protestations, eased off his incessant journeys, Charles might have to take on a more onerous role of leadership than he could well bear. Whether or not any such thoughts passed through his mind, there is something rather unpleasing about the spectacle of the happily settled brother straining every nerve to stop John following suit on the plea that it would damage the connexion. No such calculation had apparently ever concerned him in his own case. Perhaps one may charitably observe that both men easily deceived themselves with plausible reasons for doing what they wanted to do.

Perhaps Charles's fears were exaggerated (they often were). It is hard to believe that John would ever have allowed marriage to interfere with his work – certainly the marriage that did ensue never did. Marriage with Grace might still have ended in disillusionment. As it turned out, she only had ten years with Bennet, who died in 1759. Later, she became a much loved and saintly figure among the Methodists, and in 1788 she and Wesley met for the last time. Thomas Olivers, one of the preachers, discovered that she was in London. He saw her and told her that Wesley would like to see her. 'Mr Wesley, with evident feeling, resolved to visit her', and the next morning went to see her with Henry Moore. 'The meeting was affecting, but Mr Wesley preserved more than his usual self-possession. It was easy to see . . . she was a fit subject for the tender regrets expressed in those verses which I have presented' (they were attached to Wesley's private account of the affair).[44] But Grace by then was probably a very different woman from the confused widow of forty years before, and Wesley, in *A Thought upon Marriage* (1785), speaking of those youthful yearnings for happiness with a woman, now interpreted them as a substitute for waning love of God. But did he fully believe this, even when age had spent passion? Or was he simply disillusioned with marriage?

Perhaps, having come so near to success, Wesley was less inhibited in what turned out to be his approach to the marriage that did take place. Or perhaps he saw it as the only bulwark against further trouble. In his *Journal* he published the fact in terms of having for years thought he would be more 'useful' as a single man but now was as fully persuaded he would be more useful as a married one. So, by the advice of his friends, he entered on this state a few days after.[45] This was in February 1751.

Following the old rule, more or less, John informed Charles of his decision, though he took good care not to let him interfere this time. Charles was 'thunderstruck', fell into one of his depressions and 'groaned under my own and the people's burden'. The brothers had known the lady for some time – she first appears in Charles's journal (rather appropriately, one feels) as a 'woman of a sorrowful spirit'. But Charles had never suspected danger from this particular person. She was Mrs Mary (Molly) Vazeille, a widow of Huguenot extraction. Her late husband had been a London merchant. She was forty-one years old when she married Wesley, who was forty-eight. Charles could hardly object to her social status, though he distrusted her personality and the effect that the marriage would have on the societies; but one suspects he would have objected to any partner for his brother.

Wesley carefully safeguarded himself against charges of fortune-hunting by settling her £10,000 property on herself and her children by her former marriage. Financially himself he had lost his Fellowship income on marriage. The marriage day was probably precipitated by a fall which damaged his ankle. Mrs Vazeille nursed him and the marriage followed on 18 or 19 February. It is not known where it took place, despite much inquiry, and it is conceivable that to avoid publicity it was done in a private house at some unusual hour.[46]

Wesley's motives for the step must be a matter for guesswork. The gap since the Murray affair suggests that it was not the cliché case of romance on the rebound. He probably simply followed his own arguments in favour of marriage when considering the Murray case. He needed a companion and nurse and a bulwark against emotional females and scandal. Charles quotes his apologia to the London societies and the remark that 'I am not more sure that God sent His Son into the world than that it is His will that I should marry'.[47] Did he really love her or, like George Whitefield, despise such 'vanities'? His early letters to her after marriage certainly combine a characteristic mixture of concern for her spiritual welfare and work among the societies with warm satisfaction that God had made them 'helps meet for each other' and what appears to be love and affection of a simple human kind. In one he broke into a couple of lines from Sappho, imagining himself 'sitting just by you':

> And see and hear you all the while
> Softly speak and sweetly smile.

He felt, he said, that happiness which he had hoped to gain from 'his dearest earthly friend'. And he referred to her here as 'my dear love'. And, very unfortunately as it turned out, he said she could open any letters addressed to him.[48]

Mrs Vazeille's motives for marrying Wesley are more obscure. She may have been flattered, in the Methodist context, by the attention of the leader. In later years, after many quarrels, Wesley hinted that she was either mad or had married him for money and had been disappointed. She disliked Charles Wesley and apparently did resent the money settled on him from the book profits.[49]

The first symptoms of tension are already hinted at in a letter to Wesley's friend Blackwell in May 1751, saying that she had 'many trials', and by December she was showing signs of jealousy and fretted that John did not love her.[50] She showed her temper in public on many occasions, as in a confrontation with Bennet in 1752 when she told him that he was 'in the gall of bitterness, bond of iniquity and that she believed me to be a very bad man'.[51]

At first she travelled with John, though she found this a burden before too long, and Wesley of course loudly proclaimed that a Methodist preacher should not travel one mile less because of marriage.[52] This was not a very wise prescription for marriage, though it was commonly followed by the early preachers and their heroic wives.

For over twenty years Wesley's letters to his wife show a depressing, at times touching, picture of pathological jealousy, suspicion, and uncontrollable rage on her part, with patient attempts at reasoning, expostulation, claims of husbandly authority, answers to slanders and various ultimatums as the price of reconciliation on his. There were temporary reconciliations but also recurring desertions on her side. He complained that she would not let him choose his company; that she showed his private letters to the world and damaged his reputation. She scolded like a fishwife and accused him of adultery with various of his favoured female correspondents. He had tried all methods in vain, he said, to soften her natural temper. In 1777 he still hoped for a reunion after she had left him for Newcastle several years before. Curiously he recorded this, omitting her name, in his *Journal*: ' — set out for Newcastle purposing "never to return". *Non eam reliqui; non dimisi; non revocabo* ("I have not left her; I have not sent her away; I will not recall her").' Finally, in October 1778, he wrote his last letter to her, saying that she had slandered him and that if she lived a thousand years she could not undo the damage she had done him. 'And till you have done all you can towards it, I bid you farewell.'[53] She died and was buried in October 1781, but he was not informed of this until some days afterwards. On her tombstone her epitaph recorded that she was 'a woman of exemplary piety, a tender parent and a sincere friend'.[54]

Mr Wesley's marriage became one of the black legends in the Wesley canon, scarcely relieved by comedy except on the occasion when he is supposed to have legged it over the back wall of the Newcastle house as she came in at the front. The most lurid of the stories comes from John Hampson senior, who found Wesley's wife foaming with rage with her husband on the floor, and some of his hair in her hand, torn out by the roots. At the sight of those maltreated 'venerable locks', Hampson 'felt as though he could have knocked the soul out of her'.[55] It is unusual to find a more friendly estimate of her by a Methodist. Joseph Sutcliffe, however, conceded that she was a 'generous-hearted woman', her 'house and heart' open to the preachers when 'convenient' (!). She had a difficult temper, but Vazeille had known how to manage it. The fact was, Sutcliffe thought, that she had not counted the cost in marrying someone who, like Wesley, was wedded to the Lord's work.[56]

When all allowances have been made, she seems to have been a woman of a naturally jealous and possessive temperament which easily spilled over into a state of mental instability, tinged with sexual jealousy as well, for she was particularly suspicious of Wesley's relations with his female friends. She even claimed that Mrs Charles Wesley had been his mistress before her marriage.[57] According to one story she handed over doctored letters to his enemies in the Calvinistic controversy in the 1770s, though it seems they were not actually published, as she intended.[58]

If she was constitutionally neurotic, it must still be said that Wesley was the worst possible partner for her. Evangelicalism, especially of the itinerant variety, was very hard on wives, and the marvel is that more Methodist marriages did not break up. Mrs Wesley was not prepared to suffer in this way and unfortunately, given her suspicious temperament, she thought of the worst possibilities when her husband was away. Moreover, his frequent attempts to reason with her have all the usual marks of his obtuse belief that human problems can be solved by reason and logic. This and his self-contained personality were well calculated to reduce her to helpless fury.[59]

Moreover, Wesley's conduct with women gave her easy grounds for suspicion. Charges of sexual misconduct involving him were often made, and wandering preachers in excitable societies were an all-too easy target for malicious or jealous women. A few real delinquents like Westley Hall gave colour to less likely cases.[60] There is no reason to believe Wesley guilty of anything of this sort: his hesitant approach, even to marriage, would of itself make it implausible. What gave handles to his enemies and his suspicious wife was partly the nature of the Methodist classes and bands; partly his naive optimism about the regeneration of some dubious characters; and partly his affectionate spiritual correspondence with godly women.

The private nature of the bands – and of course the language of that other Methodist institution, the lovefeast – revived the usual stories of orgies which have attached themselves to new sects in all ages. The classes and bands were often seen as a kind of Popish confessional with all its suspect associations. Wesley always warned his preachers to be 'sparing' in conversation with women, 'especially young women', though he did not always follow his own advice. One hope he had of Grace Murray was that she could take over the dangerous female bands.[61] Methodist talk and hymns of love divine and the rapturous, faintly erotic language of the perfect in love easily slid (or could seem to slide) into something more earthly. In 1744 a letter of Wesley's Kingswood housekeeper Sarah Perrin shows how hard the line could be to draw: 'My heart is knit more and more unto you, and may we be filled with that manner of love wherewith Christ loved us.' In the same letter she had good reason to say that she had been cautioned 'not to write so freely because my affection has been misinterpreted; lest it should hurt the cause of God'. Just so – yet she saw no reason for refraining from speaking of the love and gratitude she felt for the blessings of Wesley's ministry.[62]

Wesley would have been well advised to have restrained himself from such correspondence after his marriage, but he did not. One might suppose that they were compensations for his miserable home life, but in fact, though they may have comforted him, they were only the continuation of an old habit. Most of these ladies were good examples of holy Methodist women, full of good works and of exemplary background and piety. But some were more equivocal. It is not surprising that Mrs Wesley was suspicious of Sarah Ryan, a later Kingswood housekeeper, who had had a spectacular career as a sinner and was at least a bigamist. But she also had spectacular visions and spiritual experiences which Wesley published in the *Arminian Magazine*.[63] Wesley clearly had no doubts about the spiritual integrity of this repentant Magdalen figure. Whatever his feelings about these ladies, some of them probably were at least a little in love with him. He innocently enjoyed their attentions and tended to be discouraging when they proceeded to marriage, though his concern here was for their spiritual health. He may have felt, however, that they would then tend to pass out of his tutelage. That he was perfectly conscious of the possibility of 'earthly' affection is shown by a remark to Ann Bolton: that he had only a 'calm, rational affection' for her.[64]

Yet Wesley was often at his best in these relationships: guiding the souls of his correspondents, urging them on to perfection, advising the more intelligent on their reading, and producing some of the simplest and most direct of his descriptions of essential Christianity for their benefit.[65]

Alexander Knox, in one of the most perceptive analyses of Wesley's character, as a friend of his last years, thought that he had 'a predilection for the female character', being 'alive to amiability' and finding in women 'a quicker and fuller responsiveness to his own ideas of interior piety and affectionate devotion'. He was therefore unusually frank in his correspondence with them. Knox thought that this also led him to exhibit his 'enthusiasm' intellectually, though his moral sentiments were always sound and aimed at virtue. This is well said and, as a modern scholar has suggested, there is a certain parallel here with a long line of Catholic saints who seem to have had the best in them brought out in correspondence with women.[66]

The idea that he was a kind of unconscious polygamist seems rather unsubtle as applied to these delicate and innocent relationships. There is nothing of erotic mysticism in Wesley's language (which, as has already been remarked, cannot always be said of some other Methodists). The late *A Thought upon Marriage* (1785), already referred to, speaks retrospectively of the youthful search for happiness in marriage and concludes that this is really an unconscious substitute for a lost love of God.[67] Was this Wesley's judgment on his own earlier love? If, in old age, the more disturbing fires died down, the warmth of friendship was still welcome, and perhaps indeed gave most of what Wesley had hoped for from marriage.

VII

Mobs and Controversies

Attacks on the Methodists and other evangelicals were broadly of two kinds: physical and verbal. The physical attacks came mainly in the form of individual and casual assaults and, more spectacularly, as mob violence. The verbal attacks came in many forms and at various levels. They could be a matter of vulgar abuse, satire in prose, verse and drama. To this should be added 'visual' attacks in cartoons and even in pottery (Whitefield's squint was a gift to caricaturists in all media as 'Dr Squintum'). At a more serious and considered level there were attacks by clergy and laity in sermons and pamphlets, which were those most generally answered by Wesley himself. Attacks could also come in the legal forms of episcopal discipline and secular court cases for violations of church order or anti-Dissenting legislation.

Mob violence produced some of the most spectacular and heroic episodes in early Methodist history and was the subject of some dramatic set-pieces in lives of Wesley, as indeed it was in his own *Journal*. Like the verbal attacks, mob attacks have been seen mainly through Methodist eyes and Wesley's responses. But it is arguable that until recently the subject has not been studied with sufficient appreciation of the reasons behind the attacks. It has been natural to assume that attacks on such harmless and indeed virtuous folk were inspired either by people of loose principles offended by the moral demands of the Revival or by rationalistic clergy confronted with a more orthodox creed. Mob violence in particular could easily be seen as mindless hooliganism, sometimes led by clergy and squires in defence of vested interests.

There is indeed truth in all these assumptions, but it is worth probing deeper. Some of the literary attacks were by men of orthodoxy and piety; some indeed by other evangelicals. The eighteenth-century mob is now often seen to have been neither mindless nor simply hooligan. In fact a study of attacks on the Revival helps us to understand the Revival itself, as well as how it was viewed at various levels of society and where its offensiveness was chiefly seen.

The discussion here will be confined chiefly to Wesley and his brand of Methodism. The mob mainly attacked the Methodists and Whitefield; Evangelical Anglicans generally escaped unless they ventured outside their parishes, like Grimshaw at Colne on one occasion, or invited Wesley to preach.[1] Evangelical Anglicans were attacked verbally for Calvinism and irregularities, and responded by reference to the Thirty-Nine Articles and Homilies, which supported their arguments against salvation by 'works'.[2] But in the eighteenth century all groups were liable to be seen indiscriminately as 'Methodists', and attacked in terms appropriate to their extremists.

1. Methodism and the mob

An entirely new perspective has been given to our view of this subject by Dr Walsh's admirable study of anti-Methodist mobs in the light of modern understanding of the eighteenth-century crowd.[3] Rioting was very common in this century, partly because there were very few legal and regular ways for ordinary people to express their grievances; partly because it was difficult to control large crowds except by calling in the military. Methodism was in any case often penetrating areas where control was at its weakest. Riots were mostly over corn prices and wages; sometimes over politics; less often over religion. Religious riots have been less studied than most and usually came in the form of 'Church and King' against Dissent, as in the Sacheverell affair of 1710 and again in the 1790s; or the Gordon Riots against Roman Catholics in 1780.[4]

The anti-Methodist riots were not usually on this scale but mostly short-lived local affairs, though they were notable for their frequent occurrence in the early years of the Revival (they came less often later). Some were not so much full-scale riots as cases of a few rowdies breaking up services, frightening women or throwing the preachers in the duck-pond. Some, however, were cases of large organized mobs, egged on by clergy or gentry, and given more scope by the failure of magistrates to act. They were not necessarily actually murderous, but could in part be intended to intimidate and frighten people off from becoming Methodists.

Such a reading of the situation of course implies that mobs were targeted, directed and controlled. This is what modern research on the subject suggests. They had leaders (the 'captain' often figures in Methodist cases) and specific objectives: corn-merchants, toll-gates, affluent Catholics, according to the occasion, and other businesses and targets were left untouched. It should be added, indeed, that mobs could get out of hand or become the cover for private vendettas or criminals, so that current fashions in interpretation should not ignore this.[5]

Before we analyse the apparent motives for anti-Methodist mobs, it is instructive to notice Methodist reactions to them. Initially these were a mixture of quite understandable alarm, frequent steadfastness and heroism. If the blood of the martyrs is not always the seed of the church when persecution is systematic, spasmodic persecution has sometimes fortified the saints, although there were also the inevitable apostasies. The 'primitive Christianity' image is once again appropriate here, for the Wesley brothers (perhaps especially Charles) sometimes approached the threat of mob violence with the exalted frame of mind of any early Christian martyr. The mob, like the convulsionaries in Bristol, seems to have given them a sense of re-living primitive Christianity, and the language of their descriptions reflects this, notably in the several days of riots at Wednesbury where they were swept up as in 'a raging sea'.[6]

However, if John Wesley's accounts can be believed, both brothers had some miraculous escapes, and from their point of view the adjective is literally correct. John several times passed through with little injury, and assaulters mysteriously stayed their hands. Unless he was exaggerating their murderous intent, one may perhaps suppose that his calm or charisma unnerved them; and sometimes mob leaders suddenly became his protectors.[7]

Methodists could also protect themselves. There is some suggestion at the first Conference that like other 'primitivists' early Methodists hesitated over whether Christians ought to go to law at least against their own brethren if not against outsiders.[8] When pressed for military service, they mostly did their duty while trying to get release, though John Nelson unusually offered passive resistance till they got rid of him. Occasionally a brawny Methodist would guard the preaching house with a strong arm.[9] Wesley soon seems to have overcome any scruples he may have had about going to law, and Whitefield even got a royal proclamation against an alleged would-be assassin.[10] Enthusiasm here was tempered with discretion, appeals to law and order, and the rights of free-born Englishmen to the protection of the King's justice.

But what stirred up the mob in the first place? Methodists often blamed the local clergy and gentry. There were certainly some cases of this kind; also stimulation by farmers and innkeepers. The Revd George White in Colne was a flagrant example: he issued a kind of mock proclamation against the Methodists.[11] A show of legality could be given to this by claiming that Methodist meetings were illegal under the Toleration Act, and of course Wesley equivocated here, because he did not wish Methodists to be branded as Dissenters. Magistrates could refuse to grant licences when applied for.[12] They sometimes failed to act against the mob, and this was taken for tacit approval. Wesley himself maintained that mobs could be quelled when magistrates firmly did their duty, but flourished when they did not.[13] He generally got more protection from the higher courts in the legal hierarchy, for at this level there was a distaste for anything that looked like persecution for merely religious reasons.

Some mobs were aggravated by threats to particular trades: alehouse keepers, musicians, actors and entertainers. These felt Methodist moralism to be a threat. It was said that harping had declined in Wales as Methodism grew, and certainly the Methodists were hostile to popular amusements.[14]

But vested interests and urging on by the local ruling class is not a sufficient explanation in all cases; and even leaders need a willing audience and followers. Criminal elements and crowd psychology offer only a partial explanation. Some cases suggest rather the reaction of a whole community against the Methodist intrusion as a threat to their values, way of life and sense of communal identity. This is indicated by the fact that some leaders regarded themselves as good churchmen, and perhaps in a conventional sense they really were. Thus at Barnard Castle, after mobbing the Methodists, the persecutors went to church and received the sacrament as if they had performed a religious exercise; certainly they must have seen themselves as defending the church. In other places the church bells were rung as a sign of triumph. In another, rioters received a hero's welcome when they were acquitted at Quarter Sessions. The bell-ringing in particular suggested triumph after repelling an invasion – which is probably how it was regarded.[15]

The root cause of such attacks, indeed, Dr Walsh suggests, lay primarily in 'the feeling of xenophobia and outraged tradition aroused by the "new religion"'. For it is important to realize how easily hostility and suspicion towards strangers could be aroused in eighteenth-century communities. This was particularly so if they arrived in a body and challenged local custom, as at fairs and wakes, like John Bennet and his friends at Islip in 1748. Here they were asked for silver and asked why they did not swear. Near Haworth that year the Methodist hymn-singing competed with drums and guns at a rush-bearing, as if the French and English armies were clashing; but uglier scenes could easily occur.[16] Individuals with strange accents, with no apparent means of support, singing hymns to gather a crowd and preaching a strange message, in some cases condemning the local clergy and popular customs, soon aroused hostility.

Those converted to Methodism locally soon seemed to stand out unpleasantly for their changed behaviour, their habit of reproving their neighbours (even their betters), looking holier than thou and meeting in mysterious private gatherings. This also upset personal and family relationships which was particularly disruptive if, as often happened, the young defied their parents and indeed tried to convert them, or wives their husbands.[17]

It was also claimed that people were led to neglect work to go to meetings.[18] Preachers, especially the more eccentric ones, could be seen as travelling cheapjacks, and their low, unlearned status was a standing challenge to the clergy with whom they were in conscious rivalry. Moreover, despite the Wesleys' warnings, preachers often openly attacked the clergy as 'dumb dogs' and 'Pharisees'. The classes and bands attracted the same kind of timeless calumnies about secret orgies and unspeakable sexual horrors that all sects have suffered in the course of history.[19]

In fact, at this level of popular feeling Methodism attracted the same dark myths and defensive savagery as other scapegoats. There are close parallels here with reactions at various times against Jews, Roman Catholics and witches. Whatever explanations may be offered for witch crazes (and modern study has not really produced a consensus here), the aura of supernatural beliefs and phenomena which clung to Methodism and its own lively sense of the diabolical made this last parallel especially significant. It could create awe, even a useful affinity with popular beliefs, but also hostility. Methodist exorcisms and healings could place preachers in fruitful rivalry to the clergy; they could earn some of them a reputation as white wizards, but they could also arouse the scapegoat complex.[20]

In terms of prevailing conventional social and religious norms Methodists could seem to be anti-religious, anti-social and, especially in times of national anxiety about war and invasion, anti-patriotic. This seems to be the explanation of why in the edgy 1740s they were suspected of being Jacobites and mob violence was especially common. Both the Methodists and Moravians were accused of Jacobitism, including Charles Wesley, who was actually hauled before a magistrate on such a charge for praying for 'God's absent ones'. Along with this went the inevitable charge of Popery, which was given colour by some Methodist practices like the class meeting and rumours about it as a confessional.[21]

So Dr Walsh sums up: 'as outsiders, adherents of a new sect that was both little known and highly organized, the Methodists were cast for the role of scapegoat, on whom could be poured the rage and . . . anxiety of their fellows. They were whipping boys for those who felt a compelling need to demonstrate in aggressive fashion their loyalty to traditional national values.'[22]

By the same token this analysis suggests an explanation for the gradual decline of persecution in its more violent forms. It died away as the Methodists ceased to be unfamiliar, mysterious and dependent on strangers. It did not suffer particularly during the American War (and Wesley, we shall see, soon wrote against the colonial rebels as well as against Wilkesites at home). They were certainly suspect of subversion in the chauvinistic, anti-radical and 'Church and King' days of the 1790s, and indeed throughout the French Wars. Then the leadership loudly protested passive obedience, but persecution by mob violence was directed rather against radical Unitarian Dissent. Where Methodism had built a chapel, acquired a few members and trustees of some social standing, or simply become a family and neighbourhood tradition, it had a place as a tolerated and recognized local eccentricity – in some places like Cornwall even the status of a 'popular' creed. Familiarity bred toleration. Above all it was no longer new or simply run by outsiders (in some areas it was largely run by the local people, despite the connexional system and itinerants). A further confirmation of this reading is that mob violence did occur on the old lines in areas where old-style preachers were a novelty, as happened with the Primitive Methodists in the early 1800s or Congregationalists in the rougher and remoter parts of North Lancashire in the same period. It was against wanderers like these that the attempt to tighten up the Toleration Act in 1811 was chiefly directed.[23]

It should be added, however, that local research is still needed to explain local variations in persecution including, perhaps, differences between town and country.

2. Methodism and its critics

Literary attacks on Methodism made more explicit the conscious reasons for the offence it caused by its teaching and behaviour.[24] The charges made can be divided roughly into five categories, though the distinctions are not precise, and in some cases the offence might cause physical violence as well. The charge of 'enthusiasm' was perhaps the commonest, and though a generalized term of abuse, it had a more precise religious meaning as well as various secular associations. Specific theological criticisms of Methodist teaching generally related to the process of salvation. Breaches of church order particularly offended the clergy. Social disruption was a recurring source of annoyance and even fear. Political subversion became a prominent charge in times of public anxiety.

'Enthusiasm' was the bugbear of decent and ordinary Anglicans, and was a charge which in many ways included all the others, for it implied not only religious excess but also social subversion. Its basic theological meaning in the eighteenth century was a claim to extraordinary revelations or powers from the Holy Spirit; and, more vaguely and abusively, any kind of religious excitement.[25] This was exactly what Bishop Butler meant when he accused Methodists of claiming special revelations which he found a 'very horrid thing'.[26] Locke said that men claim a special personal 'revelation' when they cannot account for their opinions by reason.[27] Dr Johnson defined enthusiasm as 'a vain belief of private revelation; a warm confidence of divine favour or communication'.[28] John Wesley agreed. He described enthusiasts as 'those who think themselves inspired by God and are not'. They can be detected by their contradictions of 'the law and the testimony', i.e. the Bible. In practical terms they are 'wanting the end without the means' – like the 'still brethren'.[29]

So far, so good. But how could you test such claims? Might there be genuine private revelations? Wesley's educated contemporaries thought not, and Wesley thought he could refute the charge of enthusiasm by claiming that he and his followers did not claim any *special* revelations beyond Scripture. They simply followed Scripture and the primitive church in their doctrinal teachings and the spiritual gifts and experiences they claimed, which they thought normative for all ages in the history of Christianity. By these standards, too, he could disown those who claimed prophetic and other gifts like George Bell (see below, ch. IX.2). Unfortunately for him, most of his educated contemporaries accepted that many of the charismatic phenomena of apostolic Christianity (including instant conversion) were confined to the apostolic age. In later times sober teaching, right belief and a gradual process of religious nurture and development sufficed. Anything beyond this was 'enthusiastic'. The same applied to miracles. They were acceptable to the orthodox in the early ages, but dismissed as Popish or other fakes in later times. The Deists, more logically, dismissed them all.

In defence of Methodism, Wesley played down the more extraordinary supernatural claims of his followers such as dreams, visions, healings and revelations.[30] They certainly delighted in such things as evidence of the truth of their cause and the reality of their salvation. Wesley himself allowed far more credit to them than he admitted in apologetic contexts. He publicized the convulsions in his *Journal* despite his uncertainty about them, and included many other incidents which he plainly thought confirmed the truth of his cause. Privately, to Charles, he had no doubt of divine intervention to maintain his work. Blasphemers were punished; rain stopped where he preached, and so on.[31] As Alexander Knox perceptively remarked, 'Mr Wesley would have been an enthusiast if he could', and was peculiarly prone to instant judgments and beliefs in matters supernatural.[32] This was also what contemporary critics thought. As the Revd Lewis Jones remarked in 1747:

> Is not your answer then evasive when you shift the point in question, and ask whether there be any enthusiasm in the love of God, etc.? . . . You know that censure was laid on the pretended revelations and seraphical flights in your and Mr Whitefield's journals, and on the ecstatic fits and fancied impulses, feelings and visions of some of your followers, all of which have certainly a strong tincture of enthusiasm. And as to speculative points, that censure was likewise passed on the Methodist doctrines of an imaginary new birth, an imaginary new faith and an imaginary assurance.[33]

Wesley put his finger on a problem which would have occurred even if there had been no strange fits. This was that 'whatever is spoken of the religion of the heart, and of the inward change by the Spirit of God, must appear enthusiastic to those who have not felt them; that is, if they take upon them to judge of the things which they own they know not'. Indeed we shall see that Wesley himself spoke of a class of 'spiritual senses' without which people do not grasp the things of God.[34]

For many contemporaries the strange convulsions and visions could be explained by physiological and psychological causes and discredited by comparisons with Popish and other allegedly faked phenomena. This was the line followed in Bishop Lavington's *Enthusiasm of Methodists and Papists Compared* and a similar work against the Moravians. This diatribe was originally provoked by a fake visitation charge which appeared to show him as favouring the Methodists; but his line of argument was in essence a perfectly serious and common one, and should not be simply dismissed as the bizarre result of a joke that misfired, as is usually done.[35] Rather than writing off such literature as scurrilous and unfair, one should see it as evidence of two uncomprehending world-views in collision, and in Lavington's case an 'orthodox' and not a merely rationalistic one. He accepted revelation and even (apparently) the possibility of diabolical intervention to produce the Methodists' 'effects'.

What gave an additional edge to the charges of enthusiasm in all its forms was that Methodism seemed to be reproducing the horrid and far from forgotten behaviour of the Interregnum, which had strong social and political implications as well as religious ones. In Hogarth's splendid cartoon of 'Credulity, Superstitions and Fanaticism' (1762), at the height of Methodist perfectionist claims, a fanatical preacher addressed a hysterical congregation. Tucked in odd corners were Whitefield's *Journal*, Wesley's sermons and older works on witchcraft, demonology and apparitions, while recent frauds like the woman who gave birth to rabbits or the seventeenth century boy who vomited nails also appeared.[36] Just as some attacked Methodism as an innovation, so others attacked it as a revival of old fanaticisms like the parson who compared it to Puritanism and said it was an old religion and therefore a false one.[37]

Specific doctrinal criticisms of Methodism generally related to various points in the evangelical scheme of salvation which, together with points about church order, were the subjects of Wesley's correspondence with his more serious clerical critics, such as the pseudonymous 'John Smith' (often, though improbably, identified with Archbishop Secker), John Downes, Thomas Church, Bishop Gibson and Bishop Warburton.[38]

It should be noted that in Gibson and early critics the charges made often lumped together the views of Whitefield, Wesley and the Moravians and hence created the impression that all the 'Methodists' were Calvinists and therefore undermined the need of good works – much to Wesley's annoyance. This was in fact understandable, in that strong doctrines of justification by faith common to all, especially in the early years, seemed to many critics to do away with the need of steady religious nurture and good works and led to antinomianism. Whitefield had offended not only by the impressions of enthusiasm and morbidity and pride in his journals but also by his outspoken condemnation of the *Whole Duty of Man* and Tillotson's sermons as little better than Mahometanism, a bare heathen morality. It is not clear whether Wesley endorsed this publicly at first – he may have done, since he certainly at first strongly preached justification by faith and not works against the usual contemporary views of a mixture of grace, effort and sincerity. Later he printed a version of the *Whole Duty* and by no means despised Tillotson, in strong contrast to Whitefield or Evangelicals like Henry Venn in his *Complete Duty*.[39]

At the heart of the offence here was the old suspicion which had dogged the Reformation that its emphasis on justification by faith alone and attacks on salvation by works meant that it discouraged moral effort and led to antinomianism, especially when coupled with the doctrine of predestination. This was the fear which had led to the production of the *Whole Duty* in the late 1650s, and there was always a social dimension here – a fear of undermining public order and morality. In the 1740s this fear was renewed, and to struggling saints as well as hardened sinners the idea that there was a short cut to salvation by faith alone was exhilarating, yet also potentially dangerous. Was this not salvation without any good works at all, salvation even by mere feeling?

A characteristic example of criticisms of such a supposed position may be found in Bishop Gibson.[40] Methodists are guilty of antinomianism; they teach that God has done all and left nothing for us to do but believe; they make sudden and secret impulses their guide for life. They preach justification as a sudden, instant gift with an absolute assurance of salvation; they preach 'sinless perfection'. In his 1744 *Observations* Gibson spelt out the fear that such doctrines as these would lead to people neglecting the need of good works. This was the more telling, as Gibson had also attacked those who trust to human works alone and neglect the need of grace based on the work of Christ's atonement. His view was that salvation was not by grace alone without any response of works on our part.

Breaches of church order, the creation of divisions in the church and so outright schism, were often charged on 'Methodists' of all sorts, though it was most obviously true of Wesley and Whitefield. This was also a source, as we shall see, of contention with Evangelical Anglicans.

The causes of offence can be seen in Wesley's correspondence with 'John Smith', Thomas Church and Gibson among the non-Evangelicals. The charges included hostility to the clergy and to church worship; extempore prayer; irregular preaching 'up and down'; the use of private societies; and, in general, violation of the limits of the parish system and the rights of the clergy by unauthorized preachers and meetings. Some at least of this activity was seen as arguably illegal, but in any case as being contrary to Anglican norms.[41] Wesley's reply was generally to challenge the claim that he acted illegally by various arguments (as to Bishop Butler about his status as a College Fellow), but in the last resort to say he must obey God rather than man.[42] He also denied that his irregularities meant separation by using some very minimal definitions of the church and conformity to it.[43]

Yet in fact the objections to Methodist behaviour were reasonable enough. Wesley's legal sophistry was at least open to argument; however convincing in terms of the interests of Christianity, his appeal to the high ground was not an adequate defence for an Anglican clergyman nor a plausible definition of conformity to Anglican norms. His picture of Methodism as a mere auxiliary to the Church of England was unconvincing when he allowed men of all sects and none to join his societies. His challenge in legal as well as practical terms to the Anglican parish system and Anglican clericalism and prayer-book religion was much more fundamental than he acknowledged.

Methodism was in fact a disruptive force in parish life, and peculiarly offensive and difficult to deal with, precisely because it was hard to define and confine it like Dissent. Furthermore, Methodist hostility to the clergy was often strong, and even Wesley and Whitefield offended more in this way than Wesley acknowledged in his *Journal*. The famous remarks about 'living and dying in the Church of England' were reactions, as we shall see, to recurring pressure by a section of the preachers and people to secede from the church, and in private Wesley himself was sometimes scathing about the clergy and had to concede that he could hardly answer some of the preachers' criticisms (see below, p. 298).

The criticisms about breaches in church order were not simply reactions of religious and ecclesiastical mortification. They were expressions also of social alarm and outrage. This was partly because the church and clergy were an integral part of the constitution and the ruling order in society, especially at the local level. Attacks on them and challenges to their authority even in religious terms were therefore attacks on the accepted social order. Even Whig anti-clericals were not happy about attacks of this kind from the lower orders. Attacks on unlettered lay preachers reflect not simply professional jealousy but a fear of the return to the chaos of the Interregnum and an overturning of the social hierarchy. It was also claimed that Methodism led to people neglecting their trades for preaching and so damaged the economy.[44] Wesley replied that in fact Methodism encouraged a sense of duty in one's calling and the encouragement of industry. We shall see that in his later years this led him to fear that they grew too wealthy for the good of their souls (see below, p. 366). Whatever the truth of this and speculative Weberian notions about the effects on the capitalist spirit, contemporaries saw rather its social disruptiveness; and Wesley's attacks on the rich and support for the poor encouraged this impression.[45]

Indeed the whole Methodist system with its strongly lay ethos seemed to be a levelling force, and it also divided local communities and family life. Even the plain preaching that all were equally sinners and equally needed grace could be offensive to the upper orders, as in the Duchess of Buckingham's famous comment on Whitefield's preaching. 'Their doctrines are most repulsive, and strongly tinctured with impertinence and disrespect towards their superiors, in perpetually levelling all ranks, and doing away with all distinctions. It is monstrous to be told, that you have a heart as sinful as the common wretches that crawl on the earth.[46] (She did, however, continue to hear him.) It was perhaps as well that Wesley's early experiment in 'apostolic' communism was not widely known.[47]

The disturbing secular implications of Methodism can also be seen in charges of political subversion. It has already been remarked that mob violence was easily raised against Methodism in times of national anxiety and war hysteria as an unpatriotic and subversive fifth column, its strange emissaries probably being disguised Papist Jacobites. This was particularly evident in the 1740s for obvious reasons, and tended to be confined to such tense periods. Methodist rhetoric against the corruptions of the times and immorality in high places had a certain congruity with opposition rhetoric, and some case might be made for it being in certain cases a vehicle for popular expressions of this.[48] But perhaps one should rather look to the old tendency to use slogans about the hated and feared thing as being applied indiscriminately, like the seventeenth-century charges against Quakers (of all people) as both Popish and witches or calling one's enemies with generous impartiality 'Jesuited Anabaptists'.[49]

It is fair to add that not all men of education and culture saw the Revival in totally negative terms. Lady Huntingdon's efforts produced at least a hearing from a surprising variety of the aristocracy, especially their women folk, and Evangelicals captured the Clapham Saints at the end of the century. Wesley seldom had adherents like these. Yet there were some who, even if critical of Methodism, grudgingly recognized that it had its uses as gaining a hearing for religion among the lower orders, in a style better adapted to the purpose than that of the parochial clergy. Lord Torrington, who often complained of the decay of the good old rural parish order and the absentee clergy, was quite complimentary about the effect of Welsh revivalism on the people. Dr Johnson was notoriously rude about Whitefield's vulgar manner and women preachers ('his popularity is chiefly owing to the peculiarity of his manner. He would be followed by crowds were he to wear a nightcap in the pulpit or preach from a tree'; 'a woman's preaching is like a dog's walking on his hind legs. It is not done well; but you are surprised to find it done at all.') But he observed that one could not doubt the sincerity of those who travelled without reward; that they might be able to 'excite the affections of the common people' and would impress the minds of convicted criminals – as would a Papist priest – where the regular clergy could not.[50] Late in his life Wesley was almost alarmed to find himself becoming respectable, and Charles Wesley (to shift his brother from schemes of ordination and separation) claimed that some √ of the bishops were quite friendly.[51] The rank and file often fared less well, and the respectability of the aged, venerable John Wesley was a long way from the rough pieties, anti-clerical feeling and simple emotional doctrine of local preachers.

VIII

The Rivals: Methodists and Evangelicals, Churchmen and Dissenters (1738–60)

1. Calvinistic Methodists, Whitefieldites and Huntingdonians

It was shown earlier how the development of the predestinarian dispute had an important role in the rise of Wesley's movement as a separate organization. Predestination did not then go away as an issue. Despite the often friendly relationships between Wesley and Whitefield at the personal level, their followers bickered and competed locally, and in theological terms Calvinism was on several occasions, especially in the 1770s, a major source of division within the Revival, and for some Methodists a cause of anguished episodes in their personal histories.[1]

What is often forgotten is the fact that quite apart from the powerful Welsh Calvinistic Methodist movement, there was also an English one, at least as long as Whitefield and Lady Huntingdon were alive; and that there were more Calvinistic than Arminian evangelicals in Britain as a whole. The eclipse of English Calvinistic Methodism was partly due to the personalities and policies of their leaders. Whitefield often disclaimed any intention of being more than an evangelist to all the churches, and certainly disliked being tied into the kind of routine societary supervision which made up a good part of John Wesley's life. He thought any connexion he supervised would be but a 'Penelope's web', liable to unravel as soon as woven. He also opposed the efforts of some of his admirers to set up separate societies of their own, including cases like John Edwards in Ireland. Whitefield later feared that Edwards would split the evangelical forces in Leeds by acting in rivalry to Wesley – as he did.[2]

Yet Whitefield was not consistent. It is often forgotten that he too had a 'Connexion'. 'Tabernacles' were built by his followers in several places in addition to his own in London's Moorfields; and the Moorfields Tabernacle was the headquarters of a connexion which had association meetings for several years on the Welsh model.[3] The association recorded that it had separated from Wesley over 'election, sinless perfection, perseverance and universal redemption'. Later, it was explained that 'Christ alone is our compleat righteousness, holiness and sanctification and that the very first moment we believe we stand compleatly holy and pure before God in him'. That is, in effect, we only possess holiness by 'imputation' of Christ's holiness – very like Zinzendorf's view expressed to Wesley in Lincoln's Inn Fields. Although the association added that our faith always produces good works, they are done freely and do not win us salvation.[4]

The association met in various places several times a year as in Wales, to settle doctrine and organization; to receive preachers into connexion and to allocate their stations. It was less tightly controlled and centralized than the Wesleyan organization, and effectively lacked a single controlling head. Whitefieldite 'Tabernacles' were indeed named after the mobile tent sanctuaries of ancient Israel, for Whitefield at first did not visualize that his Moorfields place would necessarily remain where it was. He was unhappy about its close proximity and obvious rivalry to Wesley's Foundery. This Tabernacle's internal organization is revealed by the minutes for 1743. It was a 'society' with 'choirs' organized by sex and marital status, as well as 'bands'. There were lovefeasts and 'letter days' for news of revival. In other words, much more Moravian influence was evident than in Wesley's organization. Indeed there was an experiment for a time with a workshop and later a kind of employment agency and a poor relief system.[5]

During Whitefield's absence in America in 1744–5 the system was run by Cennick, and then, after his departure to the Moravians in 1745, mainly by Howel Harris, with Whitefield as a nominal Moderator. In 1749 it was agreed that Whitefield would do all he could to 'strengthen their hands' and would remain 'in connexion with them', but would not 'take the immediate care of any place'.[6] The extent of the connexion is indicated by the stations appointed: London, Bristol, Gloucester, places in Wiltshire, Essex and (unexpectedly) Birmingham. Clearly it was predominantly a West-Country affair; and Whitefield had no societies in the North.

By the end of 1749 Harris had withdrawn to Wales, and what happened then is far from clear. Whitefield was being drawn into Lady Huntingdon's orbit, and without a co-ordinating and active head the connexion probably became looser. The drift to Independency strengthened, especially after Whitefield's death in 1770. The Gloucestershire churches still had their own connexion in 1781, but the 'Rodborough Connexion' in Wiltshire quickly moved to Independency; this was also the fate of the Tabernacles in the larger towns.[7] Socially, the

Tabernacles resembled Wesley's Methodism and the evangelical Independents in their composition – rather lower than Lady Huntingdon's churches.

It is possible that the decline of Whitefield's interest in his connexion in 1749 was connected with his hopes of promotion in the church through the Prince of Wales: a curious and little known episode, the basis of which in reality is hard to establish, though the attempt to penetrate the Leicester House circle of the king-in-waiting is clear enough. But such hopes were dashed by the Prince's premature death in 1751 (see further pp. 372f.).[8]

Whitefield's connexion contributed considerably to the growth of evangelical Dissent; and through Lady Huntingdon he obtained an entry into aristocratic circles denied to Wesley. Lady Huntingdon was in fact an important figure in the Revival whose full significance has never been properly evaluated, for she seems to have defeated the biographers.[9] She was a kind of godmother to the whole Revival. She appears to have come under the influence of the Methodists in 1740 through her sister-in-law Lady Margaret Hastings, who married Benjamin Ingham in 1741. She was certainly very much under Wesley's guidance at first, and is supposed to have been among the little group that seceded from Fetter Lane to the Foundery with him. She also spoke warmly for Christian perfection at this stage.[10] We have seen that she sponsored David Taylor's preaching in the Midlands, and after her husband's death in 1746 she was able to devote all her energies to the Revival.

Lady Huntingdon's drawing-room evangelism, using Whitefield's talents, drew a miscellaneous audience, mingling the pious, the curious and notorious freethinkers like Bolingbroke, whose titles and pedigrees were lovingly recorded by her snobbish biographer. The connections, if not the conversions, were impressive, and Lady Huntingdon was unsparing and uninhibited in her endeavours to save the souls of the aristocracy. She built a series of chapels, those best remembered being in watering-places and spas such as Brighton (1760), Bath (1765) and Tunbridge Wells (1769), though there were others in Worcester and Basingstoke and even Wigan. Though Wesley liked to sniff at the smartness of the furnishings and clientèle of places like this, and pointedly contrasted the 'first here first served' principle of the seating in his chapels as against her reserved and rented pews, Lady Huntingdon had a humbler end to her following as well.[11]

Lady Huntingdon, like Whitefield and Wesley, wished to avoid secession from the church. Her chapels and the ministers associated with her were notionally domestic chapels and chaplains by virtue of her peerage. But she was forced to use lay preachers, and had great difficulty in persuading bishops to ordain such questionable 'Methodists'. So, in 1768, she founded her college at Trevecka for training 'gospel ministers' for the Church of England. In the event few were actually ordained in the Church of England.[12] It seems likely that Whitefield's influence drew Lady Huntingdon into the Calvinist orbit, and although she used the Arminians Fletcher and Benson as President and Tutor of her college, they soon became embroiled in the Calvinist controversy of the 1770s and found they had to leave the college (below pp. 453ff.).

Well before her death, her connexion showed signs of dissolving like Whitefield's 'Penelope's web' and feeding Independency. Dublin already did this in 1772, and was disowned by her, as she wished for a 'general and universal' mission.[13] It is instructive to compare this with Wesley's difficulties in the same place. Both leaders feared that their following would dissipate, and we shall see that a clue is given to Wesley's motives for his ordinations in the fact that in 1782 the Countess wrote that 'an ordination *must* be soon, or the Dissenters will have all our congregations and our students also'.[14]

As it turned out, she was less fortunate or less skilful than Wesley in handling the problem. A group of evangelicals bought a former theatre in Clerkenwell and opened it for her use as Spa Fields Chapel in 1777. This could not easily masquerade as a private chapel, and though Lady Huntingdon did not wish to register it as a Dissenting meeting house, for once she came up against someone as obstinate as herself in the local incumbent, who pursued her through the courts as interfering with his parish. She was forced to choose between closure and Dissent. She chose the latter, licensed Spa Fields as a Dissenting chapel in 1782, and in 1783 formally seceded from the church. The same year she allowed her preachers to ordain a layman. One of the Anglican clergy involved justified the action, as John Wesley would soon do, by claiming that bishops and presbyters were originally of the same 'order'. But one also claimed that he could not subscribe to everything in the Prayer Book such as baptismal regeneration and the burial of sinners with the promise of 'a sure and certain hope of resurrection'.[15]

Secession at once lost Lady Huntingdon the support of Evangelicals who had acted as her chaplains, and helped to precipitate a hardening of their feelings against 'irregularities' for fear of further schisms. The Huntingdon Connexion, which now finally became a new sect, was, as Dr Welch has remarked, almost as much a missionary society as a formal denomination. Itinerancy was of the essence and at the Countess's whim: she moved preachers even faster than Wesley. But she lacked the gift of tight discipline and canny concessions by which Wesley held his army together; the misfortune of being a woman no doubt made things much more difficult. At the time of her death in 1791 she had what has been estimated as between fifty-five and eighty chapels served by her ministers, but very few were controlled by the central trust she had set up for the purpose – a fatal defect. (There were only seven such in 1791.) Shortly before her death there was a scheme for tightening up the connexion with a system of districts, but this was not carried through.[16] The connexion has survived to this day as a very small body, but most of the Countess's legacy dissolved into Independency. One example may show why some individuals left it. At Wigan, William Roby, a former Anglican, was minister in the Countess's chapel, but left for Independency partly because he could not stand an itineracy sometimes requiring moves every few months and partly because he thought that the congregation needed more discipline. He moved to Manchester in the 1790s, and became an Independent and the most fruitful minister of his generation for that denomination in Lancashire.[17] For a time the connexion retained signs of its Anglican roots in that some ministers used the Anglican liturgy; but perhaps more important, like the Independents, they were very firmly Calvinistic.[18] The fate of both Whitefieldites and Huntingdonians provides an instructive contrast with the more tightly-knit Wesleyan cohorts and their leader's endless manoeuvres to retain control of them while avoiding outright secession.

2. Anglican Evangelicals

Instructive, too, are the comparisons and contrasts between the 'Wesleyan' Methodists and Evangelicals in the Church of England.

In the eighteenth century, of course, those later to be seen as adherents of the Evangelical 'Party' in the Church of England were often labelled 'Methodists'. Indeed the distinction was often not easy to maintain at the time, and has sometimes been represented as being more clear-cut than was always really the case in the early days by later Evangelical historians anxious to avoid the stigma of un-Anglican ways and schismatic tendencies. They have perpetuated the orthodoxy that the two groups had separate and independent origins (which is broadly correct) and that they differed from the Methodists mainly on church order (which is at best only half true).[19]

Certainly it cannot be said (as some unwary historians seem to imply) that the Evangelicals were a kind of rearguard remaining in the church when the Wesleyans left it.[20] The claim for an independent origin for the party was already being made in 1834 when Henry Venn was completing a memoir of his grandfather, Henry Venn of Huddersfield, whose conversion certainly owed nothing to Methodism.[21] This seems to be typical of most of the Evangelical leaders, whose conversions were highly individual and isolated from personal or group contacts. They often owed a good deal to literature of various kinds, which illustrates the theories of background influence already discussed. Venn had been a High Church admirer of William Law; Thomas Scott had reacted against Socinian heterodoxy; Grimshaw had read Puritan writings.[22] It is true that some clergy and a good many of the rank and file were converted by Whitefield or Wesley or other Methodists, but as Dr Walsh points out, the party took its tone and outlook chiefly from leaders who had been converted independently.[23]

It followed from this casual and haphazard origin that the distribution of Evangelical clergy was also haphazard and unpredictable, and indeed defies any simple explanation in terms of ecclesiastical or social environment. There were interesting concentrations in Cornwall and the West Riding of Yorkshire, a few in the universities, and a hard patch at first in London. It is curious, for example, that there were several from an early period in Yorkshire, yet very few until much later in Lancashire.[24] The sheer accidents of patronage and individual conversion seem mainly responsible. Later on, other factors make concentrations more explicable. Evangelical patronage and Evangelical incumbents in big parishes with many chapels of ease like Halifax gave rise to crops of Evangelical curates. Rapidly growing northern towns offered openings for proprietary chapels owned by Evangelicals, and in the same places in the early nineteenth century there were openings in new, poor churches and in prison and workhouse chaplaincies.[25]

Balleine claimed that for the Methodists the world was their parish, whereas for the Evangelicals their parish was their world.[26] This is broadly correct, at least in the sense that most Evangelical clergy were parochially based. Wesley had a few clerical helpers with no parochial cure; but on the other hand men like Grimshaw and Fletcher had parishes and helped the Methodists, and so might be classified either as 'Methodists' or 'Evangelicals'. Others had parishes, but worked also outside them at least for a time, like Berridge, Venn and Simeon.

This raises the question of church order, which modern Evangelical historians have claimed to be the fundamental difference between Methodists and Evangelicals from the first. This is questionable, as some of the examples given by Charles Smyth, one of its most influential advocates, shows. Some were irregular from start to finish, like Berridge and Grimshaw; others were irregular earlier but abandoned such habits later, like Venn and Simeon. Others, again, like Walker of Truro, stuck to their own parishes and condemned irregularities from the start. The Revival, in short, was far more untidy and variable than denominational and party historians find it easy to recognize. Distinctions and divisions tended to clarify and sharpen later as a result of controversy, and in the case of the Evangelicals it is clear that fears of schism and social and political conflict made most of them more conformist and less irregular by the end of the eighteenth century. The earlier period was much more fluid.

In all this it should be observed that where church order was upheld against the Methodists, this was not in terms of high theological principle in the manner of the later Oxford Movement but rather on more pragmatic, social or simply legal grounds. The objections were basically practical: irregularities interfered with the rights and control of the parish priest; they offended propriety; they tended to schism and the reinforcement of Dissent. Walker's idea of conformity to the Church of England was not theological at all, but in terms of obedience to ecclesiastical law.[27] It was only later that some Evangelicals talked almost like High Churchmen of the invalidity of non-episcopally ordained men's ministries.[28] And indeed a number of Evangelicals, at least for a time, cooperated with evangelical Dissenters. Some attended their meetings, and laymen like John Thornton not only offered them financial support but in at least one case dissuaded one man, William Jay, from seeking Anglican orders on the ground that he would be more useful as a Dissenter.[29] Here, as with Wesley, gospel imperatives counted for more than formal church order, and one can see how, as in later times, the common gospel of justification and conversion as the mark of 'real' Christianity was felt to give all these groups a common cause against the unconverted in their own denominations.

It can be acknowledged, however, that this 'ecumenical' tendency became steadily less common as the century went on, for the reasons already stated, and that some objected to irregularity from the start – such as Walker or Adam of Wintringham.[30] Those who closely followed the full Methodist-style programme were few. Berridge and Grimshaw were rare examples of men using lay preachers – most Evangelicals eschewed them.[31] It was much more common to preach in unconsecrated buildings and other men's parishes – practices which Venn and Simeon later repented of doing, though they had shown no scruples earlier. Most of them did use religious societies, though not the inner groups of bands, and here too they usually avoided lay leaders for fear of a drift into lay preaching and schism. They preferred to take these groups themselves, rather like the old Religious Societies in Woodward's day.[32]

Evangelicals, and not least those in parish work, had two major problems to contend with. These throw a good deal of light on Wesley's attitude towards irregularities and the use of lay preachers. One was the problem of continuity. Here they were largely at the mercy of the patronage system and the custom of hiring and firing curates. They show little objection to either. This could sometimes operate in their favour, though more often it operated against them at first. The first generation had often been appointed by non-Evangelicals before their conversion, in which case they were irremovable, though some, as mere curates, were sacked.[33] If they were converted before they obtained a permanent living, their position could be precarious. But the greatest problem was of continuity. When an Evangelical died or moved he might be replaced by a non-Evangelical, and then the converts were liable to secede, as happened at Huddersfield and Truro.[34] The seceders founded what eventually became Independent churches – and Venn actually helped the Huddersfield people, though he may have thought of this as an interim measure in hope of better times. (He certainly had much to repent of when he became more conformist later.) This also explains why Wesley, quite apart from other considerations, eventually refused to abstain from having societies and visiting preachers even in Evangelical parishes, for there could simply be no certainty of continuity of their tone.[35] The only solution was to buy up benefices and put them on Evangelical trusts (this was done by the help of Henry Thornton and especially Simeon), or to found proprietary churches. But both solutions were less flexible than the Methodist method, and proprietary churches had to be financed by pew rents, and so were less open to the poor.[36]

Given the clericalist bias of Evangelicalism, the second problem was how to recruit suitable clergy, especially in a largely graduate profession. Some Oxford and Cambridge colleges and halls (St Edmund Hall, Oxford, and Queens', Cambridge, were examples) developed an Evangelical tradition. Keen young men were directed here, and at Cambridge Simeon kept them from temptation by his conversation parties and guided future ordinands (some, however, eventually found his famous 'Skeletons' or sermon outlines a stultifying influence on preaching). Local clerical societies helped to foster fellowship among the beleaguered saints, and in Yorkshire from 1777 a Clerical Education Society helped to finance young men through the universities. It was only at a later stage that theological colleges could ensure nurture in sound party principles, but even after training there was the continuing problem of obtaining ordination and livings when there were no Evangelical bishops on the bench before 1815, and not many for some years after that.[37]

One major difference between Evangelicals and Wesleyan Methodists which has probably not received sufficient emphasis in comparison with church order was doctrinal. The Calvinist controversy bulked much larger between them than is nowadays easy to appreciate. Its implications for a range of doctrines as well as a more general ethos go well beyond the single point of predestination or election. Of course there was much common ground in terms of the emphasis on grace and salvation by faith. Venn and Wilberforce waxed eloquent on the fact that grace and faith alone, and not even a mixture with works and sincerity, would enable a man to be saved.[38] John Berridge's self-composed epitaph, quoted earlier, summed up the evangelical way of salvation.[39]

But Evangelicals distrusted Methodists' alleged reliance on feeling as evidence of conversion and Wesley's idea of a special assurance from the Holy Spirit. Romaine emphasized the joy of feeling that one is in a state of grace, but Walker wrote that 'faith and feeling appear to me direct opposites, and feeling alone cannot be the witness of the Spirit'.[40] Methodist deathbeds were often marked by anxious searches for evidence of being in a state of confidence, but Evangelicals looked rather to a sense of dependence on God's election, regardless of one's feelings of inner comfort (see below pp. 429f.).

Underlying such differences were the Calvinist tradition of a strong doctrine of grace and dependence on God and a distrust of works. Wesley simplified and caricatured this position into the harshest kind of election with all its attendant risks of antinomianism. In reality the Evangelicals varied in their degree of commitment to classic Calvinism, and few had much detailed knowledge of Calvinist scholasticism. Some were not really predestinarians at all, like Edward Smyth. Venn is supposed to have been less so after the death of his first wife, and felt himself 'crucified' between the warring parties. Some, like Simeon, evaded the issue, and were 'Calvinists on their knees but Arminians in the pulpit', which was no bad description of how they often behaved in practice.[41] Their zeal for evangelism was certainly very different from the 'hyper-Calvinist' Baptists, who thought one should not evangelize at all. Their predestination was the moderate type of the Thirty-Nine Articles, and for Anglicans this was a striking and embarrassing point against Latitudinarians, High Churchmen – and Wesley.

Nor could they be accused of neglecting the necessity of good works and the drive to holiness which were strongly urged by Whitefield and Venn. A 'zeal for works truly Christian' and a 'desire to perfect holiness' were urged by Venn.[42] The trouble with Wesley was that he seemed to mingle dependence on effort with dependence on grace; that he visualized perfection as possible in this life; and that he thought men could as readily lose salvation as gain it if they did not keep up the spiritual pressure. To Evangelicals this seemed to make salvation depend too much on human effort, and by grace they believed that the truly saved would infallibly persevere to the end.

There were also differences between Wesleyans and Evangelicals on social lines. This could also be seen between Wesleyans and Huntingdonians until the Countess seceded. Generalization about the Evangelicals here is impossible, simply because as parish ministers their congregations could be as mixed according to the area concerned as other

Anglican parishes. Venn's Huddersfield and Grimshaw's Haworth congregations were much like those of the Methodists in the same kind of area.[43] The point is rather that, by virtue of their position in the establishment, it was inevitable that Evangelicals would collect an upper crust of adherents like the famous Clapham Sect group around Wilberforce, which included a few peers, classes denied to Wesley and indeed not expected by him or even welcomed (see below pp. 493ff.). The lack of clerical support meant that Wesley developed a lowly lay hierarchy and it is also the case that if Methodists followed Wesley's own attitudes, their approach to the poor was very different from the discriminating and censorious attitude which was to become common among Evangelicals (see below ch. X.3).

3. John Wesley, the Methodists and the Church of England: the early phase

A nineteenth-century Wesleyan once remarked of John Wesley's relationship with the Church of England that 'Mr Wesley, like a good oarsman, looked one way and rowed another'.[44] In his later years especially, he often made remarks such as: 'In the Church I will live and die, unless I am thrust out', and: 'If ever the Methodists in general were to leave the Church, I must leave them.'[45] Indeed he thought God would leave them too. From start to finish he denied that he was separating from the church, despite his increasing irregularities, and regularly portrayed Methodism as a mere auxiliary to the church to encourage its more 'regular' life and ministry.[46] But against this have to be set the facts that his contemporaries saw his irregularities almost from the first as a sign of separation; that he admitted Dissenters to his societies; that he was prepared to take any risk (even expulsion) to maintain his connexion in being; and that the need for frequent protests of loyalty and denials of separation in themselves revealed powerful pressures among his followers away from the church.[47]

In judging Wesley's relationship with the Church of England it is necessary to be wary of some of the more doctrinaire views expressed by later Methodists, since they have often been influenced by current denominational relationships and party attitudes to them. There have always been 'Church' and 'Dissenting' Methodists anxious to enrol Wesley for their causes, and twentieth-century ecumenism has distorted history as much as nineteenth-century sectarian strife.

Approaching the eighteenth-century situation, one has to be wary also of Wesley's own words and view them in the light of his situation and actions, as well as the ever-present forces at work among his preachers and people. One well-known example will show how easily one may be misled by taking at face value a piece of Wesley theologizing in the *Journal*. In January 1746 he read Lord King's account of the primitive church, and despite the prejudices of his High Church education thought that if King was right this meant that 'bishops and presbyters are (essentially) of one order, and that originally every Christian congregation was a church independent on all others!' At some point (perhaps even earlier than this) he had read Stillingfleet's *Irenicum*, which he said convinced him that no form of church government was divinely ordained.[48] These works are supposed to have convinced him that originally bishops and presbyters were of the same 'order' and therefore that as a mere presbyter he had the right to ordain, though in fact he was not to exercise this 'right' for another forty years. It is true that Wesley was very prone to jump to unorthodox conclusions on persons and things on the basis of reading one book: the innocence of Richard III or Mary Queen of Scots or the Montanists or the persecuted Puritans are cases in point.[49] But it is also very common for him to use respectable 'authorities' to fortify or justify positions he wished to hold for other reasons; or simply as apologias for actions he had been forced to take by circumstances. He always read his authorities very selectively to support what he wished to do or thought ought to be done, and we shall see that in the case of King and Stillingfleet he had already reached similar conclusions for other reasons. And in all this he responded to events and the needs of the moment. King and Stillingfleet had no effect on his actions in the 1740s and 1750s, and they were only used for apologetic purposes in the 1780s to support actions he had decided to take for practical and not theological reasons.

We have seen that Wesley began as a stiff High Churchman, imposing also peculiar 'primitive' customs on his people in Georgia. Though the Moravians impressed him, he developed doubts about their episcopal orders. But once the Revival began, there were soon signs of the process by which eloquent converts could take the inner call as being more important than outward order, and claim, like Mr Shaw in London in 1739, that they could administer sacraments like any ordained minister.[50] During the next few years pressure from below against the church and clergy increased in two related ways. On the one hand, the sense of righteous evangelical doctrine and life was contrasted with the defective life of the clergy and of Anglican order and worship. On the other, since the Methodist ways and preachers seemed to be superior, why should they be kept in a position of subordination to, and dependence on, the Church of England? The ambitions of some of the preachers to be ministers was a factor here, as Charles Wesley always emphasized, but it was also entirely natural for Methodists to prefer to receive their whole

Christian nurture from those they knew and trusted to be 'truly' Christian.

In the 1740s, as we have seen, criticisms multiplied over Methodist irregularities such as field preaching, lay preachers, societies dividing parishes as well as doctrinal aberrations, and all this was aggravated by the spectre of seventeenth-century styles of enthusiasm in a time of national anxiety.[51] Lay preaching in particular seemed to many critics to be so contrary to Anglican order as to constitute schism and separation. It is not therefore surprising that the early Methodist Conferences from 1744 to 1747 included much discussion of 'discipline' not only for its own sake but also in terms of relationships with the church.[52] In these discussions the striking thing is that Wesley can be seen to be testing his old stiff ecclesiastical views in the light (as he claimed) of Scripture, but even more in terms of the revival experience. In the process he produced very pragmatic and conveniently limited definitions of 'church' and 'conformity' to or 'separation' from the church, as well as a very clear sense that formal 'order' must be subordinated to the practical imperatives of the 'gospel'.

Thus in 1744 the Methodists adopted a narrow reading of Article 19 to define the Church of England as 'the congregation of English *believers* in which the *pure word* of God is preached and the sacraments *duly* administered'. This conveniently ignored the whole question of establishment, canon law and so on. They were then free to assert that membership and zeal for the church was a matter of upholding Christian truth and life; they were to obey the bishops only in 'things indifferent' and they did not separate so long as they preached the church's doctrines and attended its worship. This position Wesley would repeat many times in answer to charges of separation. If in some ways it recalls an almost Anabaptist vision of the church, in others it echoes backwards to the Anglican Puritans of an earlier period and forwards to the rebellious Tractarians of a later. At the time it clearly reflects Wesley's polemic against contemporary clergy, whom he felt were betraying the Church of England's true gospel far more than he was and therefore were practically separating from it, as he was not.[53]

In 1745 the priorities were again made clear: if bishops forbid us to preach the gospel we should obey God rather than man. And then comes an extraordinary exposition of the early development of church order in response to the question whether Episcopal, Presbyterian or Independent church order is most agreeable to reason. Wesley sketches what appears to be a historical account of how church order developed by natural processes when a preacher collected a congregation and then by stages there evolved in succession an Independent, Presbyterian and Episcopal polity. The description seems conveniently to describe how

Methodism arose: with authority vested in Wesley as the initiator of the process! Yet at the same time it appears to offer a naturalistic explanation of the rise of the Christian ministry as such, which by implication disposes of any of the main forms of church order as being of divine ordinance.

In 1746 the question was raised of the light in which our 'helpers' were to be considered; the answer was: 'Perhaps as extraordinary messengers designed of God to provoke others to jealousy' (i.e. concern or emulation).

In 1747 it was once again denied that Methodists divided from the church, but the principle was still that they obeyed the rules of the church only so far as was consistent with obedience to God. As to a 'national church', by 'church' the New Testament meant only 'a single congregation', so a national church was to be seen to be 'a merely political institution'. The implications of the 1745 sketch of church polity are confirmed by the judgment that although the threefold ministry of bishops, priests and deacons is 'plainly described' in the New Testament, there is no pattern ordained by God there for 'all churches throughout all ages'. To say that there was would be to unchurch Continental Protestant churches: 'a shocking absurdity'. Divine right of episcopacy was first asserted in the middle of Elizabeth's reign. So far had Wesley gone from his old ideals. In 1746 'John Smith' had asked where Methodist irregularities would end: surely in the madness of Interregnum days. Wesley asked what he meant by 'order': a plan of church discipline? If so, which? 'The Scriptural? the Primitive? or our own?' Then he enunciated the principle which was emerging behind his practice and in the Conference debates: 'What is the end of all *ecclesiastical order*? Is it not to bring souls from the power of Satan to God? And to build them up in his fear and love? *Order*, then, is so far valuable as it answers these ends; and if it answers them not it is nothing worth.' He then goes into the attack, in effect an attack on the defects of the parish system. 'Order' has not helped the rough places where he preached. But where the knowledge and love of God is, '*true order*' will not be lacking, and without those virtues the most 'apostolical order' is useless.[54]

In comparison with this grand imperative, questions about validity of ministry and sacraments receded into the background and would only emerge when Methodist preachers began to demand their right to administer with or without ordination. Even then, we shall see, Wesley's course of action was decided more by the expediencies of mission than by ecclesiastical niceties, though he thought he could evade a confrontation between the two principles. It is, then, curious that despite the pragmatic pronouncements of the 1745 Conference, as late as

December of that year he could write to Westley Hall in terms which still reflect a stiff High Churchmanship.[55] Here Wesley appears to defend apostolic succession and the necessity of ordination to administer sacraments by bishops in that succession in accordance with the Word of God. Such a ministry involves a form of 'priesthood' and an 'outward sacrifice' in the eucharist. Three orders of ministry were also laid down. All this Hall seemed to think Popish rather than scriptural, and he accused Wesley of being inconsistent in breaking the laws of the church by his irregularities nevertheless; but Wesley denied that he was really doing so. In any case he added the proviso of obeying only as far as conscience allowed. No doubt Hall's questions touched a sensitive nerve, though in fact there was good seventeenth-century High Church precedent for varying the demand for apostolic succession in favour of the Continental churches.[56]

It was only three weeks after this that Wesley read Lord King's book, but as we have seen, the *Journal* account (which was only published seven years later in 1753) was misleading if taken to be a sudden conversion by reading a book.[57] It was, rather, a handy confirmation for defending a position into which he had been forced by events, experiences and very probably a 'providential' sense of special call which had been developing during the past few years. The letter to Hall may be seen as an extreme response to the threat of secession by Hall himself and it is significant that it, too, was included in the part of the *Journal* published in 1753 when the preachers were pressing him hard over relations with the Church of England.

That Wesley seized upon and partly misinterpreted King suggests that he felt that he needed respectable authority to back a position forced on him by gospel imperatives. He had already probably read Stillingfleet some time in the early 1740s (and this may be reflected in the Conference debates). Stillingfleet was writing in the context of conflicts over church order in the 1660s and the policy of 'comprehension': hence he emphasized that all three main traditions had some justification in the New Testament and that none had been prescribed as of divine ordinance. But he later retreated from this to assert that dissent from the Church of England was unnecessary and undesirable. Wesley, as usual, took from the unreconstructed Stillingfleet position what he wanted for his own purposes.[58]

He did the same with King. He took two points from him: that bishops and presbyters were 'essentially' of one order; and that every congregation was originally independent of all others, as he already believed in the 1745 Conference. On various later occasions in the 1750s, 1760s and 1780s he claimed that Stillingfleet had convinced him that apostolic succession was not true; that men could preach who were not apostolically ordained and that as a presbyter he had the right to ordain, but also that such ordination did not entail separation.[59] He does not state that his reading of King in 1746 convinced him of his right to ordain, and if he did think this King did not in fact support him for, while allowing that bishop and presbyter were of the same order originally and had in the early centuries ordained, he said that they were still subject to the bishop as his agent. In fact none of these fine distinctions from the past could stand against the fact that as a presbyter of the eighteenth century Church of England Wesley had no right to ordain at all. Wesley was in fact claiming that he could ordain if he had to, according to very selective early precedents chosen by himself. Much more important was the fact that he had by now clearly enunciated the principle of gospel priorities over all considerations of 'order', and to this position he held for the rest of his life; but it was subject to two equally practical rather than theoretical constraints. One was that he would avoid secession as long as he could for the good of Methodism, and thought that he was safe by the criteria of adhering to Anglican doctrine and attendance at worship. The other constraint was that he would only exercise his supposed powers when the gospel and the maintenance of Methodist integrity demanded it: and that even if he did so he was still not separating, according to his own convenient definition. It may be held that there was another constraint – the teaching of Scripture and tradition – but though at various points Wesley was obviously influenced by Anglican conventions (as in the form of his late ordinations), he could manipulate these and the Fathers to suit his purpose, and they were apologetic devices rather than motives for action. He used precedent to clothe the nakedness of his own will, seen by signs following as the providential will of God for his mission.

For a few years after 1747 it seems that the separation issue was not acute in terms of pressure from the preachers on Wesley. The crisis really built up in the 1750s. In some cases this was mixed up with complaints about Wesley's autocratic rule. Thus in August 1751 he wrote to his brother that Charles Skelton had asked for a kind of 'aristocracy', that the Wesleys should do nothing without the consent of the preachers, and some said that John rules with 'a rod of iron'. But they also railed bitterly against the church. It was this which led John to commission Charles to purge the preachers, and early in 1752 a pact was made to maintain unity, to which Charles added a clause about keeping to the church. The purge was mainly to test the preachers' gifts and sometimes their morals, but Charles was equally concerned about disloyalty and hostility to the church, and he was almost equally afraid that if they depended too much on John for subsistence they would drift into sectarianism, for throughout the troubles that followed he thought his brother was too prone to 'enthusiasm' on the question of ordination and separation.[60] And indeed the crisis which came to a climax in 1755 showed very forcibly how far Wesley was subject to pressure from below; if Charles's cries of anguish can be trusted, he was at times on the very verge of anticipating the ordinations of the 1780s and even outright separation.

In October 1754 Charles recorded that in London Charles Perronet (the son of the Vicar of Shoreham) 'gave the sacrament to the preachers Walsh and Deaves and then to twelve at Sister Garder's'. To this, he claimed, John only said: 'We have in effect ordained already'. 'He urged me to sign the preachers' certificates, was inclined to lay on hands, and to let the preachers administer.' A few days later: 'He is wavering; but willing to wait before he ordains or separates.' Other preachers had administered, and Charles wrote bitterly to a friend that 'since the Melchisedechians have been taken in, I have been excluded his cabinet council'. John was only thinking ordination not expedient rather than unlawful, and the rebel preachers were urging that he might ordain without separation.[61] Charles pictured an unscrupulous cabal plotting against the church and for a separation through ordinations by his brother, whom he saw as fatally weak-willed. He busied himself in drumming up support for a rival pressure-group and enlisted Grimshaw, who threatened to leave the Methodists if they allowed the preachers to administer communion.[62]

The Conference of 1755 was the scene of a three-day debate on the matter which underlined its seriousness, and for this Wesley prepared a statement on 'Ought we to separate from the Church of England?', arguing the pros and cons in detail. Though he came down heavily against the expediency of doing so, he was less clear on the lawfulness of such a step, which continued to alarm Charles, and though the *Journal* is understandably reticent, letters reveal how hard the preachers pressed him and how difficult he found it to refute some of their objections to the Church of England's worship and discipline.[63]

In his prepared document Wesley rehearses the familiar definition of the Church of England in terms playing down its laws. So far as its defective spiritual courts and worship and the like are concerned one need only 'leave the evil and keep the good'. Rather disingenuously he allows that he cannot himself agree with everything in the church, but one did not need to do this except to hold a benefice. On administering the sacraments, though it might be useful to hold them together, he thought it, if lawful in itself, not expedient and therefore 'not now lawful to us'. He was also rather evasive in reply to those saying he had already separated by appointing men to preach, for he said that he had not 'appointed' but merely 'permitted' them to do so, after they began of their own accord. In any case this did not imply that he did or could appoint them to administer sacraments. Unlike preaching, this was not necessary to save souls, and the authority to preach did not carry with it authority to administer: that requires a different order of ministry.

Whether lawful or not, it was not expedient for Methodists to ordain, as this would be little less than a formal separation from the church, a step Wesley argued against for a dozen reasons. It seems significant that these were overwhelmingly practical, in terms of the damage to the Methodist mission which ordination would cause by dividing them, diverting their energies to constitution-making and prejudicing people against them, as well as damaging their special mission to the church and dooming them, like earlier rebels, to the futility of a sect. (This reveals very well the practical reasons why Wesley clung to his irregular connection with the church, and made much sense.) He agreed that Methodists should be kept in a compact body, but not in terms of separation: hence they should respect and not attack the clergy and should avoid Dissenting meeting houses. Indeed, he contrasted the dull worship and heterodox doctrines of Arian and predestinarian Dissenters with the prayers and sermons of the church, despite the criticisms made of the latter.

In a letter to Walker of Truro, Wesley explained the criticisms made of the church at the Conference: the unscriptural nature and lack of free prayer in the liturgy; the 'Popish' and 'heathen' laws and procedures of the church courts; ministers who had not received an inward call and who did not teach true doctrine. 'I will freely acknowledge that I cannot answer these arguments to my own satisfaction.' He added that Walker's argument that the essence of the church lay in its laws rather than its worship and doctrines made matters more difficult. So he fell back once again on his old formula of conformity in doctrine and worship alone. Rather than give up his 'irregularities' he would separate. Least of all would he give up the preachers whose existence Walker took to be a clear mark of schism.[64]

According to Wesley the Conference fully agreed in the end that whether it was lawful or not to separate, it was not expedient.[65] For Charles Wesley his brother was 'dissimulating', and the failure to rule the idea 'unlawful' was ominous from his point of view – if circumstances changed he might think it *was* expedient. Nor would he suspend the dissidents as Charles wished, but 'sent them in a body to Ireland' (!). Very characteristically John fell back on the principle that what mattered most was holiness and, without approving of the rebel preachers' views, prayed for more of their spirit. Nor did he approve of Charles expelling a preacher for not going to church as well as drunkenness.[66]

In terms of preserving the force of Methodism John was in fact wiser and more realistic than Charles or the Evangelicals with whom he corresponded. At the same time John's correspondence with Walker and with Thomas Adam of Wintringham showed how firmly he held to the priority of right doctrine and practical fruits against the demands of formal law and order in the church. Walker stuck to the question whether separation was lawful or otherwise rather than a matter of changeable expediency, and saw the very use of lay preachers as a key issue. Adam of Wintringham disposed of Wesley's sophistry over the distinction between 'permitting' and 'appointing' preachers and agreed with Walker that this was a clear breach of the laws of the church. Walker tried to reply to the preachers' criticisms of Anglican defects: any church and ministry had faults, and if these were grounds for separation, then there would be endless separations.[67] To Adam, Wesley reaffirmed that he would not go out unless thrust out, and (a familiar ploy) minimized his irregularities as minor 'variations' from the Church's rules for duty's sake. But he added an important fundamental justification for lay preaching which was more revealing of his real motives for accepting it. In 'ordinary' cases both an inward and outward call are necessary; but there is something far from 'ordinary' in the present case, and those called by God but not men have more right to preach than those called only by men. Many of the clergy are called by men but not by God. Wesley concluded that he knew he had not gone too far in this matter, and only wondered whether he had gone far enough in view of the 'blindness' of some clerical guides of the flock. 'Soul-damning clergymen lay me under more difficulties than soul-saving laymen!' Even the Evangelical clergy who stuck to Anglican parish conventions had little fruit: Grimshaw and Baddiley only began to save souls when they became 'irregular'. 'Can there be a stronger proof that God is pleased with *irregular* even more than with *regular* preaching?'[68]

It is no wonder that talk like this which revealed Wesley's main criterion for irregularity should have seemed like stark enthusiasm. It also underlines his divergence from his brother. To Walker in 1756, shortly before the annual Conference, Charles wrote proposing a scheme for dropping unsound preachers and preparing the sound ones as soon as possible for orders. John should also bind them and himself to keep strictly to the church, and do nothing without the approbation of the Evangelical clergy. He later acknowledged to Walker that lay preaching is a 'partial separation' and 'may, but *need* not, end in a total one'.[69] Walker wrote to John that some of the preachers should be ordained and the rest kept only as 'inspectors or readers', serving in individual societies. Charles agreed with this in substance but said that John would not agree.[70] The Conference of 1756 resolved that it was not lawful to leave the church so long as it was 'lawful and possible to continue in it'.[71] But later that year Wesley replied to Walker's proposal. He repeated his principle that he had only one point in view – to spread vital religion – and that as the preachers helped this, he would keep them. Walker's scheme would not help. He instanced Walker's own county of Cornwall: the ordained and settled would preach the people asleep for lack of change and deprive other places; the 'readers' would be crippled by unevangelical clergy. And in any case what right had he to stop people with a call from God?[72]

Meanwhile Charles was worrying away at the poor standards of the preachers and their rude remarks about the church and clergy: he confided to his *Journal* that John Hampson and others were going around calling their venerable parent 'Old Peg'.[73] Even John Wesley persuaded himself that by railing against the church a preacher in Yorkshire had damaged the society, but that he was punished by God by being press-ganged as a soldier.[74] Walker now suggested that Wesley should place his societies under the parish clergy. Wesley responded that they would suffer under unsatisfactory clergy and that withdrawing the preachers would hasten separation in such circumstances. This was a telling point in view of the secession from Walker's own congregation after his death and the appointment of his non-Evangelical successor. Indeed when Wesley tried the experiment of not appointing preachers in Henry Venn's Huddersfield parish in the 1760s, this had not stilled criticism of Methodist doctrine.[75] Obstinate and unco-operative though Wesley seemed to be, there was much truth in his belief that, given the nature of Methodist feeling, abstinence from the use of societies and preachers even in Evangelical parishes would have dissipated his connexion and hastened piecemeal secession from the church. As the fate of Walker's and Venn's congregations showed, only by the Wesley scheme could continuity be guaranteed. But underlying this was also a distrust by each party of the doctrines of the other: Calvinist versus Arminian. Charles Wesley and Walker were in any case deceiving themselves about the possibility of getting the preachers ordained, though Charles sometimes made them optimistic promises to that effect. How could he hope to succeed in persuading bishops to do so when even Lady Huntingdon often failed? He could only console himself by following the preachers round with 'buckets of water' to quench their inflammatory talk against the church![76]

Then, in 1760, the controversy over ordination and separation flared up dramatically once more.[77] In February of that year three preachers in Norwich administered the Lord's Supper of their own volition. The peculiar history of this society probably helps to explain why the revolt should have taken place here. James Wheatley had been one of Wesley's less satisfactory preachers. After some spectacular successes in Norwich he had caused scandal by seducing women and was expelled. Apparently he then redeemed himself, and he and Lady Huntingdon founded a Tabernacle for Whitefield's followers; for once they co-operated with the Wesleys even to sharing class meetings and communions. But Norwich had a strong Dissenting tradition, and the Tabernacle congregation was accustomed to receive communion from its own preacher: it seems likely that pressure from this quarter helped to precipitate the Methodist preachers' action in 1760.[78]

The Wesley brothers reacted in characteristically different fashions. John calmly set off on his travels as usual, merely sending Charles to investigate. Charles thought that the Norwich preachers would corrupt the rest and drive Methodism into Dissent. He chided John for his 'weakness' and for 'conniving' at such things too long.[79] Yet John seemed irresolute or worse, since he wished to leave a decision till Conference. Charles thought that this would allow the malcontents to poison the rest and win a majority in Conference for separation.[80]

In fact John had other thoughts in mind. Apart from his usual journeys, he was making fascinated enquiries into the numerous cases then being thrown up by a rash of perfectionist revivals in various parts of the country (see below, ch. IX.2, for this). This is what shows up most strongly in his *Journal*, and he proceeded as if there were no crisis brewing up behind him. It is very probable that this startling confirmation of his favourite doctrine outweighed in importance any little local difficulties of the kind that alarmed Charles. Providence would solve this, as Providence had given the greater work.

Charles darted off letters to his cronies and, as Tyerman remarked, seemed to be marshalling a party against his brother. He threatened to leave the Methodists. He said that if, as some claimed, an ordination could not be avoided, it should be into the Anglican Church: God would provide for this. He charged the preachers with deceit for taking licences (as some did) as Dissenting ministers and then telling the people that they were members of the church, but claiming the protection of the Toleration Act in the face of press gangs and persecutors. To John Nelson Charles wrote: 'rather than see thee a Dissenting minister, I wish to see thee smiling in thy coffin'. When Christopher Hopper asked what would happen to the preachers and their families after the Wesleys' death he replied with his usual wishful optimism that he would use his 'interest' to get them church ordination. Joseph Cownley was rightly sceptical about such a prospect, especially in terms allowing for Methodist itineracy. The prospect of ministry in one place (Anglican or Dissenting) was exactly what several of them did not want, and this, as well as the dissolution of the connexion, John Wesley always feared and resisted. But in his obsession with the church Charles appeared quite willing to see this as the lesser evil.[81]

Charles then enrolled Grimshaw in his campaign, and with his aid tried to stir up the London societies by letter with hostility to the multiplication of licensing of preachers and meeting houses as if they were Dissenters, which he claimed that John was approving. Grimshaw, too, saw the Methodists as no longer members of the Church of England but arrant Dissenters; if so, he would part company with them. Significantly, he thought the 'people' were also affected: they wanted a settled ministry and claimed that they could not conscientiously receive the church sacrament, so they wanted their own ordinations.[82] When Charles read this letter to the London societies it 'put them in a flame', and 'all cried out against the licensed preachers'; many said they should be silenced immediately. In significant and total contrast with his brother (but very much like Walker and the conformist Evangelicals), Charles declared that his 'chief concern on earth was the prosperity of the Church of England; my next, that of the Methodists; my third, that of the preachers': he would give them up for the sake of Methodism and the Methodists for the good of the church.[83] Nothing could have been more subversive of John Wesley's sense of priorities or of what was needed to sustain his mission.

Despite all this hysterical talk and intrigue, the Conference of 1760 resolved the crisis, at least for the time being. John had apparently only 'gently rebuked' the Norwich men, but he argued that preaching and administering the 'ordinances' were separate offices and that he was not clear that he had power to ordain unless they were 'wholly cut off from the Church by a public act'. Many spoke on the opposite side, saying that they were already dissenting from the church and that licensing and ordination would remove the prejudices of the Dissenters. Howel Harris, who was present, said that he and Charles were 'the rough workers' while John behaved 'more meekly', though saying that he 'could not ordain' and that he 'could renounce them in a quarter of an hour'.[84] Reading between the lines, one senses that it was not so much Charles Wesley's propaganda and threats of resignation as John Wesley's authority and *his* implied threat to desert them that carried the day. The preachers ceased to administer the sacraments and Grimshaw stayed with the Methodists. The next major crisis, with a very different result, would not arise until the 1780s.

Yet the process of licensing preachers and preaching-houses continued, and Wesley had not really changed his mind about the possibility of the power to ordain and perhaps separation in some circumstances. He had reacted very temperately to the Norwich affair, and his correspondence with Walker showed very clearly that he had no intention of following Charles' prescription for localizing the preachers by the dream of Anglican orders. In all this he almost certainly had a strong sense of Methodism's special providential mission that God would preserve. In 1761, in one of his rare moments of intimate confession, he wrote to Charles: 'I do not at all think (to tell you a secret) that the work will ever be destroyed, church or no church . . . I have done at the last Conference (of 1760) all I *can* or *dare* do.'[85] His hesitations about ordination were probably less about its legality than about its possible effect in splitting Methodism: an essentially practical concern.

If the problem in its explosive form in 1755 and 1760 did not recur for another twenty years, and then in the shadow of Wesley's increasing age and the problem of the future, the urge to obtain ordination from some apparently orthodox episcopal source continued to attract. Wesley himself appears to have felt the need for providing for more places for communion than the few where he and his brother and one or two friendly clergy provided for it. Could a few of the preachers obtain orders yet continue to itinerate? An unexpected opportunity for this seemed to offer itself in 1764–5 through the person of a supposed Greek bishop called Erasmus with the almost suspiciously appropriate title of Bishop of Arcadia.[86] Wesley befriended Erasmus and Erasmus ordained several preachers, some without Wesley's knowledge. It was rumoured that Wesley had countenanced all of them and that he was trying to get Erasmus to ordain him as a bishop. The result was an open scandal. Wesley disowned the new 'ministers' and expelled them, though two later received regular Anglican orders. The whole episode reinforced suspicions about Wesley's 'ambition'. Erasmus was probably a fraud, but in any case no such clandestine and irregular ordinations could have solved the problem of Methodist relations with the Church of England.

Apart from the general problem of Anglican–Methodist relations there was also the particular problem of relations between Methodists and Evangelicals which, as we have seen, were strained in several cases by the question of 'irregularity'. Wesley dreamed from time to time of a closer union with the Evangelical clergy, and in the late 1750s he seems to have been particularly concerned to cultivate them with the help of Lady Huntingdon. Hopes in this direction were, however, hampered by the tension over irregularities, over Calvinism and in the 1760s by the perfectionist outbreaks.[87] In 1764 he wrote a circular letter proposing co-operation on the basis of the doctrines of original sin, justification by faith and 'holiness of heart and life'. They could agree to differ on 'opinions' and 'outward order', such as 'perfection', 'imputed righteousness' and 'regular' or 'irregular' methods. But this was to gloss over as secondary what many Evangelicals saw as primary differences; nor did Wesley himself really regard the Calvinist points as optional. A revised version of the letter was sent to some forty or fifty clergy in 1766, but received only three replies.[88]

When Wesley invited some of the Evangelical clergy to the Conference in 1764 a dozen came, but the old bugbears soon divided the parties. Pawson said the clergy tried to convince them that preachers should not go where there was an Evangelical incumbent, and Charles Wesley unhelpfully said that if *he* were such a minister no preacher should preach in his parish. But some of the more outspoken Methodists like John Hampson said that he would preach without Charles's leave, 'and should think I had as good a right so to do as you had'. Charles called him a 'grievous wolf' who would 'tear the flock'.[89] By the end of the 1760s the Calvinistic controversy was finally rendering all such overtures hopeless, and Wesley's epitaph on his efforts was that he gave them up: 'they are a rope of sand'. He then turned, as we shall see, to devise plans for securing the coherence of his own connexion after his death.[90]

All these controversies and attempts at co-operation merely served to confirm the distinctiveness of the Wesleyan position, while it also raised the question of how to hold the preachers and the connexion together after Wesley's death. Separation had been avoided and the preachers kept in their ambiguous and subordinate place, but Wesley had preserved their independence of action; recognized their special calling; and in the last resort asserted his authority over the connexion against the intrigues of Charles Wesley, who was now clearly unreliable and no longer an effective partner in his labours and leadership but a kind of erratic free agent, unwilling to accept a planned place in the itinerancy yet engaging in it when it suited his pro-church purposes. John could always score over Charles by virtue of his intimate knowledge of the connexion and his superior hold over the preachers, for whom he had more respect than Charles ever showed. He could always find a use even for the less able.[91]

Neither brother was entirely consistent in his attitude to the church, and if anything Charles was less consistent than John. He, too, was irregular, yet arbitrarily prevented mere laymen from being so.[92] Subordinating the Methodists to 'order' not only made his attitude fundamentally different from that of his brother, but would have made the Methodist mission impossible and pointless. Frank Baker has suggested that all through Wesley's life there were two conflicting views of the church in him: as a historical institution linked with the apostolic age by organic ties through the apostolically-ordained hierarchy; and as a fellowship of believers using whatever means came to hand to win others and organize themselves. He had been reared in the first view; circumstances and 'providential openings' led him towards the second, but something of the earlier view persisted in him and helps to account for his fluctuating course.[93] However, it has been emphasized here that in the last resort it was the second view which ultimately prevailed and that Wesley used selected material from tradition to justify his irregular actions. Ties with the church were valued not for theoretical but practical reasons: to avoid divisions within Methodism and to avoid creating a localizing sect. It was not so much an obsession with 'order' that kept him in the church as the failure of the church to thrust him out that preserved Methodism from separation. Despite his ingenious distinctions, Wesley opposed separation as inexpedient rather than unlawful, and clearly allowed that he would separate rather than give up his system. One may well conclude that for all his skilful manoeuvering it was the failure of the authorities to expel him that enabled him proudly to 'live and die in the Church of England'. To do so at all costs was certainly not his aim.

4. 'A Catholic spirit'? John Wesley, Dissent, Roman Catholicism and toleration

It will be convenient at this point to consider Wesley's relationships with other churches and his attitude towards religious toleration.[94]

Bred in a High Church family, though with Dissenting antecedents, Wesley was naturally prone to be suspicious of Dissent and hostile towards it. It should be observed, moreover, that Dissent in the later seventeenth and early eighteenth century was not simply a matter of religious and ecclesiastical preference but a choice with strong social and political connections, and regularly seen as such. Dissent, after the Toleration Act of 1689, had developed into an underprivileged sub-culture: the defeated party after the Civil War and the legatee of the horror-stories of the Interregnum.

Something had been achieved, indeed, since that troubled time and its aftermath of persecution. We have seen that the attempt to incorporate everyone into a single state church establishment had failed, and that a measure of religious toleration had been granted.[95] Political circumstances, which had once seemed to require religious conformity as a necessary prop for social unity, now seemed to demand religious toleration to produce a social consensus. At the same time, theorists like Locke gave intellectual expression to the disgust and weariness felt after the vain attempts at forced conformity. If persecution was supposed to produce unity in the one truth that alone could save a man's soul, this was surely a fallacy. It was more likely to produce false conversions, hypocrisy and so damnation. The state, in Locke's view, should interfere with religion only for purely civil purposes: to preserve order and law. Hence it seemed logical also to except Roman Catholics from toleration.

They owed allegiance to the Pope (that foreign potentate), and it was popularly supposed that they taught that no faith need be kept with heretics. Similarly, atheists could not be tolerated as they could not be bound by oaths.[96]

After Queen Anne's reign the pressure for toleration in England gradually increased. It became a point of pride, or at least part of the settled assumptions of educated people, that persecution purely for religious opinions was contrary to nature, the laws of God and the rights of freeborn Englishmen. This was often coupled for Anglicans with the belief that such toleration should not extend to full civil rights. The sacramental test for office was necessary to preserve the status and security of the Established Church. Nor, as has been noted, should toleration be extended at all to religious positions which seemed to entail disloyalty or blasphemy against God (Unitarians were formally excluded from the Act of Toleration).

John Wesley shared in this tolerant attitude: he was glad to count on it and appeal to it when Methodists were persecuted, and quoted the King as saying he would never persecute for religion.[97] In defending Methodist irregularities he invoked not only practical arguments but also a very eighteenth-century view of Protestantism. The very foundation of a man's religion is the 'private judgment' which he makes to follow a particular church. Wesley argues in 1749 against the view he had once held that all Englishmen should belong to the Church of England: on this line of argument, he pointed out, no Protestant Reformation could have taken place, for this would 'destroy the right of private judgment, on which the whole Reformation stands'.[98] Liberty of conscience, he wrote in 1766, is a right 'by the law of God and nature' as well as the laws of England.[99]

In his earlier years Wesley had certainly shared the exclusivist episcopalian views of men like William Law and virtually unchurched Dissenters.[100] That stance, however, had been undermined for him by the imperatives of the Revival and experience and his redefinition of true Christianity. By his favourite criteria of true faith and its fruits he could not simply unchurch Dissenters nor deny the reality of the faith and life even of some Roman Catholics.

How far Wesley in addition shared the view of some liberal Anglicans that Dissenters should be relieved of the sacramental test is not clear. What is clear is that despite his growing general toleration, his attitude to organized Dissent remained distinctly equivocal.

It is possible that not only did Wesley inherit his High Church and anti-Dissenting prejudices from his parents, but they kept him in ignorance of his strong Puritan ancestry.[101] At all events he only mentions this ancestry later in life, and his knowledge of Puritanism and Dissent appears to come mainly from reading books and chiefly after his conversion. A little of this appears in the Oxford reading lists which are, however, overwhelmingly of a High Church and 'Catholic' flavour. The same is largely true of the lists of books recommended for the preachers' reading by the Conferences of 1745 and 1746, and for Kingswood School in 1748.[102] There is nothing here to prepare us for the startlingly large proportion of 'Puritan' writings in his 'Christian Library' (1749ff.). What led him to read so many is unclear, though he took advice from Philip Doddridge.[103]

Puritanism is not, however, identical with Dissent. In the 'Christian Library' Wesley was accused of having published a 'collection of mutilated writings of dissenters of all sorts'; to this he replied, not very convincingly, that in the first ten volumes there was nothing of the sort and that in the rest 'the greatest part' was from 'ornaments of the Church of England'. It has been suggested, however, that he distinguished between those forced out of the Church in 1662 and those who voluntarily became Dissenters (a distinction implied by his own attitude to how Methodist separation from the church might happen).[104] Most of the writers he used were in the ejected category, and had originally been within the Established Church. He noticeably did not include post-seventeenth-century Dissenters.

This opening up to the old Puritan divines was very probably partly due to experience as well as reading. Though it is unlikely that their irregularities influenced his own, Wesley did become aware of their views and sufferings and sympathized with them, seeing parallels with the Methodist case up to a point. The Puritans, too, had preached the gospel without fully conforming to church order and had been persecuted and ejected for it. Thus in 1739 and 1747 Wesley read Neal's *History of the Puritans*, and in the latter year commented in a letter to 'John Smith' on the treatment of Thomas Cartwright under Elizabeth. He condemned the church leaders of that day for being as much persecutors as the Catholic Queen Mary. To 'Smith', who had compared Wesley's irregularities with the Puritans, Wesley said he looked upon Cartwright and 'the body of Puritans in that age . . . to have been both the most learned and most pious men who were then in the English nation'. In 1754 he read Calamy's account of the 1662 ejections, and again compared some of the bishops to the Marian persecutors. On the other hand he deplored the holy confessors' quibbling about such minor matters as surplices and kneeling at communion.[105]

Here one can see Wesley emphasizing what he thought were the essentials, and it should be observed (especially by those who emphasize Wesley's debt to the Puritans) that he carefully edited out their Calvinism and later used John Goodwin (a rare Puritan Arminian). As with his Catholic mentors, Wesley selected only what suited his purpose and outlook, and throughout was chiefly impressed by specimens of practical divinity and biographical examples of holy living.

But if Wesley held eighteenth-century English views of toleration and appreciated some of the Puritan virtues, he was much less appreciative of contemporary Dissent. Dissenters had not been forced out of the church, but wilfully chose to separate from it. No 'sinful terms of communion' had been imposed upon them.[106] Wesley's animus – again very typical of many eighteenth-century Anglicans – comes out in his comments on Micaiah Towgood's *A Gentleman's Reasons for his Dissent from the Church of England* (1744), which he read in preparation for the Conference of 1755 when the separation issue was being debated. He found it full of 'vinegar and gall'. Wesley's reply centred on Towgood's claim that separation from the Church of England was a duty owed to Christ as the sole lawgiver in the church. This notion was not peculiar to Dissenters, but had been used by Hoadly as a blunderbuss to attack extreme High Church and Nonjuror claims to spiritual power, though it was liable to explode and damage its holder, as William Law tried to demonstrate.[107] Wesley fell back on arguments at least as old as Hooker's against the Puritans: there are 'things indifferent' which tradition, church or indeed civil authorities can fix without infringing Christ's prerogatives; and we should obey the powers that be, even on matters of worship. There was no need to separate over such things. No doubt Wesley had his own case in mind, but if so, it would follow that he felt at liberty to 'vary' as he thought fit in such matters and that the authorities had no more Christian right to expel him for doing so than they had in the Puritan case. But of course this depended on the church being as tolerant (or slack) as the eighteenth-century Church of England was proving to be in his case. Towgood might well feel aggrieved that men of principle and conscience should be condemned for not having such flexible notions of conformity as John Wesley.

In practice Wesley co-operated (cautiously) with some Dissenters more than others. How far he did so may have depended on whether they concentrated on practical religion rather than 'opinions' on church order and the like, and he sometimes preached in non-Anglican pulpits. In general he preferred Presbyterians to the rest.[108] Methodism itself was a living ambiguity since its terms of membership allowed Dissenters as well as Anglicans as long as they did not dispute on 'opinions'. When members were urged to attend communion, they went to their old denominations, though some joined in Anglican ones. Yet Wesley persisted in representing Methodism as an Anglican auxiliary, and in his address to the 1755 Conference thought it best if the preachers did not attend meeting-houses. There seems to be an implication here that by becoming preachers, even those of Dissenting background had become Anglicans. John Bennet was eventually excluded from his Presbyterian communion and sometimes attended Anglican communions. In 1779 Wesley excluded Dissenters from Methodist pulpits.[109]

In all this one should perhaps not make too much of Wesley's inherited prejudices. His attitudes were strongly conditioned by his concern to refute charges that Methodism was separating from the church, to stop the drift into Dissent and so the dissolution of his connexion. In the 1755 address he was at pains to compare Anglican worship with Dissenting worship to the disadvantage of the latter, in reply to preachers who complained of the formality and unsoundness of Anglican worship and preaching.[110] He was equally concerned with the trends in Presbyterianism towards Arian heterodoxy and its non-evangelical views of original sin and the atonement on the one hand, and the dominance of Calvinism in most of the Dissenting churches on the other.

Finally, Wesley had recurring problems with preachers who deserted him for various reasons and settled down in local churches for a local ministry. This was a major charge in his mind against Dissent. He saw itineracy and a mobile ministry as fundamental to Methodism – hence his arguments with Walker and the Evangelicals. His feelings about this (though touched also, perhaps, by Anglican snobbery) come out in his comment on Charles Skelton, one of these seceders. 'Did God design that this light should be laid under a bushel, in a little, obscure dissenting meeting house?'[111]

On Roman Catholicism Wesley was also equivocal; here he was more bound by traditional prejudices than in the case of the Dissenters. Here, too, however, he reflected the more relaxed attitudes of the eighteenth century in practice, if not in theory.[112] Three main influences affected him: first, the inherited fears and mythology of English Protestants about false Popish doctrine, deceit, cruelty and political subversion; second, the growing eighteenth-century sense of the propriety of religious toleration which often resulted in a limitation on the practical implementation of the very severe penal code against Catholics; third, the pressures induced by the fortunes and needs of the Methodist mission. A special part was played here by the interests of the mission in Ireland and by the Methodist preachers who had originated there. It is not surprising, therefore, that Wesley's attitude appears at times to be inconsistent, sentiments of sincere toleration being mingled with blood-curdling talk of Popish cruelty and disloyalty.

Wesley's debt to the Catholic tradition of spirituality has already been noted, as has the fact that some aspects of Methodist practice gave colour to attacks like that of Bishop Lavington's *Enthusiasm of Methodists and Papists Compared*. But the resemblances are easy to exaggerate, and in any case were often simply the stock-in-trade of opponents anxious to smear. Much more obvious is Methodist hostility to Catholicism, which Dr Hempton ascribes to three principal sources: the polarizing impact of religious controversy; Wesley's experiences in Ireland; and his controversial connection with the Protestant Association and the Gordon Riots. But quite apart from this, his attitudes would probably have been much the same in view of the firm Protestantism which was already part of the High Church tradition. What tempered and complicated this attitude was the force of eighteenth-century sentiments of toleration reinforced by his tendency to welcome what he took to be evidence of a common basic Christianity defined as love of God and of neighbour, to be recognized and accepted as such whatever a person's denominational label.

This last sentiment appears most clearly in one of Wesley's more surprising works: the *Letter to a Roman Catholic* of 1749. Though this was obviously influenced by recent experiences of a massive anti-Methodist riot in Cork and was therefore a bid to stop the Irish mission being ruined, it is worth noting that his 'Catholic Spirit' sermon was written about the same time. Both pieces reflect much the same sentiments as Wesley's efforts to establish common ground with Evangelicals, though in that case he could also appeal to a common stock of 'evangelical' doctrine. The remarkable thing about the *Letter* is not so much its content as the fact that it was addressed to Catholics. It is essentially an appeal for brotherly love on the basis of a few fundamental Christian beliefs, each side retaining its 'opinions'. The beliefs outlined are broadly those of the Apostles' Creed and a common morality. Agreeing on this, they should resolve not to hurt one another; speak nothing unkind of each other but use the language of love; harbour no unkindly thought or unfriendly temper; and help one another in all that aids the kingdom. It is not surprising that this piece has been reprinted in recent years as a contribution to ecumenism, but it was the product of a special situation and not at all characteristic of Wesley's writings on Catholicism.[113]

Wesley in fact shared the usual English beliefs about the Irish, being ready to cut Protestant throats as in the 1640s, and believed that Irish poverty was due to Popery. He also thought that much of the evil of Catholicism was due to the priests rather than the people. His *Short Method of Converting all the Catholics in the Kingdom of Ireland* was delightfully simple. Catholics believe that the only ministers better than their own priests were the first apostles. Hence the Church of Ireland clergy need only preach and live apostolic doctrine and the Catholics will flock to them![114]

Much more typical of his attitude when he squarely faced Catholic doctrine and practice, rather than dealing with individuals or appealing for peace, were works like *A Roman Catechism*. This was not an actual Roman catechism, but a compilation of Catholic teachings on various doctrines and practices with Protestant answers and arranged in catechetical form. It was in fact a revised version of a seventeenth-century work. This was conventional stuff, and he wrote several more polemical works of a similar tone.[115]

In 1761 Wesley answered Bishop Richard Challoner's *Caveat against the Methodists*; he claimed that its criticisms would, if true, weigh equally against all Protestantism. Challoner had argued for a church always one and under divinely appointed teachers, but Wesley argued for the whole body of those endowed with 'faith working by love', led by pastors who convert men to God. Rome did not possess these gifts, and for good measure Wesley denied that the Bishop of Rome came by uninterrupted succession from the apostles.[116]

But apart from these conventional polemics, Wesley also became involved, even if not entirely through his own fault, in the controversy over the Catholic Relief Act of 1778 and the anti-Catholic Gordon Riots which followed in 1780. The *Journal* reveals little of this. In January 1780 he recorded that he felt it his duty to write to the papers about the increase of Popery, even though some were offended by this. He does not mention the Act and was absent from London during the riots. He preached a sermon in November saying that though we should not persecute Catholics, we had a right to stop them 'doing hurt'. He visited Lord George Gordon and hoped that his captivity would do him good.[117]

These references refer to, while at the same time concealing, the series of events which began with the Act of 1778. Wesley's tract on *Popery Calmly Considered* (1779), though not referring to the Act, clearly reflects its provisions. In January 1780 his public letter defended an *Appeal* on behalf of the Protestant Association which Gordon had founded to agitate for the repeal of the Relief Act. Here Wesley claims that religion is not in question, but a government ought not to tolerate Roman Catholics because there can be no security for their loyalty – the usual Protestant line. The late Act tolerates and encourages them and so endangers English liberty.[118] Pursuing the controversy with Father O'Leary, he concludes that he would not have Catholics persecuted, but would have them enjoy the same liberties they had enjoyed for the last sixty years before the Act was passed. By this he presumably meant that while he wished to keep up the penal laws, they should be administered so as tacitly to allow peaceful Catholic worship, as had generally been the case. This seems to be confirmed by a pamphlet in 1782 denying that he advocated persecution and saying Catholics had always enjoyed 'full toleration'.[119]

Then in June 1780 the Protestant Association, led by Lord George

Gordon, organized a petition against the Act; a riot ensued which left London helpless before the mob for several days.[120] The contribution of the Methodists to this was probably more limited than was sometimes claimed. John Pawson thought that the government was suspiciously slow to act and that the Protestant Association had no hand in it, whereas many believed that the Papists themselves were active in it. The Methodists were in danger (he said) because of Wesley's writings against them.[121] What really damaged Wesley's reputation for long afterwards was O'Leary's publication of his replies to Wesley's letters in a way that seemed to imply that Wesley was also responsible for defending the Protestant Association and so was partly responsible for instigating the riots.[122] Yet although this was a misrepresentation, it is difficult to exonerate Wesley entirely. He had, after all, explicitly defended the arguments and author of the *Appeal* on behalf of the Association, and his traditionalist arguments for defensive penal laws fell a long way below his irenical *Letter* of 1749 and his frequent appeals for a 'Catholic Spirit'.

It is a sad fact that early nineteenth-century Wesleyans became notorious for their anti-Catholic sentiments and opposition to Catholic emancipation; part of the blame must be attached to the tradition which Wesley had endorsed, though there were many other factors at work as well.

It is in the light of these restrictions on charity to Catholics that Wesley's famous sermon on the 'Catholic Spirit' should be read.[123] The argument of the sermon is that men may differ in opinions and modes of worship so that external union is impossible, yet this need not prevent 'union in affection'. If men agree on belief in God, faith in Jesus Christ, love of God and neighbour, they can join, not in church government and worship but in love. This 'catholic spirit', however, does *not* mean an 'indifference to all opinions': this is the spawn of hell, not the offspring of heaven. Nor is it 'practical Latitudinarianism' – indifference to public worship. Yet while Wesley is clear about what he feels to be right and scriptural, his heart is 'enlarged' towards those who believe differently. Elsewhere he seems to go even further. 'Right opinion is at best but a slender part of religion (which properly and directly consists in right tempers, words and actions) and frequently it is not part of religion at all.' 'Whatever is compatible with a love to Christ and a work of grace I term an opinion.'[124] The qualifications are important. Without them Wesley seems to speak with the language and sentiments of an eighteenth-century Latitudinarian, and indeed the language at least is of that ilk. But behind it is probably an older Anglican tradition, distinguishing between essentials and 'things indifferent'. The problem, as always, was that one man's 'opinion' was another man's 'essential'. Wesley would have liked predestination to be an 'opinion', not breaking communion, but could not gain agreement on this and indeed often treated it as a deadly poison not to be tolerated.

It is anachronistic to see Wesley as an ecumenical pioneer in the perspective of the modern ecumenical movement. Nor were his notions of toleration simply the direct fruit of his evangelicalism. Yet for all his limitations, he was genuinely and passionately opposed to physical persecution. This he owed more than he realized to the benevolent spirit of the eighteenth-century Enlightenment.

Wesley's England: 2. Society and Revival in the Later Eighteenth Century

1. A changing society

The rather over-used category of 'revolution' has long done duty to characterize the period beginning with the last quarter of the eighteenth century and extending perhaps to the 1850s. This symbol of dramatic change has been applied variously to industry, agriculture and politics, and it is as well to remind ourselves how much, as yet, remained little altered at the time of Wesley's death in 1791. The system of parliamentary representation, the structures of the church and the divisions of society remained substantially as before. Yet the beginnings of important changes can be seen which were already affecting Methodism before Wesley's death, and even those who resist simple theories of economic causation in history may recognize that economic factors were major conditioning forces for other changes.

To begin with population: it will be recalled that between 1700 and 1750 the population rose only modestly, from perhaps 5.1 million to 5.8 million, but during the next fifty years it rose to nearly 9 million. The size and location of the largest towns altered significantly, for by 1801 the largest towns after London (which then approached one million) were Liverpool, Manchester and Birmingham. Related to these developments were the rise of the cotton industry of Lancashire, and growth in the West Riding woollen manufactures and the iron and steel trades of the West Midlands. Manchester had a population of 17,101 in 1758; 24,386 in 1774; but over 70,000 in 1801. Yet these eye-catching changes should be set alongside the fact that still only 30% of the population lived in towns of 2,500 or more persons.[1] Although the reasons for the population rise remain a matter for argument, it seems clear that much of the rise in towns like Manchester was due to immigration from country to town.

The well-worn concept of the Industrial Revolution has been questioned in some quarters, as have all such historians' shorthand terms. Cautiously accepting it, Professor Mathias sees it as indicating the result of a fundamental change in the structure of an economy, a fundamental redeployment of resources away from agriculture, and industrial production expanding at a higher and sustained rate (Rostow's famous 'takeoff into self-sustained growth'). Changes of this kind had begun to take place in the Britain of the 1780s, and marked at least the beginning of a break with the character of economic life and the pace of change in all previous centuries and in all countries. It is in this long perspective that the change in Britain becomes most obvious. The change was real, even if 'revolution' suggests too violent and rapid an image.[2]

The much-debated causes of this change need not concern us here, but it is of some importance to underline its often limited and localized nature. The spectacular growth and innovation in Lancashire cottons still allowed the industry only 1.0% of national income in 1780. In 1772 it provided only 2.3% of exports against 42.2% from woollens, though by 1800 it had 24.2% against 28.5% from woollens. Grain, meanwhile, was ceasing to be exported during the second half of the eighteenth century, and Britain became a net importer to feed its growing population, even though agriculture became more efficient. The process of growth became diffused throughout the economy, and agricultural improvements leading to the need for fewer workers helped to provide recruits for industry, even though a large work-force remained on the land. There were improvements in transport (turnpike roads, canals); more sophisticated financial instruments; and by the end of the century in advanced industries like cotton a sub-division of the old 'merchant-manufacturers' into specialist occupations was becoming visible.[3]

It appears to be of importance for understanding the progress of the Revival to appreciate the nature of industrial production and organization. Even the cotton industry (which was in any case exceptional in this regard) did not leap straight into the factory age. For years innovation chiefly affected the spinning side, and the weaving branch employed mostly handloom weavers until the 1830s. Factories were at first confined to water power and were often in villages rather than towns. Even in spinning, really large factories were a rarity until after 1800. More people were in domestic workshops or small works.

The growth and concentration of population and the proliferation of small masters and artisans meant an increase in the numbers of those places and people which had always seemed least amenable to Anglican parochial discipline and most open to Dissent and Methodism. It was the nature of early industrialization as well as sheer population increase and aggressive evangelism which underlay the growth of Methodism in the later eighteenth century.[4]

This 'more than industrial revolution', as it has been termed, produced challenging problems for law and order, social welfare, local government, politics – and religious organization.[5] Whig hegemony and the proscription of the Tories in the first half of the century gradually gave way after the accession of George III in 1760 to a more complex situation, and for various reasons a period of party instability followed.[6] Even those most sceptical about the reality and continuity of parties divided by ideology in the eighteenth century have recognized that the American revolt in the 1770s led to sharp divisions in English political life on issues of principle. Already in the 1760s the rakish John Wilkes had managed to provoke a constitutional row over his arrest by a 'general warrant' (one not specifying an individual); and again over his repeated election as an MP despite being disqualified as an outlaw. Wilkes stirred up an extra-parliamentary opposition with loud cries of 'Wilkes and Liberty' over his well-publicized grievances – an ominous precedent. By 1780 there was a movement for Parliamentary reform designed to increase county representation against what was seen as the corruption of small boroughs in the pockets of wealthy patrons. There were also attempts to cut down the number of government 'placemen' in the Commons. Conscience as well as political opportunism led to government intervention in the affairs of the East India Company, and the publicity over corruption in India led some Evangelical idealists to press for the introduction of missions (see below, pp. 474f.). Finally, working-class radicals as well as primitive trade union activity and political associations signalized the fact that something more coherent and politically sophisticated was stirring among a small section of the 'lower orders'; it was in the 1790s, too, that the language of 'class' first appeared.[7]

But perhaps the events which first polarized British opinion were those which culminated in the American Revolution. It is no accident that John Wesley, that hereditary Tory, though generally unpolitical except for recommending honest voting at elections, should have turned political pamphleteer in this period. From sympathy with the Americans he turned hostile, seeing them as allies of the rabble-rousers in England and their parrot-cries of 'liberty' (see below, pp. 376ff.). The second half of the century was indeed a troubled and divisive period, and not only in politics. More wars, more taxes, more causes for discontent were added to the strains of a changing economy and society.

Pressure on the resources of growing towns led to experiments with new organs of local government such as 'Improvement Commissioners' to deal with law and order, street lighting, cleansing and widening.[8]

There was also a new rash of voluntary organizations to educate and aid the lower orders: partly to save their souls; partly to improve their minds and bodies; partly to curb the risk of disorder. It is not an accident that the Sunday School movement took off rapidly in the 1780s, some of the schools being sponsored by town committees (see below, p. 321).

Though less conspicuous than in the towns, changes were under way in the countryside too. Enclosures of common land and small-holdings accelerated, and agricultural prosperity increased the yield of tithe and glebe to enhance the status of some of the clergy. There is a noticeable rise in the number of clerical JPs from the later eighteenth century, which had a bearing on the fortunes of rural Methodism and Dissent (see below, p. 319).

The French Revolution might have been expected to stimulate English opposition to privilege, to encourage reform and to stir up the restless plebs. But equally – or rather, as it turned out, much more – it strengthened fear of change and resistance to reform for a generation.[9] Much has been written on how and why England escaped a French-style revolution and on the alleged role of Methodism and evangelicalism more generally in this (see below, pp. 379f.). The striking fact is that the English ruling classes, reinforced by the captains of industry, rallied to the defence of property and patriotism in time of war and supported repression of the disaffected. The fascination for later historians of the friends of liberty, reform and working-class martyrs cannot obscure the fact that the ruling class kept its nerve and did not even find it necessary to make concessions to reform to avoid worse until the 1830s.

John Wesley lived long enough to see the beginning of the French Revolution, though not its most terrible fruits. His dependents, too, became more restive. He had to make concessions to their desire for greater independence of the church and to some degree to their desire for participation in leadership. But he, too, retained control. Less fortunate than he, his successors defeated rebellion only at the price of secessions. Yet Wesley adapted as well. He had reconciled himself to American Independence and accepted the idea that the American Methodists had been strangely and providentially set free to follow a more 'primitive' form of church government than that offered by the Church of England. In his only oblique references to the French Revolution he saw it in an equally providential, even millenarian, light as part of the great changes through which God would work (see below, pp. 490f). And so his 'providential optimism', which had been manifested throughout his evangelical career, persisted to the end.

2. Change and the church

At first sight the condition of the Church of England in the later eighteenth century remained much the same as it had been in the earlier period. There had been no structural reforms, and so the traditional picture of diocese and parish, the decay of formal discipline, pluralism and non-residence continued unchanged. In many rural parishes the visitation returns read much as before. The aging Parson Woodforde continued with his rural pursuits and paternalism, hardly affected by the rumbles of 'revolutionists' (especially Dissenters, he said) in Norwich.[10] In some Wiltshire villages hardly any change can be seen in clerical performance: low incomes, said the clergy, had prevented there being more than one service a Sunday since time immemorial, and a modest pluralism could not be avoided. Labourers could not be persuaded to come to Sunday morning, let alone to weekday prayers, in a pastoral economy.[11] Much the same was true in the rural parts of the more mixed county of Cheshire, though the eastern parts were showing the impact of industry.[12] In Oxfordshire the amount of pluralism and non-residence actually increased into the early century. The frequency of services and sacraments here was not greatly changed, except that more achieved the quarterly sacramental norm and fewer managed it monthly. Significant change in these and other matters can hardly be seen until after the Oxford Movement.[13] The church courts had declined further as engines for spiritual discipline, and a Chester curate in 1778 complained that citing people to them actually made matters worse when they saw that nothing more than naming of names ensued. 'They harden more and more and come at length to set us utterly at nought.' The last sign of the old régime was the closing of inns in the hours of worship.[14] Chester was notorious for its worldly, hard-drinking, fox-hunting clergy, and in the 1820s Blomfield told the tale of the clergyman so drunk that he fell into a grave before a burial.[15]

What was more ominous for the church was that while its mechanisms and routines had changed little, the world was changing around it, at least in some areas, and Methodism and Dissent took advantage of this. Rural Wiltshire incumbents could still, in the 1780s, record the presence of small bodies of Methodists without much alarm, and some of them were still uncertain whether to classify them as attached to the church or not.[16] But it was very different in large industrializing parishes in the North. It has been suggested that the separation of Methodism from the church was one cause for the apparent decline in communion attendance.[17] Whether this was so or not, the church was certainly damaged in areas where Methodism responded to industrialization and population growth. Thus in the chapelry of Birch in the large parish of

Manchester in 1789 it was observed that 'many of the lower sort of mechanics seem to have little regard for religion and seldom attend public worship', and they moved too quickly for the parson to know them. The farmers and the propertied, however, attended well. At Denton in 1804 the departure of industrial workers from the 'sobriety' and 'simplicity of manners' of the peasantry was deplored; and Methodists were meeting in cottages. At Heaton Norris it was the same: Methodist flexibility allowed them to meet in cottages, while the Anglican chapel had accommodation for only 300 in a population of 4,000.[18]

Nostalgic travellers like the Earl of Torrington attributed the decay of religion by 1790 to the departure of the gentry for spa towns, which demoralized the clergy into following suit, leaving the parish to a 'hackney curate who rides over half the county on a Sunday' to take minimal services.[19] More plausible than this view based on a past golden age is Torrington's observation that Anglican weaknesses drove people for comfort elsewhere. Religion, he thought, now lay in the hands of the Methodists. The curate at Cheltenham who augmented his stipend with his winnings at whist had allowed the sects to flourish as a result.[20]

A report from a group of Lincolnshire clergy concluded that only a third of the population attended church, and ascribed this to a variety of 'profaneness and irreligion' on the one hand and the depredations of Methodist irregularity on the other.[21] One underlying source for this alienation, apart from religious reasons, may have been the fact that agricultural improvement had brought prosperity and increased gentrification to a section of the clergy.[22] Though it enhanced their status and authority by assimilating them more closely to the gentry, it may also have distanced them from their flock, especially as an increasing number of them became JPs, with results of the kind observed by the Lincolnshire clergy.[23]

The response of the Church of England and its clergy to these various pressures took a variety of forms. In ecclesiastical terms one somewhat neglected factor is a renewal of that High Church tradition which had in any case sustained greater continuity than has always been recognized in accounts influenced by Evangelical and Tractarian propaganda. The old notions of the church's apostolicity, its independent spiritual rights, the role of tradition and the Fathers and sacramental piety survived.[24] Some of those in this tradition, like the devout wine merchant Joshua Watson, would contribute to the renewal of Anglican education, parish aids and missions in rivalry with the Evangelicals.[25] A concern to fortify the church against its rivals and in particular to draw back from the risk of seepage into Methodism and Dissent is also evident in the Evangelicals in the later eighteenth century. As we have seen, the Huntingdonian secession made some of them repent of irregularities and emphasize the beauties of episcopacy and the Prayer Book. Thus the former Methodist Cornelius Bayley in Manchester published a catechism extolling the virtues of an apostolically-authorized ministry like a High Churchman – and 'High' he certainly was in terms of his detestation of separatist Methodism and Dissent.[26] At a more vulgar as well as at a more respectable level, the bid by Dissenters to repeal the Tests around 1790, coupled with alarm at the French Revolution, led to an Anglican backlash in the 1790s and the revival of 'Church and King' mobs. Conservatives like Burke defended the church as part of the establishment, and bishops like Horsley inveighed against Methodists and other dissidents as 'Jacobins' along with political revolutionaries.

In more material terms, one solution to lack of churchgoers and competition from the sects might seem to be church-building. Although there was no national plan or public money for this until 1818, there was in fact much more building in the eighteenth century, notably in towns, than has generally been recognized.[27] The trouble was that most of these were proprietary churches financed by sales and rents from pews and burial places, with no room for the poor. It was a sign of changing times when they began to allocate cheap or free seats for the poor, though these carried the stigma of pauperism.[28]

The reforms which worried churchmen had in mind can be seen in a series of proposals from the egregious Bishop Watson at various points from the 1770s to the early 1800s. Many of them were familiar, though those towards the end of his life reflected changing times. Episcopal incomes should be made less uneven; bishops should be given more patronage to reward their own clergy; clerical incomes should be improved and tithe commuted to money payments (as a good deal already had been). A new note appears in the notion of allowing clergy in without attending the universities, and even more in a proposal in 1800 for large churches for the poor in towns and for rural clergy to live in towns. Very noticeably, Watson made no mention of strengthening the church courts (unlike Gibson in the 1730s): no solution any longer lay in this coercive direction.[29]

The old problems of plurality and non-residence continued to trouble thoughtful churchmen, and Watson's proposals were designed partly to cure the necessity for them. They were not remedied in this period, but it has been claimed that nevertheless pressure for church reform in these terms was increasing from the 1770s, as is shown by attempts at piecemeal legislation. Thomas Gilbert tried to help the financing of clergy houses; Bishop Lowth attacked resignation bonds (by which clergy agreed to give way to those favoured by patrons when required) and there were efforts to help poor curates. Pressure in other directions can also be discerned in sabbatarian legislation and campaigns for the reformation of manners.[30]

Although campaigns of this kind have been especially associated with Evangelicals, they were far from being confined to them, and they are evidence of a changing view of duty and even of belief among some of the bishops and clergy. Bishop Porteous of London, though not an Evangelical, supported their moral campaigns and was an enthusiast for sabbatarianism and the suppression of profaneness. There was a proliferation of societies for material, moral and spiritual betterment which were inspired not only by charitable and 'missionary' impulses but also by alarm at the unruliness and openness to radical propaganda of the lower orders. From another point of view they were clearly seen as necessary to supplement the formal ministrations of the church by voluntary means: very like the early eighteenth-century High Church renewal movement. Sunday Schools were one of the most important new instruments for this. Their social importance from the 1780s can be seen by the fact that some were sponsored by town committees of notables, which in Manchester even included Roman Catholics. They were difficult for the clergy to control, and by 1800 the non-denominational organizations were breaking up into denominational ones, possibly due to fears of political subversion, but certainly because of denominational suspicions about sheep-stealing. But even denominational control was difficult, and some schools like that at Stockport became popular, undenominational bodies run by ordinary laymen. Though they were often seen as having been wished on the lower orders by their betters, there is also evidence of their being the product or at least the focus of working-class self-improvement.[31]

Some of the self-searchings by the clergy about their role and duty, and changes in their attitudes to it, can be gauged from the proposals made in the Lincolnshire report already mentioned.[32] They should set an example by 'moderation in the indulgence of worldly pursuits and amusements, however lawful and innocent they may be in themselves'. They resolved to expound the 'doctrines peculiar to the Christian faith' against those preaching mere morality or those depreciating the necessity of good works (like Methodist preachers of 'faith alone'). They should catechize the youth, comfort the afflicted, advise and admonish wherever they could. They would avoid levity in dress and 'common discourse' as well as haste in the conduct of worship. They should stir up the magistrates to punish profanation of the Sabbath. They wished that the Toleration Act could be operated to make it more difficult for Dissenters to infringe it, but they also, very interestingly, wished Anglicans to be able to hold devotional meetings of their own and to allow pious persons to meet to read the Bible and devotional works approved by the Bishop.

The desire to pursue a kind of middle way between excessive emphasis on works and excessive reliance on faith alone has a familiar ring. There are indeed increasing signs of a concern to emphasize the distinctive Christian way of salvation in dependence on the work of Christ and by faith in response to it. The Revd William Jones in 1803 inveighed against pluralist fox-hunters and sympathized with poor 'journeymen' curates. But he also complained about sermons lacking the 'characteristic doctrines' of Christianity and harping on the 'watchword or catchword' of 'morality'. 'My dear hearers', he represents one preacher as saying, 'I intend to speak to you concerning Jesus Christ, a name you have seldom heard mentioned in this pulpit.'[33]

George Crabbe, the author of the sombrely realistic poem on 'The Borough' (the source of Benjamin Britten's opera *Peter Grimes*), is an interesting case. From his mother he inherited a religion deeply devout though not 'serious' as Evangelicals understood it, i.e. that they could 'be made acceptable only through the merits of the Redeemer'. In a period of depression in 1780 Crabbe meditated on Christ as the only Mediator; 'whosoever believeth shall be saved'; 'faith without works is dead'; yet it is the grace of God that works in us; we can do nothing of ourselves – almost an 'Evangelical' position. Later in life, his son says, Crabbe emphasized the doctrines as well as the practice of Christianity more and moved closer to the Evangelicals.[34] Bishop Horsley, the High Church hammer of Methodists as 'Jacobins', nevertheless received the compliment of having his visitation sermon of 1790 reprinted in the *Arminian Magazine*. He complained that for years past the clergy had been expected to press the practice rather than the doctrines of Christianity. But really 'personal holiness is the end; faith is the means'. Faith may be improved by exercise, but in the beginning is 'unquestionably a distinct gift of God'. 'We are justified by faith . . . not on account of any merit in our faith, but because faith is the first principle of that connexion between the believer's soul and the Divine Spirit on which the whole of our spiritual life depends.'[35] These were exactly Wesley's own sentiments, especially the aphorism about holiness and faith. But if, like Secker and Gibson before him, Horsley was concerned to avoid reducing Christianity to mere morality, his strictures tend to confirm the fact that an obsession with morality for the good of the individual and society continued to be a central theme of contemporary preaching.

3. The growth of the Revival

The earlier description of the origins of the Revival gave some idea of its national and international ramifications. Before sketching how it spread and diversified during the later eighteenth century, it is necessary to emphasize its fluid, untidy nature, which has often been obscured by denominational historians anxious to trace their own pedigrees. This can be misleading in at least three directions. First, as often happens in renewal movements, some groups which later became new denominations did not at first think of themselves in this light and even resisted separation. This was true of the Methodists, the Moravians and the Huntingdonians. Secondly, quite a number of converts had chequered careers leading them from one group or denomination to another, and this, together with the disruptive and confusing effects of revivalist teaching and emotion, helped to make the membership of the various groups uncertain and unstable. Methodism, as the largest of the new groups, often supplied the first halting-place on more extended pilgrimages. It was the first step out of conventional religion that was hardest to take.[36] Thirdly, there was a recurring concern among evangelicals of all sorts to co-operate with those in other revival groups, or at least for friendly individuals to help each other. After all, they often had more in common with each other than with non-evangelicals in their own denominations. A common factor in all this fluidity of allegiance was the pursuit of religious experience which disrupted old allegiances and did not at first seem clearly to define what the new ones should be. Nor were they always clear about theological definition in terms of traditional and conventional norms. Some of the results of this have already been noted in the process by which the followers of Wesley, Whitefield and the Moravians gradually came to define their positions in relation to each other through disputes about doctrine, church order and experience.

By the 1780s and often earlier, the lines of division had become more clearly drawn. Methodists still hovered uncertainly on the edge of formal separation, but were a compacted body preparing piecemeal the organs to express a *de facto* separation. The Evangelicals, as we have seen, were retreating from irregularity into greater conformity to parish norms. Yet there were at least three ways in which co-operation could be and still was maintained. First, there was a rash of societies for missionary work at home and abroad. Some of these were, indeed, denominational like the Baptist and Church Missionary Societies. But the London Missionary Society was open to others than Congregationalists, and the Religious Tract Society and Bible Society were undenominational. Secondly, in the 1790s there was a crop of organizations on a county basis for undenominational evangelism in villages. These were made up predominantly of Independents and Baptists, but with a sprinkling of Anglicans and Wesleyans. Unfortunately war hysteria, fear of revolution and the threat to Anglican hegemony scared the Anglicans off, and the Wesleyans became suspicious of undenominationalism as such.[37] Finally, there was the undenominational Sunday School movement which has already been described.[38]

If the trend after 1800 was towards a sharpened denominational consciousness, the undenominational impulse did not die easily. During Wesley's lifetime at least, these impulses deserve to be set alongside the conflicts and divisions on the Revival of which much has already been said, as well as the rise of new denominations or the refurbishing of the old, to which we can now turn.

Not much more need be said about the Evangelical Anglicans. There is no doubt that they increased in numbers, though it is impossible to quantify them. Even the numbers of their clergy are uncertain, though a figure of 500 to 800 by the end of the century has often been quoted.[39] Apart from the hardening of their conformity to the church, one of the most important developments in the party was the appearance of the so-called Clapham Sect. Because of their place in what one may call roughly the upper-middle-class ranks of society, in Parliament and in public office, they had greater influence than the clergy. No fully satisfactory account has yet appeared of the significance of the famous social reforming activities of this group.[40] Clearly it represents evangelical influence operating at a social level denied to Wesley; but the motivation is a matter for controversy, and the social work needs to be related more clearly to what was obviously a more general movement of philanthropy in this period.

Perhaps the most striking feature of the Revival in the later eighteenth century, however, apart from the continuing growth of Wesleyan Methodism, is the impact on Dissent. By the end of the century a situation had emerged here which has led historians to speak of an 'Old' and 'New' Dissent. Though useful, the distinction does not do full justice to the impact of evangelicalism in this sector. The 'New' Dissent includes new denominations thrown up by the Revival: Moravians, Huntingdonians, General Baptists of the New Connexion, the Welsh Calvinistic Methodists, and above all eventually the Wesleyans and their numerous progeny, though the Wesleyan position remained ambiguous towards Dissent for years to come. What complicated the picture was that the 'Old' Dissent – General and Particular Baptists, Independents, Presbyterians and Quakers – were also subject, though in very varying degrees and manner, to evangelical influence. The Independents and a section of the Particular Baptists were affected most in that they were transformed into expansive evangelistic forces. The Presbyterians lost out to them in numbers and often by secession to evangelical groups, but the only direct influence otherwise came through engaging figures like Richard Wright, who imitated Methodist itinerant missionary methods in the interests of a 'rational' gospel.[41] A section of the Quakers also felt some evangelical influence later, which produced at least one schism.[42] Some very unusual sectarian bodies like the Swedenborgians and Shakers which reacted in their own way against the Enlightenment also seem to have drawn off converts of the Revival into a more extreme stage of their spiritual pilgrimages.[43]

Michael Watts has remarked, with considerable truth, that 'the Evangelical Revival was initially an Anglican, not a Dissenting movement, but it was Dissent, not the Church of England, that reaped the ultimate benefit'.[44] The traditional picture of the relationship of Dissent to the Revival, which Watts largely endorses, is of an initially hostile reception followed much later by considerable recruitment. The Presbyterians and General Baptists were naturally in a state of mutual hostility with evangelicals over heterodox doctrines about the Person of Christ, the Trinity and salvation doctrine.[45] Independents and Particular Baptists were hostile to Wesley's Arminianism; and the hyper-Calvinist Particulars objected even to Whitefield's free-ranging evangelism, which they eschewed as contrary to strict election. Presbyterians and some Independents also objected to preaching by laymen who were, moreover, ill-educated by the best Dissenting standards. Like most Anglicans, many of them saw these people as 'enthusiasts'. Dissenters had particular reasons for not associating with people who often seemed to recall that shady past which hostile Anglicans never allowed them to live down.

Yet in the long run the Revival had a profound influence even on the older Dissenting bodies by a variety of processes which perhaps still require rather fuller investigation than they have received. They included a degree of traditions surviving from the past; rejuvenation from within by their own resources; and a good deal of pressure and fresh recruitment from without by other evangelical bodies and individuals.

This mixture of sources is particularly evident in the case of the Independents. Most of their churches had at least retained orthodoxy on the person of Christ and indeed on Calvinism. Men like Doddridge and Watts also conveyed something of the 'evangelistic' spirit of the Puritan tradition, and Watts's hymns were much used by evangelicals, even though Watts himself (unlike Doddridge) disapproved of Methodism. It is curious and instructive that Richard Davis at Rothwell in Northamptonshire even created a kind of local revival in the 1690s complete with lay preachers, emotional scenes and allegations of healing and demonology, though this had no wider effect.[46] More important, perhaps, was the survival of a few ministers like Thomas Cole, who co-operated with Whitefield in Gloucestershire; and of others, as well as lowly laymen, who pursued solitary pilgrimages in search of conversion before or at least independently of the new revivalists.[47]

It is the survival of traditions like this which helps to explain one important source of new Independent churches, that is, by secession from Arianizing Presbyterian ones. Cases of individual secession under the influence of evangelical preachers of all sorts occur from the 1740s: like the conversion of John Bennet and others from Chinley by David Taylor's preaching. In many other cases an Arianizing minister alienated a section of his congregation (often, apparently, members of lower social status than the trustees) who then seceded to form an orthodox Calvinist Independent church which would soon acquire an evangelical minister. There was a considerable crop of these in Lancashire where Presbyterianism had been strong and where there had been few Independents hitherto.[48] In other cases an unorthodox Presbyterian minister was replaced by an orthodox evangelical one, and the church evolved towards Independency. This was what happened eventually at Chinley after the earlier secessions.[49] There were others, as we have seen, which originated as Whitefieldite or Huntingdonian societies or seceders from Evangelical Anglican congregations who had lost their ministers to strangers (as in Truro and Huddersfield), or had seceded from Wesley's connexion (as in Leeds and Bolton).[50] And finally there was fresh Independent evangelizing, as in the notable case of Jonathan Scott, unusually ordained as 'a presbyter or teacher at large' in 1776. He founded a string of new churches in the Midlands and North-west.[51] Some of the northern churches were also supplied with ministers from James Scott's orthodox Academy at Heckmondwike, which attracted and sent out several men of evangelical antecedents.[52] By the 1750s, if not earlier, the distinction between Presbyterians and Independents in England, which had become unclear in terms of ecclesiastical polity, can most easily be made in terms of orthodoxy on the Trinity, Calvinism and evangelical sentiments on the part of Independents in contrast to Presbyterians heading for Unitarianism.

Rejuvenated Independency had changed in tone from the old. As Tudur Jones put it, the 'dignified shyness' of the old sort was being replaced by the 'militant assertiveness' of the new. Ministry to the elect congregation was replaced by ministry to outsiders. The 'respectable' congregations were replaced or invaded by colliers, artisans and labourers. Learned ministers were displaced by men from secular occupations, trained (if trained at all) in evangelism rather than the classics. Lay preaching became common, and the old, elaborately divided sermons were replaced by simple three-point discourses. Emotion and results mattered more than displays of learning. The new Academies like Scott's generally trained only preachers and used them for evangelism in the neighbourhood during training.[53] Like Whitefield, these men were Calvinists, and though vigorously evangelical, reinforced the sector of the Revival most hostile to Wesley's Methodism.

In many ways the development of evangelical Baptist churches followed a rather similar pattern under similar influences: a mixture of survival, revival and newly-founded churches.[54] I observed earlier that the old General (Arminian) Baptists had very generally developed anti-trinitarian sentiments like the Presbyterians, while parts of the old Particular branch, influenced by men like John Gill, had become 'hyper-Calvinist' and actively opposed the notion of preaching freely for conversion.[55] Both developments led to much controversy, splitting of churches, mutual suspicion and difficulty in sustaining the honourable tradition of meetings of churches in Associations for mutual help. Opposition to marrying those of other denominations or even the wrong sort of Baptist helped to hasten decline in numbers.[56]

Yet the Revival affected many Baptists in the end and especially, though not exclusively, the Particulars; and it created one wholly new group: the General Baptists of the New Connexion. The initial response was predictably hostile. Some distrusted Wesley's Arminianism but also Whitefield's 'Arminian dialect' and 'semi-Pelagian addresses'. And General Baptists disliked the trinitarian orthodoxy and strong views on sin and conversion of the revivalists.

Evangelical Particular Baptists were partly recruited from other branches of the Revival, for conversionist preaching has always produced examples of the spontaneous rediscovery of believer's baptism. If real Christianity begins with conversion, it puts in question the meaning and propriety of infant baptism; and study of the New Testament often led to the conclusion that the early Christians did not practise it. Thus David Taylor, Lady Huntingdon's protégé, was one of the founders of a group of societies in Leicestershire in the 1740s which by 1755 had been convinced by the New Testament that they should only baptize believers.[57]

Methodist influence on the new style of Baptist can be seen most clearly in the case of Dan Taylor (no relation to David). Taylor came from Yorkshire and was a Methodist in 1757 but became minister to a group of ex-Methodists in 1762. Having rejected infant baptism, he found himself in a dilemma. Since he was an Arminian, he was refused baptism by the Particulars and obtained it from the Generals in 1763. But he disliked their unorthodoxy, and so was forced to found his own 'General Baptists of the New Connexion' in 1770, 'to revive experimental religion and Primitive Christianity in faith and practice'. From Methodism he inherited a taste for association and connexionalism as well as lay preaching and itineracy. This group linked up with the Leicestershire societies and 'evangelicals' among the old General body to form a small but active new denomination with a considerable artisan membership.[58] It retained uneasy links with the old General Baptists until about 1800, by which time the old body had become ostentatiously Unitarian.[59]

But the main source of Baptist renewal seems to have been from within existing churches, however much influence played upon them from outside. Something here, as with Independency, was inherited from the past. Back in the 1690s two cousins called Mitchell and Crossley had founded a group of societies in Yorkshire and Lancashire which became Baptist, and although Crossley's reputation was later damaged by scandals, he survived as a preacher in the Manchester area in the 1740s, to correspond with Whitefield and welcome his work.[60]

But the most significant development leading to an expansive Baptist evangelism seems to have originated in religious and theological changes within the Particular Baptists in the Midlands from about 1770. At that time men like Robert Hall senior and Andrew Fuller developed a form of Calvinism which, while maintaining 'particular redemption', also allowed for what they called 'practical preaching'. They asserted that men could and should struggle against sin, and like Whitefield encouraged preaching to all with the expectation of conversions following. It was asserted that 'Every soul that comes to Christ to be saved from hell and sin by Him is to be encouraged . . . The coming soul need not fear that he is not elected, for none but such would be willing to come and submit to Christ.'[61] In practical terms this was another version of the Whitefieldite 'Arminian trend' and strongly condemned by hyper-Calvinists. But the 'Fullerites' had a powerful effect on some sections of the Baptist world, and it was from the same group in Northamptonshire that William Carey came. Backed by them, a missionary society was founded in 1792 and Carey became a notable missionary in India.

Similar influences spread elsewhere, and in 1797 an Itinerant Society was founded for village preaching; Baptists co-operated with others to penetrate the Anglican heartlands.

Baptists continued to be divided about evangelism of this kind; sturdy figures like William Gadsby (1773–1844), though founding new churches, essentially preached to the elect and drew off those suspicious of Fullerism.[62] Divided counsels and consequent hindrances to close association with other churches probably helped to limit the growth of the Baptists, but it was still considerable, and evangelicalism would mark them strongly in the coming century.

Evangelicalism in all its forms continued to grow, Methodism most of all, in the later years of the eighteenth century. Clearly it benefited greatly from population growth centred in areas where parochial weaknesses and occupational patterns favoured a relatively plebeian movement which was both well-organized and flexible. Methodism was able to benefit from being an alternative to the Church of England, yet did not alienate all those 'Church Methodists' who wished to keep ties with the church. We shall see that in Wesley's later years it was still subject to the excitements of local revivals which drew in children and fringers, if not outsiders.[63] As the Lincolnshire example showed, it could even penetrate some rural areas, and there would be more of this in new versions of Methodism after Wesley's death.

PART THREE

John Wesley and the Consolidation of Methodism (1760–91)

IX

The Enthusiasts: Methodism and Perfectionism in the 1760s

1. Dissidents: the early conflicts

It has already been shown that despite a considerable degree of common ground and attempts at co-operation, the Revival was punctuated with frequent disagreements and piecemeal secessions from the various groupings. Those possessed of a vision of 'pure' doctrine and practice were prone to separate from the 'unsound'. There were disagreements among Methodists on their relationship with the Church of England; and divisions and secessions over doctrines like Calvinism. Individuals might depart on these issues, but also leave Wesley in revolt against his autocracy or because they wished for a settled ministry in one place or stayed with him but reverted to local preaching. There was a constant trickle of local losses in this way, and it is a measure of the dynamism of Methodism that it still recorded increases of membership almost every year. Until after Wesley's death there were no major secessions to found new forms of Methodism, though there were small localized losses.

As we have seen, the main early splits were with the Moravians and Whitefieldites. After this there were a few individuals and small groups who went out on the issue of theoretical or practical 'antinomianism': denial that the moral law was binding on Christians. One especially painful example was Wesley's brother-in-law, the polygamous Westley Hall in the 1740s. There was the Wheatley case at Norwich in 1751, and a troublesome wanderer called Roger Ball turned up in various places to divide the societies for several years.[1]

Another recurring pattern was the drift to Independency, which was natural when preachers fell out with Wesley over Calvinism or the desire to have a settled ministry or both. This was what happened when John Bennet left him in the early 1750s after the Grace Murray affair, and there were several more cases during that decade. In 1751 Charles Wesley complained that Robert Swindells was inclined to Calvinism but 'teachable'; that David Trathen was a confirmed predestinarian, and that Bennet's theology was doubtful. Charles Skelton and Joseph Cownley were bitterly railing against the church.[2] Though Cownley remained faithful, the others followed Bennet separately into secession. In 1754 five preachers left for various destinations, four of them for Independency, and some of them drew Methodists off with them. There were fears that this seepage might increase, and at the 1754 Conference several preachers were persuaded to sign a pact to stay together. Wesley persuaded himself that the 'breaches lately made' had only bound them more closely together. In fact the debates on separation which followed threatened much more serious trouble, and for various reasons there were heavy losses of preachers, especially in the early 1750s. By 1751 there were or had been some eighty-five itinerants, more or less under Wesley's guidance. Of these one had been expelled; six had died in harness; ten had retired for various reasons; and sixty-eight were still employed. In subsequent years two more were expelled and forty-one left for various reasons, so that only twenty-five remained and died in the work. Of the forty-one who left, about two dozen had gone within four years of 1751.[3]

In the early 1760s a secession of a very different kind developed, predictable in a revivalistic movement, but since it was related directly to Wesley's favourite doctrine of perfection, it was peculiarly difficult and mortifying for him to deal with. This was the outbreak of extreme and 'enthusiastic' perfectionism which led to the secession of Maxfield and Bell. It was also of importance that in attempting to cope with it Wesley was led to review and refine his views of perfection in detail.

2. Perfection and enthusiasm: Maxfield and Bell

Holiness to the point of 'perfection' had always been Wesley's religious goal, and his conversion had not altered the aim, whatever it may have done to modify his ideas of the means. His passion for collecting specimens of religious experience to test and verify or confirm his beliefs had also stayed with him since the days of the Bristol convulsions. It has already been remarked that in the midst of the Norwich communion crisis in 1760 he seemed more interested in perfectionist cases than in what Charles saw as the threatened dissolution of the connexion. He was particularly excited by this, since his earlier expositions of the doctrine relied largely on the alleged scriptural evidence, and by his own account for twenty years before the 1760s the actual occurrence of living cases had been 'nearly at a stand'. But now it 'began to spread through most of England as well as Ireland and so the whole work of God increased'.[4]

There were indeed few cases recorded earlier on. Whitefield had complained about such teaching and claims, and in August 1747 some Cornish Methodists professed that they could 'live without committing sin, though not without sin remaining in them'.[5] But such cases seem to have been relatively sparse, and Wesley's own doctrine less clear at various points than it was later. Although Wesley liked to maintain that he had never altered the doctrine he had taught since 1725, as some of his critics claimed he had, it may be that Tyerman was right to suppose that Wesley had not taught until the 1760s that perfection could be obtained as an instantaneous gift by faith: probably because it was only then that he found numerous cases of it happening in this way.[6]

Just how and why the perfectionist movement spread so extensively in the 1760s is far from clear. Wesley dated its commencement from 'before Thomas Walsh's return to Ireland', which would seem to be before April 1758, though elsewhere he seems to imply that it began up to two years later.[7] Once begun, it spread rapidly, and despite the complications it produced, Wesley was persuaded that it was a work of God which increased the zeal and numbers of the societies. One of the earliest of the outbreaks was at Otley in Yorkshire. Here Wesley describes it as beginning when a group of thirty people met to pray, sing hymns and provoke each other to love and good works. Some complained of the depth of inbred sin and of their need of deliverance from it. They groaned for deliverance, some shrieking in the pains of hell, some praising God for deliverance – rather like the Bristol converts years before. Several claimed to have been 'cleansed from all unrighteousness' and, being 'poor illiterate creatures' (Wesley said), could not have been counterfeiting.[8]

Otley seems to have marked the beginning of the general spread of the work from 1760, but that the work really began early in 1758 seems to be confirmed by the fact that questions of perfection were debated at the Bristol Conference of that year. Wesley had already written in April to a Bristol woman who had been perplexed because some of the preachers (apparently James Rouquet and Thomas Walsh) had placed perfection in such a dreadful light. One of them affirmed that, 'A believer till perfect is under the curse of God and in a state of damnation'. Another said that, 'If you die before you have attained (perfection) you will surely perish.' Wesley rejected these propositions, though he acknowledged the possibility of perfect love in this life while allowing for 'infirmities' to remain. To another lady he affirmed that she could conquer sin 'little by little', but that there is also 'an instantaneous conquest'.[9]

It was in the light of the experience of these unwary preachers of the doctrine that the Conference of 1758 affirmed that perfection could co-exist with various 'infirmities, imperfections and mistakes'; that one can be saved without it; and that young preachers should be cautious in speaking about it. It consists in 'the pure love of God and our neigh-bour'.[10] The Conference of 1759 discussed the matter again, and Wesley produced his *Thoughts on Christian Perfection*. Here, too, he emphasized perfection as pure love to God and neighbour and clarified the co-existence of it with 'infirmities' by carefully defining the sin from which perfection freed people as being the 'voluntary transgression of a known law'. He also affirmed that by the testimony of the Spirit a person may be assured that he or she has the gift: in exact parallel to their original conversion. Finally, he adverted strongly to the evidence of living witnesses: without this he would have concluded that he had mistaken the meaning of Scripture on the matter.[11] This and other pieces were finally incorporated into a review of his teaching on the doctrine since 1725 in his *Plain Account of Christian Perfection* (1767) which, though designed to show that he had never changed his ideas on the question, was in fact strongly influenced by the controversies and observations of the preceding few years. Experience here was certainly fortifying, clarifying and even modifying the rather theoretical opinions he had earlier deduced from the Bible.

During 1760, despite the business over the sacraments and separation, Wesley often collected and later published experiences of perfection. In one case at Wednesbury, a young woman described how in 1758 she was 'deeply convinced there was a greater work than I had attained', and soon the preacher Mr Fugill spoke to one who had received the blessing which made her 'burn' for it till she received it.[12] It seems that in these cases the need had been felt, and then its nature clarified by deliberate preaching. This helps to show how the teaching and cases of perfection spread; it seems that some societies had hitherto remained ignorant of it. In Manchester in 1761, for example, Wesley found that when he exhorted the believers to 'go on unto perfection', 'to many of them it seemed a new doctrine'. Some here he expelled for 'quietist' teaching and was styled 'Pope John' by Byrom for doing so.[13] The work of the preachers, Wesley's interrogations and correspondence probably increased expectations, and in some places such as Wednesbury stirred up a more general local revival.[14] One correspondent even had the courage to urge Wesley to seek the gift which he never claimed for himself.[15] The Conference of 1761 evidently decided that there was no text of Scripture that would 'absolutely support instantaneous perfection', and that there is no state in this world of absolute exemption from sin, but Peter Jaco was not sure whether this would restrain John

Wesley and others who contended otherwise.[16] Here experience seemed to be in tension with the scriptural norm. There were certainly strange and contending views at large. All agreed that what some called 'the second blessing' could be obtained in a moment by faith.[17] But some spoke of a direct witness of it; others had none. Some spoke of a third blessing; and some of sanctification of the 'mind' as well as of the 'heart' as distinct experiences at different times, obtained by faith.[18]

Grimshaw, already alarmed by talk of separation, was equally disturbed by extreme perfection. In 1761 Wesley had a special conference at Leeds to clarify the doctrine, and preached especially to reassure Grimshaw at Haworth – he claimed, to Grimshaw's satisfaction.[19] But later in the year Grimshaw complained to Wesley that some of the preachers had been calling him a 'child of the devil, who dislikes the doctrine of sinless perfection'; and that 'he is no true Christian who has not attained to it': sentiments that Grimshaw correctly believed Wesley would have repudiated.[20] It was this kind of talk which helped to discredit the doctrine, and as usual one cannot judge what Methodism was really like simply by citing John Wesley's attempts at 'reasonable' presentations of it. For that matter his repeated distinctions and qualifications on the subject in the 1760s reveal clearly enough what extreme and divisive claims were being made. Yet he felt he could not deny its reality as demonstrated by the 'plain fact' of the experiences of those he saw as being the happiest and best people in the kingdom.[21]

But then, in 1762, the movement reached a climax of scandal. In Wesley's rather cool account it appears that after cases of perfection occurred in London he warned them against pride, but after his departure 'enthusiasm' broke out. Some thought their imaginations were 'impressions from God'; they fancied they could not be tempted and would not die; and finally some foretold the end of the world on a certain day. When they were disciplined, a few withdrew.[22]

The crisis was much more severe than Wesley's account implies, and his actions struck some people as being belated and not sufficiently decisive. For he was referring to the Maxfield and Bell schism, which confirmed in full measure the recurring suspicion that Methodism was simply a new version of the wild sects of the Interregnum or the more recent French Prophets. The effects, we shall see, were serious not so much in terms of the secession that followed (which was small) as in the damage it did in the long term to Wesley's favourite doctrine among some of his own followers.

It was peculiarly painful to Wesley that one of the ringleaders was the first of his own preachers as a 'son in the gospel', Thomas Maxfield. A letter of Wesley, reviewing Maxfield's career, breathes a strong air not only of injured innocence but also of outrage at the ingratitude by the revolt of one who owed his career to Wesley.[23] He had indeed given him leave to preach, obtained ordination for him, used him as an assistant and defended him when in trouble. It appears that Maxfield had encouraged perfectionists who claimed visions and superiority to others. They saw preachers in London who criticized them as having inferior gifts of grace to themselves, and began to meet separately from the rest of the society by October 1762.

George Bell was a much more recent recruit to Methodism. Born in County Durham, he had been a corporal in the Life Guards and was converted in 1758. In March 1761 he claimed sanctification, and Wesley published an account of this years later in the *Arminian Magazine*, evidently still seeing it as authentic. It had been received in a vision of Christ: 'I seemed as if my spirit was just ready to force its way out of my body.'[24] There was nothing particularly unusual in this for a Methodist, nor indeed in the fact that in 1761 Bell appeared to have cured a woman of painful lumps in the breast by prayer. This was also published by Wesley several years later in his *Journal* and he still firmly endorsed it as true.[25] As a perfectionist Bell soon gained a following. He held his own meetings, declaring that God had done with sacraments and was only to be found in the assemblies of Bell and his friends. His followers thought themselves restored to the purity of Adam and Eve and incapable of falling. They professed gifts of healing, attempting to give sight to the blind and to raise the dead; and they believed that they were exempt from death themselves. Bell himself attempted to heal a blind man by touching his eyes with spittle and saying 'Ephphatha' in imitation of Christ.[26]

Wesley, clearly convinced of the work of God in the perfectionist movement and certainly not averse to spiritual healing, was noticeably reluctant and hesitant in his approach to disciplining the prophets. Almost certainly he was afraid to hinder the perfectionist revival and indeed of fighting against the work of God. This is confirmed by his carefully discriminating account of what he observed as good and bad in Bell's proceedings. He visited them 'where I could see and hear, without being seen'. He then told Bell that he admired his fervent spirit but not his screaming, his belief that he could miraculously discern the state of people's spirits and his condemnation of his opponents. To Charles he wrote more bluntly that the proceedings in Bell's meetings were 'like a bear-garden' full of 'brawling, cursing, swearing, blasphemy'. On being removed to the Foundery they quietened down, and he found that as a number of people had been convicted or justified, good had been done. It was clearly this that, despite all the excesses, made him tolerate the meetings so long.[27]

Some of his pious correspondents like Sarah Crosby and Fletcher of

Madeley also believed the group was doing good, though Fletcher was disillusioned by Bell's and Maxfield's 'enthusiastic' letters to him.[28] At last Bell went too far. He prophesied that the world would end on 28 February 1763, and the stir that this created forced Wesley to disown him as a Methodist and to deny that the Methodists believed in the prophecy. This did not prevent a number of people from leaving London, fearing the end or at least an earthquake like that in 1750, which had produced similar effects and a flurry of sermons improving on the occasion.[29] Bell and his friends were imprisoned, and according to Southey Bell later moved from one extreme to the other, from enthusiasm to infidelity; finally he became a 'radical reformer'.[30] The whole episode showed how difficult it was to distinguish religious zeal and visionary spiritual gifts from 'pretending to special revelations' and insanity in early Methodism.

Behind Bell, it seems, was Maxfield, a more formidable figure. Wesley had had trouble with him before and had defended him against some charge in the Conference of 1761. In his usual cautious way in such cases in November 1762 Wesley had told Maxfield what he liked and disliked in him. For example, he liked his preaching of 'pure love' and perfection obtained by faith in a moment, but disliked claims of 'angelic' perfection. And he denied that instant perfection had only been taught recently: it had been taught for twenty years.[31]

Early in February, however, 'the mask was thrown off'. Maxfield claimed that Wesley did not preach perfection, and when the preachers were sent to take charge of Maxfield's meetings he took possession of Wesley's Snow's Fields chapel, refused to allow the preachers there and finally 'renounced connexion' with Wesley. He then, according to Wesley, 'spoke all manner of evil' of his old mentor and associates. It was in a letter to a friend about this that Wesley recounted Maxfield's career and complained of the ingratitude this showed to 'me, his father, his friend'.[32]

Maxfield naturally saw the affair in a different light. He thought that Wesley had tried to stifle the true doctrine of perfection and accused him of hypocrisy and double-dealing over Bell. He also claimed that Wesley had glorified himself by an epitaph quoted on Philip of Macedon:

> Here Philip lies, on the Dalmatian shore,
> Who did what mortal never did before.
> Yet, if there's one who boasts he hath more done,
> To me he owes it, for he was my son.

Wesley claimed that Maxfield had told Madan, an Evangelical clergyman, that Wesley had said to him, 'Tommy, I will tell the people you are the greatest gospel preacher in England, and you shall tell them

I am the greatest.' For refusing to do this (Maxfield said) Wesley put him away.[33] The stories could well be true, though misinterpreted by Maxfield. The Philip of Macedon verse merely reflected Wesley's injured sense of Maxwell's debt to him; and the preacher story sounds like a joke that had misfired. But in such highly personalized polemics the truth is hard to find.

The numerical losses resulting from the Maxfield secession were not large. In November 1763 Wesley found that 175 persons had separated, 106 on Maxfield's account, though other sources say 200.[34] Maxfield collected a large congregation, and later seems to have resumed friendly relations with the Methodists.[35] The revival and perfectionism continued, but the excesses of the enthusiasts forced Wesley into numerous explanations and qualifications of the claims for it. It had a more chastening effect on Charles Wesley than on his brother. At one time Charles had gone further than John in his claims for the gift as removing the 'root' of sin. But now Charles placed the achievement so high and saw it so much in terms of a prolonged and penitential discipline rather than as the result of a sudden act of faith that John complained he had made it impossible for anyone to achieve it.[36] Charles feared that these excesses would lead to a revival of the 'sect of Ranters' (an echo of the seventeenth century) and some of the preachers thought John had been far too slow to act.[37]

The affair also aggravated the rift between Wesley and the Evangelicals, who had never approved of the doctrine of perfection in any case. Wesley complained to Lady Huntingdon that they had not helped him in the crisis. He disclaimed any responsibility for the wild men, but Romaine thought that his societies were 'in confusion' and 'feared God would give them up to something still more dreadful'.[38] Grimshaw, while allowing for 'Scriptural Perfection', denied 'Sinless Perfection', and like Charles Wesley feared 'the spirit among them would drive them to Ranterism'.[39] There was really no possibility of compromise between Methodists and Evangelicals here, though it was only a year later that Wesley tried to engineer his evangelical union. To the outside world, of course, it confirmed all the old suspicions of Methodist 'enthusiasm', and it was unfortunate that it was in the early 1760s that the celebrated Cock Lane ghost was exposed by Dr Johnson: a fraud that some associated with Methodists. It was also about this time that Hogarth's savage cartoon of 'Credulity, Superstition and Fanaticism' appeared, attacking the Methodists amongst others.[40]

It is true that the perfectionist outbreaks, as Wesley claimed, did for a time at least help to stimulate more general local revivals. John Furz tells how in the early 1760s the work in Manchester which had been confined to the town for fifteen years was at last spread to the surrounding villages by means of local preachers, and that perfection was an element in this. There was also a great work in Liverpool.[41]

But the most serious effect in the eyes of Wesley and others was that the memory of the Bell excesses lingered on for years as a deterrent against the belief and preaching of perfection both among the preachers and the people. He commented on this on several occasions, and as late as 1796, after Wesley's death, John Pawson recorded a 'blessed work', but added that 'the old people are so afraid of George Bell's work returning, that they can hardly be persuaded that it is the work of God, because of a little disorder that attends it'.[42] But Wesley was not deterred. He continued to advocate the instant gift, merely defining his terms more carefully, and urged the unwilling preachers to proclaim it as well as writing much of it privately to his female correspondents; and a good many Methodists continued to hope for it. Many in fact gained it for a time, but then lost it. Reviewing the whole episode several years later, he still did not doubt that it had been a great work of God which had brought with it more general revival.[43]

How can this upsurge of perfectionism be explained? The prophetic abandon of Bell, spectacular though it was, represented only a small part of the total phenomenon. Such cases occurred inside and outside Methodism from time to time in individuals as well as in the French Prophets. Wesley mentions a couple in the 1740s, and in 1742 a Methodist preacher called John Brown appeared in Newcastle claiming he was to be king.[44] Methodism as such was not a 'millennarian' movement, and although there was more interest and activity of this kind in the troubled 1790s, it remains difficult to establish how important it was even then, despite modern attempts at social and political explanations.[45]

The question is rather why, by Wesley's account, perfectionist work should have stood still for twenty years and then erupted in such profusion in 1758–63. Indeed it was probably more of an innovation, especially in terms of instantaneous claims, than he allowed in his concern to claim that he had never changed his teaching.

Attempts at a simple explanation in terms of social and political tension seem hazardous, though they should be considered. The movement took place during the Seven Years War, in which 1759 was a significant year. In February there were rumours of a French invasion, the war was going badly for Britain and a public fast was proclaimed which was widely observed by the Methodists.[46] When matters improved at the end of the year they observed the national thanksgiving day.[47] The accession of George III in 1760 may have led to fears or hopes of change in evangelical fortunes. John Newton wrote to Wesley that another Evangelical had written to ask him about his sentiments, 'whether and how far the late changes in the State may be expected to influence the course of the gospel among us'. But he said he had nothing to say or think on this himself. He had heard that there was a bill on foot to confine the clergy to their own parishes but concluded by reflecting merely that 'the Lord reigneth'. Evangelicals often saw wars as judgments, and Wesley observed that such scares did temporarily bring in converts.[48]

But if crises like this could heighten religious concern, the specific turn to perfection probably owes more to the fact that some of the preachers had clearly been emphasizing it as early as 1758 and in ways which, as we have seen, were making people fear that without it they could not be saved at all. It was no doubt this which, despite Wesley's reassurances, built up pressure to seek the gift and produced numerous claims to it.

Debates in Conference, Wesley's writings and his own interest in the cases which reinforced his belief and advocacy for it go a long way towards explaining why the movement became general. But most of the pressure was, as so often, from below, and the Maxfield and Bell 'spectaculars' fed the phenomenon while alienating some from it. Sectarian impulses were fed by separate meetings for prayer, which would later become characteristic of the more emotional and 'primitive' Methodists despite the caution of the leadership.[49]

Furthermore, although Wesley disclaimed responsibility for the outbreaks, he helped them simply by being slow to act. It is not really surprising that among people already well acquainted with the pattern of conversion there should have been a desire for further manifestations of the spirit. The original strangeness and shock value of conversion had worn off, but perfection offered a new incentive. Wesley himself certainly saw it in this light and as an essential weapon against spiritual complacency, quietism and Calvinist antinomianism. The excitement produced could easily be the trigger for a more general 'awakening'. He saw it all as 'providential' – hence his reluctance to curb the excesses – and from another point of view his attempts to refine and define the doctrine are a good example of his role as a 'reasonable enthusiast'.

X

John Wesley and the World

1. Propagandist and cultural mediator: Wesley as preacher, author and editor

As a preacher Wesley presents a familiar problem.[1] Sermons are always more or less cold and formal in print, and it is peculiarly difficult to reconstruct the manner and effects of a revivalist preacher when one has only the apparently dull discourses surviving in print. Wesley's printed sermons clearly represent only the solid skeletons of discourses, written down and published as pieces of systematic teaching to give a framework for Methodist doctrine. In the preface to his *Sermons on Several Occasions* (1746) Wesley describes them as the 'substance' of what he preached, and his sermon record shows that some of them were preached many times, undoubtedly in variable forms.[2] Forty-four of them were finally selected together with his *Notes on the New Testament* as the standard for the doctrines to be preached in his chapels under the model deed in 1763.[3] The subjects included key doctrines such as justification by faith and perfection, but also a series on the Sermon on the Mount. In the standard editions of his works in the nineteenth century others were added to a total of 151 (a few not in fact by him). The later, relatively neglected ones include much on Wesley's deepening alarm at the effects of wealth on the spiritual life of Methodists (see below, pp. 366f.).

In practice Wesley preached extempore for an hour or more and the indications are that, like most preachers, he filled out and varied the basic material with anecdotes and illustrations, sometimes adapted to circumstances or incidents occurring during preaching. It is more than likely that he fell into anecdotage as an old man.[4] Hampson convincingly portrays him as often succeeding when he prepared but failing when he did not. 'He preached too frequently; and the consequence was inevitable' – he became trite and disjointed. But he 'made it a point to preach, if he could stand upon his legs'. Hampson adds that Wesley, when 'he fell into anecdote and story-telling, which was not seldom, his discourses were little to the purpose'; and this was generally considered as an 'infirmity of "garrulous old age"'.[5] Hampson, however, was embarrassed by the effects of this on educated audiences and Wesley was aiming at a larger public. Sir Walter Scott, at the age of twelve, heard Wesley several times, and commented that 'He was a most venerable figure, but his sermons were vastly too colloquial for the taste of Saunders.' Scott added that he 'told many excellent stories', including one of how he had rebuked a 'God damn me' soldier by telling him, 'You mean God bless me'.[6]

Wesley's ideals for preaching may perhaps be gathered from his directions to his preachers, though no doubt these were given with an eye to their besetting faults.[7] They should have a serious deportment, suit the subject to the audience, keep to plain texts, avoid 'rambling', be sparing in allegorizing, eschew quaint words, say 'hallowed' not 'hollowed' in the Lord's Prayer. After preaching they should avoid spirituous liquors and take mild ale or lemonade (this was not always observed). One can see the vices of the over-reaching self-educated reflected here. Nor should they be led off 'practical' preaching into 'what was called preaching Christ'. Here he had in mind the kind of Calvinist 'gospel preachers' whom he elsewhere condemned as 'pert, self-sufficient animals' lacking sense or grace, who bawl out clichés about 'the blood' and leave their foolish hearers saying 'what a fine gospel sermon!'[8] They should rather preach Christ 'in all his offices', and insist upon 'internal and external obedience'. Wesley often had to warn his preachers not to 'scream' – 'this is offering murder for sacrifice' – nor to preach above an hour.[9]

Wesley always stressed plain language. According to a story he told, as a young man he preached a learned sermon which left the congregation open-mouthed; tried again and left their mouths half-open. He then read the sermon to an intelligent servant, and every time Betty cried 'Stop', he wrote in a single word, until it reached a form that the congregation could understand.[10] The plain words, however, were laced with scriptural phrases and echoes and, if the published sermons are any guide (and they may not be, if Hampson is correct), with a clear structure and logical arguments.

Wesley was, in fact, using a version of the 'plain style' of preaching which had been developing since the later seventeenth century.[11] English preaching had become very different not only from the intricate discourses full of literary conceits of the age of Donne, but also from the learned and intricate subdivisions of the 'practical' preaching of the Puritans. But the evangelicals were different again. An observer in Basel in 1714 noted how the Calvinist preachers there preached 'without a book, and deliver with proper actions, keeping a medium between the

theatrical gestures of the French and Italians and the cold unattractive-
ness of our own'.[12]

It is relevant here to observe that there was a distinct tradition of
Dissenting evangelical theory and practice of preaching based on an
analysis of the way in which 'sacred oratory' should be used to appeal
to the will and the affections as well as the understanding. The passions
were to be used to excite the will. As Doddridge put it, the passions were
the 'sails of the soul', though due regard should be paid to the reason
and the avoidance of enthusiasm.[13] Wesley tacitly endorsed a similar
balanced approach. Indeed he produced a tract on 'Directions concerning Pronunciation and Gesture' (based on the work of the French
Catholic Port Royalists), taking a judicious, balanced, middle road on
these matters.[14] It has to be added, of course, that in the heat of revival
moderation of this kind was unlikely to be observed, and Wesley's advice
to his preachers tells its own tale (confirmed by other evidence) that
emotion and eccentricity of language and gesture were common.

The simplified three-point sermon seems also to have emerged
through the Revival – a memorable example is Wesley's sermon on 'The
Use of Money' ('gain all you can, save all you can, give all you can').
Even in the considered, printed versions of sermons like these, one can
gain some impression of Wesley's rhetorical style when he works up to
an application or appeal in an urgent, staccato style. Wesley himself
thought that his brother Charles beat him in 'strong pointed sentences',
whereas he himself was better in 'connexion' (connected argument).[15]
His controversial sermon on 'Scriptural Christianity' before the University of Oxford in 1744 has a damning indictment of the university, which
concludes with what some hearers felt was an almost blasphemous
invocation: 'It is time for Thee, Lord, to lay to thine hand!' This is in
the printed version, and an eye-witness account shows that Wesley
began the sermon softly and gradually raised his voice and finally his
eyes as he uttered the offending words.[16]

One thing which added to the effectiveness of revival preaching was
that such preachers sooner or later abandoned the practice of reading
sermons or even using notes. This step was often recorded as an epoch
in their lives and religious effectiveness. Wesley himself recalled in 1788
how fifty years earlier he had first done this by accident. He had come
to a London church without his sermon and left the pulpit for the vestry
in confusion. But a woman, noting this, said 'Is that all? Cannot you
trust God for a sermon?' He did so with such 'freedom to myself and
acceptance to the people' that he had never taken a written sermon into
the pulpit since.[17]

One final description of Wesley preaching, though familiar and from
an unsympathetic witness, is worth quoting, since it probably conveys

part of the truth about his manner, and perhaps indicates some of the drawbacks of which Hampson complained. Horace Walpole heard him in 1766 at Bath (probably in Lady Huntingdon's chapel).

> Wesley is a lean elderly man, fresh-coloured, his hair smoothly combed, but with a *soupçon* of curl at the ends. Wondrous clean, but as evidently an actor as Garrick. He spoke his sermon but so fast, and with so little accent, that I am sure he has often uttered it, for it was like a lesson. There were parts and eloquence in it; but towards the end he exalted his voice, and acted very ugly enthusiasm; decried learning, and told stories, like Latimer, of the fool of his college who said, 'I *thanks* God for everything.'[18]

Much must in fact have depended on the state of mind of the audience. Preaching in 1775 with the American crisis building up, Wesley so described the horrors of war that 'scarce a dry eye was seen in the large assembly'. At a more personal level, John Nelson on his road to conversion heard Wesley preach in Moorfields, saw him 'stroke back his hair', felt his heart begin to beat like a 'pendulum' and felt Wesley's eyes and message were directed at him.[19]

Wesley's voice appears to have carried well, though his claims on this are also related to the remarkable claims made by himself and Whitefield for the size of the crowds that heard them. At the age of eighty-four he was heard to speak without notes and with 'the voice of a man of thirty'.[20] At Gwennap Pit he claimed to have calculated a crowd of 12,500. More surprisingly he claimed a calculated crowd elsewhere of 20,000 in a space of forty by one hundred yards with five people per square yard; and that he could be heard one hundred or even one hundred and forty yards away.[21]

The first difficulty in estimating Wesley's achievement as an author and editor is the fact that he so frequently fused (or confused) the two functions.[22] Sometimes this is obvious, as when he published an 'extract' (usually in fact an abridgment) from a named author. But often he silently abridged, adapted and altered pieces presented as if from his own pen. Much of his output was in fact heavily derivative, though with his own characteristic touches. Thus his treatise on 'Original Sin' was really derived partly from a work by Isaac Watts. He got himself into trouble when he lifted chunks from Dr Johnson for a pamphlet against the rebellious American colonists.[23] Even allowing for relaxed contemporary standards in this matter, Wesley was remarkably cavalier in his borrowings. He seems to have taken the view that if a thing was good it should be spread further by abridgment. When dealing with his favourite Catholic saints, he omitted what he found offensively 'popish', highlighting what he saw as the essentials of perfection. Approaching the task of annotating the New Testament, he originally thought of simply setting down what had occurred to him that would benefit those lacking formal learning, but in the event came upon 'that great light of the Christian world', the Pietist J.A. Bengel. Wesley extracted the juice of his *Gnomon*, though also he added elements from other works such as Doddridge's very popular *Family Expositor*. He ingenuously decided not to acknowledge his debts in detail so as not to divert attention from 'the point in view'.[24] Abridgment, even more than translation, is a loaded art, but at least it may be said that Wesley's sympathies were a good deal wider than those of most evangelicals. He produced versions of Catholic and mystical works (despite his own strictures on 'mysticism'), bowdlerized though they might be. To them, very unlike Whitefield and Venn, he added Tillotson and the *Whole Duty of Man*. Of Tillotson he simply said that he was 'as far from being the worst, as from being the best, of the English writers'.[25] What attracted him was the useful balanced moralism to counteract the evil effects of antinomianism and Calvinism, just as he valued moral Anglican sermons more than loose 'gospel' effusions.

A few examples will suffice to show the range of his interests and the overall objectives of his writing and publishing.

The Christian Library (1749–55) was not a particularly successful project, though individual works of the same devotional kind were published more successfully. The intention was to publish specimens of 'practical divinity' from what Wesley regarded as the best body of that kind in the world: the English divines of the seventeenth and eighteenth centuries. As we have seen, some critics dismissed it as from 'dissenters of all kinds', though Wesley claimed that it was mostly from divines of the Church of England. The largest single category was in fact that of those broadly classed as 'Puritans' originally within the Establishment. There were also Anglicans as varied as Taylor, Ken, Sanderson and Tillotson; a few early Christian writers like Ignatius and Macarius; and a few foreigners like the proto-Pietist Arndt, Pascal and Molinos.

Wesley's principles of abridgment were partly in terms of style, partly for brevity, but above all to preserve what the writer said 'so far as he follows Christ'.[26] Generally he kept his word, but in the case of the Puritan writers this meant eliminating Calvinist notions of election and anything that might deter men from active preparation for salvation and the pursuit of perfection. In the mystics he brought out what he liked in them: the 'practical' love of God.[27]

A Survey of the Wisdom of God in Creation (1775), a 'compendium of natural philosophy', follows rather similar principles. Wesley aimed at a compilation of moderate size and expense; attempted to record only what was true and certain; and this in plain language, free from the 'jargon of mathematics' which is 'Greek' to ordinary readers. Above all, he wished not to minister to 'idle, barren curiosity' but rather to 'display the miraculous things of God'. Here he was using a familiar genre in the footsteps of writers like Ray and Derham. As so often, he used another work as his basis: Buddeus of Jena, though with much alteration and addition from others.[28]

There are two particular points of interest in Wesley's approach to science. One is that he did not scruple to add 'uncommon appearances of nature', since they display the wisdom of God. He balked at the mile-long Kraken, but here as elsewhere showed how he loved a wonder which, like apparitions and demonology, might show the intervention of the supernatural (see further, below pp. 387f., 431ff.). His philosophical position, as we shall see later, was that of a Lockeian empiricist with suitable modifications. Just as in his *Primitive Physick* he disowned all speculative systems and explanations of diseases and merely reported cures that apparently worked, so in natural science he avoided expla-nation in favour of description. 'I undertake barely to set down what appears in nature; not the cause of the appearances.' Facts lie within the compass of our senses, but causes do not. As Hampson said, Wesley was technically a 'sceptic' in philosophy and did not believe in any 'system'. Indeed he denied calculations of the planetary distances and the plurality of worlds: like the High Church Hutchinsonians he distrusted Newton's hypotheses, though he was equally sceptical about their own curious theories.[29] But his empiricism, too, had a religious purpose. 'God hath so done in his works that we may admire and adore; but we cannot search them out to perfection.'[30] In these terms the work could presumably be justified as an instrument for religious culture.

The same could be said of two other compendia: the *History of England* and the *Ecclesiastical History*. In the *History of England* once again Wesley complains about prolix and expensive works and attempts to remedy this by a work drawing mainly on Goldsmith, Rapin and Smollett, the first and last of who were themselves predominantly compilers of the works of others. But he also tried to remedy the faults of works 'calculated only for atheists', which did not show God 'as the supreme ruler of the earth, the disposer of all things according to his will'. Wesley's view of the use of history was inspired by classical and contemporary models together with his evangelical purpose. History should improve the mind and inspire by noble examples, but above all enable us to 'see God in all the affairs of men', 'in all civil events as well as in the phenomena of nature'.[31]

The *Ecclesiastical History* naturally followed the same principles. Eachard, Wesley said, was so dull that it sent one to sleep, and he was at a loss for a suitable candidate for his usual treatment. However, when Mosheim appeared in Maclaine's translation, Wesley said that he could remedy Maclaine's great defect by making Mosheim shorter and cheaper. Wesley also omitted many accounts of 'senseless' heresies, but above all remedied what he thought to be Mosheim's unsatisfactory account of the internal state of the church. For Mosheim seemed to treat the church like a secular object and ignored the righteousness, peace and joy in the Holy Ghost which are the real marks of the church's internal state. Wesley was in fact objecting to the sober and relatively objective approach which later critics have felt to have marked Mosheim out as the first 'modern' church historian. However, Wesley warned the 'pious reader' not to expect too many saints: they are always rare and the church showed signs of corruption from the start. In a general way he subscribed to the Protestant historiography also followed by the Evangelicals Milner and Haweis, who picked out scattered sparks of light in the dark ages of popery which preserved the truth until the Reformation dawned. His evangelicalism had by now modified the Anglican tradition of venerating the collective wisdom of the age of the Fathers.[32]

Wesley's approach in all these works, then, was a mixture of instruction, edification and apologetic. He wished to justify the ways of God to men and to build up their piety. The same aim is evident in a collection of poetry published in 1744.[33] As to his readership, he cannot have been aiming at the generality of Methodists, but rather aspired to be a semi-popular educator catering for the growing reading public of Georgian England, men of modest means eager for culture whom he no doubt hoped to capture for his view of the world.

The *Arminian Magazine* (from 1778) was designed for a more specifically religious public. As its title indicates, it first emerged in the context of the Calvinistic controversy of the 1770s and was apparently designed specifically to counter the 'miscreated relation' called *The Spiritual Magazine* and its 'twin-sister, oddly called *The Gospel Magazine*', which designed to show that Christ died only for the elect. Those organs, moreover (Wesley complained), combined the arguments of Bedlam with the language of Billingsgate. *His* magazine would be very different in tone and content. He promised items defending universal redemption; the lives of holy men of all parties; experiences of pious persons; and verses on the doctrines in view.[34] One senses that in fact the *Magazine* was seen increasingly by Wesley as having a broader function than Arminian propaganda: it was a kind of religious *Readers Digest*; a sanctified version of the *Gentleman's Magazine* for pious persons of moderate means and education, especially Methodists. He soon had to answer charges of lack of 'variety' (pressure from his reading public shows here), and occasionally there were more or less secular poems. He was also characteristically proud of its sentiments and language: obviously he wished it to be culturally respectable within its limits. He added new 'branches': his own sermons, lives of Methodists other than the preachers (whose portraits begin to appear from 1779), and extracts from his *Wisdom of God in the Creation*.[35]

It is equally characteristic that the contents came to include condensations of travel books and accounts of marvels; oddities of science and anecdotes of 'providences' as well as accounts of supernatural phenomena and apparitions and witchcraft. It is a mistake to dismiss this as peripheral to Wesley's teaching and mission. It is fully in line with his general outlook, and could indeed be justified as an aspect of the same design as his histories and science: to show God's presence and action in the world to sceptics. At the same time it illustrates the mental world of Wesley and his people (see below, 387f., 431ff.).

As an original author, Wesley's most characteristic publications, apart from his *Journal*, were sermons, 'Appeals', accounts of Methodism, 'Words' to various sorts of sinners, and controversial writings or open letters. There were also textbooks for his Kingswood school. Hymns he mostly left to Charles, though he wrote and translated some himself. To this has to be added a very large correspondence in which his passion for brevity (a necessary discipline in any case for his crowded life) sometimes reduced him to short, aphoristic replies to queries. But others, especially to pious women, include directions for study, guidance in the spiritual life and attractively simple expositions of his essential doctrine of Christian love.[36] He also wrote short tracts, usually at a penny apiece, for poor people, and these and his other writings were sold by the preachers. He complained that after all his literary labours he had only gained a debt of £500 or £600. But in later years he said he had 'unawares become rich' by these sales and was often able to give away upwards of £1000 each year from them.[37]

Hampson said that Wesley's most distinguishing characteristic as a writer was 'conciseness', as indeed it was. Judging Wesley by contemporary literary standards, Hampson went on to say that 'here he was sometimes abrupt' and 'a sort of bluntness superseded that air of elegance and ease, which, accompanied with a becoming gravity, is peculiarly pleasing', but he 'rarely fell into obscurity'. Wesley might have developed into an elegant writer, but he 'valued himself too much on logic to pay sufficient attention to the ornamental part of fine writing'. Wesley's excellence as an author lay in his controversial writings, where argument and logic were at a premium. Hampson concluded that though not in the 'first class' of English authors, Wesley was a 'laborious and useful' writer. Whitehead thought that he wrote not to please or for party purposes, but only to 'inform the understanding and warm the heart; to discourage vice and promote virtue' – an accurate enough assessment. Whitehead also noted that Wesley was not well fitted for historical or scientific work since he was apt to generalize and to place too great confidence in the 'authority of his own assertions when he himself was convinced'.[38] This is indeed characteristic of his judgments of books and other matters.

As a controversialist Wesley could be sharp and sarcastic and descend to unfair caricature, as in his treatment of Toplady (who gave even better than he got, but had some excuse in provocation).[39] To serious-minded opponents like 'John Smith' Wesley could be courteous and careful enough. He undoubtedly toned down the offensive features of Methodist 'enthusiasm' and followed the wearisome traditional methods of controversy by quotation and point-by-point refutation of his adversary. Here he was far less skilful than a Law answering Hoadly or a Newman answering Kingsley. He was a master of the traditional Oxford disputation, aiming to score points rather than discover truth; and, as his opponents complained, he not infrequently evaded the points of criticism by verbal distinctions. It is difficult to believe that any but his own supporters were ever actually convinced by this method. Wesley is really at his best both as a stylist and as a controversialist in his 'Words' and in pieces like the 'Calm Address' to the American colonists, where he puts his case crisply and cogently with perorations which are good examples of controlled but passionate appeal, like the conclusions of his printed sermons.

And then there is the *Journal*. Whatever snares it offers as a guide to Wesley's actions and motives in terms of a biographical source, and whatever questions it raises about his character, it is a unique record of the public career of a tireless traveller, evangelist and observer of men and manners.[40] It is superior as a mirror of the eighteenth century to Horace Walpole's famous letters, since if it only shows the aristocratic and fashionable world or the world of high politics from the outside, Wesley had the advantage of moving easily and without affectation between the very different worlds of the mob, the respectable artisan and tradesman, and the educated middling classes.

The *Journal* in fact became one of the instruments, along with Wesley's other writings, for a more or less conscious role as a cultural middleman – very obvious in the *Survey* and *Histories*; and at a lower level in the *Magazine*, though there are touches of this in everything he wrote. Unfortunately, beyond the evidence of reprints and sales we have little idea of what the cultural impact of all this was within Methodism and still less outside it.[41] There have been recurring claims that at least in the case of Charles Wesley's hymns we have a forerunner of 'Romanticism', and a recent study makes larger claims for Wesley's intellectual outlook as a whole and the kind of treatment he gave to the notion of 'spiritual senses'. The claim is that he had a discernible influence in preparing an audience for the Romantics and even that he had some influence on major figures among them.[42]

These claims for a capacity to join two such very different worlds seem exaggerated. It would be more plausible to maintain that to a degree at least, Wesley was in an unusually good position to act as a cultural middleman. He was an educated gentleman and a clergyman, but he was leading an irregular religious movement of the less educated, half-educated and illiterate, and he shared much of their basic supernaturalist mentality and religious tastes. He was a religious and cultural mediator from above to below, and would have liked to be a religious mediator from below to above, though in this he was less successful. But he injected an element of educated culture as well as reason and morality into the stock evangelical salvation concerns.

Wesley no doubt regarded himself as not only a man of 'reason and religion' but also as a man of taste. Indeed he wrote 'Thoughts on Taste' in 1780 for his *Magazine*.[43] This was provoked by a reading of an *Essay on Taste* by Alexander Gerard, with whose vague definition of taste as 'the improvement of the principles commonly called the powers of imagination' Wesley disagreed.[44] Wesley saw taste rather as a faculty of the mind analogous to the physical sense of taste, an internal sense 'relishing and distinguishing its proper object'. The objects may include the beauty of virtue, gratitude and disinterested benevolence. All men, . Wesley thought, may have 'taste' – for something. To have good taste is to be able to discern whatever is good in its kind. This is much to be desired, as it may increase innocent pleasures, but also qualify us to be of greater service to our fellow-creatures as well as making us more agreeable and so more profitable in conversation. Thus Wesley turns even aesthetics to religious use: the end of it all is 'the pleasing all men for their good unto edification'.

In general, indeed, Wesley reacted conventionally to beauty of various kinds, though convention was affected here by his religious concerns. He was also prone to lay down the law in response to instant conclusions of his own from scanty premises, as Alexander Knox observed, for example in the historic judgments on Richard III and Mary Queen of Scots mentioned earlier.[45] He was unashamedly pre-Romantic in his dislike of moors and mountains, and preferred nature as chastened and improved by man (but his travelling problems were not likely to endear wild and pathless areas to him in any case). He occasionally took time off to view country houses like other travelling gentlemen and recorded his appreciation, though he disliked the 'indecent' heathen statues at

Stourhead. Professor Ward points out that he may have disliked the interruption of landscape gardening by statuary. What is very obvious, however, is that he often liked to reflect with a kind of grim satisfaction on how the builders of such vain grandeur died bankrupt or prematurely – where will all this be on the last day? – and so forth.[46] But why visit and comment at all? Was it to educate his readers' taste, to point the moral, or to educate and moralize to justify his own pleasure?

Evangelicals in general and Methodists in particular were narrow in their cultural interests (as we shall see), though their degree of narrowness was influenced by background and social station. Wesley himself published a version of Henry Brooke's sentimental and pious *Fool of Quality* and is reported to have exclaimed 'O earth – earth – earth!' to a Methodist who failed to appreciate its beauties. He himself approved of it because it 'strikes at the heart', and aimed 'at inspiring and increasing every right affection'. His early Oxford days of play-reading were over, but his classical and literary reading remained in his mind for ready quotation. It comes as something of a shock to find him referring in passing to *Tristram Shandy* (of all novels!) in a pamphlet. But now all this is dedicated to religious and moral ends.[47]

2. 'He that plays as a child will play as a man': Wesley as educator

Although Wesley and his followers had a considerable concern for children and especially for the salvation of their souls, there is no discernible 'official' policy for founding schools, though some special measures were taken for children's spiritual nurture. Initiatives for founding day and Sunday schools were taken locally by concerned individuals, and were part of a growing concern for educating the poor which was not peculiar to evangelicals.[48]

Wesley's attitude to children and their nurture was influenced by his own upbringing and his overriding concern for the welfare of souls, but also by his basic perception of the problems of human nature. It was this perception which probably ultimately determined his belief, inherited from his mother, that a child's will must be 'broken' (not simply 'subdued', as Locke recommended) before it could be moulded according to its parents' wishes and so prepared for independent (correct) action later.

Late in life Wesley set down his own general principles in his *Thought on the Manner of Educating Children* (1783).[49] This was written in response to a gentleman who had objected to the severe discipline and incessant forcing of religion on children found in religious schools, which (he thought) often produced religious indifference later. He advocated instead what would now be called a child-centred approach to religious education. Wesley condemned such approaches as were based on Rousseau's *Émile*: 'the most empty, silly, injudicious thing that even a self-conceited infidel wrote'. Few religious disasters had emerged from his own Kingswood régime, and where religious schools failed, it was because either their religious or educational principles were faulty. Religion should be instilled as soon as possible because Scripture, reason and experience show that the corruption of human nature should be curbed from the first. 'The bias of nature is set the wrong way; education is designed to set it right.' This should be done by 'mildness' where this is possible, but by 'kind severity' where it is not. The purpose is to turn children from love of the world to love of God. The contrast between 'enlightened' or 'romantic' ideas of original innocence and traditional ideas of original sin is fundamental. In any case education is not enough. To Philothea Briggs in 1773 Wesley wrote that, 'All our wisdom will not even make them (children) *understand*, much less *feel* the things of God.' They need to be 'awakened' by God.[50]

Although stories were told of how much Wesley loved children and how well he got on with them, at least in his mellow old age, this trait was always subordinated to his primary concern to save their souls. He liked to record edifying child deaths, and did not hesitate to tell grieving parents that losses of children set them freer to pursue their own piety. Commonplace though this was among people of all sects who have seen heaven as being more desirable than earth, there is a lack of human feeling here which was not always shared by others who agreed with this perspective in principle.[51]

Wesley was early interested in educating the poor, as his efforts in Oxford showed. Here he reflected the ideals of the charity school movement backed by the SPCK, which included a concern for religious nurture, morals and the inculcation of habits of good order; though throughout the eighteenth century day and Sunday schools for the poor had to meet the suspicion that, far from helping to control the poor, education might make them resistant to authority and spoil them for their lowly place in the labour market.[52] For religious people, indeed, a primary hope was that children might be snatched from the devil early, and this was certainly prominent in Wesley's mind.

The same imperative also affected those individual lay Methodists who interested themselves in education, such as Miss Bosanquet or Hannah Ball, who was a pioneer of Sunday schools before Robert Raikes. More will be said about this later as an aspect of early Methodist rank-and-file social concern, for although Wesley helped to organize schools in London, Methodist initiatives in educating the poor came mainly from below and at a local level.[53] Wesley's relationship to the Sunday school movement is well expressed in a comment in his *Journal* in 1784: 'I find these schools springing up wherever I go. Perhaps God may have some deeper end therein than men are aware of. Who knows but some of them may become nurseries for Christians?' This reflected the effects of Robert Raikes's publicity, and the movement stretched well beyond the evangelical world. Although Wesley helped by printing Raikes's account and other cases in the *Magazine* and *Journal* and encouraged Methodists who joined in, he was essentially a spectator rather than an organizer in this field.[54]

Official Methodist action for child nurture took other forms. The system of class meetings included, in some places, special classes for children, though little is known about them. Preachers were urged to distribute Wesley's *Instructions for Children* to learn by heart. They should meet children weekly to talk to them, pray with them and instruct them. The *Instructions* and *Token for Children* were further examples of Wesley's adaptations from other authors.[55] Early intimations of God already in childhood were characteristic of many Methodist autobiographies, and child conversion became a feature of local revivals in the 1780s.[56]

But the educational project which was perhaps dearest to Wesley's heart, and certainly the one in which he himself was most often and directly involved, was the school he founded at Kingswood in 1748.[57] This school should not be confused with the one originally founded by Whitefield for the miners' children and taken over by Wesley amid much acrimony. By 1749 there were in fact four Methodist schools in Kingswood: day schools for boys and girls, an orphan one for girls, and the 'New House' – as Wesley called the 1748 project.[58] Although it later became a school for the sons of the itinerants, the original design was for a school for the general Christian public which would be a 'Christian' school free of the dubious educational methods and even more dubious religious and moral atmosphere of the 'great schools' (the old 'public' schools) which evangelicals were not alone in distrusting. Wesley also had an eye to future ministers: 'We design to train up children there, if God permit, in every branch of useful learning . . . till they are fit as to all the acquired qualifications for the work of the ministry.'[59] Wesley made four basic criticisms of the existing schools. They were mostly near to large towns and so to diversion and corrupting company. All sorts were admitted. Most of the masters had no more religion than the scholars. The instruction given was ill-planned: Latin and Greek predominated, to the neglect of more elementary work, and in any case were read without rational progress from the easier to the more difficult works. Thus Wesley saw himself as an educational as well as religious and moral reformer. He placed the school at Kingswood so as to have the advantages of seclusion, yet with access to Bristol; and he would take only select boarders, who would have to stay at the school throughout their course to avoid corruption and the interference of parents. The aim of this Christian education was to be that of 'forming their minds, through the help of God, to wisdom and holiness, by instilling the principles of true religion, speculative and practical, and training them up in the ancient way, that they might be rational, scriptural Christians'.[60]

The regimen of the school as Wesley described it in 1768 was that they rose at 4 a.m., spent an hour in reading, singing, meditation and prayer, met for worship at 5 and from 6 worked until breakfast. 'For as we have no play-days . . . so neither do we allow any time for play on any day.' He quotes a German proverb: 'He that plays when he is a child, will play when he is a man.' Tradition tells that when asked to allow the boys to play he responded: 'If they wish for recreation let them have a prayer meeting.'[61] On fine days they worked in the garden and otherwise in the house. Some learnt music, some did 'philosophical (scientific) experiments'. They should do all in the presence of a master. The routine continued with school from 7 to 11 a.m.; then walking or working from 11 to 12. They dined and then sang or worked till 1 p.m. Work came again from 1 to 5; then private prayer; walking or working from 6 till supper; then public worship and at 8 p.m. bed, beginning with the youngest. They slept in rooms with a light burning and a master at one end, using mattresses and not feather beds. On Sundays there was the expected diet of public worship and private devotion. The physical diet was also plainly laid down. There was porridge or gruel for breakfast; bread and butter or cheese for supper; meat and apple dumplings for dinner; and only water was to be drunk. They were at liberty (!) to fast on Fridays until 3 p.m. How far this healthful régime was rigidly adhered to is perhaps questionable, for Wesley frequently complained that the boys played even in school, and in 1782 Adam Clarke says that they not only drank beer (as would have been customary elsewhere) but also insisted on rounds of healths.[62]

As to the curriculum, boys were to be educated between the ages of six and twelve in 'reading, writing, arithmetic, English, French, Latin, Greek, Hebrew, history, geography, chronology, rhetoric, logic, ethics, geometry, algebra, physics, music'. Wesley lists the books to be studied, headed each year by a religious work: his *Instructions for Children*; Fleury's *Manners of the Ancient Christians*; Cave's *Primitive Christianity; Pilgrim's Progress*; De Renty and Law – Wesley's old favourites in fact. The lists do not include all that had been promised, such as algebra, music and French. Natural science had been seen as a form of recreation in the German Pietist schools at Halle, and the high claims sometimes made for these and the Dissenting academies as nurseries of 'modern' education in this respect can easily be exaggerated. The academies were in any case under-funded and under-staffed, and not all of them did much science.[63] What we might term the 'core curriculum' was still heavily weighted in favour of the classics, and Wesley's school was no exception. He thought little of French as a language ('no more comparable to the German or Spanish than a bagpipe is to an organ'), and his classical instruction followed the old pattern of making verses, 'themes' and 'declamations'. It was the religious grounding that stood out as an exceptional emphasis.[64] Although Wesley chose his classical authors with an eye to what he thought were the earlier and better Latin models, he was also anxious to uphold morality and to eliminate impropriety and indecency: one recalls his complaints to his brother in the 1730s about the indecency of some of the current school and university classical pabulum.[65] The Pietists agreed, though some went much further than he.

Wesley had a higher ambition, too, for Kingswood: to add a course of 'academical learning' over four years. This included the classics and modern works of science, history and literature. With characteristic self-confidence he declared that 'whoever goes carefully through this course will be a better scholar than nine in ten of the graduates at Oxford and Cambridge'.[66] In fact this part of the design was suspended until at least the late 1760s.[67] His affection and even respect for Oxford remained strong: the strictures in the University Sermon of 1744 were not against the system but against the failure to observe the rules, and he often compared universities in other countries unfavourably with those of England. But in 1768 the St Edmund Hall 'Methodists' were expelled, and although they were Calvinists and not of Wesley's connexion, his own people had trouble too. A Mr Seager was refused entry to Oxford and appeared on the Kingswood 'academical course' in 1768–9; Joseph Benson was prevented from proceeding to a degree.[68] The Methodists were not formally Dissenters, but there were ways of blocking them. It is probably no accident that the second edition of the *Short Account* (1768) expressed doubts about Oxford and included the 'academical course'. The *Plain Account* of Kingswood in 1781 had a diatribe against the Oxford system. The professorial lectures are useless; many of the tutors lack learning and religion; the public 'exercises' and 'disputations' for degrees are 'an idle, useless interruption of any useful studies' and 'shockingly superficial'. Socially, a man gains all kinds of 'company' 'except that which would do him good'. The prospect of holy orders as the reward of the system is as nothing compared with eternity. What Wesley had to offer instead was somewhat on the lines of the Dissenting academies, but what they lacked (apart from resources) was valuable social contacts, some cultural polish and of course the prospect of orders. It is difficult to say how far the 'academical' project went, for although there is some evidence of students, it is doubtful whether many went the full course. Adam Clarke's experience in 1783 was not a happy one, but partly because of the domineering wife of the headmaster.[69]

In formulating his Kingswood scheme, Wesley acknowledged that he used continental models, notably the Pietist establishment at Jena which he had visited in 1738.[70] The aphorism about play and the presence of masters at all activities come from this source. Francke, the father of the Pietist Halle establishment, was as insistent as Wesley on avoiding holidays, and for the same reason: to ensure that the school had full control of the pupils' lives. Although Francke did not ban games, there was much debate on what was permissible, and in practice emphasis was laid on walking and visits to artisans' workshops. He, too, emphasized the classics and languages and purged them for indecency, but he resisted the more extreme Pietists who would have liked to ban heathen authors altogether. Science, as already noted, was seen as a form of recreation rather than as an essential part of the curriculum.[71] The underlying pious purpose and the priority of religious nurture is the same for both men. But one may well believe that Wesley's educational vision was at bottom a combination of Epworth and Oxford, suitably modified and, in intention at least, rigorously supervised.

But this was just the problem. Wesley's ideals conflicted in any case with unregenerate juvenile nature, aggravated by the fact that he could pay only occasional visits. Everything depended on suitable staff, and these were seldom forthcoming. Wesley's judgment was not always good, his most damaging appointment for the image of the school being that bigamous if repentant Magdalen, Sarah Ryan, as housekeeper.[72] Financially, the school depended at first on fees and casual help; in 1756 the Conference proposed a subscription round the connexion, though there was not much result until 1766, when 'stewards' were appointed to manage the place, which made it more officially a 'connexional' school.[73] The preachers' sons had occasionally been sent there, but in 1788 it was ruled that the fee-payers should be reduced to ten to allow them in. After Wesley's death the school was eventually limited to preachers' sons only, though in later times this again ceased to be the case.[74]

Wesley's view of the state of the school was seldom temperate, and generally alternated between the extremes of despair and optimism – most often the former. In his *Remarks on the State of Kingswood School* (1783) he says that it has not fulfilled the ideal of a 'Christian family', mainly because the rules were not kept. The pupils lack supervision and so run up and down and fight with the colliers' children and play every day. It must be 'mended or ended' – a frequent refrain.[75] The masters were never right: either they were solemn and earnest and the boys ridiculed them, or they were adequate teachers but lacked piety and management skills.

As to religion in the school, this was as often as not also found wanting. But there was one spectacular period when Wesley's dearest wishes were gratified with a local outbreak of revival and many apparent conversions. This began in 1768 and continued on and off until 1773.[76] Though it occurred during Benson's régime – and he was nearer than most to Wesley's ideal – the chief mover (one might indeed say exploiter) of the movement was his assistant James Hindmarsh, later, like some other Methodists, to become a Swedenborgian.

According to a letter by Hindmarsh, published in the *Journal*, a 'serious concern' had become evident in some of the boys for some time, but then 'God broke in upon them' in a 'surprising manner'. On the night of 20 August 1768 'the power of God came upon them even like a mighty rushing wind, which made them cry aloud for mercy'. The whole school was affected, and several were converted, including Hindmarsh's son.[77] The revival reached another climax in September 1770 after the boys had been taken to view the body of a dead neighbour, a common enough event in evangelical circles, but one which we may suspect Hindmarsh exploited to raise the spiritual temperature. As a result of this some refused to sleep until they had been converted, and the maids were affected as well as the boys. The result, it was claimed, was a marked change in the tone of the school. Meetings were held daily for prayer and the school was worked up into a state which finally resulted in physical exhaustion. The sequel was predictable. A year later Wesley remarked that scarcely a trace of the work remained, though it started up again in 1773 under the influence of Ralph Mather, who later became a devotee of 'mystical divinity'. Wesley himself witnessed some of the scenes.[78]

One final aspect of Wesley's educational work was his concern for the mental improvement of the preachers. The 1744 Conference's thought of a 'seminary for labourers' was never fulfilled, but in that and the following year a list of recommended reading was drawn up, and in 1746 Wesley asked Doddridge for a list of 'practical divinity'.[79] In 1745 Wesley apparently envisaged the books being stocked at London, Bristol and Newcastle for his own use as well as that of the preachers. The list included natural philosophy, history and poetry as well as divinity and the classics.[80] On later occasions he sometimes collected a group of preachers to 'read over' logic and other subjects.[81] He often urged the necessity of reading to feed their preaching, and though some of them, as we have seen, dropped Latin as useless for their work, others were compulsive, candle-burning students and a few became considerable self-educated scholars, like Adam Clarke.[82] These men, after all, were acting more and more like virtual ministers except for sacramental purposes, and Wesley was anxious for them to be more than meteoric but short-lived revivalists; they were to be pastors as well. If their education was to be primarily for saving souls, Wesley had a relatively cultured idea of what this meant. Nor did he neglect ordinary members. To his favoured female correspondents he sent lists of books tailored to their intellectual capacity.[83] Oxford culture and the instincts of an Oxford tutor never really deserted him: one of his abiding characteristics was the love of directing other people's souls and improving their minds. In adapting what he had read and approved for himself to tutorial use he was once again acting as a cultural mediator as well as a religious one.

3. Holy poverty and the age of philanthropy

Large claims have sometimes been made for Wesley's influence on social reform. The very title of a book like J.W. Bready's *England Before and After Wesley* (1938) suggests that Wesley had a key role in stimulating evangelical zeal for social reform with dramatic long-term effects, if only through other evangelical bodies. It is in fact difficult, if not impossible, to believe that such complex movements as the eighteenth-century rise of philanthropy and the early nineteenth-century campaigns for protective legislation could have sprung from the efforts of one religious group, still less from those of a single individual. The sources and motives for what were certainly important shifts in public concern and activity in these fields remain rather mysterious, but the role in them of Wesley and his followers was certainly limited. Even the more obviously influential 'Clapham Sect' of upper-class Evangelicals like Wilberforce was only part of a more broadly-based impulse to philanthropy and (limited) social reform with very mixed motives.[84] In general it can be said that Wesley was neither the initiator nor the organizer of any major reform, though he often supported philanthropic efforts in various fields (mostly by his pen) when his attention was caught by them. Since he was an instinctively benevolent 'friend of mankind' and especially of the poor and suffering there is nothing surprising about this. It was poverty and the related question of wealth which most excited his concern, leading him to practical action as well as to one or two excursions into what contemporaries called 'political economy'.[85]

Wesley's attitude to the private practice of charity developed early. In a sermon of 1780 he recalled how he had been chastened when at Oxford by meeting a poor girl whom he could not help, since he had adorned his rooms at the expense of the 'blood of the poor'. Elsewhere he described how as a Fellow of Lincoln he lived year by year on £28 and gave away all the rest as his income rose. Such habits became part of the Oxford Methodist discipline and a lifelong personal one. Shortly before his death he finally gave up keeping his accounts, remarking that he simply saved all he could and then gave all he could.[86] Like many successful evangelists he was frequently suspected of lining his own pockets. In fact he confessed in later life that despite contracting debts from his projects, he had finally 'unawares become rich' by his publications, but as we have seen he gave the profits away, latterly to the tune of up to £1000 a year. Henry Moore said that Wesley disposed of £30,000 in his lifetime.[87]

The Oxford Methodists, like the old Religious Societies, but probably following 'primitive' ideals, collected for the poor as part of their regular discipline along with prison visiting and the education of the poor. Similar concerns were expressed in the rules of the bands and United Societies in terms of feeding the hungry and clothing the naked. Wesley also acted instinctively in response to local crises of dearth and unemployment. So in May 1741 the Society in London was urged to bring clothes and a weekly penny for the needy members. Wesley then proposed a regular organization to give employment in knitting at a fair price with supervisors who would also visit the sick. This led to charges that he was employing for profit.[88] Similar appeals were made in 1744 when Wesley went around begging in person, as he did on several occasions in later years; and earlier, in 1740, he had begged for the poor at large who lacked help under the Poor Law. In 1772 Methodists were said to be involved in founding the 'Christian Society' for the poor, and in 1783, at the age of eighty, Wesley begged round Bath for the poor.[89] Though the Methodist poor were perhaps a special concern, as among the Quakers, plenty of help was given for the poor at large. Charity was an accepted part of Christian duty, not least in the eighteenth century, but it was sometimes taken to extremes by Methodists, as in Wesley's case. A man who sold his clothes to feed the poor was understandably regarded as 'mad'.[90]

Compassion was also extended to the sick as in the 1741 scheme, but in addition Wesley notoriously acted as an amateur doctor. For those anxious to emphasize the more credulous aspects of his character the remedies in his *Primitive Physick* (1747) have provided plenty of ammunition (and amusement). The significance of this work will be considered later in the context of Wesley's supernaturalism, and it was remarked earlier that his approach was formally empiricist and not speculative on disease.[91] For the moment it need only be remarked that Wesley, however odd his remedies, was following the example of many Anglican clergy in offering amateur medical services to the poor, though in a wider 'parish'. For him it was an exercise in charity and compassion which included a dispensary from 1747.[92]

It has already been remarked that although Wesley supported various social campaigns, his role in them was peripheral. Thus his *Thoughts on Slavery* (1774) was a characteristically derivative work based on the famous one by Anthony Benezet, and his eloquent last letter urged Wilberforce on in his campaign against the African slave trade: 'the vilest under the sun'.[93] He occasionally visited and preached in prisons, and wrote a letter to the press giving a glowing account of the physical, moral and religious reforms in the Bristol Newgate carried out by the Whitefield convert Abel Dagge as keeper. But it was lay Methodists like the engaging Silas Told who made prison visiting their special work.[94] In a similar way, as we have seen, Wesley approved of Sunday schools, and one of the rare cases of a Methodist-originated venture in organized philanthropy, the Stranger's Friend Society.[95]

In terms of broader attitudes to society, the Rules of the various Methodist societies and bands and the injunctions of Conference are instructive. Apart from the urge to practise charity, they include a series of prohibitions on personal adornment, spirits, sabbath breaking, smuggling and so on, which show a desire to cut members off from the temptations of the world and to create a distinctive ethos. They sometimes resemble the rules of Quakers and Baptists, with a flavour of the 'sect' characteristics noted by sociologists. The most obvious sources are in fact the New Testament and 'Primitive Christianity', as can be seen in the debates in the early Conferences on whether one should go to law with the brethren or at all; and about marrying out of the society. Late in life Wesley even wondered whether he should have laid down a special dress like the Quakers: the target here was to save money that could be used for charity, as it was in his efforts to stop tea-drinking.[96] The attempt to stop vice inside and outside Methodism was typically expressed in Wesley's 'Words' to smugglers, swearers and so on.[97] It was much less typical of him to try to invoke compulsion from above, as in his support for a revived version of the Societies for the Reformation of Manners which began in 1757 and whose demise he regretted. Lay Methodists were apparently prominent in this, and Wesley also supported a 'Reformation Society' in 1779. But campaigns of this kind were more characteristic of the Evangelical Anglicans, whose lay leaders were in any case in a better position to obtain high patronage for semi-official attempts at moral reform.[98]

What is most striking about Wesley's general attitude to the poor is his ready sympathy towards them, coupled with a markedly hostile attitude towards the rich. This was certainly unusual in his day. His attitudes here were influenced by his religious purpose and the very different responses he detected among rich and poor respectively to his message. 'In most genteel religious people there is so strange a mixture that I have seldom much confidence in them. I love the poor; in many of them I find pure, serious grace, unmixed with paint, folly and affectation,' though he admitted a few exceptions among the rich. In 1748 the Conference even suggested a longer probation for membership for the rich than the poor, and Methodist chapels, unlike Lady Hunting-don's, did not offer hired seats for the better-off. Wesley thought it required 'great grace' to converse with great people, though he allowed that it was useful to convert some of them. But for himself he would prefer it to be done by others: 'If I might choose, I should still (as I have done hitherto) preach the gospel to the poor.' He also thought that 'middling people' had a great advantage in 'common sense' over the rich as there is so much 'paint and affectation', and there are so many 'scandalous customs among people of rank'.[99]

But there seems to be more here than a judgment on religious openness. Wesley was perfectly able to mix with people of all ranks and to be polite without sycophancy, but he was peculiarly sensitive to the feelings of the poor and recipients of charity. The Conference of 1744 enjoined stewards: 'Give none that ask relief either an ill word or an ill look. Do not hurt 'em if you cannot help 'em.' And in 1747: 'If you cannot relieve, do not grieve the poor.' 'Abstain from either sour looks or harsh words. Put yourself in the place of any poor man, and deal with him as you would God should deal with you.'[100] Reflecting on ministry to the sick, Wesley wrote: 'How much better is it, when it can be done, to *carry* relief to the poor than *send* it! And that both for our own sakes and theirs. For theirs, as it is so much more comfortable to them, and as we may then assist them in spirituals as well as temporals; and for our own, as it is far more apt to soften our hearts and makes us naturally care for each other.'[101] This is particularly striking, for although it seems to anticipate the 'discriminating' visitation methods of later Evangelical charities, in fact the spirit and attitude is wholly different: the point is to create tender relationships and not simply to control and weed out the unworthy.[102] The same attitude of bias against the rich and favour for the poor comes out in Wesley's exercise in 'political economy', the *Thoughts on the Present Scarcity of Provisions* (1773), when this is blamed on the greed and waste of the rich and the diversion of grain to distilling (an old Wesley bugbear) rather than on the improvidence and idleness of the poor, which was to inform so many later analyses of poverty.

There may be something here which reflects Wesley's background as the poor son of an improvident if unlucky country parson, and a Tory parson at that. His instinctive frugality may be partly rooted in the same source, as was his knowledge of the humiliations of poverty. Beyond this, some of his prejudices probably reflect old-fashioned Tory ones against wealthy speculators in stocks and shares and the City monied interest in general, though the political line in the economy was less sharply drawn than party mythology suggested. Wesley did not condemn the levying of interest as such for investment in government funds, but he was suspicious of other City practices.[103]

However, Wesley's High Church 'Catholic' and 'primitive Christian' inheritance in piety may also be significant for his attitude to poverty and charity. I commented earlier in connection with the Oxford Methodist charities that it is difficult to say how far these were the product of simple compassion and how far a studied, traditionalist 'Catholic' expression of devotional discipline. It has rightly been observed that Wesley was 'a traditionalist Catholic rather than a Protestant individualist' in his attitude to charity.[104] There is, of course, nothing inevitable or clear-cut about this kind of distinction. I also remarked earlier that John Clayton, Wesley's Manchester friend, and an extreme High Churchman, already had a discriminating attitude to the poor at Oxford and became even more sceptical about them in Manchester in later years.[105] But a modern study by Professor Pullan of the patterns of Catholic and Protestant attitudes towards the poor and treatment of them during the early modern period, while carefully noting the similarities, comes to a challenging conclusion. Can one find (Pullan asks) before the days of General Booth, a situation in Protestant Europe in which,

> the practice of mercy becomes a tactic at once in a personal quest for Christ and a war against sin, a campaign for the conquest of souls conducted by lay brotherhoods and sisterhoods, clerically inspired and bent on self-sanctification through the salvation of others in the greatest possible numbers? . . . (people) who both observe and impose an ascetic discipline in accordance with explicit man-made Rules, whose magical weapons are the sacraments, and who attack poverty in so far as it becomes not a way to salvation, but a peril to the soul?[106]

Wesley and his movement in fact provide a much closer parallel than the famous schemes of General Booth. Wesley in 1739 could say that predestination destroys our zeal for good works as it 'cuts off one of the strongest incentives to all acts of bodily mercy . . . namely, the hope of saving their (the poor's) souls from death'.[107] The classic Protestant opposition between salvation by faith and by 'works' which underlay much of the Revival was certainly modified in Wesley's case to allow for devotion and good works as a preparation for salvation.

For a time Wesley seems to have had an even more primitive and radical model for Christian social action in mind, and one which has seldom been noticed in his career. This was an experiment in 'Christian communism', which was evidently one of those recurring cases in Christian history of attempts to reproduce the picture in the Acts of the Apostles of Christians having 'all things in common'. It may owe something to De Renty and to the Moravians, though Wesley's attitude to the latter's communal economy was hostile for many years after his early enthusiasm towards it.[108] Rule 3 of the Select Societies of the 'perfect', who Wesley also hoped would be his special confidants, ran: 'Every member, till we can have all things common, will bring, once a week, *bona fide*, all he can spare towards a common stock.' The review in the letter to Perronet in 1749 only mentions the contribution to the 'stock', omitting the hope of the more radical path.[109] 'Common stock' would normally mean a fund for the poor, but in this case was intended originally only as a preliminary to a communal life.

Richard Viney, who oscillated between the Moravians and Methodists, describes how on 22 February 1744 he and Wesley wished to see a Quaker work-house, as 'that is said to be the best to take a Plan from of any in London'. 'He (Wesley) told me of an intention he and some few have of beginning a community of goods, but on a plan which I told him I doubted would not succeed.' It was that 'each is to bring what cash they have to put it together. If any owe debts they are first to be paid. Then each abiding in their dwellings and following their business as they do now, are to bring what they earn and put it into one common box out of which they are again to receive only so much as is thought necessary to maintain their families without regarding whether they put much or little into the box.'[110]

Although it seems that this plan was never carried out, there are traces of similar ideas later. In Hawnby in Yorkshire in 1757 Wesley found workers who had been turned out of their houses for their Methodism, so they had built their own 'in which forty or fifty of them lived together'. A clearer voluntary case is recorded by John Pritchard's 'band' of single men who had prayer meetings and 'lived as the Christians of old, having all things common, so that few, if any, counted anything he possessed as his own'. Community of goods was an old and sinister charge against dissident sects, and Methodism did not escape it.[111]

Wesley's sermon on 'The Use of Money' and some other observations may, however, seem to point in a very different direction, and has encouraged some to see him rather as an example of the 'religion and the rise of capitalism' theory. The idea that religious practice and ideology, especially of a Calvinist and Puritan sort, was related closely to the rise of capitalism, as in the rather different versions of Weber and Tawney, is one which has been swallowed more readily by sociologists than historians (with the exception of Marxists). It is relevant here because Weber himself thought that Wesley, like the Puritans before him, encouraged a type of asceticism conducive to capitalist accumulation.[112]

There is a certain *prima facie* plausibility about this. Methodism appealed to the industrious middling and artisan classes. It certainly taught an industrious and frugal life, and its rules strongly discouraged conspicuous consumption on adornment. As early as 1760 Wesley observed that the Methodists were becoming rich, and in the sermons of his last years he often repeated this observation and lamented the damage this did to their souls. In an almost Weberian strain he also marvelled that 'true Scriptural Christianity has a tendency, in process of time, to undermine and destroy itself. For wherever Christianity spreads, it must cause diligence and frugality which in the natural course of things must beget riches.' By 'riches', however, he meant any 'laying up treasure' beyond what was needed for food, clothing and family support.[113] We shall see that he did not exaggerate much: prosperous Methodists did appear, whether by the rise of humble folk within the society or by accession from those already well-off as Methodism became more respectable.

It is a mistake to suppose that Wesley's views necessarily determined those of rank-and-file Methodists, but a direct as well as indirect impulse towards capitalistic enterprise and acquisitiveness might seem to be evident in his sermon on 'The Use of Money', first preached in 1744 and published in 1760, which he continued to quote in later years, when warning about wealth.[114] He summed up his teaching in three crisp points: Gain all you can; save all you can; give all you can. This probably does mark a shift in tone from Puritan comments on the subject. The American John Cotton, though not spelling out the qualifications made by Wesley nor his injunctions on giving, had made the shrewd point: 'There is another combination of virtues strangely mixed in any lively, holy Christian: and that is, diligence in worldly business, and yet deadness to the world. Such a mystery as no one can read but they that know it.'[115] It is just this delicate balance that the ageing Wesley felt was being lost. The Puritans, though sometimes credited with upholding wealth as a sign of God's favour, were more subtle than this and developed a careful casuistry on these as on other moral problems. Wesley was innocent of most of these refinements, though he was as keen as his predecessors to glorify secular callings as the theatre of the Christian pursuit of holiness. Certainly there seems to be a contrast with the almost monastic seclusion of William Law, his old mentor whose models were clearly drawn from the leisured classes; but then Wesley was speaking to a very different constituency.

The first two points of the 'Use of Money' sermon seem tailor-made for the aspiring businessman in urging him to gain and save as his godly duty. Up to a point Wesley does indeed reflect the thrusting, innovative spirit of his time. He urges men not simply to follow the ways of their fathers but to be innovative, and in a remarkable sermon 'Of Former Times' he contradicts the often-repeated view that they were better than the present day not only intellectually but spiritually. Today, he says, is better: notably in religious toleration.[116] In detail Wesley carefully limits the means of gain: it must be from honest trades; he is against bill-broking and sees even investment in the Bank of England as being like burying one's talent in the earth. He is against the contracting of debts without prospect of repayment; and Methodists, like Quakers, were liable to be presumed guilty unless they could be proved innocent when they went bankrupt.[117] They must not haggle over prices (another Quaker touch), and usury (excessive interest) should not be charged. Interestingly, there was a rule that members of the society should be urged to trade with each other as 'the world will love its own and them only'.[118] In all this it seems clear that Wesley is not really encouraging the ruthless, competitive entrepreneur but the small manufacturer and tradesman with limited horizons and rather old-fashioned ways. Moreover, he is to aim primarily at providing for his family and dependants.

As to saving, the target here is the wastefulness of conspicuous consumption, which was conspicuous indeed among the eighteenth-century aristocracy whom Wesley despised. But it was the third point which was the clue to the purpose of the whole exercise: you gain and save only to give, and to give according to Wesley's own ideal of everything beyond what is strictly necessary expenditure for a modest comfort for your family, dependants and heirs. (Wesley conventionally allows for this last duty as well as for differences in dress and expenditure for different grades in society.) His only remedy in his late sermons, warning against wealth, is to give it away to the poor, though he still gave his old three-point advice, only with even more emphasis on the last point.

As an innocent encourager of capitalism, then, Wesley is an equivocal and even disappointing teacher. No doubt some of his readers were comforted by his injunctions to gain and save and failed to take his concluding advice, but it is that advice which is Wesley's real interest. He coveted more charity for the poor and not, it would seem, simply the 'deserving' poor of pious and censorious convention. The Wesleyan leadership in the early nineteenth century did not much modify its leader's advice. Though allowing for the extension of business to increase national prosperity, they saw the 1842 depression in very traditional terms as a divine judgment on excessive speculation.[119]

Apart from the attempts to assimilate Wesley to the Weberian model, there have been others which seek to place him somewhere on the line of change from restrictive 'mercantilism' to the rise of free-trade ideals from Adam Smith onwards; or as an early apostle of the late nineteenth-century social gospel.[120] Semmel is certainly right to criticize these notions as based on a very selective reading of convenient bits of Wesleyan pronouncements. For himself, Semmel sees Wesley as rejecting the communitarian ideals of the Moravians, since his central thrust is in line with the individualistic, entrepreneurial mood of commercial England. While Wesley retained some elements in the mediaeval tradition of the advocacy of the just price, opposition to usury and cornering of markets for gain, he is seen as suppressing these sentiments lest they encourage popular discontent and old-fashioned riots against hoarders. One can certainly cite evidence that suggests that Wesley modified his more old-fashioned views during his lifetime, as the abandonment of 'communism' (not noticed by Semmel) suggests. He also seems to have been half-convinced by ingenious arguments to justify charging market prices and free trade.[121] What this shows is that he reacted not so much to intellectual arguments as to the pressure of experience, partly through what he saw as an unusually well-informed observer of what was actually happening in England; partly through his knowledge of, and admiration for, his poor and middling followers and their virtues as against their betters. He was restrained in his prescriptions (such as they were) by his hereditary and biblical notions of order and obedience to constituted authority. But above all, as his sermons show, he was possessed by the idea of charity not only as an old-fashioned Christian duty and virtue but as the only way in which he could see the dangers of riches being combatted and curbed. Honest gain is good to feed the poor; and Wesley welcomed arguments which tended to help it. But restrictions on it were retained for the same purpose: the exercise of charity and the cultivation of the soul. If this helped free trade and capitalism, this was an accidental by-product.

Given this perspective, it is natural to ask whether Wesley's theology had any impact on his economics. Manfred Marquardt, in a comprehensive study of Wesley's social teaching, recognizes that Wesley's contribution to social work was only a part of the general philanthropic movement of his day, and that he was not really an initiator in this. He had only a limited insight into the sources of social evils. Marquardt ascribes these limitations to Wesley's environment, and maintains that his principles of social ethics nevertheless had more radical applications than he could have foreseen. These principles are seen as springing ultimately from Wesley's particular style of theology, his 'evangelical Arminian' idea that the love of God is offered equally to all men; and his conviction that salvation, while not dependent on our good works, must nevertheless issue in good works as part of our progress in Christian perfection. (It may be observed that Semmel's argument, too, was part of an attempt to derive 'liberal' politics and free trade from Wesley's Arminian religious principles.) The theological notion of salvation for all should logically have the social effect of respect for all ranks and a refusal to dismiss poverty as being simply the effect of divine punishment or idleness. Individual salvation has social effects through saved individuals and so on the community at large, Wesley's analysis of social problems and attempts to remedy them was influenced by his extensive journeys and knowledge of Britain.[122]

It may well be significant that Wesley's doctrines differed sharply from that of the Calvinists on predestination and perfection. If this derived ultimately from his High Church background and was confirmed by experience of what he saw as Calvinism's evil moral results, his optimism about perfection in this life, like his confidence in the economic progress of the country, was influenced by the light of experience and, perhaps, the spirit of the Enlightenment. A positive attitude to life in this world no doubt consorts well enough with cheerful injunctions to make money; and the conclusion that it should go to charity is a practical application of the life of love to neighbour as well as God. Yet Wesley's view of holiness and its scope is as limited as his view of business life. The Methodist rules may no doubt be seen as a kind of social and economic application of holy love, but Wesley had no systematic doctrine of applied perfection. And he had no better prescription for the social problems of industrial capitalism than the injunction to give wealth away for fear of corruption. His *Thoughts on the Present Scarcity of Provisions* may be read selectively as a kind of liberalizing form of economic thought. But more plausibly, it is a Wesley-style panacea based on popular prejudices against taxes plus the old Wesley hostility to distilling and luxury. His conclusion is more significant than his prescription, for it is almost millennarian: he has little confidence that anyone will adopt his remedies, for the nation is full of the contempt of religion which will only be cured when God shall 'arise and maintain his own cause'.[123]

Though modern Methodists have liked to suppose (as Marquardt also implies) that the doctrine of perfection contained within itself a great regenerative power for society, it is perhaps more plausible to suggest that the doctrine itself was related to, or at least coloured by, socially-induced changes in the ideals posited for the Christian life in the eighteenth century, as has been suggested by Professor Kent.[124] Two religious outlooks (Kent says) were existing side by side in the eighteenth century. One was the old world of asceticism as variously exemplified by the *Whole Duty of Man*, William Law and the Evangelicals. It was characterized by pessimism about man and a distrust of materialism and worldly involvement. Alongside this existed a rising outlook characterized by a more optimistic view of man, a more relaxed state of behaviour, a more positive acceptance of life in the ordinary world, and at its worst an acceptance of acquisitive materialism in business and politics. In many ways the Evangelical Revival was an attempt to revive and popularize a life characterized by rejection of 'worldliness' and the exaltation of the salvation of the soul and of a mind set on heaven. Wesley's perfectionism may then be seen as a peculiar manifestation of this attitude, combining something of the traditional Catholic and Protestant outlook. It was Catholic and almost monastic in its extreme claims for the holy life and almost mystical in its claims for unbroken communion with God; but 'Protestant evangelical' in its hope of an instantaneous perfection by faith, open to all – a kind of instant mass mysticism. It was also Protestant in its insistence that the perfect life is not to be lived by a minority in a monastery but by a substantial body of people engaged in ordinary occupations. Moreover, it was not simply a revival of the older religious view of the world, for Wesley made significant concessions to the commercial conditions of the eighteenth century. His 'gain and save all you can' in the 'Use of Money' sermon seems to be at least a practical concession to the acquisitive, market-orientated, capitalist society then developing. Yet, as we have seen, it is a limited concession for the purpose of more generous giving. Explicitly it is a remedy for the evils of acquisitiveness; implicitly, an application of holy love in a thoroughly traditional manner. If it represents an attempt to combine the old ascetic ideals with a recognition of the realities of a society moving out of the cycle of subsistence alternating with famine, Wesley's last sermons are an almost despairing cry to apply the only remedy for greed and competition which he understood. But at least his holy remnant of the perfected were expected to combine their private vision of God with service to the poor. The Evangelical Anglican legacy was to be less generous in its attitude to the poor, and its famous reforming campaigns combined selective restraints on abuses by legislation with restrictive measures on popular vices.[125]

4. Caesar's due: Wesley and politics

Perhaps the most enduring image of Wesley in relation to politics is that he was a Tory and that the Wesleyan Methodist leadership followed his lead in this well into the nineteenth century. Jabez Bunting, the 'Pope' of Methodism, is supposed to have said he 'hated democracy as he hated sin', though it is likely that he was referring to church polity rather than secular politics in doing so: very much as Wesley declared that the

Methodists were not 'republicans' in church government.[126] The question is: what did being a 'Tory' mean at various times in the eighteenth century and above all to Wesley himself?[127]

Certainly Wesley claimed to be a Tory like the rest of his family. In 1785 he rejected the charge made against his brother Charles of having been a Jacobite. 'Most of those who gave him this title did not distinguish between a Jacobite and a Tory; thereby I mean "one that believes God, not the people, to be the origin of all civil power". In this sense he was a Tory; so was my father; so am I. But I am no more a Jacobite than I am a Turk.' He admitted that he had differed on one point from his brother: John thought that exposing the King's ministers was a way of exposing the King himself; but Charles disagreed, and had not scrupled to expose Sir Robert Walpole and all other evil ministers. Ten years earlier he had expressed the same position in its ecclesiastical aspect: 'I am a High Churchman and the son of a High Churchman, bred up from my childhood in the highest notions of passive obedience and non-resistance.' In more scriptural terms he asserted in 1777: 'It is my religion which obliges me "to put men in mind to be subject to principalities and powers". Loyalty is with me an essential branch of religion.' His religious and political conduct were connected, he claimed, 'the selfsame authority enjoining me to "fear God" and to "honour the King"'[128]

Though these remarks were provoked by the strife and 'democratical' agitations over America and Wilkes late in Wesley's life, his sentiments and the religio-political theory on which they were based clearly echo the stock attitudes of the later seventeenth-century High Churchmen and the conflicts within the Church of England during the reign of Anne and the early years of George I amidst which he had grown up. But the disavowal of Jacobitism was significant. As we saw in viewing the Wesley family, old Samuel had managed to reconcile himself to loyalty to William and then to the Hanoverians, though Susanna had remained faithful to the house of Stuart and young Samuel had had very suspect connections with Bishop Atterbury. At school Charles Wesley had befriended the future Lord Mansfield against Jacobite charges. But Whig propaganda so smeared all Tories with charges of Jacobitism that modern historians still disagree about the extent to which the Tory party was Jacobite at heart and, as we have seen, the same problem, aggravated by the sour fruits of proscription from office, poisoned university life in Oxford.

Wesley's early years at Oxford in fact provide the only occasions when he showed some tendency to flirt with Jacobitism or at least with opposition to the government by indulging in the kind of loose talk 'against King George' and 'evil speaking' of Walpole in 1725 which was common enough among young members of the university.[129] There is nothing remarkable about this, and there is no sign of it continuing later. More mysterious is what Charles called John's 'Jacobite' sermon in June 1734. Since John took the precaution of getting the Vice-Chancellor's approval before preaching it, Charles said that he could 'bid Wadham, Merton, Exeter and Christ Church do their worst' (these were the Whiggish colleges).[130] Perhaps Charles was exaggerating, for it is difficult to see anything Jacobite in the surviving text of the sermon. It is on 'The one thing needful' (Luke 10.42), and is in Wesley's best Oxford Methodist style: upholding the need to exchange the image of Satan for that of God and to this end condemning pleasure, riches and preferment. But perhaps it was an oblique attack on place-seeking government supporters.[131] Yet it was only a year earlier that Wesley had claimed that a reading of Higden's *View of the English Constitution* had convinced him of the lawfulness of taking oaths to the post-Revolution monarchy, which does suggest that he had had qualms – like his mother long before.[132]

We have seen that in the 1740s the Methodists were accused of being Jacobite emissaries (so were the Moravians), and it is likely enough that some in places like Manchester had sympathies of that kind. But one Nottingham man claimed to have been converted from it to taking the oath of loyalty by Methodism (and was called 'an old Jesuit' for doing so).[133] The most picturesque incident was when Charles Wesley was hauled before the Yorkshire magistrates for praying for 'the Lord's absent ones'.[134] It was to dispel such suspicions that John Wesley proposed a loyal Methodist address to the King, and ostentatiously stayed in London when Papists were ordered to leave during the invasion scare of 1744.[135] None of this really means any more than the usual hysteria and fear of fifth columnists and strange wanderers common in times of national tension.

But if the Wesleys were loyalists, it is still possible that, as one recent historian of eighteenth-century Toryism has suggested, there was a certain 'ideological congruence' between Methodists and dissident Anglican Tories, some of whom had come of Puritan families and feared the pastoral consequences of the Whig captivity of the church.[136] Sir John Phillips, a Welsh Tory, was friendly to the Oxford Methodists, as also the SPCK; Felix Farley, the Bristol Tory, printed Charles Wesley's hymns. Professor Colley suggests that this new 'Dissent', more plebeian than the old and still attached to the church, may have acted 'as a kind of ideological Trojan horse amongst poorer Tory voters in some of the populous constituencies. The Wesleyan religious and social critique had much in common with the Tory appeal' – an observation which also helps to explain why Whitefield seems to have had hopes of support from the heterogenous opposition around the Prince of Wales in the late 1740s.[137] But Methodism soon showed itself too enthusiastic and too irregular religiously to be a suitable vehicle for political or religious oppositionists, and Wesley's *Word to a Freeholder* (1747) advocated voting for government candidates.

In fact Wesley seems to have adopted his father's Hanoverian Toryism rather than his mother's religious Jacobitism. His primary concern for religion and his scriptural loyalty to the powers-that-be led him to transfer the old 'passive obedience' to the Hanoverians. Nor was his an isolated case. It has recently been argued that new versions of divine right came to be associated with the new monarchy and that by the 1760s, with a new, less Whig-ridden King in George III, old-fashioned Tory loyalties could be focussed on their natural object.[138] Whatever earlier doubts Wesley may have had, his stance by the 1770s, especially in face of growing national divisions and popular agitations against the government and even the King himself, was an outspoken loyalty as 'an essential part of his religion' though indeed this had been evident long before in times of crisis like the mid-1740s.

Ostensibly Wesley saw himself as having no political role or competence. In 1768 he said that 'politics lies quite out of my province' and in 1782 he directly raised the question 'How far is it the duty of a Christian minister to preach politics?' and answered it in his usual confident fashion. The Bible says that you should not speak ill of the ruler of your people, yet many people do, and when the clergy rebuke them they cry out, 'O, he is preaching politics!' In this sense, however, it is a minister's duty to do so; and to defend the King's ministers, too, as the King is weakened if they are weakened. And he warned that people can seldom know what complex considerations really had to influence the judgments and actions of governments.[139]

He also acted to guide Methodist voters at elections on their duties, mainly in moral terms of not accepting bribes and 'entertainment', and publicized the fact in his *Journals*. In the *Word to a Freeholder* in 1747 he went further and advised on voting. They should go for 'one that loves God' and, failing any such, they should support one who loves 'King George who is appointed to reign over us'. Though this was in accord with his general 'scriptural' principles, it was also an anti-Jacobite stance, and in effect meant supporting the ruling Whig hegemony. This was explicit in 1756 when there were fears of French invasion, Popery and Jacobitism, which led Wesley and Whitefield to appeal to the government to raise volunteer militia; Wesley actually offered to raise a company himself. Moreover, he advised Methodists in Bristol to vote for a government candidate to keep out a 'Jacobite'. This election was in fact very much confused by local Whig divisions, partly through Dissent.[140]

In 1774 Wesley concentrated on moral criteria: vote for the person 'judged most worthy' without reward; speak no evil of his opponents or of those who vote for them. But his concern to support the King and ministry against factious opposition was strong by now.[141] Yet it may be significant that at least one Methodist leader in Bristol voted for Cruger and Burke; and Cruger, a man of American origin, supported conciliation of the American colonists.[142] Wesley at this point was about to shift from sympathy with the colonists to publicly attacking them. His most persistent attitude, particularly in his later years, was to advise voting for those who loved the King and the existing ministry, and he often defended successive monarchs against their detractors, partly because he saw them as defenders of religious toleration.[143] One can see why Wesley did not regard advice like this as 'political' at all: it was a pietist evangelical attitude to politics, acting by moral criteria and biblical injunctions to obey the powers that be as given by God with no overt party bias at all. But in practice it meant ruling out opposition groups (whatever they might happen to be) and more specifically factious 'reformers'.

Such an approach did, however, allow for intervention in the interests of moral or religious issues (such as religious liberty or slavery), and it was often by this route that conservative or unpolitical evangelicals found themselves engaged in political agitation and manipulation as time went on. So far as Wesley was concerned, he found himself involved controversially in politics from the late 1760s onwards, partly over the question of religious liberty as it involved measures to relieve Roman Catholics; partly over what he saw as factious attacks on the government; partly over the American controversy. Political as well as religious prejudices also sharpened his controversy at the same time with the Calvinists. When interpreting these developments, it is as well not to look for any profound political philosophy on Wesley's part, not to expect a very exact correlation between his political and theological views. But if, in large measure, he was reacting to events and experience as he so often did, he also carried some inherited ideological baggage which helped to condition his responses.[144]

Wesley's attitude to religious toleration and the reasons for its very selective application to the Roman Catholic case have already been discussed.[145] His strongest and most public involvement in political controversy came in the years between 1768 and 1778. The two main issues which influenced him were the libertarian and reforming noises made in the wake of the Wilkesite rows over general warrants and Middlesex elections (see above, p. 316); and the rising conflict with the

American colonies over taxation and representation culminating in the War of Independence. In his reactions to these developments Wesley not only felt instinctively antipathetic to calls from below for more democracy and the 'rights' of the 'people' and 'liberty', but also scented conspiracies and chaos as in the 1640s – Dissenters, he thought, being involved in both cases. All were revolting against appointed authority; though he sometimes acknowledged privately that wise concession to pressure might be desirable over America as it would have been before the Civil War in the 1640s.

What alarmed old-fashioned loyalists like John Wesley was the way in which Wilkes – a raffish, debt-ridden rascal anyway in the eyes of sober folks – exploited his personal problems to create mobs of non-voters to put pressure on Parliament and the government with howls of 'liberty' being under attack. In doing so he was as insulting to the King as to his ministers. Pressure from the mob was disturbing enough, and the Wilkes affair was soon followed by the American one, which split English opinion and involved further cries for 'liberty' from the Americans and their supporters.

Wesley's response to the Wilkes affair can be seen in his *Free Thoughts on the Present State of Public Affairs* (1768).[146] Wesley claims to have no party connection or interest, and interestingly does not defend General Warrants or the measures taken over the Middlesex election; nor did he defend the measures against America. But he does defend the character of the King and the rights of the Crown. The present disturbances are not due to the badness of the King and ministry but to 'French gold', ambition and unscrupulous agitators. Wilkes is like Sacheverell, the furious High Tory of the early 1700s, for both are extremist agitators; and the current agitation may have the same disastrous effects as those that preceded the Civil War of the 1640s: surely the Lord has a 'controversy with the land' for its sins.

In *Thoughts upon Liberty* (1772), Wesley enlarges on the favourite Wilkesite catch-phrase.[147] 'Liberty' is either religious or civil. God endowed all creatures with religious liberty, and it is not abridged by the present government. Civil liberty is 'the liberty to enjoy our lives and fortunes in our own way; to use . . . whatever is legally our own, according to our own choice'. This is not invaded by the King; if anything, it is endangered by the mob. What they want is liberty to rob, murder and rape. To remedy this senseless talk the press's 'licentious-ness' should be curbed. Striking at the root of claims that power originated with 'the people', Wesley denied the 'contract' theory of the Revolution Whigs and that the people had ever chosen their rulers. With considerable force, by a *reductio ad absurdum* argument he claimed that if this were true, then it could not be denied to women and juveniles, let alone to all male adults. The Bible says there is 'no power but from God', and God has given it to the King: in effect, divine right.[148] It may be observed that if this was 'Tory' doctrine, most Whigs were no more keen to allow a right of rebellion except in the one convenient case of 1688.

On the American question Wesley changed his mind in a way which caused him much trouble, especially when the change involved him in plagiarism from Dr Johnson without acknowledgment, though the attacks on him were less because of tenderness for copyright than for party reasons.[149] The passing remark in the *Free Thoughts* of 1768 that he did not defend the ministry's measures on America and that he doubted whether they could be defended 'either on the part of law, equity or prudence' were not forgotten by his enemies when he seemed to make a complete *volte-face* in his *Calm Address to our American Colonies* (1775). It has been pointed out that in this case he was mainly concerned to exonerate the current ministry from blame and to lay blame instead on Grenville, who was unpopular with the King.[150] And indeed in June 1775 he had written privately to North and Dartmouth, warning them of the strength of opposition to coercive policies and of the horrors of war. Moreover, although he believed the trouble really came from unscrupulous rabble-rousers in England and only urged concessions to confound their schemes, he also confessed that although all his upbringing and prejudices made him a 'passive obedience' High Churchman, he nevertheless thought that the Americans were 'an oppressed people' asking for 'nothing more than their legal rights, and that in the most modest and inoffensive manner that the nature of the thing would allow'.[151]

However, in public Wesley soon began to say the opposite in his *Calm Address*, the substance of his arguments being drawn from Dr Johnson's *Taxation no Tyranny*, without acknowledgment. When the Calvinist Toplady gleefully pointed out this plagiarism, Wesley ingenuously admitted it in his second edition on the grounds that he thought it good to publicize such a useful case. In fact, though Wesley used Johnson's arguments, sometimes in Johnson's own words, he greatly condensed them and recast the whole in his own style as well as adding some arguments of his own. Johnson himself seems to have been flattered by the compliment, which gave the work a larger audience, and both men were no doubt more concerned to beat the opposition than to quarrel about authorship. Wesley denied that he wrote in hope of reward and refused one when offered it, though it is possible that the government had encouraged him.[152]

The essence of Wesley's and Johnson's case against the colonists was that the English Parliament had the right to tax the colonies, and Wesley denied that there could be no taxation without direct representation since this was also the situation of many people in England. Once again he rejected what he regarded as claptrap talk about 'liberty': the Americans enjoyed as full civil and religious liberty as the English. To this he added some sharp jabs about slaves in America who really did lack liberty. At this point Wesley blamed the agitation on evil men in England and not in America, but in *Some Observations on Liberty* (1776), in answer to a tract by the radical Unitarian Richard Price, he claimed on his brother's evidence that the Americans had been talking rebellion in Boston forty years before. The notion that the Americans were being led by the nose by evil leaders of their own took increasing possession of his mind. But what really alarmed him was the notion that people like Price were stirring up revolt in England and using the Americans to further their aims. When the French joined in the American war Wesley naturally thought that the French and Popish power was joining in the plot to ruin England, and this belief was strengthened by the fears induced by the Catholic emancipation measure of 1778. And behind it all was sin – when the English began to have successes in the war after initial reverses, he attributed it to their national days of fasting and repentance.[153]

It should be remembered that the controversy over America coincided with a furious pamphlet warfare between Calvinists and Arminians (see below, p.461), and that while Wesley and Fletcher the Arminians attacked the Americans, Toplady the Calvinist sympathized with them. Other Calvinists, like the Baptist Caleb Evans and the Unitarian Price, took the same side. Fletcher claimed that these people were 'civil antinomians' who had inherited their levelling doctrines from the sectaries of the Interregnum, and Wesley saw the American rebels as the heirs of the sectarians of the last century. Though one modern historian has tried to see a theological-political rationale in this, it is probably wiser to regard it as a familiar form of smear tactics. Throughout the eighteenth century Dissenters were blackened as hereditary subversives, and Fletcher was no doubt glad to link this with Calvinist theology for the purposes of the other controversy.[154]

It is perhaps possible to see Wesley as being consistent in his political views from start to finish, the principle being the scriptural injunction of obedience to the powers-that-be, which could be glossed by old High Church and Tory views of divine right, suitably adapted to the Hanoverian dynasty. Loyalty, as he said in 1777, was for him a branch of religion; but it was also a family tradition (at least on his father's side) and reinforced to the point of making him much more open and explicit by the alarming circumstances of the latter part of his life. It was entirely characteristic of Wesley that if, as seems possible, he did have Jacobite leanings early on, he should have justified the transfer to Hanoverian loyalties in his *History of England* by actually arguing that the Hanoverians were not simply the *de facto* but actually the legitimate royal line in the remote circumstances of the Middle Ages![155] His notions of English liberty were coloured by post-Revolution English perceptions of their escape from Popery and arbitrary power.

Or should one see Wesley simply as reacting to circumstances, as was so often true of his religious ideas and actions? Or were there deeper affinities with contemporary political traditions? Or did his stance derive from his peculiar theological notions? For Dr Hempton it is not helpful to talk about Wesley's politics in party terms. Wesley, he says, accepted the defence of liberty and property given by the Whigs; hated discontent, violence and corruption; he never lost his High Church belief in passive obedience and non-resistance. His political legacy to Methodism was determined more by reactions to events than by a clear ideology; and reaction to events depended often on such factors as 'bad luck, irony, stupidity and over-confidence'. Hempton acknowledges that in Wesley's characteristic views one can detect a mixture of 'Tory' and 'Country' (anti-ministerial and anti-court) ideology, but he believes that Wesley's views were developed mainly from two sources: the Bible and his own observations on the state of the country.[156] This is perhaps to take Wesley's self-portrait of the non-politician applying biblical principles and experience too literally. One need not tie him too closely to party concerns, but his own confession about his ancestry is important. He was in fact deeply influenced by the general seventeenth-century folk-memory and by his specific upbringing, and this tended to determine the way in which he would react to any crisis in which the monarchy was attacked and the spectre of popular disorder conjured up. The rejection of the idea that power was derived from the 'people' was in line with traditional High Church Tory thinking, while the conscious consideration of the legitimacy of the Hanoverian monarchy reflected contemporary adjustments to reality. Hempton sees Wesley as becoming more self-confident in his political pronouncements in the 1770s, but he was always confident in his judgments: what happened now was that the situation became more threatening and his reactions were predictable in terms of his existing views. What he added to conventional political wisdom was a strong sense of sin and judgment on the opposition.

One must not identify Wesley's attitudes with those of Methodism as a whole, though he was not alone among the leadership in his support of the powers-that-be. But it is obvious that some thought differently, and one reason for his outbursts may have been the desire to 'enlighten' – and curb – those Methodists with other sentiments. At Plymouth in

1775 he recorded that 'some of our friends here were deeply prejudiced against the King and all his ministers', so he spoke to them and 'God applied it to their hearts, and I think there is not one of them now who does not see things in another light' – a typically optimistic assessment.[157] His clerical assistant Dr Coke appears to have believed in a 'more equal representation of the people' and in disestablishment of the church.[158] Men like Samuel Bradburn who stayed with the old connexion, as well as many who did not (like Alexander Kilham), freely used 'democratical' language about the 'rights of man' and of 'the people' in ways that Wesley abhorred; and they applied these principles to some aspects of Methodist government too. It was talk like this, coupled with a desire for Methodist sacraments and separation from the church, that alienated some 'Church Methodists' from Methodism in the 1790s.[159]

The conjunction of religious concern and political language of this kind is, however, part of an old and continuing debate about the social and political significance of Methodism. In its crudest form it has been expressed in the familiar proposition that Methodism (or evangelicalism in general) saved or helped to save England from revolution. Originally intended as a compliment, this has become the occasion for left-wing historians to condemn the movement and for others to credit it with a useful mediating role by helping to channel potentially violent and revolutionary passions into more moderate and constitutional channels. It is not always quite clear when these desirable or undesirable miracles are supposed to have happened, though presumably it was during the period between the 1790s and 1830s. As such, they are not strictly speaking the concern of a biographer of Wesley himself. The most that could be claimed is that the movement he set on foot and inspired with his ideals and practice produced the results claimed. Plainly he would have been happy to be seen as a stifler of revolution; and would hardly have welcomed the notion that he might, unconsciously, by his religious ideology, have provided material for misapplication to political 'liberalism' or working-class movements of a reformist kind. Although this is not the place for an extended discussion of the various theories proposed on this question, it is worth remarking that they have usually been characterized by generality rather than precise evidence, and indeed it is rather difficult to see what evidence would count to prove or disprove the causation of an event which never happened, namely an English revolution. It is important to realize that there seems to be little evidence for any substantial revolutionary movement needing to be emasculated by Methodism or anything else; that Methodism was neither sufficiently large a body nor sufficiently influential in the middling or lower ranks of society to have a crucial social and political role of any kind. This consideration also applies to claims that its theology was the unwitting vehicle for inculcating 'liberal' values into nineteenth-century politics.[160]

The conservative stance of Wesley's politics and that of most of the official Wesleyan leadership for many years is exactly what one would expect, and although it has often been pointed out that the so-called 'no-politics' rule in Wesleyanism was in effect weighted against reformers, it deserves to be taken seriously as being also influenced by a desire to concentrate on its religious mission. This did not prevent some Methodists from privately supporting reformist politics, and some indeed from becoming involved in more violent courses, though they were then likely to be expelled. But estimates of the weight of Methodism as a whole in favour of encouraging or discouraging particular tendencies among the sectors of the community where they were influential still depend too much on patchy evidence and insecure inferences from the supposed translation of religious teaching into political ideology to carry much conviction. What one can say with confidence is that Wesley himself became more and more explicitly opposed to anything but active loyalty to the *status quo*. It is equally clear that Methodism in the eighteenth century was regarded as a subversive and not as a kind of counter-revolutionary force. As we have seen, almost everything about it seemed reminiscent of the enthusiasm of the Commonwealth sects, and quite apart from the political and social suspicions that this suggested, the behaviour of the preachers as rivals of the clergy and the societies as dividers of the parish seemed to be a threat to the established church and so to the constitution. The image of Methodism as a counter-revolutionary bulwark of the *status quo*, a quietener of the lower orders, originated as a defensive propaganda exercise by the Wesleyan leadership against renewed suspicions of this kind in the 1790s, and as a warning to some of their own followers.

XI

The Path to Perfection: Doctrine, Devotion and Social Concern in Early Methodism

1. John Wesley and Methodist theology

There are several difficulties in the way of getting a clear picture of Wesley's theology. One is his eclecticism: since he borrowed from a wide range of Christian traditions and then interpreted them through his own selective imagination, it is all too easy for interpreters to seize on one element alone to the exclusion of the others. Furthermore, despite Wesley's repeated claims that he had not changed his views on various doctrines, there is no doubt that he did modify his teaching in significant ways throughout his life, despite some important continuities. Finally, there is a descriptive problem. Wesley composed no systematic theology; even his *Plain Account of Christian Perfection*, which deals with his most central and characteristic doctrine, is a polemical piece bringing together what he had said on the subject over the years. To lay out the ideas of such a writer in a formal, systematic shape, beginning with his teaching on God and working on in the conventional way to the last things, is peculiarly misleading.[1] Here he resembled Luther rather than Calvin, for like Luther his main concern was with the way of salvation, though if Luther focussed on the way of justification, Wesley may be said to have focussed on the way of sanctification. Both men took many traditional doctrines for granted and had nothing of fresh significance to say about them: for example on the Trinity, the person of Christ, the atonement, heaven and hell. There seems little point in exploring Wesley's thoughts on such matters, though there are odd individual observations to be found on them. For example, Wesley preached only one sermon on the Trinity (a doctrine under attack in several quarters in the eighteenth century). His conclusion was that it should be believed as a 'fact' on the evidence of Scripture but that one was not bound to a particular view of the relationship of the persons. This seems to reflect contemporary reservations about the doctrine, a distaste for disputes about 'opinions' and, perhaps, a strain of 'empiricism' in Wesley to be discussed in a moment. Or there are the last things. In his *Notes on the New Testament* Wesley printed Bengel's interpretation of *Revelation*, giving the beginning of the millennium in 1836, but only as a curiosity and without committing himself to it. Methodism was not a millennarian sect, though Wesley sometimes thought they might be living close to the 'last times' and a millennial outpouring of the gospel on earth.[2] Or again, he speculated that animals might have souls and immortality, an opinion held by a number of others in the eighteenth century.[3]

But, as Wesley himself said on Bengel's speculations, such matters were not of central concern to him. What did matter was doctrine concerned with personal salvation as the achievement of holiness to the point of perfection. This can be seen most clearly not so much in formal treatises, or even sermons and Conference pronouncements (though the attention paid to justification and sanctification in the first few Conferences is significant), but rather in a host of short, sometimes aphoristic summaries in his pastoral correspondence. Here he cut away all lesser matters to emphasize with great simplicity what was of ultimate concern. As he wrote in the Preface to his *Sermons* his concern was first to distinguish 'formal' from 'heart' religion and second to make clear the need for 'faith working by love' to those already converted. In the letters he says: 'Aim still at one thing – holy, loving faith, giving God the whole heart.' We should concentrate on two points 'Christ dying for us' and 'Christ reigning in us'. 'The end of the commandment is love . . . let this love be attained, by whatever means, and I am content, I desire no more.'[4]

This mature position was a realization of an ideal held since 1725, but it only reached this open and undogmatic formulation as a result of much conflict and searching, which included phases of much greater dogmatism and definition and re-definition.[5] In accordance with the priorities just explained, the exposition here will concentrate on Wesley's way of salvation from sin to perfection, but before we proceed to this, something needs to be said about his general intellectual position and in particular his notions of the sources of religious knowledge in the light of recent discussion. A brief word will also be in order about his view of the church as the collective aspect of salvation; and on the sacraments, because some have laid emphasis on his 'high' doctrine here as being unexpected in an 'evangelical': most modern interpretations of this seem to me to be anachronistic. Finally, the influence of the Methodists themselves on Wesley's doctrine needs to be emphasized throughout, and something has also to be said about what they made of what he taught them. Although some of the issues have already emerged in the course of the narrative so far, it will be convenient to give a synoptic view here.

Wesley was always a voracious and somewhat haphazard reader, especially in his Oxford period, but in compiling his standard set of sermons he claims that he set himself to be 'comparatively' a 'man of one book' – the Bible – as the guide to salvation. This salvation he had seen since 1725 in terms of achieving such a holiness as would realize the mind and life of Christ in the believer. The Oxford disciplines having apparently failed, he turned to the Moravian way of justification by grace through faith, but subsequent experience produced difficulties about the assurance of faith and the means by which the wished-for holiness could be developed and completed. His guides were, in his own mind, Scripture as primary, but also tradition, reason and experience. The balance of these 'authorities' varied from time to time. At Oxford, tradition – High Church and Nonjuror notions of 'primitive Christianity' – bulked large, but were then overshadowed by primacy being accorded to the Bible alone. Yet the Bible has always to be interpreted, and Wesley never entirely abandoned the use of tradition, especially for apologetic purposes; and he was a thoroughly eighteenth-century man in his desire to appeal to 'reason' and, increasingly, to experience: his own but even more that observed in others.

It has recently been claimed that although it is impossible to see Wesley as a consistent thinker if he is viewed simply as a theologian, from a philosophical point of view he held a consistent position in terms of eighteenth-century empiricism.[6] This is an important and in some ways neglected aspect of Wesley's mentality, and should be considered alongside recent attempts to relate the Revival more generally to the eighteenth-century Enlightenment rather than simply seeing these two sides of contemporary mentality as being irreconcilably opposed to each other.[7]

The anti-Enlightenment aspects of the Revival are obvious enough, and were reviewed earlier on (above, p. 167): Scripture against mere reason; grace against 'works'; original sin against benevolent views of the nature of man; and at the popular level supernatural against naturalistic interpretations of the world. Yet the eighteenth-century evangelicals retained an intellectual ballast lacking in their nineteenth-century successors.[8] The language of reason came as easily to Wesley in his *Appeals* to 'men of reason and religion' as to Law in his *Serious Call*, and for apologetic purposes against infidels evangelicals were happy enough to accept the 'evidences' of their non-evangelical contemporaries as Wesley accepted Butler's *Analogy*.[9] Wesley was more exceptional in his appreciation of sermons and treatises on practical duties, which Calvinist Evangelicals and Methodists condemned as inadequate.

Simplification of doctrine was another important contemporary characteristic. Wesley could speak in almost 'Latitudiniarian' terms of 'orthodoxy or right opinions' being 'but a very slender part of religion, if it can be allowed to be any part of it at all', though of course he had select notions of what was 'opinion' (see above, pp. 312f.). But even Calvinist Evangelicals (one of his targets in that remark) had mostly abandoned the elaborate scholasticism of seventeenth-century theologians. Scripture, reason and experience became more and more Wesley's watchwords for authority in belief, and even his appeals to 'primitive' tradition and the Reformation period in England seem mainly to be an apologetic device to establish his credentials to doubters and critics; they were not the *primary* source of his beliefs. The triple appeal to Scripture, reason and experience, though having older Anglican roots, was also very characteristic of 'Latitudinarians' like Locke and Watson. Locke's *Reasonableness of Christianity* was full of scriptural citations, and Bishop Watson, when he took to lecturing in divinity at Cambridge, ingenuously took a very 'Protestant' line by ignoring all sources but the Bible – interpreted by common sense.[10] All these men, like Wesley, had come to distrust the 'systems' of the past as being too artificial, too controversial, too much merely human. Of course they came to very different conclusions on the definitions of key concepts like justification and faith. They also had different pairs of spectacles for interpretation: Hoadly frankly interpreted the Bible by the canons of his own day; others were less conscious of doing so, and evangelicals were in fact using tradition, though of a different sort from their critics.[11]

Even ideas of God were coloured by contemporary 'enlightened' thinking. Watts's God of creation, we have seen, combined the God of the modern astronomers with the pervasive presence and control of the God of Calvin. The benevolent God of the Enlightenment coloured the more awesome God of evangelicals who, though a judge, also evoked gratitude as loving heavenly Father who showed mercy in Jesus; and evangelical piety was centred on Jesus.[12] Even the Calvinists seemed to offer this love to all who would respond in practice; and the Arminian Wesleyans did so in principle.

But in philosophical terms something much more specific can be said about Wesley: apparently he was thoroughly imbued with the contemporary fashion for empiricism and followed Locke in his approach to questions of knowledge. This is what has been argued recently by Frederick Dreyer.[13] If true, it is of considerable importance for estimating Wesley's intellectual outlook and the basis on which his teaching rested. But it should be emphasized that this is a philosophical appraisal. Wesley speaks in traditional Anglican terms about Scripture, tradition and reason. Warning himself about excessive trust in tradition, he wrote in 1746: 'The Scriptures are the touchstone whereby Christians examine all real or supposed revelations'; and in 1756, while saying that he 'reverenced the ancient church and our own', he added: 'but trying every church and every doctrine by the Bible'.[14] Reason, however, has a place, for 'religion was not designed to destroy any of our ordinary faculties, but to exalt and improve them, our reason in particular'.[15] Though this seems to move away from the pessimistic Reformation view of the fallen, darkened mind of man, Wesley in fact does not think that 'mere' reason can penetrate far into divine truth, still less bring salvation by itself. His rationalizing view of faith, challenged by his mother in 1725, and Locke's 'reasonable persuasion of the mind', were altered by his conversion into a 'disposition of the heart'. Very important for any comparison with eighteenth-century empiricism is the claim that there is a 'divine supernatural *elenchos*' (proof or test), a 'spiritual sight of God and the things of God', which gives us a knowledge of God impossible by any other means. This means that there is a 'new class of senses opened in your soul, not depending on organs of flesh and blood'. These 'senses' enable us to discover the 'spiritual objects' of the 'invisible world'. They are not natural gifts inherent in man but given by God through faith, and so one is not saved by belief and the effort of the will.[16]

The appeal to experience in terms of ordinary observation and self-analysis does become more and more important to Wesley in settling doctrine. It was this which helped to make him hostile to predestination and Moravian stillness, and to assert degrees of faith and delayed assurance. It also led him to clarify his views on perfection. Ostensibly experience merely confirmed the teaching of Scripture, but in effect it was used at least to ascertain what Scripture 'really' means. Thus on perfection he originally argued almost entirely from Scripture, but the outbreaks of the 1760s led him to say that 'if there be *no living witnesses* of what we have preached for twenty years, I cannot, dare not preach it any longer'.[17]

Dreyer's argument is that Wesley's concern was not with the 'what' but the 'how' of Christian belief, his 'doctrinal' controversies really being on points of psychology: whether belief is more than reasonable assent; whether faith can exist in different degrees; whether one can choose or resist grace. Belief as a 'sensible experience' of the Holy Ghost was the 'main doctrine of the Methodists'.[18] (One should be cautious here: this is early post-conversion Wesley, and in any case refers to the experience of the fruits of the Spirit combined with assurance. It is doubtful whether Wesley would later have seen this formula as being his main doctrine.) The evidence for this reality lies partly in the fruits of the Spirit (love, joy and peace) perceived by the ordinary senses but partly in the Holy Spirit witnessing with our own spirit, which has to be a gift given by the Spirit. Even this, however, is 'empirical' in form, since it involves a kind of 'perception', though Dreyer says that it lands Wesley in logical confusions. The same form is observed in Wesley's talk of supernatural 'spiritual senses'. Like Locke, he rejects the tradition of innate ideas and *a priori* reasoning in favour of an empiricist approach.

Here Wesley was certainly a Lockeian, though not quite a whole-hearted one. It will be recalled that though Oxford officially stuck to Aristotle, privately individuals began to read and use Locke (above, p. 65). Wesley seems to have read the *Human Understanding* as early as 1732 along with some anti-Lockeian works, and in 1781 he published extracts from the *Essay* and comments on this 'strong, weighty treatise'. He endorses Locke's condemnation of innate ideas, but sees his views on logic as being inferior to Aristotle and the old Oxford logics like Dean Aldrich's. This is very much what one would expect from an Oxford man of Wesley's generation.[19] Further evidence of Wesley's empiricism in the sense of describing phenomena without speculating on the mystery of hidden causes can be seen in his trial-and-error approach to medicine and his work on science which we have already discussed. Although this was partly on the religious grounds of the mystery of God's work, it also accords with the anti-metaphysical tendencies in the seventeenth-century search for certainty which forms the background to Locke's philosophy.[20] Even Wesley's notorious love of the supernatural, Dreyer suggests, can be seen as a form of empiricism, at least in principle, since he simply accepted stories on the evidence of honest testimony; and he certainly followed 'empiricist' principles when he accepted the stories of seventeenth-century recorders like Glanvill while remaining sceptical about their elaborate attempts to explain the *causality* of apparitions. What he did not accept was Locke's claim that the force of testimony weakens, the further it lies in the past; nor the view later to be popularized by Hume that no amount of testimony can convince us of something inherently improbable.[21]

Wesley in fact seems to have preferred the version of empiricism taught by Peter Browne which he condensed in 1730 and tried to recommend to Mrs Pendarves (Aspasia). He used Browne again to instruct some of the preachers in 1756.[22] Browne was, if anything, an even more thoroughgoing advocate of the sense-origin of ideas than Locke, but he also had a strong sense of the analogical nature of ideas about God – notions commoner in the eighteenth century than is always realized.[23]

However, one should not exaggerate the affinity between Wesley and Locke or even Browne. Dreyer admits that Wesley's ideas of faith and of 'spiritual senses' were quite different from Locke's, though he argues that the empiricist form is preserved here by postulating a 'sense' to account for spiritual experiences, very much as Hutcheson postulated a moral 'sense' to account for moral experience, as indeed Wesley did.[24] Richard Brantley goes even further in his discussion of the relationship between Wesley, Locke and Browne.[25] He would like to claim that Wesley was opening up channels for knowledge of the unseen world through the 'spiritual senses' which had already been allowed for to some extent by Locke and Browne. Unfortunately, the passages which he cites in these authors will not bear the sense that he wishes to impose upon them. Far from allowing that God might communicate directly with people today by personal revelations, this was precisely what Locke denied; and Browne confined revelations by the Holy Spirit to the written testimony of the Bible. There is little doubt that these authors would have seen Wesley and the Methodists as 'enthusiasts'.[26] The 'spiritual senses' were obviously claims to a direct knowledge of God, let alone Methodist visions and conversion experiences.

As to Wesley's supernaturalism, this will be discussed along with that of Methodism generally at a later stage (below, pp. 431ff.). In terms of the argument being pursued here it is perfectly true that Wesley doubted some of the seventeenth-century apparition stories (though he believed a great many of them, as well as those from his own day) and certainly eschewed 'explanations' of them. He believed in witches in accordance with the Bible and wise men of all ages, and especially as a knock-down argument against sceptics denying supernatural intervention in the world.[27] These things he believed, it seems, by the evidence of credible witnesses, and for the same reason he believed much else that was rejected by educated men in his day; but the Bible and the belief that what happened in the Bible could perfectly well happen in his own day were also important for his views in this area. The truth is that he shared with his followers a strong propensity to believe in such things, and saw no limitations on God's willingness as well as his ability (not to mention the Devil's) to do things contrary to the normal course of nature. He also had a strong sense of the providential work of God through Methodism, and even in his own life.[28] In all this, Wesley was going far beyond what Locke or Browne would have thought 'empirical' evidence could yield. His position was much closer to those seventeenth-century educated men who still allowed for apparitions and witches and the like; he had much in common with Richard Baxter here, and printed extracts from Baxter's collection of apparitions in the *Magazine*. But in the eighteenth century these things were no longer generally accepted by the educated as part of their world-picture, or at any rate not as a major part of it. The real difference between Wesley and them was partly that the intellectual outlook had changed to marginalize such beliefs and strand them among the lower orders; partly that Wesley added Lockeian empiricist arguments to justify them. He therefore appeared a 'reasonable enthusiast': rational in form but enthusiast in substance. He supported supernaturalist beliefs with empiricist arguments well beyond what Locke would have allowed in his more limited form of 'rational supernaturalism', which avoided Deism by allowing for truths 'beyond' but not 'contrary' to reason: such as a biblical revelation supported by miracles and prophecy, safely confined to the past.

In approaching Wesley's view of the process of salvation, one fundamental point to bear in mind is his apparently lifelong Arminianism and implacable opposition to Calvinism. God must be seen to be offering salvation to all, and all must be free to accept or reject it. Even though we are saved by grace through faith and not by our own works, we must actively pursue salvation, prepare for it, build upon the grace offered after conversion, and pursue perfection. Wesley never entirely lost this belief even in the first enthusiasm of his discovery of the Moravian doctrine, and all his experiences after that time and his conflict with the Calvinists made him emphasize it the more as necessary to morality and spiritual health. Here he was joining in a late stage of an ancient controversy which had erupted in 1739–40 and would do so again in the furious struggle with Calvinistic Evangelicals in the 1770s.

We have already seen that Arminianism came naturally to most Anglicans and especially High Churchmen by the end of the seventeenth century. On the other hand, it is not surprising that many evangelicals should have developed Calvinistic and predestinarian views as a result of their conversions: revivals of a strong doctrine of sin and grace always produce this result. The surprising thing is really that, exceptionally within the Revival as a whole, Wesley did not. We have seen how he discussed the question with his mother in 1725, and how although he does not seem, then or later, to have been personally troubled by it, he did find it intellectually puzzling and a problem because of the teaching of the Thirty-Nine Articles and that of St Paul. Susanna, we have seen, thought that God had 'elected' those whom he foresaw would respond freely to the offer of salvation. Wesley himself thought for a time that some had actually been elected to salvation indefeasibly, but that others could be added to the number, apparently by their free response to the gospel. But this he had abandoned by the early 1750s, fearing that it conceded too much to the Calvinists. In fact there seems to be no sign of this concession in his 'Free Grace' sermon against the Whitefieldites in 1739. God's only 'decree' is that he has given us a free choice of salvation by faith; and that those who are saved are those who respond to this. They can also, as he often made plain, lose salvation again by their own free choice.[29]

However, Wesley also believed in the traditional doctrines of the fall and original sin, which he spelled out in strong terms in a treatise (partly based on Isaac Watts) directed against the Arian John Taylor in 1756 (appealing, incidentally, to 'Scripture, reason and experience').[30] But how could freewill to respond be reconciled with this helpless state? Wesley's answer lay in the notion of 'preventing' or 'prevenient grace'.[31] This is emphatically not 'natural conscience', an innate quality in man as man; rather it is, though given to every man, a gift of God's grace.[32] By this theological device Wesley was able to avoid the extremes of 'Pelagianism' (human beings saving themselves by their own unaided efforts) and Calvinism's denial of freewill and fixing of the elect and damned. Along with Wesley's traditional doctrines of original sin, the atonement and the divinity of Christ it also safeguarded him against the usual smear on 'Arminians': that they were, or would end up as, outright 'Socinians' or 'Arians', people who denied not only predestination but also original sin, the substitutionary atonement and the divinity of Christ. Jabez Bunting, the Methodist 'pope' of the nineteenth century, is supposed to have testified to the special position of Wesleyanism by speaking of its *evangelical Arminianism*' with these things in mind.[33]

Wesley later pictured the process of salvation as beginning with this gift of grace, as a tendency to 'life'. If it is exercised, further grace-gifts are given which may be labelled 'convincing grace' or 'repentance', and so progress is made towards conversion expressed in 'those two grand branches': justification (by which we are saved from the guilt of sin) and sanctification (by which we are saved from the root of sin and restored to the image of God). Sanctification is both instantaneous and gradual: it begins from the moment of justification, but grows until we are cleansed from all sin.[34]

This formulation was a late one, the product of years of experience and conflict. But as early as 1746, Wesley could write that: 'Our main doctrines, which include all the rest, are three: that of repentance, of faith and of holiness. The first of these we account, as it were, the porch of religion; the next the door; the third, religion itself.'[35] This presentation is very different from Luther's placing of justification by faith and also from that of Calvinist Evangelicals.

Wesley's initial reaction to the Moravian teaching that justification comes by grace through faith alone in a moment of instant conversion bringing conquest of sin, as described in his *Journal* entry under 24 May 1738, was a review of his life which portrayed his pre-conversion experience as useless and non-Christian: it was only years later that he modified some of these harsh phrases by footnotes into the idea that he had not had 'the true Christian faith', that he had had 'the faith of a servant but not of a son'. The *Journal* and sermons show that a strong emphasis on salvation by faith and a condemnation of ideas of salvation by works was a predominant feature of his early post-conversion preaching.[36] The faith which brings justification is not a human effort but a gift of God. Justification is pardon, and is received by a faith which is a divine, supernatural 'evidence' or 'conviction' of things not discernible by our bodily senses. Justification not only means that through Christ's death God reconciled the world to himself but is also a personal sense that this was done for *me*. Wesley carefully distinguishes this from sanctification: we are not actually *made* just and righteous, but simply pardoned for our sins. To be made just and righteous is a distinct work and gift of God, though in some degree it is an immediate fruit of justification. 'The one (justification) implies what God *does for* us through His Son; the other, what he *works in* us by his Spirit.'[37]

There is no doubt that from 1738 to the end of his life Wesley adhered to this basic doctrine. But there is also no doubt that conflict and experience led him to clarify and define many times the relationship of justification to the 'repentance' which leads to it; to works before and after it; to the 'assurance' which might be regarded as a mark of its reality; to the sanctification and ultimate 'perfection' which should follow from it. There was much discussion of these matters in the first few Conferences from 1744; much writing on perfection in the 1760s; and in the 1770s Wesley appeared to have retreated so far from a rigid doctrine of justification by faith and to have come so close to salvation by works as to provoke a furious Calvinist reaction and some hasty redefinition on his part. In the process of these oscillations between the poles of Calvinism and Pelagianism Wesley, though he did not deny his original doctrine of justification by faith, certainly modified it to bring out its relationship to the process of sanctification more clearly.

The early Conferences show where the problems lay. In 1744 justification is seen as meaning that we are 'pardoned and received into God's favour' and if we 'continue therein' we shall be saved. Faith is the condition of justification, but repentance and 'works meet for repentance' must 'go before this faith'. They are also necessary for its continuance, as it may be lost by subsequent sins. Already there is a fear that this approach may have 'leaned too much' to antinomianism by the idea that the law is made void through faith. In 1745 it is said that though faith is the sole condition of justification, yet repentance and works must go before it and therefore are 'conditions' of it: to argue about this is 'mere strife about words'. It was acknowledged that at first the Methodists had come to 'the very edge of Calvinism' in their stress on grace and faith and had kept the urge to go on to perfection in the background. Faith does not supersede good works but enables them to happen. In 1746 there was a concession to the popular belief in salvation by 'sincerity' so far as to allow that those sincerely wishing to do the will of God will be given saving faith, though 'sincerity' and faith are not the same.[38] Yet the same Conference wondered whether the whole dispute about salvation by faith or works is merely one about words. 'In asserting salvation by faith we mean: that pardon (salvation begun) is received by faith producing works. That holiness (salvation continued) is faith working by love. That heaven (salvation finished) is the reward of this faith.' A degree of the love of God and holiness may go before justification, though 'abiding love of God' can only spring from 'faith in a pardoning God'.

What seems to emerge from all this is that while Wesley retained the basic notion that justification comes by grace through faith, he was constrained by experience to allow that this could be prepared for by good works which had some real value. The placing of repentance and faith as the 'porch' and 'door' to real religion as a life of holiness represents the fruit of his experience of how the Moravian formula related to his long-standing concern with holiness, which was now resuming priority. If the 1738 discovery was retained, it now took its place within the long-term project of holiness as the mark of true Christianity: justification was ultimately a means to this end, not the end in itself.

By 1770 Wesley would go much further in the light of his dread of Calvinism and antinomianism and dislike of disputes about 'words'. Sitting in his coach in December 1767, he had the following reflections, remarkable for an 'evangelical':

> That a man may be saved who cannot express himself properly concerning Imputed Righteousness. Therefore, to do this is not necessary to salvation.
>
> That a man may be saved who has not clear conceptions of it. (Yea, that never heard the phrase.) Therefore, clear conceptions of it are not necessary to salvation. Yea, it is not necessary to salvation to use the phrase at all.
>
> That a pious churchman who has not clear conceptions even of Justification by Faith may be saved. Therefore, clear conceptions even of this are not necessary to salvation. That a Mystic, who denies Justification by Faith (Mr Law, for instance) may be saved. But, if so, what becomes of *articulus stantis vel cadentis ecclesiae* (the article by which a church stands or falls)? If so, is it not high time for us . . . to return to the plain word, 'He that feareth God, and worketh righteousness, is accepted with Him'?[39]

At the Conference of 1770 it was thought they had 'leaned too much toward Calvinism' by playing down the need for and value of the works done by human beings before justification. 'And if this is not *in order* to find favour, what does he do them for?' Salvation, though not by 'merit' of works, is by works 'as a condition'. And if so, they have been disputing about words for thirty years. They have been afraid of the word 'merit', but we are 'rewarded according to our works, yea, because of our works'. 'How does this differ from *for the sake of our works*? And how differs this from *secundum merita operum* (according to the merits of works)? As our works *deserve*. Can you split this hair? I doubt, I cannot.' When people say that they have not feared God or worked righteousness before conversion we cannot be sure this is true, since such converts always undervalue themselves. Finally, talk of a justified or sanctified 'state' is misleading, leading people to trust to what is done in a moment. 'Whereas we are every hour and every moment pleasing or displeasing to God, *according to our works* – according to the whole of our inward tempers, and our outward behaviour.'[40] And a remark at the same Conference suggests a practical renewal of the old Oxford method: 'No idleness can consist with growth in grace. Nay, without exactness in redeeming the time, it is impossible to retain even the life you received in justification.'

Similarly, in *Thoughts on Salvation by Faith* (1779), Wesley asserted that to avoid Calvinism one must affirm that:

> Seeing no faith avails, but that 'which worketh by love', which produces both inward and outward good works, to affirm, No man is finally saved without this, is, in effect, to affirm, No man is finally saved without works.

Wesley had for forty years, he says, held that 'by grace we are saved through faith', yet not so as to contradict what the Apostle also says: 'Without holiness no man shall see the Lord.'[41]

In the furious controversy which followed the 1770 Minutes Wesley was driven to try to develop a scholastic argument, elaborated by Fletcher, that there is a 'double justification': the first by faith at the beginning of conversion, the second by works which is necessary to bring the Christian to a state in which he can finally be fit to be accepted by God at the end.[42]

Wesley was struggling with a problem which had dogged Protestantism since the sixteenth century and had given rise to intricate debates and definitions, particularly among Lutherans who were obsessed with the fear that they would fall into salvation by works; but there had been English debates too.[43] The Revival renewed such debates, though generally, as we shall see, with less sophistication. In conducting the debates, the protagonists used some of the old distinctions, as Wesley's comments show, but for him at least they were no more than formal counters in a symbolic game or tools for verbal demolition. His impatience with them shows what had really provoked his concern: practical considerations and the lessons of experience. The realities of pre- and post-conversion experience in moral terms; the need to make converts grow moment by moment and not to trust to one 'experience'; the threat of Calvinism and antinomianism; and the all-important objective of creating the actualities of a holy life, drove him to challenge the shibboleths of two centuries of Protestant obsessions about the 'article by which a church stands or falls', at least in terms of rigid formulas. He was, as we have seen, scathing about 'gospel sermons' full of cant and jargon which was correct but profitless and induced complacency; he preferred plain, conventional Anglican moral sermons (or the detailed, searching *Whole Duty of Man*) to these.[44] The meditations in his coach in 1767 showed his position very clearly: what matters is not formulas but the reality of observed religious experience and its moral fruits. Attain holy love by whatever means and he was content.[45] He did not deny justification by faith in his later years, but sought its reality and above all its development into perfection.

For Wesley, assurance of salvation was an essential complement to justification, though he modified his more extreme claims in later years. As we have seen, this 'assurance' was given partly by simple observation of the facts that the fruits of the Spirit were being shown, but in addition there was the 'Spirit witnessing with our spirit' that we are children of God. There are signs of such notions even before his conversion.[46] The Moravians, of course, taught him to expect it, and it was the lack of the full fruits of love, joy and peace which made him feel during 1738 that he was still not a Christian. We have seen that he tried to resolve the problem by the idea that there are degrees of faith and that assurance generally came as an experience separate from, and subsequent to, conversion. But he certainly continued to preach and teach that the experience was a necessary proof of the reality of justification having taken place – for example at the 1744 Conference, in the sermon on 'The Witness of the Spirit' in 1746, and in another as late as 1767.[47] It is said, however, that years later he recalled how he and Charles had preached that without it people were damned and that he wondered they were not stoned. Now, however, he asserted it as no more than the 'common privilege' of believers. To Dr Rutherforth in 1768 he asserted the same, allowing that it could be absent or interrupted for various reasons, including physical and psychological ones. His Arminianism showed in the fact that such assurance was only of *present* salvation: he denied the Calvinist view of an assurance of 'final perseverance' for the elect. No one can rest secure in this.[48]

'Conversion' as the experiential moment in which justification is realized and received by the individual has bulked large in the annals of popular evangelicalism. As numerous early Methodist life-stories show, they did delight in identifying this moment, and Wesley's 1738 experience has often been seen as a paradigm for it. Its earlier history has already been outlined, together with interpretations of Wesley's experience, and all that need be said here is that it was not a term he used very often. He spoke, rather, of the 'new birth': a comprehensive term for the transformation of people from a state of sin and condemnation to a state of salvation.

'New birth', however, is as slippery a term as 'conversion'. Precedents can be found for it in Puritanism and Pietism, though these are developments of the Jesus of St John's Gospel who said: 'You must be born again.' The more immediate sources for the Wesleys are likely to have been William Law and Whitefield, and we have seen that Charles Wesley was urging new birth even before his conversion. Once imbued with the Moravian idea of justification it came to be seen as a sudden experience. However, as used by Wesley it often means not simply the moment of justification but the whole process by which the believer becomes transformed from sin to holiness.[49] Wesley speaks of it as 'the great change which God works in the soul when He brings it to life; when he raises it from the death of sin to the life of righteousness'.[50] At first he seemed to see it as being associated with justification as the moment of birth into a new life through 'Christ formed in the heart'.[51] But as he came to distinguish justification and sanctification more clearly as different stages in the Christian life, so he saw justification as what God does 'for' us, and sanctification as what God does 'in us', apparently beginning with a new birth in justification but essentially a distinct work.[52] In 1748 he sees justification and new birth as 'in point of time inseparable from each other', yet of different natures. 'God in justification does something for us; in begetting us again, He also does the work *in* us.' In a sermon on 'The New Birth' he sees it as 'regeneration', and distinguishes it from 'sanctification', of which it is only part: the entrance into it.[53] Probably, as with perfection, soon after his conversion Wesley saw 'new birth' as being the inward side of justification viewed as the immediate entry into perfection; but as he separated justification from sanctification and perfection, he came to see new birth as only the beginning of the sanctifying process.

Talk of 'new birth' as the beginning of the Christian life in relation to justification and conversion of a more or less mature person always consorts uneasily with the practice of infant baptism, especially in churches or groups which believe that some form of baptismal regeneration in infants is the real beginning of the Christian life – is, indeed, the location of 'new birth'. The Book of Common Prayer contains this doctrine, and it was held to firmly by High Churchmen, including Wesley himself: certainly before his conversion and apparently afterwards, too. In 1740 Waterland preached and published on 'Regeneration' in terms evidently aimed at the Methodists. His definition of the new birth is: 'a spiritual change, wrought upon any person by the Holy Spirit, in the use of baptism; whereby he is translated from his natural state in Adam, to a spiritual state in Christ'.[54] Wesley, we have seen, thought that he had not sinned away the grace given in baptism till he went to Charterhouse. In 1756 he published a revised version of his father's tract on baptism showing that baptism washes away original sin, so that by this we are 'regenerated or born again', and a principle of grace is infused which will not be wholly taken away unless we quench the Holy Spirit by wickedness.[55]

But he did not believe baptism was essential to salvation – otherwise Quakers would, impossibly he thought, be excluded.[56] Some of his Anglican critics who doubted whether Methodist conversion had much effect on people already living good lives argued that new birth is given only in (infant) baptism.[57] Wesley never really gave up the idea that people *could* be born again in baptism, but he certainly played down the idea in later years, arguing that baptism and new birth are not the same, and that though the two events sometimes coincided, experience (that touchstone again) showed that often they were separated by many years. No matter what happened to you as an infant, the thing that really matters is the state you are in now. No matter what you once received, you have probably fallen into sin since, and so the call to all is: 'You must be born again'.[58] In his revised version of the Prayer Book for the Americans, Wesley omitted some (though not all) of the explicit 'regeneration' language in the baptismal office.[59]

It should be clear by now that for Wesley the true goal of the Christian life is sanctification, holiness, even to the point of perfection. This goal was never abandoned, and even in his first enthusiasm for justification by faith Wesley was clear about this: he simply believed that he had at last found the way to obtain it after many weary years of frustration. In any case, justification by faith always produced scandalized charges that it led to neglect of good works and antinomianism. In his sermon on the subject in 1738 Wesley was careful to reject this charge.[60] The early conferences were as much concerned with sanctification as justification; as we have seen, in 1746 this had emerged as the real objective to which justification was only the door.

But if holiness is the goal and is evidently a progressive process, what are the limits on its achievement in the present life? Notoriously, Wesley taught a doctrine of 'Christian perfection', also termed 'entire sanctification', 'perfect love', 'the great salvation', occasionally 'the second blessing'. 'Sinless perfection' was a term he rejected, though others used it.[61] Not only did this cause great controversy, misunderstanding and scandal, but Wesley had great difficulty in defining it to his own satisfaction so as to pitch it neither too high nor too low and to guard it from popular abuses.

It is fair to say, as Wesley often claimed, that the pursuit of holiness had been his original and constant aim since 1725. Claims that Christians do not commit sin and talk of perfection do occur, as we have seen, in his Oxford period, and he had portrayed the ideal Christian in his sermon on 'The Circumcision of the Heart' in 1733, though he altered the passage on faith later.[62] It has often been claimed that it was only the means for obtaining this end which changed after 1738, but in fact the injection of justification-by-faith ideas and the outbreak of perfectionism in the 1760s had a greater impact on his ideas of perfection than this statement implies.

If the ideal of complete inward and outward holiness was formulated in 1725 under the influence of Taylor and à Kempis and later of William Law, justification by faith (it was suggested earlier) seemed at first to Wesley to promise an immediate achievement of this by conquering sin. The 'conversion' of May 1738 as Wesley described it seems in fact to contain elements of justification by faith, new birth, assurance and even perfection, all in the same instant.[63] It was argued earlier that at first Wesley may well have believed that this was so, and that it was only his disillusionment with his own condition during the next few months, and his search for guidance and comfort among the Moravians and others, that made him revise his views. His first concern was to find whether the conscious fruits of the Spirit in terms of love, joy and peace were the necessary marks of true conversion and rebirth, and he persuaded himself that 'assurance' giving these might be a stage subsequent to conversion, though his later testimony seems to imply that he did not allow this in his preaching.

But there are also indications that Wesley was puzzling about perfection and whether it, too, was only given at a later stage. It was the persistence of sin that made him doubt whether he had even been converted. Tyerman suggested that he had confused the witness of the Spirit with sanctification, and the experience recorded of Arvid Gradin in 1738 seems to suggest that this is correct.[64] Wesley himself quoted Gradin's testimony in his *Plain Account of Christian Perfection* in 1767 as an example of the 'full assurance of faith', by which he here meant the gift of perfection, and says that it was the first example he had found of a living witness of this gift. Hitherto he had simply taught it as a revealed but unconfirmed 'scriptural doctrine', a significant point.[65]

Wesley always saw in the teachings and writings of others what he wished to see, and the Moravian idea of sanctification may not have been what he supposed it to be, if the conversation with Zinzendorf recorded earlier is any guide.[66] But what is certainly the case is that under the pressure of experience Wesley developed what seems originally to have been a simple notion of justification, new birth, assurance and sanctification, all achieved in a moment, into a process with several clearly defined stages, culminating in the gift of perfection. This was an answer to the problem of sin apparently remaining in believers who had been converted.[67]

The Conferences in 1744–47 explored various aspects of sanctification and perfection. Perfection is given on condition of faith, begins when faith begins and increases as it increases. To be a 'perfect' Christian is to love God with one's whole heart, mind, soul and strength. But there is no sure way of knowing who has achieved this: only 'sensible proofs' from conduct. A gradual process of the elimination of sin is visualized which will probably only be complete just before death, though the possibility is suggested of obtaining it earlier. It is allowed that few have the gift earlier and that it should be preached about cautiously to avoid targets for criticism.[68]

It is evident from this that despite Wesley's claims in the 1760s that his doctrine had always been the same, he did in fact modify it in various ways from his conversion onwards. Justification is the door into a process which is likely to be completed just before death. The basis for the teaching is essentially a particular reading of scripture, since as yet Wesley had few living models as well as a few from history – like Lopez and De Renty. There is no clear sign of the notion that perfection could come by a kind of second sudden conversion; preaching on it is to be cautious; and there is doubt as to how it is to be known to have been achieved. This cautious presentation of the doctrine perhaps accounts for the fact that Wesley could claim that despite the controversy over the doctrine, his sermon on it in 1741 had caused Bishop Gibson to see no objection to it.[69] In that sermon he had already built in qualifications about the 'perfect' not being free from 'infirmities' or from temptation; he would emphasize this more later against critics and extreme exponents of the doctrine. The sermon, however, is less cautious than the Conference discussions. In Charles Wesley's hymns more extreme views are found, which John tended to chasten or correct. In the *Plain Account* in the 1760s, when John was anxious to assert that his views had never changed, he quoted these hymns to show that he had long taught that perfection delivered from all sin; was received simply by faith; was given instantly; and could be received at any moment and not simply just before death. But it is hard to escape the impression that this was not typical of the earlier period.[70]

What made the difference was, more than anything, the sudden accumulation of large numbers of living claimants to the gift in the perfectionist revivals in the 1760s. Hitherto, only a few such cases had occurred, and Wesley himself confessed that the work had been at a standstill for twenty years. As we have seen, the whole episode was of great importance not only for Wesley's definition of the doctrine but also for his propagation of it, and for its reception among the Methodists and views of it among the public at large.

Wesley now had numerous examples of claims to the experience which he carefully investigated and often believed. They also made him place far more stress on its truth as shown by 'living witnesses' rather than simply as a doctrine which he knew in theory from the New Testament; as we have seen, he finally seems to have made this living evidence the touchstone rather than the Bible alone. Moreover, this altered at least the emphasis and perhaps even the substance of his teaching, for the idea that the gift was freely and extensively available 'now' rather than at the point of death became an insistent feature of his presentation for the rest of his life. This was clearly drawn from his observation of what was happening, rather than from the Bible, for he had confessed earlier that few cases could be found there.[71] The extreme views of some of the claimants, especially the followers of Maxfield and Bell, made him define more clearly what was and was not being claimed, as did his brother's alarmed reaction to the enthusiasts. Concentration by some on the moment of reception did not make him reject instantaneous claims, but it did make him reassert his now inbred sense that the gift should be sought by the means of grace and discipline, and even 'improved' and deepened as well as sustained afterwards by the same means. It was the same balance of faith and works as he had already applied to justification and conversion. On the same analogy, a gift of assurance through the witness of the Spirit can be obtained for perfection as well as the 'empirical' evidence of conduct.[72] And, being an Arminian, Wesley thought that it could be lost if not sustained by constant vigilance. It need hardly be said that the Calvinists rejected the whole shocking claim to perfection in this life, especially on such terms.

What Wesley seems to have done in fact is to have adapted the Moravian notion of instant conversion and assurance once again to his own purposes by applying it to this 'second conversion', while also retaining his old Oxford sense of the need for preparation and co-operative effort with God.[73] He now had an extended scenario for the drama of salvation which became distinctive of Wesleyanism, offering the believer a pilgrim's progress from sin through conviction, through conversion, to perfection and beyond; and this was also his sovereign antidote to Calvinism and quietism, as well as to those who simply trusted in instantaneous gifts and feelings alone. Yet there was plenty to please them as well, and Wesley himself loved to recount their claims to experiences of unbroken love between themselves and Christ.[74]

These multi-purpose ends were not achieved without paradox and difficulty. The allowance for 'infirmities' in the 1741 sermon had to be developed later to convince doubters that they had perfection, but Wesley had also to allow that mistakes in 'opinions' might lead to 'transgressions of the perfect law', though not to defects in love. To remedy these infirmities he claimed that the perfect had to continue to rely on Christ and his work alone, a proviso that Calvinists suspected was being left out of the picture in favour of works. On other occasions he extended this provision more consistently, from the stock evangelical point of view, by allowing that even the perfected depend at every moment, at every stage in salvation, on grace and faith.[75]

It has plausibly been suggested that Wesley was only able to assert his paradoxical doctrine of a perfection which was not perfect because he operated with two definitions of perfection, one attainable in this life and the other not; and this in turn depended on two definitions of sin. The one he preferred was 'a voluntary transgression of a known law which it is in our power to obey', and this appeared very early in his career, in a letter to Mrs Pendarves in 1731.[76] Hence if you are not conscious of such a transgression it is logical to feel no barrier between yourself and Christ, but only an uninterrupted two-way flow of love. This (together with love to humanity) was Wesley's notion of the reality of Christian perfection, and it was this which came out in descriptions of Methodist experiences of the gift. The perfection which he did *not* claim to be possible in this life was a condition in which one did not fall short in any way, consciously or unconsciously, of the perfect law of God. The moral dangers as well as the experiential attractions of the more limited definition are obvious enough, but it fitted his purpose very well, and warded off Charles Wesley's notions; to John these made perfection impossible, though some of Charles's hymns had once suggested that God could remove the very 'root' of sin. John's definitions and qualifications at least help to make his claims for the possibility of 'perfection' in love in this life intelligible.

What is beyond doubt is that the position Wesley reached in the 1760s was one which he maintained for the rest of his life, against much opposition and distaste within Methodism itself. Indeed he thought that it was Methodism's special testimony, and that if it was dropped the movement would lose its vitality (but he thought this true of other things – such as leaving the church or even the dropping of early service!).[77]

How far Methodists actually followed his teaching in theory and practice will be discussed later.

Although for the biography of Wesley it is not strictly necessary to follow the history of perfectionism beyond his lifetime, it is important to realize that its later development in Methodism and outside it has helped to colour the interpretations given to Wesley's own views.[78] To put it rather summarily, the two elements held in balance in Wesley – an instant gift and experience, and a steady progress through pious cultivation – tended to split apart into two different versions of 'holiness', the latter being less open to objection and embarrassment. Among the leaders of the next generation Adam Clarke maintained Wesley's two assertions and was favoured by revivalists for maintaining the element of the 'instant gift'. Later perfectionists and Pentecostals concentrated on the gift as an experience with little specific moral content. Richard Watson concentrated on the element of gradual progress, and it is this which has attracted those modern Methodists, with some exceptions, who have wished to see Wesley as having left a usable legacy in this area. But Wesley undoubtedly valued and believed in the instant gift, and his later correspondence is full of personal advice and urgings to seek it.

The sources of the doctrine have been the subject of the same range of disagreements as the conversion. Wesley's position as an 'evangelical' Protestant is undeniably odd, and his use of Catholic writers as well as the very language of perfection have suggested an affinity with the Catholic tradition. G.C. Cell's aphorism, 'a necessary synthesis of the Protestant ethic of grace with the Catholic ethic of holiness', has often been quoted, though this is rather a misleading indication of the general argument of Cell's book.[79] J.L. Peters elaborated it by claiming that 'the Catholic tradition provided the goal, the Protestant emphasis provided the dynamic'; adding that the content of the doctrine was adequately defined by 1733, but that the method of obtaining it was only defined after 1738.[80] Those who dislike this have preferred either to see the Catholic elements thoroughly subordinated to the evangelical after 1738 or to claim that Wesley could gain all he needed from Protestant sources.[81] Wesley's Calvinist opponents of course already instinctively suspected that Wesley was veering to Popery, and this belief was not simply vulgar abuse. What struck them was his apparent balancing of faith and works in salvation like the Council of Trent.[82]

Although it is important to recognize that Wesley never borrowed anything without setting his own interpretation upon it, and that in its mature form his version of perfection was certainly not one that can be ascribed to a Catholic writer, his ideas and language do bear a more obvious affinity to the tradition of Catholic than Protestant spirituality.[83]

The most obvious Protestant precedent in George Fox and the Quakers is unlikely to have influenced him.[84] There are clear echoes of the language of seventeenth-century French Quietism in such phrases as 'pure love' used by Wesley, and he had read a number of the writers concerned, with his usual discrimination, valuing their ideas of loving communion with God while often disagreeing with the details. Where he parted company with them was in their obsessive search for a state of 'disinterested love' in which the soul would be indifferent to its own salvation and love God alone for his own sake.[85] There was a kind of robust common-sense touched with the optimism of the Enlightenment which had already led Wesley in 1725 to balk at the morbid misery of Taylor and à Kempis in favour of the theme of 'holiness and happiness'.[86] The Catholic pursuit of disciplined progress in real, achieved holiness reinforced what he had inherited from the High Church tradition, and as we have seen, this persisted through his rediscovery of justification by faith. The idea that the gift of perfection, like that of justification, could be obtained in a moment by faith, is obviously an adaptation from the Moravian formula. The tone of optimism about the final achievement was coloured by contemporary Enlightenment ideas, but placed in a context of grace to avoid the implication of mere human achievement. But it is worth noting that the Catholic and even the mystical literature and biographies continued to attract Wesley, not least Madame Guyon with her picture of a 'short and easy method' which in a sense resembled the short cut to salvation offered by evangelical conversion, here applied to perfection as well. And the content of the state of perfect love which she described attracted him too.

Madame Guyon, too, pictured perfection as a state of 'pure love' between Christ and the soul. But Wesley always objected to passive approaches to holiness.[87] Professor Kent also seems to be right in the discussion of the social context of perfectionism noticed earlier, in saying that Wesley visualized a state of perfection to be achieved by a sizeable body of dedicated people in the world rather than a few in solitude or the monastery – an aim which also seems to be implicit in popular Quietism. But the short cut and 'simple way' for Wesley was 'Protestant' in its appeal to faith as the way rather than mental prayer. And the 'pure love' was expressed as simple love to God and man rather than as an attempt to abandon concern for one's own salvation in the extreme Quietist manner.[88]

The effects on the Methodists of these teachings will be considered later. As to the question which has intrigued students of Wesley's doctrine – why did he never claim it for himself? – this is best postponed to the end of this book, when an attempt will be made to assess his personality and personal spirituality.[89]

Two other aspects of Wesley's theology may be mentioned because of their special relevance for placing his teaching and movement in contemporary religious life. His view of the church has already been discussed in the context of his relationship with the Church of England, and more will be said about this later in the light of his late actions with regard to ordination. Here it is only necessary to underline once again the fact that here too Wesley was led by expediency and experience to move a long way from his early, High Church exclusiveness towards a simpler, practical concentration on the church as the company of believers whose chief concern should be right teaching, the pursuit of evangelism and holiness, and the development of organs for implementing these aims most effectively rather than by the niceties of church law and 'order'. Here, we have observed, he seemed to be content to adopt a selective interpretation of the definition of the church in the Articles which reflected contemporary Latitudinarianism, though with a concentration on spiritual values which seems reminiscent of the left wing of the Reformation.[90] It was suggested that if this was mainly to accommodate the 'irregularities' of Methodism without separating from the Church of England, it was nevertheless an interesting pointer to a pragmatic view of the church in contrast to the dogmatisms of some of Wesley's critics. That he failed to develop a systematic ecclesiology himself on this basis was due to the fact that he did not see himself as creating a 'church', and that he did not wish to separate, though this was as much for practical reasons as because he remained at heart a son of the Church of England. We shall see that when he did finally ordain, he adapted forms close to the Church of England seen in the light of the 'primitive church' and Scripture as he understood them, but still to practical ends.

On the sacraments Wesley changed his views less than on the doctrine of salvation, though evangelicalism did bring some significant modifications. As we have seen, he continued to maintain baptismal regeneration while making it clear that there was nothing in this to prevent all being challenged with 'you must be born again' at a later stage (above, pp. 394f.).

The problem with the Lord's Supper is to understand Wesley's views on it in relation to eighteenth-century teaching and practice as well as to the circumstances of the Methodists, and not to import anachronistic elements from the period since the Oxford Movement and the modern Liturgical Movement, for it could be argued that the Oxford Movement began a process which fundamentally altered the way in which the eucharist had functioned in Anglicanism since the Reformation.[91] It is instructive to note how Luke Tyerman, writing in the wake of the disgusted Wesleyan reaction against the 'popery' of the Oxford Movement, dismissed Wesley's continuing 'high church nonsense' after his conversion. Some twentieth-century Methodists have, however, rejoiced at this aspect of his teaching and practice.

It has not been difficult to show that Wesley's eucharistic practice was uncommonly frequent by the usual standards of his day. He seems to have communicated weekly when he could and at special seasons like Easter even daily. This is in contrast to many devout churchmen who thought monthly communion 'frequent' and the generality who communicated three or four times a year or even only at Easter. Some of the reasons for this pattern and for the varying but (by later standards) low standard of frequency of celebration have already been discussed (see above, pp. 20f.). Wesley was not, however, unique here. He was attempting a pattern pursued by Nonjurors and some other High Churchmen and members of the Religious Societies.[92] That he continued it after his conversion is further evidence of the way in which he combined old habits with new discoveries, associating disciplined devotion and the search for holiness with sudden conversion. The impact on the Methodists of his teaching of what he called 'Constant Communion', as in a sermon under that title, is another matter again, and will be discussed later: one should, as always, beware of identifying his habits and views with theirs.[93] The preaching of frequent communion is also not unique to Wesley nor indeed to High Churchmen. Anglicans of all schools of thought from Nonjurors to the most extreme Latitudinarians talked in much the same way, and answered the same objections by urging that the only preparation needed was a sincere desire to receive what Christ offered.[94]

Wesley's basic views of the eucharist were a version of the seventeenth-century High Church tradition, coloured at some points (especially of ritual, at least in his earlier period) by his Nonjuror associations. Two major issues on which the Reformation had clashed with Rome had always been the notion of 'sacrifice' and the real presence in terms of transubstantiation. There was not much difference among the Reformers on the first, though some Anglicans in the early eighteenth century, notably John Johnson in his *Unbloody Sacrifice*, had tried to develop higher views of this aspect. On the real presence all Protestants, including Anglicans, rejected the technical doctrine of transubstantiation, but apart from Zwingli most of them held a wide range of views about a spiritual real presence which conveyed the benefits of Christ's work through the rite, without being able to explain clearly how this happened.[95] Extreme Latitudinarians like Hoadly, however, taught an extreme 'Zwinglian' view of the eucharist as a mere memorial. Waterland, in his impressive *Review of the Doctrine of the Eucharist* (1737), is generally supposed to have been replying to the extremists in either direction on all aspects of eucharistic doctrine.[96]

Wesley's doctrines on sacrifice and presence are well within the range of the Anglican views of his day, though rather towards the 'higher' end, as one would expect. They are expressed most clearly in *Hymns on the Lord's Supper* (1745), to which was attached an abridgment of Daniel Brevint's *Christian Sacrament and Sacrifice*.[97] Although Charles Wesley's hymns produced startling and realistic imagery about the two main doctrines in question, John was always careful to edit work of this kind, and his version of Brevint shows what he had in mind. On sacrifice Brevint said, in good Protestant fashion, that the sacrifice of Christ cannot be repeated but he adds that the sacrament was 'a kind of sacrifice, whereby we present before God the Father that precious oblation of His Son once offered'. We offer 'the meritorious sufferings of our Lord' 'as still fresh and still powerful' for salvation, which we present 'mystically'. (Johnson, to Waterland's indignation, had gone further, to a kind of spiritual 'repetition' of the sacrifice.) All Protestants, including Brevint and the compilers of the Prayer Book, emphasized the 'sacrifice' of praise and service offered by believers.[98]

The *Hymns*, like Brevint's essay, present the full range of Anglican doctrine on this and other matters including the real presence; it is a memorial, a sign and means of grace, a pledge of heaven, and 'implies a sacrifice' and the sacrifice of our persons. As usual, the bread and wine are seen as conveying grace, though one cannot explain how:

> Who shall say how bread and wine
> God into man conveys,
> *How* the Bread His Flesh imparts
> *How* the wine transmits the Blood.[99]

What matters is that,

> The sign transmits the signified
> The grace is by the means applied.
> To every gathered soul appear
> And own Thy real presence here.

To this end the notion of *epiklesis* is invoked: the Holy Spirit descends and vivifies the elements:

> Come, Holy Ghost, Thine influence shed
> And realize the sign;
> Thy life infuse into the bread;
> Thy power into the wine.

This doctrine had been conveyed from the Eastern Church through the Nonjurors.[100]

In general the hymns are pervaded with realistic, physical language about the flesh and blood and sacrifice of Christ. The sacrifice is clearly proclaimed to be once and for all ('Once offered up, a spotless lamb' who 'did *once* atone'), yet this is now made present and effective in the eucharist, for he,

> Ever lives with God above
> To plead for us his dying love,

and along with this,

> Ourselves we offer up to God
> Implunged in His atoning blood.

In addition the Wesleys followed some of the 'Usages' which the Nonjurors adopted from the First Edwardian Prayer Book of 1549 as 'primitive' practices: the *epiklesis*; mixing water with the wine; a prayer of oblation emphasizing the sacrifice in the eucharist; and prayers for the departed. Wesley still defended the mixed cup in 1749, and the *epiklesis* appeared in his revised prayer book for the Americans in the 1780s. Prayers for the dead he defended in 1751 at least for the faithful departed, as in Anglican usage in the office for the dead.[101] But what is of much more interest is that he added one new and highly unusual notion to eucharistic doctrine after his conversion, that of it being a 'converting ordinance'. This is so unusual and has so little precedent that it is surprising that it has not attracted more comment. Normally baptism has been seen as the sacrament of regeneration, indeed conflicting with conversionist ideas, as we have seen. The eucharist has then been seen as the sacrament of sanctification – a 'confirming ordinance' – and so Wesley always saw it. He only added a 'converting' function to it after his conversion.

There was little encouragement for such a notion in tradition. Luther and Calvin admitted that the eucharist might sometimes, exceptionally, act to bring remission of sins or 'ingrafting into Christ'.[102] High Church Anglicans stuck to the 'confirming' function, though it is interesting that Waterland admitted that the eucharist might convey all aspects of Christ's work, including cleansing from sin; and Wesley may well have read this. In his 1733 sermon on 'Constant Communion' he says that it conveys 'forgiveness of our past sins'.[103]

But in fact the notion of a 'converting' ordinance could only be held when he had adopted evangelical conversion notions. Nor could he have got this from the Puritans, for it was a notion which they either rejected or only allowed in wholly exceptional cases. Independents generally only admitted the converted to communion.[104] The rare exceptions underline the contrary rule. In the 1640s William Prynne allowed for it, probably as a reaction against Independent exclusiveness, seeing it as a means of 'conversion'; so, very exceptionally, did the independent John Humphreys.[105] The most striking precedent is one that Wesley is unlikely to have known, that of Jonathan Edwards's father-in-law, Solomon Stoddard, in New England. He opened communion to the unconverted in hopes of converting them, and with some success in local revivals before the Great Awakening of the 1740s.[106] As to the Moravians, they seem to have been reluctant to admit unconverted people (like Wesley in Georgia) to their communions.[107]

What provoked Wesley into his unusual teaching was, as so often, not precedent but experience and practical need. It is certainly significant that the first mentions of cases of conversion during communion were during his controversy with the Moravians over stillness. They were publicized in his *Journal* accounts in a way plainly intended to show that using the means of grace actually led to conversion, contrary to what the advocates of stillness maintained. But he was only able to do this because the experiences occurred for him to publicize them; and it was their occurrence which evidently made him adopt this unusual doctrine.

The first hint of such a possibility appears to be in a letter by an anonymous correspondent (probably Charles Delamotte) in December 1738.[108] This merely tells how, seeking for conversion, he had a vision of the crucified Saviour but was 'afraid to venture'. The first completed experience during the eucharist appears to be that of an unidentified person, commonly thought to be Wesley's mother Susanna, in September 1738.[109] Several others are recorded in Methodist lives, and at least two non-Wesleyan ones: Howel Harris and the Evangelical David Simpson. A few are also recorded during adult baptism.[110]

If Susanna's was indeed the first case, it would have made a special impact on Wesley, and it was in connection with this case that he first categorically wrote in favour of the idea in November 1739, soon following this up with an attack on those confining the eucharist to a 'confirming ordinance' – 'for experience shows the gross falsehood' of this limitation. God gives whatever kind of grace is necessary according to need (much as Waterland had said).[111] The doctrine was also a useful weapon against those fearful of taking communion because of the excessive demands of the 'preparation' school which inhibited people from thinking they were fit to receive. For Methodists conditioned to focus on the moment of conversion, and the joy and peace it gave, this would encourage communion attendance. It is probably significant that the few references to reactions to taking communion in early Methodist biography concentrate on the feelings experienced, and it is difficult to gauge how far people actually shared Wesley's High Church views on its theology – there were no eucharistic hymns in the standard *Hymns* of 1780, for these were not designed for public worship.[112]

On doctrine as a whole, the evidence of what preachers and ordinary Methodists believed is, as one would expect, of a simple creed, centring on the process of salvation as Wesley taught it, from conviction to conversion and so to perfection. Some had struggles on the way with the seductions of Calvinism, occasionally with Deist ideas or more often with existential doubts about the reality of God. Preachers entered into controversy on Calvinism and perfection. Some added refinements of their own, like the enthusiastic advocates of totally sinless perfection and third blessings in the 1760s.[113] Michael Watts, who implies that perfection was a personal eccentricity of Wesley's due to his High Church background, is right to see it as peculiar to Wesleyanism in this period and highly controversial even within that body.[114] Most Methodists, he supposes, concentrated on the ecstasies of conversion. But this is to underestimate its appeal to the rank and file, and there are many examples of the search and claim for it, as we shall see.

A few of the preachers give simple outlines of their doctrines. Christopher Hopper said that he left 'polemical divinity to men of learning, ability and experience'; he could say little about the Calvinist and Arminian controversy. He can only say that he has been greatly humbled for his sin, and knows by experience that God is love and 'hath loved me and gave his Son for me'. He hates sin and loves holiness and pursues it.[115]

Some were more ambitious: Thomas Olivers outlined the arguments which he used to refute the Calvinist Toplady (successfully, he claimed); and William Hunter expounded perfection in Wesley's balanced way as an instant gift which could yet be improved upon.[116] Richard Rodda gave a short formal system of doctrine: the Fall; the promise of a Saviour; salvation open to all unless they refuse it; repentance and faith in Christ; and the holiness without which we cannot see the Lord. This man actually received perfection but soon lost it, and makes no further mention of it.[117] In a simple, practical, 'experimental' way such figures reflected the basic tenets of the Wesleyan form of evangelicalism. On perfection some clearly had difficulties, and Wesley equally clearly pressed them hard on this. Some were, however, enthusiastic for it, as we shall see. If these biographies represent a spiritual élite (as they do), at least that élite seems to have been well drilled in Wesley's perspective.

How should we estimate Wesley as a theologian? There have been a number of attempts by Methodists, perhaps especially in America, to claim for him a significant place in the history of doctrine, although they are arguing against the more common assumption that he is only significant as an evangelist and unwitting church founder. Cell's notion of a Catholic-Protestant 'synthesis' would be a notable achievement if true. Alexander Knox thought that Wesley had managed to combine the irresistible grace of St Augustine with the 'spiritual energy' of the New Testament – a rather similar claim.[118] More realistically, perhaps, Albert Outler claimed that Wesley's chief intellectual interest and distinction was as a 'folk theologian': he put the full Christian message in 'plain words for plain people'. He acknowledges that Wesley has 'no place in the select corpus of systematic theologians who . . . effect major mutations in the Christian mind'. But he made his own distinctive synthesis from what he inherited, particularly in his notions of justification, assurance and perfection; and this developed primarily from the exigencies of the Revival.[119] One may agree that if any distinctive claim is to be made for Wesley as a theologian, it must be on some such lines as this. 'Synthesis' is probably too flattering a term to use of what was an untidy, practical compromise between the demands of grace and the active pursuit of holiness; and Outler's 'folk-theologian', like Dreyer's 'empiricist', does not quite take sufficient account of the 'enthusiastic' streak in Wesley's composition. He was a folk-theologian in a rather less refined sense than Outler wished to allow. He was not merely transmitting a simplified version of Protestant doctrine (with some 'Catholic' elements) to an unsophisticated audience; just as much as this he was partially rationalizing what he found in the audience, and that became more obvious as the Revival proceeded. There is a case for saying that Wesley was a dangerous fanatic who released and sanctioned and could only partially control the submerged sub-culture of English popular Protestantism of the conversionist type which surfaced in times of stress like the Reformation, the Interregnum and now in the eighteenth-century Revival. Wesley did not create this, but he did help to let it loose and organized some of its results. At the same time he was a folk-religionist in the sense that he sanctioned by his own example and tolerance the more religious aspects of the darker world of popular supernaturalism in its many varieties, and we shall see that some of his followers were deeper into the world of magic than he was. The world of experience which Wesley evoked and observed could only with difficulty be clothed in the formal categories of Protestant scholasticism, and the strain shows clearly in his endless definitions and qualifications of perfection as well as in his impatience with the hair-splitting controversies over justification and with the Calvinists. Like Luther, he was at his best when he abandoned most of this jargon and concentrated on simple assertions about the achievement of faith and love.

In the perspective of Protestant history, Wesley can be said to have been trying to find a solution to the old problem of how to reconcile the notion of a salvation that depends on a divine act of grace to save fallen men with the desire for a positive and progressive attitude towards a recreation of the personality by a progressive realization of the mind of Christ in which men can take an active part. If, in a rough and ready way, Wesley brought together these two concerns, he did so in response to the practical needs thrown up by a revival situation as much as by way of a formal theological response to an old problem. In doing so, however, he mediated between the various strands of Anglican tradition with direct or indirect if highly selective and reinterpreted elements from Catholicism as well as trying to make sense of the raw religious emotions of the converts. To this task he applied some of the arts of empiricism in a practical way.

To interpret all this in terms of Wesley's 'sources' is not in the end very helpful since he used them so selectively. It is more useful to interpret it in terms of the situation: that of a High Churchman led almost accidentally by his own quest for holiness into leadership of a semi-popular religious movement in areas subject to gradually accelerating social change. Methodist teaching as Wesley visualized it was by no means a conventional form of evangelicalism, because perfection rather than justification became the real centre of his concern. As a device for dealing with the peculiar problems of the kind of people he was ministering to it worked rather well, as an ideal for cheerful ascetics making the world their monastery. But because Wesley failed to capture the Church of England at large and indeed founded a movement which separated from that church, there was never any likelihood that his theology would become significant and central even in England. Intellectually flawed though it may be, it remains of interest as the product of a special set of circumstances in the eighteenth century in a body which managed to avoid a narrow sectarianism, though the perfectionist legacy as such tended to become sectarian in other bodies.

2. Public worship and private devotion

In John Wesley's eyes Methodist meetings for preaching were not services of worship complete in themselves. They were timed so as not to clash with church service hours; Methodists were expected to attend their churches or meeting houses for ordinary services and sacraments, their own meetings being merely a devotional supplement. But in reality Methodism and its meetings became more and more a self-sufficient system which monopolized their devotion and became the sole focus of it, though there were always 'Church Methodists' who conformed to Wesley's own ideal. No doubt this trend to separateness was fostered by the growth of purpose-built preaching houses and their licensing, which would give them the apparent status and physical appearance of Dissenting meeting-houses (a term which Wesley avoided). Their status as mere 'preaching-houses' was underlined by Wesley's favourite octagon design (for acoustic purposes) which was followed in a number of places, though there were many other varieties.[120]

Methodist organization, which was described earlier in terms of a system for evangelism and pastoral care, can also be seen as a vehicle for worship and devotion. Though its formal objective was the pursuit of holiness, it also gave much scope for spontaneous expressions of feeling, lay participation and various human values of fellowship, community and personal and group identity. Apart from field preaching, the main preaching services were held early in the morning and in the evening on Sundays and weekdays to avoid clashing with Anglican services.

The form of worship was simple, consisting of short prayers, preaching and hymns – essentially a preaching service with relatively slight accompaniments. And incidentally Wesley insisted, against opposition, that men and women sit apart (a practice which may still occasionally have survived in Anglican churches of his time) and tried to stop the habit of gossiping before and after the service.[121] Then of course there were the regular meetings of classes, bands and select bands for the various grades of converts. Prayer meetings also existed and seem to have become more popular as the century went on, for they were free of the control of officials and later became sources of local revivals and even of schisms.[122] It was the variety and relative informality and high degree of ordinary lay participation which attracted those disliking the formality and parson-dominated religious culture of official Anglicanism.

In addition to these regular weekly means of grace Methodism added a number of others of a less frequent kind, some peculiar to itself.

The lovefeast was one of Wesley's most obvious direct borrowings from the Moravians. It is true that the lovefeast or *agape* had been used in the primitive church as a communal meal preceding the eucharist – hence the rather riotous scenes described in I Cor. 11. Wesley in 1748 described himself as following the 'ancient Christians' and spoke as if he had revived the lovefeast on his own initiative. But this was probably to make it respectable and to avoid mentioning the Moravians. In fact there seems no doubt that he was led to it by experiencing it with the Moravians in Georgia and in Fetter Lane.[123] The Moravians had used these groups for informal religious conversation with bread and water or bread and wine, though the latter was dropped to avoid confusion with the eucharist. As practised by the Methodists the lovefeasts were at first only for the bands, 'using a little plain cake and water'.[124] Since in 1750 Wesley says that they were confined to those who really have 'the love of God shed abroad in their hearts', they were then still confined to the bands, but the whole society was included for the first time in December 1759. By 1761 at least personal testimonies to one's own experience had been added to prayers, hymns and conversation.[125] In theory only members of the society could attend, but Wesley's insistence on this in 1777 and stories in Methodist biography suggest that non-members sometimes crept in and benefitted.[126]

The name lovefeast, and the fact that it was for members only, provoked revivals of ancient tales about nocturnal orgies and visions of silly women at midnight. Wesley replied to this partly by claiming confusion with watchnights, saying that lovefeasts seldom lasted even till 9.00 p.m.[127] On at least one occasion, however, at Fetter Lane there was an ecstatic lovefeast which extended through the night, and at 3.00 a.m. the 'power of God' broke in on the company and made them cry out for joy.[128] There were similar excitements and conversion in later years. But if Joseph Nightingale is to be believed, the lovefeast could suffer from the same boredom and tensions as the class meeting, when unwilling people felt pressured to give testimonies and were told that it was 'of the devil' when they felt unable to do so. He also said that some saints clattered down the aisle to give the cake to favoured friends – which sounds very like Mr Stiggins's temperance meeting in *Pickwick Papers*.[129] It is very probable that both favourable and unfavourable pictures are correct of different cases.

One important point about the role of the meeting in the Methodist economy is well made by Dr Walsh: that it was 'a domesticated, democratized folk sacrament'.[130] This strikes exactly the right note. Apart from its inherent attractions in these terms, the very infrequency of sacramental opportunities for eighteenth-century Methodists, especially from clergy of their own type, meant that the more frequent lovefeast was bound to assume this role – and was in any case suitably 'primitive'.

The watchnight has also been claimed, much less plausibly, as an importation from the Moravians, though again with 'primitive' precedents.[131] In 1750 Wesley claimed the precedent of 'vigils' in the 'ancient church' and the Prayer Book, but this was to give a respectable pedigree to meetings suspected of sedition and immorality.[132] At Herrnhut, watchnights were held from New Year's Eve 1733, but there is no evidence that Wesley saw one before the end of 1738, if then.[133]

In fact his own account of its origins is interesting because it shows that this was another case of spontaneous creation from below only later sanctioned by Wesley himself. And in this case there are equally interesting connections with popular custom. In 1748 Wesley describes how, apparently early in 1742, he was informed that several Kingswood Methodists met to 'spend the greater part of the night in prayer and praise and thanksgiving'. Though some pressed him to stop this for fear of the scandal of night meetings, Wesley allowed it, recalling ancient Christian precedents, and thought that it might be 'of more general use'. Then, characteristically, he took it over and regularized it to the night of the full moon (to light their way home) and it spread to the other big societies.[134] That year two hymns were published which obviously referred to the lovefeast: 'Oft have we passed the guilty night' and 'Hearken to the solemn voice'. In March he speaks of processing to a 'watch night'.[135]

The meeting later became quarterly and finally yearly on New Year's Eve: obviously an appropriate time. Nightingale says that in the North it was difficult to stop the cries for pardon and other disturbances.[136] Though it is possible that Wesley owed something to Moravian precedents which he would not be anxious to publicize (and there was a midnight meeting uncommonly like it in Kingswood as early as 31 December 1740),[137] it was very probably the guilty consciences of the Kingswood miners that set the cries off (hence the 'guilty night' hymn). It was doubly appropriate that they should have fixed on the New Year in the end for the celebration: as a spiritualized counter-attraction to that pagan folk-festival.

The Covenant Service was another rite originally held at various times but finally fixed at the New Year. But this one was imposed by Wesley from above and, uniquely among Methodist customs, drew on Puritan precedent.[138] Ideas of the covenant between God and man of course go back to the Old Testament, and were adapted in a Christian sense in the New, as the basis of God's promises of salvation in terms of his grace given to men through the work of Christ in response to faith and obedience. It became a prominent feature of Puritan theology and has been seen by some as an important element in reducing the arbitrariness of predestination by appearing to bind God to exercise his grace in predictable ways.[139] In Puritan practice the taking of private, personal covenants with God was not uncommon, and indeed there are non-Puritan Anglican precedents as well.[140] In such covenants a man bound himself to fulfil certain duties, disciplines and virtues, and periodic check-ups could be held to judge oneself by the promises made. Some eighteenth-century Methodists did the same, as did William Grimshaw, who in many ways was very like an old Puritan parson.[141]

The Independents were accustomed to 'form' their churches with a collective covenant, laying down their association as a church and often appending their forms of doctrine and church order.

It is not entirely clear when Wesley first drew on the personal covenant precedent and adapted it for Methodist use. As early as January 1748 he records that he 'strongly urged the wholly giving up ourselves to God, and renewing in every point our covenant that the Lord should be our God'; and again in July the same year.[142] This is strikingly like the language of the later service, and indeed on the second occasion he 'explained at large' 'the nature of the covenant with God'. At this point he may merely have been recommending the individual Puritan practice, and certainly nothing more of the kind appears during the next few years.[143]

The formal service appearing in 1755 has generally been accepted as the beginning of the Methodist custom. It is significant that both in 1748 and 1755 Wesley was preparing material for his Christian Library in which Puritan piety was prominent. It included the material from the Alleines which formed the basis of his own service.[144] He may also have felt it to be appropriate in 1755, when Methodism was threatened with division over the question of separation from the church, to use a rite to bind the society together.

At all events, Wesley recorded in the *Journal* for 6 August 1755 that he mentioned the joining in a covenant with God as a pious custom of their forefathers, and a few days later on 11 August celebrated the covenant in the words of 'that blessed man Richard Alleine'. On Good Friday 1757 he read over the directions for a covenant by Joseph Alleine and the next Monday they covenanted together.[145] Richard Alleine had been the father-in-law of Joseph, and both had been among the Ejected of 1662.[146] The rite was set for 1 January from 1762 and for the first Sunday in the New Year from 1780. The original service was dominated by the leader, who read the service and the covenant, the people assenting. It was peculiarly awesome in its heavy and precise recitation of sins, but even in the lightened modern versions some of the old phrases haunt the conscience: 'Put me to what thou wilt . . . put me to doing, put me to suffering . . . ' 'In some things we may please God and please ourselves, in other things we can only please God by denying ourselves.'

What is characteristic of the Methodist rite is that it took the old Puritan individual covenant and made it a collective act of self-examination and renewal of vows and dedication to God, while using words still suitable for individual acceptance within the corporate act. It neatly expressed the Methodist sense of a personal pilgrimage in company with the society of the people of God. If it seemed to assort rather oddly with the doctrine of salvation by grace through faith, it had the old Puritan notion of 'preparation' for the grace of God, which was stressed still more in Wesley's Arminian mind.

In all these Methodist services and meetings hymns played a vital role. Something was said earlier about Charles Wesley's role in providing them and the nature of his writing. But equally important is the nature and purpose of the standard *Hymns for the Use of Methodists* (1780), which distilled the contents of numerous other books.[147] The most striking thing about the book is its structure and subject-matter as compared with other books of the period. Up to a point all the evangelical books (such as Newton and Cowper's *Olney Hymns*) shared a common emphasis on salvation and personal religion, and differed strikingly from later books of all schools in their lack of attention to a 'churchly' arrangement catering for the round of rites and special occasions in church life. In the nineteenth century Anglicans structured their books on 'higher' or 'lower' versions of the Christian Year (the first example seems to be that of the Evangelical Basil Woodd in 1794).[148]

But Wesley's book has a pattern all its own. There are no sacramental hymns or hymns for church occasions at all, since this is a book for Methodist societary use, though also for private meditation. As Wesley put it in his famous preface, it was 'a little collection of practical and experimental divinity'. The structure in effect takes the user through the Methodist plan of salvation: 'Exhorting Sinners to Return to God', 'Describing the Pleasantness of Religion', 'The Goodness of God', heaven, hell, etc. Then 'Praying for a Blessing', 'Distinguishing formal and inward religion'; praying for repentance, for sinners convinced of sin; for believers rejoicing, fighting and (very important) 'groaning for full redemption' (perfection). Finally, come hymns for the society: meeting, giving thanks, departing.

Hymns, more than any other single source except the Bible, were the means by which the ordinary Methodist could obtain a knowledge of what Wesley thought Methodism taught. With characteristic confidence Wesley urged no one to try to mend his verses, because they could not (strong words from such a compulsive abridger and adapter!). Though the 'spirit of piety' mattered most, the 'spirit of poetry' would also be found (he claimed) in its admirable style. Apart from this being an expression of a touch of vanity towards the world, Wesley no doubt had an eye here to his continual side-mission as cultural mediator and tutor to the Methodist people.

But if we are rightly to gauge the impact of this and the rest of the Wesley corpus of hymns (many of them from Watts and other writers), we need to look beyond the formal collection and Wesley's aims for it, and ask how it was used by the Methodist people. This is not easy, though there are clues to be found. The Wesleys were well aware of the role of hymns in kindling emotion and 'keeping our metaphysics warm', as T.S. Eliot observed in another connection. While they did not disapprove of this, there was always a certain tension between the objects of the leader and the tastes of the led.

This can be seen most clearly in the choice of hymns and recommended tunes and the way in which they were actually used. The earliest printed Methodist tune-book, the 'Foundery Collection' of 1742, contained thirty-six tunes, mostly psalm settings and German chorales, with one secular piece from a Handel opera.[149] Later collections included some contemporary hymn tunes of a rather florid type, but even the more sober tunes were often filled out with trills and repetitions, and added 'Hallelujahs' were popular. There are also persistent stories that the Methodists, like most lively new renewal groups, were liable to adapt popular folk tunes, ballads and operatic hits, and a few appear in published collections. 'Love Divine' was set to a tune by Purcell originally used for a Dryden love poem. Charles Wesley is said to have written a hymn to fit the tune of 'Nancy Dawson', sung by London sailors. Thomas Chatterton saw the Methodists as singing in a way that 'you'd swear turns bawdy songs godly'. Horace Walpole heard children in Bath singing hymns to Scotch ballad tunes.[150]

Wesley himself did not like ornaments and Handelesque repetitions, especially if this involved people in singing different words at the same time. Indeed in his *Thoughts on the Power of Music* he claims that the reason why ancient music had electrifying effects lacking in the moderns was that they sang the melody only. Such effects now were achieved mainly in solos or folk tunes.[151] As to repetitions, he thundered 'Away with it' of a tune sung all over Cornwall in 1765 for 'Praise the Lord ye blessed ones', which was so full of 'repetitions and flourishes that it can scarcely be sung with devotion'. And at Warrington in 1781 he arrived just in time to catch and stop a 'bad custom of a few men with fine voices singing a psalm which no one knows in a tune fit for an opera', with different words sung at the same time. This he saw as 'an insult upon common sense', 'a burlesque upon public worship', 'a mixture of profaneness and absurdity'.[152] He gave an extended diatribe at the Conference on these enormities. We should speak what we feel, he told the preachers, stopping the congregation to ask them what they had sung and whether they felt it. He complained of 'complex tunes' and 'long quavering hallelujahs', repetitions and different words sung at the same time: 'the horrid abuse which runs through all modern church music', an offence to common sense and religion which indeed has 'no more religion in it than a Lancashire hornpipe'.[153] One can easily visualize the scenes he disapproved of, though visions of Methodist ecstasies may be tempered with the reflection that the custom of 'lining out' seems to have been common. The leader read a line or two of the hymn at a time which was then sung by the congregation. This was originally justified by illiteracy, though by nineteenth-century conservatives also as an aid to thinking devotion.[154]

In all this, though Wesley's directions no doubt sprang from an understandable concern to preserve devotion in emotion, they also reflect a conflict of taste between himself and his people and the inexorable pressures from below of what the people wanted.

Just as strong was the pressure to treat Methodist worship as complete within itself and not as a mere supplement to the ordered Anglican diet. In 1766, attempting to refute the charge that Methodists were Dissenters, Wesley emphasized that they were still church attenders. To those who claimed that Methodist worship was 'public worship' he allowed this only 'in a sense'. It does not supersede church worship, for it presupposes 'public prayers', and he discouraged the elaboration of prayers in connection with Methodist preaching. Methodist worship therefore lacked the 'grand parts of public prayer', nor was it connected with the Lord's Supper.[155]

All the same, Wesley was very proud of Methodist worship, and sometimes very critical of church worship. In 1757 he said that the Methodists had 'unspeakable advantages' in their avoidance of what is either 'splendid' or 'sordid'; prayers are from the heart, and serious, not careless. They are not interrupted by 'the formal drawl' of the parish clerk, the screaming of bawling boys or the 'unmeaning impertinence' of organ voluntaries. Their hymns are sung with understanding and are better than the 'scandalous doggerel' of Sternhold and Hopkins (the Anglican metrical psalms). Finally, they are sure of serious conduct of the Lord's Supper. This shows that he was not commenting on ordinary Methodist worship, but on the use of Morning Prayer and the eucharist by himself and his few clerical helpers at the London and Bristol chapels. But it is a damning indictment of Anglican worship all the same, and reflects what ordinary Methodists rebelled against.[156]

No general extension of a full Methodist adaptation of the church service outside these favoured places was possible nor indeed desirable on Wesley's plan, since it would have undermined the notion of a subordination of Methodist devotion to attendance at church. As it was, there were many examples of Methodists disobeying his injunctions to go to the church, and in his later years several compromises like the Dublin one described earlier in face of popular pressure. Wesley's concessions and the reasons for them will be discussed later in the context of the arrangements for the transition after his death. The needs of the American settlement also led to his abridgment of the Prayer Book, which sometimes seems to have been used also in England, though in the few chapels which had Morning Prayer the Anglican form was often used. But it must be emphasized that both usages were exceptional, and the natural interest of students of liturgy in such material should not be allowed to obscure the fact that the main stream of Methodist worship as it emerged from its Anglican connection lay in another direction, at least for normal, non-eucharistic Sunday worship.[157]

This brings us back to the question of Methodist eucharistic practice and attitudes. As I emphasized earlier, this cannot simply be identified with John Wesley's own practice. Ordinary Methodists had to rely mainly on the vagaries of Anglican practice which, as we have seen, ranged from quarterly celebrations in the countryside to monthly celebrations in some towns, and Methodists were sometimes repelled by the local clergy. 'Methodist' communions by the Wesleys occurred earliest in association with communion for the sick at home, and then in some preaching houses: Charles Wesley administered to the Kingswood colliers as early as 1740.[158] In the early 1740s John Wesley was able to administer in the ex-Huguenot churches he had taken over in London, and by 1745 in other London preaching-houses, but in the provinces the practice was slow to develop until after Wesley's death. Even he did not administer communion much in provincial houses until after about 1780. Since, as we have seen, he resisted pressure to ordain until late in his life and put down the occasional cases of Methodist preachers administering on their own, the result was that it was very rare for Methodists to have their own communion services outside London and Bristol.[159]

This raises the question of what Wesley really expected the Methodists to do when he spoke about 'constant communion' and, more mysteriously, what Methodists themselves actually wanted, and what part eucharistic devotion really played in the Methodist spiritual economy. This can only be understood in the light of eighteenth-century opportunities and attitudes, not in that of post-Oxford Movement and later Liturgical Movement Anglicanism. We have seen that Wesley's talk of 'constant communion' in his 1733 sermon and his answers to objections merely repeated a plea common to all schools of contemporary Anglican thought, though 'constant' rather than 'frequent' was his own choice.[160] All of these writers were anxious to counter the deterrent effects of the 'preparation' literature, and there is evidence that a good many people believed that communion could be approached safely only if one was in a high state of piety; indeed it seemed natural to view communion and preparation for it as a mark of 'serious' piety rather than as a normal part of decent worship. Scruples of this kind reinforced the pressures of tradition in favour of occasional celebration and attendance inherited from the Middle Ages, and underlined even by the enhanced norm of three times a year laid down by the Prayer Book.[161]

Wesley's urgings and the psychological effect of his 'converting ordinance' idea suggest an open attitude to attenders which was perhaps not sustained later. By 1747 admission was by class ticket or special note. This approximated to the Presbyterian (and indeed officially the Anglican) convention that communion was open to all of right belief and conduct, though membership conditions were less precise for Methodism, and Methodists certainly did not require proof of actual conversion.[162]

Even for most High Churchmen in the eighteenth century, 'frequent' communion seems to have meant monthly, except for a few extremists like Nonjurors, or John Wesley with his average of rather more than once a week.[163] It is perfectly clear that if Wesley had expected his followers to be able to communicate even monthly, a large part of them could not have done so; and to provide for them through his own preachers would have required a mass ordination of local preachers. There is not the slightest sign that he ever contemplated this even for travelling preachers, except in a few late cases for reasons to be examined later. And indeed he plainly said at an early stage that he allowed lay preaching because it was necessary to save souls, whereas no such necessity dictated ordination to administer the sacraments.[164] All that he did was to urge people to communicate as often as they could.

Ordinary Methodist attitudes can usually only be guessed at indirectly from ambiguous evidence. There are not many references to attitudes to communion in the biographies, which may suggest that it was only of special significance to a minority for their piety. Where it is mentioned, it is significant that the person dwells on satisfaction or disappointment at the feelings experienced during it.[165] Certainly there are reports of Methodists swelling attendance at Anglican services, sometimes annoying the incumbent by coming from other parishes and occasionally being repelled by him. It has even been suggested that separation of Methodists from the church later was a cause of falling attendances in Anglicanism at the end of the century.[166] But attendance at Anglican services often related to frequency of celebration: increased frequency of celebration sometimes only brought lower attendance.[167]

At strictly Methodist communions like those by Wesley and White-field, attendances could be 1000 or more.[168] On one famous occasion at Haworth when Whitefield celebrated they 'sipped away' thirty-five bottles of wine.[169] But these have to be interpreted partly in relation to the equally observable fact that in a number of places the Wesleys complained that people never went to 'church and sacrament'.[170] The reasons for both attendance and non-attendance were probably mixed, though also related to each other. Many Methodists clearly found no benefit in the church services, and believed that the church clergy were not Christians, indeed that sacraments from them were ineffective.[171] It was Methodist sacraments that they wanted. These were rare, and the reason for the large attendances sometimes recorded is obvious: they were special occasions like the one at Haworth when the Methodist leaders were present and members came from miles around.

The attempt of the preachers at Norwich and elsewhere to take matters into their own hands and administer without ordination, and the periodic pressure for an ordination, have been interpreted as due to a strong desire for more sacraments, but it is more obviously part of the pressure from below for separation and for the recognition of the preachers as a full ministry.[172] It goes along with the related pressure for services in church hours.

The fact is that eucharistic piety was not, and in fact could not be, the centre of devotion or the norm for every Sunday's worship in the eighteenth century either for Methodists or ordinary Anglicans, and it is unlikely that it ever had been. The notion that it was and should be is essentially a Tractarian invention, whatever precedents might be drawn from antiquity.[173] Even the very devout, with rare exceptions, only increased frequency without making it their weekly norm. It is in fact perfectly possible to associate relatively infrequent communions with a serious and high valuation of the rite, as the Scottish Presbyterian example shows; but this is a different pattern of seriousness, with a different place for the eucharist in the general spiritual economy. It is not the Christian's weekly or daily bread, but an occasion of special solemnity and blessing. Grimshaw exactly hit off the situation when he spoke of the memorable occasion at Haworth with Whitefield as 'a high day indeed, a Sabbath of Sabbaths'. Those large communions were great Methodist festivals, memorable for their rarity and expectation of special experience and special grace. And this in effect conformed to the usual eighteenth-century Anglican pattern of relatively infrequent celebration. What the Methodists added was their fervour, warmth, emotion, hymns – and the hope of conversion and other blessings in an especially impressive setting for the gift of Christ's coming.

But in normal circumstances these expectations were fulfilled in a variety of other meetings and services: the preaching in society, the class, the band; and the special occasions of covenant, watchnight and the lovefeast as a quasi-sacrament of a warmly informal kind.

At a more individual level the piety of the Methodists was simple enough. They studied the Bible and devotional books; said their prayers; fasted on stated occasions and perhaps on Wednesdays and Fridays; sang hymns and meditated upon them, and expressed their devotion in good works.[174] Methodist culture was, if narrow and centred on religion, also intense. For some, even if moderately literate, it meant the Bible, the hymns and Wesley's pamphlets. For others it meant something more, as for some of Wesley's favoured female correspondents whom he informally tutored.[175] Anne Reynolds of Truro read à Kempis, Baxter's *Saints' Rest*, the lives of Lopez and others (like Wesley himself; for further comments on Methodist culture, see below, pp. 446f.).[176] But the limited sale of the Christian Library tells its own tale. In an interesting study of Dissenting and Methodist 'practical divinity', Isabel Rivers has suggested that one of the sources of self-criticism in Dissent and the rise of Methodism in the 1730s was a dissatisfaction with contemporary Anglican devotional writing.[177] She thinks that it concentrated too much for all tastes on ceremonial observances (though this would not be true of the *Whole Duty* or other popular handbooks designed for various classes). What such studies did lack, as she points out, are the notes of 'experimental' and 'affectionate' piety, with guidance on the way to conversion and its fruits. Sober though they often seem, the older works of Baxter and Alleine and Doddridge's newer *Rise and Progress of Religion in the Soul* did try to chart the path to conversion, avoiding the extremes of rationalism and enthusiasm and endeavouring to engage the mind, the will and the passions.[178] As Rivers points out, these works tended, if they achieved their aims, to break down the barriers between the author and the reader so as to bring the reader into reliving the author's experience. And here one may suggest that the most effective may have been biographies (or sometimes allegories like *Pilgrim's Progress*), since they gave a living model which one could hope to follow and relive oneself. Parts of books which were rather formal guides seem to have touched off uneasiness or comfort when they appeared to describe what the reader felt he was or wished to be.[179] The force of a few books treasured and read by people of limited means and literacy could be very powerful, beyond what can now easily be imagined. It was the solitary reading of the 'Passion Hymn' by Charles Wesley – a particularly vivid and 'physical' one – that touched off a vision of Christ crucified in a Manchester woman.[180]

3. Piety and providence: religious experience and the supernatural world

Within the small but intense world of organized Methodist piety individuals pursued their own versions of what their leader laid down for them. A considerable number of these lives were recorded, though they have been relatively little studied except in the affectionate and too-little known volumes by Leslie Church.[181]

The nature and limitations of these lives need to be borne in mind. Wesley urged his preachers to keep diaries for devotional reasons and asked some of them to write narratives of their experiences, many of which, along with those of the rank and file, were published in the *Arminian Magazine* or separately. Others were written as memoirs by their friends, and vignettes of humble and obscure saints also appeared in Wesley's *Journals*. The purpose of the diaries, as of those of their Puritan and other predecessors, was to be an aid to spiritual self-development. The autobiographies and biographies were to display God's merciful, providential dealings with his people and to act as inspirations and guides to others as well as to show the world what the Methodists were really like.

Lives of this kind were really pioneered by the seventeenth-century Puritans. Indeed it is arguable that autobiographies concerned with the inner life, rather than merely outward events, were created by people like these. Those of other religious persuasions give a much more external picture. In the eighteenth century, however, autobiography and biography proliferated to disclose the outward and inward lives of a substantial cross-section of society, revealing the inner lives of much more secular-minded people.[182]

Methodist lives continued the older tradition, and it is no accident that there are close resemblances between them and the earlier Puritan type. Both were concerned to show how their subjects moved from deadness in sin through the awakening of conviction of sin, the false dawn of trying to save oneself by good works, to the experience of justification by faith through some form of personal conversion. As we have seen, this pattern of conversion, though often traced through an 'evangelical succession' from St Paul through St Augustine, Luther and Wesley, was really developed by Puritans in England and America during the seventeenth century on the model of men like William Perkins, with a parallel and related tradition in Continental Pietism.[183] The Puritan theologians developed elaborate analyses of the stages through which people prepared for and received what for them was the realization of the electing grace of God. At a less sophisticated level there are particularly close parallels to the early Methodists' life-experiences in two collections of mid-seventeenth century spiritual autobiographies collected by Henry Walker and John Rogers from their congregations which have been analysed by Michael Watts.[184] The parallel with Methodism is close in the pattern of pious upbringing, years of agonized search, dreams, visions and providences. The main difference is that Methodists often added the extra stage of the pursuit and achievement of perfection. But as Watts points out, the two collections which he analyses differ from each other on one important point. Walker followed Perkins in emphasizing that even the converted person needs to retain an element of doubt to keep him humbly reliant on grace; whereas Rogers's converts saw conversion as the ultimate religious experience and seldom show post-conversion doubts. The Walker way, Watts says, could lead to legalism and a trust in religious duties; the Rogers way to a confident antinomianism. Both problems would arise again during the Revival. Wesley's peculiar blend of High Church and evangelical piety, his stress on assurance and the pursuit of perfection gave a particular shape and tone to the Methodist pattern and made it rather different from the usual Puritan one, as well as from that of Anglican Evangelicals and Calvinistic Methodists. The difference, we shall see, comes out partly in deathbed scenes.

How far there was a direct debt of Methodism to Puritanism has already been discussed (above, pp. 175f.). It is of importance here partly because it is one of the factors to be borne in mind in assessing whether the Methodist lives describe a spontaneous development or something forced into conformity with a stereotype. In the eighteenth century some converts were searching and even finding without knowledge of the justification by faith and conversionist tradition. In other cases they certainly had guidance from Puritan models. Several read books like Alleine's *Alarm* and Baxter's *Call*, Bunyan's *Pilgrim's Progress* and *Grace Abounding*, and this affected even their style of writing.[185] But others struggled on by the light of nature, their progress punctuated by accidents of illness and bereavement, escapes from accidents and the guidance of dreams, visions or electrifying texts which were seen, at least in retrospect, as 'providential'. They used standard books of devotion like the *Whole Duty* and *Week's Preparation* in an attempt to be good Christians, but failed until they found the way of faith.[186]

In a valuable recent study Isabel Rivers has pointed out how Methodist autobiography both continued the old literature of 'pilgrim-age' and added a dimension of its own to it because of the nature of Methodist organization and culture.[187] The metaphor was an old one, though reinforced in Puritan writing and immortalized in allegorical form by Bunyan.[188] For Methodism, however, it acquired actuality from the pattern of itineracy among the preachers, and so was fed into their autobiographical model: Wesley's *Journal* naturally became a vivid large-scale example. As Rivers points out, there is also a secular parallel in the eighteenth-century picaresque novel, though not a very welcome one from a Methodist point of view. Certainly there is one Methodist autobiography which has strong elements of that genre. Silas Told was apprenticed to a slaver, captured by pirates, saw many strange sights and as a Methodist became a specialist in saving condemned prisoners. His story reads like a mixture of *Robinson Crusoe* and *Grace Abounding*.[189]

But, as Rivers points out, the picaresque hero travels from home and back again, from an uncertain to a secure place in the social order; whereas the Methodist, like Bunyan's pilgrim, travels from this world to the next, shedding worldly relationships on the way. The accidents of the picaresque journey become plainly providential; the resolution of the quest is through conversion; and security and identity are found in the closed world of the Methodist society.

Once established, this model tends to settle the shape of the personal story; and there are editorial processes to be considered as well. Only a small number of lives have survived in manuscript, and the printed versions bear the marks of Wesley's and others' editorial hand, though at least this did not de-supernaturalize the more startling episodes in the way that happened with some of the editions of George Fox's *Journal*. Some of Wesley's associates wished that he would put less material of this kind in his *Journal*, and by the nineteenth century, Wesleyan editors of the *Magazine* sneered at the strange stories recorded in James Everett's biography of Samuel Hick, the Methodist blacksmith and popular preacher. Everett replied with devastating effect by quoting similar passages in Wesley's *Journal*.[190] What was lost in transmission may rather have been the rough immediacy of style, smoothed down by Wesley.[191]

More important is the way in which the developed and expected pattern of Methodist experience unconsciously coloured the pattern laid out in the lives, even when they were based on diaries kept at the time, for most were written up years afterwards. Like all such converts the authors wrote off their parents' and their own early piety because it did not qualify as 'real' Christianity; but more important, they forced their experience into a preconceived type. A few, however, give clues to the uncertainty actually felt at the time. Duncan Wright, a Scot and former soldier, had read Puritan books, yet when God 'justified me by his grace', bringing him 'in an instant out of darkness into his marvellous light', he said that 'I did not know what to call it'. Thomas Hanby searched for the way to be good, had some contacts with the Methodists and had experiences of temptations and 'remarkable comforts but knew not what they meant'. William Ashford, of 'honest' parents but without religion, was in a group influenced by Methodist preachers which produced several cases of justification and sanctification, 'though they did not know what justification or sanctification meant'. Martha Thompson had a religious friend who felt 'pardoning love' in her last illness, and she herself felt her sin after God revealed the 'inefficacy of worldly things' to her in a dream. But it was only after meeting the Methodists in 1740 that through William Shent 'the Lord opened my understanding to know what he had formerly wrought in my heart'.[192] Even when they knew what was supposed to happen, converts might go for a long time, like Thomas Hanson, doubting whether, for example, knowledge of pardon was attainable here.[193]

Still, by whatever means, and with whatever retrospective tidying and explaining of experiences, a process was experienced which was repeated many times on broadly similar lines.

In discussing the religious origins of the Revival, I noted how many of the converts for whom we have clear evidence had a more or less marked religious background. Although they regularly remarked that their parents did not know the true way of salvation, it is clear enough that most had a distinctly moral and even devout, if conventional, Anglican or Dissenting background and upbringing. The case of Sampson Staniforth, of a family which had not 'the form, still less the power of religion', and which allowed him to grow up ignorant of morality and religion, is exceptional.[194] There follow considerable indications that what then happened to such people was that after a period of commonplace youthful misbehaviour – drinking, dancing, card-playing, swearing, Sabbath-breaking – occasional sobering thoughts and frights were succeeded by a deep sense of sin. This sounds very like the conflict between parental standards and adolescent revolt and the company of 'the world'. It is again only occasionally that one finds serious moral delinquency: Thomas Olivers and Staniforth both seduced young women.[195] There seems to be truth in the claim of Wesley's critic Lewis that most of the converts in his observation were decent enough people before. This contrasts with the claims made by Wesley and repeated since about the sinful past lives of the Methodists.[196] Of course this reflects the special and heightened sense of sin and the way of salvation by faith common to evangelicals and puzzling to outsiders, who saw only respectable and even severely ascetic persons unnecessarily and fanatically lambasting themselves. But it probably also reflects the character of the spiritual élite portrayed in the early 'Lives' rather than the anonymous generality of converts. Some of the Bristol convulsionaries may have been of the latter type, though obviously open to fear of hell.[197]

Many of these young men of reasonably good background had intimations of God from a very early age, if only occasionally. John Allen, of mixed Anglican and Presbyterian parentage, had 'serious thoughts' from the age of eight and feared hell when thunderstorms were around. He was preserved from drunkenness and 'scandalous sins', though delighting in dancing and singing.[198]

Most of the early converts had prolonged experiences of spiritual struggle and efforts at self-reformation, with frequent lapses and a growing sense of agonized failure. Their illuminations and comforts were rare until the last stages before conversion, and it was often only at that stage that they received any help from Wesley, Whitefield, visiting preachers or neighbouring Methodists. The actual conversion in a considerable proportion of cases was precipitated by some apparently supernatural experience: dreams, visions of Christ crucified or the judgment day, voices or feelings which impressed particular biblical texts on their minds as divine guidance. James Rogers dreamt that a fire from the earth burnt up the 'bad people' and his playmates who lied and cheated and played on Sundays. He saw the 'Ancient of Days' (Daniel 7 etc.). His consultation of neighbours about the way of salvation produced the replies quoted earlier about sincerity and God honouring our good efforts.[199] It was only after a long process of trying to do good that he joined the Methodists and 'found what he had never known before' 'a clear sense of pardon'. He prayed for it in company with others and finally had a vision of Christ crucified 'by the eye of faith'. In face of the gaze of Christ ('O what a look was that!'), he found his burden gone and his heart released from bondage.[200] Some felt the release so strongly that the whole world of nature was transformed for them. 'The heavens above . . . the earth beneath, both sparkled with their Creator's glory; and all creation seemed to smile upon my soul.' 'My understanding was opened to behold the power, wisdom and glory of God . . . I saw that the whole earth was full of His majesty and glory', though also 'the Ancient of Days become an infant, The Father of immortality contracted to a span' (a quotation from Charles Wesley's hymn on the incarnation).[201]

Some Methodists after conversion went through periods of temptation, doubt and fear; some were tempted to blasphemy (which they took to be the work of the devil) or, if influenced by Calvinists, had fears of not being of the elect. Only a few actually had periods of deistic scepticism like George Story, but several, like Matthew Joyce, had inexplicable temptations to blaspheme and to deny or doubt the existence of God. This is a familiar experience in the literature of conversion and should be seen as part of the psychology of this type of convert rather than as the intellectual effects of eighteenth-century scepticism and freethinking. John Valton indeed recognized that his lack of a sense of pardon was due as much to his nervous disposition as to lack of faith, and he noted that his doubts lifted when actually preaching.[202]

What these men lacked and sought for was that 'assurance', given by the 'witness of the Spirit' which Wesley so firmly taught. In some cases this came along with the experience of conversion. Thomas Walsh, the mystical Irishman, was converted during the singing of old Samuel Wesley's hymn 'Behold the Saviour of mankind', and at the same time as his sense of pardon the Spirit 'gave witness with my spirit that I was a child of God'. Richard Rodda 'received a clear sense' of 'pardoning love' within a few days of his conversion.[203] No doubt the desire for this and anxiety at its delay was aggravated by Wesley's early teaching about its necessity for the truly converted – in which some other Methodists followed him.[204] But many had to wait for it to come or never fully possessed it.

The pain caused by these post-conversion doubts is vividly illustrated by some rare examples of correspondence from early converts, some semi-literate, which incidentally throw an interesting light on their general culture (I have retained the original spelling).[205] Mary Bainton wrote to Wesley in 1742 that 'When yr Brother was preaching . . . I received the Remishon of my sins, tho I was not without Doughts and fears for three quarters of a Year, Yet the Lord was my keeper, though I was sometimes in heaviness through manifold temptations.' In 1740 John Unser wrote: 'John Westly for I cannot use any apology neither rough nor smooth seing that for several reasons I choose to deliver my Horrid sentiments to you in writing.' He had received justification and 'pardon applied to my heart' nine or ten weeks before, at which time he was 'full of love to God and man'. But now,

> the scene is quite altered and things has now another face; now all things are past away, behold all things are now become old. But not indeed properly, for I never before felt such a Hell as I now feel. I now am as very a devil as ever was or will be confined in the Everlasting chains of darkness. I now hate God, hate my brother, hate my children, hate all that is good, and what adds much to my sorrow in it, I know God and the Father and our Lord Jesus Christ love me . . . I am as proud as Lucifer, as covetous as mamon, as hateful as Beelzebub and as lustful. As for my wife, I take no more notice of her
>
> > Than I do of the spider's web
> > Swept from the wall by the gidy Maid . . .

Dr Sir, what shall I do in this condition? I am just upon the point of breaking off from God, of declaring for the Devil.

Susanna Designe, a Bristol schoolmistress, shows the influence of the old religious interpretation of the *Song of Songs* with its erotic overtones:

> O what a faint shadow is my stammering tongue able to express. I am overcome with his love . . . I can say I am coming from the wilderness leaning upon my Beloved and . . . he is a guide to my feet and a lanthorn to my path . . . When I lift up my heart to the Lord, I find such a power drawing my soul into holy Breathings to love the

Lord with my whole heart as I cannot express . . . I feel such flames of love to my Dear Saviour and to all mankind as I cannot express.

A year later, though expressing difficulties, 'in ye strength of Jesus I still am conqueror over ye world ye flesh and the Devil'. But four months later she confesses that since Wesley left Bristol she has been 'in such darkness of Heart as I never felt before', though she knows the Lord is with her as she committed 'no outward sin'. She also finds 'a greater power to reprove gainsayers' than ever she did. But she lacks love of God in her heart and longs for 'ye sweet communion I often had with Jesus'. The genuine anguish filters through the scriptural phrases, attempts at 'literary' language and self-dramatization of these letters.

Then comes the most distinctive feature of the Methodist version of the process of salvation: 'Christian perfection'. A large number of these experiences, as one would expect, occur from the period beginning with the great outbreak of the 1760s. Their frequency may be attributed partly to the publicity which this gained (though the excesses scared some off) and to Wesley's insistence on its possibility. But it is also partly the product of the experience of converts, who after the first ecstasies over the sense of sin being removed in conversion felt that they still had further to go. Perfection teaching met this need, explaining the experience of imperfection and offering a fresh goal to be aimed at. Thus William Hunter in his autobiography made no mention of perfection, but added a supplement explaining how after conversion he at first felt very happy, but then found temptations creeping in and the need for 'a far greater change', so he prayed to be 'saved from all sin' – and did not know that such a gift had been promised until he read a sermon of Wesley's.[206]

We have seen that, as fully developed, the doctrine exactly paralleled the first conversion in its preparation, reception by faith, assurance and subsequent improvement. One woman was at first only 'rationally convinced' of having the gift by the evidence of being full of love, but later had an inward assurance.[207] Another seems to have been led to hope for the assurance by reading Wesley's old favourite, Lopez.[208]

As to the content of the experience itself, sometimes it seemed as if a physical barrier had been removed to communion with Christ. Sarah Ryan, the colourful Kingswood housekeeper, said: 'it seemed to me as if something was taken out of me' when, praying against a besetting sin, she found that the sin had gone and that there was no barrier between herself and God. An 'old Mr Pritchard' testified that as 'Mr Wesley preached, I felt something across my heart like an iron bar, cold and hard. And hearing Mr Wesley insist on the word *now*, I said, Lord, here I am, a poor sinner. I believe thou canst come even *now* and give me a clean heart. Immediately that bar was broken, and all my soul was filled with love . . .'[209]

Wesley's notion of perfection as 'pure love' was what replaced the sense of barriers to be removed. A Wednesbury woman said that: 'From that moment I have felt nothing but love in my heart; no sin of any kind . . . I never find a cloud between God and me. I walk in the light continually. I do "rejoice evermore" and "pray without ceasing". I have no desire but to do and suffer the will of God . . . And I have a continual witness in myself, that whatever I do, I do it to his glory.'[210] It was a gift which could be lost through carelessness or the cares of the world or even failure to witness that one had it. (John Fletcher apparently suffered this fate for a time until he remedied it from the pulpit.) It had to be maintained by faith and the use of all the means of grace. Converts should not fall into Quietist views of being 'called to inward crucifixion, a being stript of all sensible enjoyment'. To one who talked like this, Wesley responded that we are called to 'rejoice evermore', though nervous disorders may hinder this.[211]

It has been suggested that the doctrine was a quirk due to John Wesley's peculiar High Church history and prejudices, unrepresentative of the Revival, or even of Methodism as a whole. Most converts, it could be argued, had their emotions and expectations centred on the joys of conversion.[212] Certainly perfectionism was largely confined to Methodism and controversial within it. But there is also ample evidence, even allowing for Wesley's anxiety to publicize cases, to show that a large number of Methodists at all levels sought for it and believed they had attained it, at least for a time. It was characteristic that there were crops in times of excitement, with lapses of a large proportion later. But every local revival in Wesley's later life brought more: it offered a chance of a new experience for those already converted. And in general it may at least be said that the promise helped to fulfil the role that Wesley visualized for it: of preventing the 'professors' from 'sitting on their lees'.

For preachers there was one further stage of development – the call to preach – which was often as painful and prolonged as conversion, though in some the product of accident. John Pawson was pressed to visit neighbouring societies and 'give them a word of exhortation' which at first he refused. A travelling preacher was convinced that he should preach, and pursued him with 'advice, persuasion and even threatenings of the Divine displeasure if I would not obey the call of God'. Deeply sensible of his own weakness and inefficacy, he submitted to the judgment of Wesley and the itinerants, though he continued to have doubts about his 'call', as he was 'not favoured with that freedom of mind and enlargement of heart in preaching which is so desirable'. In his dying advice to the Conference he emphasized that Methodism should continue a 'lively, spiritual, heart-searching ministry'. Hence they should 'never, no never, try to make ministers by substituting learning or anything else in the room of the call of God and those spiritual gifts and graces which He . . . will bestow upon those whom He sends . . .'[213]

Almost as important for the early Methodists as a life well lived was a death well died, and indeed a number of the short accounts of Methodist worthies in the *Magazine* were simply extended death-bed scenes with little else; blow by blow accounts of the last scenes were a prominent feature of all biographies. This kind of account has a long pedigree in Christian hagiography, and once again the old Puritans provide the closest parallel to the Methodist variety.[214] Protestantism in some ways heightened the tension of the death bed, for there was no purgatory whose pains might be shortened by prayers and masses, and most of the elaborations of Catholic death-rites had been shorn away. Here, too, the anxieties of election came to a head; if one followed the Perkins doctrine, it was wise for predestinated saints to preserve a godly doubt of themselves so as to leave room for reliance on grace. The histories of holy dyings were valued, as a later Nonconformist said, 'to perfume the name of the deceased; to console surviving mourners; to gratify descendants; and to instruct and edify the church'. They were also a proof of the truths taught by the dying saint: an important part of Methodist apologetic.[215]

It may be argued that there was a difference between Calvinists and Wesleyans here, in that the former could hold to the eternal perseverance of the elect, relying on grace alone. Thus John Newton, the old African slaver, announced himself 'packed and sealed and waiting for the post'. He had no great transports of joy, but relied on two truths: 'that I am a great sinner and Christ is a great saviour'.[216] But the Arminian Wesleyans believed that a man might be snatched from hell at the last minute (hence the interest in Tyburn ministries), though equally that saints might be lost by backsliding.[217] There is an evident note of anxious probing in Methodist death-bed scenes to elicit evidence that all was well with the dying person's soul as evidenced by actual feelings of peace and joy: exactly as in conversion and its 'assurance' experience.

Mrs Hester Ann Rogers recorded a clear example of this. A poor man had been 'enlightened respecting the way of salvation' by the Methodists. In his last illness he 'earnestly sought the Lord but his *evidence* was never clear until a little before his death'. His wife, though a backslidden Methodist, pressed him: '"My dear, how is it with your soul? Have you confidence in God?" He answered, "I am not happy, I have no *assurance*".' But shortly before death he received it. Mrs Rogers herself, incidentally, died in the expected state of confidence, and her husband carefully explained in his memoir of her that he had only questioned her about her state as a witness and a source of edification for others.[218]

Methodist devotions and duties, by accident or design, tended to monopolize the scanty free time of the members. But this they seem to have welcomed, and even members who were not preachers spent much of their time in this way. Negatively, as we shall see, many 'worldly' pursuits and 'sinful' recreations were banned; positively, a wide range of public and private exercises were expected, of the variety outlined earlier. In the case of some of the more dedicated and devout it is difficult to escape the impression that the real centre of their lives was not in their occupations and professions or even in their families, but in the life of the Spirit. Thus the young Manchester Methodist Samuel Bardsley has a diary beginning in the early 1760s which contains a few references to his work in a wine cellar, but is chiefly a record of meetings, preaching, personal encounters and reflections on his own state. The picture is of daily early morning meetings; house meetings in various parts of the town; class meetings; bands; select societies. But Bardsley added preaching in the surrounding villages at weekends. On Sundays he was active from 6.00 a.m. up to midnight. Through this runs also a tender love story with a sick girl he had visited.[219]

If Bardsley was exceptional (he later became a travelling preacher), his diary still reveals a dense sub-culture largely run by local lay people and owing little to the travelling preachers. At a later date in the same town George Lomas's life shows how he was weaned from 'worldly' commercial pursuits, if only for the sake of his family. He burned any books that were not 'useful' or religious after his conversion rather than damage anyone else by selling them. Family prayers were held three times a day; he read the Bible and religious books morning and evening; and distributed tracts.[220] The diary of John Marsden, a Manchester corn merchant, resembles that of Bardsley in its concentration on religious exercises and failure to mention business. As his modern editor remarked, from this evidence alone one would have supposed he was a minister. What concerned him was self-examination; sermons heard; class and band meetings – though also a judicious love-affair. He was concerned whether he had 'an eye to the glory of God' and whether his soul was growing 'after conformity to the image of Jesus', which was indeed the purpose of the Methodist diary as advocated by Wesley.[221]

Methodist family life and relations with children naturally included careful attention to, and anxiety about, their souls, though it is a mistake to see their attitudes as simply repressive.[222] So far as the role of women is concerned, it has already been noted that Wesley, though no feminist, was willing to break with convention in this as in other areas if he thought he could see a call of God being answered, as evidenced by 'fruits'; in this his successors were more cautious and indeed repressive where women preachers were concerned.[223] Short of preaching, however, women had considerable scope as class and band leaders and vocal members, and some, like Mrs Rogers, became notable Methodist saints. It has been pointed out that in some areas, over fifty per cent of members were women: the impact of this and of the domestic setting of many Methodist meetings has yet to be fully explored for the early period, though a beginning has been made.[224] In view of E.P. Thompson's rather melodramatic charges that Methodism stifled the natural, including the sexual impulses, or sublimated them into a holy eroticism (for which there is some evidence), there is no doubt scope for psychohistorians. Such charges are easy to make, and one of the letters on doubt after conversion quoted earlier shows the basis for similar charges often made against mystics. Conversion stories of young men also sometimes show what looks like sexual repression or anxiety.[225] But as has already been remarked, there is really no reason to suppose that Methodism prevented people from falling in love in the usual way: what inhibited them was not sexual inhibitions (except in personalities who would have had this problem anyway) but rather whether marriage was to the right partner at the right time in view of their religious duties – essentially a different problem. A recent study seems to confirm that not many Methodists shared their leader's recurring recommendation to celibacy.[226]

Through many of the lives – indeed all of them in various measures – there runs a more or less strong and overt sense of the supernatural world, divine and diabolical in its manifestations. It has already been pointed out that Wesley's own strong interest and belief in a wide range of supernatural phenomena was one secret of his hold on his followers, even though he used the forms of contemporary empiricism in his defence of his beliefs. At the rank-and-file level of Methodism, beliefs of a traditional kind with an affinity to 'popular' religion and culture were even more marked. The classic work of Keith Thomas on *Religion and the Decline of Magic* is the essential starting-point for the subject, but unfortunately it does not go beyond 1700, and Thomas's thesis of a decline after 1700 needs to be treated with caution. (Thomas himself tempered this with the admission that this may rather be a case of decline of magical and supernatural beliefs at the educated level of society and persistence at a 'popular' level.)[227] James Obelkevich's study of popular beliefs in part of mid-nineteenth-century Lincolnshire showed how persistent they were and the presumption must be that plenty existed in the eighteenth, as limited sampling confirms.[228]

The rationale for Wesley's own strongly supernatural beliefs has already been discussed, and the relationship between these and his more 'empiricist' attitudes considered (above, pp. 387f.). Attention here will be concentrated mainly on his followers. Wesley catered generously enough in his *Journal* and the *Magazine* for these tastes with accounts of wonders in nature, 'providences', dreams, visions, demon-possession, witchcraft: some as separate items, some incidental to Methodist life-histories. A rough count in the *Journal* shows over sixty such incidents in 1739–42; about ten per annum in the 1750s; and rather less in later years, though the *Magazine* made up for this. Some of his friends regretted the inclusion of such material in the *Journal*, but Wesley defended them for apologetic reasons in a sceptical generation.[229]

In doing so he was simply endorsing a common Methodist attitude, even though some of his educated lay associates were unhappy. Almost all of the recorded lives of the early preachers, for example, have a greater or lesser number of such incidents. Even Thomas Olivers, who confessed that he was prejudiced against them, records how he saw a 'ray of light, resembling the shining of a star' when his 'burden fell off'. Joseph Cownley, who was 'averse from the slightest approach of fancy and imagination in religion', and was hostile to Maxfield and Bell, was converted by words of Scripture 'suddenly and powerfully applied to his mind' – a very common occurrence.[230] It is a basic historical error and anachronism to pass over these characteristics as if they were simply contemporary aberrations of otherwise noble minds, for in fact they were an integral part of what Methodism (including Wesley's own teaching) meant and help to explain its peculiar appeal.[231] Amongst other things it appeared to confirm its claim to be true, scriptural Christianity and owned by God as such.

To take some examples of particular sorts of events: all Methodists and probably most evangelicals, it may safely be said, believed in 'particular providences' – the manifestation of the direct action of God through events which either wrought judgments on evildoers and scoffers or saved the saints or those later to be converts from danger and death. As a warning to drunkards, for example, the *Magazine* recorded how a man was drunk on the Sabbath as usual and died in his sleep. A blasphemous gardener dreamt that he met two devils and beat one of them. On waking he joined his drinking companions and later went to his hot-house. Here he was found to be on fire with his nose burnt off, his lips preserved but his blasphemous tongue burnt out of his mouth.[232]

Reviewing their lives, Methodists detected how God had preserved them from death and so from hell in their pre-conversion days as well as in their later lives. Richard Rodda, a Cornish miner, told how he had been miraculously preserved in a fall of stones, minutely detailing how he had been praying, and kneeling; how the stones fell in a particular way. Unless all these conditions had coincided he would have been killed. In a similar way, Alexander Mather as a young man caught up in the Jacobite rebellion of 1745 fled after Culloden and was nearly drowned while crossing a river. Only a large number of 'accidentally' coinciding factors ensured his escape.[233]

Nature, too, was subdued to God. Wesley quite often recorded without comment, though with obvious 'providential' implications, the fact that rain held off from his open-air preaching sessions. Sammy Hick the blacksmith agonized successfully in prayer to create rain.[234] Portents in the natural world were still taken to foreshadow great events or the judgments of God. John Morris believed that a comet betokened some great event and the Jacobite rebellion of 1745 duly ensued. Attempts at scientific explanation of earthquakes did not prevent many educated contemporaries from preaching sermons on God's judgment about the great Lisbon earthquake of 1755, the lesser London shocks of 1750 and provincial examples later. The Methodists naturally added their quota. Even the Arian Dr Percival of Manchester, having recited current explanations of these phenomena in 1777, added that whatever the secondary causes, one need not doubt that God could use them in judgment.[235] A similar view was taken of thunderstorms by sensitive souls.[236]

It is fair to say that Methodists generally avoided the extreme prophetic and healing claims of a George Bell, but they firmly believed in spiritual healing by prayer and possession by demons, though they were also perfectly capable of recognizing epilepsy and natural hysteria, and used medical means to cure diseases.[237] Wesley's *Primitive Physick* has already been mentioned as an example of his 'empiricism' in treating symptoms by trial and error and deliberately eschewing speculation on causes in terms of 'systems' in the ancient manner. The book has often been mocked for its old wives' remedies, though in fact it at least avoided the lethal remedies of contemporary medicine and had much about fresh air, cold water, exercise and the virtues of a quiet mind. It has recently had a more sympathetic consideration. One should not, of course, exaggerate: there are folk remedies of dubious virtue in it, and Wesley's famous 'modern' use of electric shocks is presented more like a quack's panacea for all ills. What is equally significant is that Wesley also used the 'sovereign remedy' of prayer: sometimes applying it instead of medicine as well as in addition to it – even, on one occasion, to his horse.[238] Dr Hempton's judgment on this dual aspect of Wesley's attitude to healing is perhaps rather flattering in its even balance, but worth pondering all the same as an assessment of his role as a cultural middleman suggested earlier. It is an example, he says, 'of how Methodism established deep roots in popular culture but did not surrender to a purely magical framework'.[239]

Methodists inhabited a world which had strong elements of dualism. The devil and his demons afflicted them during their conversion struggles, and their visions and visitations seemed vividly to symbolize the struggle for the soul between good and evil powers. And indeed Wesley himself believed in good and evil angels as agents of God and the devil.[240]

Visions and dreams were usually, though not always, distinguished by the recipients; both were taken seriously, as they might convey warnings or foreseeings of death. Visions of the judgment of the world or of the individual are quite common; but commonest of all are visions of Christ crucified and bleeding for sinners. He appeared, said Thomas Taylor, 'to the eye of my mind, as standing just before me, while ten thousand small streams of blood seemed to issue from every part of his body'.[241] From the 1770s (and occasionally earlier) a few of those seeking perfection had special visions of the Trinity seen in the distinct persons.[242] It should be said that the majority of these cases occurred in those not habitually subject to special mystical experiences. They rather seem to have been induced by the special stress of the struggle for conversion and perfection or their achievement. The visions appear to have the function of dramatizing their concerns and resolving their problems, and so marking stages in their spiritual pilgrimages. Visions of judgment brought conviction of sin; visions of the Crucified Christ brought forgiveness and joy; visions of the Trinity a kind of beatific vision open only to the perfect in love.

Beyond these specifically religious events, there was a more ambiguous world of popular belief and practice which has been vividly brought to life in Keith Thomas's book. Some of those whom the Methodists approached, including some of those whom they converted, appeared to be living in two worlds: the world of church, chapel and preaching house with its more or less orthodox plan of salvation; and the world of magic and charms, black witches and white. In such a world, a vivid realization of personified good and evil; the promise of powerful protection from evil; the prospect of various kinds of healing and vivid emotional experiences were far more attractive and far closer to their felt needs than the formal ministrations of the Church of England's clergy, whose quasi-magical rites and functions had been sharply diminished by the Reformation.[243] Charismatic or simply eccentric Methodist preachers sometimes had the reputation of being wizards, and on occasion they were effective in the role of healers or exorcists as well as agents of spiritual salvation. But as the 'convulsion' cases showed, conversion could itself be similar in its effects to possession. Tradition suggests, indeed, that some good Methodists literally inhabited two supernatural worlds: there are stories of them invoking traditional remedies for witchcraft while dutifully attending chapel.[244]

It has been plausibly argued that one reason for the success of Methodism, especially in areas like Cornwall where folklore and magic were particularly strong, was that Methodism was able to offer a fairly highly-coloured supernatural world of its own as a substitute and counter-attraction for the traditional one, which conventional Anglicanism and Dissent were unable to match.[245] In arguing for this Dr Rule indeed recognizes that there were limits to this appeal. For one thing, Methodists also attacked many aspects of 'popular' culture: its rowdy recreations and heavy drinking and dancing as well as smuggling and wrecking (see below, pp. 443ff.). Moreover, the Methodist supernatural world, officially at least, sanitized and scripturalized what was accepted: dreams, visions and healing were sanctioned; demons were exorcised; but resort to charms and witchcraft were opposed. Yet the appeal compared with conventional religion was clear enough, and at the grass roots level could go a good deal further than Wesley and his assistants were aware. A recent student of Cornish Methodism has suggested, indeed, that the symbiotic relationship between Methodism and popular belief was closer than has generally been recognized and that Methodism actually helped to fortify Cornish identity in an age of change and perpetuated its own brand of revivalistic popular religion well into the nineteenth century.[246]

An attempt has been made in this discussion of Methodist beliefs and experience to compare the ideas and ideals of John Wesley with the reality as exemplified in the Methodist people. The picture needs to be completed with some further consideration of their social service in its positive as well as negative aspects. But already a certain tension can be discerned between the image often given of a reforming, purifying, civilizing, even mildly 'modernizing' movement, taken to extremes in works like Semmel's *Methodist Revolution*, and those aspects of it which seem traditionalist and anti-rational. The division, as has been argued here, runs through Wesley himself. Professor Plumb in his chapter on Wesley and Methodism in *England in the Eighteenth Century* on the one hand acknowledges its contribution to the civilizing of the masses and perhaps to their longer-term rise into articulateness, organization and general betterment. But on the other hand (and more forcefully) he sees it as an anti-intellectual force, running counter to the rationalizing mood of the age: symbolized for Plumb by Wesley's *Primitive Physic*, seen in its most ludicrous aspects.[247]

A more measured view might be that quite apart from his suggested role as a cultural mediator, Wesley was in any case dealing with an unruly people, and that his rules were a necessary expedient to impose some order and coherence on his movement. As I have already suggested, he succeeded in many cases in internalizing various religious and moral norms as well as imposing a degree of control on a supernaturalism which merged for some into outright magic.

In morality as well as in magic Wesley's control was of course only partial. In tracts like *The Character of a Methodist* (1742) and in various apologetic works, Wesley played down not only the supernaturalist claims but also the eccentricities of his movement. Naturally he did not normally publicize his failures except when he was listing reasons why people left him or were expelled, like Bell and Maxfield. But the list already cited of reasons for leaving the class meeting (above, pp. 241f.), and the frequent purges as well as the late sermons excoriating rich Methodists for deserting their first love and old discipline, are a frank enough exposure of Methodist realities, even when allowances are made for his severe standards and an old man's disillusionment. Certainly there were moral casualties: the egregious Westley Hall and more obscure psychopaths or hypocrites really existed outside the volumes of anti-Methodist satire. A few preachers fell into sexual delinquency, like James Wheatley (above, pp. 300f.), and stories were told, apparently authentic, of Methodists guilty of actual crimes.[248] Some suffered from religious mania, though more perhaps from what their neighbours judged to be such, in a way that would have been less likely a century before.[249]

Wesley risked hostages to fortune (and got away with more than might be expected) in his public claims about the numbers of the perfected and the cases he described. Such claims were not easy to test but fatally easy to refute, and made the unco' religious – always a target for critical observation – even more vulnerable. The real vices of Methodists were, perhaps, not spectacular sins, but those Wesley himself recognized: jealousy, back-biting and malicious gossip. The affair with Grace Murray and the reactions of Methodists to it show this up only too well. Vivian Green, in his incisive assessment of the Methodist achievement, highlights the contrast between this and the high claims to perfection in love, all the more damaging when for Wesley this was the very heart and soul, the very aim of Methodism.[250] There is no way, however, of quantifying the achievement of Methodism overall. If the claims to perfection are suspect, it is still reasonable to suppose that an élite achieved a high degree of devotion as well as sacrificial service, and that a larger number achieved a more orderly, moral, civilized and indeed happier life than they would have done without their faith. Certainly there was little sign that conventional church life had achieved as much for them.

4. Saints at home: the social world of the early Methodists

As a preliminary to considering the social attitudes and activities of the early Methodists, it is as well for us to gain some idea of their numbers and social composition.

I remarked earlier (above, pp. 236f.) that we have no overall membership figures before 1766/7. In the early 1740s there are only scattered cases, suggesting that growth was rapid in some of the larger centres like London, Bristol and Newcastle, and more so in the last two than in London. In the late 1750s numbers were still very small in the Wiltshire woollen towns, though this was probably due to the strength of the old Dissent there. In Manchester they had grown from a late start in 1747 to 200 by 1756, but were halved by dissension and Dissent and obviously unstable.[251]

In national terms there were 25,911 members in 1767 and 72,476 at the time of Wesley's death in 1791 (including Ireland).[252] In England at least, membership grew every year, with minor hiccups until the secessions of the 1850s, with the exception of 1820, when losses of over 4,000 provoked pastoral self-searchings. The average annual growth rate from 1768 to 1791 was about 4%, but this masked considerable annual fluctuations between 1% and 7%, with a remarkable 13.52% in 1794. Already in the nineteenth century students of revival noted that there was a rough five-year cycle of growth, decline and growth again, though within an overall pattern of increase, and this has been endorsed by modern studies.[253] On a longer time-scale, growth continued until about 1906 in the main churches, and an even more impressive fact is that Methodism in particular was growing faster than the population at large until about the 1880s. The decennial increases for Methodism in 1771–1801 were 41.8%, 52.0% and 62.7%, as compared with the general population's 7.06%, 9.07% and 5.68%. It became less impressive later: for example only about 1% above the general increase in the 1840s. It has to be added, however, that these figures must be set against the fact that Methodism remained a tiny part of the whole population. In 1770 it was 0.35%, in 1790 0.47%, in 1801 1.04%, and by 1850 still only 2.84%.[254] Local strength, however, varied considerably. In Manchester in 1801 the Methodists probably made up about 3% of the population: nearly three times the national average.[255]

So far reference has been made to membership figures. It has always been known that there was a much larger number of adherents, some being faithful enough attenders but shrinking from full membership. A proportion often suggested is two adherents to every one member, though some would say three or more.[256] So a conservative estimate of members and adherents in 1791 might be upwards of 210,000, perhaps even near 300,000.

These people were very unevenly distributed geographically and by occupation. Long ago Maldwyn Edwards pointed out that Methodist strength lay in the industrial areas of the Midlands and North, and that the purely agricultural areas were seldom much affected, especially in the South.[257] Robert Currie made the more precise claim that Methodism was strongest in the thirteen counties where the established church was weakest. These were where the main growing industrial areas of eighteenth-century England were located: the North-east, North-west, Midlands, West Riding, London and Cornwall in 1801 held 55% of membership.[258] Currie also sought to show that this pattern differed from that of the old Dissent. He claimed that Dissent had (judging by the 1851 census figures) done best in areas of Anglican strength, but Methodism in areas of Anglican weakness. This was because Dissent had historically derived from the church, but Methodism from those whom the church failed to reach, in areas where the supervision of squire and parson was lacking.[259]

One should perhaps be cautious about these general conclusions, based on a county analysis ignoring important variations within some counties. It also leans too much on the 1851 pattern. Certainly Presbyterianism was the product of a split in the ruling class and the church, which by the eighteenth century had been sufficiently resolved in favour of episcopalianism to lose gentry support for the Presbyterians, who now became members of a mere Dissenting sect rather than of a potential established church. But Presbyterianism both before and after toleration was also strong in northern counties like Cheshire and Lancashire in circumstances where the Church of England had large and weakly controlled parishes, just as happened later with Methodism. And Methodism also drew off members of the church as well as the unchurched.[260]

Methodism also resembled Dissent in its apparently greater impact on urban rather than rural areas, and on settlements remote from the parish church and parishes without a single dominant landlord. This did not exclude some impact on villages as well as towns: again true of the old Dissent.[261] But certainly Methodism had some outstanding successes in mining and fishing communities in areas where neither Dissent nor the church had much strength: Cornwall is an outstanding example. And its growth in the later eighteenth century must owe much to the simple fact of population increase in just such areas and among populations of artisans not so directly subject to masters as agriculturalists.[262]

But who were these people in terms of occupation? There has been a persistent belief, fostered by Wesley himself, and picturesquely expressed in his brother Charles's appeal to 'harlots and publicans and thieves', that the early Methodists were predominantly among the lower orders, indeed the poor and often the outcasts. We have already seen that biographical evidence casts doubt on the depraved background of at least the solid élite. Is the image of the poor also a myth? James Hutton may have given a more realistic picture when he said the early congregations contained 'every description of persons'. 'Here thieves, prostitutes, fools, people of every class, several men of distinction, a few of the learned, merchants, and numbers of poor people who had never entered a place of worship, assembled in crowds and became godly.'[263] Wesley himself occasionally comments on 'genteel' congregations or individuals, though perhaps seeing them as exceptional. But which of these fed into membership?

Specific evidence on this is to hand in early lists of members, though too few of these give occupations. What has survived has been effectively analysed by Dr Clive Field, though there are problems here of classification. Field adapts Joseph Massie's categories of 1760, which are subject to various limitations, particularly the ambiguous category of 'manufacturers' which, while usefully distinguishing industry from commerce, does not distinguish masters from mere artisans: and in some areas 'manufacturers' were in fact 'merchants' as well. Lumping 'gentlemen' (a broad and imprecise category by now) with peers also does not help. Still, the resulting table is illuminating.[264]

		A	B	C	D	E	F
		%	%	%	%	%	%
Miscellaneous	351	2.8	4.8	8.5	10.0	54.4	19.4
Manchester Circuit (1759) (part only)	235	1.7	2.1	11.9	3.8	61.7	18.7
Keighley Round (1763)	398	0.3	1.0	19.3	4.5	65.1	9.8
W. Cornwall (1767)	589	1.2	2.2	9.3	9.8	25.5	52.0
All Methodists	1573	1.4	2.5	12.1	7.6	47.4	29.1
England (1760) (Massie)		1.2	4.4	24.8	12.1	20.9	26.6

Categories: A. Peers, gentlemen
B. Professional and military and naval officers
C. Freeholders and farmers
D. Merchants, tradesmen and innkeepers
E. Manufacturers
F. Labourers, husbandmen, cottagers, seamen, fishermen, common soldiers.

Obviously the variations in different areas reflect their dominant occupational structure: miners (under F) in Cornwall and textile workers (under E) in Keighley. But what stands out is the high proportion of people in industry compared with the country as a whole, and the low proportion of agriculturalists. On the other hand these last were not absent, and in some areas may have increased later in the century in areas affected by the growing distance between the clergy and their people where the former had prospered through enclosure and agricultural improvement, as in Lincolnshire.[265]

As regards the leadership, Dr Field has the following findings:[266]

Of 347 West Riding trustees:

Manufacturers 66%   Agriculturalists 14%   Tradesmen 13%
Professional 3%   Gentry 2%   Labourers 1%

Of 111 local preachers (miscellaneous sample):

Artisans 63%   Professional 12%   Farmers 9%
Merchants and Shopkeepers 11%   Gentlefolk 3%   Unskilled 3%

Though exact comparisons are difficult, one sees once again the dominance of 'manufacturers' of all sorts, while the categories of professionals and tradesmen bulk rather larger, as one would expect for trustees of property or those attracted by part-time local preaching, as against the risks and hardships of the itinerant.

A few local examples help to show the exact occupations behind these rather imprecise blanket categories. A partial early list of Bristol members in 1741 includes hoopers, weavers, master mariners, carpenter, serge-maker, upholsterer, baker, tobacconist, bell founder, plasterer, linen draper, haberdasher, clerk and at least one merchant.

At Congleton in Cheshire in 1759 we find: three farmers, one grocer, one shoemaker, four silk weavers, one apothecary, two ribbon weavers, one wire worker, five women.

At Bingley in 1763: one gentleman, two farmers, one yeoman, two husbandmen, one shopkeeper, two cordwainers, four spinners, five stuff makers, six women, one warehouseman, two tailors, one plasterer, one physician, one servant, one 'old man', one labourer. This reflects a textile area with farming mixed in.

At Raithby, Lincs, in 1784 (which had that rarity, a Methodist squire): one esquire, two gentlemen, three farmers, one captain, one gardener, four spinsters, two labourers, one servant.

In the large London circuit there were more professional men, artisans, shopkeepers, army officers, government officials and a number of Protestant refugees.[267]

These lists represent a selective cross-section of distinctive communities: soldiers in garrison towns, seamen in ports, miners and textile workers in their areas. Always, however, there are individual converts among pious people in less common occupations. But, as Dr Field comments, the 'proletarian influence of early Methodism has been greatly exaggerated. Although three-quarters of the early membership were manual workers, unskilled labourers were heavily outnumbered by artisans.' As to the travelling preachers, their biographies show that they were generally drawn from the ranks of craftsmen and small tradesmen, and almost all were literate, though this was not always true of local preachers.[268] Nor, as has already been remarked, do the biographies at least bear out the picture of converts from the 'unchurched masses'; on the contrary, most converts seem to have a more or less marked religious background with early concerns about religion, though they also reveal a certain detachment from the church and periods of religious carelessness.[269]

However, two cautions are necessary here. One is that in dealing with membership lists we are dealing with the more or less strongly committed core of converts, whereas the biographies deal with a spiritual élite, however humble their worldly status. It is at least possible that the social as well as the religious background of the anonymous and emotional crowds at open-air preaching as well as the adherents outside membership contained different social groups, including the labouring poor. It is perhaps plausible to suppose that those most likely to be moved by ephemeral emotions and least likely to enter into committed membership and to stay the rigours of membership and its demands on time would be the poorer, less skilled, less literate. But they could still form a kind of semi-detached and floating fringe.

The second point is that the category of 'the poor' in the eighteenth century is itself an imprecise term. It could include the skilled as well as the unskilled, and men could all too easily rise and sink. The poor that Wesley begged for in times of distress (like the prospective emigrants to Georgia) were often tradesmen down on their luck. And perhaps Gregory King was not far wrong in his high estimate of the varied groups of people, whom he saw as subtracting from rather than adding to the national wealth (above, p. 5).

One final point is worth adding. It is not uncharacteristic of religious renewal movements in their early phases to overcome, to some degree, the normal divisions of the social hierarchy. This was partly true of early Methodism: hence the alarm of critics at lay preachers and the fears of a return to seventeenth-century chaos. In movements like Methodism, although trustees were liable to be drawn from the more affluent members of the congregation, even this was not always true; and choice of preachers and class leaders was essentially in terms of spiritual qualities. At Bingley a class including a farmer and shopkeeper was led by a weaver; and even gentlemen were supervised by their inferiors. Alexander Mather was minister to a society including his old employer. Outspoken lay preachers like Sammy Hick had no inhibitions in addressing the gentry about their souls and behaviour while he shoed their horses.[270] No doubt others were more restrained by rank, and

Methodism taught obedience to superiors. But there was always the significant proviso that in proclaiming salvation the preacher, like God, was no respecter of persons.

In many respects social rank was less important than social attitudes, which tended to set Methodists apart from their fellows whatever their rank. The official standards of conduct were in effect laid down by the Rules of the United Societies published in 1743 and supplemented by various injunctions from the Conference and from Wesley himself.[271] The simple rule of entry as a 'desire to flee from the wrath to come' had an extensive sting in the tail, in the shape of the details given of the 'evidence' of this to be shown in conduct. Methodists were both to avoid evil and to do good: the first went far to make them a peculiar people; the second outlined the nature of their social attitudes and social service.

Among the evils to be avoided were: swearing, profaning the Sabbath with business, drunkenness, fighting, going to law with brethren, buying or selling smuggled goods, giving or taking loans on usury (defined carefully as 'unlawful interest'). Then there is uncharitable conversation and speaking ill of magistrates; 'doing to others as we would not they should do to us'; wearing costly jewellery or clothes; 'diversions' which cannot be defended before Christ; singing songs and reading books not tending to the knowledge of God; laying up treasures on earth; buying goods that we cannot hope to pay for.

Positively, Methodists are to care for the hungry, naked and sick: exhorting and reproving those they have dealings with; doing good especially to 'the household of faith'; being diligent and frugal; denying themselves daily and expecting that men will say 'all manner of evil of thee falsely'. Finally, there are injunctions to attend all the Methodist means of grace.

The band rules were rather similar in tone, though adding specific bans on 'spirituous liquors', pawning one's possessions, needless ornaments such as rings and ruffles, and snuff or tobacco except as medicine, for they are 'needless self-indulgence' (saving for charity rather than a mere taboo). A general ban on marriage with unbelievers was at least attempted on pain of expulsion.[272]

Although there are parallels here with other churches (such as Baptists and Quakers), the source of much of this in both cases is an attempt at 'primitive Christianity', reflected in the Conferences of 1744 and 1745, when they debated how far they could invoke the law and swear oaths. Sampson Staniforth refused to be sworn as parish constable and was allowed to serve 'in the best manner he can, according to his own way of thinking'.[273] We have seen that at first there was even a scheme for primitive 'communism' (above, pp. 364f.).

How far such rules were generally observed it is impossible to say, but some examples are known. One of the most striking is that of Thomas Willis, a Kingswood farmer and colliery owner, who in 1744 wrote to Wesley minutely, detailing how far he obeyed the Band Rules and where he found difficulties. In general he followed the principle of doing to others as he would they should do to him, and doing all to the glory of God. He observed the Sabbath except for selling milk as a work of mercy; traded without haggling; took a little tobacco before going to bed only because it helped an 'infirmity', and gave one-sixth of his profits to the poor. He diligently fulfilled all the religious exercises, including fasting on Fridays.[274]

Dress caused much trouble, and in his later years Wesley became obsessive about it as the society became more wealthy. He inveighed against women's hats and wished that he had imposed a Quaker uniform, duly censuring also those subtle folks using plain but rich materials. The point of it all was to save for the poor, though Wesley allowed for decent distinctions of rank in dress.[275]

The same concern for the poor as well as health possibly dictated his early experiments in water-drinking and vegetarianism, though 'primitive' aspirations played a part here. The ban on spirits was for health reasons, but Wesley was not a teetotaller – as a movement distinct from private tastes or vows, this American invention (or heresy as some may perhaps view it) was only imported into England in the early nineteenth century.[276] In his later life at least, Wesley had a glass or two of wine to his dinner like most other people of his class, though he obviously avoided the bottle-exploits of many of his contemporaries.[277] Some of the more curious items in his correspondence in the light of later Methodist habits are those in which on the one hand he condemns tea drinking and on the other complains (like latter-day real-ale fanatics) about the adulteration of honest English ale. Giving up tea was certainly to set an example to poorer members of the society who indulged in an expensive habit, and Brother Charles complained how such abstinence damaged sociable gatherings. What is most remarkable is Wesley's description of what happened when they gave up the lethal leaf: trembling hands, drowsiness and so on, like mild symptoms of drug-withdrawal.[278]

It has often been claimed that Wesley and his movement transformed the whole of morality and social behaviour of – in short that they civilized – the barbarous communities they evangelized, such as Kingswood. This could seem to be evidenced by the dying down of riots and assaults on Methodism itself, though as we have seen there were other reasons for this. A year after he and Whitefield had begun preaching in Kingswood, Wesley claimed that cursing, blasphemy, drunkenness, 'wars and fighting' had been replaced with peace and love. This was certainly exaggerated except for the minority of converts. It is true that such claims were not just Methodist propaganda. Joseph Priestley the Unitarian, though critical enough of Wesley's credulity, gave a handsome tribute to Methodist religious and moral services. 'By you chiefly is the gospel preached to the *poor* in this country, and to you is the civilization, the industry and sobriety of great numbers of the laborious part of the community owing; though you are a body unknown to government, and look not for your reward from men.' Wesley had often, he said, described publicly in his hearing how religion had nothing to do with 'opinions' in religion, but that all religion was 'good morals' and that 'every one who had this object was his friend'. (Priestley had obvious reasons for emphasizing this last point, and Wesley's 'latitudinarianism' and 'ecumenicalism' was rather more restricted than this implied.)[279]

It is very doubtful whether Wesley could really claim to have morally transformed whole communities quite as completely as he implied. Something of the kind was possible, at least in the short term, in some of the more monocultural New England towns in times of revival because of a higher degree of common religious tradition than obtained in more complex and divided English society.[280] So far as Wesley and England are concerned, Kingswood is a good example for testing his claims. The Kingswood miners had a reputation for being 'an ungovernable people'. Here were combined the weaknesses of an area denied the usual restraints of squire, parson and farmer together with the notoriously unruly, riot-prone and clannish community of miners.[281]

One example of the Wesleyan claims was during grain riots in 1740, when it seems that some advocated negotiation, chastened by the presence of troops in Bristol. Charles Wesley, however, claimed that although 'our colliers' were forced to join the others, he was amazed at their orderly conduct. He claimed this for the gospel influence. The colliers did invade the city in 1753, but a modern student of their activities, R. W. Malcolmson, claims that each community (Bristol and Kingswood) had its own restraints and generally avoided such outright conflict, especially in the later eighteenth century. By 1768 Wesley was claiming that they had been transformed from Indian savages to a loving, civilized people. It seems that their isolation began to break down, and in the 1750s a friendly society was founded, characterized by provisions for good order and loyalty to the government. Malcolmson attributes some of these good effects to the fact that a minority of the colliers were given a new outlook and a new set of aspirations, bringing a message of compassion to a 'people who had stood alone'. If isolation had been part of the problem, Methodism certainly brought a new kind of community linked with the like-minded elsewhere, which they had hitherto lacked. The adaptation of the pagan new year to the watch night neatly symbolized part of what had happened. But it looks as though this was only one element in a changing situation, and clearly Methodism alone was not capable of stopping riots, as Halévy had supposed.

Some local customs were too deeply rooted in popular morality for Methodism to be an effective curb outside or indeed in some cases inside its own membership. Wrecking and smuggling were cases in point, for in some coastal areas these customs were regarded as legitimate and not criminal at all. Wesley saw wrecking as 'that scandal of Cornwall', but was told in 1776 that the Methodists would have nothing to do with it.[282] His *Word to a Smuggler* (1767) was a forthright condemnation which summed up a case made by him for many years past. But the repetitions are suggestive. In Sunderland in 1757 he had to expel several members who would not promise to avoid the practice, and the problem continued after his death. John Murlin said that there was little chance of doing good on the Isle of Man because it was a nest of smugglers. John Pritchard said that they did well in the inland towns of Norfolk in the 1770s but were much troubled with smugglers on the coast: even the justices would only protect the preachers on Sundays. Richard Trewanna, a Methodist attender, was only brought to drop smuggling after a narrow escape from death in 1770.[283] John Prickard also says that robbing wrecks was prevalent in Ireland and 'many of our people' were involved, so he expelled some as an example and to counter scandal on the people of God. They were to be restored only on restitution of their takings; he claimed that this had the desired effect. It is said, however, that some Cornish Methodists compromised by abstaining from the accursed thing on Sundays (Sunday ceasing at midnight!). As late as 1846 the offenders were said to include local preachers. A recent study concludes that the numbers involved in the practice and the general influence of Methodism on fishermen and miners suggest that many were able to reconcile wrecking and religion.[284]

Apart from the general claim that Methodism civilized and moralized the people, there was the often-repeated belief that its teaching and ethos induced habits of industry and frugality which led unwittingly to wealth. Wesley himself claimed this and in his later sermons, as we have seen, reflected on the irony involved, for he saw wealth as a threat to the soul. Since he still thought it good to get money for the sake of giving to the poor, his only solution to its snares was the repeated injunction to give it away (above, p. 367). Though their main aim was, as we have seen, to save their souls, Methodists seem often to have been effective in business, and it does seem to have been the case that discipline brought prosperity or at least steadiness. The story is often quoted of how Sir Robert Peel (father of the Premier) employed Methodists as his foremen for their reliability. Wesley himself visited Peel's works in 1787 with his 'children' (the itinerants), though he characteristically remarked that it would be a wonder if Peel did not lose his soul after making so much money.[285]

Individual examples are known of Methodists who rose from humble circumstances to affluence; though not all remained Methodists. At Manchester there were three leaders who began as packers and servants and rose to be merchants; and one, by a strange chain of inheritance, who actually began as a hatter and ended as Lord of the Manor and a baronet, though he turned from Methodism to Evangelicalism.[286] Although Methodists were not prominent as innovators, they do seem to have prospered by sheer industry, and if they followed Wesley's advice they may have been helped, like the Dissenters, by exploiting their Methodist connections.[287] What is not so obvious is whether the Weberian notion is correct that the ethos of Methodism helped (as Wesley seems to have supposed) or the increasing acceptability of Methodism attracted the more affluent or that the same personality types as were successful in business were also attracted by the ethos of Methodism. Probably all three factors were involved.

There were areas of life where the Methodist moral shibboleths helped to form the contours of a distinctive evangelical culture.[288] Plays, dancing and novels were generally taboo, although arguments about them prove there were differences of opinion. Wesley himself grudgingly admitted that though plays, balls and cards were not for him, they might be allowable for others. Some Methodists had already given such things up on their way to conversion; others only after it, since they found that they deterred from the spiritual life.[289] On dancing, the opinion was commonly expressed that if not evil in itself, it led to mixed company and conformity to the world; families teaching dancing to their children were supposed to be expelled.[290] The theatre was taboo partly because of the risk of immoral plays, but perhaps above all because of immoral company and mere worldliness again – the destruction of a Bristol theatre was seen as a divine judgment. But hostility to the theatre was common to extreme High Churchmen and Evangelicals: the best known treatise against the theatre was by a Nonjuror.[291] John Wesley was exceptional in allowing that even so virtuous a novel as Brooke's *Fool of Quality* was desirable reading; and Hannah More even more exceptional in writing one, highly moral though it was. Hannah was a good deal more sprightly than her early Evangelical biographer wished to reveal. But even Wesley only allowed that very few novels might be permissible for fear that their readers might want more.[292] The need for such strictures in the eighteenth as in the nineteenth century clearly suggests that some Methodists wanted these delights. But the biographical evidence of the élite shows a determined eschewing of them, and as we have seen, John Pawson, who burnt Wesley's copy of Shakespeare as rubbish, represents one common view among the preachers and rank and file.[293] The examples of some preachers and others making themselves into self-educated scholars or at least well-read people, as well as Wesley's reading lists for them and his advice to friends on reading, are impressive, but against this has to be set the reaction of some like Alexander Mather, who saw classical learning at least as an unnecessary diversion from preaching.[294] Reading should be serious and ultimately in the service of religion and morality, though one might allow poetry and history for 'recreation'. It has also been pointed out that the early Methodists seem to have had little appreciation of natural beauty, though some cases cited earlier suggest that conversion sometimes brought a sense of a world pervaded by God speaking through nature.[295]

Methodists, then, were officially exhorted to set themselves against the common diversions and pleasures of the world, and often (though not always) obeyed. They opposed feasts, wakes and festivals, and countered them with spiritual feasts of their own. They delighted to tell of 'judgments' against the ungodly who took part in dubious amusements, like the Anglican parson who died of a mortified toe after attending Chester Races. They did not even talk in a 'gay and diverting manner'.[296]

In compensation, whether or not Methodists had the profound civilizing effect claimed for them, they did do a substantial amount of social service.[297] It has already been pointed out that Wesley himself was a lover of the poor and frequently made efforts to relieve them, but also that in the main he gave verbal support rather than taking fresh initiatives of his own for work or campaigns in this area.[298] As Stuart Andrews has remarked, 'Methodist philanthropy was a personal philanthropy and thus much less conspicuous than the large-scale philanthropic enterprises of the age.'[299] There is a contrast here with the Clapham Sect which may owe something to Wesley's traditionalist and personalized approach as well as to the fact that the Claphamites were in a social position to organize their social equals in a more extensive way.[300] The Methodists operated at a social level where it was perhaps more natural to found local groups than metropolitan ones with national pretensions.

It has already been noted that when provoked by temporary subsistence crises, especially in London, Wesley led the Methodists in creating organizations for relief, some of which probably had a longer-term existence. It will be recalled that in 1740 a few people were employed for a time in carding and spinning to support themselves: an expedient echoing workhouse schemes for profitable employment of the poor. In 1746 a loan fund was established for helping deserving persons which was still in being in 1772. Visiting the sick also became a regular office. And there is evidence that pensions for some old members of society were used in some societies.[301] Wesley's example of offering medical advice and treatment to the poor was followed by some of the preachers. Indeed when they were finally stopped from engaging in trade, one of them had to cease making money from some 'drops' of his own devising.[302] Most widespread of all, perhaps, were local schools, some day schools, mostly Sunday schools, in which Hannah Ball at High Wycombe was a pioneer several years before Raikes. Mary Bosanquet ran a kind of charity school combined with an orphanage.[303]

There were in fact some local specialized religious charitable groups such as the Female Childhood Linen Society in Lambeth and the Female Clothing Society in Halifax.[304] In other cases Wesley commended existing philanthropic societies such as the 'Christian Community', originally founded by Huguenot refugees in 1685, but apparently reorganized by Wesley in 1772 when Methodists became interested in it.[305]

But the most distinctive and most specifically Methodist organization was the Stranger's Friend Society. Strictly speaking, this was not a national organization but rather several local societies in major towns, founded and run independently but probably in imitation of each other: Bristol was the first in 1787,[306] followed by London and Manchester. It is not in fact clear that they were all originally founded by Methodists, and they may in some cases have been taken over by them. The Poor and Stranger's Friend Society of Hull was probably Evangelical, and the Manchester SFS seems to have originated in a group of Methodists seceding from an Evangelical Anglican charity society when the parson in charge wanted to restrict it to Anglicans. At all events the distinctive feature of such societies became the fact that they were run by Methodists raising funds for the relief of non-Methodists, and not members of the Society. They claimed equally to relieve 'Protestants, Roman Catholics, Strangers and Foreigners'.[307]

Prison visiting, partly in hope of ministering to and converting condemned criminals before they hanged, has already been mentioned with reference to the redoubtable Silas Told. He was not alone, but those who did this work seem to have acted individually and not as part of an organization.[308] The anti-slavery campaign also engaged the support of many Methodists, in this case through the local committees in the larger provincial towns like Bristol, Liverpool and Manchester.

Many, for example, subscribed, and some were on the particularly radical committee at Manchester which pushed the petitioning campaign and sugar boycott in which some Methodists like Samuel Bradburn joined.[309]

Methodist activity in these areas reflects that wider movement of late eighteenth-century philanthropy which has more than one source, though evangelicals of various sorts became prominent in organizing it. It was characterized by religious as well as compassionate concern, and even when done by organized societies typically engaged members in direct personal visitation. Such organizing as took place seems to have arisen partly on Wesley's own initiative, and partly on local initiatives from below. Certainly Wesley paid less systematic attention to organized charity on the kind of national scale he operated for the Methodist system as a whole. Was this for lack of time or interest, or an inherited tradition of personal charity seen as a religious duty and discipline? It may be said, indeed, that his conception of Christian holiness, as indicated by his rules for the societies, gave plenty of encouragement for such work by individuals alongside the more negative and moralizing injunctions to curb vice and rebuke evildoers.

XII

'Horrible Decrees': Methodism in the 1770s and the Calvinistic Controversy

The 1770s were among the most troubled decades of Wesley's life. They included a running battle with his Calvinist critics; the beginning of the American troubles; increasing estrangement between Charles Wesley and some of the travelling preachers; and the subscription controversy, which enhanced suspicions among evangelicals that the Anglican clergy were unsound in the faith. The American problems, coupled with radical noises at home, provoked Wesley into political pamphleteering, and helped to sharpen the antagonism between him and the Calvinist groups. Age, pressure from the preachers and the American problem made him think more urgently than before of future arrangements for perpetuating the Methodist connexion – arrangements which would take definite shape in the 1780s. And all the time the self-sufficiency and self-confidence of the Methodists increased: the formal moves of the next decade were a reluctant and partial recognition of the drift towards a separate identity which had been growing for a long time.

1. The Calvinistic controversy: the later phase

What is loosely referred to as 'Calvinism' contained a number of related issues of which sometimes one, then another, came uppermost. The death of Christ for all or some, election or salvation open to all, salvation by faith or works, assurance and perfection all came into the picture. Time and again Wesley was swayed against Calvinist doctrine by what he took to be its inevitable consequences in antinomianism (neglect of the moral law) and its liability to deter people from actively seeking for salvation. His perfectionism was his favourite antidote to it and equally a prime cause of offence to Calvinists.[1]

As we have seen (above, pp. 197ff.), the first major conflict on the question blew up very early in the Revival between Wesley and

Whitefield and their followers. It was shown that this was more than a merely personal clash and involved the opposing religious instincts of their rank and file followers and other preachers. It helped to accelerate if not initiate the process by which Wesley's connexion became a distinct body, especially when coupled with the contemporaneous Moravian conflict which Wesley saw as producing the same bad symptoms as Calvinism.

Trouble with Calvinists and antinomians seems to have been more or less endemic among the evangelical groups at a local level: sometimes as a result of individual worries; sometimes under the influence of old Dissent; sometimes from the propaganda of roving preachers like Roger Ball, James Relly and William Cudworth.[2] The opinions on both sides appear to have come more from experience than from a deep knowledge of the historical literature on these ancient and intricate questions. Puritan practical literature was another important influence, though it often only clarified or fortified the experimental source.[3] Wesley himself was probably correct in ascribing the doctrines to converts' reflection on the experience of the power of God acting upon them independently of their own efforts.[4]

Wesley, who seems simply to have inherited an instinctive revulsion against Calvinism, probably had no profound knowledge of its scholastic literature as well as little sympathy with it. He published an extract from a life of Arminius in the *Magazine*, and in a tract of 1741 quotes with apparent learning from Calvin, Peter Martyr, Zanchius and Piscator.[5] But his first-hand knowledge of these is not beyond question. Augustus Montague Toplady was the most learned on the other side, and he certainly shows a considerable knowledge of Augustine and the late mediaeval controversialists like Bradwardine as well as of Calvin and Calvinist scholastics.[6] Indeed Leslie Stephen unkindly commented that he wrote and spoke as if he were still living in that earlier mental and intellectual world untouched by eighteenth-century challenges and 'enlightenment'. Calvin and Zanchius might as well have been his contemporaries, though he also related their theological ideas to philosophical necessity.[7] He was, however, well in line with contemporary views of religious toleration and, as we shall see, in favour of the cause of America and 'liberty', unlike Wesley.

The evolution of Wesley's own views has already been traced (above, pp. 74, 388). The discussions with his mother in 1725 simply show him to be a conventional High Church Arminian, though with some intellectual (rather than existential) problems about how to reconcile the Articles with Arminianism. As we have seen, he appears to have supposed for some years that certain individuals were elected infallibly to salvation but that everyone else was free to come to salvation if they chose to do so. He only abandoned this compromise in favour of salvation as open to all, on the same terms of faith, because anything less, he thought, gave away too much to the Calvinists. This had happened by the 1750s, and seems to have been provoked by some Irish preachers who thought that he and Charles were akin to Whitefield because of their earlier hybrid position.[8] He more or less accepted the label 'Arminian', though carefully defending this from the sinister implications of unorthodoxy on the Trinity and undue dependence on human effort.[9] By the 1770s he was boldly, if not always plausibly, claiming that Scripture and the Articles rule against predestination, though conformity to the Articles on this point was always a strong point in the Anglican Calvinists' case and one which Wesley had obviously found difficult in 1725.[10]

The next major literary controversy in which Wesley was involved after the 1740s was in the mid-1750s in response to James Hervey, formerly one of his 'Holy Club' colleagues at Oxford.[11] Hervey was a consumptive, a devoted parish Evangelical clergyman, and the author of some florid but popular devotional works like *Meditations among the Tombs* (1746–7): an attempt to reproduce the 'faded charms' of the Shaftesbury school of eloquence for 'the more refined classes'.[12] One cannot easily believe that Wesley could have found the style much to his taste. However, his quarrel with Hervey, pursued beyond the latter's death, arose over another work, *Theron and Aspasio*, which he had asked Wesley to revise in 1755.[13] Fortunately the details of the unedifying wrangle which followed need not concern us here. Not for the first or last time, Wesley gave the impression of double-dealing and of making public what should have been kept as a private correspondence. His own account was that he had suggested alterations but received no reply, and therefore felt free to publish his criticisms of Hervey's views. Hervey is supposed to have prepared a response and given it to William Cudworth – a Calvinist enemy of Wesley's – to publish, but then to have asked him not to do so. Hervey's brother, however, went ahead after Hervey's death, and the published work (1765) contained some severe criticisms of Wesley's views and character and his lack of theological consistency – a point on which Wesley was always very sensitive and defensive. It should certainly not be taken for granted that Wesley was without fault in this affair.

Theron and Aspasio was a series of dialogues between a man of morality and a Christian, spelling out the conventional evangelical line on original sin and the work of Christ but more especially (and this was what aroused Wesley) the doctrine of the 'imputed righteousness' of Christ which gives us salvation. Though this did not directly raise the prime offence in Wesley's eyes of 'election', it was a doctrine which he had already discussed and criticized in the 1740s and 1750s.[14] It was in fact these onslaughts that persuaded Hervey's brother to publish Hervey's book. To put a difficult point simply, Wesley saw the doctrine as unscriptural, unnecessary and in fact misleading and dangerous. It implied, he thought, that sinners were viewed by God as being still sinners but clothed by a kind of legal fiction in the protective righteousness of Christ. This left them without any real, inherent righteousness which might be cultivated towards the achievement of real holiness and ultimate perfection. For Calvinists, however, such 'imputation' was an essential safeguard against trust in one's own goodness and merits as being capable of winning the divine favour, and to them Wesley was falling back into Popish notions of 'works'. Technical though the point was, it related to the whole Calvinist conception of salvation and clashed violently with Wesley's views. Hence his objections were not simply gratuitous trouble-making.

The perfectionist outbreaks of the 1760s, Wesley's defence of them and the reasoned development of his doctrine of perfection with its combination of sudden grace and progressive preparation both disgusted and alarmed the Calvinists and even offended such old colleagues as Grimshaw. Then came a sequence of events which precipitated several years of literary warfare. In 1768 came the notorious affair of the St Edmund Hall students in Oxford who were expelled for their 'Methodism'. As we have seen, they were in fact Calvinistic rather than 'Wesleyan', and the affair was partly influenced by hostility between the Principal (who had some sympathy with evangelical aims) and the Vice Principal, John Higson.[15] In the pamphlet war which followed, one important piece was *Pietas Oxoniensis* by the Calvinist Richard Hill, a member of an important political family in Shropshire. In this he claimed that their chief offence had been to uphold the Calvinistic and true doctrines of the Church of England, a claim rejected by Dr Nowell. In answer to Nowell, Toplady published his *Church of England Vindicated* (1769).[16]

It seems that it was in the wake of this affair that Wesley and Lady Huntingdon had increasing difficulty in placing their protégés in Oxford, and therefore both drew up plans for higher education of their own, Wesley in his scheme for an 'academical' course at Kingswood; Lady Huntingdon for her college to train ministers at Trevecka.[17] Trevecka was opened in August 1768, and by 1791 had educated at least 191 students, if only for short periods.[18] John Fletcher, the Evangelical Vicar of Madeley and a close associate of Wesley's, became President, visiting it when he could. Joseph Benson, formerly at Wesley's Kingswood School, soon became headmaster. This is not as surprising as it may seem, for despite all the friction with the Calvinists, Lady Huntingdon had worked hard in the 1760s to bring about co-operation between evangelicals of all sorts, though by now Wesley had given up hopes of a 'union'.[19] As to the lady herself – she had been an Arminian and even defended perfection in the early 1740s, but it looks as though her increasingly close patronage of Whitefield since 1749 had led her into the Calvinist camp – as a devout lay person she felt the need of clerical guidance.

But relations in the college soon turned sour. Wesley was in no mood to think well of Calvinist Evangelicals. When Fletcher complained of his lack of edification from regenerate people, Wesley replied that he was not surprised if he mixed with gentry of the Calvinist sort, even Whitefield: no good could come of preaching about 'absolute decrees' and 'infallible perseverance', nor could it come from 'genteel' Christians (a hit at Lady Huntingdon's circle); and he did not think much of the Trevecka scheme. He complained that it was '*my* college, *my* masters, *my* students' all the way.[20] Wesley compared Trevecka unfavourably with his own Kingswood foundation and his relationship to it; but he was as authoritarian as Lady Huntingdon was, and one cannot help suspecting that Lady Huntingdon's biographer may have been right, and that Wesley was jealous that she had a 'seminary for labourers' and had taken two of his lieutenants for it into the bargain.

Then in 1770, the storm broke, for Wesley's growing disquiet at the aftermath of the St Edmund Hall affair, Toplady's contribution and Wesley's distaste for Calvinist piety finally led him to produce the Conference Minutes of 1770 (above, pp. 391f.). It will be recalled that even in 1744 the Conference averred that they had inclined too much to antinomianism in their enthusiasm for the new doctrine of justification by faith alone, and much was said then about the relationship between faith and works, justification and sanctification. Now, after years of running controversy with the Calvinists and a growing and recent body of experience about the need and possibility of the pursuit of perfection by faith and action, Wesley stated his position on the disputed points with far less caution.[21] Not only did he emphasize the goal of holiness with an enhanced role for works, but he impatiently dismissed what Calvinists regarded as essential technical points about 'merit' as being mere hair-splitting and 'disputes about words'. This echoed the attitude a few years earlier in his solitary meditations in his coach.[22] What matters is the achievement of holiness whatever the means. To a Calvinist he seemed to be allowing merit to works, that we are saved at least partly by our works, even if this depends in some ultimate sense on grace. In all his oscillations between Calvinism and Pelagianism (never, indeed, ever reaching either extreme), this was the point at which Wesley came nearest to the latter position. What is most impressive is the way in which, though still struggling with the inherited language and definitions of the debaters on grace and works, he made a partial breakthrough to a position based on observation and experience of those who had, by various means, achieved the fruits of faith – to some extent even before conversion, and sometimes (like William Law) while actually denying the sovereign doctrine of justification by faith. But to his opponents this was a denial of all that the Reformation and the Revival stood for, a reversion to an unsound 'works' Anglicanism, indeed to 'Popish' salvation by works.

Several effects immediately followed. Benson had already had trouble with Calvinists at Trevecka. Now he defended the Minutes, but the Countess, having read them, banned Wesley from her pulpits.[23] Wesley urged Benson to hold fast, but the Countess dismissed him in January 1771, though with a good testimonial.[24] Fletcher tried to make peace, but found that Walter Shirley had been opposing his doctrine of a special baptism of the Holy Spirit in association with perfection. Those not attacking the Minutes were now to be expelled. So he finally resigned.[25] As an irenical gesture he recommended moderate Calvinists as possible successors, though one of them was in fact the rigorist Rowland Hill.[26]

It was while the row over the Minutes was beginning to boil up that Whitefield died on his last preaching tour in America, on 30 September 1770. Wesley then preached what became a notorious memorial sermon for him in London in November.[27] This worsened the controversy, for Wesley dwelt only on the doctrines they held in common – the new birth and justification by faith – saying that they had agreed to differ on other matters and had preserved brotherly love. It is possible, as Tyerman suggests, that this was not only a tribute to a genuine kindliness of spirit between them but also an olive branch to the critics of the Minutes. Some, however, have found it hard to reconcile the Minutes with the sermon and Wesley's private strictures on the Calvinists, including Whitefield, and hence accuse him of deliberate misrepresentation: a view certainly held by critics at the time, who thought that he falsified, or at least glossed over, Whitefield's true beliefs.[28] Though Wesley did echo Whitefield's reconciling spirit, it is hard to believe that Whitefield could have approved of Wesley's recent position in the Minutes, and in the context of the controversy Wesley was causing great offence, even if unwittingly.

Although it is clearly a mistake to imply, as has sometimes been done, that it was the memorial sermon that touched off the controversy of the 1770s, Whitefield's death was a blow which removed one of the few reconciling spirits on the question. But his survival would hardly have made any difference to Toplady and his cohorts. The Minutes were more offensive than anything that Wesley had offended Whitefield by publishing in the 1740s, and perhaps one can only reflect that Whitefield was fortunate in the day of his death, since otherwise he might well have faced a public and even permanent breach with his old colleague.

Walter Shirley and Lady Huntingdon proposed to hold a meeting of their supporters at Bristol to coincide with Wesley's Conference there in August 1771. They also proposed, since the Minutes were subversive of 'the very *fundamental* principles of Christianity', to go in a body to the Methodist Conference; to insist on a formal recantation of the offending Minutes; and in case of a refusal to sign a protest against them.[29] In the event the two parties met, and Wesley and fifty-three of the preachers signed a revised version of a document produced by Shirley, though Thomas Olivers refused. This declaration stated that the Minutes were not intended to uphold the doctrine of justification by works, and as they had been unguarded in the words used, it was declared that the authors 'had no confidence but in the alone merits of our Lord and Saviour Jesus Christ for justification or salvation either in life, death or the day of judgment; and though no one is a real Christian believer . . . who doth not good works, where there is time and opportunity, yet our works have no part in meriting or purchasing our salvation from first to last, either in whole or in part.' (The word 'salvation' is replaced by 'justification' in another version – a point of importance in the controversy which followed, when Fletcher certainly taught the necessity of works for final salvation.)[30]

On the face of it this represented a retreat from the emphasis on the necessity of good works in the Minutes, but whatever hope this offered of a reconciliation was wrecked by Wesley's action in printing a manuscript by Fletcher defending the original Minutes, despite Shirley's protests. Moreover, he said that the Minutes were 'no way contrary to that great truth of justification by faith', which Shirley certainly thought they were. Typically, Wesley claimed that they represented what he had taught for thirty or forty years and that if they had been at fault his work would not have prospered: the old test of experience once more.[31] Fletcher backed this up by claiming that Calvinism led to antinomianism and that consequently good works needed to be stressed.

The main protagonists in the literary warfare which followed were, on the Arminian side, principally Fletcher in his six *Checks to Antinomianism*, with some contributions from Wesley and from his protégé Walter Sellon, a travelling preacher who had taken orders, plus Thomas Olivers, one of the preachers. On the Calvinist side the main writers were Toplady and Richard Hill. These two indulged in a good deal of personal abuse of Wesley ('the old fox', as Toplady termed him), but Wesley, though disdaining such 'dirty' work, was quite happy to allow Sellon and Olivers to sling the mud for him. Fletcher wrote strongly but with more good temper. And Wesley himself indulged in a ploy which reduced Toplady to gibbering fury by summing up his *Zanchius* translation:

> The sum of all is this. One in twenty (suppose) of mankind are elected; nineteen in twenty are reprobated. The elect shall be saved, do what they will; the reprobate shall be damned, do what they can. Reader, believe this or be damned. Witness my hand, A – T –.[32]

This Toplady regarded as a perversion of the original, crowned by an outright forgery. It certainly represented Wesley's long-standing short way with Calvinists, and in a peculiarly offensive format.

It is impossible, and probably unprofitable, to pursue the controversy in its wearisome, blow-by-blow dissection of opponents' arguments and counter-arguments. The main issues can, however, be indicated.[33] Fletcher's *Checks* were perhaps the most solid products, though Toplady was perhaps the most learned of the protagonists: judgments on who got the best of the argument tend to depend on the judge's sympathies. Fletcher was certainly well-fitted to be Wesley's bulldog, for unlike Wesley, or indeed his opponents, he had been reared in the Continental Reformed tradition of theology, and had only at an unknown point during his subsequent residence in England turned to Arminianism.[34]

In the *First Check* Fletcher defended Wesley against the charge of Pelagianism, but while stressing that justification is a gift from God he said that repentance and the works of repentance are necessary. Since Shirley had asserted that the 'Declaration was necessary to give the correct meaning to the Minutes of 1770', Fletcher in his *Second Check* (1771) tried to reconcile the two statements. In particular he claimed that they had not renounced the doctrine of a 'second justification' – by works – which alone fits us for favourable judgment at the last day and is the necessary completion of the 'first justification' by faith. To deny this second justification is to fall into antinomianism.

Hill then joined in, and accused Wesley of teaching that works are meritorious, so that Wesley was a Pelagian. This provoked Fletcher's *Third Check* (1772). Here he dismissed irresistible grace, defended free will and defined four degrees of justification, once again stressing that salvation begins by God's grace, but needs man's subsequent co-operation for completion.

To this Hill rejoined in a *Review* of Wesley's doctrines (1772) that he taught justification by works, whereas works are only 'declarative evidence' of justification (the stock Reformation line) now and at the end, so that there is no place for a 'second justification' by works. He also denied the Wesleyan doctrine of perfection, which he shrewdly observed to depend upon a distinction between 'sins' and 'infirmities' and (a peculiarly damaging blow to Wesley) to lead to antinomianism.

He then listed statements by Wesley at various periods of his life to show his errors and inconsistencies. Wesley's *Remarks* in reply attempted in his best Oxford point-scoring and casuistic style to wriggle out of these traps by ascribing many of them to extracts from the *Christian Library* or to his brother Charles and others. Hence he could not be held responsible for them. As the Calvinists quite reasonably felt, this was a lame defence, since he habitually edited and bowdlerized these publications and must be presumed to have approved what he left.[35] In any case he reasserted the offensive notion that he could not distinguish between salvation 'according to our works' and 'as our works deserve'.

What the Calvinists suspected and plainly stated (for example Rowland Hill, Richard's brother, against Fletcher) was that Wesley and company were reasserting the Council of Trent's balanced Catholic view of salvation as the product of a co-operative enterprise between the grace of God and the good works and efforts of man.

Late in 1772 Fletcher published his *Logica Genevensis*, in which he tried to show that 'the law can be fulfilled evangelically by love, and this furthermore is Christian Perfection'.[36] And once again he expounded his notion of a second justification by works. This, he claimed, could not be reconciled with the Calvinist notion of an 'imputation' only of Christ's righteousness. But he added that man's freewill was not 'natural' – like Wesley he attributed it to 'prevenient grace', that expedient to escape both determinism and Pelagianism.

In a more technical vein Thomas Olivers, *A Scourge to Calumny* (1774), tried to revive the old categories of mediaeval and Reformation scholasticism by defending Wesley's views on merit as merit *de congruo* only (a reward exceeding the work) and not as merit *de condigno* (a reward proportional to the work). This can hardly have impressed the opposition with its flavour of old 'Popish' logic-chopping.

Fletcher's *Equal Check* (1774–5) attempted to be a reconciling gesture 'as much in behalf of free grace as of holiness'.[37] But his *Last Check* (1775) returned to his favourite subject of Christian perfection as 'the cluster of maturity of graces which compose the Christian character in the Church militant' – above all perfect love; and like Wesley he allowed for 'infirmities'.

Meanwhile there was a subsidiary controversy between Wesley and Toplady on necessity and freewill in which each tried to relate their theological positions to contemporary philosophical positions such as that of David Hartley. On a subject of this nature one must say that Toplady showed superior intellectual power. Wesley had in effect to solve the intellectual problems involved by invoking God's omnipotence to solve all problems.[38]

Fletcher continued the argument against Toplady, expounding justification by faith and works yet again and adding an exposition of his views on God's successive 'dispensations' for good measure.[39] And Wesley added his *Thoughts upon God's Sovereignty* (1777), in which he tried to combine God's absolute sovereignty with provision for freewill and God's role as an impartial judge who will not condemn for acts men could not avoid.[40] Finally, in 1778, he founded the *Arminian Magazine* as an organ to counter Calvinist publications, though as we have seen, it became a more general vehicle for educating the Methodists.

Purely in theological terms, the controversy may be regarded as inevitable; and it left the protagonists in the same entrenched positions at which they had started. Men are seldom converted to the opposite view in such controversies, which only serve to harden the lines of division; indeed in this case, along with other developments, the controversies helped to make the differences between 'Wesleyan' Methodists and the rest more distinct in the 1780s. The conflict was inevitable in the sense that all revivals of a strong doctrine of grace produce predestinarian views, and as we have seen, these were characteristic of most bodies in the Revival. Wesleyan propaganda, Methodist numerical success and the general decline of Calvinism later have helped to obscure this historical fact. Yet it is also true that this was not the hyper-Calvinism of beleaguered Baptists, for the practical 'Arminian accent' of offering the gospel to all was characteristic of both sets of protagonists; and on the other side the Methodists certainly saw themselves as upholding the claims of grace against Anglican perverters of the Reformation, despite Wesley's tortuous attempts to combat antinomianism.

Through the fog of vituperation and fine-drawn distinctions certain issues stand out. Wesley, in his thoroughly eighteenth-century instinct for the divine benevolence and human free will, and his obsessive search for holiness, went to great lengths to preserve the need for human effort. It had always been the weakness of the Calvinist and Lutheran traditions that they could never quite dispel the suspicion that election was unjust and that extreme views of justification by grace through faith led to antinomianism. But the sense of human weakness and of the almighty power and grace of God led the eighteenth-century Calvinists to have a deep suspicion of Wesley's devices for securing the drive to holiness and above all of his incredibly optimistic claims (as they saw it) about the achievement of perfection in this life.

To defend their positions, both sides were led into reviving parts of the old scholastic modes and definitions. Wesley, as we have seen, tried to preserve the framework of salvation by grace through justification by the notion of 'prevenient grace'; and by assimilating his stress on works to the notions of grades of justification and a full-blown 'second justification', apparently by works rather than grace and faith. Or at least Fletcher certainly did this, and Wesley seemed at least partly to endorse it. This was a desperate expedient, and ironical, in that in his earlier years Wesley had condemned just such notions in Bishop Bull, who in the late seventeenth century had produced by these means a view of salvation very like that of the Catholic Council of Trent. There were in fact precedents for the notion of 'double justification' in the Reformed tradition as far back as Calvin, though with the vital qualification that the good works needed for final salvation were 'imputed' only through Christ – Wesley's bugbear in his conflicts with Zinzendorf and Hervey.[41] But to Calvinists the Wesley and Fletcher version looked simply Popish and Pelagian. And if Whitefield and Venn, like Calvin before them, could speak in positive and passionate terms about the pursuit of holiness, they were always conscious of its dependence on grace alone, and were subject to the suspicion that in the end it was all 'imputed', and that perfection was a dirty and dangerous word.[42] Yet Wesley and Fletcher were not abandoning justification by faith; the difference between them and the old Reformers and the eighteenth-century Calvinists was that for them it had become the door into the pilgrimage of holiness rather than the Lutheran cradle suspending the sinner precariously by faith throughout life, or the Calvinist promise of final perseverance. It was not the real centre of their Christian existence to the same extent as for their critics.

Crow, sympathizing with the Calvinist position, sees Wesley as being in the tradition of the Anglican *via media* between mere Arminianism and mere Calvinism, pioneered by Hooker.[43] There is truth in this, but neither Wesley nor his opponents, despite their debts to traditional theologies and their use of them in polemic, were really simply living in the past. They were touched by the spirit of the moralizing and humanistic eighteenth century. This is most obvious in Wesley's impatience with scholastic categories; his pursuit of actual moral achievement; and his appeal to the lessons of experience. It is less obvious in the Calvinists, but Toplady and the Hills were not the sum total of their attitudes. As Dr Walsh has pointed out, a number of them were very moderate Calvinists and some, like some of the Methodist preachers, disliked taking sides in these controversies, feeling like Henry Venn that they were crucified between 'ranters clamouring for instant perfection' and 'antinomian abusers of grace'.[44] And the hyper-Calvinists were not wrong in detecting an 'Arminian accent' in Whitefield; as we have seen, they found the same in the Fullerite Baptists. The Revival softened the hard edges of Calvinism. Yet important though this was for the future of the Revival and the decline of the Calvinist tradition, Wesley's perfectionism, for all its inconsistencies, pointed the way towards a much more drastic revision of the centre of gravity of

Protestantism than his critics could stomach. His repeated efforts to make sense of his concerns, which were essentially practical, in terms of traditional Protestant theology were doomed to failure.[45]

Semmel, as we have seen (above, p. 377) speculated about the fact that while the Arminian Wesleyans and the Calvinist Evangelicals were locked in their theological struggle they were also on opposite sides in the 1770s on the American quarrel and the agitations for English 'liberty'. Whether a clear connection between the theological and political ideologies can be established seems doubtful. Semmel, of course, would like to see Wesleyan theology as an unconscious source for nineteenth-century liberal ideology. In historical terms, however, High Church Arminianism had been associated with seventeenth-century absolutist tendencies, and Puritan Calvinism with the overthrow of the monarchy. We have already seen how Wesley retained his stance on non-resistance and transferred it to the Hanoverian dynasty and how, in the troubled 1770s, he publicly chastized the rebels at home and abroad. On this question the Calvinists like Toplady and some Dissenters certainly sided with the Americans, and Wesley and Fletcher were not slow to draw the moral that this was a reversion to seventeenth-century rebellious type on both sides of the Atlantic. In fact the most radical of the Dissenters were men who, like Priestley, had long since abandoned Calvinism, though it may be thought significant that he had adopted a kind of secularized Calvinism in his philosophical necessitarianism.[46] But even Semmel admits that the Whig proclivities of the Anglicans arose from political reasons not particularly connected with their theology. In fact the most obvious reason why Fletcher and Toplady injected a dose of political conflict into their polemics was as a handy stick with which to beat their opponents. One should perhaps not try to be too subtle in finding inner connections between these two sets of prejudices, even though Wesley himself gave religious reasons for his politics.

2. The 1770s: the subscription controversy and plans for the future

If cries of 'liberty' helped to sharpen the Calvinist controversy, there were other areas in which religious toleration in particular could be pursued in ways unwelcome to evangelicals. We have already seen (above, pp. 309ff) how gestures towards relaxing Roman Catholic disabilities could lead Wesley into an otherwise untypical fit of intolerance. The way in which eighteenth-century instincts towards tolerance could consort uneasily with concern for orthodoxy also comes out in reactions to moves for relaxing clerical and university subscription to the Articles and Prayer Book.[47]

Proposals had been made in the 1750s for relaxation in subscription, as also for alterations in the liturgy. In 1766 Archdeacon Blackburne's *Confessional* in effect advocated abolition of subscription to the Articles, liturgy and creeds and in 1771, on his instigation, a meeting was held in the Feathers Tavern in London to draw up a petition to Parliament for abolition of subscription for Anglican clergy. The grounds for this were said to be that the Reformation stood for the natural rights of Christians to judge for themselves what could be proved from Scripture, and that they should not be bound by anything but the Scriptures alone. Some 250 signatures were obtained, but the petition was rejected by 217 to 71 in the Commons in 1772 and again in 1773 and 1774. At about the same time there was a similar move to abolish subscription in favour of a declaration of faith in the Bible at Cambridge, and some relaxation was allowed. Moves for liturgical reform were frustrated by the bishops.

What lay behind this? It was very generally suspected that the pressure came mainly from clergy tainted with heterodox views on the Trinity, a problem which had troubled a number of Anglicans and, as we have seen, a large proportion of Presbyterians, throughout the century. The Toleration Act did not allow for anti-Trinitarianism, and indeed even Dissenting ministers had to subscribe to the doctrinal part of the Articles. But since the Salter's Hall affair, an increasing number of Presbyterians and General Baptists had moved into Arian views and some, like a number of Anglicans, towards a more full-blooded Unitarianism. When the Feathers Tavern petition was rejected, a few clergy like Theophilus Lindsey honourably left to reinforce Unitarian Dissent. Although Dissenting subscription to part of the Articles may not have been universally enforced, there were moves in the 1770s to abolish it; in 1779 this was achieved, and once again the Presbyterian lead in the campaign seemed suspicious.

In fact the pressures behind these campaigns were mixed in character. Like some of the Salter's Hall Dissenters years before, some orthodox as well as heterodox Anglicans thought that Protestants whose religion was based on the Bible alone should not be bound by the words of men – Bishop Watson, it will be remembered, thought that theology should come from this source alone and not from the musty metaphysics of ancient doctors; Archbishop Herring and Archdeacon Blackburne held similar views.[48] The university agitation was partly informed by the feeling that toleration demanded relaxation for the sake of Dissenters. On the other side fears of heterodoxy were mixed with the belief that religious toleration need not extend to equality, which might damage the position of the Establishment, so intimately bound up with the integrity of the constitution; and in Oxford those for and against the relaxation of subscription tended to conform to Whig and Tory alignments of various degrees of intensity.[49]

What was the attitude of the Evangelicals and Methodists to all this? The subject has not been much explored, but there are indications of their feelings. Wesley's only comments on Blackburne refer to his tract on toleration for Papists, together with an opinion in the 1780s that the Archdeacon had decayed physically more than himself – probably through excluding the Methodists from his pulpit![50] But Tyerman, interestingly, sees Wesley's tracts on 'Liberty' and 'The Origins of Power' in 1772 in the context of the Feathers Tavern and Dissenting subscription agitations.[51] In fact the immediate occasion seems to have been the Wilkesite agitation, though he does defend English religious liberty as being so extensive that anyone who 'bawls for more religious liberty must be totally void of shame'.[52] Wesley seems to make no direct reference to the religious agitation, though Fletcher refers to it when proposing a scheme for reorganizing Methodism to be considered in a moment. Wesley, he thought, would be more likely than the Feathers Tavern gentlemen to reform without corrupting.[53] It is, indeed, probably no accident that Wesley's sermon on the Trinity (preached by request in Cork in 1775) should have been given at this time. As we have seen, he defended the 'fact' of the doctrine without speculating on the details. I have argued elsewhere that it is also significant that it was in this decade that a cluster of Methodist visions of the Trinity began to appear.[54]

The attitude of Lady Huntingdon and certain Evangelicals is more explicit and in some respects surprising. They were clearly troubled by the anti-Trinitarian associations of the agitation, and indeed Thomas Scott, an Evangelical with an unusually 'intellectual' type of conversion, seems to have been led into a further stage of the conversion process by reflection on the subject of the agitation.[55] Lady Huntingdon is described by her biographer as supporting the widest measure of religious liberty 'compatible with the public tranquillity', but as objecting to the principles of the Feathers Tavern group. In fact she exercised herself in organizing opposition to it, though in the event it was introduced into the House by Sir William Meredith, the brother-in-law of her murderous relative Lord Ferrars. However, she supported the Dissenters' petition of 1773, despite the opposition of Evangelical clergy and her own distaste for the Dissenters' religious and political opinions. Most surprisingly, she actually urged Theophilus Lindsey to remain in the church.[56]

Toplady's views are also of interest. He argued, like Burke and Lady Huntingdon, that subscription was perfectly proper for clergy in the church – after all they could go elsewhere. But he thought that the universities should allow degrees for Dissenters at least in law and medicine; and, more surprisingly, that the Toleration Act should allow for Unitarianism.[57] Here, once again, can be seen the powerful effects of the eighteenth-century Lockeian tradition of toleration which eroded the old harsh dogmatism, stopping short only at the undermining of the Anglican hegemony, or the kind of political and religious prejudices still clinging to the special case of Roman Catholics, as with John Wesley. But it seems clear that in all this the question of religious liberty was being influenced and compromised by contemporary agitations on political 'liberty', seen as demagogic and 'democratical'.

To complete the picture of this decade we have to consider Wesley's problems with the internal state of Methodism, which included the status of the travelling preachers and their relationship to Wesley's ordained associates. But with this was associated the old spectre of ordination and the increasing pressure on the ageing Wesley to make it clear what he proposed should become of Methodism and its organization after his death. Here it is best to take events in their chronological order, beginning where the earlier description of his relations with the Church of England left off, in the early 1760s.

Wesley continued to face both ways. On the one hand he still insisted that he would never leave the church; that Methodists should attend it. But on the other hand there was his strong sense of the continuing providential mission of the movement which should not be given up but should be kept united; and above all there was the pressure from below which led so many Methodists into practically abandoning the church. (Some even spoke of 'The Methodist Church' as early as 1763.) Hence Wesley was led steadily to consolidate his organization and to contemplate what ought to be done when he died.[58]

In 1760 John Haime reported that Wesley told the Conference that after his death the assistants (senior preachers in each circuit) should form a 'council' to settle matters. In the 1760s more and more preaching houses were licensed, though seldom using the term 'Methodist'. In 1763 Wesley's model deed for controlling the houses placed the succession after himself and his brother in Grimshaw, followed by 'the Yearly Conference of the People called Methodists'. In 1764 had come the episode of the dubious Greek bishop, and at the 1766 Conference Wesley had to justify his authority by the retrospective account of how he had acquired it (above, pp. 247f.).

It was in August 1769 that Wesley finally gave up dreams of an evangelical union as a 'rope of sand' and speculated on what would happen to the Methodists when he had gone. Perhaps a quarter of the preachers would take church orders; some would turn Independent. The rest should make 'a firm union', which might be done if all the travelling preachers met in London after his death, drew up articles of agreement, and dismissed those who refused them. They should choose a committee of three, five or seven, each being Moderator in turn. To lay a foundation for this now, they should perhaps draw up articles of agreement to 'devote ourselves entirely to God . . . to preach the old Methodist doctrines . . . to observe . . . the whole Methodist discipline', as in the *Large Minutes*.[59]

Yet this model, which in a sense anticipates the collective leadership with a changing president which did emerge, co-existed in Wesley's mind with the notion of a single successor who would have to be, like himself, a clergyman. This seemed to be the implication of the clerical succession in the Model Deed, and Grimshaw's death in 1763 raised a problem here. Charles Wesley was clearly unreliable, unwilling and increasingly unacceptable to the preachers. By 1773 John seems to have decided (by reason or inspiration?) that Fletcher was the man. Realistically, he wrote that some such person was essential since 'the body of preachers are not united, nor will any part of them submit to the rest; so that either there must be one to preside over all or the work will indeed come to an end'. So – 'Thou art the man!' He listed Fletcher's qualifications: his holiness, his knowledge of Methodism and even (with remarkable optimism in view of Fletcher's condition) his health. He should begin to be a coadjutor now to accustom the preachers to his position; and in his most confident tones Wesley claimed that God would give Fletcher what was needed. Fletcher held back, doubting a call to leave his parish as yet, and perhaps conscious of the difficulty of the preachers' attitude. Wesley said: 'He will not come out unless the Lord shall baptize him for it.'[60] Thus frustrated, Wesley fell back on perfecting the union of the preachers, and the Conferences of 1773–5 signed agreements on the lines suggested in 1769. But he did not give up the idea of a clerical head. According to Charles Wesley, Mark Davis, a former itinerant now ordained, might do the job, and he was paid for a time to work in London, but found unsatisfactory. But Charles also seemed to imply that Fletcher was now prepared to take on the leadership after Wesley's death, if only temporarily.[61] Or was this merely alarmed and wishful thinking on his part?

It was perhaps just as well that the Fletcher experiment was not tried, since he died before John Wesley. Even if his health could have sustained the burden, no one could inherit John Wesley's unique authority as founder, and it is doubtful whether Fletcher's style of leadership would have been effective for controlling the day-to-day running of a complex, widespread and restive organization. At Trevecka Fletcher had disrupted classes in favour of holiness meetings; and at the Conference of 1784 dissensions were resolved by Fletcher's passionate appeal for loyalty, which dissolved those involved in tears. But this was not a practicable way for ordinary occasions.[62]

The problem of succession suddenly became much more urgent in 1775. During the Spring Wesley, while in Ireland, had been struck down by illness, seemed likely to die, and had only recovered by what seemed to be literally a miracle.[63] Joseph Benson then proposed a new plan, perhaps influenced also by his own disappointed hopes for an Oxford education and ordination.[64] An inquiry should be made into the character and qualifications of all the preachers. Suitable ones should then be ordained by the Wesleys and their clerical colleagues which would make them more attached to the church, more united and more settled in their authority. The rest should either be dismissed or, where suitable, trained at Kingswood.[65]

Benson submitted the scheme to Fletcher, who approved of purging the preachers, but doubted whether the Kingswood scheme would answer; and while Methodist ordination might increase unity, it would cut them off from 'the churches of England and Scotland, which we are called to leaven'. Nor could the Wesleys decently 'turn bishops' when they had so often said they would stay by the church. They should at least try first whether the bishops would ordain the preachers, even though there would be no response. Wesley apparently allowed Benson to air his plan at Conference without result.

Fletcher now proposed a plan of his own (it was this that he recommended to show that Wesley was a better reformer than the Feathers Taverners). Methodism should be formed into 'a general society and a daughter church of our holy mother' and should only 'secede' from the church in respect of 'palpable defects'. It should be the 'Methodist Church of England', defending her against Dissent, submitting in all that is not unscriptural and attending her services and sacraments. There should be revised Articles and a corrected liturgy. They should inform Canterbury of the scheme, viewed as using the 'liberty of Englishmen and Protestants' to serve God according to the purity of the Gospel and the original design of the Church of England. The bishops should be asked to ordain suitable preachers after testing them only in what is necessary by the canons, accepting testimonials from the Wesleys and their clerical helpers; and allow placing by the Methodists as a qualification in lieu of a benefice. If this was refused, the Wesleys should themselves ordain those they think fit; make deacons of others, and keep doubtful cases on trial. The Conference would have power to suspend or degrade the unsatisfactory. On the death of the Wesleys the power of ordination should be vested in three or five of the preachers as 'Moderators' who would order the flock as the Wesleys did now. They would be guided by the 'most spiritual parts' of the Prayer

Book, the 'rectified' Articles and the *Minutes of Conference*. The 'general plan' of Methodism was to be to 'preach the doctrine of grace against the Socinians – the doctrine of justice against the Calvinists – and the doctrine of holiness against all the world'. Hence all candidates for the ministry would be questioned on these matters, and to keep them in the church they would promise not to rail against the clergy, and to submit to ordination if a bishop would give it. Kingswood School would be kept for the sons of preachers, the training of ministers and for worn-out ministers.

This combined Benson's ideas with Fletcher's desire at least to give the bishops a chance to regularize the position on Methodist terms; but it also incorporated remedies for the criticisms of the liturgy and Articles which had been expressed over the previous twenty years. In many ways it foreshadowed Wesley's action ten years later to resolve the American problem. But as yet a radical plan of this kind was exactly the kind of thing which Wesley tended to put off until forced by necessity and what he took to be the guidance of Providence through events. As yet he felt no such compulsion, and only a purge of preachers was carried out at the 1775 Conference.[66] He pursued his usual course, doing just enough to maintain the unity and momentum of the movement as need arose, and keeping the dissidents within bounds.

But this was becoming more difficult, as was shown by the case of Alexander M'Nab versus Edward Smyth which, at least in Charles Wesley's mind (always alert for 'conspiracies'), was a symptom of a general jealousy of Wesley's clerical aides and of their own ambitions. It certainly revealed the tensions which had helped to produce the Benson and Fletcher schemes.

For several years Wesley had been administering sacraments in unconsecrated Methodist buildings, but the Bristol New Room and London Foundery had been specially privileged with Prayer Book worship and a regular eucharist. Other chapels wished for this, but would have required an ordination of preachers which Wesley would not countenance. At the Conference of 1778 Edward Smyth, the choleric Irish Evangelical whom we have encountered earlier in connection with troubles in Dublin, was at this stage furious for separating from the church as corrupt (he changed his mind later).[67] It was in the following year that Smyth caused trouble by his clash with M'Nab in Bath.[68] But this was really the occasion rather than the cause of a more widespread division. In April 1779 Charles Wesley once more complained about the preachers, and with a rich irony in view of years of unpredictability, said that he and John ought to work more closely together: to curb John's defects in allowing too much rope to anti-church preachers.

The problem at this point was that Charles Wesley and other clergy were accustomed to officiate at City Road, London (opened in 1778), and monopolized the pulpit to the resentment of senior itinerants like Pawson and Rankin. Charles thought he could do more good in his declining years in this way; but they thought that he drove the congregation away with his 'dry and lifeless' preaching. He had also offended by his 'worldly' pushing of his musical sons and by his well-known distrust of itinerants, whom he also accused of pride in their demands for the pulpit. He was thought to wish that they could be dispensed with altogether in favour of the clergy. Dr Whitehead later claimed that there was a party among the preachers headed by Dr Coke (who will figure largely in the events of the 1780s) which desired total separation from the church. But Pawson claimed that they only wished for 'the lively ordinances of God' and worship at ordinary and convenient (i.e. 'church') hours, which Wesley had always resisted. However, he admitted that some believed that those called by God to preach should also be able to administer the sacraments.

The London trouble was not unique. At the Conference of 1779 it was found that London and nineteen other circuits had lost members – an unusual occurrence. It was claimed that this was due to neglect of open-air preaching; lack of preaching in new places; prejudice against the King (a significant note); but especially the increase of worldly-mindedness. (One might see these as symptoms of a missionary organization consolidating into a 'church'.) Wesley thought that London suffered from jealousy between the preachers; and now the trouble spread to Bath. Here the assistant was a Scotsman called Alexander M'Nab, a good preacher but, as Wesley said, 'too warm and impatient of controversy'. Smyth had moved to Bath for his wife's health and was asked by Wesley to preach every Sunday. M'Nab objected, saying that the preachers were appointed by Conference, not by Wesley, and that they would not allow the clergy to 'ride over their heads'. This split the congregation between the two hotheads, though the reference to the Conference raised an important issue of where authority lay. Wesley predictably read the riot act: the rules were made by him before there ever was a Conference and they were to the effect that the preachers go 'when and where I appoint'. M'Nab was suspended, and with his usual and misleading optimism Wesley claimed that almost all were 'thoroughly satisfied'.

In fact the threat to his control raised all Wesley's authoritarian instincts (especially strong in this decade). When Thomas Taylor said that M'Nab was unjustly treated, Wesley lectured him on the history of how his 'sons in the gospel' originated in dependence on him and under his direction. They had the right to leave him, but as long as they stayed must be ruled by him. It may well be, however, that as in the 1750s it was Charles Wesley who stirred his brother to a tougher line than he might otherwise have followed, though John probably did not see this as an issue in which a movement of the Spirit was in danger of being frustrated – which was what usually made him go warily. Having accompanied him to Bath and obtained M'Nab's expulsion, Charles then returned to London and prayed publicly that John be preserved from his 'rebellious sons'. Pawson says that Charles never forgave him for protesting at this and that he made John believe that M'Nab was the tool of a party plotting against John's authority. Pawson said that there was no truth in this, and although he is a prejudiced witness, exaggerated conspiracy theories always did tend to be Charles's reaction to obstreperous preachers asserting their rights and status. As in the 1750s, so in 1780, he refused to attend Conference for fear of doing no good; and as always did not trust his brother's resolution to resist calls for ordination. John, he said, was even prepared to recall M'Nab, though the Scotsman had not confessed his fault. Although in fact Charles did attend Conference, he sat in silent disapproval.

Charles claimed that M'Nab had said that the preachers were resolved to confer and settle matters among themselves like so many Americans (one sees how the secular ferment was affecting Charles, whether or not it did the others). He even claimed that M'Nab saw it as his duty to pray for John Wesley's death! And he had feared to come to Conference because he expected the separation question to be raised once more.[69] Although there was no doubt rebellious talk, it is very probable that Charles Wesley's suspicious and fertile imagination blew it up into a full-blown controversy, since he admitted to John in December 1779 that 'there is not as yet any regular plan', but a 'spirit of independence and self-seeking'. John Wesley may have erred on the side of trust and leniency in re-admitting M'Nab, but he had a far better sense of how to handle his lieutenants than Charles, and this helped to defuse the situation. As Professor Baker points out, although John continued to insist on his authority, he was also keen to build up the authority of the assistants in the circuits and, as we shall see, from 1780 there are signs of an inner 'cabinet' emerging and cases of preachers occasionally presiding at Conference in his absence.[70]

On the whole Wesley handled these crises with some skill, but almost certainly, as he claimed himself, he simply felt his way from expedient to expedient, guided by events and necessity; trying to avoid separation; retaining his overriding authority; and primarily guided by a practical desire to keep the connexion as united and therefore as effective as possible. He conceded the minimum necessary to do this at a given time, with half an eye also to grooming preachers and people for the succession, whatever that might be, after his death. In all this the pressure from below and from events outside his control became clearer, clearest of all in the American Revolution and its effects on the situation of the Methodists in America. This led directly to Wesley's last and greatest 'irregularity' – that of ordination, which had repercussions on the British situation as well.

XIII

Saints Abroad: Missions and the American Problem

1. The origins of Methodist missions

Missionary historians have always commented upon the fact that so little was thought and done by Protestants about converting the 'heathen' until the nineteenth century – the 'great century' of missions in the perspective of Latourette's triumphalist history.[1] Of course the 'Protestant' proviso has to be underlined: the Roman Catholic story in the wake of Spanish and Portuguese colonialization and trade in the sixteenth and seventeenth centuries is remarkable. It is the meagre and sporadic efforts of Protestants in the same period that is striking. And why did missionary concern among them begin to emerge during the eighteenth-century, especially at the end?[2]

Two broad categories of reasons may be suggested: material circumstances and religious attitudes. Protestantism in the sixteenth and indeed the seventeenth century was fighting for survival, and for a long time was largely restricted to the European circle – with Turks to the east and the exclusion zone of the Spanish and Portuguese in Latin America and the West Indies to the west. It has often been suggested, too, that Calvinists and Lutherans were inhibited by their theology from trying to do God's work for him. The Matthaean Christ's command, 'Go ye into all the world', was sometimes said to have been fulfilled by the apostles. Yet Calvin was not unsympathetic to missionary ideas, and circumstances may well have coloured theology here. Hyper-Calvinists in the eighteenth-century, however, did disapprove theologically of missions at home or abroad.[3]

Thus it seems more than a coincidence that the limited signs of missionary interest among Protestants come in relation to trading and colonial expansion (which is not the same thing as saying that they were simply 'caused' by them). The first signs came among the English and

471

Dutch and in the areas where their trading and colonization had taken them – North America and the East Indies – though the ban on missions by the English East India Company is a salutary reminder that there was nothing inevitable about a positive relationship between trade and colonialism on the one hand and missions on the other. And though the Dutch gave some official support, the English did not, unlike the Spanish in Latin America and the French in North America, where Christianization was part of formal policy. Although there was some concern to save the Red Indians from French Popery for security reasons, pioneer missionaries like John Eliot in New England seem to have been driven more by compassion and eschatological hopes than by anything more mundane.

Particularly relevant to John Wesley's view of missions and general English attitudes in the pre-Revival era was the founding of the SPCK and SPG in 1699–1701. Their interest in North America was suggested by English colonization there, compassion for the benighted being mingled with a prudential sense that the Indians would be even more menacing if converted by French Jesuits in the north or Spaniards from Florida in the south. This factor helps to explain the missionary element in the Georgia project which involved John Wesley and the SPG.

There has been some discussion on the degree of commitment by the SPG to an Indian mission from the first. They were certainly anxious to minister to the colonists (if only to save them from New England Puritan encroachments), but Dr Bray, one of the early promoters of the SPG and SPCK, was keen to convert Indians and negroes.[4] In the event much of their effort in the eighteenth century went into sending clergy to the whites.

In analysing the motivation behind the modest efforts in this period Van den Berg considers several elements. Politically, there was a desire to protect the colonies against attack or negro revolt. Culturally, the desire to offer a superior religion was bound up with the belief in the superiority of Western culture, though later in the century the evangelical belief that true religion opened the way to superior culture was challenged by Latitudinarians like Bishop Watson, who thought that Christianity would only be assimilated as a by-product of Westerniz-ation.[5] Protestants also had a sense of compassion for the 'poor heathen' and of a debt of gratitude to God for his grace. What had always made them wary of missions by Catholics was the real or supposed Catholic belief that such 'works' would acquire 'merit', but John Wesley, it will be recalled, went to Georgia to save his own soul even more than to save the Indians. There was, finally, an eschatological element. This was more obvious in descendants of the Puritans than in the High Church-men of the SPG and SPCK. Millennarian ideas did persist in the eighteenth century – more than used to be thought – but a distinction has to be made here between pre- and post-millennarian schemes. This refers to the traditional idea of a thousand-year rule of Christ and the saints during the end-time. Pre-millennarians thought that this would follow the Second Coming of Christ (though it was not always clear whether this would be on earth or in heaven). This was sometimes associated with militant and military sectarians in the seventeenth century. Post-millennarians thought that the millenium preceded the Second Coming and prepared for it. Daniel Whitby (1638–1726) was an influential writer, presenting eighteenth-century notions of this, which conveniently suggested optimistic views of progress in morality, religion and indeed civilization and could therefore easily take semi-secularized forms. It also accorded well with expansive evangelical ideas of mission. But the older ideas of the conversion of the Jews and heathen as signs of an imminent end or as likely to hasten it, seem to have fallen rather into the background.[6]

There seems, indeed, little doubt that one of the main impulses for the flurry of founding missionary societies at the end of the century which set off the rising enthusiasm of the nineteenth was due to the Evangelical Revival. A conspicuous example at the beginning of the Revival was the Moravian drive which took them as far as Greenland. Pietism also produced missions through Danish agency in India, and news of these ventures had reached the circles of the SPCK and SPG and Epworth rectory. It was natural that evangelicals seized with the desire to snatch sinners from hell by conversion should ultimately come to extend the gift to the heathen. But what about the Calvinist inhibitions? It is natural to suppose that Arminians would be more open to the missionary spirit, and it may be thought significant that the SPG and SPCK initiatives came from High Church Arminians like Wesley. Yet the Revival, which was responsible for the late eighteenth-century step forward, was, as we have seen, predominantly Calvinist in complexion. But it was also observed that this was very different from the inhibiting hyper-Calvinism of a John Gill. The 'Arminian accent' of a Whitefield came to be echoed in the 'Fullerite' Baptists, and it was from their circle in Northamptonshire that William Carey and the Baptists who founded the future Baptist Missionary Society came in the 1790s.[7]

Some explanation certainly seems necessary for the quick succession of missionary society foundations in the 1790s, even if the product in actual missionaries was meagre at first; and this was not confined to England. First came the Baptists in 1792, then the London Missionary Society (mainly Independents) in 1795; and what later became the (Evangelical) Church Missionary Society in 1799. The Wesleyans, as we shall see, had already been active, though their Society was only formally constituted in 1818. Although the theological changes among the Particular Baptists help to account for their part in this, as well as the aggressive evangelizing spirit among the others, circumstances of a more secular kind also favoured the initiative.

The challenge and the targets in mind were certainly helped by developments in trade and colonization. Cook's voyages suggested a field for the LMS, coloured somewhat by notions of the 'noble savage'. The anti-slave trade campaign and thoughts of colonies of freed slaves, and the promotion of 'good' trade to kill slave trading at its root, made the Clapham circle venture into what became Sierra Leone in West Africa. But India was the major target. Here the East India Company had been opposed to evangelizing for fear of creating trouble which would be bad for trade, but the loss of the American colonies and party schemes for revising the terms of the Company's government had publicized the corruptions and easy morals of the Company's servants. If there was much party interest in all this, there was also a degree of guilty conscience, and for Evangelicals the shocking spectacle of Christians complacently failing to convert the heathen and even conniving at their horrid ways. Some Company servants like Warren Hastings were sympathetic to Indian culture and, as 'enlightened' men, at times were not disposed to compare it unfavourably with Christianity, though attitudes to other religions at this time were often influenced as much by European intellectual polemics as by real knowledge or impartial curiosity.[8]

Now a very different attitude began to appear. A key figure here was Charles Grant, who had been converted to Evangelicalism in 1776, rose high in the Company's service, and began with his friends in the Clapham Sect to press for missionary work in India. In the relatively pan-evangelical spirit of the group, this also meant help for non-Anglicans and Methodists like Thomas Coke.

In 1786 the Evangelical David Brown became a Company chaplain, and in 1787 he and Grant worked out proposals for a mission. Grant took the opposite view to Bishop Watson. Westernization would not lead to Christianization: on the contrary, Christianization was the best way to assimilate Indians to their masters' culture. Not only was Christianity desirable and not only were missions a Christian duty, but they were also in the Company's interests (contrary to what had always been assumed). Indian character had been corrupted by its religion and priests, so the only way of improving it would be by converting them to Christianity. This would not only improve conditions for trade, but also bind them to their rulers through a common interest, and so secure the future of the British in India. No doubt there was a degree of calculated appeal to self-interest here in the interests of missions, as there was in some of the arguments in Wilberforce's *Practical View* for converting the English upper classes to 'real' Christianity. But there is no reason to doubt Grant's sincerity. At all events he captured the support of the Claphamites, and their well-tried pressure-group methods for anti-slave trade purposes were used in 1793, and more successfully in 1813, to place the 'pious clause' in the Company's charter. Though they did not succeed in their original aim of getting Company sponsorship for 'fit and proper persons' as missionaries in 1813 they did enable them to be allowed in voluntarily. Meanwhile, much propaganda was poured out to show the depravity of Indian religion and morals, which had a considerable long-term effect on race relations. Later, more propaganda endeavoured to highlight the alleged benefit of missions to trade.[9]

One other set of circumstances may be held to have stimulated missionary zeal, though it is played down (probably rightly) by Van den Berg. There was a renewal of millennarian interest from the 1790s, which has also excited a perhaps excessive interest from some modern historians. The startling events of the French Revolution, and especially the traumatic adventures of the Pope at the hands of Napoleon, excited fresh calculations and speculations among zealous Protestant students of the Book of Revelation, and a few new sectarians like Richard Brothers acquired a following.[10] Mainstream evangelicals did not go so far. They talked of judgment and sometimes of the near approach of the end, but in general terms; as we have seen, Wesley was non-committal about Bengel's chronology of the end-time, though some thought that he was more definite. Some Methodists, though, were keener on these speculations. So far as missions are concerned, perhaps the most we can say is that the 1790s created a certain sense of heightened expectation of great changes which might favour divine openings for evangelizing the world.[11]

What about Methodism? The formal constitution of the Wesleyan Missionary Society in 1818 is deceptive, for Methodist ventures overseas antedated this by many years. Yet the Methodist position was peculiar, and Wesley's attitude equivocal. The late eighteenth-century societies, like their Anglican predecessors, were essentially private and voluntary ventures of interested groups, and not official arms of churches, still less of governments. In this they differed strikingly from the Roman Catholics. When Coke began to agitate for Methodist missions in the 1780s, he received little official encouragement from the Wesleyan connexion, yet in 1818 the Wesleyan Missionary Society uniquely became an official organ of the emergent Wesleyan Church, and not a mere voluntary society.

Consider first Wesley's own attitude to a development which for Methodists had been growing haphazardly since about 1760. Wesley might have been expected to be sympathetic to the movement – after all he had been a missionary himself, however unsuccessfully; the Epworth household had known of the Pietist missions; and old Samuel had had his own characteristically optimistic dreams of deserting his family for the exotic East.[12] But although Wesley's attitude to missions varied, his initial reaction was distinctly negative. Here, as with Methodism at home, the initiative certainly came from others, and at first from below, from accidents of individual enthusiasm, very much as we have seen to have been the case in many localities in England.

Before we attempt to understand Wesley's attitude, it is best briefly to review the process by which Methodism extended overseas, especially in work which would normally be recognized as 'overseas missions', in the strict sense of missions to the 'heathen'. In fact it is not easy to adhere to this definition strictly. When, in 1786, Coke issued his *Address* (endorsed this time by Wesley's appeal for support for missionary work), he saw prospects for Methodism in the Gaelic-speaking Scottish Highlands and Islands; in the Channel Isles; in the West Indies; and in North America, though he also already had his eye on India. For the Methodist 'mission' was seen as being to those lacking 'real' Christianity, and this applied almost as much to those at home as to 'savages' abroad; indeed it included Roman Catholics everywhere. The West Indians were slaves transported to a white colony, though Methodism wished to get the whites as well; and the white Americans needed the gospel as much as the blacks from this point of view, as the SPG men also found. Wesley's initial feeling that there was enough to do at home is intelligible in so far as 'missions' merely meant going to largely white and nominally Christian populations who merely happened to be living abroad. There were plenty of these to evangelize at home.

America was a special case which will be considered later, as leading into the crises of the 1780s; for the moment it will be best to consider the West Indies as the first mission field for Methodists. It is in fact an excellent example (like America) of how Methodist enterprise abroad came by accidental private initiatives.

The story has often been told of how the Gilbert family became involved in beginning Methodist work in Antigua.[13] Nathaniel Gilbert was a man of estate and former Speaker of the House of Assembly on the island, but his brother Francis had been reduced to poverty by loose living and a fraudulent agent, and had fled to England from his creditors. Here he was influenced by Vincent Perronet and John Wesley, and joined the society. Nathaniel was similarly influenced through reading Wesley's *Appeal to Men of Reason and Religion* (an interesting example of propaganda reaching its intended target). He visited England, and it was at his house in Wandsworth in December 1758 that Wesley baptized his negro servant: 'The first African Christian I have known . . . But shall not our Lord, in due time, have these heathen also "for His inheritance"?'[14] Nathaniel tried to persuade Fletcher of Madeley to go to Antigua, but Fletcher refused on the grounds of lack of grace and of needing to be sure of his own conversion. So Nathaniel returned at the end of 1759, and set up as a preacher himself; and Francis later returned to help him.[15] In 1773 Francis said that they had sixty members of society, two-thirds of them black, and that almost the whole island was 'stirred up to seek the Lord'. Preachers could be used, but the island was too poor from natural disasters to afford them.[16]

By the time of Nathaniel's death in 1774 the numbers had risen to 200; Francis Asbury, the apostle of America, would have liked to go, but Wesley advised against it: 'Let the young men do the work.'[17] Then in 1778 John Baxter, a Chatham shipwright and local preacher, took up a post as storekeeper in the island and took charge of the remnant of Gilbert's work for several years. He was actually offered ordination and an Anglican living, but preferred his Methodist blacks, who by 1785 had reached 1100; Thomas Coke ordained him as a Methodist minister when they met in America. In 1786 the Conference at last agreed to send a preacher, and when Coke was accidentally driven by storms to Antigua with this man and two others destined for Newfoundland, he left all three on his own initiative, not altogether to Wesley's approval.[18]

This was a characteristically impulsive gesture of the kind that frequently landed Coke in trouble. It was also characteristic of his attitude to slavery, which was a peculiarly difficult question since the work in the West Indies and the southern American colonies was developing just when anti-slavery sentiment was developing in Britain and America. The American Conference of 1780 had condemned slavery, and in 1784, at Coke's insistence, the Conference actually threatened expulsion of slave owners; however, it was found 'prudent' to suspend this.[19] American Methodism was predominantly southern. In the West Indies, Coke modified his attitude as the price for Methodist work there. His 'Appeal' of 1786 for missions was partly in terms of justice as well as compassion towards people deprived of liberty, but he clearly saw their souls as the most important part of them to be saved. He wrote to an American preacher in 1795 that, 'If they have religious liberty, the temporal slavery will be comparatively but a small thing'. He hoped that the Lord might 'appear for them'. At this time he was influenced by revolutionary fears and an interest in apocalyptic; in the circumstances his caution is understandable, since for him the mission took priority over everything else. But at one point he went further, and actually bought slaves to work an estate given to the mission (an event seen as 'providential'). It was only later that he reverted to a harder line.[20]

Meanwhile, another area was being opened up by a mixture of private accident and official initiative. This was in British North America. Barbara Heck, the pioneer to America (below, p. 484), left New York for Montreal in 1773; British soldiers brought Methodism to Quebec in 1780; Nova Scotia was pioneered by William Black in 1775, and the cause there was strengthened by loyalist refugees from the seceding colonies.[21] Newfoundland received Methodism in a different manner when Lawrence Coughlan, a former itinerant, was ordained and sent out by the SPG in 1767. But as he said himself, 'I am, and do confess myself, a Methodist,' and he followed Wesley's 'plan'. He was also a perfectionist of the more 'enthusiastic' sort. Wesley thought that he had landed where he was 'By a various train of providences'.[22] Although his work languished through Calvinist confusers, lay Methodists arrived to help in the usual casual fashion, and in 1785 the Conference sent out a preacher and made Newfoundland an official circuit. The Americans sent two of their ordained preachers there in 1785. We have seen that the English intended two more in 1786, but that Coke detained them in Antigua. His heart was always in the West Indies, though Wesley seems to have had a special tenderness for Nova Scotia.[23]

The *Minutes* of 1785, in addition to the United States, included these figures: Nova Scotia, 300 members; Antigua, 8 whites and 1100 blacks; and in 1786, Newfoundland 100.[24]

Methodism, it might be said, had acquired her missions, like Britain her colonies, in a fit of absence of mind, coming to terms with them in an official way afterwards. The *Minutes* recognized them, like America at first, simply as new circuits which happened to be overseas and not as the field of a 'missionary society'. Official attitudes, and not least Wesley's attitude, were for a long time hesitant and indeed negative. Not that Wesley was hostile to missions as such. In 1775, though objecting to Asbury going to Antigua, he said that he had no objection to 'one or two young men willingly offering themselves to that service, though none should go unless he was fully persuaded in his own mind'. This remained his settled view: only volunteers should go, whereas for Britain he always desired to post people as he wished.[25]

In 1778 Conference actually debated the possibility of a mission to Africa for the first time. The story is that two West African princes escaped from slavery in America and, having been influenced by Methodism in England, wished preachers to go to their homeland. Two young men volunteered, but Conference thought the time not yet ripe, though a deep impression was made by a consumptive young man who volunteered to go wherever he was sent. This seems to have been Duncan

M'Callum, the other probably being Thomas Prickard; it looks as though Coke was already agitating for action and promising funds for volunteers.[26] Although the negative decision is not explained, it is usually said that Wesley was fearful of committing resources which were already overstretched at home. But Thomas Taylor said that 'the call seems doubtful', and Benson that 'the time had not arrived', which may mean that they thought that no providential signs were as yet forthcoming. It is noticeable that when impromptu missionaries showed 'fruits' – Wesley's sovereign test – he became much keener to help them.

Coke tried again in 1783–4 with a 'Plan of the Society for the Establishment of Missions among the Heathen' addressed to 'all the real lovers of mankind' with special reference to the Methodists, though the 'Plan' was not explicitly for a denominational society.[27] Subscribers of two guineas per annum could be members, and the first meeting was to be on 27 January 1784. A committee of seven would run the society's affairs between meetings. A subscription of £66.3.0 had already been raised. What happened to the society is not certain: it is usually assumed that the meeting was never held, though Mr Vickers thinks that it was. It seems clear that Wesley did not actively support it: he did not subscribe, and Coke may have hoped to 'bounce' him into accepting a *fait accompli*. Coke was a poor tactician, for this was the very time when the Deed of Declaration was being drawn up to legalize the Methodist Conference, and the new arrangements for America would soon follow: events in which Coke himself was deeply engaged. Wesley may also have disliked the idea of an independent organization. The 'providences' pointed to the American development, and practical needs, dictated the Deed. No such considerations seemed to dictate a move to the East of the kind that Coke had in mind. As Wesley said, after consulting the preachers in February 1784: 'We were unanimous in our judgment that we have no call thither yet, no invitation, no providential opening of any kind.'[28] This exactly expresses his attitude to the missionary question throughout: it was not simply or even probably mainly a prudential question of lack of resources, as is usually supposed.

But official Methodist support for missions was not far away by now, and this time Wesley's interest did become fully engaged. Coke did not give up easily. Early in 1784 he began corresponding with Charles Grant, the key figure (as we have seen) in the opening up of India for missions. This was where Coke's sights were now fixed, and although he acknowledged the practical objections made by Grant, and admitted that Methodist resources were strained to meet the demands from the West, he still hoped for an Indian project, and quoted Wesley as saying that half a dozen men would be needed if it were to be taken up.[29]

Wesley was fully associated with Coke's new *Address to the Pious and*

Benevolent in the Spring of 1786: he wrote a prefatory letter saying he 'greatly approved' of it.[30] Though the appeal was not specific in terms of organization, it was in terms of the areas in mind: the Highlands and Islands of Gaelic Scotland; the Channel Isles; the Leeward Islands; Quebec, Nova Scotia and Newfoundland. India is mentioned, but it is said that 'the providence of God has lately opened to us so many doors nearer home, that Mr Wesley thinks it imprudent to hazard at present the lives of any of our preachers, by sending them so great a distance' when there were areas already open, easier and with greater prospects of success. There was also need of work in the fallen areas of Christendom itself.

By now, of course, the Deed and American affairs had been settled, and the developments in the West already described will have convinced Wesley that providence was indeed opening the way there, and not in the East. Hence Wesley's welcome for the new proposals. Even so, he was more cautious than Coke, for example over the Highland project. Coke had recently visited Scotland, and had been struck by the heathen state of these remote areas. Providentially, a Gaelic speaker had appeared and been given 'an unlimited commission' to visit them. This was Duncan M'Callum, the consumptive volunteer for overseas, and he was sent to Ayr in 1786, though it is not clear whether this was a preliminary to a Highland mission. If so, such a mission did not materialize.[31]

The Channel Islands were a different matter. Work here was successfully begun in 1783 by Robert Brackenbury, the 'Methodist squire' and 'half-itinerant', and became a regular part of the connexion, Wesley himself visiting them (at the age of eighty-four!) in 1787.[32] The West Indian and North American work had already developed in the way described, and in 1786 Conference endorsed the sending of official missionaries.

If we wish to do so, we can therefore no doubt see 1786 as the formal beginning of Methodist missions, at least as an official project, several years before the Baptists. Yet the process as described here is obviously far more complicated and equivocal than this implies. Work in the West Indies and America had begun over twenty-five years before, and for America had been officially endorsed by Conference since 1769. From another point of view there was no Methodist missionary 'society' until 1818, and even then it was a connexional organ. 'Mission' itself was an ambiguous concept, since to Coke it included parts of Britain.

In fact three clear phases have been detected in their development.[33] The first, up to 1786, was a matter of individual and private initiatives. The second, beginning with Coke's *Address*, saw Conference sending men to designated circuits overseas. This was informally supervised by

Coke, and he was gradually given help (perhaps to curb his recklessness), for in 1790 the Conference appointed a committee of management including him, and he acted as the Conference representative. The third phase came in 1799 when the Conference declared that the Missions were fully in its care, with Coke as its 'agent'. Further organization followed, especially for finance. Finally, in 1813, in a flurry of enthusiasm, Jabez Bunting, who had assisted Coke in managing the finances, promoted the first local 'auxiliary' for fund-raising at Leeds as a 'Missionary Society of the Leeds District'. The Missionary Committee soon agreed that such groups should be formed 'at large', and they were consolidated as a national body in 1818. In part, competition for Methodist subscriptions by other formal societies (like the London Missionary Society) precipitated this.[34]

As for Wesley's attitude, it has been emphasized here that although there were good practical reasons for caution, and Coke was always reckless in his enthusiasm to commit himself and others without counting the cost, in the last resort, like Cromwell, Wesley 'followed the providences'. He stuck to the volunteer principle, but responded warmly enough when the fruits began to show, and then took the products under his official wing.[35] No doubt he felt the more confident of doing so when he had resolved other pressing problems in the mid-1780s, but there was a strong 'providential' sense throughout the process. In more mundane terms it is also clear that, like much of the early work at home, overseas missions arose mainly through initiatives from below, from the rank and file. But it is also of interest that in 1783 Wesley preached a sermon on 'The General Spread of the Gospel', in an attempt to reconcile the spectacle of the poor state of the world with the goodness and wisdom of God. He saw God as having been at work for the past half-century, for example in Methodism (which he saw as beginning in Oxford), and this work still showed no signs of abating. Now he saw it spreading through Europe and to lands where Europeans traded. But why not, he asked, to the South Seas, in areas beyond contact with the European world?[36] A mixture of euphoria at Methodist progress and increasing knowledge of the overseas world was creating a missionary vision coloured with a strong sense of providence working in history. The rising anti-slavery sentiment no doubt also fed a sense of guilty responsibility for the souls of slaves, as in Coke's comment. The belated development, after Wesley's death, of a more formal Missionary Society, does not directly concern us here, except to say that it, too, was conditioned by events initially beyond the Connexion's control. It is significant that it coincided with the opening up of India through the revised charter of the East India Company, and alarm at the competition of other denominational societies for Methodist money, as well as a general

missionary euphoria. There seems little to be said for Semmel's speculation that it was a device by the Wesleyan leadership to syphon off the
discontented for service abroad.[37]

There remains, however, the question of America, which was in fact
the most important of all the examples of overseas expansion for the fate
of Methodism in Wesley's lifetime and its settlement after his death.

2. Before the Revolution: early Methodism in America

The rise of American Methodism has to be seen in the context of the
history of the American First 'Great Awakening' which, as we have
seen, was part of the larger evangelical revival of the eighteenth century
(above, pp. 163f.). The interpretation of this cannot be followed in detail
here, and is complicated by the usual difficulties about secular and
religious causes, national differences and international connections.
Perry Miller, the *doyen* of historians of the Puritan tradition and its
aftermath, wished to claim that the American Awakening was essentially
distinct from the European movement, but although it certainly had its
own distinctive roots, it seems impossible to disregard the international
connection.[38] However, the Americans have been more fortunate than
the British in the extent and sophistication of their scholarship on the
subject of revivals, which partly reflects their greater significance for
American history.[39]

Apart from stimuli from outside America – for example from Pietist
immigrants – the New England Awakening of the early 1740s may be
traced to the tensions arising between inherited ideals and expectations
from the Puritan tradition and the failure of later generations to live up
to them. This was exacerbated and, some would say, to a large extent
caused by the stresses of an expanding and changing society.[40] Although
Jonathan Edwards's famous revival at Northampton has always had a
special place in the histories of the Awakening, this is as much because
of his powerful intellectual output and reasoned analysis of the phenomena as because of its actual importance in the movement. There had in
fact been several short-lived local outbreaks since the beginning of the
century, and then, as McLoughlin says, after 1739, parts of the whole
string of coastal colonies from Nova Scotia to Georgia 'exploded like a
string of firecrackers' from 1740 to 1745. Whitefield's visits and itinerancy seemed to give the feeling of a general awakening, and in New
England he was followed by the Presbyterian Tennants and the controversial enthusiast James Davenport, with divisive effects on the churches
between 'Old' and 'New Sides', the divisions being as much social as
religious. Dissent mushroomed as never before.

The Middle Colonies, with very different religious and social traditions behind them, were also affected. Here the Reformed tradition among Dutch and 'Scotch-Irish' immigrants was most important for revival. Itinerant preachers worked regardless of ecclesiastical propriety, and Old and New Sides Presbyterians split, with the New Siders having the upper hand in 1758. They profited from work among new immigrants in new settlement conditions.

The South was different again. Here, as Sidney Ahlstrom puts it, the Great Awakening 'was in fact not so much a revival as it was an immense missionary enterprise. Revivalism was the chief method of church extension' and its 'dynamic methods effected a radical transformation of the older religious groups in the area'. Whitefield was of less importance here than in New England, despite his base in the Georgia orphanage, and the revival owed most to less famous figures, 'less dependent upon a large semi-committed constituency'.[41] This constituency was especially among newer immigrants, particularly Scotch-Irish, behind the areas of earlier settlement. The older tidewater areas were nominally Anglican, with little to offer socially to the lower orders; and there was a general dearth of settled institutions in the back country. A group of laymen met in Harrow County, led by Samuel Morris in an irregular revival movement, later aided by Presbyterians from the North. They attacked the Anglican ministry as dead and naturally met persecution. Even more important were 'New Light' Baptists from New England led by Stearns and Marshall from 1754, who proliferated in the back country of Virginia and the Carolinas and embodied, it has been argued, elements of social as well as religious revolt in the 1760s and 1770s. They provided an element of spiritual and moral discipline as well as religious zeal in these neglected areas.[42] Even Anglicans came to be affected, especially through Devereux Jarratt, brought up under Presbyterian influence but taking Anglican orders after his conversion. In Virginia in 1763 he began an itinerant ministry which was of significance for early Methodism in this area, for when it arrived in 1772, Jarratt co-operated with them like some of his English Evangelical contemporaries. He was only disillusioned when signs of separatism began during the War of Independence.[43]

Methodism was a latecomer in this tumultuous process, and until after the War a limited and relatively insignificant one. Its greatest triumphs came late in the century, when its flexibility combined with discipline, and the exploits of its circuit riders fitted the conditions of pioneer life and a moving frontier. But at the beginning of the War there were only 3,418 members, the greater part in the South, which underlines the fact that it was the product of unplanned voluntary evangelism, particularly in that section; Wesley's influence came through the preachers whom he sent out afterwards, through the North.[44] This seems more important than the old and rather tiresome controversy about the chronological priority of the North or the South as the location of the first American Methodist society.[45]

Wesley's mission to Georgia ended in failure so far as any permanent effect is easily visible, though Methodism in the broader sense through Whitefield had more success, and there is some evidence that societies founded by him or his admirers provided a few recruits for the new wave of societies founded by Methodist immigrants in the 1760s.[46] But it is clear that the real impulse for a fresh start came by the efforts of immigrants especially of Irish origin, who had already been Methodists before they left home. There were two main groups – in Maryland and New York – which began independently at approximately the same time.[47]

Robert Strawbridge was a lively Irish Methodist who arrived in Maryland in the early 1760s and soon after began preaching and founding societies in Pennsylvania as well. In 1768 they asked for preachers to be sent from England, but Strawbridge was a magnetic figure, and he and his followers did not take kindly to direction. Strawbridge began to administer sacraments independently, and had to be tolerated when this was officially forbidden in 1773; in 1779 the Southerners formed a 'presbytery' with a view to ordination, and were only persuaded with difficulty to wait till the end of the war.

Methodism in the north began in much the same way, the pioneers being the celebrated Barbara Heck and her cousin Philip Embury, both former refugees from the Palatinate who had settled in Ireland; both had become Methodists there. In 1760 they arrived in New York. Both had been Anglican communicants, but finding this church not to their taste in New York, joined the Lutherans. For the next few years Embury, though a local preacher, did not evangelize, and according to the traditional story was only galvanized into doing so when Barbara was shocked by the spectacle of some of their community playing cards. She burst out: 'Philip, you must preach to us, or we shall all go to hell together, and God will require our blood at your hands.' This was about October 1766, and as Embury turned out to be quite effective, a class meeting was formed, some of the members of which later moved up to Albany County. Heck and others, being loyalists, moved into Canada at the approach of the American troubles in 1773, and contributed to the origins of Methodism there.

Another colourful figure in the early days was Robert Williams, a local (and occasional itinerant) preacher from Ireland who arrived in 1769. Wesley evidently regarded him as one of those useful if imperfect preachers who could only be used selectively, but he allowed him to go to America at his own expense (or rather, at that of a fellow passenger, since he was penniless). He went first to Philadelphia and then as far as Virginia, where he co-operated with Jarratt and the Southern preachers. But he, too, tended to be a law to himself, especially in publishing, which he had to be allowed to do without Wesley's permission.

Finally among the leading pioneers was the most colourful figure of all, the legendary Captain Webb – the adjective being especially apt in his case, since his varied recollections have caused much confusion to historians.[48] Webb was a former army officer who had lost an eye in 1759 during Wolfe's Quebec expedition. On his return to England he suffered from depressions, which were resolved by conversion through a vision of the suffering Christ: not uncommon among Methodists, of course, but in Webb's case the first of a series of claims to spirit-guidance. Sober Methodists found him a nuisance; John Wesley characteristically saw him as useful in some circumstances; Charles Wesley, equally characteristically, compared his peculiarities to those of the dreadful George Bell. Webb alarmed the New York Methodists in 1767 by appearing in full uniform and reputedly preached with sword as well as Bible in front of him, which certainly fits his colourful personality. But he was of great help in extending and building up societies along the eastern seaboard, as well as building the New York chapel. On his return to England in 1772, moreover, he helped to stimulate support for the American work and accompanied the preachers in 1773. Unfortunately his English and military ostentation excited suspicion that he was a spy during the war (which may or may not have been true), and after a period in prison he finally returned to England for good in 1778.

What had John Wesley been doing all this time about America? He certainly followed the events of the Awakening with interest, including Edwards's account (though in the longer term he thought his own revival more extended and impressive). He also met some evangelical visitors to England, who appreciated his preaching and Charles Wesley's hymns.[49] When Whitefield appealed for help in 1767, Wesley said that though he could not spare itinerants, some of the local preachers 'are equal both in grace and gifts to most of the itinerants'.[50] What finally induced him to help directly was the description of the work and appeal for help sent from New York in April 1768 by Thomas Taylor (an emigrant, not to be confused with the itinerant of that name). Taylor wanted legal advice on securing control of the preaching house, money and itinerants.[51] At the Conference of 1768 Wesley also read a request for help from Strawbridge and the Southern group, but action was postponed till the next year, though Joseph Pilmoor, one of those finally sent, was already feeling a vocation for the work.[52] In October 1768 a Swedish Pietist, Dr Wrangel, who had seen the work in Pennsylvania, visited Wesley at Bristol and strongly pressed him for help with preachers to those who were 'as sheep without a shepherd'.[53] Why Wesley responded at this point is not clear, but it seems reasonable to suppose that this conjunction of appeals, which seemed also to be evidence of a flourishing work, would have seemed to him to be signs of a providential calling. That winter he sent a circular to the preachers and leading laymen to publicize the New York letter and collect what money they could. In January 1769 he told Christopher Hopper that if he and Joseph Cownley 'have a mind to step over to New York' (!) he would not stop them – it would be good for their health and 'help many precious ends'.[54] Williams he now allowed to go at his own expense.

Then at the Conference of 1769 the 'pressing call' from New York was described. Richard Boardman and Joseph Pilmoor offered to go, and money was given towards the New York chapel.[55] Wesley preferred the apostolic pairing to one man alone, and these were the first of ten to be sent by him to America between 1769 and 1774. Most were relatively young and of varying degrees of experience at home. Of the first two, Boardman was the senior, though Pilmoor the more able. He was left in Philadelphia while Boardman went to New York. In Philadelphia he introduced Wesley's *General Rules* for societies, including no separation from the church, and both men tightened up the discipline of classes. They stuck mainly to the towns, though they were concerned about the country places, and appealed to Wesley for more preachers to help them here. Pilmoor complained of the 'want of ordination' to a friend and thought that they would be 'obliged to procure it by some means or other'. And he perceived a fundamental and momentous difference from Britain, deeply affecting the future of Methodism in America: 'there is no church that is Established more than another. All sects have equal authority with the Church of England.'[56] What troubled him was the difficulty of controlling local preachers and especially self-appointed itinerants like Webb and Williams, and the embryo connexion of Strawbridge in the south. Pilmoor and Boardman themselves looked settled in the cities, but in fact they do not seem to have visualized a permanent stay in America. Wesley, however, professed to be thinking of going himself (one hardly dares to speculate about the results if he had). This may have been a veiled threat to persuade others to volunteer, but at all events he thought the way 'not yet plain. I wait till Providence shall speak more clearly on one side or the other' – his usual line – and would go (health and age no bar, he told Whitefield) if he had a 'clear pressing call'.[57] In the event, at the Conference of 1771 he sent two more volunteers, one of them of signal significance, Francis Asbury, who became the Wesley of American Methodism.

Asbury was only twenty-six, with four years' circuit experience, but had a clear vision of Methodist order and priorities. He was at once disquieted at the policy of the preachers staying in the towns.[58] In fact when he arrived, Boardman and Pilmoor set off on their travels, leaving him to look after the towns. Then, in 1773, a senior preacher called Joseph Rankin arrived, which led to the first American Conference of 1773. This laid down the full Methodist discipline, though they had to tolerate Strawbridge's sacraments. Rankin found reports of American successes exaggerated, but what probably disappointed him were the numbers who were not disciplined members by his lights.[59] By now there were itinerants created from local preachers, one a native American.

Then came the War of Independence, which marked an epoch in Methodist development for England as well as America. We have seen how Wesley's private sympathy turned to hostility as he linked American rebellion with English radicalism. He urged the preachers to be 'peace-makers' and to 'addict yourselves to no party': they must keep 'full union with each other'. Charles Wesley said that he was 'of neither side, and yet of both'.[60] But of course Wesley himself took sides, and to the great damage of his American followers. Indeed he confessed in 1775 that he was in danger of losing his love for them, at least for their misguided leaders.[61] Although the preachers tried to remain neutral, most of them sympathized with the King's party, and it is not surprising that all but Asbury had left America by 1778, the last being George Shadford, who had a narrow escape from being shot.[62]

Since Asbury as a preacher felt that he could not take arms, he refused to promise to do so and retired to Delaware. The Americans were left to their own devices. Bereft of guidance from Wesley, and in an emerging nation with a parent Church of England widely regarded as being treacherous as well as corrupt, it is not surprising that they should have pressed for a kind of declaration of independence of their own. In 1779 separate Conferences met in the North and South. The Northerners suggested that Asbury should become 'General Superintendent' by virtue of his age; as Wesley's appointee; and as joined with Rankin and Shadford 'by express order from Mr Wesley', thus showing a desire for some link of authority with the parent body. The Southerners had been forging ahead in numbers and now prepared for ordination, but in 1780 the Northerners threatened to disown them, wishing to remain 'in close connection with the church'. This was probably a minority view, but Asbury and other delegates sent to the South managed to persuade them to postpone ordination for the time being. By 1784, when Wesley finally acted to give, or at least to offer, them a settlement, membership had risen to 14,988, nearly 90% south of the later Mason-Dixon line.[63] Much of this expansion began with a revival in 1775–6 in Virginia and North Carolina. Asbury had emerged as a vital link with British Methodist ideals and on his way to America his religious reading had been in the

Bible and Wesley's writings. Wesley himself was to write in 1783 that he was persuaded that 'Brother Asbury is raised up to preserve order among you, and to do just what I should do myself, if it pleased God to bring me to America.' In September 1783 he made Asbury 'General Assistant' for America and urged the Americans to keep to the British standards of the *Notes, Sermons* and *Minutes*.[64]

Asbury had indeed striven hard to keep that tradition alive. On the one hand he increasingly sympathized with the American cause, but on the other he was deeply imbued with the Wesley pattern. Yet the fact that he stayed when the other preachers left seems to indicate that he found something sympathetic in the environment for the Methodist mission. As the sequel showed, he was better fitted than Wesley to apply the old man's ideals with more pragmatism than Wesley himself would probably have shown in the new situation. He was in many ways equally autocratic, but this was tempered with a realization that the autocracy must be modified by independence so far as the relationship with England and its 'apostolic man' was concerned. We shall see that at the Conference of 1784 Wesley's plan and the appointment of his designated leaders were submitted to the decision of the preachers: a properly American independent touch. They were not simply to obey Mr Wesley's commands. 'My real sentiments,' Asbury wrote, 'are union but no subordination'.[65] This was a nice compromise at least at one point: between Wesleyan autocracy and American democracy, or rather Republican constitution-making.

But consideration of what Wesley intended for the Americans and what the Americans did with his intentions must be seen in the light not only of transatlantic needs but also of developments within English Methodism and Wesley's uneasy relationship with the Church of England and his own conscience in the 1780s.

XIV

'I Live and Die in the Church of England': Methodism in the 1780s

1. Problems of the 1780s: national anxieties and local revivals

Discussion of Wesley's life and the history of Methodism in the 1780s has understandably been dominated by the subject of his ordinations and the events which led to them. The prospect of Anglican-Methodist union in the 1960s led to a modest flurry of interest in the subject, though often informed more by twentieth-century than eighteenth-century concerns and perceptions.

Yet there was much else happening to Wesley and Methodism in this decade. There was marked expansion of Methodist numbers in England, punctuated by local revivals, and even more increase in America. The ordination question itself was only part of the more general and really more important problem of the succession to Wesley and what would happen to the connexion after his death: this became ever more urgent as his vigour visibly decayed. The old problem of the Methodist body's relationship to Church of England was involved in this. Moreover, the domestic Methodist problems had to be worked out in the context of social and political changes in England and on the continent which became explosive and even (to religious people) apocalyptic with the advent of the French Revolution during the last two years of Wesley's life. In 1779 there was the Middlesex election, which was the climax of the Wilkes agitations that had aroused all Wesley's most conservative instincts. Wyvill and his associates campaigned for more parliamentary representation for the counties against the effete electors of corrupt boroughs; and some London reformers began to talk of a wider suffrage. Burke talked of 'economical' reform, and the troubles of the East India Company and political partisanship at home helped to publicize the state of the sub-continent and was a stimulus, as we have seen, to thoughts of missions. Wesley's worst instincts about Catholics landed him in an equivocal relationship with the Protestant Association and the consequent Gordon Riots in 1780, though his controversial stance on the American revolt was followed by an apparently resigned acquiescence to the loss of the colonies as his thoughts turned to what Providence had now offered towards a settlement of Methodism there. If the French Revolution had not yet advanced to its most bloody extremes, enough had occurred by the time of Wesley's death to alarm many who had at first sympathized with it, as Burke's famous *Reflections* of 1790 showed, though conservative alarm here was much influenced by ominous rumblings of radical Dissenters and artisans at home.

What did Wesley think about all this?[1] In contrast with the 1770s – his most vocal period in politics – he was remarkably silent in the 1780s on such matters. The main exceptions are *An Estimate of the Manners of the Present Time* (1782) – a diatribe against the moral and religious degeneracy of the age – and a letter to Pitt in 1784 on taxation and suicide.[2] In the late 1780s, not surprisingly, his literary output was beginning to dry up and much of his production came in the form of sermons published in the *Magazine*. These were strongly weighted in the direction of excoriating the Methodists for their wealth and display, and their neglect of the disciplines of their first love: fasting, early services and open-air preaching. If this reflected the regrets of an old man long set in his pet ways, it also had a basis in the mature prosperity of an emerging denomination. But apart from the religious and moral themes – which could have applied in large measure to almost any period of his life – there is a striking absence of comment on current affairs.

Wesley's only references to the French Revolution are oblique yet in their way revealing. In a letter to an American correspondent in February 1790 he noted that he had had good accounts of religious progress in America. He then writes:

> One would hope the time is approaching when the earth shall be filled with the knowledge of the glory of the Lord. Indeed, the amazing revolutions which [have been] in Europe seem to be the forerunners of the same grand event. The poor infidels, it is true, who know nothing of God, have no such design or thought. But the Lord sitteth above the waterfloods, the Lord remaineth a King for ever. Meantime it is expedient that the Methodists in every part of the globe should be united together as closely as possible.

In March he wrote to William Black in Nova Scotia that,

> I have great hopes that the days of coldness and darkness are now past, and that the Sun of Righteousness is rising on Nova Scotia likewise . . . He is doing great things in many parts of Europe such

as have not been seen for many generations, and the children of God expect to see greater things than these. I do not know that England was ever before in so quiet a state as it is now. It is our part to wait the openings of Divine Providence, and follow the leadings of it.[3]

The only other relevant reference is one in his diary for 22 and 23 December 1790 to reading Burke (presumably the *Reflections*), but without comment.[4]

It looks as though the evidence of local revivalism (to be considered in a moment) coupled with the 'amazing revolutions' in Europe had induced in him a touch of 'post-millennialism' – an expectation of a notable outpouring of gospel grace and progress on earth. Rank-and-file Methodist attitudes varied. Back in 1779 a correspondent ('S.W.') had written to Wesley a letter which he published in the *Magazine* in 1789. S.W. denied that he was a Republican, and continued: 'I am convinced a Republican spirit is injurious to religion among Methodists, as I find most fallen Methodists (and perhaps some who are not fallen) are Republicans.'[5] Much more would be heard of 'Republican Methodists' in the 1790s, not simply because some were inclined that way in politics, but also because ideas and language of this kind were applied to the power struggles between the autocratic preachers' Conference and the ordinary laity demanding representation. It was in response to 'Jacobins' like these that the leadership ostentatiously proclaimed the 'loyalty' and hostility to 'reform' of the connexion. Dr Whitehead, in a memorial address for Wesley in 1791, stressed the steadying effects of Methodism, and so helped to provide part of the evidence for later 'counter-revolutionary' theories about the Methodist role.[6]

If the problems of succession and separation in Methodism dominated many minds, Wesley was probably right to imply that the expansion of Methodism was equally important. Even in his greatest difficulties in earlier years over Calvinists or Moravians, pressures for ordination and separation, he had always tended to look to signs of advance in evangelism and holiness as well as dealing tenderly with rebels and wild men who obtained 'fruits'. Nothing had ever stopped him from pursuing his basic plans for restless gospel travels. The 1780s were indeed a notably fruitful period for Methodist advance. In 1780 there were 43,830 members in Britain and Ireland and 10,139 in America. In 1790 these had risen to 71,463 and 61,811 respectively. Very soon the Americans would outstrip their parents.[7] But quite apart from this notable development which had warmed Wesley's feelings towards missions, there was also revival at home with some new features, prophetic of the future.

These revivals sometimes reproduced the phenomena of the early

1740s, with the same doubts about their origin and desirability. At Thurlton in 1782, wrote a correspondent, 'as in most revivals, a great deal of wildfire is mixed with the genuine; and it appears to me, and many others, that Satan has been permitted to work in an astonishing manner'. At Huddiscom three persons 'convinced' for some time were set at liberty. Another fell into fits, shrieking out 'as if sometimes in heaven, at other times in hell.' A brother and his wife 'suspecting this was partly affected', laboured to check such cases. They suspected them because of their 'inability to give any clear, sustained account of their conviction or conversion'. He advised careful observation of their conduct and said that 'it is our business when there is any appearance of wildness, etc., mildly to check that which is wrong, and cherish that which is of God'. Real conversions then followed.[8]

Similar experiences occurred in the Bristol Circuit in 1782–3. At one place – 'a Presbyterian town where ordinary means cannot affect them' – 'wildfire' appeared, and there would have been more conversions but for the 'unbecoming prayers' of young converts. The preacher advised prayer meetings after the service, and the power of God fell upon two or three people. After two hours of prayer 'one soul found peace with God'.[9]

At Manchester early in 1783 it was remarked that they hardly ever preached without some returning thanks 'either for a sense of pardon, or for having their backslidings healed, or for experiencing that the blood of Christ cleanses from all sin' (i.e. the gift of perfection). At a lovefeast 'the fire was kindled, so that some began to weep, others to tremble, and several to roar out for the disquietude of their souls'. People stayed to pray after the services, for they would not depart 'without a blessing', and the cries increased. The work continued, some being converted and some perfected. Though the preachers did not approve of all the symptoms, 'they durst not pluck up the tares for fear of destroying any of the wheat'. Some of the affected were ten to twelve years old, but as 'solid' as those of fifty. At Ashton one man roared like a bear and rolled on the floor for two days and nights. At Oldham much of the work was among 'those who have been in the society for some time; though some others have been awakened and converted'.[10]

In 1781–2 revival broke out in Wesley's old home town of Epworth. Here, for several years, 'some of our brethren had been crying to God to revive his work in this peculiarly dead place'. Then meetings for prayer were started in several places, and people were converted at almost all of them, in one meeting mostly children. In six weeks eighty-three members were gained, about thirty of them young men, twenty young women and several 'backsliders'. One man who had served God for thirty years was concerned about his children's salvation. He dreamed that he saw God as Judge on his great white throne, with himself and his wife on the right but the children on the left. When he told this to the children most of them were moved to rejoice in God their Saviour. Here, too, prayer meetings led to the power of God 'falling' on people, and many cried aloud for mercy. In less than three weeks over a hundred had 'peace with God', and many experienced 'full salvation'. A man sang a verse of a hymn on his knees and then some young children gathered round him and prayed for him 'in a manner that astonished the old people'. This became quite common, and one child prayed: 'Lord, keep the devil in hell, till all the people in Epworth are converted.'[11]

Epworth had acquired factories for spinning and weaving and employed young women and children. Some of these were attracted into a prayer meeting and were 'cut to the heart'. As a result (Wesley claimed) the whole atmosphere of the factories had been transformed. Such a work, he thought, had not been seen in such a short time elsewhere.[12] This was in May 1782, but just over two years later he lamented that though the work had not yet ended, there had been a 'grievous decay'. He thought that this was because the preachers following the one who had presided over the revival were not as zealous; the leaders of the converted boys did not nurture them sufficiently. One of the most helpful women had left the town and another had 'left God'. A children's group had been dropped by the preachers and so they grew cold; and others had been scattered when the factories failed and closed.[13]

Wesley found the same phenomenon of child conversion and indeed informal evangelism elsewhere, and thought it 'a new thing in the world' that God began his work in children. So it had been, he said, in Cornwall, Manchester and Epworth, and from them the 'flame spread to those of riper years'.[14]

The Cornish work was at St Just from December 1781. Here, too, there were house meetings for singing and praying which experienced outbreaks of crying and fainting, with people 'distressed for full salvation'. Meetings were held at night, and eighty were converted in a week. One convert was eighty years old, but child conversions were commoner: one aged seven was converted after being told that if children were good they went to Christ when they died, and if they were not, to the devil. Children met in several classes of their own, but 'were never met by the preachers' and so tended to fall away. Many who were not members of the society received faith before death. What was 'peculiarly remarkable' in this revival, as in the Epworth one and another in Weardale some years before, was that the travelling preachers had little to do with it. 'They were the leaders whom it pleased God chiefly (indeed almost wholly) to use' – i.e. local people.[15] Cornwall, as a recent study has shown, was to become remarkable for cycles of revival of this kind, which gathered in fringe and loosely attached adherents.[16]

The characteristic features of these revivals seem to be the prominence of children; the role of house and prayer meetings; and the fact that the work seemed to come mainly from local lay people and not the itinerants who, if anything, failed even to consolidate it. There are also strong indications that a good many of those influenced were already well in touch with Methodism, if not actually members: there were evidently good crops of perfection experiences as well as recoveries of 'backsliders'. What we are seeing here is, in part, the kind of pattern natural to a mature movement: the 'way of salvation' well known and the problem of getting the children into it becoming an anxiety to parents. Fringers needed to be brought further into the process, and one can see once again the attractions of Wesley's two-stage salvation scheme. The house and prayer meetings, and the sense that the movement was being evolved from local sources and anxieties, and not by the itinerants, marks a transitional phase from the old spontaneous revivalism to the planned revivalism of the nineteenth century. Clearly people had been praying in expectation of reviving the good old days, but the answer was still an unplanned act of God. The same was true of Primitive Methodism in the early 1800s. By the 1830s the professionals had moved in with prescriptions and special techniques which guaranteed a revival if they were followed.[17]

Wesley himself seems well aware of the new phase: he had noted the local and lay-dominated prayer meetings (in an enclosed endogenous Methodist society) at Weardale in 1772. In 1783 he observed that prayer meetings had been more useful than preaching, since there the 'flame' first came that then spread to the rest. One or two should use their 'gift' there and should pray for 'the *whole gospel salvation*' (perfection). 'Praying down' a revival would become popular, as in the great Yorkshire Revival of the 1790s.[18] But already in Wesley's approving comment one can see the shape emerging of yet another movement from below which would achieve organized form by 1812 as 'Primitive Methodism': a movement less of the famous 'camp meetings' than of lay domestic (and female) piety.[19]

For the 1780s these developments were important not only for increasing Methodist numbers but for building up the pressure for separation and independence of the church. Localized 'popular' movements like this were not only remote from the church, but a problem for the evolving 'ministry' and connexional sense of the itinerants.

2. Securing the future: (i) deeds and declarations

In the 1770s Wesley's ideas about the future control of Methodism in succession to himself seemed to be divided between a collective leadership by the body of the travelling preachers in the Conference (or a small committee of them under a Moderator) and the idea of a clerical head like himself. Benson and then Fletcher had proposed a reformed 'Anglican' structure headed by men ordained by Wesley himself if the bishops failed to oblige on his terms; and the succession to his authority would be in a small body of Moderators. Wesley was well aware that none of the travelling preachers would be accepted by the others as his successor in the solitary role of autocrat; nor, he thought, would a select number of them be acceptable. This was one reason why he thought of a clerical head as at least a final resort of authority, if not as an active peripatetic overseer like himself. Hence the provision for a 'succession' in the Model Deed, the invitation to Fletcher and the thoughts of other possible clergy, since Charles Wesley was clearly unsuitable for the proposed role. Perhaps he never quite gave up the Fletcher idea, grumbling in his usual way that that holy man spent too much time in his parish instead of travelling like himself. Fletcher realistically resisted this pressure: his health could never have stood the strain and, as has already been suggested, it is doubtful whether his style of leadership could have been effective.[20] The actions of the 1780s suggest that even before Fletcher's death Wesley was turning to other means, measures to strengthen the authority of the assistants, and the collective authority of the Conference of preachers, together with legal securities. In all this it should steadily be borne in mind that Wesley's reasoning was practical, and with practical ends in mind. The aim was to perpetuate the message and mission of Methodism which he was firmly convinced was the providential will of God; and to this end he saw it as vital that Methodist unity should be maintained, especially the unity of the preachers, with secure control of the connexion vested in them.

Before reviewing the measures he took, however, it should be observed that for personal as well as practical reasons he felt the need of a lieutenant: one more reliable than brother Charles or the reluctant and delicate Fletcher. This was something he had never been able to find: the potential partnership with Whitefield had failed to develop; sons in the gospel like Maxfield had deserted him; Thomas Walsh the Irish saint had died young. But in 1777 an apparently more promising figure joined him in the person of Thomas Coke, an ordained priest of the Church of England and an Oxford DCL into the bargain. Coke had forfeited his curacy through his 'Methodistical' ways, and thrown in his lot with Wesley as a roving clergyman.[21]

Coke became a highly controversial and suspect figure within Methodism at the time, and has remained so ever since in Methodist historiography. The picture often given is of a man too busy, too interfering, taking too much upon himself and, above all, too ambitious. He was seen as manipulating the aged (perhaps even senile) Wesley for his own ends, which allegedly included gaining a major influence in running the connexion during Wesley's lifetime, with the ultimate ambition of succeeding him as leader after his death. In addition, or as an alternative, he appeared to be nursing episcopal ambitions within Methodism or, if necessary, within Anglican missions overseas. One of the most conspicuous as well as attractive aspects of Coke's concerns was his passion for overseas missions, yet even here he was accused of ambition, pushiness and at best an irresponsible tendency to act without counting the cost.

Coke certainly gave hostages to his critics by rash statements and plans which on the most charitable reading show him to be naively self-important. He offered himself as the agent for Wesley's ordinations for America; later, as an Anglican bishop in a missionary capacity. In his journal he confessed (all too significantly, his critics have felt) that he was subject to 'foolish projects' and 'a thousand flattering dreams' and desired 'favour from men'. Such feelings were not uncommon among successful evangelicals – Whitefield felt much the same – and may be regarded as evidence of recognition of a particular temptation.[22]

But it should be realized that most of the projects and policies in which Coke was involved were highly controversial, and that the testimonies to his ambition came from those critical of the policies and not simply of the man. It would perhaps generally be agreed that he was rash and hasty and given to grandiose schemes without sufficient attention to practicalities. John Wesley himself, accepting Coke's essential integrity and his good intentions, allowed that he was too rash in this way. In his sympathetic treatment and defence of Coke, Vickers portrays him as being 'ambitious', not so much for his own personal aggrandizement as to further the causes he had at heart, especially missions. If we accept this, Coke's problem then arose from the fact that he tended always to see himself as a key figure who thought his schemes would work only if he took a leading part. To do so successfully he needed a defined status to sustain his authority: as Wesley's authorized agent, a Methodist or an Anglican bishop. It was in fact understandable that, given Wesley's scanty and rather indifferent collection of clerical helpers, the committed enthusiast Coke should have become more and more useful to him and acted as an informal or formal deputy in various tasks. But it is no doubt significant that there is no sign that Wesley suggested that Coke should be his successor as he did suggest Fletcher.

No doubt he knew both Coke and the preachers too well to hope for success in this direction. Leaving aside any question of ambition on their part or Coke's, their criteria were those of spiritual gifts and acceptability within a Methodist context: clerical status as such had no weight, as the M'Nab case had clearly shown. If Wesley's instincts still inclined him to clerical leadership where it was available, his sense of what the preachers would accept outweighed this in the end. It was what would hold Methodism together that mattered, and it became clear that neither Coke nor any other individual could achieve that.

Plans for the succession and crises over ordination and separation need to be seen in the context of the growing signs of practical separation and the consolidation of a self-sufficient Methodist 'church' life at the local level. This can be seen in such matters as the building of chapels, their registration and that of the preachers as 'Dissenting', pressure for worship in church hours and the administration of sacraments. Wesley constantly warned against even the language of separatism. Methodists should not call 'our society a church or the Church'; nor should preachers be called 'ministers' nor our 'houses' 'meeting houses (call them plain preaching houses)'. But even Wesley himself was not always guiltless of slipping into such language. In the 1770s Vincent Perronet talked about 'the Methodist Church', while Fletcher had used the term as early as 1759 and would adopt it for his scheme of 1775.[23]

The preaching houses in any case posed both legal and practical problems. There were nearly 400 of them by 1784, and when the Conference of 1783 tried to curb building to avoid debt, there were eighty-five applications for permission in three years and no doubt some unauthorized ones.[24] The practical problem was to secure the buildings on trusts which would safeguard control of the pulpit for Wesley and his appointees against any attempt by local trustees to exclude them and choose their own. The legal problem was that they were clearly not Anglican places of worship even in terms of 'proprietary' chapels (a category which would have destroyed connexionalism in any case), yet to register them as Dissenting chapels under the Toleration Act was to slide into the separatist and sectarian status that Wesley wished to avoid. However, freedom from closure under the law must be had. Wesley tried to solve the problem by advising people to register the 'house' as 'licensed for public worship', and in the 1760s and 1770s it appears that the term 'Methodist' was seldom used in applications. In Lincolnshire 'Independent' was used in a non-denominational or at least ambiguous sense, but in Yorkshire 'Protestant' or 'Protestant Dissenter', or no title at all. Since this was felt by critics to violate the spirit of the Act, there were some prosecutions, but King's Bench upheld the Methodist case, and once in Kent they got away without registering at all, much to Wesley's delight.[25]

Control was another matter. The Model Deed of 1763 secured control of the pulpit for Wesley and his designated successors, ultimately the Conference, and the trustees were to be Methodists.[26] But not all had this kind of trust, and as it turned out there would be local pitched battles with ambitious and possessive trustees.

Preachers had similar legal problems over registration. Here, too, Wesley was reluctant to let them be compromised as Dissenters. The 1763 Conference advised them only to register if 'constrained', 'and then not as a Dissenter but a Methodist Preacher'.[27] As this suggests, preachers had been registering for some time: the first extant case is dated 1758, and in the 1760s Charles objected, as we have seen, to the hypocrisy of those taking licenses as Dissenters and then claiming that they were not to their own people, while also still protecting themselves by the licenses against the press gang. Methodist opinion, by Charles's account, was split on such behaviour.[28]

The difficulties over registration of both kinds multiplied in Wesley's later years. Even the Model Deed was not thiefproof, since the 'Yearly Conference of the People called Methodists' in the formula had never been legally defined. John Pawson said that some of the 'wisest and best preachers' had suggested a general trust for all the houses, or a central collection of all deeds in London.[29] Matters came to a head in 1782, when the Birstall house was rebuilt and the new deed, like the original one of 1751, was not of the 'Model' type, for it gave the trustees power to displace preachers during Wesley's lifetime and to appoint them after his death. A sharp struggle ended with compensation for the trustees in return for an agreement for a new deed giving Conference the power of appointment.[30] Even the Deed of Declaration, to be discussed in a moment, while it cleared up the legal nicety of the definition of the 'Conference', did not settle all the difficulties. In 1787 a new chapel was built at Dewsbury, but the trustees broke their promise to put it on the Model Deed and reserved the right to reject preachers they did not like. The result of an acrimonious and unedifying quarrel was that the preacher John Atlay led the bulk of the congregation into a minor secession, and the 'loyal' survivors had to build another chapel.[31] Most remarkable of all is the fact that the trustees of the prestigious City Road Chapel in London had reserved themselves the right to approve the preachers appointed by Conference, and this was not sorted out until long after Wesley's death.[32] These tiresome and unedifying cases were important because they revealed the permanent tension within Methodism between 'Congregational' or 'Independent' and 'Connexional' ideals of the church. For Wesley's vision of Methodism, its fragmentation into little, local ministries under Dissenting 'bushels' would be the inevitable result of failure to exercise corporate control.

On registration Wesley had finally to give way both over houses and preachers. It looks as though there was a campaign in the late 1780s to deny preachers licences unless they professed themselves 'Protestant Dissenters from the Church of England': it seemed plausible, after all, to argue that they had no right to be recognized except under an Act only designed for protection of non-Anglicans. Wesley puffed loudly about 'English liberty' and 'the liberty of Christians' to Wilberforce and through him to Pitt. But of course nobody was denying him liberty – only the luxury of not conforming to the church, while avoiding Dissent as well. In the end he had to acquiesce in licensing all the houses and preachers, though on legal advice he said that this was only as 'preachers of the gospel', which he said no justice could refuse. Legally right or not, it was an evasion which could not conceal the drift into the position of a kind of *de jure* as well as *de facto* Dissent.[33] What brought on this situation by the 1790s was a double pressure: from a section of Methodism wishing for a clearer and more independent status and security; but also, and perhaps equally important, the emerging backlash of churchmen alarmed and enraged at the Dissenting campaign for repeal of the Test Act in a period of social and political tension. The Methodists seemed a kindred threat to Anglican hegemony, the more irritating for their equivocal position.

Within Methodism itself, but also underlining its growing separatism from the church, was the additional problem and provocation of cases of Methodist worship during the church hours of worship. This came from a section both of preachers and people, but was highly controversial even after Wesley's death, as 'Church Methodists' continued to oppose it.[34] The point was, of course, vital to Wesley himself as preserving at least the fiction of unity with the church, for his notion that unity only entailed belief in its doctrines and attendance at its worship would be half destroyed if Methodists failed to attend. Wesley himself was guilty of inconsistency when, as one of the preachers, Samuel Bradburn, bluntly pointed out, he had changed the Foundery service hours to coincide with those of the church. Given services and sacrament by friendly clergy, the people did not think that they were Dissenters, yet 'this had no more to do with the Church, as to real connection and subordination than with the Jews'. Hence other Methodists wanted the same privileges.[35] The practice spread to other places, and in any case there had never been any guarantee that the absence of services in church hours meant that Methodists would attend church as Wesley's ideal demanded – many clearly did not.

In fact Wesley had to take account of the fact that some objected to the Anglican liturgy and the doctrines they heard from unconverted clergy – and Calvinist Evangelicals were no better in their eyes, or indeed his own. The 1781 Conference conceded that when such clergy preached the 'absolute decrees' and ridiculed perfection they should quietly leave, though attending next time if possible.[36] What this also underlines is that with clergy varying so much, as well as Methodists, no *general* rule could have been realistic. As for Methodists of Dissenting background (a category often overlooked in discussions of this question and glossed over by Wesley himself), Wesley could only recommend them to go to their meeting houses. The growing number of Calvinistic Evangelical clergy was a particularly sore point. At Scarborough in 1786 Wesley confessed that he could not in conscience advise them to attend one of these parsons any more.[37]

That year Wesley laid down the ground rules for Methodist services in church hours: when the minister is 'a notoriously wicked man'; 'when he preaches Arian or any equally pernicious doctrine'; 'when there are not churches sufficient in the town to contain half the people'; and 'where there is no church at all within two or three miles'.[38] Yet he persisted in saying that fixing services in church hours was obliging people to 'separate from the Church or us', which was not only 'inexpedient' but 'unlawful'.[39] Thus he tried to hold the line he had laid down, very inconsistently – for on his own showing *any* meeting in church hours would have the effects he deplored. He was the more insistent because his ordinations were taken by others to mean outright separation. But it should be borne in mind throughout that, despite his protestations, unity with the church was not for Wesley an end in itself or his chief priority. There was an underlying consistency in his apparently capricious behaviour: the health and above all by now the unity of Methodism. If he needed to allow services in church hours to keep them quiet he did so; if not, not. Moreover, he argued, with considerable practical force, that such concessions if properly handled could keep people in touch with the church.

Dublin is a good illustration of these points. It was mentioned earlier in connection with Irish Methodism and the awkward and choleric Edward Smyth. The Dubliners had been repelled by the unevangelical preaching of the church and Wesley had allowed Henry Moore to hold 11.00 a.m. services, but then stopped them when Smyth began work at Bethesda. Next he compromised by allowing them except on the first Sunday of the month, on condition that people then went to church. At the 1788 Conference this led to a general ruling that the assistants could read Morning Prayer if the generality of the society agreed; provided that it was never done on church sacrament Sundays. But Wesley caused much controversy in Dublin in 1789 by allowing the assistant to read

Morning Prayer and administer the cup in communion. The Conference of that year in fact reduced the reasons for Methodist services in church hours to two: if the parson is 'notoriously wicked' or preaches 'Socinianism, Arianism or any other essentially false doctrine'.[40] The rationale of this policy of variable concessions was spelled out clearly by Wesley himself – it was 'not to *prepare* for, but to *prevent* a separation from the Church'; in support he cited the fact that more of the Dubliners, once they had their concession, went to Church and sacrament than before.[41] Of course Wesley may have been deceiving himself, and in retrospect the concessions may be seen as the first steps on the slide away from any connection with the church, but they are of importance for understanding Wesley's motives in his actions of that decade, including the ordinations.

There were indeed occasions when Wesley admitted, as in September 1788, that a 'kind of separation' was taking place. This was in *Thoughts on Separation from the Church*, and his concessions had forced him to shift his ground on attendance as a proof of belonging. 'Separation', he said, 'properly' refers to a 'total and immediate separation' ('properly' is a signal for Wesleyan wriggles out of difficulties – like his definition of sin 'properly so called' to allow for perfection). Ingham and Lady Huntingdon had formally 'separated' in this sense. But Wesley allowed that a 'kind of separation' was slowly taking place because of bad ministers.[42] One can only admire the virtuosity of Oxford logic which enabled him in effect now to claim that Methodists could do practically what they liked and still not be separating so long as they did not formally declare that they were leaving.

But these were very late thoughts, and by then two events had aggravated the situation more than Wesley admitted: the Deed of Declaration and the ordinations for America. The Deed, though in form merely a legal expedient to safeguard control of the chapels by the Conference, was also part of the process by which Methodism became a tighter corporate body and more distinct from the church, and it led to the loss of some preachers. The ordinations, however variously they may be interpreted, could only be taken by Anglicans as the final and irrevocable seal on Wesley's schism.

The Deed of Declaration was rendered necessary by the uncertainty of the legal definition of 'The Conference of the People called Methodists'. As we have seen, it had always been a body of those Wesley chose to summon to advise him: some preachers were asked and some not; sometimes other laymen were present, at least as observers. In 1766 he allowed any to come who wished but the next year only 'required' some and allowed the rest if they wished. He also tried to make sure that there were men left to man the Circuits during the sessions, and took good care not to invite trouble-makers during crises.[43] As long as he lived, he was determined to exercise control, and challenges like the M'Nab affair made him lay down the law to Thomas Taylor on the old lines: the preachers had originally asked for his direction; this was how it had been ever since. The Conference was originally summoned only to advise him and still was. You have liberty to disagree, but if so you leave; and so on.[44]

But the M'Nab affair, if not the iceberg tip of a conspiracy, as Charles Wesley claimed, certainly showed an increasingly restive and 'democratical' mood. In 1780 Wesley reverted to his earlier practice of only inviting a select number of preachers, and apparently not allowing others to come. He also called Fletcher and Coke and probably four of the lay preachers to form a kind of 'cabinet' to guide the business, while deliberately conceding more days for debate. That year a preacher presided temporarily for the first time.[45] But he avowedly retained his rights of control to the end: if there were concessions they were to *be* concessions, not an allowance of 'rights'; nor would he be controlled by the preachers or held responsible to them. Contentious people were deliberately left out, and he admitted as much: a 'packed' Parliament in fact.[46] It is not surprising that the old charges of 'Pope John' kept recurring: the Moravians repeated their old view of this bluntly to each other when Charles Wesley tried abortive negotiations for a reconciliation in 1784.[47]

The legal Deed of 1784 was not intended to delegate or derogate from Wesley's power, nor did it. What it did, apart from making it easier to control the trusts, was to restrict the legal Conference to a named body of men instead of a haphazard selection at Wesley's whim; and this was also done with an eye to the succession after his death. The circumstances in which this was done gave rise to controversy because of the party views involved, the suspicions of Coke's alleged intrigues, and the resentment of those left out of the newly-defined magic circle.

Coke obtained a legal opinion from a fellow-Welshman, a barrister called John Madocks, while the Birstall case was going on. But he also said that he quoted to the 1783 Conference an opinion by Madocks that 'the law could not recognize the Conference in the state which it stood at that time, and consequently that there was no central point which might preserve the connexion from splitting into a thousand fragments after Mr Wesley's death'. There is uncertainty about the exact course of events which followed, but eventually Madocks proposed fixing the sense of 'Conference', its powers and its mode of continuing in succession. Wesley should enrol the definitions in a Chancery deed, naming the members and the mode of filling vacancies, with the minutes as evidence. Coke reported this to the 1783 Conference, which asked Wesley to draw up the deed, and the 'mode of doing it was entirely left to his judgment and direction'. The matter was suddenly made more urgent when Wesley was taken ill during the Conference (he was now eighty years old) and seemed likely to die. He asked Coke and an attorney to draft the deed, but what turned out to be the really controversial point was Wesley's own work: the hundred named persons who were to constitute the newly-legalized body.[48]

The Deed was drawn up and enrolled during February and March 1784. It is uncertain whether Wesley intended to keep the details secret until the Conference, but in the event Coke took it upon himself to send copies to all the assistants to show to their colleagues, with a covering letter claiming that he 'had no hand in nominating or omitting any of my brethren'. Wesley himself then authorized other copies to be sent. It was in this way that at least one of the nominated hundred – Samuel Bradburn – received the news of his appointment.[49] This looks like a confusion of counsels, or at least a lack of good sense or even good manners, which made a difficult situation worse. There are in fact contradictory accounts even of the process by which the deed was drawn up: in *Thoughts upon Some Late Occurrences* Wesley gives the impression that he did all the business with the lawyers and Coke is not mentioned; but Coke's account implies that *he* did all the negotiating. Since neither man was a conscious liar, one must suppose that defective memory, unconscious self-importance and (very possibly) a decent desire by each to divert some of the criticism over the affair from the other combined to create two different versions. It is most probable, as Baker suggests, that there is some truth in both. The one thing that Coke plainly did *not* want to claim responsibility for was the naming of the names; indeed he said that he had suggested that all the travelling preachers should be nominated. Wesley in fact claimed sole responsibility here, and there is no reason to doubt this. He thought at first of having only ten or twelve, then decided there was safety in numbers and put one hundred: he did not include them all because some would be needed in the circuits during Conference. He chose those whom he thought most suitable, and to those who thought others might have been more suitable replied, 'True, if I had thought as well of them as they did of themselves' – a remark reflecting the bitter recriminations which followed.[50]

Wesley's motives for his choices are open to debate. What caused offence was the fact that he had obviously not gone by seniority but chosen in terms of suitability regardless of age and experience, and so some seniors were omitted and juniors included. The suspicion was that he left out men of independent mind (or, if one prefers, trouble-makers). A more idealistic biographer could see this as a judicious mixing of young and old to ensure balanced counsels. In view of Wesley's 'packing'

of Conference earlier, the first interpretation seems at least equally
likely.[51] The charge that Coke influenced the old man is probably
groundless. Pawson thought that Wesley had 'no improper design' but
that he acted 'without due consideration, not foreseeing the consequences which would follow', and he acquitted Coke of any improper
influence too.[52]

Some of the senior men excluded from the list were naturally furious,
in particular John Hampson senior (who had a long record of annoying
Charles Wesley by attacking the Church). In *An Appeal to the Reverends
John and Charles Wesley* he spoke for the 'excluded ninety-one', urging
them to come to Conference and throw out the offending document. At
the Conference in 1784 Fletcher, now near to death, staged one of
his spectacular entries and dissolved the assembly into tears. A few
itinerants resigned, including the two Hampsons and Pilmoor the former
missionary to America. The younger Hampson later took Anglican
orders and might be said to have had his revenge in his biography of
Wesley, though in fact this is arguably, for all its bias, one of the better
readings of Wesley's character (see below, pp. 536f.).

The Deed, after defining the Conference as the one hundred named
men and 'their successors for ever, to be chosen as hereafter mentioned',
lays down fifteen regulations for the conduct of the Conference.[53] The
Conference is to meet annually at London, Bristol or Newcastle (by a
later amendment other places could be chosen) for a minimum of five
days and a maximum of three weeks. The quorum is to be forty and
decisions are to be by majority vote. A President and Secretary are to
be chosen annually, after vacancies in the one hundred have been filled.
The Conference should settle the President's powers; it has power to
expel members who forfeit their places if absent for more than two years
without dispensation. Those elected as members must have been in
connexion for at least twelve months. The Conference has power to
admit into connexion those whom it approves as preachers. It can only
appoint preachers to its chapels who are members and in connexion
with it, and for not more than three successive years. For chapels in
Ireland or outside Britain, Conference could send delegates with full
powers. If Conference failed to meet for three successive years or fell
below forty members for that length of time it would be extinguished
and its chapels left to the trustees, who could then appoint what
preachers they desired. Most important, none of these provisions was
to extinguish, lessen or abridge the 'life-estate' of John and Charles
Wesley in the chapels. Among the other significant points were provisions to limit stays in the circuits, majority votes in Conference and
the remarkably low qualification of twelve months' service to qualify for
Conference membership, rather than some form of seniority. This was

in line with Wesley's original selection of members, but in practice his successors stuck to electing senior men.

Nothing was said about relationships with the church nor indeed about doctrinal standards. The latter, however, had already been defined in the Model Deed of 1763 as being taught in Wesley's *Sermons* and *Notes*, though no list of doctrines was specified. As to the relationship with the Church of England, Professor Baker is surely right to say that setting up a legal body of this kind for spiritual purposes never approved of by any ecclesiastical court, of laymen not accountable to episcopal or parish authority, in buildings held in trust for a private organization not subject to the established church, was bound to appear to many to mean that the notion of Methodism as an 'unseparated arm of the church' was a legal fiction.[54]

The new Deed made little difference to the actual functioning of Conference for the time being, except that Wesley now appeared in the *Minutes* as 'President' with Coke as 'Secretary'. Although he occasionally allowed others to take the chair, the letters already quoted from 1785 make it clear that he summoned only those preachers he wished to the Conference. He declared that 'No power which I have enjoyed is given up by the Declaration Deed', and said that no such thing could have been supposed but for 'that improper and ambiguous word life-estate'. There were also fears that the 'Legal Hundred', as it was later termed, might use its powers to exclude others from the Conference discussions. In April 1785 Wesley wrote a letter to be read in the first Conference after his death, 'beseeching you by the mercies of God' not to use the Deed to assume any 'superiority over your brethren', but to keep things as far as possible as in his lifetime and not to show any respect of persons in making appointments.[55] While he lived, he would behave as before, though when he was absent briefly during a session of Conference in 1785 he accepted a decision made by the preachers with which he disagreed, saying, 'I will not run my head against all the Conference by reversing what they determined.'[56] The force of the preachers, Wesley's age and his avowed intention of accustoming the people to accept the preachers' authority when he had gone – all this helped to soften the assertion of his absolute power over them. But not much. His primary concern remained to keep the connexion together and to avoid whatever (at least in his eyes) would constitute an outright separation from the church during his lifetime. At the same time he was quite prepared, as before, to take whatever measures he thought necessary to secure the first objective even at the expense of the second. It is in this light, however paradoxical and perverse his actions may seem to be, that one should view the second and far more controversial decision of 1784: the new arrangements and ordinations for the Methodists in America.

3. Securing the future: (ii) 'But who laid hands on him?' Wesley's
ordinations

Wesley's first ordinations were part of a scheme for American Methodism designed to give it an independent church life on lines which would
combine the values of the Church of England with those of Methodism.
At the same time he evidently hoped to keep the Americans 'in connexion'
with him and indeed subject to his final authority as far as possible.
Ostensibly this left the British situation unchanged, though in subsequent years Wesley did several ordinations for Scotland and a very
few for England. Apart from the controversy this aroused inside as well
as outside Methodism, the ordinations are perhaps less important in
themselves than for the light they throw on the larger questions of
Wesley's 'plan' for Methodism; on conflicting views of its relationship
with the church; on the question of the status of Methodist preachers in
their own eyes and those of the people; and on the problems of holding
Methodism together as a body. None of these problems were new, but
they naturally became increasingly urgent as Wesley's death
approached.

The question of ordination had of course been on the agenda for years,
and Wesley had mentally prepared for himself a reserve position to
justify it when necessary by his convenient manipulation of the King
and Stillingfleet arguments back in the 1740s, along with dropping the
myth of the apostolic succession. But he resisted the demand for
ordination, though under great pressure in the 1750s, mainly on practical
grounds as not 'expedient' and (as he then thought) 'little less than a
formal separation' from the church.[57] In the 1780s he would deny by
some ingenious and characteristic sophistries that ordination meant
separation, for separation was something he did wish to avoid – again
for practical reasons. During the intervening period some elements of
practical separation had been developing. Various reasons might be
given for this. Wesley himself professed to believe that it was due to the
recruitment of Dissenters to Methodism who corrupted the rest with
their hatred of the church, and Methodist historians have often said the
same.[58] This is not very plausible, and in case impossible to verify
statistically. There is no reason in any case to suppose that those in favour
of separation and those against divided in terms of their Dissenting or
Anglican background. The process came about essentially because of the
development of a self-sufficient Methodist way of life and organization
which owed little to the church and expressed a fundamentally different
ethos and set of priorities.

In formal terms of worship, ordination and sacramental ministrations,
Wesley himself admitted that 'a kind of separation' was taking place in

the 1780s, but he narrowed down his definition of such an event from denying the church's doctrines and absenting oneself from its worship to that of proclaiming a formal secession as a body: like Lady Huntingdon's action. In these terms he could still deny he had done any such thing, even by his ordinations (at least so he claimed).[59] On various occasions preachers had taken the matter of sacraments into their own hands and simply administered without any ordination at all, perhaps relying on their status as preachers, as in Norwich in 1760. Some in later years had at least indulged in taking baptisms and burials. Wesley seems to have made no great fuss about burials, but he objected to baptisms. In 1783–4 he threatened to expel those doing it (several had), but by 1787 he was merely saying that they should go 'slow and sure' on it.[60]

Wesley was adamant that his euphemistic 'permitting' of men to preach (for which he allowed that they had an 'inward call' which, if anything, was better than the 'outward call' and ordination of many church ministers) did not carry with it the 'priestly' power of administering sacraments, particularly the eucharist. Some form of ordination was necessary for this, if only his own. Some of the preachers, even those with a sense of ecclesiastical propriety, nevertheless thought a man might in extreme circumstances take it upon himself to administer without ordination. Francis Gilbert, contemplating his isolated West Indian situation in 1760, thought that a lay preacher 'may lawfully give the sacrament, without the imposition of a bishop's hand', though he thought that Methodists should not. But if he was in a distant land where there was as yet no church, it might be right to do so.[61]

Wesley's concern was to keep Methodism as an evangelizing body with a mobile corps of travelling preachers. He had argued in the 1750s that this mission required allowing laymen to preach so as to save souls, but whereas preaching was essential for salvation, the eucharist was not.[62] Although this was a tactical argument to edge the preachers away from demands for ordination, it also represented Wesley's lasting view of their role and that of Methodism. As his arguments with Walker had shown, he dreaded ordination because it was likely to destroy itinerancy, if not Methodism itself. Nor did his advocacy of 'constant communion' ever lead him to contemplate mass authorization or ordination to secure it for Methodists: on his system of semi-dependence on the church they already had it available. But, as we have seen, the pressures for ordination and Methodist sacraments had at least as much to do with status, self-sufficiency and antipathy to Anglicanism as to a simple desire for more eucharistic worship.

In America the situation was similar yet different. It will be remembered that Strawbridge in Virginia had drifted into administering communion without authorization, exactly like the English rebels. The disruptions of the American Revolution and the flight of loyalist Anglican clergy aggravated rather than created a situation in which ordination seemed desirable, if not necessary – for obtaining sacraments at all or for maintaining Methodist stability. But here again the really alarming problem for Wesley and for some of his American disciples was the severing of links with their parent by the war. This, we shall see, was not a problem peculiar to Methodism, for American Episcopalians were also in confusion and less free to act than the Methodists. They were indeed driven to consider expedients almost as radical as Wesley's.

Wesley made more than one attempt to persuade the Bishop of London (whose jurisdiction extended formally to North America) to ordain men for work there. The Bishop's reply – that there were already three in Canada, which was the subject of one of Wesley's requests – has been seen as ludicrous.[63] But he was being asked, presumably, to ordain Methodists (no easy matter even for England), and when Wesley used the refusal as an excuse to do his own ordinations he (Wesley) must really have been relieved that he was free of the complications of episcopal jurisdiction in the emerging United States. The utopian scheme proposed by Fletcher in 1775 (which its author fairly clearly thought unlikely to be accepted) for Methodists ordained by the bishops but subject to Conference, was a solution without prospect of success, hence Fletcher proposed the possibility of acting independently instead (above, p. 466).

Shortly after the peace treaty was signed with the Americans in September 1783, Wesley replied to an American preacher, Edward Dromgoole, who had appealed for more preachers. His reply was that he hoped that when 'the Government in America is settled', some preachers would go, but 'First let us see how Providence opens itself'. It was in the same letter that he said that he was persuaded that 'Brother Asbury is raised up to preserve order among you, and to do just what I should do myself if it pleased God to bring me to America'.[64] In October 1783 he appointed Asbury 'General Assistant' for America, and urged the preachers there to keep to the Methodist doctrine and discipline as defined in England. He also warned them to beware of preachers coming from England without full authorization from himself. They should not receive any who were unwilling to be subject to the American Conference; above all he feared the infiltrations of Calvinists.[65] This was a holding operation. Wesley was tacitly accepting American political independence despite his earlier hostility, while trying to retain a slender link of authority and conformity over the transatlantic connexion, pending further action.

It has been suggested by Professor Baker that in October 1783 Wesley discussed his plans for a 'Methodist Church of England' in the United States: a church with its own doctrine, discipline, ministry and liturgy; a system of Methodist ideals within an Anglican framework, yet without Anglican control and only the lightest of English Methodist supervision.[66] He had talked sometimes of going to America himself – he was talking of this as late as October 1783.[67] But he seems already to have had Coke in mind as his representative. This was natural enough, and the possibility arises that their respective involvements in the scheme that followed may have been rather similar to those in devising the Deed of Declaration. Unfortunately the sources and interpretations of the American scheme are bedevilled by the same problems of second-hand accounts, faction fighting and diverse views and suspicions of Coke's character and 'ambition' as in the other scheme.[68]

According to a rather vague later account, derived from Coke, Wesley (probably in October 1783 but possibly earlier) 'informed Dr Coke of his design of drawing up a plan of church government and of establishing an ordination for his American societies. But, cautious of entering on so new a plan, he afterwards suspended the execution of his purpose and weighed the whole for upwards of a year.' The 'little sketch' referred to in a letter to the Americans in September 1784 was presumably drawn up at some point between then and the Conference of 1784.[69] The complete scheme provided for two 'joint Superintendents' for 'North America'; two 'elders' to administer the sacraments; and a revised liturgy based on the Prayer Book for use on Sundays.

This liturgy was published as *The Sunday Service of the Methodists in North America, with other occasional services.* It included also a revised version of the Thirty Nine Articles, reduced to twenty-four. There has been learned discussion of the sources, principles and antecedents of this revision, which cannot be entered into in detail here.[70] Wesley, like the Anglican Evangelicals, regarded the Church of England as the 'best-constituted National Church in the world' and its liturgy as having 'more of a solid, scriptural, rational piety' than any other.[71] But, like the Puritans before them, some of the preachers had already complained in the 1750s about its unscriptural defects and Wesley did not disagree. Fletcher had proposed a revised liturgy as part of his scheme in 1775.[72] Indeed there were recurring grumbles about the liturgy in the eighteenth century and several projects for revision, with at least one of which Wesley was acquainted.[73] Though these were partly concerned with abbreviation and objections to the damnatory Athanasian Creed (a problem felt also by Fletcher and other orthodox men), the main characteristic of such schemes had generally been a desire by Arians to purge the book of Trinitarian language. This was why Fletcher thought that Wesley would make a better job of reform than the Feathers Taverners.

Wesley claimed that he only made 'little alterations' except for removing most of the holy days; shortening the Sunday Service; omitting some sentences in the offices for baptism and burial; and leaving out many psalms and parts of psalms as 'highly improper for the mouths of a Christian congregation' – very like Isaac Watts here. In fact he made more extensive alterations than this, both in omitting services such as Confirmation, and tinkering with individual services. There is also a complicated bibliographical story of how Wesley apparently included the manual acts in the Eucharist and Coke omitted them.[74] As to the Articles, he omitted some old enemies like XIII on works before justification and XVII on predestination. The significance of these changes is open to various interpretations. It is not plausible to suppose (as some have suggested) that Wesley borrowed from eighteenth-century Arians or from the Puritan Savoy Conference scheme of 1661. Some of the changes simply reflect the book's American purpose. Some may reflect a desire to avoid offence to Dissenters there (such as no rubric about kneeling at communion). To imagine Wesley solemnly conning and collating liturgies is anachronistic: Professor Baker's picture of him simply slashing and annotating a Book of Common Prayer exactly catches his usual method. The changes in fact reflect the objections he and other Methodists had felt for years; and there is a touch of eighteenth-century (though in his case 'orthodox') 'Scripture and common sense' attitudes too. The book does not seem to have been very widely used in Britain or America except for the Lord's Supper and Morning Prayer (some chapels in any case used the Prayer Book version). Many Methodists preferred their own plain service.

It seems that the conversation with Coke in October 1783 may only have been in terms of a proposal for a plan of church government and an ordination of preachers, presumably by Wesley assisted by Coke and others. For in February 1784 Coke seems to have been taken aback when Wesley proposed that he should ordain Coke as a superintendent or bishop. This became so controversial later as part of an already sufficiently controversial scheme that it has muddied the evidence with the claims of contending parties, some all too ready to suspect that Coke's 'ambitions' were the source of the whole scheme. Some did not hesitate to see him as pressurizing a senile Wesley into actions which Wesley afterwards regretted. Wesley's letter to the Americans in September 1784 seems to imply that he acted alone – as he implied he had done for the Deed of Declaration. It is not surprising, in view of the suspicions about him, that Coke claimed that he was taken aback when Wesley in February 1784 proposed to make him a 'bishop'. The most damning evidence against him comes (as it too often did) from his own pen. For two of his letters seem to show him as a busy, ambitious little man, badgering Wesley in his own interest.

According to Coke's biographer Drew, who appears to have heard this from Coke himself, Wesley, keeping his eye as usual on the Bible and 'the ages of unadulterated Christianity', had admired the way in which the early church of Alexandria for two hundred years used presbyters to ordain their bishops. He then asked Coke 'to accept such (episcopal ordination) at his hands, and to proceed in that character to the continent of America, to superintend the societies in the United States'. This was when Coke was taken aback, but after taking time off to study the early authorities he was able to concur with 'the absolute lawfulness of the measure which had been proposed'.[75]

However, in April 1784 Coke wrote in a still extant letter, in terms which seem to consort oddly with this account, for while it made plain that he had been discussing with Wesley a forthcoming visit to America, he seems to imply that the terms of his commission had not been settled; he even appeared to be pressing for a mission that had not yet been settled, if proposed at all.

> If some one in whom you could place the fullest confidence and whom you think likely to have sufficient influence and delicacy of conduct for the purpose were to go over and return, you would then have a source of sufficient information to determine on any points or propositions.

Wesley might well outlive him and Coke might lack the qualifications for the job. 'Otherwise, the possibility of my surviving you would render my taking such a voyage expedient.' Besides, if they both lived many years, Coke's journey would give Wesley fuller information than mere correspondence could do; it would facilitate a 'cement of union between the societies of preachers in the two countries'; and if Wesley died before him,

> it is almost certain, for many reasons which might be given, that I should have business enough of indispensable importance on my hands in these kingdoms.[76]

Perhaps too much should not be read into this. It seems as if Coke so far was trying to persuade Wesley to let him go to America to re-establish contact and collect information, with no request for authority to ordain or anything else, though the last sentence may sound like at least an expectation of being a leading figure in the connexion on Wesley's demise, which he might naturally expect to be.

In letters before the Conference Wesley canvassed for volunteers (his

usual policy for work overseas), and at the Conference, though mainly
concerned with the Deed of Union, he proposed to send Coke and others
to organize the American societies. Whatcoat and Vasey were chosen.
But Wesley only revealed his ordination plan to his 'cabinet'.[77] This was
a stormy occasion. According to Pawson, a member of the group, 'the
preachers were astonished when this was mentioned, and, to a man,
opposed it. But I plainly saw that it would be done, as Mr Wesley's
mind appeared to be quite made up.' Rankin, the former assistant in
America, suggested that Coke should get the help of American clergy
to ordain: not a very likely source. Fletcher was consulted, advised
trying the bishops first, but said that in any case Wesley should give
'letters testimonial' of the act.[78]

According to Whitehead (a prejudiced witness), Wesley knew that
no bishop would oblige (which was true enough) and so was inclined to
do it himself, yet seemed 'so languid if not wavering' that Coke thought
it necessary to use further means. Hence his letter of 9 August, which
will be quoted in the next paragraph. James Creighton, who was a
clerical aide of Wesley's (and another unreliable witness who later
claimed that Wesley repented of his ordinations) said that Wesley
consulted a group of clergy in Leeds including Fletcher and the anti-
Calvinist gladiator Walter Sellon. Creighton said: 'They did not approve
of the scheme, because it seemed inconsistent with Wesley's former
professions respecting the Church.' Upon this, the meeting was 'abruptly
broken up by Mr Wesley's going out'.[79] This was often his reaction when
meeting opposition. Charles Wesley, understandably, was not consulted
at all.

Wesley was evidently still hesitating about ordination, not through
senility, but because of the problems which he knew would arise in
relation to the church and indeed within Methodism. It was then, on 9
August, that Coke wrote to him in terms which have once again played
into the hands of his critics, for he appeared to be pushing Wesley to a
decision, ambitiously, for his own ends. But it is clear that Wesley
already had the scheme in mind and that if Coke was pushing him, it
was to make up his mind to implement it. He wrote:

> The more maturely I consider the subject, the more expedient it
> appears to me that the power of ordaining others should be received
> by me from you, by the imposition of your hands, and that you should
> lay hands on Brother Whatcoat and Brother Vasey, for the following
> reasons. 1. It seems to me the most scriptural way, and most agreeable
> to the practice of the primitive churches. 2. I may want all the
> influence in America which you can throw into my scale.

This was because he had heard that Asbury had written that:

he should not receive any person deputed by you to take any part of the superintendency of the work invested in him' . . . (Hence) it is well to provide against all events, and an authority *formally* received from you will be fully admitted by the people, and my exercising the office of ordination without that formal authority may be disputed, if there be any opposition on any other account . . .

Coke assured Wesley that he would only use the authority so far as necessary 'for the prosperity of the work', and rejected Rankin's argument that omitting it would avoid odium. If it were known, Wesley would be bound to 'acknowledge that I acted under your direction, or suffer me to sink under the weight of my enemies, with perhaps your brother at the head of them'.[80]

Whitehead commented that on Wesley's own argument for presbyteral ordination, Coke had as good a right as Wesley to ordain. Indeed he might have spared Wesley the odium of it by acting with other clergy himself. We do not in fact know whether Wesley needed much persuading by now, and to argue about Coke's equal right is to miss the real point, which in fact is clear enough in the letter and very cogent, as well as offering a clue to what Wesley's motives and concerns really were. No doubt Coke was anxious for his own skin and anxious to get Wesley's support visibly committed to him; maybe he was ambitious. But the real point was, as he said, that he needed all the authority he could get at home and in America to convey Wesley's authority and control over the new church. The symbolic act of ordination to a superior and supervisory capacity, whatever it might mean in terms of ecclesiastical or Anglican tradition, was a clear symbolic act for the conveyance of *Wesley's* authority through Coke over the American branch of the connexion: in this respect Coke's equal status with Wesley as an Anglican priest had no real significance.

In view of his later comments on Wesley's repentance of the act, it is worth noting that James Creighton was associated with Wesley and Coke in the ordinations which took place in Bristol on 1 and 2 September 1784. The published *Journal* simply records that Wesley 'appointed Mr Whatcoat and Vasey to go and serve the desolate sheep in America'. In a passage omitted (by accident or design) in the second 1789 edition, he wrote: 'I added to them three more.' The diary, however, records that on 1 September he 'ordained' Whatcoat and Vasey and on 2 September 'ordained' Coke.[81] The discreet *Journal* references then conceal the fact that he ordained Whatcoat and Vasey on successive days as deacons and 'elders' or presbyters, with Coke as 'superintendent' on the second occasion – hence 'adding to them three more'. Their letters of orders included the claim that for lack of Anglican support, 'I,

John Wesley, think myself to be providentially called at this time to set apart some persons for the work of the ministry in America.' So he set them apart ('as Elders' added above the text) 'by the imposition of my hands and prayers'. In later cases the term 'presbyter' was used. They were 'fit persons' to feed the flock and administer the sacraments 'according to the usage of the Church of England'. If Wesley used his new prayer book, the form will have been very similar, apart from the titles of the offices, to that of the Book of Common Prayer.[82]

Wesley's official view of the American scheme was expressed in a letter to the Methodists there on 10 September 1784. 'By a very uncommon chain of providences,' he began, 'many of the Provinces of North America are totally disjoined from their Mother Country . . . The English Government has no authority over them, either civil or ecclesiastical.' He then says that Lord King's book had convinced him many years ago 'that bishops and presbyters are of the same order, and consequently have the same right to ordain'. But he had resisted pressure to ordain travelling preachers 'not only for peace' sake, but because I was determined as little as possible to violate the established order of the National Church . . . ' 'But the case is widely different between England and North America.' They lack bishops and even parish ministers, and so the sacraments. So 'I conceive myself at full liberty, as I violate no order and invade no man's right by appointing and sending labourers into the harvest.' He then says that he has 'appointed' his superintendents and elders and prepared a liturgy which he 'advises' them to use. He concludes by answering the advice to ask the bishops to ordain some of the preachers for America. He could not persuade the Bishop of London to act; it would also be too slow. But he also says (more importantly) that if they ordained, 'they would likewise expect to govern them. And how grievously would this entangle us!'

As the Americans are now disentangled from the state and the hierarchy, 'we dare not entangle them again either with the one or the other. They are now at full liberty simply to follow the Scriptures and the Primitive Church. And we judge it best that they should stand fast in that liberty wherewith God has so strangely made them free.'[83] He repeated his claim to be 'as much a Christian bishop as the Archbishop of Canterbury' in a private letter a few months later. But he had resolved never to use his power 'except in case of necessity'. 'Such a case does not (perhaps never will) exist in England. In America it did exist.' But he still asserted that he was 'now as firmly attached to the Church of England as ever I was'.[84]

It is not always sufficiently recognized that Wesley was not alone in his problems with America or in the 'providences' which seemed to set him free to act. Since they had never had resident bishops, the American

Episcopalians had always depended for ordination either on individuals voyaging to England to gain it or on clergy coming from England. Now the Revolution had cut them off, and American independence destroyed the jurisdiction of the English Crown and hierarchy. In response to this crisis there was more than one reaction: the romantic story of Samuel Seabury's pilgrimage in search of episcopal consecration is only half of it, and perhaps not the most interesting half, even if for some the most comforting and correct.[85] That other half has a bearing on Wesley's apparently eccentric, if not outrageous, action.

The Episcopalians were not only bereft of episcopal help but devastated by the accidents of war and the loss of loyalist refugees as well as being divided by the infiltration of Latitudinarian and Socinian views, not unmixed in some cases with 'republican' views of church government. In 1782 William White, a Philadelphia clergyman, drafted a scheme for a federal church structure and even proposed a presbyterian ordination until an episcopate could be established. In Maryland in 1783, Dr William Smith convened a meeting of clergy which declared that a Protestant Episcopal Church existed, and elected Smith as bishop, though he still had to find consecration. Moreover, some of the Maryland clergy, hearing of Wesley's scheme, either just before or during the Christmas Conference of 1784 which inaugurated the new Methodist body, invited Coke and Asbury to consider a merger of the Methodists and Episcopalians, recommending the 'very simple' and 'rational' plan of the Marylanders for a convention of an equal number of laity and clergy with a bishop as president. Coke might be consecrated as a bishop and they could 'see no impropriety in having two bishops in one state, one of whom might always be elected from among the people called Methodists, so long as that distinction should be kept up amongst them'. Coke was not encouraging, and one of the Episcopalians was probably right in seeing it as 'an indispensably necessary' point among the Methodists that 'Mr Wesley be the first link of the chain upon which that church is suspended'.[86]

Meanwhile White proceeded with his schemes, and proposed a general convention which met in 1785. But the Connecticut High Churchmen were alarmed at these Latitudinarian and republican noises, and chose Samuel Seabury to seek consecration. Failing to find it in England, if only because of the legal and constitutional confusion in the wake of the peace, he finally received it at the hands of Scottish Nonjuror bishops in November 1784; he also hoped to introduce their version of the Prayer Book into America. White and his friends would have liked to revise the Book in other directions. Their party finally persuaded the English government to legislate to allow the English episcopate to consecrate bishops for America independently of the

Seabury group, and in February 1787 bishops were consecrated for Pennsylvania and New York. The two groups were united by a compromise in 1789.

Thus, as Professor Ward concludes, the English Methodist disputes about ordination were 'not so much the end-product of a long course of ecclesiastical irregularity in England, as part of a larger disagreement in the Anglican world about the unprecedented situation across the Atlantic'.[87] Certainly the final crisis was precipitated and the old problems were placed in a new dimension by this larger problem. And the Latitudinarian party in American Episcopalianism is an important reminder of the extent to which Wesley's actions and attitudes were related to the variety of Anglican opinion in the eighteenth century – they have too often been judged simply by later notions of theological propriety.

Coke and his companions arrived in New York in November 1784 and travelled to Philadelphia.[88] When Coke met Asbury and revealed Wesley's plan to him, Asbury expressed doubts, but added, 'it may be of God'. More significantly, he at once insisted that his own appointment as Superintendent should be left to the preachers, and it was agreed that there should be a General Conference in Baltimore at Christmas 1784 to debate the scheme. Asbury's attitude was as practical here as Wesley's, for though he was almost as authoritarian as the old man himself, he had a more realistic sense of what the Americans, especially after Independence, would accept. As Asbury recorded it, the Conference resolved to 'form ourselves into an Episcopal Church and to have superintendents, elders and deacons', and that he and Coke were 'unanimously elected to the superintendency of the church'. Asbury was then ordained successively as deacon, elder and superintendent.

At the ordination Coke preached a sermon to justify it and to explain the 'character of a Christian bishop'. One of those present explained that 'with us the Superintendent answers to the Bishop, who is to have the management of all, and we think it a better scheme, because *modern* Bishops being Lords are generally devourers of the flock and a curse to the people, and the very name conveys a disagreeable savour'.[89] Coke himself in his sermon dwelt on the politicized nature of past experience of bishops as 'hireling shepherds'. He justified the right to ordain by presbyters, citing 'primitive' precedents and the arguments of Bishop Hoadly (whom he had read on the way across the Atlantic) and the Dissenter Calamy. He defended 'moderate episcopacy' as best in terms of its practical role for securing unity and executive force – essentially Wesley's priorities. He then expounded the character of a Christian bishop with a special emphasis on humility.[90]

At the Conference, despite Asbury's insistence on his election by that body rather than simply following Wesley's appointment, the Americans were gratifyingly anxious to acknowledge their links with the founder and adopted his disciplinary code and the liturgy and articles. But they were discriminating about his authority. 'During the life of the Rev. Mr Wesley', they resolved, 'we acknowledge ourselves his sons in the gospel, ready in matters of church government to obey his commands. And we do engage after his death to do everything that we judge consistent with the cause of religion in America and the political interests of these States to preserve and promote our union with the Methodists in Europe.'[91]

What this meant was revealed in 1786, when Wesley summoned a General Conference to meet at Baltimore in 1787 for making two of the preachers superintendents. The Americans had already made their own arrangements and refused to comply. They also forced Coke to restrict his episcopal functions to America (i.e. not to control them from England), and denied that Wesley had power to post Asbury elsewhere. As Asbury said, 'For our old Daddy to appoint Conferences when and where he pleased, to appoint a joint superintendent with me, were strokes of power we did not understand.'[92] Within a few years they had not only adopted the title 'Methodist Episcopal Church' (which might pass as an allusion to the link with Anglican tradition), but altered 'superintendent' to 'bishop' and in 1789 added insult to injury by recording in their Minutes: 'Who are the persons that exercise the episcopal office in the Methodist Church in Europe and America? Wesley, Coke and Asbury.'[93]

Wesley observed and disliked these developments. To Asbury in September 1788 he wrote to define their different relationships to the Methodists: 'You are the elder brother of the American Methodists; I am under God the father of the whole family.' He 'naturally' cared and provided for them all, and what Coke gave them he could not give 'but for me'. Then, more intemperately, he went on to say that Asbury and Coke differed from him in that 'I study to be little; you study to be great. I creep; you strut along . . . How can you, how dare you suffer yourselves to be called Bishops? I shudder, I start at the very thought. Men may call me a knave or a fool, a rascal, a scoundrel, and I am content; but they shall never by my consent call me Bishop!'[94] He also objected to them erecting a school and calling it a 'college', and this, coupled with the tone of the other remarks, seems to suggest that what he was really objecting to were the symptoms of pride rather than niceties of ecclesiastical order and definition. In fact all of these arguments were less important than the obvious fact that the Americans were compelled by circumstances and sentiment to develop their own structures in effective independence of Wesley and England, even though they had incorporated some of the traditions of English Methodism in their own.

They effectively limited Coke's pretensions too, and his fantastic project for a reunion of American Methodists and Episcopalians in 1791 (though possibly coloured by his alarm at political and Methodist problems there) only served to discredit him further on both sides of the Atlantic.[95]

There was, inevitably, controversy in England too. Whitehead, seeking to discredit the affair as much as possible, quoted two 'old preachers' opinions on it as those of the 'uninfected itinerants'. One doubted the ordinations till he read the *Minutes*, and exclaimed: 'a new mode of ordination to be sure – the Presbyterian plan! – in spite of a million of declarations to the contrary!' He saw it as coming not from a 'multitude of councillors' but 'obstructed upon the Conference'. 'Who is the Father of the Monster?' He scoffed at the 'black-robed boys' and the 'few favourites' behind the scheme. Another said: 'I wish they had been asleep when they began the business of ordination: it is neither Episcopalian nor Presbyterian but a mere hodgepodge of inconsistencies.'[96]

It was predictable that the most outraged and furious opposition should have come from Charles Wesley. He had obviously been deliberately kept in the dark about the affair and only heard of the *fait accompli* from one of its Bristol opponents. He frankly thought that Coke had taken advantage of his brother's senility: 'He thought he could do what he would with the Doctor; but the Doctor has done what he would with him.'[97] Characteristically, his most bitter remarks were in verse:

> So easily are Bishops made
> By man's or woman's whim?
> W– his hands on C– hath laid,
> But who laid hands on him?

> W– himself and friends betrays,
> By his good sense forsook,
> While suddenly his hands he lays
> On the hot head of C–.

Of Coke's ordination of Asbury he wrote:

> A Roman emperor 'tis said,
> His favourite horse a consul made:
> But Coke brings other things to pass,
> He makes a bishop of an ass.[98]

He wrote to a friend that his old school-fellow Lord Mansfield, the eminent lawyer and Lord Chief Justice, had said that 'ordination is separation', but that John could not or would not see this. So 'our partnership is finished, though not our friendship'. The Methodists would become a new sect of Presbyterians.[99] Once the American ordinations had been carried out, he thought, the English preachers would not rest until John followed suit with them, and as Charles lived to see the Scottish ones, he seemed to be right. John's response was sharp, since he quoted Charles's own intemperate lines about obedience to 'heathenish priests and mitred infidels'. He repeated his old views about the true definition of the church and of separation and denied that he had separated even now, he continued to 'vary' from the church according to need. He allowed that he would ordain still, only not allowing those ordained to 'use the power they receive while in England'.[100] In the end the brothers had to agree to differ: John maintaining that he had not separated, Charles averring that he had.[101] Charles consoled himself with letters to American Episcopalians. James Creighton, apparently repenting of his part in the ordination, asked Charles to approach Mansfield with a view to asking the bishops to get an ordination. A letter, possibly by Coke, outlined a scheme for recognizing Methodists as 'extraordinary missionaries', gaining ordination for some and making John Wesley a bishop, perhaps to ordain during his lifetime and through some of the preachers after his death. Otherwise there would be separation in England as in Scotland.[102]

And indeed Charles Wesley's prophecy of separation creeping into Britain seemed to be fulfilled when Wesley ordained preachers for Scotland in 1785. The circumstances and reasons for this were discussed earlier (see above, pp. 230f.); Wesley justified the propriety of his action by claiming that as in America, though for different reasons, the Church of England establishment's writ did not run there. So once again he was not 'separating from the Church'. In any case (more to the point in terms of his real priorities), 'I dare not avoid doing what good I can while I live, for fear of evil that may follow when I am dead', a quotation from his remarks at the first Conference of 1744.[103]

The justifications for the American and Scottish ordinations might seem to imply that extending the system to England would indeed be 'separation'. Wesley annoyed the preachers ordained for Scotland by insisting that they dropped their gowns and bands and sacramental work when they were posted back to England; and Pawson annoyed him by allowing a kind of 'presbytery' to be set up in one Scottish town. The logic seemed to be that whatever Wesley's 'orders' meant, in practical terms they were primarily an expedient to keep the Scots Methodists in union with himself and the connexion (like the Americans).

But Wesley's rather specious arguments for acting where the Anglican writ did not run were eventually undermined. In 1786 he was urged to ordain a man for 'a desolate place in Yorkshire', but this was rejected by a majority in Conference.[104] That the plan was for a 'desolate place' is significant for estimating Wesley's motives. Here was a parallel to the needy sheep in America: a shred of justification might be found where the church, though nominally in charge, was not effectively present. But in 1788 he broke his own embargo by ordaining a senior preacher, Alexander Mather, and although the evidence is ambiguous, it appears as superintendent as well as deacon and elder – certainly Mather claimed later that Wesley had done this as part of his plan for the future.[105] Then, in 1789, he ordained two more men who remained in England: Rankin and Moore.[106] Though he had no clear plan yet for England, a reasonable interpretation of these acts might be that he was preparing for some kind of succession through a group of older and younger preachers after his death. This was what some of those concerned thought, as the sequel was to show, though it is difficult to see how this could be reconciled with the corporate authority of Conference, legally secured, unless they simply acted as agents on its behalf. It may equally well be the case that he simply continued the process of 'varying' here and there as needs arose, though the ordinations for England manifestly shot his earlier sophistries to pieces.

Altogether Wesley ordained twenty-seven men as presbyters plus two (Coke and Mather) as 'superintendents.' It is not always noticed that Coke continued to ordain after Wesley's death, apparently making Pawson a 'bishop' in 1794; and these ordinations included men for England. It is not strictly true, as is often stated, that formal ordinations of this kind were dropped, except for the mission field, until Conference revived them in 1836.[107]

Wesley is supposed to have said later that he was 'overpersuaded' about the Scottish ordinations and that no good came of it but much evil. He is even said to have repented of the whole business of ordinations and 'with tears expressed his sorrow both in public and private', for example at Conference in 1789.[108] The source for this is James Creighton and has to meet the difficulty that a few days after that Conference Wesley ordained Rankin and Moore, that is, unless one supposes that he really was senile (and there is really no evidence for mental, only for physical deterioration apart from loss of memory at the end). The source of these remarks was James Creighton and, as Professor Baker suggests, he may have taken Wesley's regret over the Scottish cases (because they did not produce good practical effects) as a general repentance. Maybe Wesley did occasionally regret the acts for the trouble they brought, but Creighton is not an unbiased witness, for in a sense he was covering himself for his own indiscretion in taking part. In any case, there is no sign that Wesley changed his mind on his *right* to ordain: that had been settled fifty years before; the whole of the proceedings in the 1780s emerged from his judgment of expediency, and it was perfectly reasonable to doubt from time to time whether he had judged correctly in those terms. Many of the objectors were really horrified at his claim to a 'right' – like Charles Wesley.

Although events after Wesley's death early in 1791 do not strictly concern us here, indirectly they are of some importance as illustrating the different views held not only of the course of action to follow but also of what Wesley's intentions had really been. They also show very clearly what the pressures and divisions were with which he had to contend and which he kept more or less in check as long as he lived.

The Conference of 1791 followed the Deed of 1784 and elected a President and Secretary. Coke hurried back from America and clearly expected to play an important role, perhaps indeed as President, to judge by a letter he wrote as if in anticipation of being 'President of the European Methodists'.[109] In the event, a meeting of preachers at Halifax resolved not to have 'another King in Israel', but in any case to have a 'king' appeared impossible by the Deed. They suggested that the vacancies in the Hundred be filled by seniority; that the President be elected for one year only; and that the circuits should be grouped in several Districts, each with a committee and 'president' or chairman. This was more or less what was done at the Conference later that year. William Thompson was elected President and Coke Secretary. It is natural to see this as a snub to Coke's 'ambition', but it was also a snub to other seniors, notably Mather as a presumptive 'bishop' designated by Wesley. Pawson certainly thought that Wesley had intended Coke and Mather to continue the ordinations in a kind of episcopal church.[110] More would be heard of this claim later, but whether or not it was correct, it did not really settle the question of authority in the connexion or the relationship of any bishops to the Conference. And in fact the Conference had an anxious and variable course to follow during the next few years because it had not only to establish its own authority but also to accommodate the rival views of various parties on ordination and the administration of sacraments. With this was bound up the whole question of relationships with the Church and the question of separation. In addition there was the question of the authority of the Conference as a purely travelling preachers' body and the claims of Methodist 'democrats'.[111] All this, too, in the context of a period of social and political anxiety. One cannot, perhaps, simplify the contenders into 'Church' Methodists wishing to avoid Methodist sacraments altogether and what might be called 'Dissenter' Methodists wanting ordination and sacraments. There were certainly some who saw 'Mr Wesley's plan' (and with some justice) as a matter of piecemeal concessions as need arose – a process which might presumably continue for a long time and without any formal secession or need to break off all relations with the church locally and individually in terms of attendance.

William Thompson spoke for the straitest of church Methodists in rejecting ordination as offensive to the church, perverting the priestly office and a denial of ecclesiastical discipline. But Pawson was very like Wesley in speaking of the Methodists as always having followed the leadings of Providence, as they should still do. He did not think that their future depended on staying in the church for evermore; but neither did he wish for a 'formal separation'. So the people and preachers should be allowed to worship in church hours and have the sacraments where they wished.[112]

The Conference modified its attitudes from year to year on the sacramental question, though it forbade the freelance ordinations indulged in by some of those already ordained.[113] Pawson complained that they 'really had no government' and that Coke and Mather should be 'allowed to be what they are, bishops' and ordain two others who should act with them at any rate for a year from four centres.[114] Then, in April 1794, Coke, Mather, Pawson and five others met secretly at Lichfield to concoct an 'episcopal' plan for Methodism. There should be an order of 'superintendents' appointed by Conference and subject to annual reappointment, and they would maintain Methodist discipline, each in his own district. In addition there would be an ordained ministry of elders and deacons. The Lord's Supper would be administered where the society wished for it, unless the trustees were against it. Not very tactfully, the group chose all but one of the proposed superintendents from their own number. This made it look like yet another 'cabal', with the egregious Coke involved as usual. The Conference turned down the plan as creating 'invidious and unhallowed distinctions among brethren'.[115]

Meanwhile an even more unhallowed row had been developing in Bristol where the Portland chapel, opened in 1792, had become a focus for those wishing for a formal Methodist ministry and sacraments. In 1792 two preachers read prayers in surplices and gowns and bands there and in 1794 Coke and Moore administered the sacrament. The New Room trustees took this as a deliberate provocation to Church Methodists like themselves, and barred their pulpit to Moore. There were also charges by their opponents that the 'High Church party' favoured the rich, which suggests the kind of social divisions which emerged between churches in some town circuits later. There was a similar conflict between the new Salford chapel founded in 1791 and its old, more Church Methodist partner in Oldham Street, Manchester.[116]

The Plan of Pacification (1795) resolved these problems with a compromise by which, amongst other provisions, chapels could have the sacraments if the trustees and leaders agreed, subject to Conference permission. Clashes should still be avoided, however, with the church sacrament Sundays. This in fact gave the trustees a blocking vote, so it was seen by some as a victory for them. Still, the option was taken up widely and from one point of view might be said to have led to a gradual and piecemeal 'separation' from the church, though of course there was much else involved in this.[117]

Although John Wesley is often said to have had a genius for organization, he had certainly not made all his intentions clear to his successors. His ordinations and superintendents had confused the apparently clear structure left by the Deed of Declaration, and divisions over relations with the church and oral traditions about his intentions through interested parties had ensured conflict and confusion. On the other hand, the Conference might be said to have muddled its way through by 1795 to the kind of untidy but practical concessions to necessity which, in a sense, had always been (under Providence) 'Mr Wesley's Plan'. Though there was a secession in 1797 by those wanting a more 'democratic' Conference and government, the Wesleyans did not do too badly. Very much worse conflicts were, however, ahead of them, but it is doubtful whether any structure devised by man could have evaded these, since they depended on factors other than purely Methodist ones in any case.

How in fact should we understand Wesley's ordinations and his 'plan' for Methodism (if there was one)? There seems little point in denying that from an Anglican point of view ordination must mean separation in formal ecclesiastical terms: but many had thought that this had been the situation, despite all Wesley's wrigglings, re-definitions and sophistries, ever since his 'irregularities' began after his conversion. His use of lay preachers alone had made this plain. The ordinations were really a final symbol of a process that had been going on for years. Yet Wesley, despite his perverse definitions, could claim some pragmatic truth in his contention that in practical terms the separation was not a complete breach so long as some Methodists continued to retain links of worship with the church, and this continued in some areas long after his death. Here was not a simple and clear-cut schism like that of Lady Huntingdon.

Although it is possible to devise theories in order to try to justify Wesley's ordinations as being somehow 'valid' in terms of ecclesiastical precedent or higher authority, they could certainly not be justified in terms of *Anglican* order.[118] Wesley's citations of King and Stillingfleet were flimsy and hardly true to their authors or their original context; nor, as has been argued here, were they the real justifications for his action when it finally came: but that is a separate question. The idea that Wesley acted as an 'apostolic man' can hardly be sustained as a serious ecclesiastical justification; if it is a claim to a kind of belated Pauline type of status, it is material for theologians rather than historians, and uncomfortably close to the kind of wilder sectarian claims that Wesley would certainly not have wished to be associated with.[119] The most that could be said is that Wesley did feel he was acting in response to divine guidance: not by a voice from heaven, however, but by Cromwell-type 'providences', the guidance of events which he believed did show that God had a purpose for his movement and himself.

The pattern Wesley chose to follow offers some clues. As far back as the Conference of 1745, it will be recalled, he had offered a striking historical sketch of how church government had developed which seemed to show that successive elements of Independency, Presbyterianism and Episcopalianism had emerged by a natural process in answer to need: none had been laid down by God.[120] This also seemed to reflect and justify the process by which he had acquired authority within Methodism and appointed preachers. Had he chosen to argue along these lines, he would have had a better basis for justifying his later actions than dubious arguments from King and Stillingfleet – though hardly to justify his position as an Anglican priest indulging in such things.

But how does this relate to the ordinations Wesley performed and the form he chose for them? The titles of 'deacon', 'elder' or 'presbyter' and 'superintendent' were clearly chosen deliberately as being comparable to the traditional and Anglican threefold ministry, but adjusted to 'primitive' terminology. The title of 'superintendent', though an alternative translation of 'bishop' (rejected when used by the Americans), was probably chosen partly to reduce offence but also to avoid 'lordly' associations and perhaps above all to express the primary intention of the office which Coke and others would be exercising. This would be a 'primitive' and pastoral 'episcopacy', an improvement in his eyes on the contemporary Anglican article. It may still be asked why, if presbyters and bishops are really of one order, Wesley needed to add an apparently distinct office. 'Validity' he had settled in terms of his appeal to primitive presbyteral ordination; 'succession' he had rejected as a 'fable'. But superintendency, and a recognized authority from Wesley acceptable to *Methodists*, were needed. For this he naturally fell back on a version of the superior order recognized by tradition. Complete ecclesiastical propriety and logicality Wesley could hardly achieve in the circumstances, but for the practical purposes he had in mind the ordinations fulfilled their purpose, even though not all Methodists approved. Ecclesiastical archaeologists might wish to explore other possibilities, but Wesley by now was no longer much of an ecclesiastical archaeologist, except for apologetic purposes. He was more concerned to hold Methodism together: he even denied (unlike almost everyone else then and since) that ordination meant separation – in his new and convenient definition of a formally proclaimed schism.

It is true that in his 1755 'Ought we to separate?' address Wesley emphasized the need for formal ordination to a superior priestly order to administer the sacraments, and he repeated this as late as the notorious 'Korah' sermon of 1789.[121] This somewhat confused utterance seems to have been designed less with a theoretical than a practical purpose in mind. Though it repeated his old High Church contention that the preachers were preachers only, and that this did not convey a right to administer sacraments, it also reflects another old obsession – and a more important one: the fear that by desiring orders they would settle down (whether as Anglican, Dissenting or Methodist ministers) and lose their peculiar glory and usefulness as *travelling* preachers. This was why he had always resisted schemes like Walker's or his brother's to get the preachers Anglican ordination and attach them to parishes. It was this, too, which had made him heave an implicit sigh of relief when the Americans did not get Anglican orders and were set free to act in a 'primitive' fashion – under *his* guidance. For this was the other vital consideration in his mind. Methodists must be mobile, united and (for his lifetime at least) under his own control, with transmission of control to the Conference (with or without 'superintendents') after his death.

In fact all the concessions which to Wesley's critics seemed to make for separation were made not to create but to stave off a formal separation. This was how Wesley explained his permission for church hour services in Dublin: 'not to *prepare for* but to *prevent* a separation from the Church.'[122] By this means he hoped not only to satisfy Methodist demands for their own services at ordinary times but also to obtain occasional attendance at church in return. All his concessions were made with the same end in view, even the ordinations: this was why he did not make them general, any more than he gave permission to have services during church hours. There were just enough concessions to solve local problems and to stave off a movement for general secession or piecemeal disintegration of Methodism into a loose collection of localized and ineffective Dissenting chapels.

It is worth observing that Lady Huntingdon faced exactly the same problem. Like Wesley she thought that she might be forced into an ordination to save her connexion from dissolving; but unlike him she was forced into schism by the Spa Fields affair – which gave Wesley a nice precedent for *not* separating by formal secession. Apart from holding

Methodism together, he wished to avoid separation with its religious and social 'taint of dissent', and to avoid further losses.

All of Wesley's schemes and concessions, then, had the same purpose: to maintain unity, his own authority over the whole body, and the force of the mission. This was the nature of his consistency, pursued by means which often from other and more formal and ecclesiastical points of view seemed inconsistent. He may also be seen as having had a 'plan' in terms of the way in which he treated the Americans and Scots, as is indicated by a hint in the Deed of Declaration. One clause in that document allows for Conference to appoint delegates to chapels 'in Ireland or other parts out of the Kingdom of Great Britain', with full powers from Conference for their acts to be treated as if they were its own. This was in fact how Coke acted for Wesley at the Irish Conference. This delegated authority could also be seen as extending to America and was no doubt intended to (Asbury was also a member of the Legal Hundred), though the Americans frustrated its purpose. Professor Ward suggests that the 'plan' was for a system of subordinate, regional Conferences bound together at the summit with each other and the yearly Conferences by travelling bishops or superintendents. The ordinations, then (Ward argues), were not a final sign of separation but the latest of a series of attempts to maintain unity and control. What Wesley failed to reckon with was American nationalism.[123]

Certainly this accords with the view taken here of Wesley's underlying and consistent priorities. The last words may be left with him. In 1790 he wrote that the purpose of Methodism was to 'spread life among all denominations' and that Methodists would do this till they separated. A little earlier, and even more to the point: 'I have only one thing in view – to keep all the Methodists in Great Britain one connected people'.[124]

4. 'In age and feebleness extreme': Wesley's old age and death

Wesley clearly intended to die in harness. He was still travelling and planning his usual spring itinerary at the time of the beginning of his last illness in February 1791. In 1789 his tour included Ireland and Cornwall for the last time. In 1790 the round ran much as usual: the London area – Bristol – the Midlands – Cheshire, Lancashire and Yorkshire – via Newcastle to Scotland – back via Yorkshire and Lincolnshire to Bristol for the Conference in August – South Wales–Bristol again – the Isle of Wight and so back to London for the winter. Although he had been confined to the British Isles ever since 1738, despite talk in the 1780s of visiting America, in 1783 he took a trip to Holland which he repeated in 1786. This was a kind of working holiday, since he made contact with Pietists there to cultivate the 'Catholic spirit'.[125] In 1787, at the age of eighty-four, he visited the Channel Isles, where Methodism now had a foothold. His *Journal* continued to the end to show the same mixture of evangelical adventures and wide-ranging curiosity: he viewed a pelican in 1790 and duly dismissed the legend that it fed its young on its own blood.[126]

Wesley in old age had become a venerable figure with white hair and an apostolic mien. He still rose early (between 4.00 and 5.00 a.m.) and still preached in the open air: the last occasion was beneath a tree at Winchelsea in October 1790, when he was aged eighty-seven.[127] As to his appearance, we may recall Walpole's description of him in early old age (so to speak) in 1766 as clean, fresh coloured, his hair 'neatly combed, but with a little soupçon of curl at the end'.[128] At a later date John Hampson says that his figure showed his 'temperance and continual exercise': he only weighed 8 stone 10 pounds (55.3 kg.) and is said to have stood only 5 feet 3 inches (1.53 m.). Hampson continues:

> His step was firm, and his appearance, till within a few years of his death, vigorous and muscular. His face, for an old man, was one of the finest we have seen. A clear, smooth forehead, an aquiline nose, an eye the brightest and most piercing that can be conceived, and a freshness of complexion scarcely ever to be found at his years, and impressive of the most perfect health, conspired to render him a venerable and interesting figure . . . In his countenance and demeanour, there was a cheerfulness mingled with gravity; a sprightliness, which was the natural result of an unusual flow of spirits, and was yet accompanied with every mark of the most serene tranquillity. His aspect, particularly in profile, had a strong character of acuteness and penetration. In dress, he was a pattern of neatness and simplicity. A narrow plaited stock, a coat with a small upright collar, no buckles at his knees, no silk or velvet in any part of his apparel, and a head as white as snow, gave an idea of something primitive and apostolical; while an air of neatness and cleanliness was diffused over his whole person.

As to his 'manner in private life', Hampson says that it was:

> the reverse of cynical or forbidding. It was sprightly and pleasant to the last degree; and presented a beautiful contrast to the austere deportment of many of his preachers and people who seem to have ranked laughter among the mortal sins. It was impossible to be long in his company without partaking his hilarity . . . His cheerfulness continued to the last.[129]

As regards his health, he had had many illnesses, and more than once expected to die prematurely. But as he wrote to Charles in 1760, 'I have been preternaturally restored more than ten times'.[130] During Charles's own last illness he still hoped that prayer as well as other remedies would restore him.[131] At the end of 1753 John was so ill that he even wrote his own epitaph (see below, p. 533). But as he grew older he felt that his health improved, though he still had some serious illnesses. In 1773 he was operated on for a hydrocele, and though he put an optimistic face on it, the trouble did not clear up easily.[132] In 1775 he had a violent fever in Ireland and his recovery was signalized, so it was said, by some miraculous accompaniments. A company of praying friends gathered round him and prayed that he might be spared for fifteen more years like Hezekiah (II Kings 20.6; Isa. 38.5). One then rose from her knees and cried 'The prayer is granted!' and he duly survived as predicted. Alexander Mather, then in England, had heard that Wesley was dead but did not believe it. Opening his Bible at the Isaiah passage he prayed that this would be fulfilled for Wesley.[133]

In 1776 Wesley wrote on his birthday:

I am seventy-three years old, and far abler to preach than I was at three and twenty. What natural means has God used to produce so wonderful an effect? (1) Continual exercise and change of air, by travelling above 4,000 miles in a year; (2) constant rising at 4.00; (3) the ability, if ever I want, to sleep immediately; (4) the never losing a night's sleep in my life; (5) two violent fevers and two deep consumptions . . . causing my flesh to come again, as the flesh of a little child. May I add, lastly, evenness of temper? I *feel* and *grieve*; but, by the grace of God, I *fret* at nothing.[134]

He was still marvelling at his health being so much better than in his youth into the 1780s, and in 1784 did not attribute this to 'secondary causes, but to the Sovereign Lord of all'.[135] But by this time he was regularly taking a chaise and not a horse for his journeys.

Annual reviews of his health became a feature of these years in his *Journal*, observed with a mixture of the clinical and curious with an underlying note of religious wonder. In 1785 he was still saying that he had not felt weariness for eleven years; even though his vision and strength failed, he claimed to feel 'no sensation of weariness'.[136] In 1788 he thought that his good health was owing to natural means, the power of God and 'the prayers of his children'. But he acknowledged that he was not so agile, his sight was a 'little damaged' (meaning that he could hardly see out of his left eye), and his memory was clearer for long-ago events than recent ones: yet he still felt no weariness in travel.[137] Only in June 1789 did he finally acknowledge that 'I now find I am old'. He could not read small print except in a strong light; his strength had decayed; his memory had deteriorated.[138] Finally came the sad confession of 1 January 1790. 'I am now an old man, decayed from head to foot. My eyes are dim, my right hand shakes much, my mouth is hot and dry every morning, I have a lingering fever almost every day, my motion is weak and slow. However, blessed be God, I do not slack my labour. I can preach and write still.'[139] On his birthday that year he claimed that for above eighty-six years he had felt none of the infirmities of old age, but that last August (in 1789) he had found a 'sudden change'. Now 'it seems nature is exhausted'.[140] Henry Moore, reading this entry, was astonished, for he said the old man still rose at 4.00 and went through his daily duties, 'not indeed with the same apparent vigour, but without complaint and with a degree of resolution which was astonishing'.[141] It was evidently a triumph of will and spirit over matter.

Wesley's memory had certainly decayed; more, probably, than he allowed. At the 1790 Conference Pawson said that 'he was now nearly worn out, and his faculties evidently were very much impaired, especially his memory'. Atmore heard him preach in May that year and noted that: 'He appears very feeble . . . his sight has failed so much that he cannot see to give out the hymns; yet his voice is strong and his spirit remarkably lively.'[142] 'For several years preceding his death,' recorded Whitehead (who was physician as well as preacher), 'this decay was more visible to others than to himself; particularly by a more frequent disposition to sleep during the day; of a growing defect in memory, a faculty he once possessed in a high degree of perfection; and of a general diminution of the vigour and agility he had so long enjoyed.'[143] Whitehead would probably have liked to believe that Wesley's late ordinations were the work of a bewildered old man, pressurized by unscrupulous colleagues. No doubt the picture of physical decay is correct, but the *Journal* and letters show no decay of mental power, and it seems best to attribute his last actions more to the pressures of the situation than to any serious failure in his clarity of mind. Clearly he had a strong constitution, and he was no doubt right to suppose that a sensible diet and an active life, mingled with intellectual activity, had seen him through. His vegetarian experiment and abstinence from wine in Georgia had been dropped, then resumed for a couple of years, but then dropped again in the 1740s on medical advice. The same thing happened with his dropping of tea to save money. In his later years at least, according to Hampson, he took wine with his dinner, though in moderation.[144]

By Wesley's own account, too, he was free from emotional upheavals: a point of some importance which will be considered in connection with his spiritual experience (see below, p. 540). He may well have achieved a tranquillity in old age which had been less evident in his youth. Like all old men, he suffered the experience of outliving his friends: Vincent

Perronet (who lived to be ninety-one), Fletcher who died in 1785 and his brother Charles who died in 1788. It was certainly Charles's death that stirred him most deeply. They had often disagreed yet remained friends; and Charles was the confidant of some of his more intimate thoughts as well as being the last link with the days of the Oxford Methodists. A fortnight after Charles's death he tried to give out one of his hymns – 'Come O thou Traveller Unknown' – and at the words

> My company before is gone
> And I am left alone with Thee

he broke down in tears.[145] There had been no such reaction, understandably, at his wife's death seven years earlier, though one may still wonder a little at the bare record in the *Journal* that he was only told of it some days afterwards, actually after her funeral.[146]

But while nature slowly decayed, Wesley's compulsive, habitual journeys continued. More and more they became a kind of triumphal progress. At Falmouth in August 1789 he recalled how forty years before he had been mobbed there as in a den of lions. But now 'high and low . . . lined the streets, from one end of the town to the other, out of stark love and kindness, gaping and staring as if the King was going by'.[147] He had become a legend in his lifetime, a kind of national institution, his eccentricities often tolerated despite the continuing controversies over the ordinations. Charles Wesley, in an optimistic letter, claimed that the bishops had let them alone for fifty years to do as they wished. 'At present some of them are quite friendly towards us, particularly towards you. The churches are all open to you.'[148] The point of this remark was in fact to deter John from further ordination, but there was truth in it, as the *Journals* confirm. At King's Lynn in 1790 almost all the clergy came to hear him. At Diss the clergyman hesitated to invite him, but was told that Bishop Horne (a critic of Methodism) had said that he had no objection. There was a comic incident here when Wesley's friends supposedly hustled him away when a question was asked about the ordinations; but if they feared indiscretions, the explanation may be the prosaic fact that he had (as usual) another engagement to fulfil.[149]

Plainly many people were taking their last opportunity to see a historic figure and many remembered it all their lives, including several non-Methodists. The testimony of Crabbe was quoted at the beginning of this book, and one final and rather similar picture may be added here. Henry Crabb Robinson, a 'rational Dissenter', as a boy of fifteen heard the old man at Colchester in October 1790 a few days before Crabbe the poet. Wesley was pleased at the singing and said a few words of prayer at the end of each section of his sermon. At the end he spoke in favour of association with other varieties of religionists. 'If they fear God

and work righteousness and keep His commandments we have nothing
to object to.' This naturally pleased Robinson. The old patriarch stood
with a minister on either side holding him up. 'His feeble voice was
barely audible. But his reverend countenance, especially his long white
hair, formed a picture never to be forgotten. There was a vast crowd of
lovers and admirers. It was for the most part a pantomime, but the
pantomime went to the heart. Of its kind I never saw anything
comparable to it in later life.'[150]

Wesley was soon to close his accounts with God and his own people.
Literally so in one respect, for in July 1790 he recorded that 'For upwards
of eighty-six years I have kept my accounts exactly. I will not attempt
it any longer, being satisfied with the constant conviction that I save all
I can, and give all I can, that is, all I have.'[151] The last entry of the
Journal written up for publication was dated 24 October 1790, but the
diary continued until the beginning of his final illness. On 23 February
1791 he preached his last sermon, in the house of a friend at Leatherhead,
and the following day wrote his famous last extant letter, urging
Wilberforce on in his mission to end the slave trade.[152] Next day he
entered his house in City Road for the last time.

Wesley was proud of the way the Methodists died, and as we have
seen, their last days and deaths were carefully recorded as examples to
be followed, but also as a reassurance that in the sometimes anxious
Arminian scheme of things there had been no last-minute faltering of
faith (see above, p. 429). Inevitably, Wesley's last days and death were
carefully recorded, and many were anxious, if not to be present, at least
to be edified by the story of an end which blended peace with triumph.
Wesley's old friend and correspondent Miss Elizabeth Ritchie took
charge, acted as his nurse, and at the request of his physician Dr
Whitehead wrote a detailed account of events. Whitehead read a
shortened account after the funeral sermon for Wesley, and this was
circularized in a fuller version later.[153]

The concerns felt on these occasions are well expressed in Miss
Ritchie's description of how they prayed that if Wesley did not fully
recover, he might be aroused so that 'we might at least receive his dying
charges, and enjoy the comfort (amidst this awful scene) of hearing him
seal, with his latest breath, the blessed truths we had long been
accustomed to receive from God through him. We were indulged
herein . . . ' And so to a minute account of words and actions unfolded
in a series of 'pleasing, awful scenes'. Even Wesley did not quite escape
the pressures put upon dying Methodists. Having quoted a hymn used
during an earlier illness ('I the chief of sinners am, But Jesus died for
me'), Miss Ritchie said: 'Is this the present language of your heart, and
do you now feel as you then did?' and he replied, 'Yes'.

Some Methodists had visionary experiences of heaven on their death-beds, but this was denied to Wesley, and would not really have been in character. His mind seems mainly to have run on old favourite hymns. Almost at the end he was understood to say that he wished his sermon on the love of God to be printed and given away to everybody. Henry Moore very appropriately recorded him as saying: 'How necessary is it for everyone to be on the right foundation.' 'We must be justified by faith and then go on to full salvation' (perfection).[154] He cried out twice, 'The best of all is God is with us.' During his last night he frequently tried to repeat Isaac Watts's hymn 'I'll praise my Maker while I've breath', but his last word is said to have been simply 'Farewell'. And then, 'without a lingering groan', he passed over on Wednesday 2 March 1791. Mr Rogers then prayed 'for the descent of the Holy Ghost on us, and all who mourn the general loss to the Church Militant sustained by the removal of our much-loved Father to his great reward'. It is said that the event had a good effect on the London society: chapels were crowded, classes and bands 'exceedingly lively'. In May one hundred new members were found and nearly an equal number 'who had . . . tasted of the *pardoning* or the *pure* love of God'.[155]

The burials of great men were often attended with a great deal of pomp, ceremony and display, but there had always been those who sought to cut this down, some for religious reasons. This was particularly true of evangelicals, who often carefully specified what should and should not be done. Wesley's old enemy Toplady had forbidden the customary use of gifts of mourning rings, scarves and hat-bands, a monument or even a funeral sermon.[156] It was often difficult to persuade friends to obey. Wesley, as might be expected, was also careful to lay down his conditions. In his will he had stipulated that he should be buried wrapped in wool, and twenty shillings should be given to each of six poor old men to carry his body to the grave (a pleasantly old-fashioned custom). 'I particularly desire that there may be no hearse, no coach, no escutcheon, no pomp except the tears of those that love me and are following me to Abraham's bosom. I solemnly adjure my executors in the name of God, punctually to observe this.' They were to receive 'no recompense till the resurrection of judgment'. Wesley left few legacies – what money there was would come from his literary properties – but volumes of his sermons were to be given to his preachers. His private papers went to his executors and led to an unedifying series of squabbles about the writing of his biography, which considerably affected the first crop of lives in the 1790s.[157]

It was difficult, as always, to resist the feelings of survivors that much should be made of the funeral of such a man. Tradition has it that Wesley's body lay in state in the City Road Chapel on the night before the funeral, dressed in full canonicals and 'an old clerical cap', with a Bible in one hand and a handkerchief in the other; but Henry Moore, as an eyewitness, denied this.[158] To avoid crowds, the funeral was held at 5.00 a.m., but large numbers still gathered. When the officiating minister came to the words in the burial service, 'Forasmuch as it hath pleased Almighty God to take unto Himself the soul of our dear *brother*', he substituted 'our dear *father*' and the congregation dissolved into tears.[159] Methodists did not venerate the saints in any formal sense, but their funeral sermons and biographies, like those of their Puritan predecessors, acted as a kind of Protestant icon, models for holy living and dying to be revered and imitated. But there is a curious story that each attender at Wesley's funeral was given a biscuit in an envelope with a portrait of the patriarch dressed in canonicals and surmounted with a halo and crown. The whole chapel was draped in black, the material carefully chosen so that it could be re-used to provide 'decent dresses' for sixty poor women. It is also said, and appropriately, in view of some of Wesley's late scorching sermons on dress, that the only woman in that darkly-clothed assembly to wear a ribbon in her bonnet realized the enormity of it, tore off the offending thing, and ground it under her feet.[160]

John Wesley was buried in a vault in the burial ground behind City Road chapel. He had abandoned belief in the need for consecrated ground for burials as a 'popish conceit'. Charles, characteristically, had insisted on being buried in Marylebone churchyard, though John said that City Road ground was as '*holy* as any in England, and it contains a large quantity of "bonny dust"'. It is perhaps a final ironic comment on Charles's career that in fact the Marylebone churchyard had not been consecrated.[161]

John could not escape epitaphs. Like other religious men, when he thought he was dying in 1753, he had composed his own to escape eulogies:

Here lieth the body of John Wesley, A Brand plucked out of the burning; Who died of a consumption in the 51st year of his age, not leaving, after his debts are paid, Ten Pounds behind him. Praying, God be merciful to me, an unprofitable servant! He ordered, that this, if any, inscription should be placed on his tombstone.[162]

In 1791 he could not escape so easily, and perhaps in the end it was more fitting that his admirers should have been allowed to express their feelings rather than being bound by such conspicuous humility.

On his tombstone is written:

To the memory of the venerable John Wesley, A.M., late Fellow of

Lincoln College, Oxford. This great light arose, by the singular providence of God, to enlighten these nations, and to revive, enforce and defend the pure apostolical doctrine and practice of the Primitive Church, which he continued to defend, both by his labours and his writings, for more than half a century, and who, to his inexpressible joy, not only beheld their influence extending, and their efficacy witnessed in the hearts and lives of many thousands, as well in the Western world as in these Kingdoms, but also, far above all human power or expectation, lived to see provision made, by the singular grace of God, for their continuance and establishment, to the joy of future generations. Reader, if thou art constrain'd to bless the instrument, give God the glory. After having languished a few days, he at length finished his course and his life together, gloriously triumphing over death, March 2, anno Domini 1791, in the 88th year of his age.[163]

But perhaps Wesley might have been content with the plain record on his coffin which simply recalled his Oxford days:[164]

> Johannes Wesley AM
> Olim Soc. Coll. Lin. Oxon.
> Ob. 2d. die Martii 1791
> An. aet. 88.

POSTLUDE

Reckonings

1. John Wesley's personality and piety

Wesley's physical appearance has already been described, and in Hampson's description an impression is given of his behaviour and acceptability in general society (above, p. 527). It may certainly be said that in terms of general social intercourse few men of his time had such opportunities or capacity for mingling with so wide a range of social groups, both high and low, at least below the very highest. What hampered him here – and this has a bearing on any estimate of his personal relationships – is that he had to work to a more or less rigid timetable. This, combined with early rising and incessant travelling, along with his large correspondence, enabled him to keep his fingers on the pulse of his movement. Hampson calculated that he must have travelled well over 200,000 miles and preached over 40,000 sermons.[1] But the cost in human terms of social intercourse and even more of personal relationships was heavy. Dr Johnson's famous judgment exactly illustrates the point. 'John Wesley's conversation is good, but he is never at leisure. He is always obliged to go at a certain hour. This is very disagreeable to a man who loves to fold his legs and have out his talk, as I do.'[2] Wit shows in Wesley's writings, but a sense of humour was probably denied him.[3] One has a strong impression that he always conducted social and personal relationships on his own terms, and he certainly habitually judged that the disciplines that he found useful for himself would be useful for others, regardless of circumstances and temperament. Everybody should rise early; everybody should travel incessantly; everybody would find good for their health what he found good for his. Moreover, if his pet prescriptions and disciplines (like early services) were not followed, Methodism would decay. His fastidious neatness and tidiness were obsessive and extended from his person to

535

his personality. They were wished upon others: the contrast with Johnson is, of course, particularly marked, and one can guess what Wesley thought of Johnson's untidy ways and household, though he must also have appreciated Johnson's deep moral and religious integrity. Of course all this was necessary for his religious mission, and to this in the end all was subordinated. Such people, though admirable, are usually uncomfortable to live with; and it may be counted to Wesley's credit that he still found time for general culture, even though this too, as we have seen, was viewed in a religious light. Like many evangelicals, his interest in things and people was ultimately directed towards saving their souls and using them for his higher purposes.

To penetrate the inner springs of this personality is not easy, and most difficult of all in terms of Wesley's spiritual experience. On these matters we are largely at the mercy of his own writings and the observations of those who were closest to him in his later years. His writings, as has frequently been pointed out in this study, can easily deceive, especially when he is surveying himself from a later perspective: the *Journal* is coloured by propaganda purposes and the diaries reveal less than might be expected. As contemporary evidence the letters are more useful, but also conditioned by their purpose and the correspondents concerned: usually John is at his most candid to his brother. Hostile witnesses are of course valuable when their bias is allowed for, but the most intimate portraits come from those who knew him within the movement, and not less so because some broke with him later. Chief among these are the assessments by Hampson, Whitehead and Moore, together with the remarkable essay by Alexander Knox. All of these people, however, knew him only in old age and they knew the young Mr Wesley only through such documents as were accessible to them, though in Moore's case there were also Wesley's own confidences to him. Their evidence is therefore less useful for his early life and character; in many ways the modern student knows the young Mr Wesley – a much less tranquil figure than the old Mr Wesley – better than they did. And all these men had their own prejudices and purposes which coloured their judgments. Since a good deal will be drawn from them in what follows, something should be said about each.

Hampson was the younger of the two preachers who left Wesley over their exclusion from the Legal Hundred and he later took Anglican orders. He disapproved of Wesley's ordinations and disliked his 'superstition'. Yet he sees Wesley as an essentially good man, devoted to his religious mission, achieving much good but flawed by a consuming desire for power, as well as eccentric in doctrine (notably on Christian perfection). (The lust for power or 'ambition' in Wesley was perpetuated in Southey's picture of him, and though Alexander Knox seems to have convinced Southey of his error here, Methodist biographers constantly lamented that he did not live to retract the charges in a later edition of his *Life*.) Hampson was also critical, as we have seen, of Wesley's preaching and his literary achievements. On the whole his is in many ways an admirable portrait, mixing criticism with appreciation and unjustly dismissed by Wesleyan critics.[4]

Whitehead's *Life* and reactions to it were complicated by controversies over the possession and use of Wesley's manuscripts.[5] His treatment of Wesley was also influenced by his views of the Deed of Declaration and the ordinations. To some extent he drew the sting from the charge of power and ambition by rightly recognizing the need to hold the connexion together, and condemned rather the aggrandizement of power by the preachers after Wesley's death: a reflection of the controversies of the 1790s described earlier. Like Hampson he also attributed much blame to intriguers like Dr Coke and to Wesley's supposed senility. Like Hampson, too, he was scornful about Wesley's superstition; but the most curious point is that despite his own knowledge of Wesley, he drew largely on Hampson in describing his character.

Knox's elaborate character study of Wesley is much more independent.[6] He wished to defend Wesley against Southey's charge of 'ambition', and while he disapproved of Wesley's credulity and erratic and hasty judgments in this area, he was also anxious to dissociate him from the wilder kind of 'enthusiasm' associated with early Methodism and the seventeenth century. As a kind of bridge figure himself between Wesleyan perfectionism and Tractarian concerns for the pursuit of holiness, he was well fitted to appreciate this side of Wesley's legacy, though he disapproved of its more eccentric aspects. In many ways his remains one of the most acute and penetrating studies of Wesley's character and theology.

Moore had collaborated with Coke in a hastily produced *Life* in the 1790s, but his more considered and better attempt was as late as 1824–5. He aimed to undo what he saw as the bad effects and errors of the earlier lives, especially Whitehead's.[7] The picture that emerged was of Wesley as a faultless paragon, the leader of a wholly beneficient movement. The controversies over the Deed, the ordinations, Coke, 'ambition', 'superstition' are all placed in a favourable light. What seemed to give this picture special authority was the use of Wesley's manuscripts, and Moore's own friendship with the old man and the recollections and explanations he had obtained from him, including some on his early life. Moore should have been Wesley's Boswell, but he was scarcely that, and it is again curious that he often silently relied on Whitehead's material, while setting it in an uncritical framework which helped to establish an orthodoxy for Methodist views of Wesley. And on Wesley's theology, though he adhered to the old man's perfectionism, the perspective of justification by faith controlled his whole negative estimate of Wesley's pre-conversion life.

All these lives, then, were strongly influenced by the controversies of Wesley's later years and of the 1790s, in which the Methodists and ex-Methodists as well as their critics had been participants or prejudiced observers. They were not very forthcoming on Wesley's personal spirituality except that in general they accepted that Wesley was a holy man, marred only by some faults of character (the selection of these varying according to taste): morally, of course, he was impeccable, though Hampson had some interesting reservations about his conduct of personal relationships.

Some of the leading features of Wesley's character and the charges to which they gave rise may now be considered. 'Ambition' was one which had dogged Wesley ever since the days of the Moravian controversy, as we have seen. The grip he kept on his increasingly extensive connexion, and the Deed and ordinations, only confirmed this in many people's minds. In most of his numerous controversies Wesley looked as though he was always anxious to be master, beating down opposition and expelling dissidents. Obviously 'ambition' in conventional eighteenth century church terms could not apply to him: he neither sought nor expected preferment, and clearly behaved in a way that rendered its achievement impossible. What was really meant by the charge was that he was seeking power over other people in the context of his movement, the submission of all within it to his personal will. Southey says: 'However he may have deceived himself, the love of power was the ruling passion of his mind.' This power, says Hampson, was 'absolute and despotic'; and he never thought his authority safe unless it was exercised absolutely. It was also the chief source of the defection of his friends. Whitehead was more cautious. Wesley, he says, always denied the charge, but he concedes that he 'always considered his power as inseparably connected with the *unity* and prosperity of the societies over which he presided . . . on this account only he was so tenacious of it'. Moreover, he exercised it very moderately and protected the people against abuses by the preachers. The real danger lay in the preachers' abuse of it after his death.[8] The point about unity is well made, though Wesley also had a strong 'providential' sense of his role in Methodism and in public justified his control by the terms on which he said the preachers had always asked him to employ them.

Knox went to great lengths to refute the charge.[9] He rightly saw that Wesley had no preconceived plan of seizing power, but merely took expedients to meet exigencies as they arose: 'this, in fact, was his great talent'. It was exercised for his leading purpose of spreading truth. He allowed that Wesley's natural feelings were 'gratified by the progress of his society' and as a partial parent he was 'liable to palliate its imperfections, and to overestimate its good effects'. He also had a natural pleasure in exercising the talents given to him. In fact (he says), Wesley, though tenacious of power, did not love it for its own sake but rather regarded it as a providential deposit which he had no right to part with; and he knew of no one in his societies who could fitly share it. Knox also thought that Wesley's criticisms of the Methodists in his old age were not the thoughts of a man complacently regarding the fruits of his work; nor was his peace of mind characteristic of grasping power-seekers. Whatever one's final judgment is on the question of Wesley's pursuit of power, there can be little doubt that much of the success of Methodism did depend on his keeping it in relative unity by holding the threads of control in his own hands to the end. His purpose in doing so was practical, but at the same time he reacted to challenges with traditional assertions of hierarchical control, natural to a man of his generation and background. Underpinning it all, as has been often emphasized in this study, was a sense of providential guidance through circumstances.[10]

That eye to 'providences' was, of course, only one aspect of Wesley's conspicuous and much criticized 'superstition', his strong sense of the supernatural intervention of God, his 'enthusiasm'. Southey, Hampson, Whitehead and Knox all deplored this in varying measures; Moore and other early Methodist writers defended him and the tradition lingered on, though more equivocally, in Tyerman's reaction; but there had been Methodist critics of his excesses in this matter even in his lifetime. The stock intellectual defence can be seen in Watson's reply to Southey, also used by Moore: Wesley was not simply credulous; he exposed old wives' tales; on apparitions and the like he was not peculiar; he judiciously followed the positive views of the learned as well as the ignorant in all ages, based on respectable testimony.[11] Knox was more judicious: Wesley was too credulous, yet he did not go all the way with 'enthusiasm'; he allowed due place to reason. 'I even think he would have been an enthusiast if he could', but 'there was a firmness in his intellectual texture which would not bend to illusions'.[12] This was perceptive – Wesley certainly had tendencies this way and he had once written to Charles saying that he had 'much constitutional enthusiasm', and that Charles had more. What he was objecting to here was Charles's habit of claiming convenient 'guidance' for his erratic choices of places where he wished to preach without planning with his brother.[13] But he also acknowledged that he thought he had been 'preternaturally' healed many times, and that providence would not suffer Methodism to be defeated.[14] What Knox wished to do was to dissociate Wesley from the

wild spirits of the seventeenth century or the more recent excesses of a
George Bell. He was right to do so: Wesley saw 'providences' rather in
events than voices, much like Cromwell, but this was 'enthusiastic'
enough for his time. Knox hit off Wesley's peculiar 'reasonable' enthusiasm well. His general intellectual position between the traditional and
'enlightened' ways has already been discussed, and its relevance to his
spirituality will be noted later.[15]

Knox associated Wesley's 'credulity' with his general intellectual
propensities, which he saw as especially exhibited in Wesley's correspondence with women. Here, he says, all Wesley's 'peculiarities are in fullest
display: his confident conclusions from scanty and fallacious premises;
his unwarranted value for sudden revelations of the mind; his proneness
to attribute to the Spirit of God what might more reasonably be resolved
into natural emotion, or illusory impressions'.[16] Hampson commented
on Wesley's 'excessive attachment to particular opinions' and, in
argument, his desire to win rather than to seek truth: a tendency which
was related, as we saw earlier, to the Oxford school of argument in
which he was reared. But it was also a trait of his personality. Hampson
interestingly says that when outfaced by opposition Wesley would turn
it off by telling a story, starting a hymn or ending a conversation (and
sometimes he simply walked out). Was this peacemaking or simply an
evasion of defeat?[17]

Wesley's emotional temperament, as observed by those who knew
him as an old man, seemed to be a miracle of calm, controlled serenity.
Indeed Wesley himself, as was noted earlier, remarked complacently
on his capacity for easy sleep and the fact that though he '*felt* and
grieved he did not *fret*'.[18] Almost certainly he exaggerated, though this
was probably truer of his later than his earlier life. Moore quotes
someone who thought that Wesley's behaviour on his death-bed showed
the power of sixty years' habits of praying and preaching, but Moore
himself was sure that Wesley had reached this state only by long
struggles against the corruptions of his nature, and that more would be
known of this if Mrs Wesley had not carried off his journals. There may
be truth in this; Hampson remarked of Wesley's apparent 'placibility'
that: 'His temper was naturally warm and impetuous'. Religion had,
'in a great degree, corrected this, though it was by no means eradicated.'
He would still brook no opposition and showed a high degree of
indignation when his authority was called in question, though he easily
forgave when the offenders submitted.[19] This whole question of the
strength of his feelings and his control over them also has a bearing on
his inward spirituality.

But apart from Wesley's treatment of his subordinates and of opposition, what were his more personal relationships like? He was often

thought, especially by his brother Charles, to be a poor judge of character; but there is not a consensus on this. Charles certainly thought him made for scoundrels to profit by, but part of the reason behind judgments like this (and not least in Charles's case) was that the critics disapproved of Wesley's choice of advisers. Another reason was that John certainly tended to take people at their face value, especially if they were repentant sinners, or claimants to perfection, or showed apparent success as converters. Examples of the first were Sarah Ryan the bigamous housekeeper, and there were many in the other categories, such as George Bell. If Wesley examined people carefully he often saw what he wished to see. But on the other hand he had a realistic appreciation of what he needed to keep Methodism going; and this conflicted with the orderly notions of Charles and others.

Knox said that Wesley was 'apt to conceive strong attachments; and they who were thus distinguished by him did not always appear to impartial persons worthy of that preference'. In 1780 John wrote that, 'My brother laughs at me and says, Nay, it signifies nothing to tell you anything, for whomever you once love, you will love through thick and thin.' What really offended Knox was that in old age this habit of John's led him under the influence (as he saw it) of designing men.[20] Hampson had similar motives for distrust of Wesley's judgment, and went further by accusing him of surrounding himself with flatterers: the standing temptation, indeed, of autocrats.[21] More generously, and perhaps more perceptively, Whitehead saw Wesley as a man 'remarkably free from jealousy or suspicion and therefore very open to imposition'. He was reluctant to believe the worst of anyone, and readily believed sinners if they repented.[22] John Pawson thought that Charles Wesley was wrong. He read him as being of a 'very suspicious temper' (true enough where intrigues against the church were in question). But John, says Pawson, 'had far more charity in judging persons in general (except the rich and great) than his brother had'. It was not even true (Pawson went on) that he was easily taken in by plausible men. 'He was well able to form a judgment of particular persons, and was as seldom mistaken as his brother.' Pawson had heard John say: 'My brother suspects everybody, and he is continually imposed upon, but I suspect nobody, and I am never imposed upon.'[23] This was typically optimistic, but perhaps at least partly true. Pawson, however, was one of the targets of Charles's suspicions, and took different views of the late events of Wesley's life and their sequel from the critical biographers.

Hampson, in any case, saw Wesley as harsh and indifferent towards those who left him.[24] And he was right in saying that Wesley could be extremely harsh even with trusted and faithful preachers who challenged his authority. When Benson had a disagreement with him in 1769, apparently based on rumours (and Wesley was prone to believe such things without sufficient care), he told Benson that 'honour and power had done him no good'. Benson then stood up for himself and accused Wesley of only honouring sycophants who showed complete submission to him, especially if they claimed perfection:[25] precisely Hampson's charge.

It is hard to escape the impression that Wesley behaved most graciously to those who were either submissive to his guidance or were in various ways naturally inferior to him; and that when he conceived an affection for people (especially, perhaps, women) he was liable to see in them idealized versions of what he wished to see: as in the case of those potential ideal wives, Sophy Hopkey and Grace Murray. He continued to like the old tutorial relationship, suitably adapted and seen essentially as a relationship between superiors and inferiors. Those female friendships have already been analysed (above, pp. 267ff.) and their limitations suggested. What about other sorts of personal relationships?

Hampson is once again sceptical, even on an aspect of Wesley which was singled out earlier as unusually benevolent in the eighteenth century: his concern for the poor, even for their feelings (above, p. 363). This, Hampson says, had given him a reputation for being 'a man of much softness and sensibility', which he thought was not the case. 'His charities rather seem to have been the result of a sense of duty, than of any peculiar tenderness of nature.' This is harsh and difficult to verify. But Hampson is perhaps on stronger ground when he says that Wesley 'had no attachments, so far as we have been able to discover, that partook of the genius of friendship. His regard for some individuals, proceeded less from personal than from public considerations. All his views were of this kind. His first object was the success of Methodism'; and so Hampson worked round to the theme of 'power' once more.[26]

The picture is an unpleasant one, and not wholly just. Wesley was in a solitary position, forbidding to intimacy and inhibiting undue sharing of his inward feelings and concerns, except sometimes with Charles. But even allowing for this, Hampson had perhaps discerned something in Wesley which has escaped most of his biographers except for Vivian Green. Green remarks on Wesley's position as an essentially lonely man, despite his vast range of human contacts; and he comments on how few of his closest associates stayed with him to the end.[27]

What is really disquieting about Wesley is the evidence of his insensitivity to ordinary human feelings, particularly in matters like the death of children and wives. The most searing example of this appeared in writing to his sister Martha (married to Westley Hall) in 1742: 'I believe the death of your children is a great instance of the goodness of

God towards you. You have often mentioned to me how much of your time they take up. Now that time is restored to you and you have nothing to do but serve our Lord till . . . you are sanctified . . . '[28] This is not an isolated instance, nor was it confined to his earlier and in some ways harshest period either. In 1755 Wesley told Christopher Hopper, whose wife had just died, that 'The Lord gave and the Lord hath taken away, and wise are all his ways.' The great point is to carry on with the mission and dedicate oneself to it. Everything that helps this is good. 'Consider yourself as now more than ever married to Christ and his dear people.'[29] At the very end of his life, in 1791, he told Adam Clarke, who had just lost a child, that when he spoke of grieving so much for it, it was a case of 'inordinate affection'.[30]

Now of course it will be said, quite correctly, that this attitude of 'the Lord giveth and taketh away' has been common enough among all classes of serious Christians, Catholic and Protestant, in past times: it was conspicuous among Puritans and eighteenth-century Evangelicals. It reflected a perspective which is hard for modern Christians to understand, in which eternity and eternal life matter more than the present. Children may even be better off dying before sin creeps in. Moreover, it may even be a judgment on their parents. There are many records of such views, but the important point is that in some cases at least (one can see it in the Mathers in America or in the lay Evangelical and celebrated agriculturalist Arthur Young at the death of his daughter 'Bobbin'), this co-exists with agonizing pangs of human loss, conflicting with inherited theology. No such conflict is discernible in Wesley, nor any hint that he perceived its possibility. In the case of his sister he shows a truly monumental lack of understanding of the conflicting feelings of a mother harassed by infant demands and the pangs of grief.[31] It is true that some of Wesley's followers shared his view: one cannot simply attribute it to Wesley's lack of experience of fatherhood (he once momentarily wondered if he was somehow defective in his understanding of child nature for lack of this, but not for long).[32] But Clarke evidently felt his loss deeply, and even old John Nelson, after a dreadful conjunction of family losses, and being accused of hard-heartedness for resigning himself to the mysterious will of God, initially reacted with: 'How shall I bear it, now the Lord has taken them . . . ?'[33] It is significant that Charles Wesley, an affectionate father, and with a warmer pastoral heart than John, should have written a model letter of consolation to Joseph Cownley on the death of his wife. 'It is the Lord', he begins; but he goes on to explain how Cownley can submit and be patient until he comes to know the comfort of the Father in 'this severe affliction'.[34]

Once again Vivian Green is most perceptive about Wesley's character.

'His charm and grace cloaked an iron will; he was granite in aspic.' Like many Christian saints, he was 'self-regarding'. Under God's guidance he was himself the real centre of his interest. His life was 'built around his own experience, an experience glazed and insulated from the outside world by his confidence in God and himself. Completely selfless and yet completely egotistic, he had come to identify himself with his own creation.' Green goes on to ask what the famous *Journal* was really for: if for his own edification, it ministered to his pride; if for posterity, it pandered to self-glorification. A harsh dilemma indeed! On this point the truth is rather more complicated, as was suggested earlier, but on the rest Green's hard judgment must be faced. If John Wesley was a saint (a subject on which various views may be held), he certainly had many of the uncomfortable qualities of that character. In personal relations it is hard to fault Green's 'granite in aspic' and his perception that it was this which reduced some, including Wesley's wife, to helpless fury.[35]

Although it may be felt that only by his hard-core character and commitment could Wesley have achieved what he did for Methodism, the human cost remained severe. Like Queen Elizabeth as Gloriana, he acquired the love of a distant multitude but exasperated even those who adored at closer quarters.

Most elusive of all is Wesley's inner life, especially after the Oxford period and the apparently revealing months of the conversion struggle and its aftermath up to the beginning of 1739. His outward practice is obvious enough. His high rate of sacramental observance has already been noted, as of course his incessant preaching, in and out of churches. There is every reason to suppose that, as the diaries surviving early and late after the Oxford period show, he maintained a routine of prayer and meditation three or four times a day, but the obsessive 'grids' for intense self-examination had gone. There would hardly have been time for them anyway, and he now saw Christian achievement in a different perspective. But the basic notion of an ordered life of piety was part of his whole personal and Methodist ethos as well as an ingrained habit. Gambold said: 'He thought prayer to be more his business than anything else; and I have seen him come out of his closet with a serenity of countenance that was next to shining.'[36] The picture reflects that of Moses coming down from Sinai, and is not of course direct evidence for Wesley's state of mind.

What Wesley most conspicuously lacked was, as Clayton had remarked in 1738, a 'spiritual guide'; or, failing that, a 'religious friend' of the kind he had hoped for and to some extent found at Oxford.[37] Even in more mundane matters he lacked real confidants, as we have seen: he particularly lamented the loss of Thomas Walsh, for whom he had a special affection, and Coke was only a partial substitute.[38] Though he found consolation in some of his female correspondents and there are some slight clues, as we shall see, that he shared some of his own feelings with them, he really needed a person able to examine and guide him; these were hard indeed to find within the Methodist circle.

The *Journal*, as we have seen, has to be used with caution as evidence of Wesley's inner state at a given time, but even this virtually ceases to be informative on such matters after the final outburst of self-criticism in January 1739 (with one or two exceptions to be considered in a moment). It was suggested earlier that unless this silence was simply prudential, it is possible that either his doubts were resolved or at least that he learnt to live with them when he became involved in the business of revival. Also, it will be argued that reassurance came partly through the evidence of the truth of his message through results on other people: very conspicuous in the early days in Bristol. It is significant that in a letter from this period he noted that he still felt 'cold' except when speaking. Other Methodists found that their 'nerves' disappeared when doing this.[39]

The letters are a little more revealing, but not much. There is no clear evidence that Wesley ever received the kind of 'assurance' that he was looking for after his conversion in May 1738 and had still failed to find after the briefly warmed heart. A letter to Charles in 1747, criticizing the idea that one is not saved unless one has this assurance, seems to speak as if, like others, he had 'peace with God' 'frequently' before the special 'sense of pardon', but probably only implies momentary experiences before and after his conversion.[40] To Bishop Lavington in 1751 he was anxious to play down exaggerated accounts of his 'enthusiasm' based on his self-critical expressions earlier on. He describes them as what 'serious divines mean by desertion', and says that Lavington does not know how long this continued, nor can he infer Wesley's present state of mind from what it was then.[41] To Elizabeth Hardy in 1758 Wesley confessed that, like her, he ('a few years ago') 'felt the wrath of God abiding on me. I knew myself to be the chief of sinners' and 'all sin and corruption', though innocent in the sight of others. But he implies that the solution is the sense of Christ as our advocate, who died for our sins, to whom we look and are saved.[42] To Mrs Ryan later that year he wrote: 'As to myself, I am still cold and faint, though (as I told you) a little revived since I wrote freely' – interesting evidence of his need of a confidant.[43]

The most startling evidence of John's inner feelings comes in a letter to Charles Wesley on 27 June 1766. It was originally published with the more personal passages omitted, and these (partly in shorthand) were only restored in Telford's edition of the letters in 1931. The relevant parts are as follows (shorthand passages and translations in square brackets):

In one of [my] last [I] was saying [I] do not feel the wrath of God abiding on [me]; nor can I believe it does. And yet (this is the mystery) [I do not love God. I never did.] Therefore [I never] *believed* in the Christian sense of the word. Therefore [I am only an] honest heathen, a proselyte of the Temple, one of the φοβούμενοι τὸν θεόν. [Those that fear God.] And yet to be so employed of God! and so hedged in that I can neither get forward nor backward! Surely there never was such an instance before, from the beginning of the world! If I [ever have had] *that faith*, it would not be so strange. But I never had any other ἔλεγχος [proof] of the eternal or invisible world than [I have] now; and that is [none at all], unless such as faintly shines from reason's glimmering ray. [I have no] *direct* witness, I do not say that [I am a child of God], but of anything invisible or eternal.

And yet I dare not preach otherwise than I do, either concerning faith, or love, or justification or perfection. And yet I find rather an increase than a decrease of zeal for the whole work of God and every part of it. I am φερόμενος [borne along], I know not how, that I can't stand still. I want all the world to come to ὃν οὐκ οἶδα [whom I do not know]. Neither am I impelled to this by fear of any kind. I have no more fear than love. Or if I have [any fear, it is not that of falling] into hell but of falling into nothing.[44]

This astonishing confession seems at first sight to be a throwback to the dark days of self-doubt and self-excoriation in the months immediately following his conversion, which may seem to confirm the view that the famous warmed heart was indeed a passing glow, relatively insignificant in Wesley's spiritual development.

To find Wesley repeating assertions of this kind, in very strong language, at the height of his career as an evangelical leader, has disconcerted and embarrassed his admirers. Telford clearly found it surprising, but merely commented on Wesley's discipline and the severity he exercised on himself. But others have found it so disturbing as to require explanation. It has usually been taken to be a momentary and entirely untypical depression due to especially stressful circumstances. It has been pointed out that he was having much trouble with his wife and that there were difficult problems in the connexion. The forthcoming Conference would be discussing separation from the Church, Wesley's authority and the disciplining of the preachers (though he commented that 'a happier Conference we never had' when the time came). He was exasperated at lack of help from Charles and was still feeling the effects of a severe accident the previous year. But in referring to this he spoke cheerfully of evangelistic prospects, and his greetings to his wife suggest he was on good terms with her.[45]

Though all these problems may seem more than enough to induce depression, in fact they are typical of many other periods. Two considerations suggest another interpretation. One is that the resemblance to the self-examinations of 1738–9 is superficial. The passage in the 1766 letter does not appear to be an outburst of despair but rather an example (like his descriptions of his physical condition in his last years) of Wesley's empirical curiosity about the phenomena of spiritual experience, usually applied to his followers, but in this case to himself. It is almost as if, with detached curiosity and fascination, he was analysing another person. He marvelled that he could lack almost any sensible experience of God or the unseen world, yet could not restrain himself from preaching the truth he could not feel; preaching with zeal, yet without fear or love.

The second point to observe is that this state of mind was not simply an isolated and momentary aberration. The hints already quoted over a period of years show at least that he was subject to periodic moments of pain about his spiritual state long after the 1738–39 period. In 1772 there was a famous outburst to Charles: 'I often cry out, *Vitae me redde priori* [Give me back my former life!] Let me be again an Oxford Methodist! I am often in doubt whether it would not be best for me to resume all my Oxford rules, great and small. I did then walk closely with God and redeem the time. But what have I been doing these thirty years?'[46]

What exactly did Wesley think he was lacking? Some of his bolder associates had the courage (or possibly, of course, obtuseness) to express their suspicions that he did not feel all the experiences he preached, and although such opinions may have been wide of the mark, they do suggest that those who looked for the popular raptures of Methodist experience did not find them visibly forthcoming from their leader and suspected that he lacked them. In September 1766 Wesley wrote with unusual frankness to his close friend Sarah Crosby, whose circle was evidently critical of his spiritual experience. He began by saying that he had decided to write without reserve (incidentally confirming that he was often more cautious). Sarah had evidently said that he lost authority with the people by not 'living closer to God'. Wesley replied that they only knew by 'surmisings with which God is not well pleased' and by his 'outward walking' on which he is 'bold to say they know nothing but what might become Gregory Lopez' (his favourite Mexican hermit). He then added that Sarah knows something of the closeness of his walk with God by his own testimony, but others do not. The charge has been made that he was little affected by things which would make others 'run mad', but to this he responded that if he *felt* such things as many do, he would be incapable of the work that God had called him to do. He added that perhaps the temper and behaviour she blamed was one great means whereby he was capacitated for carrying on this work. This is very much in line with the remark quoted earlier to the effect that he '*feels*' but does not '*fret*'.[47]

Suspicions about Wesley's spiritual state from this point of view had occurred earlier and were clearly not simply a reflection of a bad patch in 1766. Thus in 1750 Wesley's book steward William Briggs wrote to him:

> I think you have the *knowledge* of all *experience*; but not the *experience* of all you *know* . . . partly by the information of others and partly from experience; but I think your *experience* is *buried* in your extensive *knowledge*. I think you *feel not abidingly* a deep sense of your own spiritual *weakness*, the *nearness* of Christ to save, or a *sweet communion* with God by the Holy Ghost. You have the *appearance* of all Christian graces; but they do not, I think, spring from a *deep experience* or change of *nature*.[48]

In April 1761, during the great outbreak of perfectionism, a Miss B wrote almost as boldly to Wesley, giving him a lesson in how to obtain this experience instantaneously: 'Do *you* seem to be a great way off? You are not out of God's reach . . . all He asks of you is to *claim your right* . . .' Then, possibly repeating a revelation of his defects to her, or perhaps her own, she says: 'All you say of wanting desire and earnestness, I can say with regard to a farther blessing.'[49]

The problem which seems to lie behind these hints and the plainer statements of the early *Journal* and the letter of 1766, as well as the other correspondence, is that Wesley generally lacked the kind of direct emotional experience of the presence of God, the supernatural world and an inward assurance of salvation of the kind that so many of the converts valued and about which he and they spoke so often as being open to all. A lack of a capacity for such experiences seems to have been a fundamental feature of his constitution. As far back as 1734 at the end of his *Reflections upon the Conduct of Human Life . . . from Mr Norris* he quotes Norris on reading books which 'warm, kindle and indulge the affections and awaken the divine sense in the soul', as he is 'convinced by every day's experience that I have more need of heat than of light'. The last phrase was to be repeated by Wesley more than once in later years.[50] In 1745 to 'John Smith' he again made the remark, though adding, 'but now I know not which I want most'.[51] The problem persisted to the end of his life, for to Elizabeth Ritchie he wrote in 1786: 'Almost ever since I can remember I have been led in a peculiar way. I go in an even line, being very little raised at one time or depressed at another.' He quotes Zinzendorf as saying that some are led by reason, some by Scripture, some by experience. 'I am very rarely led by impressions, but gently by reason and by Scripture. I see abundantly more than I feel. I want to feel more zeal and love for God.'[52] (One can see what Briggs suspected here.) In 1789 Wesley repeated his three-fold formula for guidance and warned against impressions as being open to diabolic as well as divine influence; he said that for himself he was led by the Spirit through reason.[53] To Henry Moore he said the same, though adding that at times God led him through all three ways concurring; and Moore believed that it was a great mistake to suppose that Wesley was 'wholly led by impressions and inward feelings'.[54]

Of course many outsiders thought the opposite of Wesley, but in comparison with his followers he must have seemed a cold fish. Alexander Knox thought him too prone to draw fallacious conclusions from scanty premises, and that he 'would have been an enthusiast if he could', but even he admitted that Wesley was restrained compared with some, and that he did not profess that he had attained the 'witness of the Spirit'.[55] What gave the impression that Wesley was a simple enthusiast professing special revelations was in fact his habit of accepting the claims of others and seizing on events and success as signs of providential guidance; but this was more the result of observation than anything like an inward 'revelation'.

In the light of this lifelong temperamental pattern, the May 1738 experience, though significant for Wesley's teaching in the ways explained earlier (and this is perhaps the really important point about it), must be seen as being wholly exceptional for him in its emotional quality. The Moravian promise and the brief moment when it seemed to have been achieved, coupled with the evidence of the many who seemed to have acquired it, may well have given him a hope, persisting for years, that he might have it too; and the lack of it sometimes gave him pain. The self-doubts and laments at the lack of direct experience of God and the assurance of salvation by the evidence of his feelings show him searching for such experiences and searching in vain. The 1766 letter is therefore best seen as a confirmation of an old pattern, though a particularly frank analysis of the problem. But it also seems to suggest that by then Wesley was beginning to be able to accept it with greater tranquillity as the way in which God had chosen to deal with him. It seems to have been the case that, as one might expect, there were also a few occasions when he had moments of greater apparent warmth as in 1750, when he wrote to John Bennet that he had not 'found God so present with me for so long a time, ever since I was twelve years old'.[56]

It is not surprising that the same pattern of urging others to seek the experience Wesley did not possess himself is repeated in his teaching on perfection. In 1767 he recalled how he had described the character of a Methodist some twenty-five years before, but had avoided the suspicion that this was a panegyric on himself by writing 'not as though I had already attained . . .' He made it clear that he still did not claim to have attained this perfection.[57] Occasional claims by Methodists to have identified a moment when Wesley had in fact obtained the gift fall foul of these denials unless one supposes that he was simply wary of giving hostages to his enemies or, following his own teaching, one supposes that he might once have tasted of it and then lost it. (The supposed occasion might be an apparently ecstatic experience in December 1744.)[58] On one occasion in 1781 Wesley was asked privately by Samuel Bradburn what *his* experience was. The old man responded by saying that 'his experience might almost any time be found in his brother's hymn "O Thou who camest from above"'.[59] But even if this is authentic there is an ambiguity: the words can be read as aspiration rather than achievement.

No doubt in all this Wesley was judging himself, as of old, by remarkably exacting standards. One need not deny that he had moments of 'sensible devotion': what he felt that he lacked was the full measure of the sensible consciousness of the divine presence of which he taught. There is much in his beliefs and behaviour to suggest that his 'assurance' came not from the 'inward witness' of his frequent teaching but rather from the 'empirical' yet at the same time 'providential' evidence of the results that he saw in his followers. This was what fortified his belief in the truth of perfection above all: and it looks very much as though it fortified his personal faith as over the years he gradually came to terms with the limitations of his own nature. The 1766 letter may be taken to be a rare moment of revelation about this.[60] And here we may see, at the most personal level, another example of what has often been emphasized in this study: that if Wesley sustained Methodism (and at great cost to himself), Methodism in an important sense sustained him by confirming to him the truth of what he preached.

2. Achievement and legacy

Wesley's most obvious and measurable achievement and legacy must necessarily be the Methodist churches worldwide, which, even allowing for the notoriously slippery nature of ecclesiastical statistics, total some tens of millions of members or adherents, making them among the largest Protestant bodies, especially in the USA. Methodism is also rare among the large denominations in claiming a single founder

(Lutheranism is the only comparable case). Wesley was, in fact, a church founder *malgré lui*, and this alone would have ensured him a place in the history books. Ironically, of course, this is the kind of distinction and recognition that he would have most detested.

So far as Wesley had a conscious aim from the first, it was to 'revive the nation, and especially the church – and to spread scriptural holiness through the land'. In these terms he has to be reckoned to have failed. Manifestly Methodism did not 'revive the church', though Methodists have often assumed that it did. For one thing, it gradually separated from the church, and the Evangelical party within the church was not a Methodist 'rearguard' but, as we have seen, essentially a distinct movement, and far from a dominant one. The renewal of the Church of England during the nineteenth century – a complex and varied process – was not the work of Methodism, nor indeed solely of the Oxford Movement (another venerable myth).

If Methodism did not revive the church, neither did it revive the nation. It remained essentially a minority body, patchy also in its geographical and social coverage. What it did do (and again rather unwillingly so far as a section of its Wesleyan branch was concerned) was to become an important and in some ways distinctive part of Evangelical Nonconformity in the nineteenth century and hence had effects (still subject to debate) on the social, cultural and political contours of the time.

In its original eighteenth-century setting it was certainly much less significant than this, yet its achievement was not negligible. It almost accidentally identified and captured a religious minority which might otherwise have been lost to organized religious life altogether; gave its members satisfactions denied them elsewhere; more remarkably, organized a national connexion in a period of localized church life; and most remarkably of all, Wesley created a considerable sense of common doctrine and purpose among his itinerants, despite their differences over policy before and after his death.

One of Wesley's major failures, however, was that the structure of discipline and piety which he had constructed seemed incapable of holding together the Methodists even in England. In America he lost control almost from the start, and the Americans had their own divisions in the nineteenth century – between black and white, North and South – in response to the tensions within American society. In England the tensions already evident in Wesley's lifetime erupted into schism on many occasions during the next sixty years. Splits, secessions and revivals created a family of rival Methodist churches – New Connexion, Primitives, Methodist Reformers and others – as well as the continuing Wesleyan body. The forces behind these splits and controversies con-

tinue to be a subject for debate. If, as is likely, social and political
tensions in one of the most troubled periods of English history played
an important part, one should not ignore the fact that from another
point of view the divisions within the Methodist movement represented
the splitting apart of two sides of Wesley's legacy, indeed of two sides of
his policy and personality.

On the one hand there was the concern for the pursuit of evangelism,
regardless of formal church order, which had led the High Church
Wesley into irregularities and pragmatic improvisations and a strong
tincture of 'enthusiasm'. On the other hand, there was the concern for
pastoral care, supervision, good order and organization in Methodist
terms, which reflected his drive for progressive holiness as well as initial
conversion. A benevolent pastoral despotism was not only the hallmark
of Wesley's piety but also of the structures he devised to achieve it.

The quarrelsome, divided Methodist bodies of the nineteenth century
could all claim some portion of Wesley's spirit, though usually expressed
in a more one-sided fashion than he would have approved. Thus the
Primitives recalled many aspects of the early, ecstatic and irregular
habits of the first Methodist generation, and as the last great flare-up of
the movement which had begun in the 1730s had a special claim to the
'primitive' inheritance of the movement. Hugh Bourne, though a very
different personality from Wesley, had some of the organizing and
indeed autocratic instincts of his predecessor (so indeed did William
Booth, the ex-Methodist founder of the Salvation Army, another 'primitive' movement).

The Wesleyans were more mixed than has always been allowed. They
did not lack a revivalist element, but what struck critics was their
conservative, authoritarian style of ministry. There was a good deal of
the old Wesley in this, too, but without his flexible response to pressure
from below and his eye for providential guidance through the work of
his followers. Yet the concern for pastoral care, however heavy-handed,
was also an authentic Wesley emphasis. Part of the problem that
haunted Methodists throughout the nineteenth century was that their
founder had devised a system well fitted to remedy the deficiencies of
the old parish system in a time of accelerating change. But it had already
shown signs of fossilizing itself in Wesley's lifetime, and it did not prove
much more successful than the parish system in coping with the problems
of the Victorian city. The skeleton of the original system has persisted
in Methodism to the present day.

Of theology and spirituality it is harder to speak. If Wesley's perfectionism, the product partly of his own make-up, partly of the special
circumstances of the early eighteenth century, was his most distinctive
contribution to the Christianity of his day, he certainly left a legacy, but

once again an ambiguous one. As an instant second blessing it was to be perpetuated in certain forms of nineteenth-century revivalism and ultimately as an .element in the Pentecostalist movement and other bodies. As a progressive, cultivated pursuit of holiness, it might be said to have appeared in another form in the Tractarian Movement, though not through his influence. For later Methodism it was often an embarrassment, or at best was watered down to obscure the awkwardness of its two uneasily combined aspects.

Socially and culturally, Methodism outgrew the mould into which Wesley tried to pour it. By the end of the nineteenth century the Anglican Evangelicals had fossilized into a more rigid version of their forefathers' attitudes, whereas Methodists, like other Nonconformists (and some High Churchmen), responded in greater or lesser degree to the pressures for social reform and a degree of cultural emancipation. It is difficult to say how far this can be said to represent something in the ethos Wesley had tried to instil into them, or how far it was simply a response to their peers in their various environments.

Perhaps, as Gordon Rupp once remarked, what is really distinctive about Methodism is not particular bits and pieces of doctrine and practice, some of which have come to be shared with other churches, but rather a particular history. If so, this is a history made up of a particular blend of traditions, an inherited ethos and way of behaviour, the remains of a vision of a people pursuing inward religion in company rather than alone, informally rather than formally. There was also a vision of a Christianity which could embrace the rough energies of the vulgar (in the non-pejorative sense of the word), while holding before them aspirations for self-improvement, both spiritual and cultural. Together with this was the notion of a religious movement organized on pragmatic lines, attempting to preserve the dynamic of religious revival without degenerating into its characteristic weaknesses of ephemeral emotion and individualism; and the values of a disciplined and organized religious life without degenerating into finicky ecclesiastical niceties. And in all this there was the ideal of joining together all who agreed on a few fundamentals: an attractive, if elusive, conception. Nor should one forget the implicit ideal for church order as something to be improvised in response to, and in the service of, religious truth and religious mission rather than settled by dogmatic presuppositions. Perhaps this is a lesson which has still to be learned.

As to Wesley himself, he retains, one supposes, a secure if perplexing place in the history books. The paradox of a 'reasonable enthusiast', of a precise clergyman reaching and organizing the submerged religious frustrations of his time, remains. Although one can still glimpse something of his neatness, rationality and sense of order in the simple elegance of the curving rails on the stairs of the Bristol New Room pulpit, the sighs and cries and convulsions of the people he addressed there have long since fallen silent. Wesley's achievement, and it was not a small one, was to bring some parts of those two sides of Georgian England together. Few, if any, of his successors have achieved as much.

Bibliographical Note

A complete list even of the works used for writing this book would have extended its length yet more intolerably, and lists without comment are not very helpful. Readers in search of information on particular topics are advised to consult footnotes at the beginning of the relevant sections, where the main works are usually listed. Not all such information will be repeated here, but only a select guide to some of the literature in books and articles, almost all in English, with some emphasis on recent work where this is available. The list is also largely confined to the English Revival and English Methodism.

Novices in the English history of the period may find it helpful to read recent surveys such as W.A. Speck, *Stability and Strife. England 1714–60*, Edward Arnold 1977, and I.R. Christie, *Wars and Revolutions. Britain 1760–1815*, Edward Arnold 1982. Much of the detailed research has been on the Industrial Revolution and party politics, other matters being relatively neglected, but the newer social history can now be approached through Roy Porter, *English Society in the Eighteenth Century*, Penguin Books 1982 (which is stimulating, though rather breathless) and J.A. Sharpe, *Early Modern England 1550–1750*, Edward Arnold 1987; E. Royle, *Modern Britain 1750–1985*, Edward Arnold 1987 (more sober and measured).

The religious history of England in this period has been sadly neglected. There are some useful documents in E.N. Williams (ed.), *The Eighteenth-Century Constitution*, Cambridge University Press 1965, ch.V. The only recent general survey by E.G. Rupp, *Religion in England 1688–1791*, Clarendon Press 1986, concentrates on ideas and spirituality, and does not tackle the more social approaches now customary for other periods. The old C.J. Abbey and J.H. Overton, *The English Church in the Eighteenth Century*, Longmans 1878 (two volumes), still has value for its use of a wide range of printed sources. For the Church of England, Norman Sykes's *Church and State in England in the Eighteenth Century*, Cambridge University Press 1934, has been the most influential of his various works and gives a sympathetic view of the workings of the establishment. This should be supplemented by the social approach of A.D. Gilbert, *Religion and Society in Industrial England 1740–1914*, Longmans 1976, which cites much unpublished and other scattered work. G.V. Bennett, *The Tory Crisis in Church and State 1688–1730*, Oxford University Press 1976, illuminates the political and religious world in which Wesley grew up. A. Warne, *Church and Society in Eighteenth Century Devon*, David and Charles 1969, and D. McClatchey, *Oxfordshire Clergy 1777–1869*, Oxford University Press 1960, throw light on local situations, and A.T. Hart, *Clergy and Society 1660–1800*, SPCK 1968, on the clergy generally. James Woodforde's famous diary can be sampled in the Oxford World's Classics selection. Worship and spirituality have been little studied. The old work of L.G. Wickham Legg, *English Church Life from the Restoration to the Tractarian Movement*, Longmans 1914, concentrates on High Church survivals and may be supplemented by Richard Sharp's essay in G. Rowell (ed.), *Tradition Renewed*, Darton, Longman and Todd 1986. But F.C. Mather, 'Georgian Churchmanship Reconsidered', *JEH* XXXVI, 1985, is a stimulating fresh approach which should be followed up. W.K. Lowther Clark, *Eighteenth Century Piety*, SPCK 1944, ch.I, gives some ideas on devotional literature.

Work on the theology of the period has concentrated rather too exclusively on the Deist controversy. G.R. Cragg, *Reason and Authority in the Eighteenth Century*, Cambridge University Press 1964, covers the ground conventionally, and J.M. Creed and J.S. Boys Smith, *Religious Thought in the Eighteenth Century*, Cambridge University Press 1934, gives a documentary accompaniment. Of the numerous works on Deism, R.E. Sullivan, *John Toland and the Deist Controversy*, Harvard University Press 1982, stands out for its awareness of the social as well as intellectual context.

On Dissent, M. Watts, *The Dissenters*, I, Clarendon Press 1978, supersedes all previous treatments. For the main denominations, see R.T. Jones, *Congregationalism in England 1662–1962*, Independent Press 1962; R. Brown, *The English Baptists of the Eighteenth Century*, Baptist Historical Society 1986; R.M. Jones, *The Later Periods of Quakerism*, I, Macmillan 1921; R.T. Vann, *The Social Development of English Quakers 1655–1755*, Harvard University Press 1969; J. Goring et al., *English Presbyterians*, Allen and Unwin 1968. On Roman Catholics J. Bossy, *The English Catholic Community*, Darton, Longman and Todd 1976, is fresh if controversial; see also E. Duffy (ed.), *Challoner and his Church*, Darton, Longman and Todd 1981.

For a fresh view of the evangelical element in the old Dissent before the Revival see G.F. Nuttall, 'Methodism and the Older Dissent', in *United Reformed Church Historical Society Journal* II, 1981. There is no comprehensive history of the Revival as yet, though some are likely to appear before too long. For the Continental background there is not much in English. For the Pietists see F.E. Stoeffler, *The Rise of Evangelical Pietism*, E.J. Brill 1965, and *German Pietism in the Eighteenth Century*, E.J. Brill 1973. For new approaches see W.R. Ward, 'The Relations of Enlightenment and Religious Revival', in *SCH* Subsidia 2, 1979, and 'Power and Piety', *Bulletin of the John Rylands Library* LXIII, 1980. For America there is a long-term survey in W.G. McLoughlin, *Revivals, Awakenings and Reform*, University of Chicago Press 1978.

There is little on the origins of the English Revival, but there are important essays by John Walsh on 'The Origins of the Evangelical Revival' in G.V. Bennett and J. Walsh (eds.), *Essays in Modern English Church History*, A. & C. Black 1966, and 'Elie Halévy and the Birth of Methodism' in *TRHS*, Fifth Series XXV, 1975.

On Methodism, for a detailed bibliography see K.F. Rowe (ed.), *Union Catalogue*, Scarecrow Press 1981ff., which has reached letter 'I'. For Wesley, see R.G. Green, *Works of John and Charles Wesley*, London 1895, which will be replaced by F. Baker's edition in the Bicentennial Edition of the *Works*. *HMCGB*, IV contains a full bibliography and there are wide-ranging annual ones by Clive Field in *PWHS*. Selections of Wesley's writings can be found in A.C. Outler, *John Wesley*, Oxford University Press 1964, and F. Whaling, *John and Charles Wesley*, SPCK 1981.

Some comment was made in the Introduction about modern works on Wesley and in the chapter on his personality on the early ones, but the recommendation of Tyerman, Green and Heizenrater may be repeated here for their special virtues. The five volumes by J.S. Simon do not really replace Tyerman for documentation, but his first volume on *John Wesley and the Religious Societies*, Epworth Press 1921, is useful on them. Stanley Ayling, *John Wesley*, Collins 1979, is the most recent one-volume life, readable but not advancing on Green for interpretation. To explore Wesley's personality it is still best to read his letters (more than the *Journal*). For Charles Wesley there is no replacement for Thomas Jackson's old *Life*, London 1841, and his rather inadequate edition of the *Journal*, but there is some fresh material in the early *Journal* edited by Telford (1909) and an excellent brief life based on new letter material by F. Baker, Epworth Press 1948.

Only a small selection of special studies on Wesley can be listed. On his theology Colin Williams, *John Wesley's Theology Today*, Epworth Press 1946, is comprehensive, but H. Lindstrom, *Wesley and Sanctification*, Epworth Press 1946, centres on the main theme for Wesley himself. Controversy over his 'conversion' may be followed in the discussion in the present work. On social matters see S. Andrews, *Methodism and Society*, Longmans 1970, which has documents and commentary, but there has been a good deal to add since. B. Semmel, *The Methodist Revolution*, Heinemann 1974, attempts to see Methodist ideals as the unwitting preparation for nineteenth-century 'liberalism'. E.P. Thompson's splendid and moving (though highly controversial) *The Making of the English Working Class*, Penguin Books 1968 (with answers to his critics at end), should be read for its attack on Methodism for its counter-revolutionary and emotionally crippling effects, but the debate goes on. Those with German may try M. Marquardt, *Praxis und*

Prinzipien der Sozialethik Wesleys, Vandenhoeck und Ruprecht 1977. For politics D. Hempton, *Methodism and Politics in British Society*, Longmans 1984, ch.I, is good on Wesley in his context.

On the perennially arguable question of Wesley's relationship with the Church of England, Frank Baker, *John Wesley and the Church of England* Epworth Press 1970, is fairly exhaustive and detailed. I agree with Baker's emphasis on Wesley's practical motivation, which is obscured by debates about the nicer ecclesiastical aspects of his ordinations; and for a forthright approach to this see J. Kent, *The Age of Disunity*, Epworth Press 1966, ch.VI. There is good material on this and other matters in J.M. Turner, *Conflict and Reconciliation*, Epworth Press 1985, chs. I and II. J.C. Bowmer, *The Lord's Supper in Early Methodism*, Dacre Press 1951, is representative of the usual view of Wesley's surviving High Church ideals in this area, but a different approach will be found in my treatment of it.

Too little work has yet been done on the Methodists as distinct from Wesley. The preachers can be encountered in the clutch of autobiographies in T. Jackson (ed.), *Lives of the Early Methodist Preachers*, six volumes, 1872, or the slightly different version edited by J. Telford as *Wesley's Veterans*, seven volumes, 1912. But two neglected works give a collective profile based on a mass of early material: Leslie Church's *Early Methodist People*, Epworth Press 1948, and *More About the Early Methodist People*, Epworth Press 1949. A modern critical approach is badly needed. Some idea of what this might mean can be found in D.M. Valenze, *Prophetic Sons and Daughters*, Princeton University Press 1985, and some essays in J. Obelkevich (ed.), *Disciplines of Faith*, Routledge 1987. On the subject of the supernatural, the classic work of Keith Thomas, *Religion and the Decline of Magic*, Penguin Books 1973, is compulsory reading, but has not been followed much past 1700. I have attempted to open up some aspects in my 'Doctors, Demons and Early Methodist Healing', in *SCH* XIX, 1982, and elsewhere, and hope to pursue this further. On Methodism and 'popular' religion see J. Rule, 'Methodist Popular Beliefs and Village Culture in Cornwall 1800–50', in R.D. Storch (ed.), *Popular Culture and Custom*, Croom Helm 1982. Satirical attacks on Methodism are surveyed in A.M. Lyles, *Methodism Mocked*, Epworth Press 1960; and a fresh approach to physical attacks can be found in J. Walsh, 'Methodism and the Mob', *SCH*, VIII 1972, pp. 213–27. Unfortunately the first volume of *HMCGB* was largely a lost opportunity, although it has a useful survey of Methodist organization by Frank Baker and a fine and wide-ranging essay on 'Methodism in the later Eighteenth Century' by John Walsh. More study is needed of the social composition of early Methodism, but some myths are dispelled by Clive Field, 'The Social Structure of English Methodism', in *British Journal of Sociology* XXVIII, 1977, pp. 199–225. A modern history of Methodist missions is another gap, but the early stages can be gleaned from John Vickers, *Thomas Coke*, Epworth

Press 1969. For America a short list of books will be found in the notes to my sketch above.

There is room for more study of the Revival in the old Dissent. The best survey is again to be found in Watts and the relevant parts of the denominational histories already mentioned, with fresh angles in Nuttall's article (also already mentioned). The Moravians badly need a new history and G. Wauer, *Beginnings of the Brethren's Church in England*, ET London 1901, is still useful. Two articles add a little more: J. Hutton, 'The Moravian Contribution to the Evangelical Revival', in J. Tait (ed.), *Historical Essays*, Manchester University Press 1902, and J. Pinnington, 'Moravian and Anglican', in *Bulletin of the John Rylands Library* 1969. C.W. Towlson, *Moravian and Methodist*, Epworth Press 1957, places too much stress on personal factors in the split. But still the most illuminating opening to the early Moravian work may be D. Benham, *Memoirs of James Hutton*, London 1856, which uses much material from the early diaries. A.J. Podmore in *PWHS* XLVI, 1988, pp. 125–53, and his forthcoming Oxford thesis will add much here.

Whitefield and Lady Huntingdon have largely defeated their biographers. A. Dallimore, *George Whitefield*, two volumes, Banner of Truth Trust 1970, 1980, does not fully replace the old and worthy work of L. Tyerman, two volumes, 1876; and for Lady Huntingdon and her connexion (the most neglected of all) the old A.C.H. Seymour *Life*, two volumes, 1844, is inaccurate and irritating but indispensable. C. Welch, *Two Calvinistic Methodist Chapels* (London Record Society XI, 1975) reprints the Minutes of Whitefield's and Lady Huntingdon's London chapels and of the English Calvinistic Methodist Connexion with a valuable introduction. But it may be best to approach Whitefield through his autobiography and journal edited by I. Murray, Banner of Truth Trust 1960, though this only covers his early career.

On the Anglican Evangelicals there is not much critical work. The old survey (still useful for names and lives) by G.R. Balleine, *History of the Evangelical Party in the Church of England*, new edition Church Army Press 1951, has not yet been replaced, though it may be soon. There is a fuller account in L. Elliott-Binns, *The Early Evangelicals*, Lutterworth Press 1953. C. Smyth, *Simeon and Church Order*, Cambridge University Press 1940, includes several biographies of early figures which do not entirely bear out his claim that the difference between Methodists and Evangelicals was over church order; on this see C.G. Brown, 'Itinerancy and Loyalty', *JRH* VI, 1961. A local group is studied in G.C.B. Davies, *Early Cornish Evangelicals*, SPCK 1951. There is a good biography of *William Grimshaw* by F. Baker, Epworth Press 1963; for another irregular figure see A.S. Wood, *Thomas Haweis*, SPCK 1957. P.F. Streiff, *J.G. de la Fléchère*, Lang 1984 (in German), is the best life of this famous saint.

The Clapham Sect has attracted attention, much of it either uncritical or doctrinaire in approach. E.M. Howse, *Saints in Politics*, Allen and Unwin 1952, is useful as a factual survey only. F.K. Brown, *Fathers of the Victorians*, Cambridge University Press 1961, has interesting material, but scents too many conspiracies. The latest biography of *Wilberforce* by J.C. Pollock, Constable 1977, has new material, but defends him at all points. The best biography of a rather unusual Evangelical is by M.G. Jones of *Hannah More*, Cambridge University Press 1952, which peels off some very dishonest early biographical veils. (Her correspondence with Horace Walpole, in W.S. Lewis's edition, is worth reading here.) D. Rosman, *Evangelicals and Culture*, Croom Helm 1984, is a valuable study. The anti-slave trade campaign has attracted a large literature, but for a combination of economic, political and religious analysis, R. Anstey, *The Transatlantic Slave Trade and British Abolition*, Macmillan 1971, is especially helpful (though not the last word). On missions, Howse's uncritical approach should be supplemented with C.A. Embree, *Charles Grant*, Allen and Unwin 1962. A critical study of the Evangelicals' social work in the context of late eighteenth-century philanthropy is clearly much to be desired; a start has at last been made in B. Hilton, *The Age of Atonement*, Clarendon Press 1988, which was too late to be used here.

Additional Bibliographical Note (1992)

The pace of research on eighteenth-century England is quickening, and covers a greater variety of areas than used to be the case. The following very selective list deals only with recent works on religion, the Revival and Methodism, plus one or two older works accidentally omitted in the original edition.

On the Church of England: J. Spurr, *The Restoration Church of England 1646–89*, Yale University Press 1991, helps to explain the attitudes of the next generation. P. Virgin, *The Church in an Age of Negligence*, James Clark 1989, gives a statistically-based account of the working of the establishment with vignettes of individuals. R. Hole, *Pulpits, Politics and Public Order in England 1760–1832*, Cambridge University Press 1989, argues for the positive influence of religion on political ideas and includes Wesley's views. S. Wright (ed.), *Parish, Church and People*, Unwin Hyman 1988, includes essays on the local working of the church. Horton Davies, *Worship and Theology in England*, III, Princeton University Press 1961, covers all denominations.

On religion and doctrine: the background to the more charismatic elements in the Revival is illuminated by C. Garrett, *Spirit Possession and Popular Religion*, Johns Hopkins University Press 1987. I. Rivers, *Reason, Grace and Sentiment*, I, Cambridge University Press 1991, is an important study of Latitudinarians, Deists and Wesley; while A.C. Clifford, *Atonement and Justification*, Clarendon Press 1990, analyses the Calvinist tradition along with Tillotson and Wesley. G.F. Scholtz, 'Anglicanism in the Age of Johnson', *Eighteenth Century Studies* V, 1988, pp. 182–207, explains the conventional Anglican view of salvation in this period.

On Dissent: J. E. Bradley, *Religion, Revolution and English Radicalism*, Cambridge University Press 1990, argues for local Dissenting influence on the radical tradition.

On the Revival: W.R. Ward, *The Protestant Evangelical Awakening*, Cambridge University Press 1992, at last offers a general survey, particularly of the Continent; while T.A. Campbell, *The Religion of the Heart*, University of South Carolina Press 1991, argues for a movement of 'inward religion' well beyond the Protestant world. D. Bebbington, *Evangelicalism in Modern Britain*, Unwin Hyman 1989, has a good chapter on the eighteenth century. Social analyses of a local revival can be found in T.C. Smout, 'Born Again at Cambuslang', *Past and Present* XCVII, 1987, pp. 114–27, and N. Landsman, 'Evangelists and their Hearers', *Journal of British Studies* LXXVIII, 1989, pp. 120–49. D.L. Morgan, *The Great Awakening in Wales*, ET Epworth Press 1988, analyses Welsh religious experience. M.J. Crawford, *Seasons of Grace*, Oxford University Press, New York 1991, covers the origins of Anglo-American revivalism, and D.W. Lovegrove, *Established Church, Sectarian*

People, Cambridge University Press 1988, shows how itinerant preachers penetrated the Anglican countryside.

On Methodism: bibliographically there is now C.D. Field, *Anti-Methodist Publications of the Eighteenth Century*, as *BJRL* LXXIII (2), 1991. Among the newer volumes in the Bicentennial Edition of Wesley's *Works* are all the *Sermons; Hymns for the Use of Methodists; The Rules of the Methodist Societies;* and three volumes of the *Journals* (with a remarkable Introduction in volume I by W.R. Ward). New studies of Wesley include J. Stacey (ed.), *John Wesley: Contemporary Perspectives*, Epworth Press 1988, with essays of variable merit; R.P. Heitzenrater, *Mirror and Memory*, Abingdon Press 1989 (especially on Wesley's piety and his early post-conversion development); W.S. Gunter, *The Limits of 'Love Divine'*, Abingdon Press 1989 (on perfection and changes in Wesley's doctrine); R.N. Flew, *The Idea of Perfection in Christian Theology*, Oxford University Press 1934; and H. Abelove, *The Evangelist of Desire*, Stanford University Press 1990, which usefully, though speculatively, explains the sources of Wesley's authority and describes some characteristics of his followers. D. Hempton, 'Methodism and the Law 1740–1820', *BJRL* LXX (3) 1988, pp. 93–108, throws some light on an obscure subject; and J.Q. Smith, 'Occupational Groups among the Early Methodists of the Keighley Circuit', *CH*, LVII, 1988, pp. 187–95, adds local detail on Methodists' social status. P.W. Chilcote, *John Wesley and the Women Preachers of Early Methodism*, Scarecrow Press 1991, gives a surprisingly long list of them.

On Dissent and Revival: H.D. Rack, 'Survival and Revival: John Bennet, Methodism and the Old Dissent', in K.G. Robbins (ed.), *Protestant Evangelicalism*, SCH Subsidia VII, Blackwell 1990, pp. 1–24, explores one example of an important theme. Finally, the Moravians receive fresh study by C.J. Podmore in *PWHS* XLVII, 1990, pp. 156–86 (on Fetter Lane), and by E. Welch (ed.), *The Bedford Moravian Church in the Eighteenth Century*, Bedfordshire Record Society, LXVIII, 1989 (with a useful general introduction).

Notes

Introduction

1. George Crabbe, *The Life of George Crabbe*, Cresset Press 1947, p. 128.

Prelude Wesley's England: 1. Society and Religion in the Early Eighteenth Century

1. E.A. Wrigley and R.S. Schofield (eds.), *The Population History of England 1541–1871*, Edward Arnold 1981, pp. 207–10; see B.R. Mitchell and P. Deane, *British Historical Statistics*, Cambridge University Press 1962, for other estimates.

2. Mitchell and Deane, *Statistics* (n.1), p. i; P.J. Corfield, *The Impact of English Towns*, Oxford University Press 1982, p. 7.

3. Corfield, *Impact* (n.2), p. 15.

4. *EMP*, V, p. 56.

5. R. Porter, *English Society in the Eighteenth Century*, Penguin Books 1982, p. 56.

6. Daniel Defoe, *A Tour Through England and Wales*, Dent (Everyman) nd, I, p. 31 (Letter VI); H.A. Lloyd-Jukes (ed.), *Bishop Secker's Visitaton Returns* (1738), Oxfordshire Record Society XXXVIII, 1957, pp. 24f.

7. D. Vaisey (ed.), *The Diary of Thomas Turner*, Oxford University Press 1984, pp. xxixf.

8. G.S. Holmes, 'Gregory King and the Social Structure of Pre-Industrial England', *TRHS* XXVII, 1977, pp. 41–68; P. Mathias, 'The Social Structure in the Eighteenth Century: A Calculation by Joseph Massie', *Economic History Review* X, 1957, pp. 30–44; P. Mathias, *The First Industrial Nation*, Methuen 1983, ch. 2.

9. Holmes, 'Gregory King' (n.8), pp. 53, 64; table in Mathias, 'Massie' (n.8), pp. 42–5.

10. A. Briggs, 'The Language of Class', in A. Briggs and J. Saville (eds.), *Essays in Labour History*, Macmillan 1960, pp. 43–73.

11. See Porter, *English Society* (n.5), p. 68, for what follows.

12. For what follows see the recent challenge to exaggerated ideas of 'openness' by L. Stone and J.C.F. Stone, *An Open Elite? England 1640–1880*, abridged edition, Oxford University Press 1986.

13. Porter, *English Society* (n.5), p. 65.

14. For what follows see especially R.W. Malcolmson, *Life and Labour in England 1700–1800*, Hutchinson 1981, pp. 11–14, 108f., 130ff.

15. William Wilberforce, *A Practical View*, London 1797, ch. VI; cf. a writer in 1715 quoted by Malcolmson, *Life and Labour* (n.14), p. 17.

16. For this see G. Rudé, 'The Pre-Industrial Crowd', in his *Paris and London in the Eighteenth Century*, Fontana Books 1969, pp. 17–34.

17. E.P. Thompson, 'Eighteenth Century English Society: Class-Struggle without Class?', *Social History* III(2), 1978, p. 158.

18. Porter, *English Society* (n.5), pp. 358–62.

19. For descriptions of the system see: J. Brooke, *The House of Commons 1754–90*, Oxford University Press 1964; B.W. Hill, *The Growth of Parliamentary Parties 1689–1742*, Allen and Unwin 1976; id., *British Parliamentary Parties 1742–1832*, Allen and Unwin 1985; G.S. Holmes, *British Politics in the Age of Anne*, Macmillan 1967.

20. For good examples of Newcastle's church patronage letters see E.N. Williams (ed.), *The Eighteenth Century Constitution*, Cambridge University Press 1960, pp. 353–5, 357–62.

21. Summarized by J.A. Sharpe, *Early Modern England*, Edward Arnold 1987, pp. 269f.

22. For a long-term survey see J.F.C. Harrison, *The Common People*, Fontana 1984 esp. ch. V; Sharpe, *Early Modern England* (n.21), Part III; Malcolmson, *Life and Labour* (n.14), ch.IV; Porter, *English Society* (n.5), ch. VI.

23. See e.g. J.H. Plumb, *The Commercialisation of Leisure*, Reading University Press 1973.

24. S.P. (Symon Patrick?), *Brief Account of the New Sect of Latitude Men* (1661), Augustan Reprint Society No. 100, University of California Press 1963, p. 7. For the working of the Establishment see N. Sykes, *Church and State in England in the Eighteenth Century*, Cambridge University Press 1934; A.D. Gilbert, *Religion and Society in Industrial England*, Longmans 1976, ch. I.

25. J. Fortescue (ed.), *Correspondence of George III*, Macmillan 1927, I, pp. 33–44.

26. A. Hartshorne (ed.), *Memoirs of a Royal Chaplain 1729–63*, Bodley Head 1905, p. 266; for a particularly bad example, E. Chalmers (ed.), *Lives of Pocock, Pearce, Newton and Skelton* II, London 1816, p. 169.

27. Gilbert, *Religion and Society* (n.24), p. 5.

28. Ibid., p. 7; S.L. Ollard (ed.), *Archbishop Herring's Visitation (1743)*, Yorkshire Archaeological Society LXXI, 1928, p. xii.

29. J.A. Savidge, *Queen Anne's Bounty*, SPCK 1955; G.F.A. Best, *Temporal Pillars*, Cambridge University Press 1963; for examples of stability only slowly achieved cf. J. Booker, *History of Ancient Chapel of Birch*, Chetham Society XLVII, 1859, pp. 150–2; id., *History of Ancient Chapel of Denton*, Chetham Society XXXVII, 1856, pp. 51–70 (struggles with lack of endowment and Dissenting intrusions).

30. G. Holmes, *Augustan England*, Allen and Unwin 1982, ch. IV (on the clerical profession).

31. For all this see G.V. Bennett, *White Kennett*, SPCK 1957; id., *The Tory Crisis in Church and State 1688–1730*, Oxford University Press 1975; id., 'Conflict in the Church', in *Britain After the Glorious Revolution*, ed. G. Holmes, Macmillan 1969, pp. 155–75. On the survival of divine right ideas, see G. Straka, 'The

Final Phase of Divine Right Theory', *EHR* LXXVII, 1962, pp. 638–68; J.C.D. Clark, *English Society 1688–1832*, Cambridge University Press 1985, ch. III.

32. But caution is necessary here. The subject has not been properly researched, and a sampling of Lancashire cases (Correction Books in CRO. EDV 1/72–105, 1701–79) shows cases continuing patchily throughout, though with fewer actual punishments later. Financial cases continue better than moral. Much depended on local initiative, and in Manchester in 1742 there had been none for a dozen years because of quarrels between officials (ManchCL M39/2/7/3, 5, 6).

33. For this see Bennett, 'Conflict' (n.31), and *The Tory Crisis*; G. Holmes, *The Trial of Doctor Sacheverell*, Eyre-Methuen 1973.

34. Gilbert Burnet in H.C. Foxcroft, *A Supplement to Burnet's History*, Oxford University Press 1902, p. 497; and see his *Pastoral Care* (1692).

35. G.V. Portus, *Caritas Anglicana*, Mowbrays 1912; F.W.B. Bullock, *Voluntary Religious Societies in Great Britain 1520–1799*, Budd and Gillatt 1963, pp. 109–50, 160–85; D.W.R. Bahlmann, *The Moral Revolution of 1688*, Yale University Press 1957; T.C. Coats and W.A. Speck, 'The Societies for the Reformation of Manners', *Literature and History* III, 1976, pp. 45–61; Rack, 'Religious Societies', pp. 588f.

36. Gilbert, *Religion and Society*, (n.24), p. 8.

37. For details and a sympathetic account of their problems, see Sykes, *Church and State*.

38. For published early eighteenth-century examples see *Bishop Secker's Visitation* and *Herring Visitation*. For a local study, A. Warne, *Church and Society in Eighteenth-Century Devon*, David and Charles 1969; A.T. Hart, *Clergy and Society 1600–1800*, SPCK 1968.

39. *Herring Visitation*, pp. 71, 72, 75, 79; *Secker Visitation*, p. 78.

40. *The Spectator*, No. 112, 1712.

41. J. Beresford (ed.), *Diary of James Woodforde*, The World's Classics, Oxford University Press 1949.

42. A. Macfarlane (ed.), *Diary of Ralph Josselin*, Oxford 1976, passim.

43. F.G. Stokes (ed.), *The Blecheley Diary of William Cole*, Constable 1931.

44. N. Sykes, *Edmund Gibson*, Oxford University Press 1926, ch. IV; id., *From Sheldon to Secker*, Cambridge University Press 1959, pp. 192–202.

45. J. Wickham Legg, *English Church Life from the Restoration to the Tractarian Movement*, Longmans 1914; F.C. Mather, 'Georgian Churchmanship Reconsidered', *JEH* XXXVI, 1985, pp. 255–83.

46. St Ann's, Manchester (1712), had morning and evening prayers daily; St John's (1769) twice a week (C. Bardsley, *Memorials of St Ann's Church*, Manchester 1877); Act of Parliament for St John's (1769), see Wickham Legg, *English Church Life* (n.45), ch. IV.

47. *Secker Visitation*, pp. 6, 10, 42, 58, 69, 155.

48. For what follows see *Secker* and *Herring Visitations* and Mather.

49. Tillotson case in *Granville Letters*, Surtees Society XXXVII, 1860, p. 176 n. For post-Restoration difficulties see J.II. Overton, *Life in the English Church, 1660–1714*, Longmans 1885, pp. 166–8. Chester case in R.V.H. Burne, *Chester Cathedral*, SPCK 1958, p. 89.

50. T. Secker, *Visitation Charge* (1741), in *Eight Charges*, London 1763, pp. 62f.

51. See above n.45 and for Samuel Wesley see p. 53.

52. For an example at Holy Trinity, Hull, see *Herring Visitation*, II, p. 78.

53. Bennett, 'Conflict' (n.31), pp. 157, 159.

54. See the remarks in P. Collinson, *The Religion of Protestants*, Oxford University Press 1982, pp. 207–14, especially p. 210.

55. W. Burkitt, *Poor Man's Help*, London [27]1749, pp. 82ff.; M. Ransome (ed.), *Wiltshire Visitation*, Wilts Record Society XXVII, 1971, p. 238; R. Warren, *Daily Self-Examinant*, London [7]1724, p. 107; John Wesley's sister in Tyerman, *OM*, pp. 39f.

56. J. Tillotson, 'A Persuasive to Frequent Communion', in *A Collection of Cases*, London 1698, III; B. Hoadly, in *Works*, London 1773, III, pp. 843–903; John Wesley, 'Constant Communion', Sermon CI in *Works*, VII.

57. For an extract from Tillotson's sermon 'His Commandments are not Grievous' see E.N. Williams, *Constitution*, pp. 378–81; Bishop Joseph Butler in *Charge* (1753), quoted in B. Dobree, *English Literature in the Eighteenth Century*, Oxford University Press 1959, pp. 302, 291.

58. For some discussion see W.K. Lowther Clarke, *Eighteenth Century Piety*, SPCK 1944, ch. I.

59. For its disputed authorship (Richard Allestree is most likely) see P. Elman, 'Richard Allestree and the Whole Duty of Man', *The Library*, Fifth Series, VI, pp. 19–27.

60. Wesley, *Works*, XIV, p. 231; *Diary of Thomas Turner*, pp. 107, 136f., 184.

61. 'Diary of a Manchester Wig-Maker', in J. Harland, *Collectanea*, Chetham Miscellany, OS, LXVIII, pp. 172–208; there is another in ibid., pp. 236–9.

62. E.L. McAdam (ed.), *Works of Samuel Johnson I*, Yale University Press p. 10.

63. R. Parkinson (ed.), *John Byrom's Journals*, Chetham Society, OS, XXXII, XXXIV, XL, XLIV, 1854–8; abridged by H. Talon, Rockliff 1950.

64. See 'Ralph Mather's Account' for a kind of spiritual gazetteer, in C. Walton, *Notes and Materials for . . . William Law*, London 1854, pp. 595f. For Mather see J.F.C. Harrison, *The Second Coming*, Routledge 1979, p. 233 and note. For Swedenborgianism see below, p. 325.

65. Note 35 above.

66. For differing views on this see Rack, 'Religious Societies', 584.

67. K. Thomas, *Religion and the Decline of Magic*, Penguin Books 1973, especially ch. XXII; Malcolmson, *Life and Labour* (n.14), pp. 83–93; B. Bushaway, *By Rite*, Junction Books 1983; J. Obelkevich, *Religion and Rural Society*, Clarendon Press 1976, ch. VI.

68. M. Spufford, *Small Books and Pleasant Histories*, Cambridge University Press 1981, pp. 196f.; G.H. Jenkins, *Literature, Religion and Society in Wales 1660–1730*, Cardiff 1980, pp. 35ff. (82% of Welsh books).

69. Clark, *English Society* (n.31), Introduction. For a fine illustration of the mixture of old and new in France see J. McManners, *Death and the Enlightenment*, Clarendon Press 1981.

70. Above, note 24.

71. See the remarks on faith and reason in John Smith, *Select Discourses* (1673), pp. 2–4; Henry More, *Explanation of the Grand Mystery of Godliness* (1660), in P.E. More and F.L. Cross (eds.), *Anglicanism*, SPCK 1957, pp. 223ff., 641f.

For the relationships with debates about materialism internationally see R.L. Colie, *Light and Enlightenment*, Cambridge University Press 1957.

72. Sermon in *Works* II, pp. 406ff.; Rack, 'Hoadly versus Law'.

73. T. Birch, *Life of Tillotson*, in *Works* I, London 1820, p. cclxxxiii.

74. J. Locke, *Essay*, Book IV, xvii, 24; cf. id., *The Reasonableness of Christianity*, paras. 22, 181, 167, 172, and *Essay* IV, xviii, 10.

75. For this idea see E. Duffy, 'Primitive Christianity Revived', *SCH* XIV, 1977, pp. 287–300.

76. For a fresh view of the continuity of the High Church tradition see R.L. Sharp and P. Nockles in G. Rowell (ed.), *Tradition Renewed*, Darton, Longman and Todd 1986.

77. For a specimen of his work see *Review of the Doctrine of the Eucharist*, London 1737, and on him R.T. Holtby, *Daniel Waterland*, Holtby 1966.

78. Walsh, 'Origins', pp. 132–62.

79. D. Bisse, quoted in C.J. Abbey and J.H. Overton, *The English Church in the Eighteenth Century*, Longmans 1878, I, p. 325.

80. E. Gibson, *Second Pastoral Letter* (1730).

81. T. Secker, *Charge* (1758), in *Eight Charges*, London 1769, p. 238, cf. pp. 235–7.

82. *JWJ*, II, pp. 275ff.

83. *EMP*, IV, p. 277.

84. Egmont, *Diary* I, pp. 123f.

85. He was apparently from an Independent family: J. Hayes, *Thomas Gainsborough*, Tate Gallery 1980, p. 15.

86. Quoted in Whitefield, *Journals*, p. 327, cf. 314.

87. G. Bull, *Harmonia Apostolica*, London 1670; *JWJ*, II, p. 470.

88. C.F. Allison, *The Rise of Moralism*, SPCK 1966, pp. 178ff., 199ff.

89. Birch, *Tillotson* (n.73), p. ccxxvii.

90. Whitefield, *Letters* I, p. 505 (18 January 1740), attributes this originally to Wesley in a 'private society'. But Wesley certainly softened his view later, as Whitefield is also alleged to have done.

91. Gibson, *Second Pastoral Letter* (1730); Secker, *Charges*, p. 236. Wilberforce, *Practical View*, ch. VI; similarly Wesley in the preface to his version of the *Whole Duty*, *Works* XIV, p. 231.

92. H.G. van Leeuwen, *The Problem of Certainty in English Thought 1630–90*, Nijhoff, The Hague 1963. Cf. Locke, *Essay*, IV, xv.

93. Not specified in the account in the *Essay*, but noted by James Tyrrell in his copy in the British Library: so M. Cranston, *John Locke*, Oxford University Press 1985, pp. 140f.

94. *Essay* IV, xvii, 23.

95. M.C. Jacob, *The Newtonians and the English Revolution 1689–1720*, Harvester Press 1976.

96. R.E. Sullivan, *John Toland and the Deist Controversy*, Harvard University Press 1983, chs. V, VIII; J. Kent, *The Unacceptable Face*, SCM Press 1987, p. 77.

97. A.R. Winnett, 'Were the Deists Deists?', *Church Quarterly Review* CLXI, 1960, pp. 70–7; Sullivan, *John Toland* (n.96), ch. VII.

98. For surveys, see P. Gay, *The Enlightenment*, two vols., Weidenfeld and Nicholson 1967, 1970; J. Redwood, *Reason, Ridicule and Religion*, Thames and

Hudson 1976; and the older work of Leslie Stephen, *English Thought in the Eighteenth Century*, two vols., London 1878.

99. David Ogg, *England in the Reigns of James II and William III*, Clarendon Press 1955, p. 533.

100. See below, pp. 383f.

101. M. Watts, *The Dissenters*, Clarendon Press 1978, supersedes all previous treatments. For the main denominations see also: R. Brown, *The English Baptists of the Eighteenth Century*, Baptist Historical Society 1986; R.T. Jones, *Congregationalism in England 1662–1962*, Independent Press 1962; C.G. Bolam et al., *English Presbyterianism*, Allen and Unwin 1968; Rufus M. Jones, *The Later Periods of Quakerism* I, Methuen 1921; R.T. Vann, *The Social Development of English Quakers*, Harvard University Press 1969.

102. H. Kamen, *The Rise of Toleration*, Weidenfeld and Nicholson 1967; R.B. Barlow, *Citizenship and Conscience*, University of Pennsylvania Press 1962; for Locke see *Epistola de Tolerantia*, ed. R. Klibansky and J. Gough, Clarendon Press 1968.

103. Holmes, *Politics in the Age of Anne* (n.19), p. 107 and note; Brooke, *House of Commons* (n.19), pp. 169f. Egmont recorded the belief that there had been 170 at the Restoration but were only 20 by 1741 (Egmont *Diary* III, p. 226).

104. E.D. Bebb, *Nonconformity and Social and Economic Life*, Epworth Press 1935, pp. 50–3, 82f. Watts, *Dissenters* (n.101), p. 483.

105. J.E. Bradley, *Whigs and Nonconformists: Presbyterians, Congregationalists and Baptists in English Politics 1715–90*, University of California PhD 1981.

106. Watts, *Dissenters* (n.101), pp. 267ff., 490ff.

107. Bebb, *Nonconformity*, p. 45; Gilbert, *Religion and Society* (n.24), p. 16.

108. A. Everitt, 'Nonconformity in Country Parishes', *Agricultural History Review* XVIII (Supplement), 1970.

109. Holmes, *Augustan England* (n.30), pp. 111–14.

110. T.S. Ashton, *The Industrial Revolution*, Oxford University Press 1948, pp. 17ff.; E. Hagen, *On the Theory of Social Change*, Homewood 1962, pp. 305–8; D. McClelland, *The Achieving Society*, Princeton University Press 1961; D.S. Landes, *The Unbound Prometheus*, Cambridge University Press 1969, p. 73f.; Mathias, *First Industrial Nation* (n.8), pp. 142–8.

111. G.F. Nuttall, 'Assembly and Association in Dissent', *SCH* VII, 1971, pp. 289–310; there is a local example in A. Gordon, *The Cheshire Classis Minutes*, London 1919; for Baptists, see Brown, pp. 34ff., 85ff.

112. For interpretations of this episode see Goring, *English Presbyterianism* (n.101), pp. 155–65; Watts, *Dissenters* (n.101), pp. 374ff.; R. Thomas in G.F. Nuttall and O. Chadwick, *From Uniformity to Unity 1662–1962*, SPCK 1962; id., 'The Non-Subscription Controversy', *JEH* IV, 1953, pp. 162–86.

113. For examples see D. Coomer, *Hanoverian Dissent*, Epworth Press 1946, pp. 16–18. For 'hyper-Calvinism' see P. Toon, *The Emergence of Hyper-Calvinism in English Nonconformity 1689–1765*, The Olive Tree 1967.

114. J.B. Williams, *Matthew Henry* (1828), reprinted Banner of Truth Trust 1974, p. 110.

115. E.g. Doddridge, see J.D. Humphreys (ed.), *Correspondence and Diaries of Philip Doddridge*, London 1829–31, V, pp. 275ff.; James Clegg, *Diary, passim*.

116. For Watts see A.P. Davis, *Isaac Watts*, Independent Press 1948; for Doddridge, G.F. Nuttall (ed.), *Philip Doddridge*, Independent Press 1951; R.L.

Greenall, *Philip Doddridge, Nonconformist and Theologian*, University of Leicester Adult Education Department 1981; M. Deacon, *Philip Doddridge*, Northants Libraries 1980.

117. Nuttall, *Doddridge*, p. 134.

118. G.F. Nuttall, 'Methodism and the Old Dissent', *United Reformed Church Historical Society Journal* II, 1981, pp. 259–74.

119. Watts, *Dissenters* (n.101), p. 440.

120. See, among recent works, M.D.R. Leys, *Catholicism in England 1559–1829*, Longmans 1961; there are stimulating and controversial new perspectives in J. Bossy, *The English Catholic Community 1570–1850*, Darton, Longman and Todd 1976; E. Duffy (ed.), *Challoner and his Church*, Darton, Longman and Todd 1981; short survey in Rupp, 180–97.

121. Birch, *Tillotson*, pp. xixf.

122. Letter translated and printed in E.N. Williams, *The Eighteenth Century Constitution*, pp. 340f.

123. For these numbers and the following paragraph see Bossy, *Catholic Community* (n.120), ch. VIII; for local examples see J. Bossy, 'Catholic Lancashire in the Eighteenth Century', in J. Bossy and P. Jupp (eds.), *Essays Presented to Michael Roberts*, Blackstaff Press 1976, pp. 54–69; G.P. Connolly, *Catholicism in Manchester and Salford 1770–1850*, Manchester PhD 1980.

124. For example the West-country Clifton diocese: C.M.D. Appleby, *The English Catholic Community 1850–90: Catholicism in the West of England*, Bristol MA 1978.

125. For this see Duffy, *Challoner* (n.120), ch. IV.

126. Manchester Sunday School Minutes 3 October and 7 November 1785; 6 July 1789; 2 August 1790; 4 April 1796; MS in Chetham's Library, Manchester; Infirmary Trustees in F.J. Faraday, 'J.L. Phillips', *Manchester Literary and Philosophical Society Transactions* 1890, p. 30.

127. Bossy, *Catholic Community* (n.120), pp. 391–401.

I. A Country Living: Epworth (1703–20)

1. W.B. Stonehouse, *The Isle of Axholme*, London 1839, for the area. For the population, Samuel Wesley in 1701 reported above 1100: E. McClure (ed.), *A Chapter in English Church History. SPCK Minutes 1698–1704*, SPCK 1884, p. 343; *Speculum Lindoniensis*, Lincolnshire Record Society IV, 1913, p. 157, gives 300 to 340 families, which suggests 1350–1530 persons; Tyerman, *SW*, p. 203, gives about 2,000 in 1866.

2. Tyerman, *SW*, pp. 203f.; Stonehouse, *Axholme* (n.1), p. 165.

3. R.B. Mannering, *The English People and the English Revolution*, Penguin Books 1978, pp. 151, 206, 260; and disturbances as late as 1718–19 are noted (information from unpublished MS on Hoole of Haxey by the late Alan Keighley).

4. *Speculum Lindoniensis*, p. 157, says sixty 'Anabaptists' and twenty Quakers, with three licensed meeting houses. Samuel in 1701 said that he had about forty Quakers and above seventy Anabaptists, and a hundred of little or no religion: McClure, *Chapter* (n.1), p. 344.

5. Clarke, pp. 103–10; Stonehouse, *Axholme* (n.1), pp. 170f.

6. Tyerman's account in *SW*, pp. 65–77, is now supplemented by H.A.

Beecham, 'Samuel Wesley: New Biographical Evidence', in *Renaissance and Modern Studies* VII, 1963, pp. 78–109. The scandalous story of the Calf's Head Club, repeated by Tyerman, may be black propaganda by the Grub Street hack, Edward Ward: see *Bishop Nicholson's London Diary*, ed. C. Jones and G. Holmes, Clarendon Press 1985, p. 321 and n.; cf. J.P. Kenyon, *Revolution Principles*, Cambridge University Press 1977, pp. 76f.

7. For this story see John Wesley, *History of England* IV, p. 75; see also loose note in *MCA* Brown Folio III of Charles Wesley correspondence. Rupp, p. 69, thinks that it might be true. The speech was generally believed to have been 'ghosted', but Samuel Wesley is not mentioned as a possible co-author by G. Holmes, *The Trial of Dr Sacheverell*, Eyre Methuen 1973, p. 196. See also Green, *YMW*, p. 47 n.

8. An account of his misfortunes and appeal for funds to Oxford University is printed in HMC, *Kenyon*, pp. 434f.

9. *Speculum Lindoniensis*, p. 157; Tyerman, *SW*, pp. 411–15; Sykes, *William Wake*, Cambridge University Press 1957, I, pp. 173f. Cf. his ideals in *Address to a Young Clergyman*, printed in Jackson, *CW*, II, pp. 499–534.

10. See below, pp. 48f.

11. Rupp, p. 346; 'the inward witness' quoted by John Wesley is in *JWL (B)* II, pp. 288f.; the death-bed description by Charles Wesley in Priestley, pp. 51ff., does not mention this.

12. See Beecham, 'Samuel Wesley' (n.6), pp. 92–100, for details.

13. See Tyerman, *SW*, p. 198, corrected on p. 467, for the story; Green, *YMW*, p. 44 and n.

14. Green, *YMW*, p. 44. For Normanby, later the Duke of Buckinghamshire, see *DNB*, s.v. 'Sheffield, John'. Normanby's family was related by marriage to the Annesleys; see *Nicholson's Diary* (n.6), pp. 579 n, 281, 284.

15. John Dunton, *Life and Errors* I, London 1818, pp. 166. The best biography of Susanna is John Newton, *Susanna Wesley and the Puritan Tradition in Methodism*, Epworth Press 1968.

16. For this figure see F. Baker, 'Susanna Wesley', *Epworth Review*, IX, 1982, pp. 40f., who has worked out the family tree accurately.

17. The error came from Jonathan Crowther: for the true details, see *JWL (B)* I, p. 180 n. Incidentally, the name 'Wesley' was probably pronounced 'Wessley', judging by the old spelling 'Westley' (as by Lord Egmont). However, an untraced claim for 'Wezley' as a pronunciation approved by Wesley has been made; see *PWHS* XXXIV, 1963, pp. 48f.

18. Green, *YMW*, p. 46.

19. *Wesley Banner* IV, 1852, p. 283, in Newton, *Susanna Wesley* (n.15), p. 87.

20. Clarke I, ²1836, p. 198f. Cf. the shorter account in *AM*, 1786, p. 606; Newton, *Susanna Wesley* (n.15), pp. 87f.

21. *PWHS* XXIX, 1953, pp. 50ff; Newton, *Susanna Wesley* (n.15), pp. 89–93.

22. Green, *YMW*, pp. 49f.

23. *Speculum Lindoniensis*, IV, pp. 157, 175. Green, *YMW*, p. 48, says £130 and £50. Samuel in a letter of 1737 says that Wroot yielded hardly £50 normally, and in some years not enough to pay expenses for the curate at £30 (Clarke, p. 208). In the 1730s he said to Susanna that Epworth was supposed to be £200, but seldom yielded above £100, of which he allowed £20 to a curate (his son-in-law Whitelamb): Clarke, pp. 154f.

24. HMC, *Kenyon*, pp. 434f.; Clarke, pp. 87–94, 99–111.
25. Clarke, I, ²1836, p. 391.
26. Clarke, pp. 53f., 149–55.
27. Clarke, p. 250.
28. *JWL (B)* I, p. 160; Clarke, p. 387.
29. Clarke, p. 266; Newton, *Susanna Wesley* (n.15), p. 85.
30. Newton, *Susanna Wesley* (n.15), p. 84.
31. Clarke, pp. 283–313, 316–27.
32. Green, *YMW*, p. 51.
33. Tyerman, *OM*, p. 378.
34. Rupp, p. 344.
35. Clarke, p. 466; *JWL (B)* I, p. 159 n.
36. *AM*, 1778, pp. 183f.; Clarke, pp. 475f.; *JWL (B)* II, p. 80. Cf. an unfeeling letter on his death by Wesley in *JWL*, V, p. 151.
37. Clarke, p. 483.
38. Clarke, pp. 487f.; *JWL (B)* I, pp 151 n, 176 n; Clarke, pp. 501–10.
39. *JWL (B)* I, pp. 201–5.
40. Clarke, pp. 511–37.
41. Green, *YMW*, p. 46.
42. Tyerman, *SW*, pp. 411ff.; *Speculum Lindoniensis*, p. 157; Tyerman, *SW*, pp. 237f.; letter on the weekly communion quoted in ibid., pp. 427f.; 'Letter to a Young Clergyman' in Jackson, *CW*, pp. 531f.
43. Tyerman, *SW*, p. 213.
44. McClure, *Chapter* (n.1), pp. 57, 140, 143, 273, 283; Clarke, pp. 96–8; Tyerman, *SW*, pp. 295ff.; *JWJ*, III, p. 33.
45. McClure, *Chapter* (n.1), pp. 178–82.
46. Ibid., p. 344; Tyerman, *SW*, p. 417.
47. *JWJ*, III, p. 24.
48. Clarke, pp. 327–36.
49. Clarke, pp. 256f., 261–7; *JWJ*, III, pp. 134–9; Sermon on 'Obedience to Parents', *AM*, 1784, pp. 462–4, cf. *JWL (B)* I, pp. 330f.
50. L. Stone, *The Family, Sex and Marriage in England 1500–1800*, abridged edition Penguin Books 1979, pp. 125f., 254–6, 256, 273, 297f.
51. P. Greven, *The Protestant Temperament*, Knopf, New York 1977, pp. 14–20, 122, 126, 136–43.
52. Linda A. Pollock, *Forgotten Children. Parent-Child Relations from 1500 to 1900*, Cambridge University Press 1983, e.g. p. 120.
53. Baker, *CW*, p. 109; cf. Newton, *Susanna Wesley* (n.15), p. 115.
54. J.L. Axtell (ed.), *The Educational Writings of John Locke*, Cambridge University Press 1971, pp. 138, 218, and passim.
55. Ibid., pp. 130 and n., 215ff., 227f., 229, 239.
56. E.g. Sermons XV, XCVI, in *Works* VII.
57. *JWL (B)* I, p. 331.
58. Greven, *Protestant Temperament* (n.51), pp. 53ff., 93.
59. Sermon XCVI, section I, iv.
60. Heitzenrater, *EMW* I, pp. 38–43, for Wesley's composite account of his mother's and his own recollections, originally published in *AM* 1778; and a discussion of how the 'providential' interpretations of Wesley's special 'call' grew up around the event. The best contemporary account seems to be by

Susanna in letters to Samuel Wesley Jr on 14 February 1709 and to Mr Hoole on 24 August 1709, five days and six months respectively after the event: G.J. Stevenson, *Memorials of the Wesley Family*, London 1876, pp. 106f. See also Samuel Wesley to the Duke of Buckinghamshire; Stevenson, pp. 107ff.

61. Susanna Wesley MSS, Wesley College Bristol, quoted by Newton, *Susanna Wesley* (n.15), p. 111.

62. Heitzenrater, *EMW* I, pp. 38–43.

63. Cf. e.g. the letter to Charles in *JWL* IV, p. 108: 'I care not a rush for ordinary means. Only that it is our duty to try them.' All God's dealings with them had been extraordinary; he had been 'preternaturally healed' ten times. Though cf. *JWL (B)* II, p. 527.

64. Moore, I, p. 116.

65. *JWL* IV, p. 106 and n.; Stevenson, *Wesley Family* (n.60), London 1876, p. 330.

66. Tyerman, I, p. 18, quoting Clarke II, ²1836, p. 321.

67. Ibid.

68. Ibid. Moore, II, p. 292, has: 'I suppose he would not do anything *non etiam crepitare*', which sounds like a coarser original placed in the 'decent obscurity of a learned language' by Moore and then bowdlerized in English by Clarke.

69. This seems to have been the end of this patronage, which no doubt dried up when the Duke lost his court offices a few months later on the accession of George I. See *DNB* under 'Sheffield, John'.

70. Tyerman, I, pp. 19f.

71. Letter to Coke and Moore by 'An Old Member of Society', quoted by Tyerman, I, 20; a more flattering version in Stevenson, *Wesley Family* (n. 60), p. 483.

72. *JWJ* I, p. 465.

73. *JWJ* I, p. 466; *JWL* III, p. 30.

74. Moore, I, p. 117.

75. *AM*, 1784, pp. 548–50, 606–8, 654–6; accounts published by Priestley and reprinted by Clarke, pp. 159–200; cf. also Heitzenrater, *EMW* I, pp. 43ff.

76. Wesley, *Diary*, 13 September 1726.

77. Clarke, p. 183.

78. E.g. Clarke, p. 199; Tyerman, I, pp. 23f. is more cautious.

79. Green, *YMW*, p. 59.

80. Cf. J. Obelkevich, *Religion and Rural Society*, Clarendon Press 1976, ch. VI.

81. Green, *YMW*, pp. 55, 59f.

82. See *JWL (B)* I, p. 143, for his first extant letter, in a scholarly hand unlike his later style, about a muddle over his exhibition money.

II. A Holy Experiment: Oxford (1720–35)

1. E. Gibbon, *Autobiography*, The World's Classics, Oxford University Press 1907, pp. 36–45.

2. T. Hearne, *Remarks and Collections*, ed. H.E. Salter, Oxford Historical Society, Oxford University Press 1885–1921, X, p. 205.

3. C.E. Mallet, *History of the University of Oxford* III, Methuen 1927, p. 2.

4. For what follows I have drawn on V.H.H. Green, *Religion in Oxford and*

Cambridge, SCM Press 1964; id., *A History of Oxford University*, Batsford 1974; and on the latest and fullest work by L.S. Sutherland and L.G. Mitchell (eds.), *Oxford University in the Eighteenth Century*, Oxford University Press 1986 (volume V of a new history, hereafter cited as *History*). For politics see also W.R. Ward, *Georgian Oxford*, Oxford University Press 1958.

5. Mitchell in *History*, p. 3.

6. Ibid., p. 467.

7. For details see Ward, *Georgian Oxford* (n.4), passim.

8. *History*, pp. 106f.; Sykes, *Gibson*, Appendix B, p. 399. For attacks on the church in the 1730s see T.F.J. Kendrick, 'Sir Robert Walpole, the Old Whigs and the Bishops 1733–6', in *Historical Journal* XI, 1968, pp. 421–5; and on the university, *History*, ch. V.

9. *History*, pp. 313f.

10. C. Wordsworth, *Scholae Academicae*, Cambridge University Press 1877, pp. 216–31; *History* (Sutherland), pp. 169–91.

11. For all this see Wordsworth, *Scholae Academicae* (n.10), pp. 124–6.

12. Yolton in *History*, pp. 570–6, 595.

13. For his syllogisms see e.g. *JWL (B)* I, p. 421 (on not leaving Oxford); on Locke and logic see *Remarks upon Mr Locke's 'Essay'*, in Works, XIII, p. 460; and see below, pp. 384ff., for his philosophical position.

14. *History*, p. 519; poems in *JWL (B)*, I, pp. 147, 190–3; Moore, I, 118–20; Whitehead, I, pp. 382–4.

15. Mallet, *University of Oxford* (n.3), pp. 56–62, 128f.

16. Example cited in ibid., pp. 63f.

17. Whitefield, *Journal*, pp. 51, 57.

18. Mallet, *University of Oxford* (n.3), pp. 65f.; Green, *Oxford University* (n.4), p. 118 and n.

19. Green, *YMW*, p. 195.

20. Green, *Oxford University* (n.4), pp. 115, 119.

21. Thomas Warton in *The Student* (1750), quoted in Green, *Oxford University* (n.4), pp. 110, 354–6.

22. *History*, pp. 389–91.

23. *History*, chs., VII, XVIII.

24. Ward, *Georgian Oxford* (n.4), p. 21.

25. Green, *YMW*, pp. 29f., 122f., 147f.; *History*, pp. 435–8, and for the political implications Ward, *Georgian Oxford* (n.4), pp. 145f.

26. For Wesley's Oxford career see above all Green, *YMW*, and his *Commonwealth of Lincoln College*, Oxford University Press 1979. For his religious development and the so-called 'Holy Club', Heitzenrater, *OM*.

27. Green, *YMW*, ch. IV. See now *PWHS* LXVII, 1989, pp. 29–37.

28. For all this see Ward, *Georgian Oxford* (n.4), pp. 2–3; Ch. III, pp. 106ff.

29. Hearne, *Remarks etc.*, XI, p. 55.

30. *JWL (B)*, I, pp. 144–59, 150f., 154–6, 190f.

31. E. Harrison, *Son to Susanna*, Nicholson and Watson 1937. For the identification of Sally rather than Betty as Varanese see ibid., pp. 66f., firmly endorsed by Green, *YMW*, p. 207n. But for an apparent flirtation with Betty as well see the letter in Tyerman, I, pp. 49f.

32. *JWJ*, I, pp. 466f.

33. *JWL (B)*, I, pp. 149, 152–7, 157–60.

34. Contradicting Heitzenrater, *EMW*, I, p. 50.

35. Wesley, *Diary*, 14 April 1725. The entry is clearly squeezed in later alongside the formal record of daily actions. For Emily's letter see *MCA*; *Wesleyan Methodist Magazine*, 1845, pp. 359–62; G.J. Stevenson, *Memorials of the Wesley Family*, London 1876, pp. 262f. Her remarks about Wesley's marriage prospects appear to be merely a warning about a purely hypothetical situation in the light of her own real problems, which were the main concern of the letter.

36. *JWL (B)* I, p. 431 (13 May 1735).

37. *JWJ*, I, pp. 48–51; Heitzenrater, *EMW*, I, p. 51; *Diary*, January 1726; *JWJ*, I, pp. 52, 57 (facsimile of MS diary).

38. *JWL (B)*, I, p. 160.

39. *JWJ*, I, p. 467.

40. *JWL (B)*, I, pp. 83, 168.

41. F. Baker, in *PWHS* XXXVII, 1969, pp. 78–82, in contrast to the chronology in *Plain Account of Christian Perfection*, para. 4, in *Works* XI.

42. *JWL (B)*, I, p. 168.

43. Heitzenrater, *OM*, p. 57 n.; *JWL (B)*, I, pp. 208f., 214.

44. *Diary*, and cf. *JWJ*, I, pp. 48, 49, for the idea that this was from the Charterhouse period; Heitzenrater, *OM*, pp. 59f.

45. *JWJ*, I, pp. 466f.; *Works*, XI, pp. 366f.; *JWL*, IV, pp. 298f.; Outler, p. 79.

46. *JWL (B)*, I, pp. 162–6, 171.

47. *JWL (B)*, I, pp. 167–73.

48. *JWL (B)*, I, pp. 174–89.

49. *JWL (B)*, I, pp. 171, 176f., 180–3, 189; see Green, *YMW*, pp. 76–80 on the whole story. The younger Thorold became a freelance evangelist later: Green, *Commonwealth*, p. 325 n.

50. *JWL (B)*, I, pp. 193f.

51. *Works*, VIII, p. 121.

52. Green, *Commonwealth*, pp. 190 and n., 348; letter to S. Wesley Jr in *JWL (B)*, I, 693f., and n.; *CWJ*, I, p. 194. The death of his older brother may have stopped him in 1739. See also *JWJ*, II, pp. 468f.

53. Green, *YMW*, App. II, pp. 320f., and *Commonwealth*, p. 327 and n.

54. *JWL (B)*, I, pp 286f. and n. For Morley and Isham see Green, *Commonwealth*, pp. 306, 307.

55. Moore, I, pp. 148f.; Whitehead, I, 412.

56. Green, *Commonwealth*, p. 304.

57. Green, *YMW*, p. 100n.

58. *JWL (B)*, I, pp. 213f., 216f. for Mrs Wesley's contrary opinion.

59. Heitzenrater in *PWHS* XXXVII, 1970, pp. 110ff.; cf. XL, 1975, pp. 7ff.

60. Green, *YMW*, App. I.

61. *JWL (B)*, I, p. 196.

62. Wesley, *Diary*, 6 November 1725; 1 June 1726; 6 October 1726.

63. *Diary*, June to August 1726, passim.

64. *JWL (B)*, I, pp. 246 n., 286 n.

65. Green, *YMW*, pp. 208f.

66. *Diary* 14 October 1726. (Green, *YMW*, p. 213 wrongly reproduces this as a dialogue; Heitzenrater *EMW*, I, p. 54, sees it correctly as a monologue by Varanese.)

67. *JWL (B)*, I, p. 247.

68. *JWL (B)*, I, p. 201, 210; cf. 211f.

69. Mary Wesley to John, 20 January 1727: Stevenson, *Wesley Family* (n.35), p. 290; Kirkham to Wesley, Tyerman, I, pp. 49f.

70. Green, *YMW*, p. 106; *Diary* 3 June 1726.

71. *Diary* 3 June, 3 July, 13 August 1726.

72. *JWL (B)*, I, pp. 246ff., passim.

73. Green, *YMW*, pp. 208–11, gives the most convincing interpretation.

74. *JWL (B)*, I, pp. 201–6; cf. 151 n., 159f., 172.

75. *JWL (B)*, II, p. 381.

76. Cf. *JWL (B)*, I, 440 to Burton on Georgia.

77. *JWL (B)*, I, p. 193.

78. *JWL (B)*, I, pp. 208f.

79. *JWL (B)*, I, pp. 208–23.

80. *JWJ*, I, 41ff.

81. For these see *JWJ*, I, pp. 48f., and in part (more correctly) Heitzenrater, *EMW*, I, pp. 51f., who asserts that this was in 1725 and adds that year to the MS text.

82. *JWL (B)*, I, p. 214 and n. For examples of these resolutions and reflections on them see *Diary* at end of January 1726; Good Friday 1726; cf. *JWJ*, I, pp. 52, 57; 54, 56; Green, *YMW*, p. 103 n.

83. Green, *YMW*, App., pp. 305–19.

84. Ibid., pp. 135, 137.

85. For the text of the letter to Morgan see *JWL (B)*, I, pp. 335–44, from a contemporary transcription by Charles Wesley which differs in detail from John's version in *JWJ*, I, pp. 87–105; also Heitzenrater, *EMW*, I, pp. 63f. For other accounts see *Works*, VIII, pp. 300, 348. There is no reference at all to the group in the 24 May 1738 retrospect.

86. For his identity see n. 102 below.

87. *Works*, VIII, p. 348; Schmidt, I, p. 102 n.; see the review in *PWHS* XLII, 1980, p. 120 for other cases.

88. Samuel Wesley in Moore, I, p. 171.

89. *JWL (B)*, I, p. 278.

90. *JWL (B)*, I, p. 379.

91. *JWL (B)*, I, p. 352.

92. The relationship between the rise of Methodism and the Religious Societies will be discussed later (below, pp. 186, 221).

93. *JWL (B)*, I, p. 356 n.; Green, *YMW*, pp. 185, 269f.: note especially the Fox family.

94. Richard Graves, see above, p. 66.

95. Jackson, *CW*, II, pp. 389f.; *JWL (B)*, I, pp. 233–9; Baker, *CW*, pp. 10–17.

96. *JWL (B)*, I, pp. 229–32; Baker, *CW*, pp. 10, 11f.; *JWL (B)*, I, p. 234; Green, *YMW*, p. 139, suggests that John may also have been entangled.

97. *JWL (B)*, I, pp. 234–6.

98. Green, *YMW*, pp. 147f. and n.; for the motives see *JWL (B)*, I, p. 235.

99. *JWL (B)*, I, pp. 233–9; Baker, *CW*, pp. 10–16, 15f. on Stanton.

100. For De Renty, see *PWHS*, XVIII, 1931–2, pp. 43ff.; M. Schmidt in *Theologia Viatorum*, V, 1953.

101. *JWL (B)*, I, p. 240.

102. See Heitzenrater, *OM*, pp. 87, 95, for the usual identification; Green, *YMW*, p. 155 and n. suggests Francis Gore.

103. *Short History of Methodism* in *Works*, VIII, pp. 347–51.

104. Heitzenrater, *OM*, pp. 25–46; id., *Methodist History*, XII, 1974, pp. 10–35; summary in *PWHS* XLII, 1979, pp. 90f.; cf. Green, *YMW*, pp. 156ff., 177 for indications already of meetings in different places; also *JWL (B)*, I, pp. 385ff.

105. See Green, *YMW*, ch. VII for a detailed survey of his actions in this field from 1729–35.

106. *JWL*, VII, p. 78; Heitzenrater, *OM*, p. 109.

107. For details of this and other cases see Green, *YMW*, pp. 178–81, 190–4.

108. *JWL (B)*, I, pp. 357–62.

109. *JWL (B)*, I, pp. 364–71, 374–6, 379–82, 385f. For a sensible assessment of the whole story see Green, *YMW*, pp. 194–200.

110. *JWL (B)*, I, pp. 337–9 for Samuel's letter; and for earlier examples Green, *YMW*, p. 157.

111. Set of questions for the Castle work: *JWL (B)*, I, pp. 339f.

112. *JWL (B)*, I, pp. 339–42. Hoole later moved to Manchester, where he was associated with the Clayton and Byrom circle and the Nonjurors, though he himself was a more moderate High Churchman. It is to be hoped that information on this from Mr Keighley's MS may be published.

113. *AM*, 1798, pp. 117–21, 168–72.

114. E. Duffy, 'Primitive Christianity', *SCH* XIV, 1977, pp. 287–300; Rack, 'Religious Societies', p. 588. For Clayton on the authority of the primitive church see *JWL (B)*, I, p. 352.

115. For Wesley and Law, see Baker in *PWHS*, XXXVIII, 1969, pp. 78–82. For Clayton's idea, see *JWL (B)*, I, p. 334.

116. *JWL (B)*, I, pp. 331ff., 336 n.; Heitzenrater, *OM*, pp. 169–74; Green, *YMW*, pp. 166, 173.

117. *JWL (B)*, I, pp. 342f.

118. Heitzenrater, *OM*, p. 167.

119. *JWL (B)*, I, pp. 327, 331.

120. For Clayton's later severe view see J. Clayton, *Friendly Advice to the Poor*, 1755, in a Manchester controversy. Discussed by G.B. Hindle, *Provision for the Relief of the Poor in Manchester 1754–1826*, Chetham Society, Third Series, XXII, 1975, pp. 22ff.

121. *JWL (B)*, I, p. 333.

122. See *JWL (B)*, I, pp. 357–64 on Morgan's illness.

123. See e.g. C.L.S. Linnell (ed.), *Thomas Wilson's Diary*, SPCK 1964, p. 81.

124. For a sensible judgment on this see Green, *YMW*, pp. 170f.

125. For the *Fog's Journal* letter see *WMM*, 1845, pp. 237–9; there is an unexpurgated text in Heitzenrater. *EMW*, I, pp. 29–31. For Law's alleged authorship, see Heitzenrater, *OM*, p. 208 n.; *PWHS*, XIX, 1934–5, pp. 181–3, XX, 1935–6, pp. 30–2; J.S. Simon, *John Wesley and the Religious Societies*, Epworth Press 1927, pp. 97f.

126. For examples of the alternative slander of 'orgies' see N. Cohn, *Europe's Inner Demons*, Paladin Books 1976, pp. 1–4, 19 etc. See below, p. 436 and n. 249, for problems of stories of self-mutilation of early Methodists, but there were occasional cases of suicide from religious despair.

127. Sermon XVII in *Works*, V, 202–12; for the alteration see para. I.7 of the sermon.

128. See below, pp. 165, 216f.

129. *JWL (B)*, I, pp. 350–2.

130. Heizenrater, *OM*, pp. 240ff., while recognizing these influences, emphasizes, rather, a pattern drawn from Wesley's own practice. However, Mr Keighley (unpublished MS) shows convincingly how strongly he was influenced by Spincks and Nelson. Cf. also the 'Scheme of Self-Examination' in *Works*, XI, pp. 521–3, from a scheme of 1733–4 (?).

131. *JWL (B)*, I, pp. 437n.; Schmidt, I, pp. 140ff.

132. *JWL (B)*, I, pp. 382–5, 386–8, 391–3.

133. *JWL (B)*, I, pp. 437f.

134. For the correspondence concerning this see *JWL (B)*, I, pp. 395–423.

135. *JWL (B)*, I, p. 442 and n.

136. *JWL (B)*, I, pp. 395–410.

137. *JWL (B)*, I, pp. 411, 414, 416, 417, 420.

138. Schmidt's attempt to deny this and to give a theological defence of Wesley is not convincing (Schmidt, I, pp. 119–22). Cf. also Rupp, pp. 348ff., for the more usual view.

139. *JWL (B)*, I, pp. 435, 439–42. Schmidt, I, pp. 131ff., again gives a refined theological explanation. This seems unconvincing, though one need not deny that Wesley genuinely believed he was doing what was best for others as well as himself.

140. Heitzenrater, *EMW*, I, pp. 58f.

141. *JWJ*, I, pp. 55, 56.

142. Heitzenrater, *EMW*, I, pp. 59–62, and scheme in *Diary*, April 1734.

143. Clayton in *JWL (B)*, I, p. 392; Heitzenrater, *EMW*, I, p. 73.

144. *Plain Account of Christian Perfection*, paras. 10–11, 1–6, in *Works*, XI.

145. *JWJ*, I, pp. 466–70. The 'contemplative man' was identified by Curnock as Joseph Hoole, the Rector of Haxey and later in Manchester (see n.112). But the details better fit James Garden who also figures in Byrom's Journal as a mystic (*Byrom Journal*, Chetham Society XXXIV, 1855, I(2), pp. 519f.; G.D. Henderson, *Mystics of the North East*, Spalding Club 1934, p. 60.) I owe this identification to Mr Keighley's MS. But William Law is possible, too.

146. Heitzenrater, *EMW*, I, pp. 94–6; Outler, pp. 441–7. Curnock (*JWJ*, I, pp. 418–24) inserted this into the original printed *Journal* from Whitehead, II, pp. 54–6, who followed Moore, I, pp. 198–202. The MS (in Wesley College Bristol) has the Greek text and includes Nonjurors in the title.

147. Schmidt, I, p. 160.

148. *JWL (B)*, I, pp. 162–4, 165.

149. For 'holiness and happiness' see e.g. to Ann Granville in *JWL (B)*, I, p. 386 (1731): 'I lay it down for a rule that I can't be too happy and therefore holy', ibid., pp. 289, 294. Hannah More the Evangelical thought similarly. For the historical precedents see Schmidt, I, p. 101 n.

150. *JWL (B)*, I, pp. 168–70, 172–3.

151. *JWL (B)*, I, pp. 244f., 318, 319. Samuel Wesley Jr argued that 'sincerity' was 'sufficient', ibid., p. 325. For the contemporary usage of the term see Rack, 'Hoadly versus Law', p. 283; Rupp, p. 98 n. It was opposed by Henry Venn,

Complete Duty of Man, London 1763, Preface, but reasserted by Wesley later against the Calvinists (see Minutes of 1770, below, pp. 391f., 454).

152. *JWL (B)*, I, p. 369.

153. *JWL (B)*, I, pp. 373, 363f., cf. 377.

154. *JWL (B)*, I, p. 377.

155. Sermon XVII, para. I. 6–9 note.

156. *JWL (B)*, I, pp. 352, 355f., 393, 438. For Georgia and after see below, pp. 119, 188, 394f.

157. On Wesley and the mystics see Orcibal in *HMCGB*, I, ch. III; R.G. Tuttle, *Influence of Roman Catholic Mystics on John Wesley*, Bristol PhD 1969; D.D. Wilson, *Influence of Mysticism on John Wesley*, Leeds PhD 1968 (with very different conclusions). Tuttle's *John Wesley*, Paternoster Press 1979, is a curious pastiche 'autobiography' of Wesley with some direct discussion of the mystical influence, with firmly 'evangelical' conclusions, but he ignores Wesley's later development.

158. *JWL (B)*, I, pp. 391f.; cf. *Byrom Journal* (n.145), I, p. 252; (Talon, pp. 82 and note, 97 and note, 104f. [with Law]). See in general R.L. Colie, *Light and Enlightenment*, Cambridge University Press 1957.

159. *JWL (B)*, I, p. 392; Green, *YMW*, p. 318. Wesley was reading Malebranche in 1733.

160. Green, *YMW*, pp. 305–19 passim; *JWL (B)*, I, p. 372. De Renty was also read by Pietists of a mystical cast like Gottfried Arnold: Schmidt, I, p. 213 n. For Scougal see *JWL (B)*, I, p. 345 (1732), though the diary suggests perhaps August 1732 and again in 1734.

161. *JWJ*, I, p. 468, see above n. 145.

162. *JWL (B)*, I, p. 345; Schmidt, I, p. 48.

163. Outler, pp. 9–10 and n. on Macarius' identity and pedigree.

164. *JWL (B)*, I, pp. 487–90 and n.

165. Byrom *Journal*, I (2), pp. 616–19; II (1) pp. 112f., 181–3 (Talon, pp. 155–7, 174f., 185f.).

166. Moore, I, p. 246.

167. So Moore throughout, e.g. I, p. 348.

168. Heitzenrater, *OM*, p. 408 and *EMW*, I, pp. 73f.; *JWL (B)*, I, p. 440; Whitefield, *Journals*, p. 56.

169. Cf. Walsh, 'Origins', p. 143.

170. Heitzenrater, *OM*, pp. 423, 426.

171. For details see Green, *YMW*, chs. XIII, XV; id., *Religion in Oxford and Cambridge* (n.4), pp. 203, 205ff.; see Tyerman, *OM*, for the careers of various members. For Methodists and Evangelicals at Oxford see *History* (Sutherland), pp. 405f.

172. *JWL*, VI, p. 6.

173. *JWJ*, VI, p. 213.

174. *Works* VIII, pp. 292f., 293ff. See further below, p. 357.

III. Serpents in Eden: Georgia (1735–37)

1. K. Coleman, *Colonial Georgia. A History*, Scribners 1976, pp. xiii–xv.

2. D.J. Boorstin, *The Americans*, I, *The Colonial Experience*, Penguin Books, 1965, pp. 89, 102.

3. A.A. Ettinger, *James Edward Oglethorpe, Imperial Idealist*, Oxford University Press 1936, p. 110; Coleman, *Colonial Georgia* (n.1), pp. 1, 11f.

4. Ettinger, *Oglethorpe* (n.3), chs II and III; P. Spalding, *Oglethorpe in America*, University of Chicago Press 1977, pp. 3f., 38.

5. Egmont *Diary* I, pp. xii, xv, xvi; 264 for attack on the City.

6. Ettinger, *Oglethorpe* (n.3), pp. 118f.; Coleman, *Colonial Georgia*, pp. 18–20; Egmont *Diary*, I, p. 273.

7. Spalding, *Oglethorpe in America* (n.4), pp. 60f.

8. Ibid., pp. 48–51; Ettinger, *Oglethorpe* (n.3), pp. 150f.

9. Spalding, *Oglethorpe in America* (n.4), pp. 66f., 72, 74.

10. Coleman, *Colonial Georgia* (n.1), pp. 129f.; Spalding, *Oglethorpe in America* (n.4), p. 38.

11. Egmont, *Diary*, II, pp. 132f.

12. Coleman, *Colonial Georgia* (n.1), pp. 144–8; E.L. Pennington, 'John Wesley's Georgia Ministry', *CH*, VIII, 1939, p. 232.

13. Egmont, *Diary*, I, p. 30; II, p. 194; Pennington, 'Georgia Ministry' (n.12), pp. 233f; *Georgia Historical Quarterly*, XI, 1927, pp. 158–65.

14. Egmont, *Diary*, II, pp. 182, 194, 196, 200. On Hall's career see Green, *YMW*, pp. 238–41, 291f., and see below, p. 295 and above, pp. 52, 99.

15. *JWL (B)*, I, pp. 441f.

16. *JWL (B)*, I, pp. 437, 444.

17. *JWL (B)*, I, pp. 435f.; *JWJ*, VIII, pp. 285–8.

18. Ettinger, *Oglethorpe* (n.3), pp. 129, 134, 140f.

19. Egmont, *Diary*, II, p. 201; Ettinger, *Oglethorpe* (n.3), pp. 150f.; *JWJ*, I, pp. 106, 109.

20. Jackson, *CW*, II, p. 390, to Doctor Chandler in the 1780s.

21. For a discussion (only partially followed here) see F. Baker in *Methodist History* VIII, 1970, pp. 25–32, and *PWHS*, XLII, 1980, pp. 93–5; and see the BE of the *Journal* by W.R. Ward, volume I, Introduction. For examples of Wesley's varying accounts of Georgia events see Heitzenrater, *EMW*, I, pp. 75f., 85, 89f.

22. *JWJ*, I, p. 112f., 117, 132, 136.

23. E.g. *JWJ*, I, pp. 140, 142–3.

24. *JWJ*, I, pp. 150–5, 159f.; Schmidt, I, pp. 152f. quoting Spangenberg's diary.

25. Egmont, *Diary*, II, p. 112; *JWJ*, I, p. 371.

26. *JWJ*, I, pp. 401–9.

27. *JWL (B)*, I, p. 447.

28. For what follows see *JWJ*, I, pp. 188f.

29. *CWJ (T)*, esp. pp. 35–41, 60–64.

30. *CWJ (T)*, pp. 40f.; *JWJ*, I, p. 213 diary and n. John saw Charles as almost miraculously recovering from illness on his own arrival, but Charles's account is less dramatic (*JWJ*, I, p. 193, cf. *CWJ (T)*, p. 33). Hampson suggests natural emotional causes (Hampson, I, p. 179), and an element of psychomatic illness is very likely in Charles's condition in Georgia, as in early 1738 in England.

31. *JWJ*, I, pp. 260–6; Schmidt, I, p. 194, quoting Töltschig's diary.

32. *JWL (B)*, I, pp. 492–4.

33. *JWJ*, I, p. 197.

34. See below, ch. XIII.1.

35. Letter in *Gentleman's Magazine* III, 1733, pp. 413–15, quoted by L. Church, *Oglethorpe*, Epworth Press 1932, p. 245; Oglethorpe to Samuel Wesley in November/December 1734, in *Henry Newman's Letter Book*, pp. 315–21, quoted by Spalding, *Oglethorpe in America* (n.4), pp. 83–5.

36. *JWJ*, I, pp. 238, 239, 245–50; *JWL (B)*, I, pp. 454–6.

37. *JWL (B)*, I, p. 474.

38. *JWJ*, I, pp. 367f., 407f.

39. *JWJ*, I, 238, 297f.; Egmont, II, p. 312; *JWL (B)*, I, pp. 491, 467–9.

40. *JWJ*, I, pp. 350f., 352, 345f.

41. *JWJ (B)*, I, p. 462.

42. *JWL (B)*, I, pp. 486f., 497.

43. Egmont *Diary*, II, pp. 312, 370; *JWL (B)*, I, 504f.

44. *JWL (B)*, I, pp. 502–4, 509f., 514f.

45. *JWJ*, I, pp. 212f., 386f., 166f. (a baptized child recovered from illness 'from that hour'), 210f. The *Herring Visitation* in Yorkshire (1743) shows clearly how this discipline of giving notice had become obsolete.

46. *JWJ*, I, pp. 213f., 273f.

47. *JWJ*, I, pp. 197–205 and notes; pp. 226–32 and notes.

48. *Concise Ecclesiastical History*, London 1781, IV, p. 175.

49. *JWJ*, I, p. 198 n.

50. Schmidt, I, pp. 191f. and n.; H. Bett in *PWHS* XVIII, 1931, pp. 43–5.

51. *JWJ*, I, pp. 234, 385f.

52. *JWL (B)*, I, pp. 452f.

53. *JWL (B)*, I, pp. 473ff.; *JWJ*, I, pp. 274–8; for the old man, p. 224.

54. *JWL (B)*, I, pp. 449f., 477–83.

55. *JWJ*, I, pp. 151, 170f. Not ordained bishop as Wesley said: *JWJ* (BE) I, p. 151 n. 59.

56. For what follows see Schmidt, I, pp. 169ff., 179ff.

57. For this view see N. Sykes, *The Church of England and Non-Episcopal Churches in the Sixteenth and Seventeenth Centuries, Theology Occasional Paper*, SPCK ²1949; id., *Old Priest and New Presbyter*, Cambridge University Press 1956, which convincingly shows this attitude. For the Moravian position, Schmidt, I, p. 162; *JWJ*, I, p. 277 n.; *CWJ (T)*, p. 113; W.G. Addison, *Renewed Church of the United Brethren*, SPCK 1932, pp. 91–102.

58. Schmidt, I, p. 138 n. 152, for patristic authority, Spangenberg's account of the conversations and his question about Wesley's faith. For Wesley and the Salzburgers see Schmidt, I, pp. 169, 179f.

59. Schmidt, I, pp. 161f., quoting Töltschig's diary.

60. *JWL (B)*, I, pp. 479–83.

61. *JWJ*, I, p. 151 and n.; Schmidt, I, p. 156.

62. See J.L. Nuelsen, *John Wesley and the German Hymn*, ET A.S. Holebrook (1938) 1972, and for the Charleston Hymn Book, ibid., pp. 28, 71; *JWJ*, I, p. 349 (diary 18 April 1737).

63. Nuelsen, *John Wesley* (n.62), pp. 27, 71 and App. II; *JWJ*, I, pp. 212, 220 n.; Schmidt, I, pp. 166f.

64. *JWL (B)*, I, p. 454.

65. *CWJ (T)*, p. 67.

66. See the accounts of Williams and Stephens, below, nn. 81, 84.

67. Hampson, I, p. 192.

68. Whitehead, II, p. 30.
69. Moore, I, pp. 311, 312 n.
70. Cf. Heitzenrater, *EMW*, I, ch. IV: Curnock confuses this with his synthetic account.
71. Heitzenrater, *EMW*, I, pp. 78–89, for extracts; cf. *JWJ*, I, pp. 378ff.
72. The narrative comes mainly from Wesley's most intimate account.
73. *JWJ*, I, pp. 337 n., 347f. For Williamson see *Egmont Diary* III, pp. 65, 119, 120, 125.
74. *JWJ*, I, p. 330 (diary), and Heitzenrater, *EMW*, I, p. 83.
75. *JWJ*, I, p. 376.
76. Moore, I, p. 335.
77. *JWJ*, I, pp. 383–5.
78. *JWJ*, I, p. 385f.
79. *JWJ*, I, pp. 387f.; *JWJ*, VIII, pp. 308–10; cf. F. Baker, *From Wesley to Asbury*, Duke University Press 1976, pp. 22ff.
80. *JWJ*, I, p. 391.
81. W. Stephens, *Journal of the Proceedings in Georgia*, I, pp. 9–40, passim; *Georgia Colonial Records*, XXII, pp. 32–41; cf. Pennington, 'Georgia Ministry' (n.12), pp. 247–50, 251–3.
82. *JWJ*, I, p. 392.
83. *JWJ*, I, pp. 393, 396, 399f.; Moore, I, pp. 331f. suggested that the magistrates probably deliberately let him go.
84. *JWJ*, VIII, pp. 256ff. and Heitzenrater, *EMW*, II, pp. 55ff.; JWJ, I, p. 296 and VIII, pp. 304ff.; *JWL (B)*, II, pp. 83–5, 88–90; Pennington, 'Georgia Ministry' (n.12), p. 246.
85. *JWL (B)*, I, pp. 496f. and n., 507f.
86. Egmont, *Diary*, II, pp. 450f.
87. *JWJ*, I, pp. 437, 438, 440; Egmont *Diary*, II, pp. 450f., 467f., 473, 481.
88. *JWJ*, I, pp. 421–4.
89. *JWJ*, I, p. 435.
90 Whitefield, *Journal*, p. 157.
91. *JWL (B)*, I, pp. 519f.; Pennington, 'Georgia Ministry' (n.12), p. 281.
92. Baker, *Wesley to Asbury* (n.79), ch. I; cf. the account of Whitefield's mission in Georgia in Coleman, *Colonial Georgia* (n.1), pp. 151ff.
93. *Plain Account of Christian Perfection*, para. 7; *Short History of Methodism* in *Works*, VIII.
94. *JWJ*, I, pp. 470f.
95. *JWJ*, I, pp. 414–18.
96. First printed in Whitehead, II, pp. 54–6; as from a 'private paper' in Moore, I, p. 342. Original in Wesley College, Bristol and printed in Heitzenrater, *EMW*, I, pp. 94–6.
97. Schmidt, I, pp. 207–12.
98. Green, *YMW*, pp. 278f. gives a judicious summary.

IV. The Road to Aldersgate Street: The Wesleys' Conversion (1738)

1. Green, *YMW*, p. 266, is one of the few to pose this problem.
2. Schmidt, I, p. 226.
3. Green, *YMW*, ch. XIII.
4. For other examples see Walsh, 'Cambridge Methodists'.

5. *CWJ (T)*, pp. 114f., 117, 121, 123, 126–8, 133–7.
6. *JWL (B)*, I, pp. 532–4.
7. Green, *YMW*, pp. 257, 269f.
8. Schmidt, I, p. 228; cf *JWJ*, I, p. 441.
9. *JWL (B)*, I, p. 526.
10. Schmidt, I, pp. 224f., 226.
11. For what follows see Schmidt, I, pp. 228–35.
12. J.P. Lockwood, *Memorials of Peter Böhler*, London 1868, p. 67.
13. *JWJ*, I, p. 440; Schmidt, I, pp. 235ff. and note.
14. *JWJ*, I, pp. 442, 448.
15. *JWJ*, I, pp. 442, 448. For the debate see J. McManners, *Death and the Enlightenment*, Oxford University Press 1981, pp. 191–7. Cautionary tales were told of those who reformed, but cheerfully returned to vice on being reprieved. For Silas Told see *Life of Silas Told by Himself*, 1786, reprinted Epworth Press 1954.
16. For this last point see C.W. Towlson, *Moravian and Methodist*, Epworth Press 1957, p. 53, who also notes that 'Scotch Will' Darney advised William Grimshaw in very similar terms (quoting W. Miles, *Life and Writings of William Grimshaw*, London 1806, p. 18).
17. *JWJ*, I, pp. 454f.; Schmidt, I, 239.
18. *JWJ*, I, p. 457.
19. Schmidt, I, pp. 241f.; letter in *JWJ*, I, pp. 461f.
20. *JWJ*, I, pp. 458f.; D. Benham, *Memoirs of James Hutton*, London 1856.
21. *JWJ*, I, p. 458 n.; Schmidt, I, pp. 244f., and estimate in Rack, 'Religious Societies', p. 583. For a fresh account, published since this article was written, see C.J. Podmore, *PWHS* XLVI, 1988, pp. 125–53.
22. *JWL (B)*, I, pp. 538f.
23. *JWJ*, I, p. 449.
24. *JWL (B)*, I, pp. 540–50.
25. For Law generally see A.K. Walker, *William Law*, SPCK 1973; there is a lucid summary of his 'Behmenism' in Rupp, pp. 232–40. For Wesley and Law see J.B. Green, *John Wesley and William Law*, Epworth Press, 1945; E. Baker, *A Herald of the Evangelical Revival*, Epworth Press 1948. Schmidt, I, pp. 246–54, gives a sympathetic account of the controversy, though explaining the differences.
26. *CWJ (T)*, pp. 120, 122.
27. L. Wiseman, *Charles Wesley*, Epworth Press 1933, p. 36.
28. William Law, *Christian Perfection*, in *Works* III, London 1762, p. 188.
29. Whitefield, *Journals*, pp. 81, 85; *CWJ (T)*, p. 121. For Ingham's conversion see JRUL Eng. MS 1062, p. 5.
30. *CWJ (T)*, pp. 134–40.
31. *CWJ (T)*, pp. 142f.
32. *CWJ (T)*, pp. 146–9.
33. *JWL (B)*, I, pp. 550f.
34. *JWJ*, I, pp. 472–6; *JWL (B)*, I, pp. 550f. The passage from Luther's *Preface to Romans* is identified by Schmidt as 'Faith is a divine work in us', etc. For another translation see e.g., J. Dillenberger (ed.), *Martin Luther*, Doubleday 1961, pp. 23f. Some have surmised that it was really from Luther's *Galatians* and perhaps the same as that read by Charles Wesley earlier: cf. Curnock in *JWJ*, I, p. 467 n.

35. For example, Moore in his *John Wesley* writes firmly from this standpoint.

36. Schmidt, I, pp. 305–9.

37. Green, *YMW*, ch. XIV; cf. the view of George Every, *The High Church Party 1688–1718*, SPCK 1956, p. 173–7.

38. St Paul might be said to have been converted from Judaism to Christianity; St Augustine from paganism to Christianity; Luther from a Catholic to a proto-Protestant type of salvation doctrine; Wesley from High Church Anglican to Moravian views of salvation, at least for the time being.

39. See, e.g., P. Miller, 'Preparation for Salvation', in *Nature's Nation*, Harvard University Press 1957; J.C. Brauer, 'Conversion from Puritanism to Revivalism', *Journal of Religion* LVIII, 1978, pp. 227–43; B. Citron, *New Birth*, Edinburgh University Press 1951; N. Pettit, *The Heart Prepared*, Yale University Press 1966; E.S. Morgan, *Visible Saints*, New York University Press, 1963; P. Caldwell, *Puritan Conversion Narratives*, Cambridge University Press 1983.

40. P. Miller, 'Solomon Stoddard', *Harvard Theological Review* XXIV, 1921, pp. 277–320; R. Middlekauff, *The Mathers*, Oxford University Press, New York 1971, pp. 124–38.

41. Schmidt, I, pp. 140ff.

42. For a full exposition of this interpretation see below, p. 393.

43. On the early converts see below, p. 424.

44. *JWJ*, II, pp. 89–91, 125f.

45. Reviews of 29 January 1738 and 24 May 1738 in *JWJ*, I. On doctrine see also below, pp. 389ff. For the modifying notes see Outler, pp. 48 n., 49 n., 60 n., 62 n., 63n., 65 n. For Cell's criticism and rejection of their authenticity see G.C. Cell, *The Rediscovery of John Wesley*, Henry Holt 1935, pp. 179f.

46. Heizenrater in *PWHS* XLIII, 1982, pp. 173–6.

47. T. Källstad, *John Wesley and the Bible, A Psychological Study*, Nya Bokforlags Aktiebolaget, Stockholm 1974.

48. J.W. Fowler, 'John Wesley's Development in Faith', in *The Future of the Methodist Theological Traditions*, ed. M.D. Meeks, Abingdon Press 1985, pp. 172–92.

49. R.L. Moore, 'Justification Without Joy', *History of Childhood Quarterly*, II, 1974, pp. 31–52, and id., *John Wesley and Authority*, Scholar Press 1979.

50. Moore, 'Justification', pp. 48f.

51. Apparently first suggested in R.D. Urlin, *Churchman's Life of Wesley*, SPCK 1880, pp. 12f. and Appendix IV, and then by J.A. Léger, *La Jeunesse de Wesley*, Paris 1910, but best known from A. Piette, *John Wesley in the Evolution of Protestantism*, ET Sheed and Ward 1938, pp. 240–5, 305–9, though not as clearly as is sometimes implied. Green, *YMW*, ch. XIV follows a similar line with some refinements.

52. *Plain Account of Christian Perfection*, paras. 5–7; *Short History of Methodism*, para. 10. When he mentions or implies 1738 in later years it is a change in teaching, not his personal experience, that is cited.

53. *JWL (B)*, II, pp. 82f. (a rare reference specifically to 24 May); *JWJ*, V, p. 116 (1765) and see J.E. Rattenbury, *The Conversion of the Wesleys*, Epworth Press 1938, pp. 19–24. He refers back to his holiness teaching from 1725 or to his distinctive missions from 1738 without reference to the 'conversion' experience.

54. *Minutes of Some Later Conversations* in *Works*, VIII, pp. 275–98, passim.

55. See below, p. 393.
56. *JWL*, V, pp. 358f., and see below, p. 393.
57. *JWL*, V, p. 366.
58. *JWL*, V, pp. 243f.; cf. *Minutes* I, pp. 95f. (1770); *Works*, VIII, pp. 337f., and see below, p. 391.
59. See below, pp. 388ff.
60. A.C. Outler, *John Wesley*, Oxford University Press 1964, p. 52.
61. See n.45 above and Cell, *Rediscovery* (n.45), pp. 179f., who is anxious to emphasize what he calls Wesley's 'Calvinism' (i.e. early Reformation doctrine) on justification by grace through faith.
62. Cell, *Rediscovery* (n.45), pp. 360, 361: 'the necessary synthesis of the Protestant ethic of grace with the Catholic ethic of holiness'.
63. E.G. Rupp, *Principalities and Powers*, Epworth Press 1952, p. 82, quoted in C.W. Williams, *John Wesley's Theology Today*, Epworth Press 1960, p. 176.

Interlude. Converting Fires: The Origins of the Evangelical Revival

1. For discussions of the meaning of the term and developments in it see J. Kent, *Holding the Fort*, Epworth Press 1978, ch. I; D.H. Luker, 'Revivalism in Theory and Practice: the Case of Cornish Methodism', *JEH* XXXVII, 1986, pp. 605–7; R. Carwardine, *Transatlantic Revivalism 1790–1865*, Greenwood Press 1978, p. xv; W.G. McLoughlin, *Modern Revivalism*, Ronald Press 1959; id., *Revivals, Awakenings and Reform*, University of Chicago Press 1978, p. xiii.
2. *JWL*, VI, pp. 339f.
3. *JWJ*, V, pp. 465ff.
4. Kent, *Fort* (n.1), p. 15; cf. P. Boyer and S. Nussbaum, *Salem Possessed*, Harvard University Press 1974, p. 25, who point out that there were signs even in the worst affected areas in the 1690s of the possibility of channelling these emotions into the more benign direction of religious revival.
5. Kent, ibid. For an example see the Richard Davis revival in Northamptonshire in the 1690s; and for an interesting contrast with the New England witch craze see the case of the 'Surey Demoniac' in Lancashire in the same decade. Here Dissenters failed to raise a witch scare though they saw some signs of religious renewal: T. Jollie and J. Carrington, *The Surey Demoniack*, 1697, pp. 38, 48, 49, 60; J. Carrington, *The Surey Demoniack*, 1697, pp. 48ff.
6. Luker, 'Revivalism' (n.1), p. 606; Kent, *Fort* (n.1), p. 16, and see below, p. 494.
7. For this see Kent, *Fort* (n.1), pp. 16ff.; McLoughlin over-stresses the significance of Finney as a pioneer here.
8. Luker, 'Revivalism' (n.1), and see below, pp. 491ff.
9. Kent, *Fort* (n.1), p. 16. This judgment might perhaps be modified in the light of his remarks in *The Unacceptable Face*, SCM Press 1987, pp. 110–11, where he sees Methodism as merely a reorganization of part of the 'religious sub-culture'; see below p. 424 for the problem of the apparently marked religious background of many of the members.
10. The only substantial treatment in English is F.E. Stoeffler, *The Rise of Evangelical Pietism*, Brill 1965, and id., *German Pietism During the Eighteenth Century*, Brill 1973. See also M. Fullbrook, *Piety and Politics*, Cambridge University Press 1983. For international aspects of the Revival see G.F. Nuttall, 'Continental

Pietism and the Evangelical Movement in Britain', in *Pietismus und Reveil*, ed. J.P. van den Berg and J.P. van Doren, Brill 1978, pp. 207–36.; E. Duffy, 'Correspondence Fraternelle', *SCH* Subsidia 2, 1979, pp. 251–80; W.R. Ward, 'The Relationship of Enlightenment and Religious Revival', ibid., pp. 281–306; id., 'Power and Piety', *BJRL* LXIII, 1980, pp. 231–52; M.J. Crawford, *The Invention of the American Revival: The Beginnings of Anglo-American Religious Revivalism 1690–1750*, Boston PhD 1978.

11. Ward, 'Power and Piety' (n.10), passim.

12. F.E. Stoeffler, *Continental Pietism and Early American Christianity*, Eerdmans 1976.

13. Ibid.

14. For Frelinghuysen see Stoeffler, *Continental Pietism* (n.12), pp. 47f., but for controversies about his role see F.J. Schrag, 'T.J. Frelinghuysen, the Father of American Pietism', *CH* XIV, 1945, pp. 201–16; H. Hermelink, 'Another Look at Frelinghuysen and his "Awakening"', *CH* XXXVII, 1968, pp. 423–38.

15. W.G. McLoughlin, 'Revivals', for recent literature; P. Miller, *Errand into the Wilderness*, Harvard University Press 1956. For social interpretations see e.g. J.P. Greene and J.R. Pole (eds.), *Colonial America*, Johns Hopkins University Press 1984, pp. 238ff., 317–44.

16. M. Clement, *The SPCK and Wales 1699–1740*, University of Wales Press 1954; G.H. Jenkins, *Literature, Religious and Society in Wales 1660–1730*, University of Wales Press 1978.

17. For Davis see P. Rehakosht, *A Plain and Just Account*, 1692; R. Davis, *Truth and Innocency Vindicated*, 1692; N. Glass, *Early History of the Independent Church at Rothwell*, Northampton 1871. For the Baptists, see F. Overend, *History of Ebenezer General Baptist Church Bacup*, 1912, pp. 22–4; W.T. Whitley, *Baptists of North West England*, London 1913, pp. 77–80; G.A. Weston, *Baptists of the North West*, Sheffield PhD 1969; J.H. Turner, *Halifax Books and Authors*, Bingham 1906, pp. 36f.; and for the Whitefield connection *Christian History* (1743), V, ii, p. 52; VI, i, p. 35. For Dissenting itineracy see e.g. J.B. Williams, *Life of Matthew Henry*, London 1825, pp. 114, 139f.

18. Crawford, *American Revival* (n.10).

19. See below, pp. 284ff.

20. See below ch. V, 2, n.128.

21. See below, pp. 217–19.

22. See below, ch. VIII.2.

23. See below, p. 325.

24. See E. Isichei, *Victorian Quakers*, Oxford University Press 1969 on the 'Beaconites'; Watts, pp. 461ff.

25. See below, pp. 226ff., and for Ireland, below, pp. 231ff.

26. Watts, p. 440.

27. See e.g. Miller in *Errand into the Wilderness*, Harvard University Press 1956, pp. 156f.

28. Quoted in C.H. Smyth, *Simeon and Church Order*, Cambridge University Press 1940, p. 198.

29. *HMCGB*, I, xxxvi.

30. Ward, 'Power and Piety' (n.10 above).

31. *Acta Fratrum*, London 1749, p. 83, quoted by A.J. Lewis, *Zinzendorf, Ecumenical Pioneer*, SCM Press 1962, p. 71.

32. O. Chadwick, in *Christian Spirituality*, ed. Peter Brooks, SCM Press 1975, pp. 215f.

33. Stoeffler, *German Pietism* (n.10), ch. V.

34. See below, p. 325 for Swedenborgianism.

35. J. Delumeau, *Catholicism Between Luther and Voltaire*, ET Burns Oates 1977, pp. 189f., and on 'missions', pp. 189–202; cf. S. Gilley, 'Catholic Revivalism in the Eighteenth Century', *Epworth Review* XXV, 1988, pp. 72–8.

36. By the time this book is published promised studies of revivalism by Louis Billington and of Evangelicalism in England from 1738 by David Bebbington should be in print. Professor Ward is working on a general study.

37. E. Halévy, *The Birth of Methodism* (1906), ET University of Chicago Press 1971.

38. For an excellent critique and further suggestions see Walsh, 'Halévy'.

39. R. Currie, *PWHS* XXXVI, 1967, pp. 67f.

40. Whitefield, *Journals*, p. 216; *JWJ*, III, 288.

41. Thomas Taylor in *EMP*, V, p. 56.

42. A.D. Gilbert, *Religion and Society in Industrial England 1740–1914*, Longmans 1976, p. 89, but cf. Watts, p. 409, though he uses only the lives of travelling preachers.

43. E.P. Thompson, *The Making of the English Working Class*, Penguin Books 1968, pp. 427ff., 919f. Contrast E. Hobsbawm, 'Methodism and the Threat of Revolution', in *Labouring Men*, Weidenfeld and Nicholson 1964. For the relative lack of exact correlation between economic fluctuations and revival see Carwardine, *Transatlantic Revivalism* (n.1), 54–6; for the view that such factors heighten internal rhythms see Julia Werner, *The Primitive Methodist Connexion*, University of Wisconsin Press 1984, pp. 32–44.

44. See G. Holmes, 'The Achievement of Stability', in *The Whig Supremacy*, ed. J. Cannon, Edward Arnold 1981, ch. I, esp. p. 6.

45. Walsh, 'Halévy', pp. 10f.; earthquake sermons, *CWJ*, II, pp 68–70; *JWJ*, II, pp. 453, 456f.; the earthquake sermon no. CXXIV in *Works*, VII, pp. 386–99 is by Charles, not John. See also Watts and Guyse, Preface to Edwards' *Narrative* (1737); *Christian History* (American ed.), I, pp. 15, 114.

46. See below, p. 197.

47. Walsh allows some influence to this in 'Halévy', p. 5; cf. Watts, pp. 438ff. E.D. Starbuck, *Psychology of Religion*, Scribner 1903, and J.B. Pratt, *Religious Consciousness*, Macmillan, New York 1926, emphasized conversion as an adolescent phenomenon, but they were looking at the descendants of the evangelical tradition who expected conversion then.

48. The following account is based on Walsh, 'Origins'.

49. For examples cf. *EMP*, I, pp. 21f.; V, pp. 223ff.; ibid., p. 88, for later Tom Paine influence; for the sense of loss and temptation to blaspheme see *EMP*, V, pp. 230f.; II, p. 283, 268f.; IV, pp. 241ff.; I, p. 52. This is very much in the seventeenth-century Puritan tradition, and not influenced by Deism.

50. See above, Prelude, n. 90, and below ch. VII, n. 39.

51. H. Venn, *Life of Venn*, London 1839, pp. 19–21.

52. See above, Prelude, n. 66; and below, pp. 186, 221.

53. *DNB*, 'Burkitt, William'. His father was an ejected minister of 1662.

54. Walsh, 'Halévy', p. 5.

55. Ibid.

56. G.F. Nuttall, 'Methodism and the Older Dissent' (see above, Prelude, n. 18).

57. *EMP*, II, pp. 107f.; V, p. 136; II, p. 158; V, pp. 1–2; II, pp. 277f., 282f.

58. Walsh, 'Origins', p. 157; *PWHS* XLV, 1985, pp. 67–79.

59. R. Gough (ed. D. Hey), *History of Myddle*, Penguin Books 1981, p. 43; *EMP*, I, pp. 109f., 111; Whitefield, *Journals*, p. 315 (found as waste paper); cf. Walsh, 'Origins', p. 159.

60. *JWL (B)*, II, pp. 262f. in 1747; *JWJ*, VI, p. 273; cf. Watts, p. 422.

61. E.g. *JWJ*, IV, p. 203 (though not understood until he became a Methodist); Cennick in 1737 (*PWHS*, XXX, pp. 30f.); and a local revival in Lakenheath c. 1718, *JWJ*, IV, p. 295; Cornish Evangelicals in G.C.B. Davies, *Early Cornish Evangelicals*, SPCK 1951, ch. II and p. 58; Nuttall, 'Older Dissent', for Dissenting examples.

62. See below, p. 441.

63. See S. Durden, 'A Study of the First Evangelical Magazines', *JEH* XXVII, 1976, pp. 255–75.

64. W. Batty, *Church History* (1779), p. 4.

65. Walsh, 'Halévy', pp. 19f.; id., 'Religious Societies', p. 593, and see below, 372.

66. J. Wesley, *Farther Appeal*, in *Works*, VIII, Part I, passim; Sermon LVII, 'The Reformation of Manners', in *Works*, V, eg. II.1; *JWL (B)*, II, p. 36; Lewis in ibid., p. 363.

67. Though see the evidence of contacts via the SPCK: E. Duffy, 'Correspondence Fraternelle' in *SCH*, Subsidia 2, 1979; W.O.B. Allen and E. McClure, *Two Hundred Years*, SPCK 1898, p. 122 n.; *JWJ*, III, p. 347.

68. K.S. Pinson, *Pietism and the Rise of German Nationalism*, Columbia University Press 1934.

69. Watts, pp. 436–9.

70. Cf. above, Prelude, n. 96.

71. S.T. Bindoff, *Tudor England*, Penguin Books 1950, p. 224.

72. For further development of these points see J. Kent, *The Unacceptable Face* (n. 9), pp. 107–19.

73. See below, p. 494 and n. 16.

V. 'A New Species of Puritanism': The Emergence and Expansion of Methodism

1. See Heitzenrater, *EMW*, I, pp. 17, 59, 85 for the question of his hair; Hampson, III, pp. 168f. for his later appearance. See I. Milner and T. Hawers, *History of the Church of Christ*, Nelson 1840, pp. 1063f. for the 'cast' story, which does not appear elsewhere. Was this a confusion with Whitefield? Height: see below, p. 639 n. 129.

2. E.R. Hassé, *The Moravians*, London 1912, p. 75.

3. *JWJ*, I, p. 481.

4. Priestley, *Letters*, pp. 67ff., 75ff.; cf. Tyerman, I, pp. 189f; Heitzenrater, *EMW*, II, pp. 66–8.

5. *JWJ*, I, pp. 429–31.

6. Benham, p. 40, apparently accepted by Heitzenrater, *EMW*, II, p. 68; Hampson, I, p. 320; cf. *JWJ*, II, p. 11 n. If the Count was the Count of Solms, Wesley did find that the family dressed and ate very plainly (*JWJ*, II, p. 12).

7. *JWJ*, II, pp. 13f.

8. *JWJ*, II, pp. 25–47; Schmidt, I, pp. 286–96 for a commentary on the shades of difference between them.

9. *JWJ*, II, p. 49 and n.; *Plain Account of Christian Perfection*, para. 8; cf. Moore, I, pp. 396f.

10. *JWL (B)*, I, p. 562; *JWJ*, II, pp. 82f. Bedford befriended Whitefield for a time: Whitefield, *Journals*, p. 82.

11. *JWL (B)*, I, pp. 556–62.

12. *JWL (B)*, I, pp. 566f., 574; *JWJ*, II, p. 496; see also the comment by C.W. Towlson, *Moravian and Methodist*, Epworth Press 1957, pp. 74f.

13. *JWL (B)*, I, p. 616. Usually attributed to Hervey, but by Baker to Clayton, doubted by Rupp, p. 362; cf. Whitefield, *Letters*, I, p. 105.

14. For a full discussion see my 'Religious Societies', pp. 279–302.

15. *JWL (B)*, I, pp. 570f.

16. *JWL (B)*, I, pp. 572, 601f., 568, 579, 583.

17. *JWJ*, II, pp. 101, 131f., 140–3, 145; *JWL (B)*, I, pp. 606f.

18. *JWJ*, II, pp. 136, 214f.; *JWL (B)*, I, p. 658; *CWJ (T)*, pp. 215, 236–9; *JWJ*, II, p. 131. For the history and significance of the French Prophets see H. Schwartz, *The French Prophets*, University of California Press 1980.

19. *JWJ*, II, pp. 108–11. Curnock suggests that this letter was by Delamotte.

20. *JWJ*, II, pp. 123–5. Curiously, Charles does not record this in his *Journal*.

21. *JWJ*, II, p. 135.

22. Benham, pp. 40f., 46f.; *JWJ*, II, pp. 146, 157f; *JWL (B)*, I, p. 611. See E.P. Crow Jr, *John Wesley's Conflict with the Antinomians*, Manchester PhD 1964.

23. *JWL (B)*, I, pp. 586, 588, 590–3, 595.

24. *JWL (B)*, I, pp. 599, 613, 609.

25. *JWL (B)*, I, pp. 614–17; *JWJ*, II, p. 216 (January 1739), by which time he had begun field preaching.

26. *JWJ*, II, pp. 89–91, 115f., 125f.

27. Benham, p. 47, partly reprinted in Heitzenrater, *EMW*, II, pp. 69f.; *JWL (B)*, I, 588f.; Källstad, pp. 270f., 276, 342.

28. *JWL (B)*, I, pp. 605, 612.

29. *JWJ*, II, pp. 156–8; *JWL*, II, p. 245; Moore, I, p. 438; *CWJ (T)*, p. 227.

30. *JWJ*, II, pp. 167f.

31. *LyH*, I, p. 197. The reference to Trapp fixes this no earlier than 1739. For Continental views see Ward, 'Power and Piety', p. 248 and n. For the later case see the J.L. Fricker letter in K.C.E. Ehmann, *J.L. Fricker*, Tübingen 1864, p. 21.

32. See e.g. Murray's introduction to Whitefield, *Journal*; J.C. Ryle, *Christian Leaders of the Last Century*, London 1868. For Whitefield, see *Works*, six volumes, London 1771; *Letters*, three volumes, London 1772 and facsimile with additions of Vol. I, Banner of Truth Trust 1976 (but see Nuttall in *JEH*, XXVIII, 1977, p. 427 for omissions). Lives: J. Gillies, *Memoirs of Whitefield*, London 1772; Tyerman, *Whitefield*, Dallimore. For Whitefield's connexion E. Welch, *Two Calvinistic Methodist Chapels*, London Record Society XI, 1975.

33. For what follows see *Short Account of God's Dealings with George Whitefield* in *Journals*.

34. Whitefield, *Journals*, p. 62.

35. Ibid., p. 81. See above, p. 143 for a discussion of his and Charles Wesley's use of 'new birth'.

36. Walsh, 'Halévy'; Whitefield, *Journals*, p. 200 and n. says that this first occurred to him when rooms became full, forcing him into the churchyard.

37. *PWHS* VI, 1907, pp. 102f., 124–7.

38. Whitefield, *Journals*, p. 562ff. for a famous account of preaching in America.

39. For *Minutes* and account of this see Welch, *Methodist Chapels* (n.32).

40. Whitefield, *Journals*, p. 241.

41. *JWJ*, II, pp. 172f., 175–9.

42. Whitefield, *Journals*, pp. 240, 242, 243, cf. 231.

43. *JWJ*, II, pp. 180–6, 189f.

44. *JWJ*, II. p. 203.

45. *JWL (B)*, I, 645f.; Cennick in *PWHS* VI, 1907, p. 109; J. Kent, *Holding the Fort*, p. 47 (but the account is not by Wesley himself, as he says, cf. *JWJ*, IV, p. 332 n.).

46. *JWJ*, IV, pp. 334–48; cf. *LyH* I, pp. 397f.; *JWL (B)*, II, p. 113, in 1744; *JWJ*, IV, p. 331 (1759); V, pp. 465ff.

47. *AM*, 1778, pp. 179ff.; cf. *PWHS* VI, 1906.

48. James Robe in *Christian History* (American ed.), I, ii, pp. 11–14.

49. Cf. the argument on sixteenth- and seventeenth-century French cases: R. Mandrou, *Magistrats et Sorciers*, Paris 1968; D.P. Walker, *Unclean Spirits*, University of Pennsylvania Press 1981.

50. See *JWJ*, II, pp. 298–300, where a girl had given herself to the devil and was violent when Jesus was mentioned. This parallels the New Testament to observers, cf. p. 271 ('the enemy began to tear him'); p. 291 ('torn by the devil'). For a spectacular case see George Lukyns (discussed in my 'Doctors', pp. 147f.)

51. *JWJ*, II, p. 186; cf. p. 203 for suggested natural explanations.

52. *JWL (B)*, I, pp. 680, 682–4, 688–90.

53. *CWJ*, I, pp. 243, 247, 314, 316; Cennick in *PWHS*, VI, 1907, pp. 108f.

54. *JWJ*, II, p. 184, cf. *JWL (B)*, I, pp. 639ff., where the 'providential' reference is more explicit; there is another case in *JWJ*, II, p. 188.

55. *JWL (B)*, I, pp. 694, 695; *JWJ*, II, pp. 84, 202.

56. *JWJ*, III, pp. 60, 69; *JWL (B)*, II, pp. 113,71; *JWL*, V, p. 366.

57. *JWL (B)*, I, p. 639; *JWL*, II, p. 240; *JWL (B)*, I, p. 672. Whitefield makes no reference to this in his *Journals*.

58. B. Holland, *PWHS* XXXIX, 1973, pp. 77–85.

59. W. Sargent, *Battle for the Mind*, Heinemann 1957.

60. Watts, pp. 406ff.

61. *JWL (B)*, I, p. 639.

62. *JWJ*, II, p. 184; *JWL (B)*, I, p. 649; *JWJ*, II, p. 203; *CWJ (T)*, pp. 239f.; *JWJ*, II, pp. 288f.; *CWJ*, I, p. 188; *JWJ*, II. p. 353.

63. *CWJ*, I, p. 247.

64. *JWL (B)*, I, p. 662; Whitefield, *Letters*, I, pp. 155–7.

65. *JWL (B)*, II, p. 31.

66. *JWL (B)*, II, pp. 31–3; *CWJ*, I, pp. 250, 254, 255, 263f.

67. *JWL (B)*, II, pp. 48f.; Whitefield, *Letters*, I, p. 133; *JWJ*, II, pp. 21f., 426–34; *JWL (B)*, II, pp. 46f. and nn.51f.; *CWJ*, I, pp. 265–76.

68. *Works*, VII, Sermon CXXVIII; Whitefield, *Journals*, pp. 569–88.

69. Whitefield, *Journals*, p. 568n. and *Works*, II, p. 466.

70. Whitefield, *Journal*, pp. 240, 243; *JWL (B)*, I, pp. 638f., 702, 667.

71. *JWL (B)*, II, p. 59; *JWJ*, II. pp. 194f. For this 'communism' see below, pp. 364f.

72. *JWL (B)*, II, p. 66. For an abortive conference in August 1743 to reconcile the differences see Tyerman, I, p. 420; *JWJ*, III, p. 88 and n.

73. *CWJ (T)*, p. 228.

74. *JWJ*, II, pp. 216, 220, 222f., 274.

75. Schmidt, II, pp. 240 n. 244; he says that the Herrnhut MSS cast no light on Molther's character.

76. Benham, pp. 53f.

77. *JWJ*, II, p. 312.

78. *JWJ*, II, pp. 313–16.

79. *JWJ*, II, pp. 329–31.

80. *JWJ*, II, p. 343; cf. *JWL (B)*, II, p. 249; Towlson, *Moravian and Methodist* (n.12), p.84, surely correctly.

81. *JWJ*, II, pp. 344f., 335, 354–51.

82. *JWJ*, II, pp. 365–71; *LyH*, I, p. 36, but cf. Baker on Maxfield in *PWHS* XXVII, 1949, pp. 3–5. First letter to Wesley, October 1741, in *JWL (B)*, II, p. 67.

83. Byrom *Journal*, Chetham Society XLIV (1857), II (2), pp. 629–31 (Talon, pp. 281f.); *Life of John Morris* in *AM*, 1795, pp. 18ff. There is no mention of this in Wesley's *Journal*.

84. Jackson, *CW*, I, pp. 273, 278; *LyH*, I, p. 41; *JWJ*, II, pp. 418, 424; *JWL (B)*, II, pp. 52, 56f., 67.

85. Benham, p. 75.

86. Crow, *John Wesley's Conflict* (n.22), ch. III, pp. 74–5; cf. also e.g. 91, 92–5, 99.

87. See above, pp. 27f.

88. For the complicated history of this episode cf. *JWJ*, II, 478 and n.; *JWL (B)*, I, pp. 693f. and n.; for the sermon, Sermon LXXXIV, in *Works*, VII, and Sermon II in *Works*, V; also *JWJ*, II, p.470, on Bull's view of justification, described without comment. See Bull, *Harmonia Apostolica* (1669–70), and on Fletcher's and Wesley's later view of 'double justification', below, pp. 459f.

89. *JWJ*, II, pp. 451f.

90. Schmidt, II, pp. 41f.

91. *JWJ*, II, pp. 488–90, together with a letter originally written in August 1740. For Latin conversation translated see Moore, I, pp. 481–3, and Outler, pp. 369–72.

92. See Towlson, *Moravian and Methodist* (n. 12), ch. VII; on the lot in the Oxford period, Heitzenrater, *OM*, p. 300 (in 1735). For Whitefield's bands, letter days, choirs, etc. see Welch, *Methodist Chapels* (n. 32), pp. 1, 14f.

93. Baker in *PWHS*, XLII, 1980, p. 95; *CWJ*, I, p. 197, Jackson in his edition of *CWJ* omits at least one of these attacks by preachers (MS in *JRUL* at 26 October 1756).

94. Quoted by Tyerman, *Whitefield*, I, pp. 317f.; *CWJ*, I, pp. 133, 135.

95. *JWL (B)*, I, p. 633.

96. *JWL (B)*, I, p. 634; *CWJ (T)*, pp. 230f., 238, 239.

97. See Whitefield, *Journals*, pp. 218, 221, 222, cf. 228 for a card-playing parson.

98. Ibid., pp. 249f., 259, 293, cf. 300–2.

99. *CWJ (T)*, pp. 240f.; *JWL (B)*, p. 660 and n.

100. Whitehead, II, pp. 118–21: Moore, I, pp. 413–15; included by Curnock in *JWJ*, II, pp. 256f. For the new text Baker in *PWHS*, XLII, 1980, pp. 93–100.

101. For Wesley's view and an indecisive discussion of the legal position see Outler, *John Wesley* (n.91), p. 21 n.; *PWHS*, XX, 1935–6, pp. 64ff., 93f.; XXI, 1936–7, 31f.; cf. XI, 1938, pp. 82–93. cf. *Farther Appeal* in *Works*, VIII, pp. 112ff. Baker, *JW*, pp. 103f. notes cases proposed for prosecution under the Act of Uniformity which were thought not likely to succeed. Green, *YMW*, p. 303, seems to accept the validity of Wesley's claim as a Fellow to preach anywhere.

102. *JWL (B)*, I, pp. 616, 677, 692f., 660f.

103. *JWJ*, II, p. 335. Wesley wrongly quoted his definition as Article 20. For Latitudinarian views see Rack, 'Hoadly versus Law'.

104. *JWJ*, VIII, p. 93; *Works*, VIII, p. 311.

105. Moore, II, p. 11; *JWL (B)*, II, p. 73; Baker in *PWHS*, XXVII, 1949, pp. 7–15; cf. *JWL (B)*, II, p. 56 and n. For Richards and Westell, ibid., pp. 638 n., 627.

106. Dr Walsh's phrase.

107. *JWL (B)*, II, p. 46 n.

108. *PWHS*, VI, 1907, pp. 108f.

109. *JWL (B)*, I, p. 700.

110. *JWL (B)*, II, p. 56 and cf. 29, 39; *JWL (B)*, I, p. 661; *CWJ*, I, p. 259.

111. *JWJ*, II, pp. 194–7 with illustration; lost journal record quoted by Whitehead, II, p. 125; *JWJ*, II, p. 316 and n. Account of her death in *JWL (B)*, II, p. 82. For her 'conversion' see *JWJ*, II, p. 267; and see in general John Newton, *Susanna Wesley and the Puritan Tradition in Methodism*, Epworth Press 1968, ch. VI. For the controversy over her attitude to the new Methodism see Clarke, pp. 339–55.

112. *JWJ*, II, pp. 429–33, 442, 443, and *JWL (B)*, II, p. 55.

113. For all these Rules see *Works*, VIII, pp. 269–74, but for variations over the years see the Methodist Societies volume in BE, IX.

114. *JWJ*, II, p. 119 n., where Curnock points out that talk of 'thousands' in a church cannot be true. But for examples of Wesley calculating numbers see below, p. 346.

115. *JWJ*, II, pp. 433, 398, 371.

116. J. Walsh, 'Cambridge Methodists'.

117. *JWL (B)*, II, p. 86.

118. F. Baker, *William Grimshaw*, Epworth Press 1963, pp. 150f.; cf. D. Hempton, *Methodism and Politics in British Society*, Hutchinson 1985, pp. 14–16.

119. *JWJ*, II, pp. 482–6.

120. *JWJ*, II, p. 464 and n., and R.C. Swift, *Lively People: Methodism in Nottingham 1740–1979*, University of Nottingham Department of Adult Education, 1983; *CWJ*, I, pp. 309, 319; *JWL (B)*, I, p. 702 n.; II, p. 75 n. (April 1742): when Sympson had left the Moravians but was 'not quite at ease'.

121. *JWJ*, III, pp. 9–11; *JWL (B)*, II, pp. 76f., 79.

122. *JWJ*, III, pp. 11–14; *PWHS*, V, 1906, p. 148.

123. See the new fragment of Charles Wesley's *Journal* printed in *Methodist History*, XXV (1), 1987, p. 51, which allows more effect to the Hall visit.

124. *JWJ*, III, p. 15; Nelson, *EMP* I, pp. 59f.; CW to JW in *JWL (B)*, II, p. 86; *JWJ*, III, pp. 50, 53f., 55; 68–71 and a similar list in MCA Bennet *Letter Book*, p. 42 (for details see below, pp. 241f.).

125. J. Ellis, 'A Dynamic Society: Social Relations in Newcastle 1660–1760', in *The Transformation of English Provincial Towns*, ed. P. Clark, Hutchinson 1984, pp. 190–227, esp. pp. 208–12.

126. *JWJ*, III, pp. 18–20.

127. William Batty's MS *Church History* (= *CH*), p. 4 in MCA; 'An Account of Benjamin Ingham and His Work by William Batty written from Benjamin Ingham's Diary', JRUL MS Eng. 1062, p. 7. Both appear to be based on lost diaries by Ingham and others. The *Church History* is dated 1779; Eng. 1062 is a later copy of a more detailed narrative. Diary for 1733–4 ed. R. P. Heitzenrater as *Diary of an Oxford Methodist*, Duke University Press 1985; travel journal to Georgia in Tyerman, *OM*, pp. 63–80. In addition to Tyerman's account in *OM* see D.F. Clarke, *Benjamin Ingham and the Inghamites*, Leeds MPhil, 1971 and id., *PWHS* XXXVIII, 1972, pp. 170ff.

128. *JRUL* Eng. MS 1062, pp. 2, 3; Ingham MS *Diary* in MCA, p. 23; cf. letter of 27 February 1734 in Tyerman, *OM*, pp. 57f.

129. Eng. MS 1062, pp. 5, 9.

130. Ibid., p. 6.

131. Ibid., pp. 7, 8, 10.

132. Ibid., p. 13; John Bennet *Diary* in MCA, 1–7 May 1742.

133. Batty, *CH*, p. 6; Eng. 1062, p. 10.

134. For the story see Eng. 1062, p. 8; MS notes on life of Okely in JRUL Eng. 1062, pp. 44–6; and for a full account Walsh, 'Cambridge Methodists'.

135. E.E. Titterington, *Historical Sketch of Moravian Church in Dukinfield*, London 1910, pp. 8ff.; JRUL, MS Eng 1066 'Dukinfield'; Benham, p. 120. For the result of his work as contributing to the General Baptists of the New Connexion see below, p. 327.

136. *EMP* I, p. 38. This so-called *Journal* is in fact an autobiography based on lost journals with few dates.

137. James Clegg, *Diary* (in JRUL now edited by V.S. Doe for Derbyshire Records Society, three volumes, 1978ff.) 8 October 1741; 4 January 1742; J. England, *Short Sketches of . . . Moravian Church in Lancashire, etc.*, Leeds 1888, quoted by E.A. Rose, 'Methodism in Cheshire', *Lancashire and Cheshire Antiquarian Society* LXXVIII, 1975, p. 22. Taylor was born in Leicestershire but moved to Cheshire. Bennet stayed at 'Mr Taylors' in 1743: Bennet *Diary*, 3 July 1743. Bennet begins with an autobiographical account merging into the diary, though this volume was written up from the original diary extant in a slightly fuller version from the same point. Some pages missing from the autobiography can be supplied from a summary in Everett's *Methodism in Manchester*, Manchester 1827. The date given for his conversion by him is January 1741 but this is almost certainly an error (probably due to old style dating) for 1742.

138. *EMP* I, *Journal*, pp. 14, 18.

139. Ibid., p. 55.

140. Ibid., pp. 56, 59; *JWJ*, III, pp. 11, 17.

141. This account is based on Baker, *Grimshaw* (n.118), pp. 94f.

142. Baker, *Grimshaw* (n.118), ch. II; cf. an old-style Dissenter similarly in B. Hanbury (ed.), *Joseph Williams*, London, enlarged edition 1815, pp. 6, 24, 225f., for his meeting with Grimshaw.

143. *AM*, 1797, Supplement pp. 44–6, 46–8; *JWL (B)*, II, pp. 263f., 268f. for some of his journeys in 1747; Baker, *Grimshaw* (n.118), chs. VII and X, e.g. 109f., 148ff., for the Quarterly Meeting and see below, p. 246.

144. There is no biography of Bennet. The main sources are the diaries already mentioned (incomplete) and a letter-book. See also Rose, 'Methodism in Cheshire', and my 'Survival and Revival' (details on p. 562 above).

145. Bennet, *Diary*, 18, 20 October 1748; F. Baker, *PWHS*, XXXV, 1965, pp. 1–4.

146. Bennet, *Diary*, 1–2 April 1952; *JWJ*, IV, pp. 14f.

147. For this see *Diary*, 4 August 1752; Whitefield to Bennet, 11 February 1754 in MCA; references in Caleb Warhurst *Diary* in ManchCL and my forthcoming account.

148. JRUL MS Eng. 1062, p. 8; Benham, pp. 63f., 110.

149. MS Eng. 1066: bundle of Dukinfield notes; Titterington, *Historical Sketch* (n.19), p. 8.

150. JRUL MS Eng. 1062, pp. 16, 19f., 23.

151. Baker, *Grimshaw* (n.118), pp. 243–5.

152. See the early context in J. Everett, *History of Methodism in Manchester*, I, Manchester, 1827; the fullest account of beginnings is in C.D. Little, *PWHS* XXV, 1945–6, pp 116–22; XXVI, p. 478, pp. 17–22, 33–5, but this needs to be supplemented from Dissenting sources.

153. P.W.J. Higson, 'Some Leading Promoters of . . . Lancashire Chapelries', *Lancashire and Cheshire Antiquarian Society* LXXV–VI, 1966, pp. 123–63; J. Booker, *History of the Ancient Chapel of Birch*, Chetham Society, XLVII, 1859; id. *History of the Ancient Chapel of Denton*, Chetham Society XXXVII, 1856. B. Greeves, *Analysis of the Spread of Methodism in Yorkshire*, Leeds MA 1961, ch. IV, says that Leeds was penetrated from outlying townships.

154. For Bagshawe see R. Mansfield, *The Development of Independency in Derbyshire*, Manchester MA 1951. James Clegg's and Bennet's Chinley church was one of his foundations. For the Manchester case see Everett Scrapbook, pp. 412–14, in MCA.

155. *JWJ*, III, p. 443. For the history of this society see Everett, *Methodism in Manchester*, I (n. 152), p. 139–74.

156. *Wesleyan Methodist Magazine*, 1823, p. 204.

157. *CWJ*, I, pp. 321, 323, 329.

158. Ibid., p. 325.

159. *JWJ*, III, pp. 132, 181.

160. *CWJ*, I, p. 376.

161. For what follows see G.C.B. Davies, *Early Cornish Evangelicals*, SPCK 1953, pp. 32ff., 34ff., 61.

162. *CWJ*, I, p. 369.

163. Davies, *Cornish Evangelicals* (n. 161), chs. II, III; for Hervey, cf. *Herveiana*, London 1822, p. 43.

164. J.C.C. Probert, *Sociology of Cornish Methodism*, Cornish Methodist Historical Society 1971; J. Rule, 'Methodism and Popular Religion', in R.D. Storch

(ed.), *Popular Culture and Custom in Nineteenth-Century England*, Croom Helm 1982; D.H. Luker, 'Revivals and Popular Religion', *JEH* XXXVII, 1986, pp. 603–19.

165. For a brief sketch see G.T. Roberts, 'Methodism in Wales', in *HMCGB*, III, pp. 253ff.; Rupp, pp. 453ff. drawing on D.L. Morgan's history, which was translated too late for use here. See also Watts, pp. 376f., and refs. For the Calvinistic Methodists see: G.M. Roberts (ed.), *Selected Trevecka Letters*, Carnarvon 1956; M.H. Jones (ed.), *Trevecka Letters*, Carnarvon 1932; B. La Trobe, *Brief Account of the Life of Howel Harris*, 1791; Eifion Evans, *Howel Harris*, University of Wales Press 1974; G.F. Nuttall, *Howel Harris, the Last Enthusiast*, University of Wales Press 1965. For the English connexion see C. Welch (ed.), *Two Calvinistic Methodist Chapels*, London Record Society XI, 1975. For the background see G.H. Jenkins, *Literature, Religion and Society in Wales 1660–1730*, University of Press 1978.

166. Whitefield, *Journals*, pp. 228f.

167. *JWJ*, II, pp. 223f., 292ff, 341f., 395 n.

168. *CWJ*, I, pp. 225ff., 255ff.

169. Ibid., pp. 287, 294; *JWJ*, II, pp. 505–10.

170. C.V. Wedgwood, *The King's Peace*, Collins 1955, pp. 109f.; Watts, pp. 139f.

171. Jenkins, *Literature* (n.165).

172. *JWJ*, II, p. 296.

173. Jenkins, *Literature* (n.165), eg. pp. 305–9.

174. See M.G. Jones, *The Charity School Movement*, Cambridge University Press 1938, pp. 38–41; M. Clement, *The SPCK and Wales*, SPCK 1954; Watts, pp. 424–7; Jenkins, *Literature* (n.165).

175. Watts, pp. 397, 416f. For Trevecka see below, pp. 453f.

176. On this and what follows see especially Jones, *Trevecka Letters* (n. 165), pp. 216f., 238f., on the origins of society ideas in Wales.

177. Nuttall, *Howel Harris* (n.165), e.g. pp. 26f.

178. For the associations see Jones, *Trevecka Letters* (n.165), pp. 257–94; and for the Whitefield and English connexion later Welch, *Methodist Chapels* (n.165) and below, p. 283.

179. See MS *Minutes*, 1743, 1749.

180. Welch, *Methodist Chapels* (n.165), introduction.

181. *HMCGB*, III, pp. 255–7.

182. For what follows see A.L. Drummond and J. Bullock, *The Scottish Church 1688–1843*, St Andrews Press 1973, chs. I–III.

183. M.J. Crawford, *The Invention of the American Revival*, Boston University PhD, 1978, ch. I; R. Middlekauff, *The Mathers*, Oxford University Press 1971, pp. 274ff.

184. Drummond and Bullock, *Scottish Church* (n.182), pp. 50, 51; D. Stevenson, 'The Radical Party in the Kirk 1637–45', *JEH* XXV, 1974, pp. 135–66.

185. *JWL (B)*, I, pp. 688–70.

186. A. Fawcett, *The Cambuslang Revival*, Banner of Truth Trust 1971; the older D. Macfarlane, *The Revivals of the Eighteenth Century*, Edinburgh 1827, ch. IX has interesting accounts of conversions.

187. Macfarlane, *Revivals* (n.186), pp. 34–6.

188. Ibid., 58, 92 n.; Whitefield, *Letters*, I, 401, 407f., 437.

189. Macfarlane, *Revivals* (n. 186),p. 32; *Christian History* (American ed.), I, ii, pp. 11–14.

190. Whitefield, *Letters*, I, pp. 128, 139, 262, 267, 317, 402, 508; Dallimore, II, ch. V.

191. Whitefield, *Letters*, I, pp. 409f.; Macfarlane, *Revivals* (n.186), pp. 76f.

192. *JWL (B)*, I, p. 680; II, pp. 16, 48, 92.

193. Ibid. II, pp. 124, 128f.; *JWJ*, III, pp. 178–80.

194. For what follows see also A. Skevington Wood in *HMCGB*, III, pp. 265–71; W.F. Swift, *Methodism in Scotland*, Epworth Press 1947.

195. *CWJ*, II, pp. 91ff.; *EMP*, I, p. 206; *JWL*, IV, p. 295 (years later).

196. Wood in *HMCGB*, III, p. 266.

197. *JWJ*, V, p. 168; VI, p. 19; VII, p. 387; VIII, p. 67.

198. *EMP*, II, pp. 189–94, and for other examples *HMCGB*, III, pp. 268f.

199. J. Vickers, *Thomas Coke*, Epworth Press 1969, pp. 140f. and see below, p. 480.

200. *HMCGB*, III, p. 270; reply by Wesley to Erskine in *JWL*, V, p. 91.

201. *EMP*, IV, p. 55.

202. *JWJ*, V, p. 169; VI, p. 19.

203. *JWL*, VIII, pp. 135f.; Tyerman, III, pp. 581f.

204. *EMP*, IV, p. 56; *JWL*, VIII, p. 105; Tyerman, III, pp. 534, 549.

205. *HMCGB*, III, pp. 270f., quoting D. Wilson, *Methodism in Scotland*, Aberdeen 1850, p. 105.

206. Figures in J. Hall (rev. T.G. Hartley), *Circuits and Ministers*, London, nd, appendix. For Ireland see: C.H. Crookshank, *History of Methodism in Ireland*, three volumes, London 1885–6; *HMCGB*, III, pp. 232ff. for a brief sketch. There is a valuable analysis of secular and religious factors in Methodist growth in D. Hempton, 'Methodism in Irish Society 1770–1830', *TRHS*, Fifth Series, XXXVI, 1986, pp. 117–42.

207. C.S. Phillips, *History of the Church of Ireland*, Oxford University Press 1933, III, pp. 182, 199.

208. Ibid., pp. 233f.

209. For figures based on returns in the 1730s see ibid., p. 161 n.

210. Ibid., p. 224.

211. Whitefield, *Journals*, pp. 180–5; *LyH*, II, pp. 148f.

212. Hassé, *Moravians* (n.2), p. 88.

213. *JWJ*, III, p. 472; *CWJ*, I, p. 457.

214. *JWL (B)*, II, pp. 256n., 278n., 673f.; *LyH*, II, p. 149 n.

214. *JWJ*, III, p. 314.

216. *CWJ*, I, pp. 456ff.; II, pp. 1 –10; *JWJ*, III, p. 342.

217. 'Letter' in *Works*, X (reprinted in 1968); D. Hempton, *Methodism and Politics in British Society, 1750–1850*, Hutchinson 1984, p. 35.

218. *JWL (B)*, II, p. 310; *JWJ*, III, p. 395.

219. *JWJ*, III, pp. 281–318 passim and 281 n.

220. *LyH*, II, p. 152; Whitefield, *Letters*, II, p. 451; *JWJ*, IV, pp. 67, 95. For possible motives behind Whitefield's distaste for organization at this stage see C.E. Watson, 'Whitefield and Congregationalism', *Transactions of the Congregational Historical Society*, VIII, 1923, pp. 171ff., 237ff. esp. 238; Rack, 'Religious Societies', pp. 591ff.

221. *LyH*, II, p. 189 n.; D.A. Akenson, *The Church of Ireland 1800–85*, Yale University Press 1971, p. 37.

222. *LyH*, II, pp. 189ff.; Tyerman, III, pp. 241f.

223. *JWJ*, VI, pp. 262f. and below, pp. 468ff., for the Bath case; *PWHS* IX, 1914, pp. 135ff.; Tyerman, III, p. 313.

224. *JWJ*, VII, pp. 285ff., 294; *JWL*, VIII, pp. 63, 146f.

225. Tyerman, III, p. 313.

226. *JWL*, VIII, pp. 146f.; *LyH*, II, p. 213; for his Manchester career see the Everett Scrapbook in MCA, pp. 435, 517; C. Hulbert, *Memoirs*, privately printed 1852, p. 152.

227. See Hempton, 'Methodism in Irish Society' (n. 206), for what follows.

228. Ibid., p. 125 n.

229. *EMP*, III, p. 82. Irish was his native tongue, ibid., p. 14.

230. Hempton, 'Methodism' (n.206), pp. 134f.

231. See N.W. Taggart, *The Irish in World Methodism 1760–1900*, Epworth Press 1986; Hempton, *Methodism and Politics* (n.217), passim.

232. Tyerman, II, p. 130; *JWL*, IV, p. 104.

233. *JWJ*, III, pp. 153, 96, 97.

234. R. Currie, A. Gilbert and L. Horsley (eds), *Churches and Churchgoers*, Clarendon Press 1977, p. 139.

235. The best description of a sometimes complex development is by Frank Baker in *HMCGB*, I, ch. VII, 3; see also his *JW*, passim.

236. *Plain Account of . . . Methodists*, especially para. 2, in *Works*, VIII; Sermon on 'God's Vineyard' in *Works*, VII, pp. 206f.; cf. MS. *Minutes*, 1746.

237. On this see below, pp. 250, 293.

238. On this see H.D. Rack, in *PWHS* XXXIX, 1973, pp. 12–20, and W.W. Dean, *PWHS* XLIII, 1981, pp. 41–8.

239. Rack, 'Religious Societies', pp. 589, 594.

240. *Rules of the United Societies* in *Works*, VIII, pp. 269–71; and for the discipline implied see below, p. 442.

241. C. Perronet in *AM*, 1781, pp. 604f.

242. In *Works*, VIII, pp. 272f.

243. Baker in *HMCGB*, I, p. 228.

244. *Works*, VIII, pp. 223f.; MS *Minutes*, 1744; *HMCGB*, I, p. 224 and nn. 38, 39.

245. MS *Minutes*, 1744.

246. *JWL (B)*, II, p. 44. This was earlier than the first reference by Wesley in his diary for 20 May 1741.

247. *Plain Account of . . . Methodists*, *Works*, VIII; *JWL*, II, pp. 292–311; *Thoughts upon Methodism, 1786*, in *Works*, XIII, para. 7. In the *Plain Account* Wesley confuses the chronology by describing the classes, bands and select bands as developing in that order.

248. For the story see *JWJ*, II, pp. 528, 535; III, p. 97; *Works*, VIII, pp. 252f.; XIII, p. 259; *PWHS*, III, 1899–1900, pp. 64f.; XIX, 1915–16, pp. 64f.; *HMCGB*, I, pp. 222–4.

249. I have examined the Manchester Society Account Book (transcript in my possession) from 1752 which shows, as might be expected, fluctuations and no clear relationship between the numbers of members and the notional sums expected of them.

250. *EMP*, VI, p. 258 and see below, p. 365 for early 'communism'.

251. For this and what follows see Rack and Dean on class meeting (n.238 above).

252. *JWL (B)*, II, pp. 94f.

253. *JWJ*, IV, p. 350; V. p. 84.

254. *JWJ*, II, pp. 70f.; for a slightly different list John Bennet, *Letter Book* in MCA, p. 42, possibly dated 1749–50, but maybe a defective copy of Wesley's (or vice versa!).

255. *Works*, VIII, p. 275; cf. MS *Minutes* 1744 for further details.

256. *Agenda* in MS *Minutes* 1744.

257. Ibid.

258. For a version of this see *Works*, VIII, pp. 299–338. For the various editions of this see *Minutes* I, London 1862, pp. 444–675.

259. For later problems over trusts see below, p. 498.

260. This was, however, clarified at the 1745 Conference when 'helper' appears for the travelling lay preachers and 'assistant' for fifteen of those most trusted; these soon became the superintending preachers of the 'circuits', see below, 244.

261. For this and what follows, see *HMCGB*, I, pp. 230f.

262. *JWL*, VII, p. 9.

263. Baker in *PWHS* XXVII, 1949, pp. 75f.; cf. his *JW*, pp. 203f.; Rupp, pp. 396f.

264. *JWL*, IV, p. 257.

265. J.S. Simon, *John Wesley. The Last Phase*, Epworth Press 1934, pp. 181f.

266. D.M. Valenze, *Prophetic Sons and Daughters*, Princeton University Press 1985; for the early phase cf. Church, *MA*, ch. IV.

267. *HMCGB*, I, pp. 236–8.

268. See his advice and directions in *Works*, VIII, pp. 290ff., 304ff., including *Rules of a Helper*. For advice on preaching and cultural achievements see below, 344 and 351., 446f.

269. Examples from Manchester Circuit account book (in my possession in transcript).

270. *HMCGB*, I, pp. 233–6.

271. *EMP*, IV, p. 27.

272. *JWL*, III, p. 195, e.g.

273. For what follows see Baker in *HMCGB*, I, p. 239; also in *London Quarterly Review*, January 1949, pp. 28–37; *PWHS* XXV, 1965, pp. 1–4; Bennet, *Letter Book*, in MCA, pp. 33f.

274. MS *Minutes*, 1748, 1749.

275. Bennet, *Letter Book*, pp. 29, 31 in MCA.

276. Bennet, *Diary*, 18 and 20 October 1748.

277. MS *Minutes*, 1749; Baker in *PWHS* XXXV, 1965, pp. 11ff.

278. B. Perkins, *Methodist Preaching Houses and the Law*, Epworth Press 1952; *HMCGB*, I, pp. 229f.

279. *JWL (B)*, II, p. 592.

280. Charles Wesley said that he ruled with a rod of iron (Baker, *JW*, p. 160); for the courageous preacher see Rodda MS on Conference of 1790 in MCA.

281. *EMP*, IV, p. 26; *JWL*, V, p. 196; Atmore MS quoted in *JWJ*, VII, p. 5 n.

282. See below, pp. 502ff.

283. *JWL*, VIII, p. 196. For his political views see below, ch. X.4.

284. *Minutes*, I, pp. 60–2; *Works*, VIII, pp. 298–301; Tyerman, II, pp. 577ff.

285. Above, p. 6; on the relationship to Methodism see J.C.D. Clark, *English Society 1688–1832*, Cambridge University Press 1985, p. 67, and the reference to A.D. Gilbert, *Religion and Society in Industrial England* 1740–1914, Longmans 1976, p. 114.

286. For association in Dissent see G.F. Nuttall, 'Association and Assembly', in *SCH*, VII, pp. 289–310. For an example see A. Gordon (ed.), *The Cheshire Classis Minutes 1698–1745*, London 1919; Brown, pp. 85ff., 91f., 111ff.

287. H.R. Niebuhr, *The Social Sources of Denominationalism*, Shoe String Press, reprinted 1954, p. 53.

288. F. Dreyer, 'A "Religious Society under Heaven": John Wesley and the Identity of Methodism', *Journal of British Studies* XXV, 1986, pp. 62–83; for the idea of the 'denomination', see Niebuhr, *Denominationalism* (n.287), pp. 69–74. However, Methodism fits uneasily into this typology; see D. Martin, 'The Denomination', *British Journal of Sociology* XII, 1962, pp. 1–14; M. Hill, 'Methodism as a Religious Order', *Sociological Yearbook of Religion* IV, SCM Press, 1973, pp. 91–9. Dreyer sees it as an eighteenth-century 'club', but if so, it fell foul of dubious social and political associations, as Samuel Wesley Jr pointed out in the Oxford period (above, p. 84).

289. Cf. J. Kent, *The Age of Disunity*, Epworth Press 1966, ch. 1.

VI. Brothers in Love

1. *CWJ* includes a selection of letters, often undated. The early *Journal* for 1735–39 was re-edited by John Telford (1909) with some shorthand passages restored.

2. Baker, *CW*; *CWJ*. The attempt to give Charles a larger place in Methodist history by F.C. Gill, *Charles Wesley, The First Methodist*, Epworth Press 1964, is rather uncritical, and does not supersede Jackson, *CW*, for detailed documentation.

3. Moore, I, p. 152 and n.; cf. II, pp. 368f.

4. Gambold in *AM*, 1798, pp. 117ff., 168ff.; extracts in *JWJ*, VIII, pp. 265ff., and Heizenrater, *EMW*, II, p. 37.

5. Baker, *CW*, p. 12.

6. For Samuel Wesley Jr see *PWHS* XI, 1918, pp. 25ff. and passim.

7. Baker, *CW*, pp. 54f.

8. Ibid., p. 58. These verses were later altered for the *Hymns and Sacred Poems* (1749) to remove the personal reference.

9. For a more sympathetic account of Mrs Whitefield's problems see Dallimore, II, pp. 101ff. For Berridge see *LyH*, I, p. 389, and *Works*, 1838, pp. 508f.

10. Baker, *CW*, pp. 60f.; *CWJ*, II, p. 52.

11. *CWJ*, II, p. 44, and 44–56 for negotiations.

12. *JWL (B)*, II, pp. 346f. Mrs Gwynne was probably persuaded partly by a letter from Vincent Perronet, the 'Methodist' Vicar of Shoreham, who vouched for the book profits: Gill, *CW*, p. 139.

13. *CWJ*, II, pp. 56f.

14. Baker, *CW*, pp. 109–14; cf. *CWJ*, II, pp. 140–56 for accounts of Charles's sons.

15. Baker, *CW*, pp. 114–16.

16. *LyH*, I, p. 389.

17. Tyerman, II, pp. 271f.; cf. Jackson, *CW*, II, pp. 135–7.

18. *JWL (B)*, II, p. 472. For what follows see also Baker, *CW*, chs. III and VIII and below, pp. 296–305.

19. *JWL (B)*, II, pp. 527, 528.

20. *JWL*, V, p. 16.

21. See below, p. 468, for the complaint.

22. Baker, *CW*, pp. 20f., 25.

23. D. Davie, *A Gathered Church*, Cambridge University Press 1976, p. 53; see also his *Purity of Diction in English Verse*, Chatto and Windus 1952, ch. V for Charles's 'classicism'. For a less complimentary view R.D. Stock, *The Holy and Demonic*, Princeton University Press 1982. For other aspects of the hymns H. Bett, *Hymns of Methodism*, Epworth Press [3]1945; B.L. Manning, *Hymns of Wesley and Watts*, Epworth Press 1942.

24. B.L. Manning, *The Hymns of Wesley and Watts*, Epworth Press 1942, p. 83.

25. The account (in the British Library) seems certainly to be by Wesley though not in his own hand except for some amendments and verses at the end. It was edited with a full commentary by J.A. Léger as *Wesley's Last Love*, London 1910. See also the letter to Charles on 25 September 1749, giving a retrospect of his views on marriage, with other letters to Thomas Bigg (?) and Bennet: *JWL (B)*, II, pp. 380ff., 377ff., 388f., 391f. E. Harrison, *Son to Susanna*, Nicholson and Watson 1937, chs. XXIII–XXXI, has a highly-coloured account. For the complex legal questions about betrothal and 'bigamy', see F. Baker, 'John Wesley's First Marriage', *London Quarterly*, October 1967, pp. 305–15; criticized by F.E. Maser, 'John Wesley's Only Marriage', *Methodist History* XVI, 1977. For Bennet's version, see *Diary* in MCA, 3 October 1749. Also W. Bennet, *Memoirs of Grace Bennet*, Macclesfield 1803; article in *Methodist Recorder (MR)*, Christmas 1902, by Curnock.

26. See Léger, *Last Love* (n. 25), pp. 15–60, for her early life and religious experience.

27. *CWJ*, I, p. 224; Léger, *Last Love* (n. 25), p. 10 and n. 1; Bennet, *Memoirs* (n. 25), p. 18; *MR*, pp. 24, 25.

28. Léger, *Last Love* (n. 25), p. 40.

29. Ibid., pp. 1, 5; Baker in *JWL (B)*, II, p. 378 n.

30. *MR*, p. 25; Léger, *Last Love* (n. 25), p. 3.

31. *JWL (B)*, II, pp. 353f., 657.

32. *MR*, p. 25; Léger, *Last Love* (n. 25), p. 5; *JWL (B)*, II, p. 377 n.

33. Léger, *Last Love* (n. 25), pp. 5f.; *MR*, pp. 25f.

34. Léger, *Last Love* (n. 25), pp. 7–9; *JWL (B)*, II, pp. 377–9.

35. Léger, *Last Love* (n. 25), pp. 62f.

36. Ibid., pp. 81–8.

37. *JWL (B)*, II, pp. 389f., 391–3; Baker, *CW*, p. 74.

38. *JWL (B)*, II, pp. 380, 388f.

39. Baker in *London Quarterly* (n. 25).

40. For Sarah Wesley's interpretation and Curnock's initial acceptance of it as showing that the BL MS was corruptly interpolated by Noah Vazeille see *MR*, pp. 28f., 26.

41. Bennet, *Diary*, 3 May 1742, 6 and 12 September 1742 for earlier hopes and dreams.

42. Egmont, *Diary*, gives some startling examples of this.

43. Baker, *CW*, p. 72.
44. Moore, II, p. 171.
45. *JWJ*, III, p. 512; cf. 513 n. for what follows; Baker, *CW* pp. 74f.
46. *JWJ*, III, notes on pp. 513–16.
47. *JWJ*, III, p. 515 n. Charles could not face being present on this occasion, though he was formally reconciled to John and his wife a fortnight later. In 1790 John Wesley wrote that he married because he needed a home to recover his health, but that he 'did not seek happiness and did not find it': *JWL*, VIII, p. 223. However, this does not accord with his early letters to his wife.
48. *JWL (B)*, II, pp. 451, 453–8, 454 n.
49. *JWL*, VI, p. 102, and letter quoted in Baker, *CW*, p. 76; *JWL*, V, p. 74; Baker, *CW* pp. 76f.
50. *JWL (B)*, II, p. 461 n. from MS journal.
51. Bennet, *Diary*, 1 April 1752.
52. *JWJ*, III, p. 517.
53. *JWL*, IV, pp. 41, 61, 75–8, 89, 101, 152; VI, pp. 87, 90, 98–102, 273; *JWJ*, V, p. 400 and n.; *JWL*, VI, p. 321.
54. Telford, *John Wesley*, p. 260.
55. Hampson, II, p. 127; Tyerman, II, p. 110.
56. Sutcliff, *History of Methodism* (MS), I, p. 402, quoted in *JWL*, IV, p. 74; cf. also Harrison, *Son to Susanna* (n.25), ch. XXXII for a fair estimate of all parties.
57. Tyerman, II, p. 110.
58. Watson, *Works*, 1848, V, pp. 203f., quoted in Rupp, p. 404.
59. Green, *JW*, p. 141, notes this possibility.
60. For Wheatley see *JWJ*, III, pp. 531–3; Tyerman, II, pp. 121–6; J. Brown, *History of Congregationalism in Norfolk and Suffolk*, London 1877, pp. 189–97; for Hall *JWJ*, VIII, pp. 147f.; *JWL (B)*, II, 269–73; Lavington's charge about misconduct to a maid in *JWL*, III, pp. 88f.
61. *JWL (B)*, II, 385.
62. *JWL (B)*, II, pp. 108f.
63. *AM*, 1779, pp. 296ff. and passim; Tyerman, II, pp. 285ff.; *JWL*, IV, pp. 4, 22.
64. See J. Banks, *Nancy, Nancy*, Leeds 1984, pp. 49–51, for Ann Bolton. For Wesley's self-examination finding only 'calm, rational affection' for her: *JWL*, VI, p.73.
65. For example see *JWL*, .VI, pp. 110, 111, 132, 133 to Elizabeth Ritchie who 'managed' his deathbed; Miss Bishop, Miss March, Elizabeth Briggs.
66. A. Knox, *Remarks* in R. Southey, *Life of John Wesley* (ed. M.H. Fitzgerald), Oxford University Press 1925, II, p. 339; similarly Rupp, pp. 396–8, who compares these relationships with those of Catholic saints and holy women.
67. I believe that the idea of 'polygamy' came in a review of Stanley Ayling's *Wesley*. An answer was attempted by M. Edwards, *Dear Sister*, Manchester 1975. For Wesley's late thoughts on marriage see *Thoughts on Marriage* in *Works*, XI, pp. 463f.

VII. Mobs and Controversies

1. For Grimshaw and the Colne and Roughlea affair led by the vicar George White see *JWJ*, III, pp. 369ff.; IV, p. 31; *JWL (B)*, II, pp. 324ff.; F. Baker, *William Grimshaw*, Epworth Press 1963, pp. 130–41, 205f.

2. For attacks on Evangelicals see e.g. Bishop Randolph, quoted in E.N. Williams (ed.), *The Eighteenth Century Constitution*, Cambridge University Press 1965, p. 382; for one of the best defences of their orthodoxy see John Overton, *True Churchman Defended* (1800), which carefully distances them from the more irregular brethren (Hill and Haweis no doubt in mind).

3. J. Walsh, 'Methodism and the Mob', in *SCH*, VIII, 1977, pp. 213–27.

4. See G. Holmes, *Trial of Dr Sacheverell*; R.B. Rose, 'The Priestley Riots', *Past and Present*, XVIII, 1960, pp. 68–88; G. Rudé, 'The Gordon Riots', *TRHS*, Fifth Series, VI, 1956.

5. For modern analyses see G. Rudé, in *Paris and London in the Eighteenth Century*, Fontana Books 1969, passim; E.P. Thompson, 'The Moral Economy of the English Crowd', *Past and Present* L, 1971, pp. 76–136. For a late example of a 'Church and King' mob see F. Knight, *The Strange Case of Thomas Walker*, Lawrence and Wishart 1957, ch. IX.

6. Heitzenrater, *EMW*, I, pp. 125–33; II, pp. 71–81, for this attitude and cf. John's and Charles's accounts, *JWJ*, III, pp. 98–104, 117–19; *CWJ*, I, pp. 347ff.

7. For example: *CWJ*, I, p. 340; *JWJ*, II, 190.

8. MS *Minutes* 1744.

9. Everett Scrap Book, MCA, p. 440.

10. Tyerman, *George Whitefield*, II, pp. 365–9.

11. Baker, *Grimshaw* (n.1), p. 135.

12. Baker, *JW*, pp. 316f. This happened to John Bennet when he turned Independent and sought a licence: *Diary* under 1754.

13. Bennet, *Diary*, 20 February 1748.

14. C.B. Andrews (ed.), *The Torrington Diaries*, Eyre and Spottiswoode 1934, I, p. 142.

15. Quoted in Walsh, 'Mob' (n.3), p. 222; cf. also Bennet, *Diary*, 2 March 1747; and 'Huzza boys! Well done! Stand up for the Church' by the Wednesbury mob in 1744: *CWJ*, I, p. 346.

16. Bennet, *Diary*, 2 June and 3–4 August 1748.

17. *EMP*, IV, pp. 9f., but cf. VI, p. 152, for an easier converting of the family.

18. *JWL (B)*, I, pp. 596f.

19. N. Cohn, *Europe's Inner Demons*, Paladin Books 1976, pp. 1–4, 19, 38.

20. Walsh, 'Mob' (n.3), p. 225 and my 'Doctors'.

21. *CWJ*, I, pp. 327, 356, 358–62.

22. Walsh, 'Mob' (n.3), p. 227.

23. B. Nightingale, *Lancashire Congregational Union*, Manchester 1906, ch. III; H.B. Kendall, *The Origin and History of the Primitive Methodist Church*, London nd, I, pp. 229, 238–40; J. Werner, *The Primitive Methodist Connexion*, Wisconsin University of Press 1984, pp. 98–100.

24. For the satirical attacks see A.M. Lyles, *Methodism Mocked*, Epworth Press 1960.

25. See U. Lee, *Historical Backgrounds of Early Methodist Enthusiasm*, New York 1931. R. Knox, *Enthusiasm*, Oxford University Press 1951, is a well known history from a partisan standpoint: surprisingly, the chapter on Wesley is one of the best.

26. *PWHS*, XLII, 1982, p. 97.

27. J. Locke, *Essay Concerning Human Understanding*, IV, xix, 'Of Enthusiasm'.

28. Johnson, *Dictionary*, s.v. 'Enthusiasm'.

29. *JWL*, II, p. 204; *JWJ*, II, p. 130; *Works* VIII, p. 106.

30. *Farther Appeal, Works*, VIII, pp. 76–134; *JWL (B)*, II, p. 230; *JWL*, IV, pp. 33f; II, pp. 204ff.

31. *JWL*, IV, p. 108; *AM*, 1782, p. 490; 1787, p. 26; *JWL*, IV, p. 321; *JWJ*, V, p. 387; IV, pp. 414, 463. Horse episode in *JWJ*, III, p. 236.

32. A. Knox, 'Remarks', in Southey *John Wesley* (ed. Fitzgerald), Oxford University Press 1925, II, p. 339, and see below, pp. 539f.

33. *JWL (B)*, II, 263.

34. *JWJ*, II, p. 319 and see below, pp. 385–7.

35. J. Lavington, *Enthusiasm of Methodists and Papists Compared*, three volumes, 1749–51 (and ed. Polwhele 1820); *PWHS* XXXIII, 1962, pp. 109ff.; XXXIV, 1962, pp. 17–41; XLII, 1980, pp. 101–11, 134–8 for the circumstances; Wesley's reply in *JWL*, III, pp. 259ff., 295ff.

36. For the history of this piece and background, R. Paulson, *Hogarth* II, Yale University Press 1971, p.298, 301, 354–8.

37. *EMP*, II, p. 134.

38. For the 'Smith' correspondence see Moore, II, pp. 475–576, and reprinted in *JWL (B)*, II, passim and p. 138 n. for a convincing case against Secker's authorship. For Downes, *JWL*, IV, pp. 325ff.; Church, *JWL*, II, pp. 175ff., 212ff.; Gibson, *JWL*, II, pp. 277ff.; Warburton *JWL*, IV, pp. 338ff. Gibson's observations are mainly in *Observations* (1744) and *Charge* (1747).

39. Whitefield, *Journals*, pp. 404, 407, cf. 438, 462; *Letters*, I, pp. 505f.; Dallimore, I, pp. 482f.; II, p. 47 for retraction. Whitefield said that the offending phrase was first used by Wesley in a private meeting: *Letters*, I, p. 505. For Wesley's preface to the *Whole Duty* in *Works*, XIV, p. 231; contrast Henry Venn in *Complete Duty of Man*, 1763, Preface.

40. Gibson, *Pastoral Letter* (1739) and *Observations* (1747); see N. Sykes, *Church and State in England in the Eighteenth Century*, Cambridge University Press 1934, pp. 307ff., 313ff.

41. For the legality question see above, pp. 208ff.

42. See Wesley's reply to his old college friend Hervey in *JWL (B)*, I, pp. 677, 692f.

43. See below, p. 293.

44. *JWL (B)*, I, 596f.

45. Walsh, 'Halévy', pp. 18f. and see below, pp. 362ff.

46. *LyH*, I, p. 27.

47. For this, see below, p. 365.

48. See below, p. 372.

49. M. Spufford, *Contrasting Communities*, Cambridge University Press 1974, pp. 285, 295f.

50. *Torrington Diaries* (n.14), I, p. 141; II, p. 130; Birbeck Hill and L.F. Powell (eds.), *Boswell's Life of Johnson*, Clarendon Press 1934ff., III, p. 230; II, pp. 79; III, p. 409; I, p. 463.

51. See below, p. 530.

VIII. The Rivals: Methodists and Evangelicals, Churchmen and Dissenters (1738–60)

1. Examples of Calvinistic agonizings in *EMP*, VI, pp. 22, 25f.; II, p. 185 (a split); see below, pp. 333f., for losses of preachers over this.

2. 'Penelope's web' *JWL (B)*, II, p. 327; Whitefield, *Letters*, II, p. 451; III, p. 143, on Edwards. But already in 1742 Whitefield wished 'no people to be called after my name', *JWL (B)*, II, p. 97.

3. For these see E. Welch (ed.), *Two Calvinistic Methodist Chapels*, London Record Society XI, 1975.

4. Ibid., pp. 19, 21f.

5. Ibid. pp. 1, 14.

6. Ibid., p. 14.

7. For the Rodborough Connexion see C.E. Watson in *Transactions of the Congregational Historical Society* X, 1927–9, pp. 277–86 and Tudur Jones, *Congregationalism in England*, Independent Press 1962, pp. 149f.

8. *LyH*, I, pp. 175f.

9. *LyH* contains indispensable material but is notoriously inaccurate and ludicrously (though sometimes usefully) snobbish over pedigrees. M. Francis, *Lady Huntingdon and her Connexion*, Oxford BLitt 1957, adds little.

10. *LyH*, I, pp. 36f. On her support for perfection *JWL (B)*, II, 67 and n.

11. For history of chapels see Francis, *Lady Huntingdon* (n.9). On paying for pews see *JWL (B)*, II, p. 14: the development of Methodist pew rents has not been studied. Occasional cases of pews in consideration of building subscriptions occur early: e.g. Manchester Circuit accounts in 1750s (transcript in my possession).

12. For Trevecka see *LyH*, II, ch. XXXI; G.F. Nuttall, 'Students of Trevecka College 1768–91', *Transactions of the Honourable Society of Cymmrodorion*, 1967, pp. 249–77, and below, pp. 453f.

13. *LyH*, II, p. 162.

14. *LyH*, II, pp. 423, 466f. and n.

15. *LyH*, II, pp. 304–13, 436–50; C. Welch, 'Lady Huntingdon and Spa Fields Chapel', *Guildhall Miscellany* IV, 1972, pp. 175–83.

16. *LyH*, II, pp. 483ff.

17. W.G. Robinson, *William Roby and Lancashire Independency*, Manchester PhD 1951; id., *William Roby*, Independent Press 1954.

18. For the doctrinal articles *LyH*, II, pp. 441–3.

19. For an influential exposition of this view C. Smyth, *Simeon and Church Order*, Cambridge University Press, 1940.

20. E. Halévy, *History of the English People*, I, ET Penguin Books 1938, p. 56.

21. H. Venn (ed.), *Life and Letters of Henry Venn*, London [6]1839, pp. xf.

22. See in general Walsh, 'Origins'; F. Baker, *William Grimshaw*, Epworth Press 1963, pp. 44f.; T. Scott, *The Force of Truth*, [3]1795.

23. *HMCGB*, I, pp. 289f.

24. G.R. Balleine, *History of the Evangelical Party*, new edition Church Army Press 1953; G.C.B. Davies, *Early Cornish Evangelicals*, SPCK 1951; L. Elliott-Binns, *The Early Evangelicals*, Lutterworth Press, 1953.

25. H.D. Rack, 'The Providential Moment: Evangelicals and Methodists in Manchester in the later Eighteenth Century', in *Transactions of the Historic Society of Lancashire and Cheshire* LXX, 1992 (forthcoming).

26. Balleine, *Evangelical Party* (n.24), p. 41.

27. Walker and Wesley in Davies, *Cornish Evangelicals* (n.24), chs. V and

VI; also *JWL (B)*, II, pp. 582–613; *JWL*, III, pp. 192, 221 and 584 for the point about conformity.

28. Cf. e.g. C. Bayley, 'Questions for Children upon the Ministerial Office', Manchester 1796. (Bayley was an ex-Methodist.)

29. C.G. Brown, 'Itinerancy and Loyalty', *JRH* VI, 1971, pp. 232–45; for the Jay case see G.B. Redford and J.A. James (eds.), *Autobiography of William Jay*, London 1854, pp. 41–3.

30. See above n.27 and Davies, *Cornish Evangelicals* (n.24); for Adam, *JWL (B)*, II, pp. 603ff., 609ff.

31. For another example: John Baddiley of Hayfield in Derbyshire: *AM*, 1779, p. 375.

32. Walsh, 'Religious Societies', pp. 295–302.

33. Walker and Grimshaw survived censure; for an example of an expelled curate, see Bennet, *Diary*, 10 January 1750.

34. *Life of Venn*, pp. 162ff.; see Davies, *Cornish Evangelicals* (n.24), pp. 212f. for a view on the Huntingdon secession.

35. Wesley to Walker, *JWL*, III, pp. 221ff. See below, p. 300.

36. For example, B.F.L. Clarke, *The Building of the Eighteenth-Century Church*, SPCK 1963, ch. XIV. The first free seats for the poor in Manchester (or rather Salford) were by an Evangelical at St Stephen's in 1794 (CRO, EDA/2/p. 214).

37. J.S. Reynolds, *Evangelicals in Oxford 1738–1877*, new edition Marcham Manor Press 1975; Smyth, *Simeon* (n.19); Davies, *Cornish Evangelicals* (n.24), pp. 74–87; Balleine, *Evangelical Party* (n.24), p. 64.

38. Venn, *Complete Duty*, Preface; cf. W. Wilberforce, *Practical View*, London 1797, ch. IV, sec. vi.

39. Smyth, *Simeon* (n.19), p. 198.

40. E.g.W. Romaine, *The Walk of Faith*, 1771, ch. VII; cf. Welch, *Methodist Chapels* (n.3), p. 21 (Minutes of Association 1745).

41. Venn, *Life* (n.21), pp. 29–32, 497; Smyth, *Simeon* (n.19), p. 185; Walsh in *HMCGB*, I, p. 290.

42. Venn, *Complete Duty* (n.38), Preface, p. xxxi.

43. Venn, *Life* (n.21), pp. 39ff. (old members met by Henry Venn Jr).

44. B. Gregory, *Sidelights on the Conflicts of Methodism*, 1899, p. 161.

45. *JWL*, VIII, p. 58; VII, p. 163.

46. *Works*, VIII, p. 299 ('Not to form any new sect; but to reform the nation, particularly the church and to spread scriptural holiness over the land').

47. The best study of Wesley's relationship with the church is Baker, *JW*, to which I am indebted.

48. *JWJ*, III, p. 22; *JWL*, III, p. 181, cf. *JWL*, IV, p. 150. Baker, *JW*, pp. 145f., argues for the early 1740s as the likely period for Wesley reading Stillingfleet.

49. *JWJ*, V, p. 322; 257, 348; VI, p. 490; *AM*, 1785, 35f., 112, 285f.

50. CWJ, I, pp. 147, 149.

51. Gibson, *Charge* (1739) and *Observations* (1744), cf. N. Sykes, *Edmund Gibson*, Oxford University Press 1926, pp. 312ff. Sykes perhaps exaggerates Gibson's early sympathy with Methodism. This amounted to refusal to interfere rather than anything more positive, though it is fair to say that he was almost as much concerned as Wesley to move the teaching of the clergy beyond mere morality. For 'Smith's' criticisms see *JWL (B)*, II, pp. 189f.

52. For what follows see MS *Minutes* (1744–7).

53. The clergy who do not preach the gospel are really the worst Dissenters from the church: *JWJ*, II, p. 335.

54. *JWL (B)*, II, pp. 205f. 'Smith' was not convinced.

55. *JWL (B)*, II, pp. 173–5; *JWJ*, III, pp. 229–31; Baker, *JW*, pp. 146f.

56. Cf. Sykes, *Old Priest and New Presbyter*, Cambridge University Press 1956; id., *The Church of England and Non-Episcopal Churches, Theology* Occasional Paper SPCK, 1949.

57. *JWJ*, III, p. 232.

58. Baker, *JW*, pp. 141–9. For 'comprehension' schemes see N. Sykes, *From Sheldon to Secker*, Cambridge University Press 1959, ch. III; *JWL*, III, p. 181.

59. *JWL (B)*, II, p. 572; *JWL*, IV, p. 150; VII, p. 21.

60. *JWL (B)*, II, pp. 470–6, 479–90; Charles Wesley MS, quoted by Baker, *JW*, p. 160 ('The Preachers 1751', in MCA); Baker, *CW*, p.85; MS Conference *Minutes*, 29 January 1752; Baker, *CW*, p.91. Further pacts in 1754 and 1756.

61. Tyerman, II, pp. 202f. and n.; Baker, *CW*, pp. 92f. 'Melchizedechian' is a reference to the mysterious priest-king in Gen. 14.14; Heb. 7.1–4, who had no recorded ecclesiastical pedigree.

62. F. Baker, *William Grimshaw*, Epworth Press 1963, pp. 249f.

63. Reprinted in Baker, *JW*, pp. 326–40; abbreviated version as *Reasons against Separation* in *Works*, XIII, pp. 225–32.

64. *JWL*, III, pp. 144–7.

65. *JWJ*, IV, p. 115.

66. Baker, *JW*, pp. 168f.; *JWL*, III, pp. 132, 133; *JWL (B)*, II, p. 574.

67. *JWL (B)*, II, pp. 582–6, 592–6, 603f.; *AM*, 1779, pp. 371–3; *JWL (B)*, II, pp. 606f.

68. *JWL (B)*, II, pp. 609–11.

69. Tyerman, II, pp. 244f.; Baker, *CW*, pp. 95f.

70. E. Sidney, *Samuel Walker*, London [2]1838, p. 207–12, 216–20; Tyerman, II, pp. 245–8; copy of Charles Wesley letter in *PWHS* XV, 1925, pp. 70f.; Baker, *JW*, p. 171.

71. *JWJ*, IV, p. 186; Baker, *CW*, p. 96.

73. *JWL*, III, pp. 192–6.

73. *CWJ*, II, p. 114; Baker, *CW*, pp. 96f. For Charles Wesley cf. *EMP*, II, p. 24. *CWJ*, MS *Journal* in MCA at 26.10.1756 (omitted in Jackson ed.) where Hampson and others refer to the church as 'Old Peg'.

74. *JWJ*, IV, pp. 232, cf. p. 223.

75. *JWL*, III, pp. 221–6; IV, pp. 215–18.

76. *CWJ*, II, pp. 96f.

77. For what follows see especially Baker, *CW*, pp. 97–103; id., *JW*, pp. 175–8.

78. J. Browne, *History of Congregationalism in Norfolk and Suffolk*, London 1877, pp. 189ff.; Tyerman, III, pp. 121–6; 189f., 325f, 381–8; Baker, *CW*, pp. 81, 83; *JWJ*, IV, pp. 302f. and n., 352; V, p. 36; Baker, *JW*, p. 129; Tyerman, II, pp. 527f.

79. Substance of two letters to John in March 1760 in Tyerman, II, p. 381; Baker, *CW*, p. 98.

80. Baker, *CW*, p. 99.

81. Tyerman, II, pp. 382–4, 387; Jackson, *CW*, II, p. 184; Baker, *CW*, pp. 99, 102; Baker, *JW*, pp. 175f., 177f.
82. Jackson, *CW*, II, pp. 188, 191.
83. *WMM*, 1845, p. 1205 quoted in Tyerman, II, 387f.
84. T. Beynon, *Howel Harris*, Carnarvon 1958, pp. 79f., 82f.; Baker, *JW*, p. 178.
85. *JWL*, IV, p. 162.
86. For this episode see *JWL*, IV, pp. 287–90; Baker, *JW*, pp. 200f. and references; *PWHS* XXXVIII, 1971, pp. 82–7.
87. For these efforts and the action following see Baker, *JW*, ch. XI.
88. Baker, *JW*, pp. 191f., 193; *JWL*, IV, pp. 235–9 and *JWJ*, V, pp. 60–6.
89. Pawson, *Short Account*, MCA, pp. 31f. The account in Pawson's *Life* in *AM*, 1806, p. 845 and *EMP*, IV, p. 28 tactfully omits the exchange between Charles Wesley and Hampson.
90. Beynon, *Howel Harris* (n.84), p. 79; *JWL*, V, pp. 143–5.
91. *JWL (B)*, II, pp. 470–3.
92. J.W. Etheridge, *Life of Thomas Coke*, London 1860, p. 151.
93. Baker, *JW*, pp. 137f.
94. J.M. Turner, *Conflict and Reconciliation*, Epworth Press 1985.
95. For an admirable survey to 1700 see H. Kamen, *The Rise of Toleration*, Weidenfeld and Nicholson 1967; for the eighteenth century in England R.B. Barlow, *Citizenship and Conscience*, Princeton University Press 1962.
96. See R. Klibansky and J.W. Gough (eds.), *John Locke: Epistola de Tolerantia*, Oxford University Press 1968.
97. Sermon CVII, 'God's Vineyard', IV, ii in *Works*, VII; cf. *JWL*, VI, p. 72.
98. *JWL*, IV, pp. 152f.; *JWJ*, III, p. 72; Sermon XXXIX, 'The Catholic Spirit', in *Works*, V, para. I, x.
99. *JWL*, V, p. 22.
100. For Law, see his letters to Hoadly in *Works*, 1762, I; Rack, 'Hoadly versus Law'.
101. F. Baker in *London Quarterly Review* CLXXXVII, 1963, pp. 180–6.
102. For Oxford reading see Green, *YMW*, Appendix; for the preachers' and Kingswood list see MS *Minutes* 1745, 1746, 1748.
103. For the Puritan influence see R.C. Monk, *John Wesley: His Puritan Heritage*, Epworth Press 1966, and J. Newton, *Susanna Wesley and the Puritan Tradition in Methodism*, Epworth Press 1968, passim. For the Doddridge letter see *AM*, 1778, pp. 419–25; Monk, *Wesley*, pp. 45f., and Appendix I and II for list of works in the *Christian Library*.
104. Monk, *Wesley* (n.103), pp. 37ff.
105. *JWJ*, II, p. 205; III, pp. 285f.; *JWL (B)*, II, pp. 212, 235; *JWJ*, IV, p. 93.
106. *Farther Appeal*, Part II (1745), in *Works* VIII; *JWL*, VII, p. 326; Sermon CIV, 'On Attending the Church Services', para. 25, in *Works*, VII.
107. *JWL*, III, p. 251. For the contemporary context see Rack, 'Hoadly versus Law'.
108. Baker, *JW*, pp. 133–5.
109. Ibid., p. 338; Bennet to Charles Wesley, 30 July 1745 (in MCA). He also hoped for the Wesleys to come more often to administer communion. Anglican refusal: Bennet, *Diary*, Easter 1750.
110. Baker, *JW*, pp. 339f.; *JWL*, VI, 326.

111. *AM*, 1779, p. 95.
112. For an excellent discussion of Wesley's view of Catholicism see D. Hempton, *Methodism and Politics in British Society, 1750–1850*, Hutchinson 1984, pp. 30–43, to which I am indebted.
113. *JWL*, III, pp. 7–14; Hempton, *Methodism and Politics* (n.112), pp. 34–43.
114. Hempton, *Methodism and Politics* (n.112), pp. 36f.; 'A Short Method' in *Works*, X along with his other writings on Catholicism in the same volume.
115. All in *Works*, X. For the origins of the catechism see T. Jackson, *Recollections*, London 1874, p. 236.
116. *JWL*, IV, pp. 135–41.
117. *JWL*, VI, pp. 267, 299f., 301, 302.
118. *JWJ*, VII, p. 267; *Works*, X, 'Letter to a Priest'.
119. 'Disavowal of Persecuting Papists', *Works*, X.
120. G. Rudé, 'The Gordon Riots', *TRHS*, Fifth Series, VI, 1956, pp. 93–114; J. Stevenson, *Popular Disturbances in England 1700–1870*, Longmans 1979, pp. 15f., 76–9.
121. *EMP*, IV, p. 48; cf. Hempton, *Methodism and Politics* (n.112), pp. 39f.
122. Hempton, *Methodism and Politics* (n.112), pp. 41f.
123. Sermon XXXIX (1749, printed 1750), in *Works*, VI.
124. *JWL*, IV, p. 347, cf. p. 297.

Interlude Wesley's England: 2. Society and Revival in the Later Eighteenth Century

1. P. Corfield, *The Impact of English Towns 1700–1800*, Oxford University Press 1982, pp. 7–11. For Manchester, see A.P. Wadsworth and J. de L. Mann, *The Cotton Industry in Industrial Lancashire*, Manchester University Press 1931, Appendix A.
3. P. Mathias, *The First Industrial Nation*, Methuen ²1983, pp. 1–4.
3. Ibid., pp. 15f., 88; M.M. Edwards, *The Growth of the British Cotton Trade 1780–1815*, Manchester University Press 1967, chs VII and VIII.
4. On this point see A.D. Gilbert, *Religion and Society in Industrial England 1740–1914*, Longmans 1976, pp. 110–15.
5. The phrase is Professor Harold Perkin's.
6. For recent discussions see B.W. Hill, *British Political Parties 1742–1832*, Allen and Unwin 1985; F. O'Gorman, *The Emergence of the British Two-Party System 1760–1832*, Edward Arnold 1982.
7. A. Briggs, 'The Language of Class', in *Essays in Labour History*, ed. A. Briggs and J. Saville, Macmillan 1960, pp. 43–73.
8. See S. and B. Webb, *English Local Government*, Longmans 1922, ch. IV on Improvement Commissioners; A. Redford, *History of Local Government in Manchester* I, Longmans 1939. J.H. Plumb, *England in the Eighteenth Century*, Penguin Books 1950, pp. 86f., rightly calls attention to the importance of this.
9. There is a now classic treatment of this, moving if controversial, in E.P. Thompson, *The Making of the English Working Class*, revised edition, Penguin Books 1968; see A. Goodwin, *The Friends of Liberty*, Hutchinson 1979 for sober detail. On the dubious prospects of revolution see M. Thomis and P. Holt, *The Threat of Revolution in Britain*, Macmillan 1977; I.R. Christie, *Stress and Stability in Late Eighteenth-Century Britain*, Oxford Univerity Press 1984.

10. Woodforde, *Diary*, 25 May 1796, 'The World's Classics', Oxford University Press, pp. 528.

11. M. Ransome (ed.), *Wiltshire Returns to the Bishop's Visitation Questions*, 1783, Wiltshire Record Society 1972, pp. 35, 59.

12. R.B. Walker, 'Religious Change in Cheshire 1750–1850', *JEH* XVII, 1966, pp. 77–94.

13. D. McClatchey, *Oxfordshire Clergy 1777–1869*, Oxford University Press 1960, pp. 31f., 44, 86ff., 119f.

14. Walker, 'Religious Change' (n.12), p. 80.

15. Ibid., p. 79; A. Blomfield, *Memoirs of Bishop Blomfield*, ²1864, pp. 77f.

16. Clearly recognized as separate in *Wiltshire Returns* (n.11), passim, but confusion is caused by the prolific Whitefieldite and Huntingdonian societies. However, the Cheshire returns of 1778 and even 1789 still show uncertainty because of Methodist church attendance (*Lancashire and Cheshire Wesley Historical Society* 6, 1967, 86–9).

17. Walker, 'Religious Change' (n.12), p. 82.

18. Visitation Returns in CRO, EDV 7/2/143; 7/3/156, 232.

19. C.B. Andrews (ed.), *Torrington Diary* II, Eyre and Spottiswoode 1934, p. 238.

20. Ibid., I, p. 13; II, p. 238.

21. *Report from the Clergy . . . of Lincolnshire*, ²1800, pp. 18–22, though it is noted that some of the Methodists still attended church.

22. For this see W.R. Ward, 'The Tithe Question in the Early Nineteenth Century', *JEH* XVI, 1965, pp. 67–81; E.J. Evans, *The Contentious Tithe 1750–1850*, Routledge 1976.

23. Evans, *Tithe* (n.22), p. 10, but he also notes the poor curates; see also McClatchey, *Oxfordshire Clergy*, pp. 110ff.

24. See the essays by Sharp and Nockles in G. Rowell (ed.), *Tradition Renewed*, Darton, Longman and Todd 1986.

25. For Watson see E. Churton, *Joshua Watson*, Oxford 1863; A.B. Webster, *Joshua Watson*, SPCK 1954.

26. C. Bayley, *Questions for Children*, Manchester 1796.

27. For a partial survey see B.F.L. Clarke, *The Building of the Eighteenth-Century Church*, SPCK 1963. For regional examples the essays by R. Leese and myself in E. Royle (ed.), *Regional Studies in the History of Religion*, Humberside College of Higher Education, nd.

28. See, for example, St Stephen's Salford in 1794, CRO, EDA, 2/9, p. 214.

29. R. Watson, *Anecdotes*, 1818, I, pp. 156ff.; II, pp. 155f.

30. G. Best, *Temporal Pillars*, Cambridge University Press 1963, ch. IV esp. pp. 131–47.

31. A.P. Wadsworth, 'The First Manchester Sunday Schools', *Bulletin of the John Rylands Library*, XXXIII 1951, pp. 299–326; W.R. Ward, *Religion and Society in England 1790–1850*, Batsford 1972, pp. 212–16; W.T. Laqueur, *Religion and Respectability*, Yale University Press 1976; D. Hempton, *Methodism and Politics in British Society, 1750–1850*, Hutchinson 1984, pp. 85–9.

32. *Report from Lincolnshire Clergy* (n.21), pp. 17ff.

33. O.F. Christie (ed.), *Diary of the Revd William Jones*, London 1929, pp. 158f, 263.

34. G. Crabbe, *Life of G. Crabbe*, reprinted Cresset Press 1947, pp. 93, 77, 95.

35. *AM*, 1792, p. 360.

36. See Walsh, 'Cambridge Methodists' for examples.

37. For later eighteenth-century developments see Walsh in *HMCGB*, I, pp. 275–316. See W.R. Ward, 'The Religion of the People and the Problem of Control 1790–1830', *SCH* VIII, 1972, pp. 237–57, for the view that undenominationalism was succeeded by a sharper denominationalism.

38. Above, p. 321.

39. *HMCGB*, I, p. 292.

40. For a factual but uncritical survey of their activities see E.M. Howse, *Saints in Politics*, Allen and Unwin 1953; the conspiracy theory is in F.K. Brown, *Fathers of the Victorians*, Cambridge University Press 1961. For individuals see J.C. Pollock, *William Wilberforce*, Constable 1973; M. Hennell, *John Venn and the Clapham Sect*, Lutterworth Press 1958; M.G. Jones, *Hannah More*, Cambridge University Press 1952; S. Meacham, *Henry Thornton*, Harvard University Press 1964. B. Hilton, *The Age of Atonement*, Clarendon Press 1988, marks a fresh critical approach which appeared too late to be used here. On anti-slavery, from a large and growing literature, R. Anstey, *The Atlantic Slave Trade and British Abolition*, Macmillan 1975, stands out for the combination of economic, political and religious analysis.

41. For Wright, see Richard Wright, *A Review of the Missionary Life . . . of Richard Wright*, London 1825; S. Mews, 'Reason and Emotion in Working Class Religion', *SCH* IX, 1972, pp. 365–82. The Unitarian Methodists later added an 'evangelical' note to the tradition which affected Unitarian city missions: see H. McLachlan, *The Methodist Unitarian Movement*, Manchester University Press 1919.

42. See I. Isichei, *Victorian Quakers*, Oxford University Press 1969 for the 'Beaconites'.

43. R.J. Lineham, 'The English Swedenborgians 1770–1840', University of Sussex DPhil 1978; W.R. Ward, 'The Swedenborgians: Heresy, Schism or Religious Protest?', *SCH* IX 1972, pp. 303–9: a parallel to the 'Church' and separatist Methodists. For the Shakers see E.D. Andrews, *The People Called Shakers*, revised edition, Dover Books, New York 1963.

44. See Watts, p. 440 and ch. VII, for the impact of the Revival on Dissent.

45. Ibid., pp. 450ff.

46. See above, pp. 583 n. 17 for references.

47. G.F. Nuttall, 'George Whitefield's Curate', *JEH* XXVII, 1976, pp. 369–86; B. Hanbury (ed.), *Extracts from the Diary etc. of Joseph Williams*, London 1815; G.F. Nuttall, 'Methodism and the Older Dissent', *Journal of the United Reformed Church Historical Society* II, 1981, pp. 259–74.

48. R.T. Jones, *Congregationalism in England 1662–1962*, Independent Press 1962, ch. IV; B. Nightingale, *Lancashire Nonconformity*, six volumes 1890–3.

49. R. Mansfield, *The Development of Independency in Derbyshire*, MA Manchester 1951, p. 145 (in 1782).

50. For Walker's congregation see G.C.B. Davies, *Early Church Evangelicals*, SPCK 1951, pp. 212ff.; for Venn's, H. Venn (ed.), *Life and Letters of Henry Venn*, London [6]1839, p. 162; for Edwards, above p. 234 and n. 220; for Bennet, above pp. 219f.

51. Nightingale, I, p. 256; Jones, *Congregationalism* (n.48), pp. 155f.

52. H. McLachlan, *English Education under the Test Acts*, Manchester University Press 1931, pp. 192f.

53. Jones, *Congregationalism* (n.48), pp. 162–8; McLachlan, *English Education* (n.52); J.I. Milner and T. Haweis, *History*, London 1840, p. 1058.

54. Watts, pp. 454ff.; Brown, chs IV–VII.

55. P. Toon, *Emergence of Hyper-Calvinism in English Nonconformity 1689–1765*, The Olive Tree Press 1967. But there were exceptions; for these and further developments see Brown passim.

56. Brown, pp. 60–3.

57. Brown, pp. 67f.; Watts, pp. 454–6.

58. Brown, pp. 67–70; Watts, pp. 454–6.

59. There is an account of the complications of this in Brown, pp. 105–7.

60. Watts, p. 389; J. Horsfall Turner, *Halifax Books and Authors*, Bingham 1906, pp. 36, 37; *Christian History*, V (1743), ii, 52; VI (1743), i, 35. The Baptist church in Manchester provided some of the members for the Independent church founded in the 1750s.

61. John Martin quoted in Brown, p. 90; Watts, pp. 458–60.

62. J. Gadsby, *William Gadsby*, London 1844.

63. See below, pp. 491ff.

IX. The Enthusiasts: Methodism and Perfection in the 1760s

1. See *JWL (B)*, II, pp. 269ff. for Hall; for Wheatley, ibid., pp. 464ff.; Ball, *CWJ*, II, pp. 129–32, 137; and for a comparison between his preaching and Charles Wesley's by an Independent see Caleb Warhurst, *Diary*, in ManchCL M185, Box 1. See also B. Semmel, *The Methodist Revolution*, Heinemann 1974, pp. 43ff., 24 January and 16 March 1758 for the antinomians.

2. Jackson, *CW*, I, pp. 583; Baker, *CW*, pp. 83–7.

3. Tyerman, II, pp. 126f.

4. *JWJ*, V, pp. 40f.; *Works*, VIII, p. 350; cf. *JWJ*, IV, p. 532.

5. Whitefield in *JWL (B)*, II, pp. 32, 43, 66; J.C.C. Probert, *Methodism in Redruth*, nd, p. 5; *JWL (B)*, I, pp. 201, 318.

6. Tyerman, II, pp. 417, 444.

7. *JWJ*, IV, pp. 365f.; *Short History of the People Called Methodists*, paras, 80, 81, in *Works*, IX, p. 473.

8. *JWJ*, IV, p. 365.

9. *JWL*, IV, pp. 10ff.; cf. p. 167f., where he allows for 'involuntary' defects which still need the grace of Christ; ibid., p. 46, at Sheffield.

10. MS *Minutes* 1758; Tyerman, II, p. 307; *Plain Account of Christian Perfection*, para. 17.

11. *Plain Account*, para. 19.

12. *JWJ*, IV, pp. 367–70.

13. *JWJ*, IV, p. 446; Byrom *Journal*, Chetham Society XLIV (1857), II (2), pp. 629–31 (Talon, pp. 181–3); *Wesleyan Methodist Magazine*, 1863, p. 1104.

14. *JWJ*, IV, pp. 372, 445, 439, 442, 468, 477, 518f. There were also first conversions: *AM*, 1780, p. 496.

15. *AM*, 1781, p. 390; Tyerman, II, pp. 418–22.

16. MS *Minutes*, 1761; *JWL*, IV, p. 163.

17. This term became popular in the nineteenth century but was already current in the eighteenth. Wesley was equivocal about its use, and though he once deprecated it (quoted Outler, p. 304), he occasionally used it: *JWL*, III, p. 216; V, p. 315, 337; VII, p. 116.

18. Tyerman, II, p. 422.

19. *JWJ*, IV, p. 445 and n.; 469f.

20. Tyerman, II, pp. 423f. quoting Whitehead, II, p. 297.

21. Tyerman, II, pp. 424, 426; *JWL*, IV, pp. 169, 186. For a MS questionnaire about experiences of perfection, attributed to Wesley, see *PWHS* XXXIV, 1963, pp. 29ff.

22. *Plain Account*, paras, 20, 22, 25.

23. *JWL*, IV, p. 209; Moore, II, pp. 218–32; Tyerman, II, p. 432.

24. *AM*, 1780, p. 674.

25. *JWJ*, II, pp. 481f. Southey suspected fraud, but Coleridge posited what would now be termed a psychosomatic explanation and a cure by 'suggestion': Southey, *John Wesley* (ed. Fitzgerald), Oxford University Press 1925, II, pp. 179f. and note. See Rack, 'Doctors', p. 150 and n.

26. *AM*, 1790, p. 42; Tyerman, II, p. 434; Southey (n.25), II, p. 180.

27. *JWJ*, IV, pp. 539, 540–42; *JWL*, IV, pp. 196, 199, cf. 338.

28. Tyerman, II, pp. 436f.

29. *JWJ*, V, pp. 4, 9; for the 1750 earthquake see *CWJ*, II, pp. 68ff. Sermon CXXIX on 'The Cause and Cure of Earthquakes in *Works*, VII is by Charles, not John.

30. Southey (n.25), II, pp. 183f.; Tyerman, II, p. 438.

31. *JWL*, IV, pp. 192–4; *JWJ*, IV, pp. 535–8.

32. *JWJ*, V, pp. 5–7, 10–13; *JWL*, IV, pp. 201f., 208–11.

33. Tyerman, II, pp. 440f; *JWL*, IV, p. 211.

34. *JWJ*, V, p. 40 and n.

35. Ibid., and Tyerman, II, p. 446.

36. *JWL*, IV, pp. 188f.; V, pp. 20ff., cf. IV, p. 187, which has the same letter duplicated for September 1762; Jackson, *CW*, II, p. 210.

37. *EMP*, II, pp. 26–8.

38. *JWL*, IV, pp. 205f.

39. MCA, *Wesley Family Letters*, II, pp. 94f.

40. For the story see R. Paulson, *Hogarth*, II, Yale University Press 1971, pp. 355–8 (see above, p. 277).

41. *EMP*, V, pp. 127ff.

42. Ibid., V, pp. 23f.; *JWL*, IV, p. 245; V, pp. 38, 49; Tyerman, II, pp. 443f.

43. For Manchester gains and losses see *JWJ*, V, 162 and n. Examples of gain and loss in *EMP*, II, pp. 188–94; *JWJ*, V, pp. 40f.

44. H. Schwartz, *The French Prophets*, University of California Press 1980; *JWJ*, III, p. 239; III, p. 54.

45. J.F.C. Harrison, *The Second Coming*, Routledge 1979; W.H. Oliver, *Prophets and Millenialists*, Auckland/Oxford University Press 1978; C. Garrett, *Respectable Folly*, Johns Hopkins University Press 1975.

46. *JWJ*, IV, p. 299; *LyH*, I, p. 395; *CWJ*, II, p. 209.

47. *JWJ*, IV, p. 361.

48. *AM*, 1780, p. 443; F. Baker, *William Grimshaw*, Epworth Press 1963, pp. 193ff.

49. See D.M. Valenze, *Prophetic Sons and Daughters*, Princeton University Press 1985 and below, pp. 491ff., on revivals in the 1780s.

X. John Wesley and the World

1. On Wesley as a preacher see W.L. Doughty, *John Wesley, Preacher*, Epworth Press 1955; Horton Davies, *Worship and Theology in England*, III, Oxford University Press 1961, ch. VII; Schmidt, II, ch. VI; Outler in BE *Sermons*, I, Introduction, pp. 13–29.

2. For the sermon register (1747–61) see *JWJ*, VIII, pp. 171–252.

3. See E. Sugden in *Standard Sermons I*, Epworth Press 1921, pp. 13–26, 331–40, for the significance and scope of these 'standards'.

4. For some accounts see Heitzenrater, *EMW*, II, 83–9; *PWHS* XL, 1975, p. 92. 'Entirely devoid of expansion and imagery' and unimpassioned in delivery, said William Jay disappointedly of the elderly Wesley preaching: W. Jay, *Autobiography*, London 1854, p. 414.

5. Hampson, III, pp. 169–71.

6. H.J.C. Grierson (ed.), *Letters of Sir Walter Scott V*, Constable 1933, pp. 340f. (this would have been in 1783).

7. *Large Minutes, Works*, VIII, question 37; MS *Minutes*, 1747.

8. *JWL*, p. 82; VI, pp. 326f.; cf. V, p. 345.

9. *JWL*, III, p. 97; V, p. 347; VI, pp. 186, 308; VIII, p. 190.

10. Telford, *John Wesley*, pp. 315f.

11. Outler, *BE* edition of *Sermons*, I, pp. 20–6.

12. From Abraham Stanyon, *An Account of Switzerland* (1714), p. 170, quoted by C.L. Hubert-Powell, *J.J. Wetstein*, SPCK 1938, p. 2.

13. I. Rivers (ed.), *Books and Their Readers*, Leicester University Press 1982, pp. 129–33.

14. *Works*, XIII, pp. 518–27; and for the source T. Jackson, *Recollections*, London 1874, p. 236.

15. *JWL*, V, p. 16.

16. *Sermon*, IV, iv, 10, 11; Kennicott extract in Heitzenrater, *EMW*, II, pp. 8ff.

17. *WMM* 1825, p. 105, quoted in Tyerman, III, p. 563.

18. W.S. Lewis (ed.), *Letters of Horace Walpole*, XXXV, Yale University Press 1973, p. 119.

19. Chester Chronicle, quoted in *PWHS* XL, 1975, p. 92; *EMP*, I, p. 16.

20. *Gentleman's Magazine*, 1787, II, p. 732.

21. *JWJ*, VII, p. 112; V, p. 182; IV, p. 68; Telford, *John Wesley*, p. 317.

22. I have not seen T.W. Herbert, *John Wesley as Editor and Author*, 1940, which appears to be the only full treatment.

23. The *Original Sin* was partly from Watts' *Ruin and Recovery*: so A.P. Davis, *Isaac Watts*, Independent Press 1948, p. 44. For the Johnson affair see below, p. 376.

24. *Notes on the New Testament*, Preface.

25. Preface to Tillotson's sermons in *Works*, XIV, p. 233; and for the implied defence of the *Whole Duty* against evangelical criticisms see Preface in *Works*, XIV, p. 231 (contrast Venn in *Complete Duty*, London 1763 Preface).

26. Preface to *Christian Library* in *Works*, XIV, pp. 222f.; cf. *JWL*, IV, p. 9,

where he says that he does not care who speaks, but what is spoken; cf. R.C. Monk, *John Wesley and his Puritan Heritage*, Epworth Press 1966, p. 37.

27. Monk, *Puritan Heritage* (n. 26), pp. 32–6, 54–63; cf. his remarks on the Quietist Mme Guyon when he praises parts of her work but criticizes her for violations of Scripture and reason and trusting too much to 'impressions': *Works*, XIV, pp. 275–8; *JWL*, VI, p. 44.

28. *Works*, XIV, pp. 300–3.

29. Hampson, III, p. 175, cf. Whitehead, II, p. 465; for the Hutchinsonians see *JWJ*, V, p. 149, on Jones of Nayland, who he thinks disproves Newton, though whether he established his own hypothesis was another matter. On the Hutchinsonians see A.J. Kuhn, 'Glory or Gravity: Hutchinson versus Newton', *Journal of the History of Ideas*, XXII, 1961, pp. 303–22.

30. *Works*, XIV, p. 301.

31. *Works*, XIV, pp. 272–5; cf. *JWL*, VI, p. 67: 'My view in writing history (as in philosophy) is to bring God into it.'

32. *Works*, XIV, pp. 296–9. Cf. J. Walsh, 'Joseph Milner's Evangelical Church History', *JEH*, X, 1959, pp. 174–87. Milner judged by the incidence of justification by faith in his authors, but found it in some surprising places.

33. Letter to Lady Huntingdon about this scheme in *JWL (B)*, II, pp. 114f. and n.

34. Preface to *A.M*, 1778, p. 3; *Works*, XIV, pp. 278-79.

35. *AM*, 1779, p. 3; 1780, p. 3; *Works*, XIV, pp. 281–7. For a secular poem see e.g. 'Henry and Emma' by Matthew Prior, his favourite poet, in *AM*, 1780, p. 11.

36. See, for example, the letters to Miss Ritchie and Miss Bishop and other women in *JWL*, VI, passim. On Wesley as a letter writer see Baker, Introduction to *JWL (B)*, I.

37. Tyerman, III, p. 616; Telford, *John Wesley*, pp. 330f.

38. Whitehead, II, pp. 486, 491ff.; cf. Hampson, III, pp. 145, 150, 151.

39. See biography of Toplady in his *Works*, I, London 1825, pp. 100f., and below, p. 457.

40. For Green's criticism of its egotistic character see his *JW*, p. 141, but see above, p. 113 for the reasons and purpose in writing it.

41. For Methodists and culture see below, pp. 446ff.

42. R.E. Brantley, *Locke, Wesley and the Method of English Romanticism*, University of Florida Press 1984; also the older work of F.C. Gill, *The Romantic Movement and Methodism*, Epworth Press 1937. But for a criticism of Brantley see *PWHS* XLV, 1985, pp. 63–5. For the survival and revival of the supernatural and 'demonic' in eighteenth-century literature see R.D. Stock, *The Holy and Demonic*, Princeton University Press 1982. For Wesley and 'empiricism' see below, pp. 383ff.

43. *AM*, 1780, p. 662, reprinted in *Works*, XIII, p. 465.

44. For Gerard see *DNB*, s.v. The identity is clear from references in Wesley's essay.

45. Alexander Knox in Southey, *John Wesley* (ed. Fitzgerald), Oxford University Press 1925, II, p. 339. For the references to the historic figures see above, p. 292 and n. 49.

46. *JWJ*, V, p. 368; VI, p. 361.

47. Brooke's work in Wesley's version was called *The History of Henry Earl*

of Moreland (1780). For the story in the text see Tyerman, III, pp. 342f. Adam Clarke attempted to palliate the enormity of publishing a novel by saying that Wesley regarded it as substantially a true history of real persons. For Tristram Shandy see *Works*, XI, p. 31.

48. For the subject generally see A.H. Body, *John Wesley and Education*, Epworth Press 1936; Schmidt, II, ch. IX; P. Sangster, *Pity My Simplicity: The Evangelical Revival and the Education of Children 1738–1800*, Epworth Press 1963. For rank-and-file responses see Church, *EM*, ch. VI; and below, p. 448.

49. *Works*, XIII, pp. 474–7.

50. *JWL*, VI, p. 39.

51. For examples see Church, *EM*, pp. 236–41; see below, p. 453, for the question of his defects for lack of experience as a father.

52. For attitudes to charity schools see M.G. Jones, *Charity School Movement*, Cambridge University Press 1934; and her *Hannah More*, Cambridge University Press 1952, for that lady's restrictions on educating the poor.

53. For these schools see below, p. 448; for Sunday Schools, above, p. 321.

54. *JWJ*, VII, p. 3; *AM*, 1785, p. 41; *JWL*, VII, p. 364; *JWJ*, VIII, pp. 71, 20.

55. *HMCGB*, I, p. 222; MS *Minutes* 1748; *Works*, VIII, p. 293; *JWL*, VI, p. 19.

56. See below, p. 493.

57. For this see the accounts in *Works*, VIII; Three Old Boys, *The History of Kingswood School*, London 1898 (*History*).

58. *JWJ*, III, p. 392; *History*, p. 20.

59. *History*, p. 13; MS *Minutes*, 1748.

60. *Plain Account of Kingswood School*, para. 11, in *Works*, XIII.

61. The account of the system is in *A Short Account of the School in Kingswood*, 1768 in *Works*, XIII, with a few extra points in *Plain Account*. I cannot trace the source of the prayer-meeting story, but it has an authentic ring.

62. *History*, pp. 55, 77, 79; *Remarks on the State of Kingswood*, in *Works* XIII.

63. For Francke's approach see G. Kramer, *A.H. Franckes Pädagogisches Schriften*, 1876; for Doddridge, J.D. Humphreys (ed.), *Diary and Correspondence of Philip Doddridge*, London 1829–31, IV, p. 404; H. McLachlan, *English Education under the Test Acts*, Manchester University Press 1931, pp. 148, 149.

64. *JWJ*, IV, p. 188.

65. *Plain Account*, para. 14; *JWL (B)*, I, p. 444.

66. *Short Account*, ad fin. For the original scheme covering five years see MS *Minutes* 1748.

67. For what follows see *Plain Account*, paras. 16–23.

68. *History*, pp. 101, 57; J. McDonald, *Memoirs of Joseph Benson*, London 1822, p. 13.

69. *History*, p. 52 and ch. IX.

70. C.W. Towlson, *Moravian and Methodist*, Epworth Press 1957, pp. 238–43; *JWJ*, II, pp. 58–61.

71. Kramer, *Pädagogische Schriften* (n. 63).

72. See above, p. 268.

73. *Minutes*, I, pp. 46, 56; *JWJ*, V, p. 183.

74. *History*, pp. 44, 83; *Minutes* of 1773, 1788, 1796.

75. *Works*, XIII, pp. 301f. The other examples are in *JWJ*, V, pp. 149, 159; VI, p. 134.

76. *History*, ch. VII, and *JWJ*, V, pp. 249, 388.

77. *History*, p. 58 n., and *DNB*, s.v. 'Hindmarsh, Robert'.

78. *JWJ*, V, pp. 430, 526. For Mather see e.g. *JWL*, VI, p. 10; J.F.C. Harrison, *The Second Coming*, Routledge 1979, pp. 21–3, 233 (for details and his 'gazetteer' of theosophical readers).

79. *JWL (B)*, II, p. 190 n. which sees Doddridge's advice as for the *Christian Library*; but in *AM*, 1778, pp. 419–25 for young students of divinity.

80. MS *Minutes*, 1745.

81. *JWJ*, III, pp. 284 (young men), 398 (preachers).

82. Alexander Mather in *EMP*, II, pp. 191, 192; M. Edwards, *Adam Clarke*, Epworth Press 1942; I. Sellers, *Adam Clark, Controversialist*, Wesley Historical Society 1975, privately printed 1976.

83. E.g. *JWL*, V, pp. 220, 241, 286; VI, pp. 125f., 205. But he was wary about their attraction to mysticism: VI, pp. 43f., 136, 232f.

84. See above, pp. 291f., 324.

85. The most recent general study of Wesley's social attitudes is M. Marquardt, *Praxis und Prinzipien der Sozialethik John Wesleys*, Vandenhoeck & Ruprecht 1977, with full bibliography; E.M. North, *Early Methodist Philanthropy*, New York 1914; K.W. McArthur, *The Economic Ethics of John Wesley*, Abingdon Press 1936; R. Hayward, 'Was John Wesley a Political Economist?', *CH* XXXIII, 1964, pp. 314–21; T.W. Madron, 'Some Economic Aspects of John Wesley's Social Thought Revisited', *Methodist History*, IV, 1965–6, pp. 33–43; C. Elliott, 'The Ideal of Economic Growth', *Land, Labour and Population in the Industrial Revolution*, ed. E.L. Jones and G.E. Mingay, Edward Arnold 1967; B. Semmel, *The Methodist Revolution*, Heinemann 1974, pp. 71–9; also the older work of W.J. Warner, *The Wesleyan Movement in the Industrial Revolution*, Longmans 1930.

86. Sermon LXXXVII 'On Dress', LXXXIX 'The More Excellent Way', in *Works*, VII; *JWJ*, VIII, pp. 80 n., 85.

87. *JWL*, VI, pp. 207, 334–8; VIII, p. 76; Sermon LXXXVII, 'The Danger of Riches', in *Works*, VII; Telford, *John Wesley*, pp. 330f.; Moore, II, p. 434. See also above, p. 350.

88. *JWJ*, II, p. 454; Tyerman, I, p. 357.

89. *JWJ*, III, pp. 117, 122, 125, 501; IV, pp. 29f., 298; II, p. 333; VI, pp. 450, 451; V, p. 495.

90. Whitefield, *Journals*, p. 267.

91. See above, pp. 347f., on his *Survey of the Wisdom of God*; and below, p. 387. For the *Primitive Physic* in relation to his view of the supernatural see my 'Doctors'.

92. *JWJ*, III, p. 273.

93. *JWL*, VIII, p. 265. On Benezet and Wesley see R. Anstey, *The Transatlantic Slave Trade and British Abolition 1760–1810*, Macmillan 1975, pp. 239–42.

94. *JWL*, IV, pp. 227f.; for Told, see *The Life of Silas Told written by Himself* (1786), reprinted Epworth Press 1954; T. Wood, *Biographical Sketch of . . . James Bundy*, London ³1824; W.R. Williams, *The Prisoner's Friend*, London 1880.

95. For Sunday schools see above p. 321, and below, p. 348. For the Stranger's Friend Society, see below, p. 448.

96. MS *Minutes* 1744, 145; Sermon LXXXVIII 'On Dress', in *Works* VII; on tea, below, p. 443.

97. For the 'Words' see *Works*, XI.

98. See Sermon LII, in *Works*, VI, for most of the details; *JWJ*, V, pp. 101, 159; VI, p. 223. For later Evangelical attempts see R.I. and S. Wilberforce, *Life of William Wilberforce*, I, London 1838, pp. 130–8; in general E.J. Bristow, *Vice and Vigilance*, Gill and Macmillan 1977; Rack, 'Religious Societies', pp. 590f.

99. *JWL*, III, p. 229; *JWJ*, IV, pp. 259, 358; MS *Minutes* 1748; *JWL*, VI, pp. 20ff.; *JWJ*, IV, pp. 222, 276f.

100. MS *Minutes*, 1744; *JWJ*, III, p. 301.

101. *JWJ*, IV, p. 422. Seen as done from duty rather than a warm heart by Hampson, III, p. 199 (see below, p. 542).

102. For later Evangelical attitudes see H.D. Rack, 'Domestic Visitation', *JEH*, XXIV, 1973, pp. 357–76.

103. Cf. H.T. Dickinson, *Bolingbroke*, Constable 1970, pp. 187–91, for his bid for the support of the gentry and small tradesmen against the moneyed men. For Tory attitudes Linda Colley, *In Defiance of Oligarchy*, Cambridge University Press 1982; *Minutes*, I, p. 90 (1770: preachers are not to trade, but may hold shares in ships), cf. *JWL*, IV, pp. 270f.

104. D. Hempton, *Methodism and Politics in British Society 1750–1850*, Hutchinson 1984, p. 233, following John Walsh, who will be publishing on this theme.

105. Above, p. 91. William Law was much more traditional in charity without strings, and the stream of beggars to King's Cliffe annoyed his neighbours: J.H. Overton, *William Law*, Longmans 1881, pp. 244ff.

106. B.S. Pullan, 'Catholics and the Poor in Early Modern Europe' in *TRHS*, Fifth Series, XXVI, 1976, p. 34.

107. Sermon CXXVIII, 'Free Grace', *Works*, VII.

108. On the Moravian settlements and Harris's Trevecka community see *JWJ*, IV, pp. 5f., 232; cf. V, p. 25; VI, p. 428. For De Renty, see *Life* (ed. Wesley), 1741, pp. 39, 47.

109. MS *Minutes*, 1744; *JWL*, II, 304. The 'common stock' alone appears in 1748.

110. Richard Viney, *Diary*, 22 February 1744 (MS in Moravian Archives, photocopy in JRUL MS Eng. 965).

111. *JWJ*, IV, p. 223; *EMP*, VI, p. 258; A. Jephson, 'A Friendly and Compassionate Address to all Serious and Well-Disposed Methodists', London 1760.

112. M. Weber, *The Protestant Ethic and the Spirit of Capitalism*, ET Talcott Parsons, Allen and Unwin 1930, pp. 139–43; cf. also Warner, *Wesleyan Movement* (n. 85). Weber drew only on German secondary works and missed the 'Use of Money' sermon, but he noted the affinities and differences between Wesley, the Puritans and the Pietists.

113. *JWJ*, IV, p. 417; Sermon CXVI, 'Causes of the Inefficacy of Christianity'; Sermon LXXXVII, 'The Danger of Riches'; Sermon CVIII, 'On Riches' (all in *Works* VII).

114. Sermon L, in *Works*, VI.

115. P. Miller (ed.), *The American Puritans*, Doubleday 1956, pp. 171ff.

116. Sermon CII, in *Works*, VII.

117. *Works*, VIII, pp. 308, 309; there is a case of expulsion for debt in *EMP*, I, p. 166.

118. Rules in *Works*, VIII; *Notes on the New Testament* (1754), at Luke 19.23.

119. On this and Wesley's economics in the light of Weber's theory see Elliott, *Economic Growth* (n. 85); for an older treatment, Warner, *Wesleyan Movement* (n. 85). For a nineteenth-century biography associating Christian and business virtues, see B. Gregory, *The Thorough Business Man*, London 1871.

120. Semmel, *Methodist Revolution* (n. 85), pp. 71–9.

121. *JWJ*, VI, pp. 125f.; *PWHS*, IV, 1904, p. 209.

122. Marquardt, *Sozialethik* (n. 85), ch. X.

123. *Works*, XI, p. 79.

124. J. Kent in H. Cunliffe-Jones (ed.), *A History of Christian Doctrine*, T. & T. Clark 1978, pp. 473–80.

125. But for a more positive view of the social legacy at least of American evangelicalism see T.L. Smith, *Reconstruction and Social Reform*, Johns Hopkins University Press 1980.

126. Maldwyn Edwards, *After Wesley*, Epworth Press 1935, p. 154, quoting James Everett.

127. For an older comprehensive account of Wesley and politics see M. Edwards, *John Wesley*, Epworth Press 1933; the most recent account, incorporating the present understanding of eighteenth-century party politics, is in Hempton, *Methodism and Politics* (n. 104), pp. 30–49. For the 'Methodism and revolution' theories see n. 160 below.

128. *JWL*, VII, pp. 305f.; VI, 156, 161, 267.

129. Green, *YMW*, pp. 78f. and n.

130. T. Jackson, *CW*, I, p. 331; Tyerman, I, p. 99; Green, *YMW*, p. 78.

131. Sermon V, in *Sermons of the Late Reverend Charles Wesley*, London 1816, pp. 81–94. Like others in this volume, it is a copy of John Wesley's sermon. For the identification see Heitzenrater, *OM*, pp. 274, 276.

132. *JWL*, III, p. 32; Green, *YMW*, appendix, p. 317.

133. *CWJ*, I, p. 355.

134. *CWJ*, I, pp. 356, 358–61.

135. *JWJ*, III, pp. 123f. The address was not presented, as Charles objected that it would make the Methodists seem a separatist body. Cf. also the loyalist sentiments in *JWL (B)*, II, pp. 152f., 162–4; for staying in London *JWJ*, III, p. 122.

136. For what follows see L. Colley, *In Defiance of Oligarchy*, Cambridge University Press 1982, pp. 112–15, 171f.

137. See e.g. Rack, 'Religious Societies', pp. 591–3; G.F. Nuttall, 'Howel Harris and the "Grand Table"', *JEH* XXXIV, 1988, pp. 531–44.

138. J.C.D. Clark, *English Society 1688–1832*, Cambridge University Press 1985, pp. 173ff., 179.

139. *Works*, XI, pp. 15, 154f.; *JWL*, VI, p. 283.

140. *A Word to a Freeholder*, in *Works*, XI, pp. 196–8; *JWL*, III, pp. 165f.; for the Bristol contest see G. Skelton, *Dean Tucker*, Macmillan 1981, pp. 148–55.

141. *JWJ*, III, p. 305; *Works*, XI, pp. 196–8; *JWJ*, VI, p. 40; *JWL*, III, pp. 165f.; Tyerman, II, pp. 235f.

142. *JWJ*, III, p. 40 n.

143. *JWL*, VIII, p. 173; see *JWJ*, IV, p. 417 on the death of George II ('when will England have a better Prince?'); and on George III especially *Free Thoughts*, *Works*, XI, pp. 16ff.

144. See especially Hempton, *Methodism and Politics* (n. 104), pp. 30–49, for what follows, though I allow more than he does for the family tradition of Tory sentiments.

145. Above, ch. VIII.4.

146. *Works*, XI, pp. 14ff. For the Wilkes affair see G. Rudé, *Wilkes and Liberty*, Clarendon Press 1962.

147. *Works*, XI, pp. 34ff.

148. *Thoughts Concerning the Origin of Power* (1772), in *Works*, XI.

149. For what follows see Tyerman, III, pp. 185–92; Semmel, *Methodist Revolution* (n. 85), pp. 63–71; A. Raymond, ' "I Love God and Honour the King": John Wesley and the American Revolution', *CH*, XLV, 1976, pp. 316–28; Clark, *English Society* (n. 138), pp. 237–40; see chs. III, IV.3, for adaptations of divine right to the Hanoverian dynasty.

150. Raymond, 'American Revolution' (n. 149), p. 317.

151. *JWL*, VI, pp. 155–64.

152. For what follows see Tyerman, III, pp. 186, 188f., 191; Raymond, 'American Revolution' (n. 149), pp. 321f. It is said that Wesley was offered favours for himself or the Methodists and that he finally accepted some money for charity, but denied that he had asked to be made a royal missionary and to have the privilege of preaching in any church. See *JWL*, VI, pp. 192f., for a denial of writing for favours but only to 'quench the fire' of agitation.

153. *Works*, XI, pp. 99ff., 119ff., 134f.

154. Semmel, *Methodist Revolution* (n. 85), pp. 69–71. He wishes to see Arminianism as a source of 'liberalism', but the traditions of the seventeenth century have more generally been seen as ultimately producing reformist and republican sentiments from Puritanism against the conservative paternalism of Arminianism.

155. Semmel, *Methodist Revolution* (n. 85), p. 210.

156. Hempton, *Methodism and Politics* (n. 104), p. 48.

157. *JWJ*, VI, p. 78.

158. J.W. Etheridge, *Thomas Coke*, London 1860, p. 152.

159. For an example of Bradburn's rhetoric see a letter in Hempton, *Methodism and Politics* (n. 104), p. 61. For suspicions of his political radicalism which helped to influence a 'Church Methodist' to leave the connexion in the 1790s see Everett Scrapbook in MCA, p. 453.

160. In addition to Semmel and Hempton see the survey in S. Andrews, *Methodism and Society*, Longmans 1970; E.P. Thompson, *The Making of the English Working Class*, Penguin Books 1968, ch. XI and the Afterword; E. Hobsbawm, *Labouring Men*, Weidenfeld and Nicholson 1964, ch. III; H.J. Perkin, *Origins of Modern English Society 1770–1880*, Routledge 1969 (for Methodists and others helping to create a 'viable class society'); P. Stigant, 'Wesleyan Methodism and Working-Class Radicalism in the North 1792–1821', *Northern History* VI, 1971, pp. 98–116; for a regional study see A.D. Gilbert, 'Methodism, Dissent and Political Stability in Early Industrial England', *JRH* X, 1978–9, pp. 381–99. See also above, p. 317, for the likelihood or otherwise of a 'revolutionary' situation.

*XI. The Path to Perfection: Doctrine, Devotion and Social Concern in Early
Methodism*

1. Schmidt, II (2), p. 7, remarks that he lacked system.

2. Sermon LV, 'On the Trinity', *Works*, VI, p. 206; *Notes on the New
Testament* (at the end of 'Revelation'); *JWL*, VIII, pp. 63, 67; see below, p. 491.
Some Methodists were more speculative, especially in the 1790s and after, e.g.
Coke in J. Vickers, *Thomas Coke*, Epworth Press 1969, p. 330.

3. Sermon LX, 'The General Deliverance', *Works*, VI. For other examples
of this and its significance see K. Thomas, *Man and the Natural World*, Penguin
Books 1984, pp. 138–41.

4. Preface to *Sermons*, 1748; *JWL*, VI, pp. 113, 134; II, p. 75.

5. For treatments of Wesley's theology see, most systematically and
comprehensively in terms of subjects, C. Williams, *John Wesley's Theology Today*,
Epworth Press 1960; but most fully in terms of his salvation and perfection
doctrines H. Lindstrom, *Wesley and Sanctification*, Epworth Press 1946; and in
terms of justification by faith, W.R. Cannon, *Theology of John Wesley*, Abingdon
Press 1946. See A.C. Outler, *John Wesley*, Oxford University Press, New York
1964, for selected documents and introduction. See M. Schmidt, *John Wesley*,
for a 'theological biography', and ch. VII on him as a theological writer. The
older work of G.C. Cell, *The Rediscovery of John Wesley*, Henry Holt 1935, represents
a kind of Barthian interpretation, though allowing for 'Enlightenment' elements.
H.A. Snyder, *The Radical Wesley*, Inter-Varsity Press 1980, is an interesting
attempt to relate him to Reformation 'radicalism' (i.e. the Anabaptist tradition).

6. F. Dreyer, 'Faith and Experience in the Thought of John Wesley',
American Historical Review LXXXVIII, 1983, pp. 12–30; cf. also R.E. Brantley,
Locke, Wesley and the Method of English Romanticism, University of Florida Press
1984, chs. I–III, who also relates Wesley to Locke and Browne. For criticism
see H.D. Rack, 'Methodism and Romanticism', *PWHS* XLV, 1985, pp. 63–5.
Dreyer, p. 21 n., notes that H.B. Workman (in *New History of Methodism*, ed.
Workman et al., London 1909, I, pp. 7, 16–19) related Wesley to contemporary
empiricism; and one could add G. Eayrs, *John Wesley as Christian Philosopher and
Church Founder*, Epworth Press 1926. These men were influenced by the
contemporary vogue for Schleiermacher and William James.

7. For what follows see H. Willmer, 'Evangelicalism 1785–1835', unpublished Hulsean Prize Essay (1962), in Cambridge University Library; D.
Rosman, *Evangelicals and Culture*, Croom Helm 1984; W.R. Ward, 'The Relationship of Enlightenment and Religious Revival in Central Europe and the English-
speaking World', *SCH Subsidia* 2, 1979, pp. 281–306.

8. This was even more marked in Scotland, for example in Thomas
Chalmers: see D.F. Rice, 'Natural Theology and the Scottish Philosophy in the
Thought of Thomas Chalmers', *Scottish Journal of Theology* XXIV, 1971, pp.
23–46; H.D. Rack, 'Chalmers', *Theologische Realenzyklopädie* XII, pp. 676f.

9. *JWJ*, III, p. 232. See later J.B. Sumner, *A Treatise on the Records of
Creation*, London 1816, which also draws on Malthus.

10. R. Watson, *Anecdotes* I, London 1818, pp. 62ff.

11. Hoadly, in his *Works* III, London 1773, p. 844 ('the common rules of
speech in like cases'); cf. pp. 847f., 850f.

12. For the later seventeenth-century evidence from 'popular' literature see

M. Spufford, *Small Books and Pleasant Histories*, Cambridge University Press 1981, pp. 207–10. This may help to explain the response to revival preaching.

13. See above, n. 6.

14. *JWL*, II, p. 117; III, p. 172.

15. *Notes on the New Testament* on I. Cor. 14.20.

16. Contrast Locke, *Human Understanding*, IV, xvii, 24; *JWL (B)*, I, pp. 175, 179; *Works*, VIII, p. 276; MS *Minutes*, 1744. One may perhaps contrast here the barer 'enlightened' views of reason with the more spiritualized ones of the Cambridge Platonists, who somewhat resemble Wesley at this point (above, pp. 24f.).

17. *JWL*, V, p. 41; cf. *Thoughts on Christian Perfection* (1759), at the end of *Plain Account*.

18. Dreyer, 'Faith and Experience' (n. 6), p. 15, quoting *JWJ*, I, p. 476; *JWL (B)*, II, pp. 181f.

19. *JWL*, III, p. 105.

20. See above, p. 30.

21. *JWJ*, V, pp. 266, 311; *Works*, XIII, p. 463; cf. R.M. Burns, *The Great Debate on Miracles*, Associated Universities Press 1981.

22. *JWL (B)*, I, p. 251 and n.; *JWJ*, IV, p. 192; cf. Dreyer, 'Faith and Experience' (n. 6), and Brantley, *Locke, Wesley* (n. 6).

23. P. Browne, *Procedure, Extent and Limits of Human Understanding*, London ²1729, pp. 141f. Cf. William Law in his *Case of Reason*; and for the use of analogy in this period, D. Cupitt, 'Analogy in the Age of Locke', *Journal of Theological Studies*, NS XIX, 1968, pp. 186–202.

24. *Works*, V, pp. 135f.; Dreyer, 'Faith and Experience' (n. 6), pp. 26f.

25. See Brantley, *Locke, Wesley* (n. 6) and my criticism (n. 6).

26. Locke, *Human Understanding*, IV.ix.5; Browne, *Procedure* (n. 23), II, 7–9.

27. *JWJ*, V, pp. 265ff.; *JWL (B)*, II, p. 364; cf. *AM*, 1790, pp. 607f., on the 'magic art'; *JWJ*, VI, p. 24, for the only case of him encountering possible witchcraft.

28. E.g. *JWL*, IV, p. 108.

29. *JWL (B)*, I, p. 176; II, pp. 498f.; Sermon CXXVIII, in *Works*, VII, pp. 373–86; see Whitefield's reply in *Journals*, Appendix, pp. 564–88.

30. In *Works*, X. For the Watts element see above, p. 346 and n. 23.

31. For the possible influence of William Tilly see *PWHS* XXXV, 1960, pp. 137–41; cf. *JWL (B)*, I, p. 438 but Rupp, p. 348, doubts its importance.

32. Sermon XLIII, para. I,2; Sermon LXXXV, para. II,1, in *Works*, VI; Sermon CV, paras I, 4–5, in *Works*, VII; Williams, *Wesley's Theology* (n. 5), pp. 41–6.

33. T.P. Bunting, *Life of Jabez Bunting*, London 1887, p. 742.

34. Sermon, LXXXV, para. II, 1, in *Works*, VII.

35. Letter to Church (1746), in *JWL*, II, p. 268.

36. As in Sermon V, para.III, 5; IV, 3; Outler, pp. 126ff.

37. Sermon I, para. II, 5; IV, 4, 5; II, 1.

38. On 'sincerity' cf. Rack, 'Hoadly versus Law', pp. 283, 291; Rupp, pp. 97f.

39. *JWJ*, V, pp. 243f. (published 1771).

40. *Minutes* 1770, in *Minutes*, I, p. 96; *Works*, VIII, pp. 337f.

41. *Works*, XI, pp. 488f.

42. See below, pp. 459f.

43. C.F. Allison, *The Rise of Moralism*, SPCK 1966.

44. *JWL*, V, p. 83; VI, pp. 326f.; cf. the Preface by Wesley to *Whole Duty*, in *Works*, XIV, p. 231.

45. *JWL*, II, p. 75.

46. *JWL (B)*, I, pp. 169f., 174f.; *JWJ*, I, pp. 424; cf. Williams, *Wesley's Theology* (n. 5), p. 103. On faith he drew on the definition of Richard Fiddes, whose view was similar to Locke's.

47. MS *Minutes*, 1744; Sermons X, XI, in *Works*, V.

48. Southey, *Wesley* (Fitzgerald ed., p. 641 n. 6), I, p. 210. *JWL*, V, pp. 358f.; *AM*, 1786, pp. 52ff.

49. See Rupp, pp. 419–21, for examples.

50. Sermon XLV, para. II, 5, in *Works*, VI.

51. Sermon I, para. II, 7, in *Works*, V; cf. Lindstrom, *Wesley and Sanctification* (n. 5), pp. 83ff.

52. Sermon V, para II, 1, in *Works*, V.

53. Sermon XIX, Introduction 2, in *Works*, V; Sermon XLV, para. IV, 3, in *Works*, VI.

54. Quoted in Tyerman, I, p. 330.

55. *A Treatise on Baptism* in *Works*, X; cf. Williams, *Wesley's Theology* (n. 5), p. 117.

56. *JWL*, III, p. 36.

57. See, e.g., John Lewis in *JWL (B)*, II, p. 265.

58. Sermon XLV, paras. IV, 1–2, 4, in *Works*, VI.

59. A.R. George, in *HMCGB*, I, pp. 268f. and refs.

60. Sermon I, paras. III, 1, 2; II. 7, 6 in *Works*, V.

61. Criticism in Outler, p. 304; but cf. *JWL*, III, p. 212; V, pp. 315, 333; VI, p. 116 ('properly so called') for Wesley using it.

62. Sermon XVII, para. I, 7, in *Works*, V.

63. Rupp, p. 422, notes all these elements but the last.

64. Tyerman, I, pp. 202f.; cf. also Williams, *Wesley's Theology* (n. 5), pp. 115 and n., 170; Sugden (ed.), *Sermons of John Wesley*, I, p. 446; II, p. 44.

65. *JWJ*, II, pp. 47–9; *Plain Account*, para. 8, in *Works*, XI.

66. See above, p. 206.

67. So, for example, in Sermons XIX, XIII, in *Works*, V.

68. MS *Minutes*, 1744–7, passim; *Works*, VIII.

69. *Plain Account*, para. 12; Sermon XLV, in *Works*, VI.

70. See above, p. 335, for the few early examples.

71. *Minutes* 1745, 1747, in *Works* VIII; though he claimed texts to support the doctrine.

72. *Thoughts upon Christian Perfection* (1759), in *Plain Account*, para. 19.

73. F. E. Stoeffler, *Continental Pietism and Early American Christianity*, Eerdmans 1976, pp. 195f., takes a similar view; pp. 184–96 is a good discussion of the 'Catholic' elements in Wesley's theology. See also *HMCGB* I, pp. 81–112.

74. See below, pp. 427ff., for examples.

75. *Plain Account*, paras. 19, 25, questions 9–11, in *Works*, XI, pp. 394ff., 417f.

76. *JWL (B)*, I, pp. 289, 318; Williams, *Wesley's Theology* (n. 5), p. 170; and MS *Minutes*, 1758.

77. *JWL*, VIII, p. 238.

78. For this history see J.L. Peters, *Christian Perfection in American Methodism*, Abingdon Press 1956; J. Kent, *Holding the Fort*, Epworth Press 1978, ch. VIII.

79. Cell, *Rediscovery* (n. 5), p. 361.

80. Peters, *Christian Perfection* (n. 78), p. 21.

81. Williams, *Wesley's Theology* (n. 5), pp. 174–6; he quotes E.G. Rupp, *Principalities and Powers*, Epworth Press 1952, p. 82.

82. See, for example, R. Hill, below, p. 458.

83. Caution in accepting Wesley's valuations of his Catholic borrowings is well expressed by J. Kent in *The Unacceptable Face*, SCM Press 1987, pp. 223f.

84. Cf. B.B. Warfield, *Perfectionism* (abridged edition by S.G. Craig), Presbyterian and Reformed Publishing Co., Philadelphia 1958, pp. 251f. and n.

85. Cf. J. Orcibal in *HMCGB*, I, pp. 81–113; J. McManners, *Death and the Enlightenment*, Oxford University Press 1981, pp. 211–16, for examples of this. For Wesley's early doubts about it see *JWL (B)*, I, pp. 168, 174; *JWJ*, II, pp. 494, 498f.; to Lavington in *JWL*, III, p. 304; to Robertson *JWL (B)*, II, pp. 517f.

86. *JWL (B)*, I, pp. 168, 174.

87. One of Mme Guyon's translators makes the same distinction between two kinds of perfection as those asserted by Williams for Wesley and sees Mme Guyon as approximating to the same view: Dugald Macfadyen (ed.), *A Method of Prayer*, Clarke, London 1902, pp. 202, 206. But the phrase 'pure love', used also by Wesley, does not refer to a love for God for himself alone, regardless of one's own salvation: see the passages in n. 85 above. Contrast a Methodist letter in Tyerman, II, p. 419 with Wesley's warnings in *JWL*, V, pp. 341, 342; VI, pp. 39, 43, 44, 125, 233, to correspondents attracted by Quietist 'pure love'.

88. Cf. J. Kent in H. Cunliffe-Jones (ed.), *History of Christian Doctrine*, T. & T. Clark 1978 p. 477, on the 'simple way'.

89. See below, p. 550.

90. Cf. above, pp. 250, 293, and Snyder, *Radical Wesley* (n. 5).

91. For Wesley on the sacraments generally see J.R. Parris, *John Wesley's Doctrine of the Sacraments*, Epworth Press 1963; I have not seen O. Borgen, *John Wesley on the Sacraments*, Zurich 1972. On baptism, see B.G. Holland, *Baptism in Early Methodism*, Epworth Press 1970. On the Lord's Supper see J.E. Rattenbury, *The Eucharistic Hymns of John and Charles Wesley*, Epworth Press 1948, which reprints their collection, and Wesley's abridgement of Brevint; J.C. Bowmer, *The Lord's Supper in Early Methodism*, Dacre Press 1951; and for Anglican doctrine in this period C.W. Dugmore, *Eucharistic Doctrine from Hooker to Waterland*, SPCK 1942; for practice see above, pp. 19ff. I hope to write further on this elsewhere.

92. For this see J. Wickham Legg, *English Church Life from the Restoration to the Tractarian Movement*, Longmans 1914, chs. II and III.

93. See below, pp. 417ff.

94. See above, pp. 20f., for Tillotson and Hoadly.

95. For seventeenth-century examples see P.E. More and F.L. Cross, *Anglicanism*, SPCK 1935, 1967, ch. XIII, 2, 3.

96. See Dugmore, *Eucharistic Doctrine* (n. 91), and R.T. Holtby, *Daniel Waterland*, Holtby 1966.

97. For the hymns and Brevint see the reprint in Rattenbury, *Eucharistic Hymns* (n. 91).

98. Brevint, VI in Rattenbury, *Eucharistic Hymns* (n. 91), p. 187.

99. This and the following quotations are from *Hymns for the Lord's Supper*, nos. lvii, lxxi, cxvi, lxxii, cxxxvii.

100. Bowmer, *Lord's Supper* (n. 91), p. 86; Rattenbury, *Eucharistic Hymns* (n. 91), p. 183.

101. *JWJ*, I, p. 419; *JWL*, III, p. 326; Bowmer, *Lord's Supper* (n. 91), pp. 26f., 92.

102. Luther, as quoted in Waterland, *Review of the Doctrine of the Eucharist* (1737), Clarendon Press 1868, p. 225 n.; Calvin, *Institutes*, IV, xvii, 33, as quoted in B.A. Gerrish, *The Old Protestantism and the New*, T. & T. Clark 1982, p. 112; cf. Waterland, *Review* (n. 102), p. 244.

103. Waterland, *Review* (n. 102), ch. IX; Wesley, Sermon CI, para. I, 2, in *Works*, VII.

104. G.S. Wakefield, *Puritan Devotion*, Epworth Press 1957, p. 39.

105. Prynne, quoted in W.M. Lamont, 'Episcopacy and Godly Discipline 1641–6', *JEH* X, 1959, p. 88; Humfrey in W.W. Biggs, *Transactions of the Congregationalist Historical Society* XVI, 1949–51, pp. 178–89.

106. P. Miller, *Errand into the Wilderness*, Harvard University Press 1956, pp. 159f.; R. Middlekauff, *The Mathers*, Oxford University Press 1971, pp. 126–9.

107. Zinzendorf to Wesley in 1736; *JWL (B)*, I, pp. 481, 482.

108. *JWJ*, II, p. 109.

109. So Curnock, referring also to remarks in November 1739: *JWJ*, II, pp. 207, 315. For Susanna Wesley's alleged criticisms of John's new way and her acceptance of it, see above, p. 212 n. 111.

110. For Harris see B. Latrobe, *Brief Account of . . . Howel Harris*, 1791, pp. 10ff.; for Simpson, Tyerman, III, p. 165; for baptismal conversion cases *JWJ*, III, p. 135; *CWJ*, I, p. 358.

111. *JWJ*, II, pp. 361f.

112. See further below, pp. 417ff.

113. See above, p. 337.

114. Watts, pp. 433f.

115. *EMP*, I, p. 151; IV, p. 147, 167; for Mitchell, *EMP*, I, p. 257.

116. *EMP*, II, p. 87, 250, 259.

117. Ibid., II, pp. 317f. It is perhaps significant that though he describes receiving perfection, he also says he lost it after three weeks and does not mention it later, ibid., pp. 303f.

118. Alexander Knox in Southey, *John Wesley* (ed. Fitzgerald), Oxford University Press 1925, II, p. 339.

119. Outler, pp. vii, 119.

120. For the licensing problem see below, pp. 497f. For early Methodist chapel architecture see G. Dolbey, *The Architectural Expression of Methodism*, Epworth Press 1964. For worship see John Bishop, *Methodist Worship in Relation to Free Church Worship*, Epworth Press 1964; Church, *MA*, ch. VI.

121. *Works*, VIII, p. 332. For separate Anglican seating at least in Charles I's reign: R.V.H. Burne, *Chester Cathedral*, SPCK 1958, p. 104.

122. See below, p. 494.

123. *JWL*, II, p. 302. On the lovefeast, see F. Baker, *Methodism and the Lovefeast*, Epworth Press 1957; and for the Moravian source C.W. Towlson, *Moravian and Methodist*, Epworth Press 1957, pp. 209–16.

124. *JWL*, II, p. 302.
125. *JWL*, III, p. 33; *JWJ*, IV, p. 361, 439, 480; V, p. 379.
126. *JWL*, VI, p. 265.
127. *JWL*, V, p. 55.
128. *JWJ*, II, pp. 121–3.
129. J. Nightingale, *Portraiture of Methodism*, London 1807, pp. 201ff.
130. Walsh, 'Religious Societies', pp. 288f.
131. Towlson, *Moravian and Methodist* (n. 123), pp. 216–20, leans to a Moravian origin. He rightly dismisses Overton's hopeful claim that like the class meeting it was simply derived from early church practice (though no doubt this confirmed Wesley's desire to adopt it): J.H. Overton, *John Wesley*, London 1891, p. 30.
132. *JWL*, III, p. 287.
133. Towlson, *Moravian and Methodist* (n. 123), pp. 216f. interprets it as connected with the excitable lovefeast in Fetter Lane on 31 December–1 January 1738–9. If correct, this would explain the late hour.
134. *JWL*, II, p. 299.
135. *JWL*, II, pp. 534ff. The first in London was 9 April 1742 (*JWJ*, II, p. 136).
136. Nightingale, *Portraiture* (n. 129), pp. 214ff.
137. *JWJ*, II, p. 412.
138. F. Hunter in *London Quarterly*, 1939, pp. 78–87; *PWHS* XXII, 1940, pp. 126–31; Baker in *London Quarterly*, 1955, pp. 215–20; D. Tripp, *The Renewal of the Covenant in the Methodist Tradition*, Epworth Press 1969.
139. See e.g. Perry Miller, *Errand into the Wilderness*, Harvard University Press 1956.
140. Rupp, p. 292, notes the case of Horneck, one of the founders of the Religious Societies.
141. Baker, *William Grimshaw*, Epworth Press 1963, ch. V; Church, *MA*, pp. 274–7.
142. *JWJ*, III, pp. 328, 361.
143. That 1748 was not the beginning of the Methodist Covenant Service has been generally accepted (Tripp, *Renewal* [n. 138], p. 12), but the problem might be resolved by supposing that Wesley in 1748 was recommending individual covenants and in 1755 a collective one.
144. Monk, *John Wesley and his Puritan Heritage*, p. 105 and n.
145. *JWJ*, IV, pp. 126, 200.
146. A.G. Matthews (ed.), *Calamy Revised*, Clarendon Press 1934, pp. 6f. for the Alleines.
147. For the latest critical edition see *Works*, BE, Vol. VII, ed. Hildebrandt and Beckerlegge; unfortunately not compared with other eighteenth-century books.
148. The *Olney Hymns* (1779) contains some curious pieces, allegorizing various natural phenomena in the manner of seventeenth century 'emblem' poems. For Woodd's collection see C.B. Phillips, *Hymnody Past and Present*, SPCK 1937, p. 193.
149. I have used the facsimile edition by B.F. Spinney (n.d.).
150. Information partly from N.F. Adams, *Musical Sources for John Wesley's Hymns Books*, Union Theological Seminary New York thesis 1980 (copy in

MCA). For other examples see T.B. Shepherd, *Methodism and the Literature of the Eighteenth Century*, Epworth Press 1940, p. 236; F.C. Gill, *Charles Wesley. The First Methodist*, Epworth Press 1964, pp. 210f. The use of popular tunes in religious movements like Methodism is common throughout history.

151. *Works*, XIII, pp. 470–3.

152. *JWL*, IV, pp. 311f.; *JWJ*, VI, p. 312.

153. *Works*, VIII, pp. 318f.

154. P. Scholes, *Oxford Companion to Music*, Oxford University Press [8]1950, p. 412.

155. Tyerman, II, pp. 575f.; *Works*, VIII, pp. 321f.

156. *JWL*, III, p. 226; Baker, *JW*, p. 173, says that the reference is to use of the Anglican liturgy – undoubtedly this is correct.

157. See below, p. 510, for his adaptation of the 'Sunday Service' for America.

158. *CWJ*, I, pp. 243, 245.

159. A.R. George in *HMCGB*, I, pp. 264ff.; Baker, *JW*, pp. 213f. and n. 51.

160. See above, p. 403.

161. See above, pp. 19f.

162. Bowmer, *Lord's Supper* (n. 91), pp. 115ff.

163. Ibid., pp. 51–6; cf. L.G. Wickham Legg, *English Church Life from the Restoration to the Tractarian Movement*, Longman 1914, pp. 21–35, for Nonjurors and others.

164. *JWL*, III, p. 186; cf. 'Ought We to Separate?' in Baker, *JW*, p. 332.

165. *EMP*, IV, p. 176; V, p. 144; VI, pp. 138f. (all before conversion); III, p. 303 (informal eucharist with John Fletcher); IV, p. 27, 56, 60f. (Methodist ones).

166. R.B. Walker, 'Religious Changes in Cheshire', *JEH*, XVII, 1966, p. 82.

167. D. McClatchey, *Oxfordshire Clergy 1777–1869*, Oxford University Press 1960, p. 86.

168. For example 1,600 at Manchester in 1790: *JWJ*, VIII, p. 57.

169. Baker, *Grimshaw* (n. 141), pp. 183f.

170. *JWL*, IV, p. 271; *JWJ*, IV, p. 407; Bowmer, *Lord's Supper* (n. 91), pp. 73f.; *CWJ*, II, p. 137.

171. 'Ought We to Separate?', in Baker, *JW*, pp. 328, 334.

172. Recognized by John Lawson in *HMCGB* I, p. 208 n. 193, as against Bowmer, *Lord's Supper* (n. 91), p. 188, cf. pp. 193ff.

173. A. Härdelin, *Tractarian Understanding of the Eucharist*, Studia Historico-Ecclesiastica Upsaliensia VIII, Uppsala 1965, pp. 268–80.

174. Church, *MA*, pp. 268–85.

175. See above, p. 268.

176. I owe this illustration to Mr Darrian Gay.

177. I. Rivers, 'Dissenting and Methodist Books of Practical Divinity', in id. (ed.), *Books and Their Readers in Eighteenth Century England*, Leicester University Press 1982, pp. 127–64.

178. See above, p. 345.

179. *EMP*, II, p. 62; V, p. 82.

180. *JWJ*, III, p. 374.

181. For samples of lives of travelling preachers see T. Jackson (ed.), *The Lives of the Early Methodist Preachers*, six volumes, London [4]1872; another version

is edited by J. Telford as *Wesley's Veterans*, seven volumes, London 1912. The only collective study of the rank and file is by L. Church, *The Early Methodist People*, Epworth Press 1948, and *More About the Early Methodist People*, Epworth Press 1949.

182. For discussion of these developments see P. Delany, *British Autobiography in the Seventeenth Century*, Routledge 1969; D. Ebner, *Autobiography in Seventeenth-Century England: Theology and the Self*, Mouton 1971. For the eighteenth century see D.A. Stauffer, *The Art of Biography in Eighteenth-Century England*, two volumes, Princeton University Press 1941. Professor Ward places Wesley's *Journal* in a European context in his introduction to volume I of BE *Journal*.

183. For the conversion tradition and literature see above, pp. 147f.

184. H. Walker, *Spiritual Experiences of Sundry Believers* (1652), and John Rogers, *Ohel or Beth-Shemesh. A Tabernacle for the Sun* (1653). I have only been able to examine Rogers's book. For a discussion and analysis, see Watts, pp. 174–9.

185. For Haime, see *EMP*, III, p. 211; Taylor, *EMP*, III, pp. 373, 375; Pawson, *EMP*, IV, p. 8.

186. *EMP*, II, p. 113; IV, p. 177.

187. I. Rivers, "'Strangers and Pilgrims': Sources and Patterns of Methodist Narrative', in *Augustan Worlds*, ed. J.C. Hilson et al., Leicester University Press 1978, pp. 189–203.

188. W. Haller, *The Rise of Puritanism*, Columbia University Press 1938, ch. IV; O.C. Watkins, *The Puritan Experience*, Routledge 1971.

189. *The Life of Silas Told by Himself* (1786) reprinted Epworth Press 1954.

190. For the bowdlerizing of Fox's *Journal* see J.L. Nickalls (ed.), *Journal of George Fox*, Cambridge University Press 1954, Preface. For Everett and Hick and the reviewers see J. Everett, *The Village Blacksmith*, [11]1848, pp. 176ff., 187 n.

191. There is an example from the Told edition in Rivers, "Strangers and Pilgrims" (n. 187), pp. 200 and 203 n.

192. *EMP*, II, pp. 111–17; V, pp. 297f.; *AM*, 1783, p. 468.

193. *EMP*, VI, p. 203.

194. *EMP*, IV, p. 110. For examples of religious upbringing see *EMP*, IV, p. 1; V, p. 108; II, pp. 158, 277; VI, p. 249.

195. *EMP*, III, pp. 50f.; IV, p. 116; *AM*, 1779, p. 296 and passim; Tyerman, II, p. 285.

196. *JWL (B)*, II, pp. 262f.

197. But John Haydon, one of the most spectacular, was a pious man, cf. *JWL (B)*, I, pp. 646f.; *JWJ*, II, pp. 180, 189. Watts, pp. 417f., 427, on the basis of *EMP*, emphasizes that very few had a really bad moral background, but though this would also be true of the known rank and file, he fails to note the élite character of these lives.

198. *AM*, 1778, pp. 277, 517; *AM*, 1779, p. 633.

199. *EMP*, IV, p. 277 and see above, pp. 27f.

200. *EMP*, IV, pp. 274–86.

201. *EMP*, V, p. 252; II, p. 299. There were several other examples of this.

202. *EMP*, V, pp. 218–33; IV, pp. 242–7; VI, pp. 34, 36, 46, 48, 51, 52.

203. *EMP*, III, pp. 59f., 63f.; II, p. 299; cf. *AM*, 1778, p. 228 for another case.

204. Cf. Alexander Mather in *EMP*, IV, pp. 167, 224.

205. *MCA* Colman Collection and printed in S. Dimond, *The Psychology of the Methodist Revival*, Oxford University Press 1926, pp. 167, 172, 175ff.

206. *EMP*, II, pp. 246–9.

207. *AM*, 1781, p. 282. Mrs Ruth Hall also had assurance simultaneously with the gift of faith, ibid., p. 497.

208. Tyerman, II, pp. 419–21.

209. *AM*, 1779, p. 306; 1781, p. 336.

210. *JWJ*, IV, pp. 367f. Others in *EMP*, I, p. 151; II, pp. 83, 102, 313; IV, p. 142 and many others in *AM*. For a case shortly before death in the 1760s see William Smith of Norwich who found that 'The Lord filled his soul with love . . . He had stamped His image on his heart': Thomas Mitchell to John Wesley in MCA, Wesley Family Letters, II, pp. 70ff.

211. Mrs Bathsheba Hall to John Wesley in *AM*, 1781, pp. 197f. For the Fletcher story see D. King and C. Ryskamp (eds.), *Letters and Prose Writings of William Cowper*, Oxford University Press 1979, I, pp. 565f. This was by no means unique, but Fletcher may have had more influence than Wesley on the nineteenth-century models of perfectionism.

212. Watts, pp. 433f.

213. *EMP*, IV, pp. 23f., 89f.

214. See my 'Evangelical Endings', *BJRL* LXXIV (I), 1992.

215. J.B. Williams (ed.), *Life of Matthew Henry*, London 1828, p. 164; and preface to *Life of Philip Henry*, pp. xxxviff. (Both reprinted by Banner of Truth Trust 1974.)

216. J. Bull, *John Newton*, Religious Tract Society 1868, p. 358.

217. Catholics and Protestants were equally dubious about death-bed conversions: J. McManners, *Death and the Enlightenment*, Oxford University Press 1981, pp. 191ff. For Methodist Arminians they were logical enough.

218. *The Experience and Spiritual Letters of Mrs H.A. Rogers*, London 1835, pp. 164–6, 203. For an unhappy and controversial case of a Methodist saint with doubts at the end see Thomas Walsh in *EMP*, III, pp. 278–85.

219. *Diary* of Samuel Bardsley in MCA, passim.

220. G. Marsden, 'Memoir of Mr George Lomas', *WMM*, 1811, pp. 481–91.

221. Extracts from diary of John Marsden in A. Ponsonby (ed.), *More English Diaries*, London 1927, pp. 140–6 (this diary now appears to be lost).

222. For this see Church, *EM*, ch. VI and above, p. 56. For Methodist education see Church, *EM*, pp. 256ff.; *MA*, pp. 186f, and above, pp. 353ff.

223. For women preachers see above, p. 244.

224. For this point see D. Hempton, *Methodism and Politics in British Society*, Longmans 1984, pp. 13f.; for the role and significance of women in Methodism later see D.M. Valenze, *Prophetic Sons and Daughters*, Princeton University Press 1985.

225. E.P. Thompson, *The Making of the English Working Class*, Penguin Books 1968, pp. 401–9; Walsh, 'Halévy', p. 5, notes sexual anxiety as a factor in conversion.

226. Some illuminating material showing that Wesley's penchant for celibacy was not shared by many early Methodists and balancing Thompson's rather extreme reading can be found in H. Abelove, 'The Sexual Politics of Early Wesleyan Methodism', in *Disciplines of Faith*, ed. J. Obelkevich et al., Routledge 1987, pp. 86–98.

227. See above, pp. 23f. For the controversial but fashionable subject of 'popular culture' see P. Burke, *Popular Culture in Early Modern Europe*, Temple Smith 1978, Part III for changes in this period. For Methodism, see J. Rule, 'Methodism, Popular Beliefs and Village Culture in Cornwall 1800–50', in *Popular Culture and Custom in Nineteenth Century England*, ed. R.D. Storch, Croom Helm 1982, pp. 48–70; there is a more positive valuation of the Methodist influence in D.H. Luker, *Cornish Methodism, Revivalism and Popular Belief c.1780–1870*, Oxford DPhil 1988.

228. J. Obelkevich, *Religion and Rural Society*, Clarendon Press 1976, ch. VI.

229. *JWL*, VI, pp. 81f.

230. *EMP*, II, pp. 60, 27, 4.

231. Cf. the slighting attitude of Outler in M.D. Meeks (ed.), *The Future of the Methodist Traditions*, Abingdon Press 1985, p. 36 (the *Arminian Magazine* as 'that marvellous montage of jewels and junk').

232. *AM*, 1782, p. 581.

233. *EMP*, II, pp. 304f., 159f.

234. *JWJ*, VI, p. 158; V, p. 275; VI, p. 282; Everett, *Village Blacksmith* (n. 189), pp. 177ff.

235. *Life of John Morris* in *AM*, 1795, pp. 181f.; for the Lisbon earthquake and its effects see T.C. Kendrick, *The Lisbon Earthquake*, Methuen 1956; *CWJ*, II, pp. 69f.; T. Percival, *Works* IV, London 1807, pp. 416ff.

236. Cf. e.g. *EMP*, II, p. 317; III, pp. 195, 233 n.

237. John Valton, in *EMP*, VI, pp. 40, 88f.; Valton MS *Diary* in MCA for 30 January 1788; 2 May 1788; 17, 18 and 30 June 1788. See Rack, 'Doctors', pp. 149f. for a demoniac, and for the Evangelical Hannah More's disgust: W.S. Lewis (ed.), *Letters of Horace Walpole* XXXI, Yale University Press 1973, pp. 279ff., 335 – 'Poor reason, when wilt thou come to years of discretion.'

238. *JWJ*, IV, p. 187; VI, p. 334.

239. Hempton, *Methodism and Politics* (n. 224), p. 29.

240. *AM*, 1784, pp. 101, 160; Sermon LXXI, LXII, in *Works*, VI, 361f;, 370ff.; Tyerman, III, p. 306.

241. *EMP*, II, p. 76; IV, p. 122; V, p. 11, and several others.

242. For a full discussion see my 'Early Methodist Visions of the Trinity', *PWHS* XLVI, 1987, pp. 38–44, 57–69.

243. For this see K. Thomas, *Religion and the Decline of Magic*, Penguin Books 1973. For the attraction of a healing type of ministry in various periods and contexts see *The Church and Healing*, SCH XIX, 1982. The warning not to distinguish 'magic' from 'religion' too sharply is well made by R.L. Fox, *Pagans and Christians*, Penguin Books 1988, pp. 36–8.

244. J.T. Barker (ed.), *Life of Joseph Barker*, London 1880, pp. 3, 19–22; Rule in Storch, *Popular Culture* (n. 227), pp. 65ff.

245. Ibid.

246. Luker, *Cornish Methodism* (n. 227).

247. J. H. Plumb, *England in the Eighteenth Century*, Penguin Books 1950, pp. 95f.

248. Baker, *CW*, pp. 119f.; Bennet, *Letter Book*, to N. Haughton, 4 July 1752, p. 107.

249. See M. Macdonald, 'Religion, Social Change and Psychological Healing', in *SCH* XIX, 1982, pp. 101–26. But although such cases as self-mutilation

have been documented in sectarian religion and elsewhere, one must be wary of fantasies by enemies: see A. Warne, *Church and Society in Eighteenth-Century Devon*, David and Charles 1969, p. 117.

250. Green, *YMW*, p. 102.

251. See above, pp. 213, 236f., for early figures; Walsh, 'Halévy', p. 11f.; *CWJ*, II, p. 129 (1756).

252. *Minutes* 1767, 1791; Hall, *Circuits and Ministers*, revised edition, London (nd), p. 607; R. Currie et al. (eds.), *Churches and Churchgoers*, Clarendon Press 1977, p. 139.

253. Ibid., p. 39.

254. These figures (for England and Wales only) are calculated from population estimates and the 1801 census in B. Mitchell and P. Deane, *British Historical Statistics*, Cambridge University Press 1962, pp. 5, 6; the Methodist figures from Currie, *Churches and Churchgoers* (n. 252) pp. 139f., including all the Methodist bodies for the later years.

255. Membership figure only from 1799.

256. A Salford example might suggest 2:1. See Charles Atmore's *Journal* (MCA), 22 December 1826, 7 April 1817, recording communicants and attenders (*Journal of the Lancashire and Cheshire Historical Society* 8, 1968, pp. 132f.); J.C.C. Probert, *Sociology of Cornish Methodism*, Redruth nd, p. 5, says 3:1; for the later nineteenth century A.D. Gilbert, 'Methodism and Political Stability', *JRH* X, 1978–9, p. 394, says 3:1.

257. M. Edwards, *After Wesley*, Epworth Press 1935, pp. 142f.

258. R. Currie, 'A Micro-Theory of Methodist Growth', *PWHS* XXXVI, 1967, p. 67.

259. Ibid., pp. 68f.

260. Watts, ch. IV.2, pp. 267–89 and Appendix.

261. A. Everitt, 'Nonconformity in Country Parishes', *Land, Church and People*, ed. J. Thirsk, *Agricultural History Review*, Supplement xviii, 1970, pp. 178–99, emphasizes the substantial rural membership of Dissent, but in a largely rural society the high urban proportion is all the more striking. M. Spufford, *Contrasting Communities*, Cambridge University Press 1974, pp. 298–318, casts doubt on theories by Everitt and others that Dissent (and Methodism has been seen similarly) is especially associated with particular types of landholding and ownership.

262. See above, pp. 315f.

263. Tyerman, I, p. 236.

264. C. Field, 'The Social Structure of English Methodism in the Eighteenth to Twentieth Centuries', *British Journal of Sociology* XXVIII, 1977, pp. 199–202, 213, 216 for the eighteenth century. I am indebted to Dr Field for allowing me to use these figures; he wishes to make it clear that he would now refine the categories and add further material. However, this version is adequate for the general points made here.

265. See above, pp. 318, 319, for Lincolnshire and Cheshire.

266. Field, 'Social Structure' (n. 264), p. 213; Church, *MA*, pp. 105–31; W.J. Warner, *The Wesleyan Movement in the Industrial Revolution*, Longmans 1930, p. 259.

267. Church, EM, pp. 2–4. For the 'Methodist squire', ibid., pp. 117–25; the Manchester Circuit membership list for Congleton is in MCA.

268. Warner, *Wesleyan Movement* (n. 266), ch. VIII.

269. See above, pp. 176, 424.

270. Everett, *Village Blacksmith* (n. 190), pp. 96ff.; *EMP*, II, p. 166.

271. *Works*, VIII, pp. 269–71.

272. Ibid., p. 263, cf. 295f.

273. MS *Minutes*, 1744; 1745; *EMP*, IV, pp. 140f.

274. *AM*, 1778, pp. 273–7; *JWL (B)*, II, pp. 116–18; Church, *EM*, ch. V.

275. Sermon L, 'The Use of Money', *Works*, VI; *Works*, XI, p. 477; Church, *EM*, pp. 196ff.

276. See B. Harrison, *Drink and the Victorians*, Faber 1971, for the full story.

277. Hampson, III, p. 184.

278. *JWL (B)*, II, pp. 208, 267; *JWJ*, III, pp. 245f.; *JWL*, VIII, pp. 165–8; *Works*, X, p. 393.

279. *JWJ*, II, pp. 322f.; J. Priestley, 'Address to the Methodists', in *Original Letters*, pp. xvii, xix, xxii; see above, pp. 365ff., for Wesley's economics.

280. J. Kent, *Holding the Fort*, Epworth Press 1978, pp. 15, 30, 36f.

281. R.W. Malcolmson, 'A Set of Ungovernable People', in *An Ungovernable People: The English and the Law in the Eighteenth Century*, ed. J. Brewer and J. Styles, Hutchinson 1980, pp. 85–127; *JWJ*, II, p. 322.

282. *JWJ*, VI, p. 123. 'Wrecking' here means collecting the spoil of wrecks rather than the sinister legends of luring ships on to the rocks.

283. *JWJ*, IV, p. 220; *EMP*, III, p. 298; VI, pp. 267f.; *Memoir of Richard Trewanna*, pp. 56–64, quoted in Church, *EM*, p. 194, with other examples.

284. *EMP*, IV, pp. 186–8; J. Rule on wrecking in D. Hay et al., *Albion's Fatal Tree*, Penguin Books 1977, p. 185.

285. *JWJ*, VII, p. 305; *Wesley Banner*, 1850, p. 114, quoted in Tyerman, III, p. 499.

286. *Lancashire and Cheshire Wesley Historical Society Journal*, II (3), 1971, p. 56; Everett Scrapbook in MCA, p. 453; cf. also *JWJ*, V, p. 452; VII, p. 303, for a Manchester hatter who turned 'worldly' and left Methodism.

287. For Dissenters and industry see above, p. 36; advice to Methodists in *Rules of the United Societies*, para. 5, *Works*, VIII, p. 271.

288. D. Rosman, *Evangelicals and Culture*, Croom Helm 1984, passim; H.D. Rack, 'Wesleyanism and the World', *PWHS* XLII, 1979, pp. 3ff. For the relaxation of Dissenting rigour see examples in G.W. Pilcher (ed.), *The Revd. Samuel Davies Abroad*, University of Illinois Press 1967, pp. 38f., 102, 106, 110.

289. Sermon LXXXIX, 'The More Excellent Way', para. V.2–5, in *Works*, VII; *EMP*, VI, pp. 235f.

290. *JWL*, VII, pp. 227f.; Minutes, I, p. 256; A. Clarke in *AM*, 1792, pp. 264–72.

291. Jeremy Collier, *A Short View of the Profaneness and Immorality of the English Stage* (1698). For Methodists and the theatre see *PWHS* XX, XXI, 1942, 1943; see M.G. Jones, *Hannah More*, Cambridge University Press 1952, pp. 191ff., 232ff. for her 'Coelebs'. Dr Johnson was shocked that Hannah had read *Tom Jones*, ibid., p. 52.

292. *JWL* VII, pp. 227f. For Brooke's novel see above, p. 353.

293. H.B. Workman et al. (eds.), *New History of Methodism*, London 1909, p. 32; F.L. Wiseman, *Charles Wesley*, Epworth Press 1933, pp. 187ff.; cf. *JWJ*, V,

p. 368; VI, p. 361 for Wesley's own reactions (and for his taste see above, pp. 352f.).

294. *EMP* II, pp. 192f.

295. Above, p. 425.

296. John Bennet at a festival in the Cotswolds reminded the revellers of sin, *Diary*, 2 January 1748; for the parson's toe, ibid., 29 May 1752; James Wood, *Address to the Members of the Methodist Societies*, 1799; John Wesley, *Advice to the People Called Methodists*, in *Works*, VIII, p. 354.

297. For examples see Church, *MA*, ch. V; S. Andrews, *Methodism and Society*, Longmans 1970, pp. 49–53; E.M. North, *Early Methodist Philanthropy*, New York 1947; J.W. Bready, *England Before and After Wesley*, Hodder and Stoughton 1938, grossly exaggerates the Methodist and even the Evangelical contribution to social reform.

298. See above, pp. 361f., for Wesley's part in all this.

299. Andrews, *Methodism and Society* (n. 297), p. 49.

300. For the Evangelical societies see the list in F.K. Brown, *Fathers of the Victorians*, Cambridge University Press 1961, pp. 329–40, but note that he exaggerates the number they founded or infiltrated.

301. *JWJ*, II, pp. 453f.; III, pp. 117, 122, 125; Tyerman, I, p. 357; Church, *MA*, pp. 180f.; Andrews, *Methodism and Society* (n. 297), p. 50. For the pensions and restrictions due to trade depression see Manchester and Circuit Minutes 20 February 1806 in Manch. CLA.

302. Rack, 'Doctors', p. 146.

303. Church, *MA*, pp. 182ff.

304. G.J. Stevenson, *City Road Chapel*, London 1873, p. 547; *Methodism in Halifax*, quoted in Church, *MA*, p. 190.

305. *PWHS* XX, 1935–6, pp. 98–100; Tyerman, III, p. 134.

306. For Bristol see Church, *MA*, pp. 194f. quoting *Life of Elizabeth Rhodes*; *JWJ*, VIII, p. 49, where Wesley suggests using it for religious mission as well. For a detailed study of the Manchester SFS see G.B. Hindle, *Provision for the Relief of the Poor in Manchester*, Chetham Society, Third Series, XXII, 1975, pp. 78–89.

307. But for its origin in a breakaway from an Evangelical society confined to Anglicans see C. Bayley, 'Rules of a Benevolent Society', in *Sermons, Tracts and Prayers*, Manchester 1830. The Hull case is revealed in *Society for Bettering the Condition of the Poor. Report*, I, 1800, pp. 295–302; see also *AM*, 1798.

308. Church, *MA*, pp. 195–202; *Life of Silas Told by Himself* (1786), Epworth Press 1954.

309. Church, *MA*, pp. 203f.; E.M. Hunt, 'The Anti-Slave Trade Agitation in Manchester', *Lancashire and Cheshire Antiquarian Society* LXXX, 1977, pp. 46–72.

XII. 'Horrible Decrees': Methodism in the 1770s and the Calvinistic Controversy

1. For accounts of the controversy in historical perspective see A.P.F. Sell, *The Great Debate*, H.E. Walter 1982, ch. III; E.P. Crow Jr, *John Wesley's Conflict with Antinomianism in Relation to the Moravians and Calvinists*, Manchester PhD 1964, which carefully goes through the pamphlet warfare. B. Semmel, *The Methodist Revolution*, Heinemann 1974, ch. II, has a useful summary as part of

his thesis relating Methodist Arminianism to social and political change. P.F. Streiff, *Jean Guillaume de la Fléchère*, Peter Lang 1984, chs. XIX–XXI (in German), is the latest and by far the best biography of him. I have not seen A. Coppedge, *John Wesley and the Doctrine of Predestination*, Cambridge University dissertation 1976 (Rupp, p. 370 n.). The discussion in the text is intended only to indicate the main points in controversy and to explain their significance for Wesley and his connexion and the Revival.

2. Semmel, *Methodist Revolution* (n. 1), pp. 45–8.

3. Toplady, one of the main protagonists, was converted from Arminianism to Calvinism by reading a Puritan work: A.M. Toplady, *Works* I, London 1825, p. 10.

4. 'Predestination Calmly Considered' (1752), in Wesley, *Works*, X.

5. See especially ibid. and 'Dialogue between a Predestinarian and his Friend' (1741), in *Works*, X.

6. Cf. especially his *Historic Proof of the Calvinism of the Church of England* (1774), and translation of the *Life of Zanchius* in *Works* I, II, V, London 1825.

7. L. Stephen, *History of English Thought in the Eighteenth Century II*, reprinted Rupert Hart-Davis 1962, ch. XII, para. 105.

8. *JWL (B)*, II, pp. 498f., and for a comparison with Zwingli, Rupp, p. 347; Tyerman, II, pp. 144f.; cf. also 'Predestination Calmly Considered' in *Works*, X, which was a reply to the Irish arguers.

9. 'The Question "What is an Arminian?" Answered', *Works*, X.

10. *JWL (B)*, I, pp. 175f.; 'Some Remarks on Mr Hill's "Review"' (1772); 'Remarks on Mr Hill's "Farrago Double-Distilled"', in *Works*, X. It is no doubt significant that he omitted the offending Article XVII from his abbreviated Articles for the Americans in 1784 (see below, p. 510).

11. For Hervey see Tyerman, *OM*, pp. 201–333; 'J.C.', *Herveiana*, Scarborough 1822.

12. Stephen, *English Thought* (n. 7), ch. XII, paras. 116–17, but the genre would repay further investigation.

13. For this tangled tale see the preface to 'Treatise on Justification . . . from John Goodwin', in *Works*, X; Wesley to Hervey in *JWL*, III, p. 371 n. and refs; Crow, *Antinomianism* (n. 1), pp. 172–84.

14. MS *Minutes*, 1744, and *Works*, VIII; 'Predestination Calmly Considered' (1752) and 'Letter to a Gentleman' (1758), in *Works*, X.

15. See above, p. 105, and W.R. Ward, *Georgian Oxford*, Oxford University Press 1958, ch. XV, pp. 239–42, 243ff., on the connection with the Subscription Controversy (see below, pp. 462ff. and n. 49).

16. Crow, *Antinomianism* (n. 1), pp. 86–9.

17. See above, p. 357.

18. List in G.F. Nuttall, 'The Students of Trevecca College 1768–91', *Transactions of the Honourable Society of Cymmrodorian*, 1967, pp. 249–77, which extends that in *LyH*., II, p. 112 n. For an account of the college see *LyH*, chs. XXXI, XXXII, and refs. in Nuttall. For Fletcher's role see Streiff, *de la Fléchère* (n. 1), chs. XVIII, XIX.

19. See above, pp. 303f.

20. *JWL*, V, pp. 83f., 88, 166; cf. 165. See *LyH*, II, pp. 234f., on Wesley's alleged jealousy.

21. *Minutes*, 1770, and reprinted in *LyH*, II, pp. 232–50; Tyerman, III, pp. 72f.

22. *JWJ*, V, pp. 243f.

23. *JWL*, V. pp. 166, 202–4; Harris, *Journal*, 29 March and 12 April 1770, and Walter Shirley, *A Narrative of the Painful Circumstances Relating to the Revd Mr Wesley's Late Conference*, Bristol 1771, p. 5 quoted in Crow, *Antinomianism* (n. 1), pp. 212, 211.

24. *JWL*, V, pp. 211f.; *LyH*, II, p. 106.

25. Crow, *Antinomianism* (n. 1), p. 216; *JWL*, V, p. 228; *LyH*, II, p. 238. Benson may also have been teaching this 'Spirit' doctrine which became common in the nineteenth century.

26. L. Tyerman, *Wesley's Designated Successor* [Fletcher], London 1882, pp. 177f., 186; Crow, *Antinomianism* (n. 1), pp. 218–20.

27. Sermon LIII, in *Works*, VI.

28. Tyerman, *Successor* (n. 26), p. 174; *JWL*, III, p. 77; Crow, *Antinomianism* (n. 1), p. 215.

29. Tyerman, III, pp. 93f.; *LyH*, II.

30. Tyerman, III, p. 100 and n.; *LyH*, III, p. 242.

31. *JWL*, V, pp. 274f.

32. *JWL*, V, p. 304; 'The Doctrine of Absolute Predestination Stated and Asserted by the Revd. A— T—', in *Works*, XIV.

33. For a full analysis see Crow, *Antinomianism* (n. 1), chs. V, VII, VIII and ch. VI on the 1770 *Minutes*.

34. Streiff, *de la Fléchère* (n. 1), p. 235.

35. Crow, *Antinomianism* (n. 1), p. 257, quoting Wesley's Sermons on 'The Lord our Righteousness' and 'The Wedding Garment', nos. XX and CXX in *Works*, V, VII.

36. Fletcher to Charles Wesley, 5 July 1772, quoted by Crow, *Antinomianism* (n. 1), p. 262.

37. Crow, *Antinomianism* (n. 1), pp. 272–83.

38. Wesley, *Works*, X, pp. 457–90, especially pp. 473f.; 'Scheme of Christian and Philosophical Necessity' (1775).

39. Fletcher in *Works*, London 1806–7, V; Crow, *Antinomianism* (n. 1), pp. 285–9, 292.

40. In *Works*, X, pp. 457–74.

41. 'Remarks on Hill's Farrago', *Works*, X, pp. 414, 415, 427. For Calvin see *Institutes*, III, xvi, 1; xvii, 5, 10; R. Stauffer in M. Prestwich (ed.), *International Calvinism*, Oxford University Press 1985, p. 34; F. Wendel, *Calvin*, ET Collins 1969, pp. 269f.; Rupp, p. 419. For Wesley on Bull's *Harmonia Apostolica* see *JWJ*, II, p. 470.

42. For Calvin on 'perfection' see *Institutes*, III, xvii, 15 end; H. Venn, *Complete Duty of Man*, Preface, for holiness language.

43. Crow, *Antinomianism*, ch. IX.

44. Walsh in *HMCGB*, I, p. 290; H. Venn, *The Life and Letters of Henry Venn*, London ⁶1839, pp. 244, 179, 193, 497; for Simeon and Wesley see *JWJ*, VIII, p. 39.

45. For an illustration of the confusions in which ordinary Methodist preachers found themselves when arguing for their version of grace and salvation see H. Crabb Robinson, *Diary* (ed. T. Seddon), London 1869, II, p. 48.

46. Semmel, *Methodist Revolution* (n. 1), pp. 65–71.

47. This movement still requires full modern critical treatment. See C.J. Abbey and J.H. Overton, *The English Church in the Eighteenth Century I*, Longmans 1887, pp. 431–42; N. Sykes, *Church and State in England in the Eighteenth Century*, Cambridge University Press 1934, pp. 381ff. R.B. Barlow, *Citizenship and Conscience*, University of Pennsylvania Press 1962, chs. IV and V; A. Lincoln, *English Dissent*, Cambridge University Press 1938, ch. VI; L. Elliott-Binns, *Early Evangelicals*, Lutterworth Press, ch. IX.

48. G.G. Perry, *History of the Church of England* III, London 1864, p. 376; *Gentleman's Magazine* LXIX, 1799, p. 915.

49. W.R. Ward, *Georgian Oxford*, Oxford University Press 1958, pp. 239–42, 243ff.; L.S. Sutherland and L.G. Mitchell (eds.), *Oxford University in the Eighteenth Century*, Oxford University Press 1986, pp. 161–74.

50. *JWJ*, VII, p. 160.

51. Tyerman, III, p. 146.

52. *Works*, X, p. 41.

53. *JWJ*, VIII, pp. 339f., 333.

54. Sermon LV in *Works*, VI; H. Rack, 'Early Methodist Visions of the Trinity', *PWHS* XLVI, 1987, pp. 65f., 69.

55. T. Scott, *The Force of Truth*, ³1795, pp. 30f.

56. *LyH*, II, pp. 288–90.

57. A.M. Toplady, *Theological Subscription Not Grievous* (1772).

58. For this and what follows see F. Baker, *JW*, pp. 199–204.

59. *JWL*, V, pp. 143–50.

60. *JWL*, VI, pp. 10–12, 33f.; Moore, II, pp. 258–61.

61. *PWHS* XXIII, 1945, pp. 7–14; Baker, *JW*, pp. 207f.; Baker, *CW*, pp. 129f.

62. *LyH*, II, pp. 102f.

63. Tyerman, III, pp. 202–6; for these stories see below, p. 528.

64. See above, p. 357 and n. 68.

65. For this and what follows see J. Macdonald, *Memoirs of Benson*, London 1822, pp. 12–49; *JWJ*, VIII, pp. 328–34 passim.

66. *JWJ*, VI, pp. 22f.

67. For Smyth in Dublin and his subsequent career see above, pp. 234f.

68. For this and what follows see Tyerman, III, pp. 296–313; Baker, *JW*, pp. 215–17; Baker, *CW*, pp. 132f.

69. Baker, *CW*, pp. 132f.

70. *EMP*, I, p. 219; Baker, *JW*, pp. 209, 220f.; and see above, p. 347; below, p. 505.

XIII. Saints Abroad: Missions and the American Problem

1. K.S. Latourette, *History of the Expansion of Christianity*, Eyre and Spottiswoode 1938–46, titles to volumes III to V.

3. See especially J. van den Berg, *Constrained by Jesus' Love: An Inquiry into the Motives of the Missionary Awakening . . . Between 1698 and 1815*, Kampen 1956. On the Anglican societies see H. Cnattingius, *Bishops and Societies*, SPCK 1952.

3. R. Brown, *English Baptists of the Eighteenth Century*, pp. 72ff., 115f.

4. Cnattingius, *Bishops and Societies* (n. 2).

5. R. Watson, *Anecdotes*, I, p. 321. For motives and later modifications see van den Berg, *Missionary Awakening* (n. 2), pp. 93–105.

6. See L.E. Froom, *Conditionalist Faith of our Fathers*, four volumes, Revival Herald Press, Washington, DC 1946–54, which despite its Adventist perspective is valuable for compendious information.

7. For the Fullerites see above, p. 328.

8. See P.J. Marshall, *The British Discovery of Hinduism in the Eighteenth Century*, Cambridge University Press 1971; D. Pailin, *Attitudes to Other Religions*, Manchester University Press 1984, pp. 1–6, who shows the influence of internecine European religious conflicts on perspectives; for Sir William Jones and others see P.J. Marshall, 'Warren Hastings as Scholar and Patron', in *Statesmen, Scholars and Merchants*, ed. A. Whiteman et al., Clarendon Press 1973, pp. 242–62.

9. W.A. Embree, *Charles Grant and British Rule in India*, Allen and Unwin 1952. E.M. Howse, *Saints in Politics*, Allen and Unwin 1952, ch. IV, explains the Clapham concerns, but without seeing the implication of Grant's approach.

10. See above, p. 341.

11. van den Berg, *Missionary Awakening*, pp. 144–64; *Gentleman's Magazine*, 1788, I, p. 557, and cf. *JWL*, VIII, pp. 63, 67. But Thomas Walsh and Vincent Perronet were more inclined to detailed prophecy: *EMP*, III, p. 233; *AM*, 1799, p. 161; for Coke see below, p. 477.

12. See above, p. 53; Tyerman, *SW*, pp. 295f.

13. See in general G.G. Findlay and W.W. Holdsworth, *History of Wesleyan Methodist Missions* I, London 1921. For the Gilberts, see Tyerman, II, pp. 297f., 535; III, pp. 151, 173; for subsequent developments see J. Vickers, *Thomas Coke*, Epworth Press 1969, ch. X.

14. *JWJ*, IV, pp. 227f., 293. This was published in 1764.

15. The Gilbert family was intimate with Fletcher: *AM*, 1780, p. 387; 1783, p. 329; 330; *WMM*, 1854, p. 58; Tyerman, II, pp. 297–302.

16. *AM*, 1786, p. 567; Tyerman, III, p. 151.

17. *JWL*, VI, p. 148; Tyerman, III, p. 195.

18. *AM*, 1788, p. 383; Tyerman, III, pp. 273f.; Vickers, *Coke* (n. 13), pp. 99, 146, 149f., 153. Wesley seems to have thought the keeping of the missionaries was providential, though obviously disliking having his plans altered.

19. Vickers, *Coke* (n. 13), p. 150.

20. Ibid., pp. 170–2.

21. Ibid., pp. 144ff. For Black see *EMP*, V, pp. 242–95, and *JWL*, VII, pp. 168f., 224f.; cf. his account of a case of demon possession in Nova Scotia: *EMP*, V, pp. 271ff.

22. *AM*, 1785, p. 491; *WMM*, 1851, p. 869; *JWL*, V, p. 101; Tyerman, III, pp. 25–7.

23. For these developments see Tyerman, III, pp. 452f.; Vickers, *Coke* (n. 13), pp. 146–8.

24. *Minutes*, 1785.

25. *JWL*, VI, p. 148.

26. Vickers, *Coke* (n. 13) p. 37; *JWJ*, VI, p. 206 and n.; Tyerman, III, pp. 272f; *EMP*, IV, p. 184; J. Macdonald, *Memoirs of Joseph Benson*, London 1822, p. 75. There is no reference to these proceedings in the *Journal* or Conference *Minutes*.

27. For details and reaction to the plan see Vickers, *Coke* (n. 13), pp. 133–5.

28. *JWJ*, VI, p. 476.

29. *AM*, 1792, pp. 83ff.; 331ff.; Vickers, *Coke* (n. 13), pp. 135f.

30. *JWL*, VII, p. 322.

31. Cf. above, p. 230; also D. Wright in *EMP*, II, p. 123. Wesley urged him to brush up his Gaelic to speak to Highland immigrants in Perth.

32. See Vickers, *Coke* (n. 13), pp. 139–44 and refs.

33. N.A. Birtwhistle in *PWHS* XXX, 1955, pp. 25–9.

34. Vickers, *Coke* (n. 13), pp. 352–4.

35. *JWL*, VII, pp. 168f., 224, 232; VIII, p. 68; and see n. 28 above.

36. *AM*, 1783, for Sermon LXIII in *Works*, VI.

37. On this see B. Semmel, *The Methodist Revolution*, Heinemann 1974, pp. 148–69, but Semmel is effectively criticized by D. Hempton, *Methodism and Politics in British Society*, Heinemann 1974, pp. 96–8, and S. Piggin, 'Halévy Revisited: The Origins of the Wesleyan Methodist Missionary Society', *Journal of Imperial and Commonwealth History* IX, 1980, pp. 7–32. For the element of competition with other missionary societies involved in the formation of the Wesleyan one see *PWHS*, XLII, 1979, pp. 81–7.

38. P. Miller, *Errand into the Wilderness*, Harvard University Press, 1956, pp. 156f.

39. For the background and course of the Awakening and interpretations of it see above, pp. 163f.; and for references W.G. McLoughlin, *Revivals, Awakenings and Reform*, University of Chicago Press 1978, chs. II, III.

40. F.E. Stoeffler, *Continental Pietism and Early American Christianity*, Eerdmans 1976; the classic study of the transition from Puritanism is P. Miller, *The New England Mind from Colony to Province*, Harvard University Press 1953; but for social and political interpretations see e.g. J.P. Greene and J.R. Pole (eds.), *Colonial British America*, Johns Hopkins University Press 1984, passim.

41. McLoughlin, *Revivals* (n. 39), p. 59; S. Ahlstrom, *A Religious History of the American People*, Yale University Press 1972, pp. 314f.

42. Rhys Isaac, 'The Evangelical Revolt', *William and Mary Quarterly*, Third Series, XXXI, 1974, pp. 345–68.

43. For Jarratt, see D. Jarratt, *Life of Devereux Jarratt*, Baltimore 1806.

44. For Methodism in America see R.M. Cameron, *Methodism and Society in Historical Perspective*, Abingdon Press 1961; W.W. Sweet, *Methodism in American History*, Abingdon Press ²1954; W.C. Barclay, *Early American Methodism 1769–1844*, two volumes, Methodist Board of Missions 1949–5; E.S. Bucke (ed.), *History of American Methodism*, three volumes, Abingdon Press 1964. For a view of the unity of the British and American traditions in the earliest period see F. Baker, *From Wesley to Asbury*, Duke University Press 1976, to which I am indebted.

45. Baker, *Wesley to Asbury* (n. 44), p. 34 and n., 40.

46. Ibid., pp. 25–7, 30–2.

47. For what follows especially Baker, *Wesley to Asbury* (n. 44), chs. III and IV.

48. Best unravelled by ibid., IV.

49. *JWL (B)*, II, pp. 128 and n.; *JWJ*, IV, p. 101; G.W. Pilcher (ed.), *Samuel Davies Abroad*, University of Illinois Press 1967, p. 132; *JWJ*, IV, pp. 125f., 149f., 194f.

50. *JWL*, V, pp. 44f.

51. For the versions of the letter see Baker in *Methodist History* VIII, 1965, pp. 3–15, and *Wesley to Asbury* (n. 44), pp. 73–5.
52. Baker, *Wesley to Asbury* (n. 44), pp. 80f.
53. *JWJ*, V, p. 290; Sweet, *Methodism* (n. 44), p. 47 and n.
54. *JWL*, V, pp. 126, 123.
55. *JWJ*, V, p. 330 and n.; *Minutes*, I, p. 86.
56. *Methodist History* X, 1972, p. 57.
57. *JWL*, V, pp. 182, 183, 212.
58. Baker, *Wesley to Asbury* (n. 44), p. 93.
59. Ibid., pp. 95f., quoting Asbury's *Journal*. *EMP*, V, p. 193.
60. *JWL*, VI, pp. 142f., 150, 155.
61. *JWL*, VI, pp. 179f.
62. *EMP*, VI, pp. 171–5.
63. Sweet, *Methodism* (n. 44), p. 79.
64. Baker, *Wesley to Asbury* (n. 44), pp. 116, 128.
65. Ibid., p. 129.

XIV. 'I Live and Die in the Church of England': Methodism in the 1780s

1. For an approach to the relationship between Evangelicalism and the French Revolution see V. Kiernan, 'Evangelicalism and the French Revolution', *Past and Present* II, 1952, pp. 44–56.
2. *JWL*, VII, pp. 234–6.
3. Ibid., VIII, pp. 199f., 204.
4. *JWJ*, VIII, pp. 117, 118 ('revolution' as a cyclical change in history).
5. *AM*, 1789, pp. 613; Maldwyn Edwards, *John Wesley*, Allen and Unwin 1933, p. 93, wrongly cites this as a remark by Wesley himself.
6. *Monthly Review* V, 1791 p. 356, quoted by Edwards, *Wesley* (n. 5), pp. 93f. See also D. Hempton, *Methodism and Politics in British Society*, Longmans 1984, ch. III, and above, pp. 379f.
7. *Minutes*, 1780, 1790.
8. *AM*, 1790, p. 385.
9. *EMP*, VI, pp. 103–10.
10. *AM*, 1781, p. 664.
11. *AM*, 1784, pp. 46–9, 103–6.
12. *JWJ*, VI, pp. 351–3.
13. *JWJ*, VI, pp. 520f.
14. *JWJ*, VI, pp. 514f.
15. *AM*, 1784, pp. 211, 266f.; *JWL*, VII, pp. 138, 143, 145. For the Weardale Revival, which was also an example of an excitable outbreak in a long-established society see *JWJ*, V, pp. 465–72.
16. Cornwall was especially noted for a cycle of revivals every few years well into the nineteenth century: see D.H. Luker, *Cornish Methodism, Revivalism and Popular Belief 1780–1870*, Oxford DPhil 1988; id., *JEH* XXXVII, 1986, pp. 601–19.
17. For the later revival tradition see W.G. McLoughlin, *American Revivalism*, Ronald Press, New York 1959 (though he exaggerates the influence of Finney). See also J. Kent, *Holding the Fort*, Epworth Press 1978, ch. II; R. Carwardine, *Transatlantic Revivalism*, Greenwood Press 1978.

18. *JWJ*, V, p. 466; *JWL*, VII, p. 162. For the Yorkshire revival see J. Baxter, 'The Great Yorkshire Revival 1792–6', in M. Hill (ed.), *Sociological Yearbook of Religion in Britain*, SCM Press 1974, pp. 46–76.

19. See D.M. Valenze, *Prophetic Sons and Daughters*, Princeton University Press 1985; J. Werner, *The Primitive Methodist Connexion*, University of Wisconsin Press 1984.

20. See above, pp. 465f.; P.F. Streiff, *J.G. de la Fléchère*, Lang 1984 (in German), ch. XXIX.

21. Of the older biographies the most useful are S. Drew, *Memoirs of the late Revd. Thomas Coke*, London 1816, and J.W. Etheridge, *Life of the Revd. Thomas Coke*, London 1860, but they are largely superseded by J. Vickers, *Thomas Coke. Apostle of Methodism*, Epworth 1969, who attempts to defend him against the long-standing charges of ambition.

22. Moore, II, pp. 530ff.; Vickers, *Coke* (n. 21), pp. 341ff., 344 n.

23. Baker, *JW*, p. 198.

24. E.B. Perkins, *Methodist Preaching Houses and the Law*, Epworth Press 1952, p. 14; Baker, *JW*, p. 293.

25. *PWHS*, XVIII, pp. 113–20; *JWL*, IV, pp. 99f.; Baker, *JW*, pp. 174, 198f.

26. Perkins, *Preaching Houses* (n. 24), pp. 32–8.

27. *Minutes*, I, p. 604; *JWJ*, V, pp. 278f.; on Methodism and the Conventicle Act see *PWHS* XI, 1907–8, pp. 82–93, 103–8, 130–7; Baker, *JW*, pp. 198f.

28. Baker, *JW*, pp. 174–6.

29. Tyerman, III, pp. 420f.

30. *The Case of Birstall Preaching House* in *Works*, XIII; *JWL*, VII, pp. 148–51; *JWJ*, VI, pp. 437f.; Tyerman, III, pp. 381–3; Perkins, *Preaching Houses* (n. 24), pp. 25ff.

31. Perkins, *Preaching Houses* (n. 24), pp. 53f.; Tyerman, III, pp. 551–60.

32. Perkins, *Preaching Houses* (n. 24), p. 54.

33. *JWL*, VII, pp. 336f., 339; VIII, pp. 10f., 78, 230; *JWJ*, VII, p. 339; Baker, *JW*, pp. 316–19.

34. For what follows see Baker, *JW*, pp. 288–303, to which I am indebted for much of the detail.

35. S. Bradburn, *The Question, Are the Methodists Dissenters? Fairly Answered*, London 1792, pp. 10f. quoted in Baker, *JW*, pp. 289f.

36. *AM*, 1786, pp. 92f., 152f., 377f.

37. *JWL*, VII, pp. 326.

38. *Minutes*, 1786.

39. *JWJ*, VII, p. 217.

40. *Minutes*, I, p. 547.

41. *JWJ*, VII, pp. 481f.

42. *AM*, 1789, pp. 45f.; *JWL*, VIII, p. 92.

43. *Minutes*, I, p. 61.

44. *JWL*, VI, 375f.

45. *JWJ*, VI, p. 330; *Minutes*, I, p. 503; Baker, *JW*, pp. 220f.

46. *JWL*, VII, p. 279, though he seems to have again asked the other preachers to attend for the rest of the 1785 Conference: perhaps as observers? Indeed lay people other than preachers sometimes attended 'open' sessions of the Conference.

47. Johann Lortz to Benjamin LaTrobe, 12 July 1786, printed in W.G. Addison, *The Renewed Church of the United Brethren*, SPCK 1932, Appendix E, pp. 194–224, especially 222, 226. See also C.W. Towlson, *Moravian and Methodist*, Epworth Press 1957, pp. 157ff; Vickers, *Coke* (n. 21), pp. 107–11.

48. *Minutes*, I, p. 181. For the illness see Tyerman, III, p. 403. On the circumstances and content of the Deed see Baker, *JW*, pp. 222–30, 384f.; Vickers, *Coke* (n. 21), pp. 62–5.

49. Drew, *Coke* (n. 21), p. 39; *PWHS*, X, 1906–7, p. 111; Baker, *JW*, p. 230; Vickers, *Coke* (n. 21), p. 63.

50. Coke, *Address*, p. 7; Wesley, *Works*, XIII, p. 236.

51. J. Crowther, *Life of Coke*, Leeds 1815, p. 121; J.S. Simon, *PWHS* XII, 1908–9, pp. 81ff.

52. *EMP*, IV, pp. 52f.

53. *JWJ*, VIII, App. XXXI, pp. 335–41.

54. Baker, *JW*, pp. 229f.

55. *Works*, XIII, pp. 237f.

56. *JWL*, VII, p. 286; Baker, *JW*, p. 233.

57. 'Ought We to Separate?', in Baker, *JW*, Appendix, p. 334.

58. Whitehead, II, p. 501, quoting a memorandum of Wesley's dated December 1789. For an assessment of the reasons, playing down this element, see Rupp, pp. 444ff.

59. *Thoughts on Separation from the Church* (1788), in *Works*, XIII, pp. 263f. For discussion of the separation see A.W. Harrison, *The Separation of Methodism from the Church of England*, Epworth Press 1945; Baker, *JW*, passim; J. Kent, *The Age of Disunity*, Epworth Press 1966, ch. VI; J.M. Turner, *Conflict and Reconciliation*, Epworth Press 1985, ch. II.

60. *JWL*, III, p. 133; VII, pp. 179, 203, 213; VIII, p. 23.

61. Gilbert to Wesley (in 1760) printed in *PWHS* XXVII, 1950, p. 147.

62. See above, p. 298.

63. *JWL*, VII, pp. 30, 239.

64. Baker, *JW*, p. 240, quoting W.W. Sweet, *Religion on the American Frontier* IV, *The Methodists*, Chicago University Press 1946, pp. 12–15; cf. *PWHS* XXVI, 1948, pp. 27f.

65. *JWL*, VII, p. 191.

66. Baker, *JW*, pp. 241.

67. Vickers, *Coke* (n. 21), p. 75, quoting MS letter in Wesley's Chapel, City Rd, London.

68. See Baker, *JW*, pp. 241f., 263ff.; Vickers, *Coke* (n. 21), pp. 275ff.

69. T. Coke and H. Moore, *Life of John Wesley*, London 1792, p. 458; Moore, II, p. 326; *JWL*, VII, p. 238; Baker, *JW*, pp. 241f. The 'sketch' has not survived and its contents can only be gauged from the letter to the Americans of September 1784.

70. F. Hunter, *PWHS* XXIII, 1945, pp. 124–33; W.F. Swift, *PWHS* XXIX, 1953, pp. 12–20; H. Barton, *PWHS*, XXXII, 1960, pp. 97–101; J.C. Bowmer, *The Lord's Supper in Early Methodism*, Epworth Press 1970, Appendix, pp. 206–15; but the most sensible account is in Baker, *JW*, ch. XIV.

71. *JWL*, VII, p. 239.

72. Above, p. 466; and 'Ought We to Separate?', in Baker, *JW*, p. 331.

73. *JWJ*, III, pp. 490f.

74. *JWL*, VIII, pp. 144f.; Barton, *PWHS* XXXII, 1960, pp. 97–101.

75. See Etheridge, *Coke*, p. 100 and n. (who says that Drew probably received the statement from Coke himself).

76. *MCA*, Coke to Wesley (17 April 1784) printed in Vickers, *Coke* (n. 21), p. 76 and Etheridge, pp. 101f.

77. *JWL*, VII, pp. 224f.; Baker, *JW*, p. 264.

78. Pawson MS, *Life of Whitehead*, quoted in Tyerman, III, p. 428.

79. Whitehead, II, pp. 415–17, who also refers to consulting the clergy. Creighton's account is from a letter to Bradburn in 1795 allegedly printed but not traced – so Baker, *JW*, pp. 265, 394 n. 47, 399 n. 117.

80. Whitehead, II, p. 417; cf. Moore, II, pp. 330–2.

81. *JWJ*, VII, p. 15; Baker, *JW*, p. 266.

82. Baker, *JW*, pp. 267f.; facsimile in *JWJ*, VII opposite p. 16; Baker, *JW*, pp. 395f, n. 66.

83. *JWL*, VII, pp. 238f.

84. *JWL*, VII, p. 262; cf. pp. 284f.

85. For these events see W.R. Ward, 'The Legacy of John Wesley', *Statesmen, Scholars and Merchants*, ed. A. Whiteman et al, Oxford University Press 1973, pp. 323–50.

86. Vickers, *Coke* (n. 21), pp. 90f.

87. Ward, 'Legacy' (n. 85), p. 331.

88. For what follows see Vickers, *Coke* (n. 21), ch. VI.

89. Quoted in ibid., p. 271.

90. Ibid., pp. 88ff. For Hoadly and Calamy see Rack, 'Hoadly versus Law', p. 176.

91. F. Baker, *From Wesley to Asbury*, Duke University Press 1976, p. 151. 'Europe' may be a euphemism for England here.

92. Vickers, *Coke* (n. 21), pp. 116ff.; Ward, 'Legacy' (n. 85), p. 335.

93. Vickers, *Coke* (n. 21), p. 118 and n.; Baker, *JW*, p. 271.

94. *JWL*, VIII, p. 91.

95. Vickers, *Coke* (n. 21), pp. 176ff.; Ward, pp. 334f.

96. Whitehead, II, pp. 418–20.

97. Baker, *CW*, pp. 134–7; id., *JW*, p. 273.

98. Quoted by Vickers, *Coke* (n. 21), pp. 101f., from F. Baker, *Representative Verse of Charles Wesley*, Epworth Press 1961, pp. 367ff. and F. Asbury, *Letters*, p. 65.

99. Jackson, *CW*, II, p. 392; Tyerman, III, pp. 439f.

100. *JWL*, VII, pp. 284f. The last sentence is quoted in MS *Life of Benson*, II, p. 1388 according to Telford in *JWL*, VII, p. 285 n.1; *AM*, 1786, pp. 50f.

101. Jackson, *CW*, II, pp. 396–8; *JWL*, VII, pp. 288f.

102. Creighton to Charles Wesley, 6 October 1787, in MCA, quoted in Baker, *JW*, pp. 279f.

103. *Works*, XIII, pp. 243f.; *JWL*, VII, p. 321.

104. Baker, *JW*, p. 279.

105. For discussion of this evidence see Baker, *JW*, pp. 280f.

106. Baker, *JW*, p. 281.

107. *PWHS* XXXIII, 1962, pp. 118–21; Vickers, *Coke* (n. 21), pp. 197f., 200f. and n., 372f. As he points out, this shows that the common view that ordinations by laying on of hands ceased until 1816 except for missionary cases

is incorrect. See also Bowmer in *PWHS* XXXVI, 1967, pp. 36–40, for ordinations between 1796 and 1813.

108. Creighton, quoted by Baker, pp. 279, 282 n., 397 n., 399 n.

109. Vickers, *Coke* (n. 21), p. 192.

110. Vickers, *Coke* (n. 21), p. 195; Pawson to Atmore 13 December 1793, in MCA, and Tyerman, III, p. 443.

111. For various views on these developments see: J. Kent, *The Age of Disunity*, Epworth Press 1966, chs. II, III, V; J.C. Bowmer, *Pastor and People*, Epworth Press 1975; W.R. Ward, *Religion and Society 1790–1850*, Batsford 1972, ch. VI; id., *Early Correspondence of Jabez Bunting 1820–9*, Camden Society 1972.

112. Pawson to Benson, 4 May 1791, in MCA, quoted by Hempton, *Methodism and Politics* (n. 6), p. 60.

113. Harrison, *Separation* (n. 59); Hempton, *Methodism and Politics* (n. 6), ch. III; Vickers, *Coke* (n. 21), ch. XIII.

114. Pawson to Atmore 13 December 1793 in MCA, quoted by Vickers, *Coke* (n. 21), p. 198.

115. For the plan and its reception see Vickers, *Coke* (n. 21), pp. 199f.; Hempton, *Methodism and Politics* (n. 6), pp. 45–8.

116. Hempton, *Methodism and Politics* (n. 6), pp. 43ff.; Vickers, *Coke* (n. 21), pp. 205ff. For the Manchester and Salford dispute see Everett Scrapbook in MCA, pp. 437f.

117. Harrison, *Separation* (n. 59), pp. 48–57 with list of points, p. 55; Vickers, *Coke* (n. 21), pp. 205–11; Hempton, *Methodism and Politics* (n. 6), pp. 63–6.

118. Discussions in e.g. Bowmer, *Lord's Supper* (n. 70), ch. XI; A.B. Lawson, *John Wesley and the Christian Ministry*, SPCK 1963; E.W. Thompson, *John Wesley, Apostolic Man*, Epworth Press 1957; Baker, *JW*, ch. XV; A.R. George in *HMCGB* I, ch. IV, with bibliography on p. 143 n.1. For a different approach see John Kent, *Age of Disunity*, ch. VI; also Ward, 'Legacy' (n. 85), stressing the transatlantic context. J. Walsh in *HMCGB* I, pp. 278–82, is especially judicious.

119. Thompson, *Wesley* (n. 118), criticized by Kent, *Fort* (n. 17), pp. 169–76.

120. MS *Minutes*, 1745; see above, pp. 293f.; Kent, *Fort* (n. 17), pp. 47ff., 171ff.

121. Sermon CXV in *Works*, VII; Baker, *JW*, p. 313, for view of this.

122. *JWL*, VII, p. 483.

123. Ward, 'Legacy' (n. 85), pp. 330f., 337.

124. *JWL*, VIII, pp. 211, 205.

125. *JWJ*, VI, pp. 416ff.; Tyerman, III, pp. 393f.; *JWJ*, VII, p. 195.

126. *JWJ*, VIII, p. 95.

127. *JWJ*, VIII, p. 102.

128. W.S. Lewis (ed.), *Letters of Horace Walpole* XXXV, Yale University Press 1973, p. 119.

129. *PWHS*, III, 1903, p. 185, though J. Telford, *John Wesley*, says just under 5 ft 6 ins (1.66 m), following family tradition. But Wesley is always described as a very small man. For the description Hampson, III, pp. 166–8, 178f., repeated in part by Whitehead, II, pp. 484f.

130. *JWL*, IV, p. 108.

131. *JWL*, VIII, p. 46.

132. *JWJ*, VI, p. 8; *JWL*, VI, pp. 66, 81, 114.

133. Tyerman, III, pp. 203f.

134. *JWJ*, VI, pp. 112f.
134. *JWJ*, VI, p. 521, cf. *JWL*, VII, p. 204.
136. *JWJ*, VII, pp. 97, 175.
137. *JWJ*, VII, pp. 408f.
138. *JWJ*, VII, pp. 514f.
139. *JWJ*, VIII, p. 35.
140. *JWJ*, VIII, pp. 35, 76, cf. *JWL*, VIII, p. 201.
141. Moore, II, p. 379.
142. *EMP*, IV, p. 58; *JWJ*, VIII, p. 63 n.
143. Whitehead, II, pp. 451f.
144. Tyerman, I, pp. 117, 525, 521–3; *JWL*, II, p. 158, 285; Hampson, III, p. 184.
145. Tyerman, III, pp. 526, 527.
146. *JWJ*, VI, p. 337.; see above, p. 266.
147. *JWJ*, VIII, p. 3.
148. Tyerman, III, p. 446.
149. *JWJ*, VIII, p. 108 and n.
150. Letter of 18 October 1790 in T. Seddon (ed.), *Diary etc. of H.C. Robinson* I, London 1889, pp. 19f. For a similar account on the same tour see George Crabbe, above, p. xi.
151. *JWJ*, VIII, pp. 80 n., 83. Similarly in his account book earlier in the month.
152. *JWJ*, VIII, pp. 128, 134; Tyerman, III, p. 650; *JWL*, VIII, p. 265.
153. Account printed in *JWJ*, VIII, pp. 131–44; some further details in a letter in *PWHS* XXXVI, 1968, pp. 155f.
154. Moore, II, p. 389.
155. James Rogers, quoted in *JWJ*, VIII, p. 144n.
156. A.M. Toplady, *Works*, I, pp. 135f. Cf. the attempt at a 'plain' funeral by Wilberforce, which was frustrated by public demand: R.I. and S. Wilberforce, *Life of William Wilberforce* V, London 1838, pp. 373–5.
157. Text of will in *JWJ*, VIII, pp. 342–4; and for the controversy over his papers and biography see Whitehead, I, Advertisement and II, pp. 462f.; Moore, I, Preface; II, p. 396 n.; also Hampson, I, Preface.
158. Southey, *John Wesley* (ed. Fitzgerald), Oxford University Press 1925, II, p. 333 following Hampson; Moore II, p. 394n.
159. Moore, II, p. 394.
160. G.J. Stevenson, *City Road Chapel*, London 1872, p. 114 quoted by Church, *MA*, p. 253.
161. *JWL*, VIII, pp. 52, 57. But Susanna was buried in Bunhill Fields among the Dissenters.
162. *JWJ*, IV, p. 90.
163. For the epitaph, following a model by Adam Clarke, see Heizenrater, *EMW*, pp. 156–8. For another on the wall of the chapel see Southey, II, p. 410.
164. 'John Wesley A.M. Formerly Fellow of Lincoln College Oxford, died 2 March 1791 in his 88th year'. See Southey, *Wesley*, ed. J.B. Atkinson, London 1893, p. 543.

Postlude Reckonings

1. J. Hampson, *Memoirs of John Wesley*, three volumes, Sunderland 1791.

2. G.B. Hill and L.F. Powell (eds.), *Boswell's Life of Johnson*, Oxford University Press 1934–50, III, p. 230.

3. So Green, *JW*, p. 70. I incline to agree. Wit and sarcasm are not infrequently shown in the *Journal* and writings, but there seems little sign of much beyond this.

4. Hampson, III.

5. J. Whitehead, *Life of John Wesley*, two volumes, London 1793.

6. Alexander Knox, 'Remarks on the Life and Character of John Wesley', reprinted in full in C. S. Southey (ed.), *Southey's Life of Wesley*, Longmans 1893, II, pp. 293–360; omitting the theological discussion at the end in the Fitzgerald edition, Oxford University Press 1925, II, pp. 338–72.

7. See above, p. 532 n. 157.

8. E.g. Hampson, III, pp. 203–5; *Southey* (Fitzgerald [n. 6]), II, p. 81; Whitehead, II, pp. 475–7.

9. See Knox in *Southey* (Fitzgerald [n. 6]) II, pp. 351–6, 360, for what follows.

10. Cf. Green, *JW*, pp. 69–71, 123, 125; cf. *JWL*, IV, p. 108, for the sense of guidance.

11. E.g. Hampson, III, pp. 196, 198; Moore, II, pp. 444–5, quoting Watson for defence.

12. Knox (n. 6), II, pp. 356f.

13. *JWL (B)*, II, p. 527.

14. *JWL*, IV, p. 108.

15. See above, pp. 384ff.; below pp. 546ff.

16. Knox (n. 6), II, p. 339.

17. Hampson, III, pp. 196f. Cf. Charles to John in 1746, saying that it is 'utterly in vain' for him to write on anything on which they are not already agreed. 'Either you set aside the whole by the short answer that I am in ill humour, or you take no notice at all of my reasons but plead conscience': *JWL (B)*, II, pp. 207f.

18. *JWJ*, VI, p. 113.

19. Moore, II, p. 458; Hampson, III, pp. 179f.

20. Knox, (n. 6), p. 358, cf. *JWL (B)*, II, pp. 526, 527; *JWL*, VII, p. 40.

21. Hampson, III, pp. 200f.

22. Whitehead, II, p. 470.

23. Pawson MS *Memoir of Whitehead* quoted in Tyerman, III, p. 297.

24. Hampson, III, pp. 199f.

25. *JWL*, V, pp. 157f.

26. Hampson, III, p. 199.

27. Green, *JW*, pp. 125, 127.

28. *JWL (B)*, II, pp. 90f.

29. *JWL (B)*, II, pp. 587f.

30. *JWL*, VIII, p. 253. He cited his favourite De Renty's reaction to the death of his wife as an example; cf. Schmidt, I, pp. 215–17.

31. L. Pollock, *Forgotten Children*, Cambridge University Press 1983, pp. 27ff.; D.E. Stannard, *The Puritan Way of Death*, Oxford University Press 1971, pp.

51ff.; M. Betham-Edwards (ed.), *Autobiography of Arthur Young*, London 1898, pp. 277–99 for his long grief.

32. *JWL (B)*, II, p. 457.
33. *EMP*, I, p. 28.
34. Quoted in Baker, *CW*, p. 123.
35. Green, *JW*, pp. 70, 127, 141.
36. Moore, I, p. 241, quoting Gambold in *AM* (1798), p. 168 (in the 1730s).
37. *JWL, (B)*, I, pp. 538f.
38. *JWL*, IV, p. 132; V, pp. 164f.; VII, p. 289.
39. *JWL (B)*, I, p. 633 cf. *EMP*, VI, p. 72.
40. *JWL (B)*, II, p. 255.
41. *JWL*, III, pp. 308f.
42. *JWL*, IV, p. 20.
43. *JWL*, IV, p. 45.
44. Telford transcribes it almost accurately in *JWL*, V, pp. 15f. I have checked it with the original in MCA, Wesley Family Letters III, p. 28, and print it here with a few minor alterations to the brackets in Telford.
45. Telford, *JWL*, V, p. 15; Outler, p. 81; Heizenrater, *EMW*, I, pp. 198–200. Reference to Conference in *JWJ*, V, p. 182; Letter of 28 February 1766 in *JWL*, IV, p. 322; *JWL*, V, p. 10 on illness. Outler wrongly says that there is no other trace in his letters of this time about such feelings – see *JWL*, IV, p. 322, also to Charles.
46. *JWL*, VI, p. 6.
47. *JWL*, V, pp. 25–7.
48. *JWL (B)*, II, p. 415.
49. Tyerman, II, pp. 418f.
50. *JWL (B)*, II, p. 161n.; F.J. Powicke, *Dissertation on John Norris*, London 1894, p. 16, ascribing the saying to him.
51. *JWL (B)*, II, p. 161.
52. *JWL*, VII, p. 319.
53. *JWL*, VIII, ɩ. 154.
54. Moore, II, p. 294.
55. Knox (n. 6), pp. 339, 356f.
56. *JWL (B)*, II, p. 408.
57. *JWL*, V, p. 43.
58. *JWJ*, III, p. 157.
59. This was in 1781: S. Bradburn, *Select Letters of John Wesley*, London 1837, p. xxiv; cf. also Tyerman, III, p. 658.
60. Orcibal in *HMCGB*, I, p. 109, sees Wesley as, like Fénelon, expounding the ideal of perfection without having attained it himself by 'transferring it to the intellectual plane,' but here it is argued that Wesley believed this (like much else) on the evidence of the experience of others. The psychological interpretation of Robert L. Moore (see above, p. 152) similarly implies confirmation of truth from observation of others rather than of his own experience, though with reference mainly to his post-conversion doubts in 1738–9.

Abbreviations

Note

The Bicentennial Edition (BE) of Wesley's Works will eventually replace all previous editions, but at the time of writing very few volumes have appeared. It has therefore seemed best generally to cite the old fourteen-volume edition. Since the pagination varies in different printings I have tried to cite only volume numbers and paragraph numbers where possible. Where page references are unavoidable I have used the last Conference edition of 1872 (reprinted by Zondervan). The 'Standard' edition of the Journals has been used (but some volumes of BE are now available). For the letters I have, however, used Frank Baker's BE for letters up to and including 1755. This has the immense advantage not only of new material and an immaculate text, but also of printing generous selections from Wesley's correspondents. For 1756 onwards and some earlier 'open' controversial letters I have used Telford's 'Standard' edition. Outler's BE of the Sermons is now complete, but I have generally used the 1872 edition and its numbering, though referring occasionally to Outler where necessary; similarly with other volumes of BE.

AM	*Arminian Magazine* (later *Methodist* and *Wesleyan Methodist Magazine*)
Baker, *CW*	F. Baker, *Charles Wesley as Revealed by his Letters*, Epworth Press 1948
Baker, *JW*	F. Baker, *John Wesley and the Church of England*, Epworth Press 1970
BE	Bicentennial edition of Wesley's *Works*
Benham	D. Benham, *Memoirs of James Hutton*, London 1856
Bennet, *Diary*	John Bennet's MS *Diary* in MCA
Bennet, *Letter Book*	John Bennet's MS *Letter Book* in MCA
BJRL	*Bulletin of the John Rylands Library*
BL	British Library
Brown	R. Brown, *English Baptists of the Eighteenth Century*, Baptist Historical Society 1986
Church, *EM*	L. Church, *The Early Methodist People*, Epworth Press 1948
Church, *MA*	L. Church, *More About the Early Methodist People*, Epworth Press 1949

CH	*Church History*
Clarke	A. Clarke, *The Wesley Family*, London [1]1823
CRO	Chester County and Diocesan Record Office
CWJ	T. Jackson (ed.), *Journal of Charles Wesley*, two volumes, London 1849 reprinted Beacon Hill Press 1980
CWJ (T)	J. Telford (ed.), *Journal of Charles Wesley*, London 1909
Dallimore	A. Dallimore, *George Whitefield*, Banner of Truth Trust, two volumes, 1970, 1980
DNB	*Dictionary of National Biography*
Egmont, *Diary*	*Diary of the Earl of Egmont* (HMC), three volumes, 1920, 1923
EHR	*English Historical Review*
EMP	T. Jackson (ed.), *Lives of the Early Methodist Preachers*, six vols., London [4]1872
ET	English translation
Gilbert	A.D. Gilbert, *Religion and Society in Industrial England 1740–1914*, Longmans 1976
Green, *YMW*	V.H.H. Green, *The Young Mr Wesley*, Arnold 1961
Green, *JW*	V.H.H. Green, *John Wesley*, Nelson 1964
Hampson	J. Hampson, *Memoirs of John Wesley*, three volumes, Sunderland 1791
Heitzenrater, *EMW*	R. Heitzenrater, *The Elusive Mr Wesley*, two volumes, Abingdon Press 1984
Heitzenrater, *OM*	R. Heitzenrater, *John Wesley and the Oxford Methodists*, Duke University PhD 1972
HMC	Historical Manuscripts Commission
HMCGB	E.G. Rupp, A.R. George and R.E. Davies (eds.), *A History of the Methodist Church in Great Britain*, four volumes, Epworth Press, 1965, 1973, 1983, 1988
Jackson, *CW*	T. Jackson, *Life of Rev. Charles Wesley*, two volumes, London 1841)
JEH	*Journal of Ecclesiastical History*
JRH	*Journal of Religious History*
JRUL	John Rylands University Library, Manchester
JWJ	N. Curnock (ed.), *Journal of John Wesley*, eight volumes, reprinted Epworth Press 1938
JWL	J. Telford (ed.), *Letters of John Wesley*, eight volumes, Epworth Press 1931
JWL (B)	F. Baker (ed.), *Letters of John Wesley*, two volumes, Oxford University Press 1980–81 (BE, XXV, XXVI)
LyH	A.C.H. Seymour, *Life of Lady Huntingdon*, two volumes, London 1844
ManchCL	Manchester Central Library Archives
MCA	Methodist Church Archives in JRUL
Minutes	*Minutes of the Methodist Conference 1744–*, Vol. I, London 1862
Moore	H. Moore, *Life of John Wesley*, two volumes, London 1824
MS *Minutes*	Manuscript Minutes of early Conferences 1744, etc., to be published as BE, X
NS	New Series

OS	Old Series
Outler	A.C. Outler (ed.), *John Wesley*, Oxford University Press 1964
Priestley	J. Priestley, *Original Letters of John Wesley*, etc., Birmingham 1791
PWHS	*Proceedings of the Wesley Historical Society*, 1893–
Rack, 'Doctors'	H.D. Rack, 'Doctors, Demons and Early Methodist Healing', in *SCH*, XIX, 1982
Rack, 'Hoadly versus Law'	H.D. Rack, '"Christ's Kingdom Not of This World". The Bangorian Controversy Revisited', *SCH* XII, 1976
Rack, 'Religious Societies'	H.D. Rack, 'Religious Societies and the Origins of Methodism', *JEH* XXXVIII, 1987
Rupp	E.G. Rupp, *Religion in England 1688–1791*, Clarendon Press 1986
SCH	*Studies in Church History*
Schmidt	M. Schmidt, *John Wesley, A Theological Biography*, English translation, three volumes, Epworth Press 1962–73
Telford, *John Wesley*	J. Telford, *John Wesley*, reprinted Epworth Press 1947
TRHS	*Transactions of the Royal Historical Society*
Tyerman	L. Tyerman, *Life and Times of John Wesley*, three volumes, London 1872
Tyerman, *GW*	L. Tyerman, *Life of George Whitefield*, two volumes, London 1890
Tyerman, *OM*	L. Tyerman, *The Oxford Methodists*, London 1873
Tyerman, *SW*	L. Tyerman, *Life and Times of Samuel Wesley*, London 1866
Walsh, 'Cambridge Methodists'	J. Walsh, 'The Cambridge Methodists', in P. Brooks, (ed.), *Christian Spirituality*, SCM Press 1975
Walsh, 'Halévy'	J. Walsh, 'Elie Halévy and the Birth of Methodism', in *TRHS* XXV, 1975
Walsh, 'Origins'	J. Walsh, 'The Origins of the Evangelical Revival', in G.V. Bennett and J. Walsh (eds.), *Essays in Modern English Church History*, A. & C. Black 1966
Walsh, 'Religious Societies'	J. Walsh, 'Religious Societies, Methodist and Evangelical, 1738–1800', in *SCH* XXIII, 1986
Watts	M. Watts, *The Dissenters*, I, Clarendon Press 1978
Wesley, *Diaries*	*John Wesley's Diaries*, MSS in MCA
Whitefield, *Journals*	I. Murray (ed.), *George Whitefield's Journals*, Banner of Truth Trust 1960
Whitefield, *Letters*	*George Whitefield's Letters*, Vol. I, reprinted Banner of Truth Trust 1976; II and III, London 1772
Whitehead	J. Whitehead, *Life of John Wesley*, two volumes, 1793, 1796
WMM	*Wesleyan Methodist Magazine* (formerly *AM*)
Works	*Works of John Wesley*, London 1872

Index

Arabic numerals refer to pages, Roman numerals to chapters (sometimes followed by subsections, e.g. X.1).

CW = Charles Wesley; JW = John Wesley; SW = Susanna Wesley